FRENCH WOMEN WRITERS

Edited by EVA MARTIN SARTORI
and DOROTHY WYNNE ZIMMERMAN

University of Nebraska Press
Lincoln and London

for Ann and Mary
and
for Anne, Jenny, and Leo

Originally published as *French Women Writers: A Bio-Bibliographical Source Book* by Greenwood Press, an imprint of Greenwood Publishing Group, Inc., Westport, CT. Copyright © 1991 by Eva Martin Sartori and Dorothy Wynne Zimmerman. This edition by arrangement with Greenwood Publishing Group, Inc. All rights reserved.

First paperback edition: 1994
Most recent printing indicated by the last digit below:
10   9   8   7   6   5   4   3   2   1

Library of Congress Cataloging-in-Publication Data
French women writers / edited by Eva Martin Sartori and Dorothy Wynne Zimmerman.
p.   cm.
Originally published: New York: Greenwood Press, 1991.
ISBN 0-8032-9224-4
1. French literature—Women authors—Bio-bibliography.   2. Women authors, French—Biography—Dictionaries.   3. French literature—Women authors—Dictionaries.
4. Women and literature—France—Bibliography.   I. Sartori, Eva.   II. Zimmerman, Dorothy Wynne, 1925–   .
PQ149.F73   1994
840.9′9287—dc20
[B]
93-39753   CIP

∞

CONTENTS

PREFACE

Dorothy Wynne Zimmerman
Eva Martin Sartori

This contributor volume aims to acquaint the reader with the lives and works of some of the most important women writers in the history of French literature. Like the other bio-bibliographical source books published by Greenwood Press, it is intended for the general reader as well as for students and scholars. Fifty-one of the chapters cover the lives and works of individual writers with an emphasis on their experiences as writers, a discussion of their major themes, and brief surveys of critical reactions. Each is followed by a bibliography of primary works, a list of titles translated into English, and a selection of critical studies. An additional chapter describes the trobairitz, the women troubadours of the twelfth and thirteenth centuries. Too important to exclude, they were too numerous and our knowledge of their lives too fragmented to justify a chapter on each. The volume ends with a chronology featuring the dates of events and trends of special significance to French women. The chronology serves also to place their writings in the context of important literary movements and alongside the productions of their usually better-known male contemporaries.

The names of many of the writers included here will be familiar to students of literature, for they have long been included in the French literary canon—indeed, they are part of the literary canon of Western civilization. But some of these writers will be recognized only by students of French literature, while others will be unknown even to the specialist. Both those long canonized and those emerging from obscurity have been reread by our contributors, who have brought to their readings new perspectives and have included in their reviews of the criticism summaries of the work of other contemporary critics. From these new perspectives, the contributors have examined the manner in which these authors have used traditional genres and probed the influence of gender on the choice and handling of themes.

In assembling this collection, we have given a broad interpretation to the term "French women writers," taking it generally to mean European women who have written in French and who have identified with French culture. A few of the authors included were not born in France and have, indeed, scarcely lived there. Marguerite Yourcenar, for example, was born in Belgium and lived much of her adult life on an island off the North American coast. Isabelle de Charrière was born in Holland in the eighteenth century and lived most of her adult life in Switzerland, but her writing in French and interest in all things French have led to her traditional inclusion in histories of French literature. A few authors were not born in Europe at all—Marguerite Duras, Hélène Cixous, and Andrée Chedid among them—but authorship in French and an adult life lived in France permit their inclusion as "French women writers." Thus we have solved a traditional labeling problem in the broadest way, by considering French those who have written in French and identified themselves with French culture and intellectual life.

From all the possible French women writers between the twelfth century and the late twentieth, it was difficult to choose. Some choices were obvious: one could not exclude Lafayette, Sévigné, or Colette, nor of course would one want to. In addition to these well-known writers, there are those who were formerly obscure but who, as a result of the resurgent women's movement in the 1970s, have attracted increasing attention. Although other candidates for inclusion suggest themselves—for instance the sixteenth-century mother and daughter poets Madeleine and Catherine des Roches—our selection was influenced by the availability of scholars and, of course, by the limitation of a single volume. It would not have been difficult to compile a list of twice as many writers, but in general there was agreement among our contributors concerning the writers to be included here.

A major criterion for inclusion was that the author have created a substantial body of work, whether published during her lifetime or not. Thus we have omitted some writers we would have liked to include, such as the revolutionaries Olympe de Gouges and Théroigne de Méricourt, whose work covers relatively few surviving pages. We have excluded also the Saint-Simonian feminists of the first half of the nineteenth century. Most of their work was journalistic and appeared in rather ephemeral papers. With the exception of Simone Weil, we have chosen "belles-lettristes," women who wrote or are writing novels, poetry, plays, letters, and memoirs (the last two increasingly seen as forms of fiction), over writers of expository prose.

A few of the authors we have included would not pass a test for feminist "political correctness." Manon Roland was not interested in her contemporaries Olympe de Gouges and Théroigne de Méricourt, and Lucie Delarue-Mardrus regretted the decline of chivalry and what we would call the "feminine mystique." Simone Weil would not have been interested in women's rights as opposed to human obligations. But, as others have observed, throughout most of European history it was subversive for women to write at all, and almost all these authors provide a woman's voice and point of view, directly or indirectly.

Some editorial decisions need to be explained.

We view the often extensive bibliographies appended to the entries as important contributions to this work. However, because the volume often threatened to spill over into a second, we had to impose restrictions on the length of the bibliographies of well-known authors. We have allowed longer bibliographies for writers who have no published or extensive bibliographies elsewhere. Where extensive bibliographies already exist, the contributors have been more selective.

The authors' works in the bibliographies are listed in the order in which they were published, to give the reader a sense of the writer's development. The order of translations reflects the original order of publication. The bibliographies of secondary works are in alphabetical order by author.

Within the text an asterisk preceding an author's name indicates that she is discussed in a separate chapter in the volume. Titles of authors' works are given in French in the text, followed by an English translation in parentheses. The English version of a French title is not italicized unless it is the title of a published English translation of the work.

We have chosen the form of the author's name which we believe will be most easily recognized by the reader. This means that in some cases we have preferred a pseudonym (George Sand, Rachilde, Colette) and in others the actual name (Marie d'Agoult rather than Daniel Stern). Most of the choices coincide with the entries preferred by Library of Congress, but those that do not (for example, we use Delphine Gay de Girardin rather than Mme Emile de Girardin, and Marie d'Agoult rather than Daniel Stern) are cross-referenced in our index and in library catalogs.

ACKNOWLEDGMENTS

We wish to state here our obligation and gratitude to the authors of the chapters in this volume, without whom there would be, of course, no book. We thank them not only for their fine contributions and for the years of scholarship that made these contributions possible, but also for their enthusiasm for this project, which made it easier for them to bear with us in our tasks as editors over the past several years. We are also very grateful to Diane Marting, editor of a similar volume on Spanish-American women writers, who suggested that we undertake this work and who, in true sisterly fashion, shared her experiences with us and was unfailingly generous with advice.

We would like to acknowledge also the advice and support of Susan Rosowski, Robert Knoll, Louis Crompton, Brenda Hosington, Inge Worth, and Tom Carr—friends and colleagues who helped with their expertise as writers and editors. Margaret Jane Slaughter was kind enough to review the chronology prepared by Julia Lauer-Chéenne. The Department of English at the University of Nebraska-Lincoln has supported Dorothy Zimmerman's part in the project in every way, and a semester's residence at the Camargo Foundation in 1986 helped her lay the groundwork for the volume. A research leave from the University of Nebraska-Lincoln Libraries in 1988–1989 enabled Eva Sartori to organize the project and write her chapter on Madame de Tencin. The UNL Libraries administration, particularly Kent Hendrickson, Joan Giesecke, and Linda Parker, could not have been more wholehearted in their support. One person in the Libraries deserves special mention: Barbara Turner, secretary in the department of Central Reference Services, did much of the typing of the correspondence and assisted in the preparation of the manuscript. Without her always timely help it is hard to imagine that this project would have come to completion.

Eva Martin Sartori
Dorothy Wynne Zimmerman

INTRODUCTION

In the nineteenth century George Eliot declared with some envy that "in France alone woman has had a vital influence on the development of literature . . . in France alone, if the writings of women were swept away, a serious gap would be made in the national history" (54). While serious gaps would also exist in English literature without the works of Jane Austen, the Brontës, and George Eliot herself, her statement dramatizes the vitality and importance of women's writing in the history of French literature. France can claim authors of international reputation—Marie de France, Mme de Sévigné, Mme de Lafayette, for example—from periods when women in other European countries were able to write only religious works, letters, translations, and miscellaneous fragments.

The lives and works of the women described in this volume help explain the emergence of great writing by women from the medieval period on. The biographies and reviews of works consistently reveal energy and versatility. Often unconventional in their personal lives, many of these authors had careers in addition to their writing—as salon hostess, actress, educator, painter, musician, preacher, or labor organizer. Women did not wait for Simone de Beauvoir to tell them that they should make existential choices and have "projects in the world."

Certainly it has not been easy for women to become writers in France. Lack of education and leisure except among the most wealthy and the shame of doing the unconventional and the "inappropriate" have been critical factors in the lives of women approaching writing. Not until the late nineteenth century did education for women become free and compulsory. And even among the wealthy the education of women was a sometime activity, for convent instruction provided little in the way of real knowledge. Ridicule was also a potent social weapon easily used against women by the most foolish fop, as the sixteenth-century woman of letters Marie de Gournay angrily remarked. Outright discrimination also dampened the enthusiasm of all but the most determined. English Showalter has documented the difficulties Mme de Graffigny experienced in attempting to have her plays staged. Nevertheless, women in France have been writing since the early days of literary history, and the fact that much of this literary production has survived means that, to some degree at least, a supportive environment, one which promoted the empowerment of women, was part of the social fabric of the culture.

As far back as the twelfth century we find evidence that in certain places and in certain situations women in France were held in high esteem. Although women had few legal rights during the Middle Ages and sexual relations were often brutal, a literary tradition of women-worship called *fin'amors* or courtly love appeared in the twelfth century in the south of France. Scholars have developed numerous and often conflicting theories about its appearance and significance. Some have seen it as an early manifestation of feminism, others as an ingenious way of keeping women more firmly in their place. As defined by Gaston Paris in 1883, the term "courtly love" refers to an illicit relation marked by a mystical devotion to a lady whose moral superiority the lover acknowledges. Because it emphasized relations of choice rather than relations of power, and because it promoted self-examination, the development of refined feelings, and the arts of persuasion rather than force, the concept of courtly love must have had important consequences, though they may have made themselves felt very slowly. While the power conferred by the "pedestal" is ambiguous at the very least, it is certainly possible that, in the words of Emily James Putnam, "every lady who listened to troubadour or *jongleur* . . . was furnished with the material for constructing a fresh estimate of her own importance" (quoted by Bogin, 65). And finally, it empowered women to add their voice to debates about love, for it brought forth a spirited response from the trobairitz, the women who wrote poetry that was a counterpart of that of the troubadours. In the *cansons* (solo songs) and *tensons* (a discussion between two people, usually, but not always, between a man and a woman) that they in turn addressed to their lovers, the women responded to men's worship by making their own demands, often startlingly physical, for equality in love. As expressed in the love lyric written in the vernacular (the Provençal of southern France), the poetry of courtly love marks the first time in the history of French literature that we find a reevaluation of the relations between the sexes accompanied by literary and linguistic innovation.

The tensions between the courtly ideal, which valorized women, and a strong misogynist tradition came to a head in the fourteenth century with the *querelle des femmes*, or quarrel about the nature of women. The champion of women was Christine de Pizan, the first woman in France to write in a variety of genres. By that time innumerable books had been written, mostly by men, arguing either for or against women's merits, either attacking or defending them. Tired of these arguments in which women had no voice, Pizan wrote *La Cité des dames (The*

City of Ladies), in which she enumerated the many famous women, both mythological and historical, whom she considered a credit to their sex, protested the misogyny of much of the literature of her time, and pleaded for the right to education for women. She was probably the first woman writer to make a living by her pen, receiving annuities for her literary productions.

Although the Renaissance may not have been as favorable to the development of women as of men, as the historian Joan Kelly has argued, some women at least experienced the revitalization of the new learning. Women both at court and at its periphery took an active role as both writers and patrons of writers. At the French court, Renée de France, Diane de Poitiers, and Marguerite de Valois all wrote memoirs. But the most accomplished and productive woman of her era in France was Marguerite de Navarre. At the French royal court, where she often resided, and at her own court in Navarre, Queen Marguerite gathered about her many of the luminaries of her generation, including the writers Melin de Saint-Gelais and Jacques Amyot, and protected writers of Protestant leanings. Known as a brilliant conversationalist, Marguerite of Navarre was not content to talk but also wrote poems, religious meditations, and her most famous book, the collection of stories known as the *Heptaméron*, published under her own name in 1559.

The education of women had been advocated by some of the most famous humanists of the time, including Erasmus, but primarily in order to enable them to carry out their domestic role with more intelligence, not in order to present themselves better on the world's stage. The writer Marie de Gournay, however, intoxicated by the love of learning, argued that men and women were equal in their ability to study and to learn, and she defended women writers against those who ridiculed their literary aspirations. She was one of the earliest writers to proclaim that equal education would eliminate the intellectual differences between men and women.

The Renaissance love of learning and of the arts was felt in the provinces as well as in Paris. In La Rochelle, Anne and Catherine de Parthenay wrote plays, and Marguerite and Catherine des Roches in Poitiers and Marie de Romieu in the Vivarais wrote poetry. In Lyons in particular, where the Italian Renaissance was strongly felt, a taste for letters and conversation flourished. Louise Labé, Pernette du Guillet, and Clémence de Bourges were part of the school of poets called the *école lyonnaise*. Labé's salon was one of the most frequented of the locality. In her garden or library, depending on the weather, the habitués read their verse and discussed literature, science, and morals. Labé was particularly concerned with the question of gender. In her poetry she claimed the right of women to participate in the new learning and urged women to pay more attention to their education than to their jewelry.

In the early seventeenth century the development of the salon as a locus of conversation and sociability was further institutionalized and codified by Mme de Rambouillet. Because she believed that the society at court was not sufficiently refined, she withdrew from court life in 1609 and began to receive at her house in Paris an elite group of distinguished writers, not all aristocrats, and others who were to become distinguished, including Madeleine de Scudéry, Mme de Lafayette, and Mme de Sévigné. The distinguishing feature of these salons is the importance they accorded to women. "Each salon leader," writes Joan DeJean, "set the tone and determined the membership and, in large part, the subjects of discussion. . . . This is the only time in the history of the French literary tradition that a powerful phenomenon, a movement with important literary, social, often even political implications, was initiated by women. It remained under female control for nearly two centuries" (299).

The development of the salon in the early seventeenth century coincides with the brief flowering of the *précieux* movement. Many of the *précieuses* who frequented these salons were aristocrats but, as Carolyn Lougee has shown, many were also members of the high bourgeoisie seeking admittance into aristocratic circles. They had in common an interest in language, a yearning for education, a desire for autonomy, and a belief in the active participation of women in the world. As in the case of troubadour literature, we note at this moment in French literary history a conjunction between sexual politics and language.

As Peter Brooks has pointed out, the "polite sociability" of the salon found expression in a corresponding literature, written by women as well as men. In the Parisian salon the spirit of equality and the requirements of good manners did not entirely mask the real power inherent in masculine control of religious and political institutions, but they did give women freedom to express themselves both in conversation and as authors. The salon was productive of letter writing as well as talk. It was a fairly short step from conversation to letter writing, which also implies an interested and sympathetic recipient; thus the fine and voluminous epistolary collections of Sévigné, du Deffand, Lespinasse, and others.

From the sixteenth through the eighteenth centuries, the institution of the salon, with its opportunities and limitations, is the source of much of women's writings in France. The "portrait," based on the classical example of Theophrastus, was originally a salon genre, its composition being a kind of parlor game, in which Scudéry and Lafayette excelled in the seventeenth century. The genesis of the modern novel in France in the same period owes much to the salon atmosphere and to the women who wrote. Scudéry's novels, *Le Grand Cyrus* and *Clélie*, are based on conversations about love, with disguised portraits of the author's friends as characters. Lafayette's famous *La Princesse de Clèves* was read aloud to her friends as it progressed, and they assisted with the historical research. This novel bears the imprint of the salon as well as the court in its oral qualities, made up as it is in large part of conversational gatherings, anecdotes related, and letters written, lost, and rewritten *à deux*, and its general sense of a social group from which it is difficult to escape. It could be said that the novel is really *about* the process of talking, of misunderstanding, of masking in language and the choice of speaking or not speaking.

As developed in France by women in the seventeenth and eighteenth centuries, the novel provided alternatives to the usual life-script for women—courtship, marriage, and silence. Mme de Villedieu wove stories of women into the events of public life in her fiction, influencing the direction of the French novel by mixing history and romance. Mme de Lafayette's heroine, the Princess de Clèves, confounded her contemporaries by refusing to marry the Duc de Nemours even though her husband's death had freed her to marry. This refusal of the ''script for women'' aroused controversy over the novel that continues to this day. Mme d'Aulnoy, whose first novel was published in 1690, made use of many complicating features—cross-dressing and disguises—which confused the traditional love plot. Her heroines were always given strong central roles even when the titles would indicate a hero at the center—*Le Comte de Warwick*, for example, or *Jean de Bourbon*. The fictions of Mme de Tencin had a strong feminist content in their resistance to arranged marriages and enforced religious vocation, the latter especially meaningful for her since her parents had placed her in a convent from which she escaped only by unremitting perseverance. And Mme de Graffigny wrote the *Lettres d'une Péruvienne*, in which the heroine at the end refuses to marry either Aza or her French tutor. This conclusion was considered so unnatural that sequels were written in which the heroine does marry after all. And finally, Mme de Charrière, at the end of the eighteenth century, created a number of resisting heroines.

Women writers who headed salons themselves or were active participants in the activities of the salons of other women include Mlle de Scudéry and the Mmes d'Aulnoy, de Lafayette, de Tencin, de Graffigny, de Duras, de Genlis, Roland, and de Staël. But although the aristocratic salon gave impetus to women's writing and helped to protect the social status of those who wrote, it is a mistake to think that all women writers belonged to the aristocratic milieu. Marie de Gournay, who became the editor of Montaigne's *Essais* and who wrote her own works from a strong feminist viewpoint, came from the minor nobility and made her living by writing—with annuities from, among others, Marguerite de Valois. Villedieu began by writing poetry for the aristocratic circle where her mother was a lady's maid, but she later became a playwright and popular novelist who lived by her pen. She was snubbed by the ladies of Brussels because, we are told, she was an author and an ''adventuress.'' Mme Riccoboni, who made an important contribution to the development of the novel, was born to a poor mother and was put upon the stage at an early age, where she supported herself as an actress for twenty-six years. Only after her retirement did she write her popular novels.

At the end of the eighteenth century, during the Revolutionary period, the lives and experiences of two women illustrate the choices women made and the difficulties they could suffer if they wanted to be authors. Manon Roland, the bourgeois daughter of an engraver of metals, chose not to write for publication, but Germaine de Staël strongly and uninhibitedly decided to write and to publish. In her *Mémoires*, written when she was in prison, Roland noted that although she had done much writing, which piled up in a dusty corner of her room, she did not attempt to publish because "I perceived very early that a woman who acquires that title loses far more than she has gained. The men do not love her, and her own sex criticize her. If her works are bad, they ridicule her; and they are right! if they are good, they ascribe them to someone else; if they are forced to acknowledge that she has discovered merit, they sift so maliciously her character, her morals, her conduct and her talents, that they balance the reputation of her genius by the publicity which they give to her errors" (277). She published almost nothing in her lifetime but wrote many articles, speeches, and letters for her husband, Jean-Marie Roland, who was active in Revolutionary politics on the side of the Girondins. But when she was imprisoned for her role as hostess for the Girondins, she was happy to pen, at last, her memoirs, with the hope that they would be published and read. She was now beyond considerations of respectability, and the question of whether others would approve of her was moot.

Although Germaine de Staël began her publishing career anonymously, she signed her name to all major works beginning with the pamphlet *Réflexions sur la paix* (Reflections on the Peace, 1795). She frequently wrote on the necessity of education for women and devoted the preface of the 1814 edition of her *Lettres sur les ouvrages et le caractère de Jean-Jacques Rousseau (Letters on Rousseau)* to defending women's right to education and, in the case of exceptional women, authorship. Though widely respected in Europe for the originality and political importance of her works, she was exiled by Napoleon who did not care for her democratic ideas or intellectual superiority in a woman.

As the eighteenth century closed, some of the social forces that supported women's writing in France all but disappeared. Women continued to write during the years of the Revolution and during Napoleon's ascendance, whether in exile or at home, including those who welcomed the Revolution: Staël and Charrière. But these last writers came to deplore the violence that followed and opposed the execution of Louis XVI and Marie Antoinette.

Radical feminists began to appear during this period—Théroigne de Méricourt, for example, who organized Revolutionary clubs for women and made speeches that have survived, and Olympe de Gouges, who wrote plays, pamphlets, and a Declaration of the Rights of Women. Both eventually paid for their audacity with sequestration (Méricourt) and death by the guillotine (Gouges). The Revolution had raised hope for equality in the new world to come, but the aims of feminists were totally dashed when the Convention disbanded the women's clubs in 1793. These are Chaumette's words when he proposed the dissolution: "Nature says to woman:" be a woman. The tender cares due to children, the sweet duties of maternity, these are your work. But your occupations merit a recompense and you shall have it. You will be the divinity of the domestic sanctuary, you will reign over all which surrounds you by the invincible charm of your grace and virtue. Imprudent women who wish to become men, are you not well enough endowed? What more do you want? You reign over our senses! The legislators are at your feet" (quoted in Sullerot, 77, translation ours).

In the phrases "domestic sanctuary" and "invincible charm" one hears the language that would dominate the lives of most French women in the nineteenth century. The reaction to the disorders of the Revolution brought about a stifling of any rights women might have had and any reforms they had hoped for. The new Social Code (Napoleonic Code), whose writing Napoleon had supervised, reduced women to the status of minors; they could not engage in a professional activity without their husband's consent, nor could married women manage their property or any income they might earn. Such deprivation was not auspicious for women as writers. As Germaine Brée writes in *Women Writers in France*: "The Napoleonic code tied the French woman firmly down to the family, making her in every manner a minor, economically and legally dependent on man; and a stigma was attached by that society to the woman who did not conform. . . . Literary and social circles no longer reinforced one another in the same way. This conjunction affected the woman writer's position adversely; social respectability and literature parted company" (40). The French salon as it had existed for centuries effectively disappeared. Félicité de Genlis, who during the period of the Consulate presided over what was perhaps the last of the author-hostess salons in the pre-Revolutionary style, complained about the lack of manners and the differences in tone between the pre- and post-Revolutionary gatherings.

Salons continued to exist in the nineteenth century but proved overall less productive of anecdote and literature. Marie d'Agoult had her "Tuesdays" in Paris for many years, and George Sand assembled around her a brilliant group of friends, which included at various times Chopin, Liszt, Delacroix, Marie Dorval, and others. They met in Paris and were guests at her country house at Nohant. But the French salon as a steadily productive social-literary institution dominated by women seems to have ended with the Revolution.

In spite of obstacles, French women continued to write in the nineteenth century, supporting themselves by their efforts and by their other occupations in the world. More women of the lower classes and of the bourgeoisie joined the republic of letters, expanding the subject matter and themes of writing. Marceline Desbordes-Valmore, the popular poet, was an actress for twenty-five years and wrote about children, relations between women, and social conditions. Flora Tristan, who suffered the double stigma of illegitimacy and separation from her husband, was a labor organizer as well as a writer. George Sand, who has given her name to the "era of George Sand," was involved in most of the political and artistic movements of her time, managed her estate at Nohant, maintained a voluminous correspondence, and wrote sixty novels as well as essays, plays, travel books, and an autobiography. Her innovations included positive portrayals of workers and peasants. Marie d'Agoult was a historian as well as a novelist. Sophie de Ségur created children's books while managing her estate in Normandy and documented the changes wrought by the Industrial

Revolution on class relations. Women also entered the world of publishing as editors and as journalists. Delphine Gay de Girardin was a successful playwright as well as a journalist and described the daily life of Paris over a ten-year period in the *Lettres parisiennes* for her husband's newspaper. Marie d'Agoult wrote articles on politics, history, literature, music, and art. Judith Gautier covered the cultural scene and also wrote travel pieces. Rachilde, in addition to writing the infamous "decadent" novel *Monsieur Vénus*, launched with her husband the review *Mercure de France*, a leading publisher of symbolist work, and wrote plays, literary criticism, and poetry as well as novels.

In the twentieth century the world has opened up for women writers as many of the social gains so vehemently sought by the feminists of the nineteenth and early twentieth centuries have been realized. Vestiges of prejudice against women as writers no doubt remain. Colette was considered a scandalous creature in her early years as an author and music-hall performer, carrying on the nineteenth-century tradition of women authors as marginal, but by mid-century she was revered as the *grande dame* of French literature. Simone de Beauvoir's first book was rejected by Gallimard because, as Sartre reported to her, "the house of Gallimard did not understand books written by women of my generation and background, that modern France and French publishing houses were not yet ready to deal with what women thought and felt and wanted; that to publish such a book would brand them as a subversive publishing house and they couldn't risk offending all sorts of patrons and critics" (Bair, 207). But Beauvoir went on to her well-known long and brilliant career in spite of this initial obstacle.

Women in France now write and publish freely, generally in expectation of a fair hearing. In addition to writing, they launch and support journals (for example, the *Nouvelles questions feministes*, *Cahiers du GRIF*), own and direct theater groups (Adriane Mnouchkine's Théâtre du Soleil), own publishing houses (notably the Editions des femmes), write and direct films (Marguerite Duras, for example), and are in the forefront of experimentation with new literary forms.

Yet the *querelle des femmes*, begun during the Middle Ages, continues as women probe questions of gender, sexuality, and language. What is the nature of women's identity? If there is a female nature, to what degree is it determined by the female body? To what extent are women's perceptions of the world structured by a language—linear, discursive, goal-oriented—which avant-garde writers such as Kristeva, Cixous, and Irigaray believe to have been elaborated by a male consciousness? As their ancestors the trobairitz and the *précieuses* have done before them, modern French women writers are developing new language and new literary forms to create and express a new social and political reality.

BIBLIOGRAPHY

Bair, Deirdre. *Simone de Beauvoir: A Biography*. New York: Summit Books, 1990.
Bogin, Meg. *The Women Troubadours*. Scarborough, England: Paddington Press, 1976.

Brée, Germaine. *Women Writers in France: Variations on a Theme*. New Brunswick, N.J.: Rutgers University Press, 1973.

Brooks, Peter. *The Novel of Worldliness*. Princeton, N.J.: Princeton University Press, 1969.

DeJean, Joan. "The Salons, 'Preciosity,' and the Sphere of Women's Influence." In *A New History of French Literature*. Ed. Denis Hollier. Cambridge, Mass.: Harvard University Press, 1989.

Eliot, George. *Essays of George Eliot*. Ed. Thomas Pinney. New York: Columbia University Press, 1963.

Lougee, Carolyn C. *Le Paradis des Femmes: Women, Salons, and Social Stratification in Seventeenth-Century France*. Princeton, N.J.: Princeton University Press, 1976.

Roland, Mme (Marie-Jeanne). *The Private Memoirs of Madame Roland*. Ed. Edward Gilpin Johnson. Chicago: A. C. McClurg, 1900.

Showalter, English, Jr. "Writing Off the Stage: Women Authors and Eighteenth-Century Theater." *Yale French Studies* 75 (1988): 95–111.

Sullerot, Evelyne. *Histoire et sociologie du travail féminin*. Paris: Editions Gonthier, 1968.

MARIE D'AGOULT
(1805–1876)

Kathryn J. Crecelius

BIOGRAPHY

Marie de Flavigny, who wrote under the pen name Daniel Stern, was born in Frankfurt am Main, Germany, on December 31, 1805. Her father, the Viscount Alexandre de Flavigny, was a French émigré; her mother, Marie-Elisabeth Bethmann, was the daughter of the founder of one of Europe's most prestigious banks. Raised in France, Marie married the count Charles d'Agoult, fifteen years her senior, in 1827. Her first daughter was born the following year, the second in 1830. Intelligent, well read, and well connected socially, Marie decided to open a salon. Her salon would remain a focal point of her social and intellectual life throughout her tumultuous existence.

Marie met Franz Liszt for the first time in 1832 and was electrified by this twenty-six-year-old genius with sea-green eyes. Soon they became lovers. Marie's marriage had never been emotionally satisfying. How could it be, when she and her fiancé had only met a month before the wedding? They quickly learned they had nothing in common. Yet, despite the difficult position in which Marie was to put him and his daughter, Charles d'Agoult behaved with complete courtesy and tolerance toward the woman who legally remained his wife until his death in 1875.

In 1835 Marie left her husband and remaining daughter, Claire (her first-born, Louise, having died five months earlier), to join Liszt in Switzerland. This was the beginning of a tumultuous nine-year liaison whose drama would be played out in four European countries. Marie bore Franz three children: Blandine, Cosima (named for her birthplace, Italy's Lake Como), and Daniel. Cosima later became famous as the wife of Richard Wagner and the doyenne of Bayreuth. Since none of the children's birth certificates listed the mother's name, Liszt was their sole legally recognized parent. After the breakup of their relationship,

Liszt used this privilege, part of Europe's patriarchal legal system, designed to protect bloodlines and inheritances, against Marie to prevent her from seeing her own children. This abuse of paternal power caused the relationship of Marie and Franz to be prolonged well beyond the point of their separation in 1844 and does not show Liszt in a very favorable light. It should be noted, however, that animosity toward Liszt was and remains the rule among Marie's partisans, while supporters of Liszt have largely execrated Marie and her influence. The quarrelsome relationship between the two lovers lives on in the critics' camps.

Yet the bitter parting should not be allowed to obscure the joyous beginning, for Marie and Franz's story starts like that of any other pair of lovers. Their elopement to Switzerland was romantic and carefree. The early years of their liaison are closely associated with George *Sand, Marie's friend and mentor, whose example of personal freedom inspired Marie to leave her husband and who encouraged Marie to write. In many ways, Marie's friendship with George Sand parallels her relationship with Liszt: early enthusiasm and mutual understanding gave way to jealousy and recriminations. To a certain extent, this pattern was unavoidable with George Sand. Each woman saw the other immediately as a peer, as someone with a similar educational background, artistic interests, and desires for self-expression. Yet beyond the similarities were vast differences. Marie remained ever the aristocrat, while Sand, though of no lower birth, was more egalitarian in style. Sand enjoyed broad humor, whereas Marie's tastes were more refined. Marie disapproved of Sand's easy-going sexuality, which allowed Sand to have more than one lover at a time. Finally, Marie became jealous of Sand, suspecting that she might have designs on Liszt. Although there is much evidence that Sand and Liszt shared many interests, as well as a genuine camaraderie, there is nothing to indicate the remotest romantic involvement. Here, Marie was allowing her imagination to influence her observations. As Sand and Chopin became romantically linked and were happy together just as Marie and Liszt were experiencing difficulties, Marie turned completely against Sand. Artistic jealousy also fueled Marie's anger, for Sand was a famous author before Marie even thought of publishing; furthermore, Sand had more talent.

Sand was not entirely blameless in the souring of the friendship, for during a visit by Balzac to Nohant, she recounted Marie and Franz's story to him, out of which was born Balzac's novel *Béatrix*, in which Marie is portrayed as cold and manipulative. The final blow was given to the friendship when Marie's acid comments about Sand were revealed to George by their mutual friend Carlotta Marliani. Although Mme Marliani's motivations were most likely not malicious, the result of her foolish meddling was the impossibility of George and Marie's reconciling. The two rarely crossed paths after their relations ended, although as major social and artistic figures each remained aware of the other's activities.

In evaluating Marie and George's friendship, several circumstances must be taken into account. First, they became friends almost too rapidly, without taking the time to notice and acknowledge their dissimilarities. Yet they cannot be blamed for quickly taking to each other, for the number of women in their society who were truly their intellectual equals was very limited, given women's restricted status. Sand and Marie were two women who, with a larger circle of female friends to choose from, probably never would have been more than acquaintances. This assertion underscores another important issue that needs to be addressed when discussing Marie and George's friendship, or indeed the relationships between any famous women. It is usually expected that famous women either be friends or foes, and their relationship is generally put in these terms; when they do not get along, this is seen as diminishing the accomplishments and humanity of both parties. Men are almost never considered in this way; their friendships, quarrels, and liaisons are ancillary to their work. Too often, we overdetermine women's relationships with other women, as well as with men, expecting more of these attachments than they can legitimately bear. Like Marie's affair with Liszt, her friendship with George Sand has produced two antagonistic groups, each championing its heroine. Perhaps the time has come to say, simply, that they were friends, but events and their own personalities drove them apart. In her *Histoire de la Révolution de 1848* (History of the Revolution of 1848), Daniel Stern is complimentary of Sand's actions during the Revolution, while George Sand sent Marie a touching condolence letter after Marie's daughter Blandine died in 1862. Although they were never reconciled, a certain sympathy always remained, along with a good dose of ambivalence.

After leaving Liszt definitively in 1844, Marie continued the writing she had begun some time earlier, and resurrected her Paris salon. Even in Geneva, where she and Liszt first settled, Marie had consoled herself for the social exile the straitlaced local society imposed on her, the wife of one man and the mistress of another, by inviting to her home a select group of men unabashed by her company. There, Charles Simonde de Sismondi, the historian and friend of Germaine de *Staël, the poet Louis de Ronchaud, who became her lifelong friend, and Adolphe Pictet, author of a humorous account of Marie, Franz, and George Sand's trip to Switzerland, formed her society. Marie's Paris salon, which met in the rue Neuve-des-Mathurins, included Henry Bulwer-Lytton, Bernard Potocki, and Charles-Augustin Sainte-Beuve. After Louis-Napoléon's coup d'état in 1851, Marie's salon, now situated in the "Maison rose" ("Pink House"), became a meeting place for the democratic opposition. Her guest list reads like a who's who of art, literature, and politics, and featured Alexis de Tocqueville, Jules Michelet, Ivan Turgenev, and Emile Littré. Marie pressed her contacts for eyewitness accounts when writing her history of the Revolution of 1848, and utilized her salon to premier some of her own works. Her daughter Claire, now a mother and separated from her husband (Marie's own disastrous marriage not having prevented her from allowing her daughter to make the same mistake), was an accomplished artist and helped her mother as salon hostess.

During the thirty years following her break with Liszt, Marie wrote steadily, publishing fiction, history, travel literature, plays, and numerous articles. She traveled widely, often to gather material for her books. As her children by Liszt reached adulthood, she was able to have more contact with them and to follow their busy lives and those of her grandchildren. Her later years were increasingly marked by the depressions that had manifested themselves early in her life, but after each episode she was able to regain her mental equilibrium. She died quietly in 1876, at the age of seventy, and was buried in Père-Lachaise cemetery.

MAJOR THEMES

If Marie's biography has taken up so much space, it is because her art is inseparable from her life. While this is true of many writers, it is particularly the case for Daniel Stern. Without the rupture from her past life as wife and mother that her flight with Liszt provided, Marie d'Agoult would in all likelihood never have become the kind of writer she was. She might have written her memoirs, like so many countesses before her; she might even have written for Emile de Girardin's newspaper, *La Presse*, as his wife Delphine did. But to remain Madame la comtesse d'Agoult and to write fiction or a history of the Revolution of 1848 would not have been possible. To be a woman writer in nineteenth-century France meant being outside the mainstream; one has only to think of George Sand, once Marie's friend and role model, Hortense Allart, another friend of Marie's and a single mother, or Flora *Tristan, whose *Peregrinations of a Pariah* bears a title indicative of her social status, to measure the gulf between Marie d'Agoult and Daniel Stern. She herself wrote in her private notebook that the meeting with Liszt had been decisive: "If I hadn't met on my path a very young man, very handsome, very ardent, very high-strung, very pious like myself, full of genius, who could take me out of my world, I would have died there" (Dupêchez, 283).[1]

Daniel Stern was born in December 1841 when Emile de Girardin published an article in *La Presse* called "La Nouvelle Salle de l'Ecole des Beaux-Arts peinte par M. Paul Delaroche" (The New Room in the School of Fine Arts Painted by M. Paul Delaroche) under the byline Daniel Stern. In the posthumously published *Mémoires*, Marie recounts her choice of name, goaded by Girardin. Daniel came to her automatically, without reflection. It was her two-year-old son's name, and also that of the biblical hero. Then, she thought of Wahr, German for truth, but decided on Stern, or star, for she hoped she had a lucky star. Thus, according to her, was her bilingual, masculine pseudonym born. Like her contemporary George Sand, Marie's gender was an open secret, her nom de plume merely a smokescreen to protect her noble family from seeing their name in print and to allow her more freedom of expression. Daniel Stern was the writer, and Marie d'Agoult the woman.[2] Nothing speaks more eloquently of the tensions in her life than this split nomenclature.

As Daniel Stern, Marie published widely. Her articles appeared in all the major French periodicals of the time, and her subjects included art, history, literature, politics, and music. Indeed, she had long written on music, having since 1837 composed the "Lettres d'un bachelier" (Letters of a Music Student) for the *Gazette musicale* as a ghostwriter for Franz Liszt. Many of Daniel Stern's articles, especially those of the 1840s, concern German art and culture and deal with such German contemporaries as Heine, Georg Herwegh, and Bettina von Arnim (whom Stern pilloried). In 1858 she was involved in starting the *Revue germanique*, designed to facilitate cultural understanding and exchange between France and Germany and to make France more aware of new developments in German culture. Not only did Daniel Stern write for the *Revue germanique*, but so did her daughters Claire and Cosima.

While her publications in the press spanned her entire writing career, Daniel Stern's foray into fiction writing is limited to the period 1842–1845, with the exception of one novella published in 1859. Daniel Stern's fiction is not the most successful part of her oeuvre, but it is the most personal, and therefore worthy of study. After publishing two novellas in *La Presse*, Daniel Stern had a *succès de scandale* with *Nélida* (1846), a thinly disguised version of her romance with Liszt. The title is an anagram of her new pen name and ties the birth of Daniel Stern the writer with Marie's liaison.

Nélida provided Marie with a kind of catharsis and was written almost in a fever, as she indicated in a letter to a friend in 1850: "This novel was not *composed* with premeditation; it burst out of me like an eruption, like measles" (J. Vier, ed., *Lettres républicaines* [Republican Letters], 20). While the eponymous Nélida plays Marie's role in the novel, Mother Ste. Elisabeth, abbess of the convent in which Nélida received her education, is an even more compelling figure. Where Nélida represents Marie's real life, Mother Ste. Elisabeth would seem to embody Marie's fantasies. A headstrong, intelligent girl, Elisabeth chooses religion over marriage, for she sees the convent as offering her opportunities to lead a community and to have an impact on others. "I couldn't imagine any other happiness than that of command; my heart only beat at the thought of a great destiny" (*Nélida* [1846], 263). Later, she leaves the convent and lives among the workers in Lyons, becoming a sort of prophetess or Saint-Simonian.

Elisabeth's desire for power, to play a role in society beyond that prescribed for women, is echoed in the longings of Daniel Stern's other fictional characters. Valentia, heroine of the 1847 novella of the same name, takes opium to end her life after an unhappy love affair. She dies as the Revolution of 1830 breaks out, wishing that she could have fought for a great cause. This poignant need for action betrays a cruel lack in the lives of nineteenth-century women, whose possibilities for self-actualization were sorely limited.

Valentia also shows the dark alternative to this dream of social participation, which was the temptation of suicide. While a common theme in Romantic literature, it is nonetheless significant that suicide should appear in four out of five of Stern's fictional works. Alice's husband, in *La Boîte aux lettres* (The Post Box), challenges his wife's lover to a duel that is really a self-immolation; in the novella that bears his name, Julien attempts suicide, as does Nélida. Stern's characters feel useless, without connection or outlet, and so are tempted by annihilation. Although Marie d'Agoult herself was not suicidal, she suffered from severe depressions throughout her life. While depression can have many physical and psychological causes, it is not untoward to hypothesize that Marie's own unfulfilled desire to play a role in the world was one source of her depressions. Her sense of being denied access to the field of action is expressed in her motto: "In Alta Solitudine" (In High Solitude).

Like Marie herself, Daniel Stern's heroines value learning, and often their education (in the broad sense of the word) is detailed in Stern's fiction. Elisabeth reads widely and finds role models in books. From Madame Roland's memoirs, she discovers with pleasure that "women could be great, strong, be something at last!" (*Nélida*, 259). Yet what good was the education patiently acquired by these fictional characters if they could not act on it? Surely Marie d'Agoult had asked the same question as she sought to find a niche for herself. Ultimately, writing became her means of "being something." Whether it was the most appropriate use of her talents is another issue; given the constraints on women at the time, Marie had few other choices. Victim of her class's prejudices as much as of her gender, Marie's only acceptable outlet was writing. One does not imagine her touring France to organize workers into unions, as Flora Tristan did. Today, Marie d'Agoult would have many options; law or politics might be her chosen field. Literature would probably not tempt her, although other forms of writing might.

Yet fiction provided a useful training ground for Daniel Stern's masterwork, her *Histoire de la Révolution de 1848*. If as a fiction writer Daniel Stern was not the equal of her contemporaries, male or female, as the chronicler of the major event of the nineteenth century she was ahead of her time. Indeed, her book is the first modern history written by a Frenchwoman. She calls herself a historian (using the masculine form to agree with her pseudonym) and employs what today would be considered proper research techniques: interviewing eye-witnesses and consulting primary sources. Each of the three original volumes includes copies of historical documents, among which are lists of names, autograph proclamations of the Provisional Government, enumerations of professions of members of the Ateliers Nationaux (National Workshops), and excerpts from Olympe de Gouges's "Déclaration des droits de la femme" (Declaration of the Rights of Woman), a key document from the French Revolution. Despite its scholarly underpinnings, Stern's *Histoire*, which proceeds day by day, sometimes hour by hour, is very evocative and lends an immediacy to the events recounted. The reader has the feeling of being in the middle of the action as it unfolds, and finds the narrative so compelling that the lengthy volumes of the original edition that had seemed so daunting instead are quickly devoured. The descriptions of the street combats and of the casualties these battles produced are exceptionally well handled. Perhaps because of her eloquence, Stern's writing has been appropriated by other historians of the revolution, making plagiarism the highest form of praise.

Stern's purpose in writing her history was to chart the evolution of the social revolution that had its roots in the eighteenth century, began in earnest with the French Revolution, gained momentum in the first half of the nineteenth century, came to a head in 1848 all over Europe, and culminated in France in the election of Louis-Napoléon Bonaparte, the future Emperor Napoléon III. Significantly, the last chapter is called "La Réaction" (The Reaction, often used in the sense of repression) and details the rather discouraging results of the revolution. Stern's sad and warning message is worth heeding even today: "Is nineteenth-century democracy doomed, as they say, to the pathetic destiny of the Roman plebes? Incapable of rising up to freedom, does democracy have no other ideal than bread and spectacles, no other end than invasion by barbarians?" (Desanti, ed., *Histoire*, 736).[3] She castigates the bourgeoisie for its failure to educate the masses about what democracy and freedom really mean. Stern ends, though, on a note of hope, affirming her faith in the future and in the ultimate attainment of freedom by all people, thanks to the "social instinct of the people and the political know-how of the literate classes" (737).

Liberty for all, according to Stern, included freedom for women, which would come as a consequence of greater social enlightenment. This freedom would come both from without, extended by men, and from within, as women of the lower classes, who, Stern asserts, did not know inequality, set the example for their aristocratic sisters. While Stern held an idealistic and romantic view of the working classes' nobility and of the lack of inequality she perceived in those women's lives, it is important to note that she sympathized with a group of whom her aristocratic and bourgeois peers were plainly afraid: "Working classes, dangerous classes," said the common wisdom of the time. It is also true that to a woman so constrained by her class, the working class and peasant woman's active role in the workshop and field, as well as the home, may have seemed attractive, although the working women would probably have gladly traded places with Marie d'Agoult.

It is in this context of class and historical period that Daniel Stern's "feminism" must be evaluated, both in her *Histoire* and in her writings in general. I have already indicated that Stern looked forward to all women's greater participation in society at all levels. Yet she was not an emancipationist; in her history, she ridicules the efforts of women's clubs to vote or to put their names on the ballot. Like George Sand, she takes a longer-term view and insists that women need time and education in order to become full citizens. In her 1847 *Essai sur la liberté considérée comme principe et fin de l'activité humaine* (Essay on Liberty Considered as the Source and Goal of Human Activity), she discerns three problems within the family as constituted at the time: the legal inferiority of women, the indissolubility of marriage, and the absence of state intervention in children's education. She had had personal experience of the first two strictures herself, and always insisted that they must be changed if women's status was to improve.

Yet Stern also says in this same chapter (vol. 2, chap. 15, "La Femme") that women are more frail, with "a temperament that retains something of a child's" (96); furthermore, she declares that "the highest regions of speculation are, if not unattainable, at least of difficult access for her" (96). To be fair, she does go on to maintain that these physical and mental differences are not apparent in the practice of daily life. The modern reader cringes, though, at the repetition by this strong and cerebral woman of essentialist arguments that continue to be used against women's full self-realization. Yet we cannot impose our views and the benefits of hindsight on the nineteenth century; it suffices to point out the limitations of Stern's thought while lauding the boldness and coherence of many of her ideas. On children's education, for example, Stern was ahead of her peers in advocating state-supported education of girls and boys of all social classes.

Daniel Stern was consistent in the themes her writings explore, whether fiction, history, or essay. She demonstrates a faith in the human spirit's nobility and a striving for freedom and social inclusion. Although she never achieved the fame and importance she craved, Stern was known and read throughout Europe. She was not afraid to tackle imposing subjects like revolution and liberty, and it must be said that her writings did them justice. Daniel Stern deserves to be better known and better read, and to be accorded her rightful place in nineteenth-century cultural history.

SURVEY OF CRITICISM

Daniel Stern's critical fate follows that of contemporaneous women writers. Known and read in her time, she became the subject of several critical appraisals and biographies in the 1930s when women authors were briefly back in vogue. Scholars then did not share the disdain or ignorance of women writers that would result over the ensuing decades in women writers almost disappearing from the curriculum. While such works as those by Monod and Gugenheim are serious and contain some useful information, they are by and large dated. Jacques Vier's six-volume biography, published from 1955 to 1963, remains the standard work.

Curiously, the revival of interest in women writers in the 1970s and 1980s, especially those who were "lost" or at the least went unread, has not touched Daniel Stern to the same degree as her contemporaries. Historians have shown more awareness of Stern's work than literary scholars. This critical silence may constitute a recognition that Stern's fiction is of interest more to specialists than to students or casual readers, but the omission remains striking, since many women writers of limited talent have attracted champions. The lack of articles is particularly puzzling. Only Dominique Desanti, fresh from having written on Flora Tristan, attempted to rehabilitate Stern. While bringing Stern criticism up to date, *Daniel, ou le visage secret d'une comtesse romantique* (Daniel, or the Secret Face of a Romantic Countess) is not Desanti's best work nor the best appraisal of Daniel Stern's life and writings. Desanti has also reedited Stern's *Histoire de la Révolution de 1848*, making this key text available again in an accessible format. More recently, Charles Dupêchez published a biography called *Marie d'Agoult*. The result of much research, Dupêchez's book includes unpublished material and paints a coherent portrait of Marie d'Agoult's life. He brings out in a more consistent way than past writers the depressions d'Agoult suffered. Ultimately, though, despite his professed sympathy for her, Dupêchez's attitude at times borders on the contemptuous and mars our belief in his authority. Dupêchez has also recently reedited *Nélida* and is working on an edition of Stern's autobiographical writings, left unfinished at her death.

Clearly, there is much still to be done on Daniel Stern. In particular, her place as a historiographer of the Revolution of 1848 remains to be defined. It is to be hoped that she will attract more critical notice in the years to come.

NOTES

1. All translations are my own.

2. Throughout this chapter I maintain the distinction between Marie d'Agoult the woman and Daniel Stern the author.

3. Even though Desanti's edition does not include the historical documents and has been cut, I quote from it rather than the original because her edition is more easily obtained by the reader.

BIBLIOGRAPHY

Major Works by Daniel Stern/Marie d'Agoult

Nélida. Paris: Amyot, 1846. Ed. Charles Dupêchez. Paris: Calmann-Lévy, 1986.
Lettres républicaines du Second Empire. Paris: N.p., 1848. Ed. J. Vier. Paris: Editions du Cèdre, n.d. [1951].
Essai sur la liberté considérée comme principe et fin de l'activité humaine. Paris: Amyot, 1847.
Histoire de la Révolution de 1848. Paris: G. Sandré, 1850–1853. Ed. Dominique Desanti. Paris: Balland, 1985.
Jeanne D'arc, drame historique en cing actes et en prose. Paris: Michel Lévy frères, 1857.
Dante et Goethe, dialogues. Paris: Didier, 1866.
Histoire des commencements de la république aux Pays Bas, 1581–1625. Paris: Michel Lévy frères, 1872.
Mes Souvenirs, 1806–1833. Paris: Calmann Lévy, 1877.
Valentia; Hervé; Julien; La Boîte aux lettres; Ninon au couvent. Paris: Calmann Lévy, 1896.
Mémoires, 1833–1854. Introd. Daniel Ollivier. Paris: Calmann-Lévy, 1927.

Translations of Daniel Stern/Marie d'Agoult

No evidence has been found that Daniel Stern's work has ever been translated into English.

Studies of Daniel Stern/Marie d'Agoult

Desanti, Dominique. *Daniel, ou le visage secret d'une comtesse romantique*. Paris: Stock, 1980.

Dupêchez, Charles. *Marie d'Agoult*. Paris: Perrin, 1989.

Gugenheim, Suzanne. *Madame d'Agoult et la pensée européenne de son époque*. Florence: Leo S. Olschki, 1937.

Monod, Marie Octave. *Daniel Stern, comtesse d'Agoult*. Paris: Plon, 1937.

Stock-Morton, Phyllis. "Daniel Stern, Historian." *History of European Ideas* 8, no. 4–5 (1987): 489–501.

Vier, Jacques. *La Comtesse d'Agoult et son temps*. 6 vos. Paris: Armand Colin, 1955–1963.

MARIE-CATHERINE LE JUMEL DE BARNEVILLE, COMTESSE D'AULNOY (1650/51–1705)

Lewis C. Seifert

BIOGRAPHY

Marie-Catherine Le Jumel de Barneville was born in either 1650 or 1651 in Barneville-la-Bertrand (Normandy) and, judging from the few accounts that remain, had a tumultuous early life. After her marriage at age fifteen or sixteen to the baron d'Aulnoy, who was more than twice her age, the baronne acquired a reputation for scandalous (sexual) conduct among some of her contemporaries. Indeed, she herself repents for having had "an immoral affair" (quoted in Roche-Mazon, *En Marge de l'Oiseau bleu*, 18) in one of the confessional pieces from the end of her life. By far the most serious of her purported improprieties occurred when she conspired to have her husband denounced for *lèse-majesté* against the king, for which she was imprisoned. Very little is known about her existence beyond the resulting separation from her husband, his decision to strike her from his will just before his death, a possible trip to Spain, and her death in January 1705 in Paris.

Aulnoy came to writing relatively late in life (at age thirty-nine or forty) with the publication of her first novel, *Histoire d'Hypolite, Comte de Duglas* (*Hypolitus Earl of Douglas*, 1690), which had an instant and lasting success. That a fairy tale is embedded in this text suggests the generic variety of her production; for, while Aulnoy wrote two collections of fairy tales, *Les Contes des fées* (*Tales of the fairies in Three Parts, Compleat*, 1697–98) and *Les Contes nouveaux ou les fées à la mode* (New Tales or Fairies in Fashion, 1698), the vast majority of her corpus consists of novels, novellas, and "pseudo"-memoirs with "exotic" settings. With her *Mémoires de la cour d'Espagne* (*Memoirs of the Court of Spain*, 1690), the *Relation du voyage d'Espagne* (*Travels into Spain: Being the Ingenious and Diverting Letters of the Lady *****, 1691), her *Nouvelles espagnoles* (Spanish Novellas, 1692), and the two frame-narratives in *Les Contes des* *fées—Don Gabriel Ponce de Léon* and *Don Fernand de Tolède*—she built on her reputation as a novelist/memorialist with a predilection for Spain. Aulnoy's foreign settings also include England, as her *Histoire d'Hypolite*, the *Mémoires de la cour d'Angleterre* (*Memoirs of the Court of England*, 1695), and her last work, *Le Comte de Warwick* (The Count of Warwick, 1703), certainly suggest. Even when the hero is French, as is Carency in *Histoire de Jean de Bourbon, Prince de Carency* (*The Prince of Carency*, 1692), the action is almost immediately shifted to Spain, the Mediterranean Sea, and Morocco. Only in her paraphrases of two Psalms, *Sentiments d'une âme pénitente* (Impressions of a Penintent Soul, 1691) and *Le Retour d'une âme à Dieu* (A Soul's Return to God, 1692), *Le Nouveau Gentilhomme bourgeois* (The New Bourgeois Gentleman)—the frame-narrative in *Les Contes nouveaux ou les fées à la mode*—and the *Nouvelles ou mémoires historiques* (Historical Novellas and Memoirs, 1693) are traces of such "exoticism" mostly absent.

In contrast to the dominant perception of Aulnoy as a novelist and memorialist in her own time, today she is almost exclusively remembered for her fairy tales. Paradoxically, what is less well known is the important role these texts played in the "vogue" of literary *contes de fées* (fairy tales) written for adults in France between 1690 and 1710. Not only was the untitled tale in *Histoire d'Hypolite*, often called "L'Ile de la félicité" (The Island of Felicity), the first to be published, but Aulnoy also proved to be the most prolific of all the fairy-tale writers in this period, with twenty-five *contes* to her credit. Even though her tales and those of six other women writers dominated the genre numerically, literary history has overwhelmingly favored the texts of Charles Perrault and has often given not the slightest hint of the existence of any others.[1]

But if Perrault was able to attain a public renown (as a member of the French Academy and a "modernist" polemicist in the Quarrel of the Ancients and the Moderns) that Aulnoy, as a woman, could never have hoped for, her status was nonetheless far from inconspicuous. Her writings earned her a place in the Academy of Ricovrati of Padua, where she was given the titles "Clio, the Muse of History" and "the Eloquent," as well as praise in reviews by contemporary literary journals (the *Mercure galant* and the *Histoire des ouvrages des savants*, among others). Moreover, several of her novels and memoirs had just as much success in England and other countries, where they were translated almost immediately after their publication in France. The personal contacts she had with other writers indicate that she was far from unknown to her contemporaries; for instance, she held a salon that was frequented by authors such Charles de Saint-Evremond and was a friend of Henriette-Julie de Murat and Marie-Jeanne Lhéritier, fellow women fairy-tale writers. What literary history has refused her, Aulnoy had already gained in her own time through both her novelistic writings and her fairy tales.

MAJOR THEMES

As in the narrative fiction of many of her contemporaries, the single most important theme in Aulnoy's writing is love. Although her psychological analyses of the birth, development, and obstacles to desire between a (heterosexual) couple are quite conventional, certain recurrent features of her writing may be considered as subversive or deviant renderings of the theme. For example, the many instances of characters taking disguises and, specifically, of sexual or class cross-dressing often problematize the traditional plot of heterosexual love between aristocratic characters. At the end of *Histoire d'Hypolite*, disguise is used to destabilize the very notion of sexual identity when the heroine, Julie, is forced to dress as Sylvio, a man traveling as a helpless pilgrim, to escape an aggressive and undesirable suitor. When a marquise falls in love with Sylvio, the jealous husband discovers his wife's affections and has the pilgrim arrested and tried, at which point the disguise is discovered. Later, however, as Julie is about to leave to be married to Hypolite, the marquise asks her to cross-dress once again:

"Don't refuse my request," she said, "give me one last time the sight of my conqueror in the same dress in which you caused my passion." Since she was alone, Julie was willing to comply with her desire; she put on her pilgrim's outfit and went to the marquise. No sooner did she catch sight of her than she felt like fainting. "Alas!," she cried, "I find my illness where I hoped to find a cure. Sylvio, adorable Sylvio, you now only have a place in my soul, for everything I can conceive of you is but a chimera that can neither flatter nor cure my pain." (*Hypolitus Earl of Douglas*, 255; translation modernized)

Although it is ultimately repressed, the deviance of the marquise's phantasm, Julie's willing compliance with it, and, especially, the insistence placed upon it in the text (this scene takes place two pages from the end, for instance) call into question a simplistic representation of heterosexuality and gendered identity.

In Aulnoy's fairy tales, it is through the common folkloric features of metamorphosis and transformation that sexual roles can be explored. In "L'Oranger et l'abeille" (The Orange Tree and the Bee), for instance, the heroine, Aimée, transforms herself into a bee, and the hero, Aimé, into a tree to escape an ogre. The reversal of gender roles through this metamorphosis becomes apparent when a princess, enamored with the anthropomorphic tree, tries to cut some of its flowers, for Aimée immediately reacts as would a knight defending his lady: "The vigilant Bee darted out, buzzing among the leaves where she kept watch, and stung the princess with such force that she thought she would faint" (*Les Contes des fées*, in *Nouveau Cabinet des fées* [hereafter cited as NCF], 3: 344).[2] Through these metamorphosed forms, the text also presents an erotic scene that flies in the face of the almost exclusively psychological description of love in seventeenth-century narrative forms. "You will find on my flowers a pleasant dew," says Aimé to the heroine, "and a liqueur sweeter than honey from which you can take nourishment. My leaves will be your bed of repose where spiders will not harm you." When Aimée responds to this invitation, she emphasizes the displaced nature of such pleasures: "You will see me fly around you incessantly, and you will know that the Orange Tree is no less dear to the Bee than Prince Aimé was to Princess Aimée." Finally, Aimée moves from words to action: "Indeed, she enclosed herself in one of the biggest flowers as if in a palace; and true tenderness that finds resources everywhere did not fail to acquire its own in this union'' (343).

While the activities of Aimée and Julie are, on the whole, exceptional moments in Aulnoy's thematics of love, a much more common feature is the centrality of the heroine. This is hardly an unusual trait in narrative fiction of the time, and especially in works of other contemporary women writers, but perhaps more uncommon are the ways that Aulnoy emphasizes the roles of her female characters. In her novels, the heroines are sometimes given a central role even when the hero's seems to be privileged. From the perspective of length, for instance, the titles *Jean de Bourbon* and *Le Comte de Warwick* turn out to be misnomers since the adventures of Casilde (*Jean de Bourbon*) and the countess of Devonshire (*Le Comte de Warwick*) occupy a greater part of the text than the adventures of the heroes. Similarly, in Aulnoy's *contes de fées*, the heroine's role is often highlighted just as much or even more than the hero's, and thus undermines the male-dominated plot of many fairy tales (in which an active hero pursues a passive heroine). "Finette-Cendron," for example, bears witness to just such a "feminization" of the plot. While combining the Tom Thumb and Cinderella folkloric motifs treated separately by Perrault, the hero of the first tale is transformed into the clever Finette who, unlike the despised heroine of the second one, becomes a resolutely active character. Over and beyond this valorization of heroines, Aulnoy makes an emphatic use of fairies (*fées*, who are always female), featuring them strikingly more often than Perrault does. Thus, contrary to his version of Tom Thumb ("Le Petit Poucet"), "Finette-Cendron" provides a fairy godmother for Finette and, in this way, further reinforces a heroine-dominated plot with a supernatural female presence. To be sure, "evil" fairies also appear in her tales, but even more frequent are the "good" fairies who protect and guide the (male and/or female) protagonist.

At the same time as representing the complexity of heterosexual relations and reaffirming the role of women in narrative, Aulnoy's writing also demonstrates how a female writing subject can be empowered by manipulating genre, setting, and history. By sometimes conforming to generic conventions but deviating from them at other times, Aulnoy maintains an ambivalent relation to the dominant literary aesthetic of her day. Her use of the genres of memoir, novel, and novella, for instance, is representative of a vast narrative production at the end of the seventeenth century, in which women writers (such as *Lafayette and *Villedieu) played an especially significant role. At the same time, however, Aulnoy combines certain elements of the "new" novel of the end of the century (limited length, historical characters and settings from a recent past, narrative claim to historical "truth") with others reminiscent of heroic novels of the period before 1660 (idealized, superlative characters; intricate plots with unusual catalysts, such as kidnappings, duels, false messages, nocturnal rendezvous; predominantly happy endings). Her fairy tales display a similar knowledge and admixture of generic boundaries, for they integrate motifs and structures from folklore with widely used conventions and *topoï* of the novel (such as the exchange of portraits, embedded letters and poems, extended, sentimental conversations between the heroic couple) and observe the period's cliché that all works should not only "please" but also "instruct" (*plaire et instruire*) by regularly including a versed moral at the end of the narrative.

Besides expanding the possibilities for writerly innovations, Aulnoy's conjunction of genres (folk or fairy tales with other narrative forms and the "new" with the heroic novel) creates a strategic juxtaposition of fictional and "real" worlds. This is, of course, most apparent in the fairy tales, whose marvellous setting is not only a transposition, but also a transformation, of discursive "reality." Reflecting a detailed knowledge of aristocratic pastimes, the references to courtly danses, games, or operas in "La Princesse Belle-Etoile et le Prince Chéri," "Le Prince Lutin," or "Le Serpentin vert" (The Green Serpent) glorify and idealize the elite classes of the time. Yet, the humor and irony with which she treats the supernatural in many of her tales can also be used to create a fictional alternative to an unjust "reality." When, with the help of a fairy, the hero in "La Grenouille bienfaisante" (The Benevolent Frog) goes to extraordinary lengths to liberate his wife from a dragon, the narrator pokes fun at both the remote, magical setting of the tale *and* certain men of Aulnoy's time: "A husband who follows this course of action to get his wife back is most certainly from the days of the Fairies, and his conduct is sufficient to reveal the time-setting of my tale" (*Les Contes nouveaux ou les fées à la mode*, NCF, 4: 334–35). That Aulnoy's humor is directed against unfaithful husbands is premised on a feigned belief in fairy-tale magic, but also suggests that the supernatural feats of the hero are the fulfillment of the woman writer's wish to reorder gender relations. By recourse to the marvellous setting of the fairy tale, Aulnoy is able to conceive of female protagonists who express and act on their sexual desires (Laidronnette/Discrète in "Le Serpentin vert" and Chatte Blanche in the tale named for her) and/or assume the active role normally reserved for heroes (Finette; Printanière in "La Princesse Printanière") as well as male characters who do not dominate and oppress women, but who are put in a position of activity that is equal—Torticoli in "Le Rameau d'or" (The Golden Bough)—or sometimes even inferior to that of the heroine—the prince in "Le Mouton" (The Sheep).

In her pseudo-memoirs, Aulnoy affirms the power of the female writing subject by depicting historical events, settings, and personages. Alongside much of the historiographically based factual information in her first-person *Mémoires de la cour d'Espagne*, *Relation du voyage d'Espagne*, and *Mémoires de la cour d'Angleterre*, Aulnoy also creates fictional characters and settings, exaggerates descriptive details, invents omniscient psychological analyses of historical figures, and gives real events spurious causes. In the *Relation du voyage d'Espagne* this idiosyncratic rewriting—if not questioning—of history is carried even further with the insertion of four digressions, which ambiguously resemble short novellas, at different points in the text. By means of these transmutations of history, Aulnoy's writerly "I" draws attention to its creative (because transgressive) force.

However, the oppositionality of Aulnoy's writing is not without its limits. Her textual self-empowerment is tempered by the not infrequent plagiarisms in the pseudo-memoirs. Furthermore, the "exotic" settings in these works can occasion Aulnoy's ethnocentrism: "Without doubt, if I were to tell you all the tragic events I learn every day, you would agree that this country is the stage for the most horrible scenes in the world" (*Relation du voyage d'Espagne*, 446), says the "I" in describing the inhabitants of a country where, as she puts it, "reason has hardly any control at all over emotions" (464–65). Likewise, in Aulnoy's fairy tales, males who are empowered by the marvellous sometimes inflict violence on women, as do the heroes in "Le Prince Marcassin" and "Le Dauphin," and/or repress female sexuality. In other tales, the explicit moral of the narrative reaffirms certain misogynistic clichés (e.g., the condemnation of female curiosity in the moral at the end of "Le Serpentin vert").

In the final analysis, however, the hegemonic aspects of Aulnoy's texts— aristocratic and heterosexual prejudice, ethnocentrism, suppression of female sexuality—are similar to those that beset all women writers of the period, who worked within a patriarchal culture. Although reflecting this conflicted position, Aulnoy's resisting treatment of love as a theme and her strategic manipulation of genres, settings, and history empower her to inscribe the desire of a woman to come to writing and to mark her texts as distinctive creations.

SURVEY OF CRITICISM

Judging from the republications, translations, and critical reception of her works, Aulnoy achieved great success from the beginning of her career. During her lifetime, however, it was especially her novels and memoirs that received public adulation. "We have not for a long time seen a book have as much success and be as enjoyable to read as *Les Mémoires d'Espagne*," proclaimed the *Mercure galant* in March 1692 (quoted in Storer, 22). Another contemporary noted in 1703: "Madame d'Aulnoy . . . wrote the *Mémoires de la cour d'Espagne* and the *Voyage d'Espagne*, and these curious and pleasing works were extremely satisfying to the public" (quoted in Storer, 39). Of her novels and memoirs, *Histoire d'Hypolite* and *Relation du Voyage d'Espagne* were the most popular, based on re-editions and translations, with this first work being republished thirty-seven times. While Aulnoy's fairy tales were also well received at the time of their publication, it was not until the nineteenth century that they eclipsed her novels and memoirs in popularity. Concomitant with this privileging of her fairy tales, however, was what might be termed a "decanonization." Whereas during the eighteenth century most critics portrayed her fairy tales in a very positive light (some even preferred them to Perrault's), beginning in the nineteenth century it became a commonplace to assert their ultimate inferiority to Perrault's (and to neglect her other writings). "If you want to grasp the poetic value of Perrault's tales, compare them to the other collections of fairy tales composed in our country, best of all, for example, Mme d'Aulnoy's," declared one nineteenth-century critic, only to continue with a comparison that identifies Aulnoy with an allegedly inferior fabulist: "Reading a tale by Mme d'Aulnoy after a tale by Perrault is like reading a fable by Florian after a fable by La Fontaine" (Montégut, "Des Fées . . . ," 663). Yet, even if devalorized, Aulnoy was never completely forgotten, unlike many women writers of this period and others.

Only in the twentieth century, however, have Aulnoy's text—novels, memoirs, and fairy tales—received extensive critical attention. A definitive biography of her life and bibliography of her works was not published until 1926 with Foulché-Delbosc's "Madame d'Aulnoy et l'Espagne," which was supplemented by Roche-Mazon's *En Marge de l'Oiseau bleu* (1930), an account of the writer's supposed plot against her husband. Aulnoy's works have been of interest to a wide variety of scholars: her novels and memoirs have been examined in large measure by specialists of Spanish and English literature, while experts of French literature have concentrated almost exclusively on her fairy tales. Among her novels and memoirs, it is the *Relation du voyage d'Espagne* that has provoked the most critical scrutiny as a (possible) testimony of seventeenth-century Spanish life (Foulché-Delbosc; Maura Gamazo). Even before its consideration as a primary historical source, however, critics such as Taine praised its stylistic qualities (although not without a sexist bias): "It is well written; Mme d'Aulnoy belongs to the literary *Grand Siècle* . . . she speaks correctly and naturally . . . she has all the qualities of a talented and well-mannered French woman—good sense, a spontaneous wit, an assured tact, a slightly mocking grace, a constant and leisurely politeness" (Taine, 1). The studies devoted to Aulnoy's novels and/or memoirs by Wenke-Streckenbach (1931), Beeler (1964), and Palmer (1971) demonstrate that her texts rewrite Cervantes, La Fontaine, and extant histories of England, France, and Spain, and include her in the seventeenth-century female literary tradition best represented by Villedieu and Lafayette.

By far the greatest number of studies on Aulnoy's writings have been devoted to her fairy tales. The first monograph on the *contes de fées* was Krüger's *Die Märchen der Baronin Aulnoy* (1914), which opened a panoply of questions pursued by subsequent scholars: the relation of the tales to seventeenth-century literary history (Storer, 1928; Robert, 1982), their treatment of folkloric sources (Robert), their use of thematic elements (Mitchell, 1978; Robert) and stylistic elements (Di Scanno, 1975). While all of these provide useful perspectives on Aulnoy's *contes*, Robert's rigorous study is especially important since it complements these divergent critical approaches with structural and sociological analyses to show the specificity of Aulnoy's narratives in these different contexts and in the broader production of fairy tales in the seventeenth and eighteenth centuries. Of the several recent studies that have explored the fairy tales in terms of ego psychology (Hubert, "Le Sens du voyage dans quelques contes de Madame d'Aulnoy," 1973; Sterckx, 1981; and DeGraff, 1984), DeGraff's is the most thorough and suggestive in its analyses of the self-development of several protagonists. Finally, of the few articles informed by feminist criticism, Farrell's "Celebration and Repression of Feminine Desire in Mme d'Aulnoy's Fairy Tale: *La Chatte Blanche*" (1989) is the most thought-provoking since it builds on Robert's analyses to examine the representation of female sexuality and to highlight the tensions of class and gender that result from Aulnoy's rendering of the genre.

While Aulnoy's works continue to be studied by a relatively small number of scholars, a far greater number of children read or are read her fairy tales. Indeed, of all of Aulnoy's texts, currently the most readily available are several of her *contes de fées* included in children's anthologies. Yet, given that these, like her other texts, were originally intended for adult readers and that they treat many themes of interest to feminism and to current literary studies, surely the time has come to save the body of Aulnoy's writing from oblivion. Just as the narrator in "La Chatte Blanche" preserves the storytelling of the tale's heroine to counteract the negligence of her secretary, "who was an old cat, [and who] wrote so poorly, that even though her works have been preserved, it is impossible to read them" (*Les Contes nouveaux ou les fées à la mode*, NCF, 4: 467), so too we can retrieve Aulnoy's texts by republishing and (re)reading them. So doing, we could capitalize on the ambivalent uses of sex roles, settings, and history in Aulnoy's works to further reflect on how gender differences are constructed and what differences they make in writing and society at large.

NOTES

1. The *conteuses* (female storytellers) included, besides Aulnoy, Catherine Bernard, Louise d'Auneuil, Catherine Durand, Charlotte-Rose de La Force, Marie-Jeanne Lhéritier de Villandon, and Henriette-Julie de Murat, and they wrote two-thirds of all of the fairy tales published during this "vogue." The male fairy-tale writers (or *conteurs*) at this time were l'abbé de Choisy, François de la Mothe-Fénelon, Eustache Le Noble, Paul-François Nodot, le chevalier de Mailly, Jean de Préchac, and Charles Perrault.

2. Unless otherwise noted, all translations are my own.

BIBLIOGRAPHY

Works by Mme d'Aulnoy

Histoire d'Hypolite, Comte de Duglas. 1690. Geneva: Slatkine Reprints, 1979.
Mémoires de la cour d'Espagne. 2 vols. Paris: Claude Barbin, 1690.
Relation du voyage d'Espagne. 3 vols. The Hague: Bulderen, 1691.
Sentiments d'une âme pénitente. Paris, 1691.
Le Retour d'une âme à Dieu. Paris, 1692.
Histoire de Jean de Bourbon, Prince de Carency. 3 vols. Paris: Claude Barbin, 1692.
Nouvelles Espagnolles. Par Madame D***. 2 vols. Paris: Claude Barbin, 1692.
Nouvelles ou Mémoires Historiques. Contenant ce qui s'est passé de plus remarquable

dans l'Europe, tant aux Guerres, prises de Places, & Batailles sur terre & sur mer, qu'aux divers interests des Princes & souverains qui ont agy depuis 1672, jusqu'en 1679. Par Madame D***. 2 vols. Paris: Claude Barbin, 1693.

*Mémoires de la Cour d'Angleterre. Par Madame D. . . . 2 vols. Paris: Claude Barbin, 1695.

Les Contes de fées. 4 vols. Paris, 1697–1698. Rpt. in vols. 3 and 4 of *Nouveau Cabinet des fées.* 18 vols. Geneva: Slatkine Reprints, 1978. Partial rpt. of *Le Cabinet des fées; ou collection choisie des contes des fées, et autres contes merveilleux.* 41 vols. Amsterdam, 1785–1786; Paris, 1788.

Contes nouveaux ou les fées à la mode. 4 vols. Paris: Veuve de Théodore Girard, 1698. Rpt. in vols. 4 and 5 of *Nouveau Cabinet des fées.* 18 vols. Geneva: Slatkine Reprints, 1978. Partial rpt. of *Le Cabinet des fées; ou collection choisie des contes des fées, et autres contes merveilleux.* 41 vols. Amsterdam, 1785–1786; Paris, 1788.

Le Comte de Warwick. Par Madame d'Aulnoy. Paris: Compagnie des Libraires Associez, 1703.

Modern Editions

Relations du voyage d'Espagne. Ed. R. Foulché-Delbosc. Paris: Klincksieck, 1926.

Translations of Mme d'Aulnoy

Hypolitus Earl of Douglas. 1708. Intro. Josephine Grieder. New York: Garland, 1973.
Memoirs of the Court of Spain. 1692. Wing English Books 1641–1700 (Microfilm, 80:5).
Travels into Spain: Being the Ingenious and Diverting Letters of the Lady ****. 1715. Intro. R. Foulché-Delbosc. New York: McBride, 1930.
The Prince of Carency. 1719. Intro. Josephine Grieder. New York: Garland, 1973.
Memoirs of the Court of England in 1675. Ed. George Gilbert. Trans. Lucretia Arthur. London: Routledge; New York: Dutton, 1913.
The Tales of the Fairies in Three Parts, Compleat. 1715. Intro. Michael Hearn. New York: Garland, 1977.
Beauties, Beasts and Enchantment: Classic French Fairy Tales. Ed. Jack Zipes. New York: NAL-Penguin, 1989.

Studies of Mme d'Aulnoy

Barchilon, Jacques. "Madame d'Aulnoy, reine dans la féerie." In *Le Conte merveilleux français de 1690 à 1790. Cent ans de féerie et de poésie ignorées de l'histoire littéraire.* Paris: Honoré Champion, 1975.
Beeler, James R. "Madame d'Aulnoy, Historical Novelist of the Late Seventeenth Century." Diss., University of North Carolina, Chapel Hill, 1964.
DeGraff, Amy Vanderlyn. *The Tower and the Well: A Psychological Interpretation of the Fairy Tales of Madame d'Aulnoy.* Birmingham, Ala.: Summa Publications, 1984.
Di Scanno, Teresa. *Les Contes de fées à l'époque classique (1680–1715).* Naples: Liguori Editore, 1975.

Farrell, Michèle. "Celebration and Repression of Feminine Desire in Mme d'Aulnoy's Fairy Tale: *La Chatte Blanche.*" *L'Esprit Créateur* 29, no. 3 (Fall 1989): 52–64.

Foulché-Delbosc, R. "Madame d'Aulnoy et l'Espagne." *Revue hispanique* 67 (1926): 1–152. Rpt. in *Relation du voyage d'Espagne*, by Madame d'Aulnoy. Ed. R. Foulché-Delbosc. Paris: Klincksieck, 1926.

Hubert, Renée Riese. "L'Amour et la féerie chez Madame d'Aulnoy." *Romanische Forschungen* 75 (1963): 1–10.

———. "Poetic Humor in Madame d'Aulnoy's Fairy Tales." *L'Esprit créateur* 3, no. 2 (Fall 1963): 123–29.

———. "Le Sens du voyage dans quelques contes de Madame d'Aulnoy." *French Review* 46 (April 1973): 931–37.

Krüger, Kurt. *Die Märchen der Baronin Aulnoy.* Leisnig: Ulrich, 1914.

Maura Gamazo, Gabriel. *Fantasias y realidades del viaje a Madrid de la condesa d'Aulnoy. Criticado historicamenta por Ag. Gonzàlez de Amezua.* Madrid: Ed. "Saturnina Calleja," 1944.

Mitchell, Jane Tucker. *A Thematic Analysis of Mme d'Aulnoy's Fairy Tales.* University, Miss.: Romance Monographs, 1978.

Montégut, Emile. "Des Fées et de leur littérature en France." *Revue des deux mondes* (April 1, 1862): 648–75.

Palmer, Melvin D. "Madame d'Aulnoy in England." *Comparative Literature* 27 (1975): 237–53.

———. "Madame d'Aulnoy's Pseudo-Autobiographical Works on Spain." *Romanische Forschungen* 83 (1971): 220–29.

Robert, Raymonde. *Le Conte de fées littéraire en France de la fin du XVIIe à la fin du XVIIIe siècle.* Nancy: Presses Universitaires de Nancy, 1982.

Roche-Mazon, Jeanne. *En marge de "l'oiseau bleu."* Paris: L'Artisan du Livre, 1930. (Rpt. as "Madame d'Aulnoy et son mari," in *Autour des contes de fées.* Paris: Didier, 1968, 95–150.)

———. "Le *Voyage d'Espagne* de Madame d'Aulnoy." In *Autour des contes de fées.* Paris: Didier, 1968, 7–20.

Sterckx, Christiane. "Le Passage au stage adulte dans cinq contes de Madame d'Aulnoy." In *Recherches sur le conte merveilleux.* Ed. Georges Jacques. Louvain-la-Neuve: Université Catholique de Louvain, 1981.

Storer, Mary Elizabeth. *Un Episode littéraire de la fin du XVIIe siécle. La Mode des contes de fées (1685–1700).* 1928. Geneva: Slatkine Reprints, 1972.

Taine, Hippolyte. "Madame d'Aulnoy, *Voyage en Espagne.*" In *Dernier essais de critique et d'histoire.* 6th ed. Paris: Hachette, 1923. 1–57.

Welch, Marcelle Maistre. "Le Devenir de la jeune fille dans les contes de fées de Madame d'Aulnoy." *Cahiers du Dix-septième: An Interdisciplinary Journal* 1, no. 1 (Spring 1987): 53–62.

Wenke-Streckenbach, Maria. "Madame d'Aulnoy, ihre Novellen und Romane." *Romanische Forschungen* 45 (1931): 145–256.

SIMONE DE BEAUVOIR (1908–1986)

Yolanda Astarita Patterson

BIOGRAPHY

Simone Lucie Ernestine Marie Bertrand de Beauvoir was born on January 9, 1908, at 103, Boulevard du Montparnasse. All of her subsequent addresses in Paris throughout her life were within a very small radius of this building, whose livingroom windows looked out on the Boulevard Raspail. Her mother, Françoise Brasseur de Beauvoir (1885–1963), was an attractive and devout provincial from Verdun whose happiest childhood years were those spent attending a small convent school. Her father, Georges de Beauvoir (1878–1941), was a lawyer by profession, a bon vivant who enjoyed acting in amateur theatrical productions, and an agnostic. The adult Simone later attributed her independence of spirit to the dichotomy of beliefs represented by her parents as she was growing up.

Simone's sister Hélène, nicknamed ''Poupette'' by the family, was born on June 9, 1910. The author asserts in her autobiography that having a sibling taught her how to communicate. She enjoyed teaching Poupette everything she herself was learning at her private Catholic school, the Cours Adéline Désir, and decided at an early age that she would much prefer teaching to the routine domesticity in which she saw her mother enmeshed. When family finances dwindled as a result of World War I, Françoise de Beauvoir was obliged to take on household chores that had previously been performed by servants. The repetitiveness and dullness of these chores did not escape the eye of the young Simone, who had no regrets when told that there was no family money for dowries but rather welcomed the opportunity to pursue a career outside of the home.

With her best friend and classmate Zaza ''Mabille'' Lacoin, the adolescent Beauvoir discussed the relative merits of bringing nine children into the world, as Zaza's mother had done, and of writing books, which Simone considered an infinitely more valuable type of creativity. Zaza's mother came to represent for

Simone the manipulative, guilt-producing approach to motherhood that she associated with the socially conventional bourgeoisie, and undoubtedly had much to do with Beauvoir's predominantly negative pronouncements about maternity in *Le Deuxième Sexe (The Second Sex)* and elsewhere.

A major trauma in the young Simone's life occurred when, at age fifteen, she lost her faith in the existence of God and in the validity of the Catholic religion in which the devout Françoise de Beauvoir had conscientiously raised her two daughters. It was several years before she could bring herself to admit her loss of faith to her mother, an admission that wedged a barrier between them that was not removed until the final weeks of the latter's life, and then only partially so. Simone de Beauvoir was very much aware of the gap left in her life by her loss of religious faith and sensed that she had sought in literature, in her own writing, in her relationship with Jean-Paul Sartre, and even in bar-hopping the kind of mystical communion she had once found in the Catholic Church.

First through her father and then through her cousin Jacques "Laiguillon" Champigneulles, Simone de Beauvoir was introduced to the world of literature. Jacques lent her books by such authors as Alain-Fournier, Jean Cocteau, Henry de Montherlant, Maurice Barrès, Paul Claudel, André Gide, and Paul Valéry. Grateful to him for revealing a whole new realm of existence to her, Beauvoir intermittently believed herself to be in love with her cousin and at times was convinced that marrying him would solve all of the problems that had emerged during her adolescence between her and her parents and would recreate the comfortable, affectionate family atmosphere of her childhood. Cousin Jacques, however, was interested in the pursuit of a secure financial future. When Simone learned that he had decided to marry the sister of one of his wealthy friends, she was disillusioned about this bohemian hero of her teenage years who had turned out to be a far cry from the Grand Meaulnes of Alain-Fournier's fanciful story, with whom the Beauvoir sisters had frequently compared him.

After receiving two baccalaureate degrees, Simone de Beauvoir went on to study philosophy at the Sorbonne. Her research, conducted under Léon Brunschvicg, focused on German philosopher Gottfried Wilhelm von Leibniz. At the Sorbonne she was befriended by a married classmate, René Maheu (André Herbaud in the memoirs), who was later to become director of UNESCO. Noting the similarity between the family name "Beauvoir" and the English word "beaver," as well as his friend's conscientious approach to her studies and to life in general, Maheu assigned the nickname "Castor," the French word for "beaver," to Simone de Beauvoir, and "Castor" she remained for the rest of her life to her most intimate friends. One night Beauvoir was invited by Maheu to join a study group that included a fellow student of formidable reputation, Jean-Paul Sartre. When the results of the 1929 examinations for the *agrégation* in philosophy were posted, Sartre's name headed the list and Simone de Beauvoir was in second place. She was the youngest person ever to receive the *agrégation* in philosophy. The juxtaposition of her name and Sartre's on the list of successful candidates for that degree was the first official record of an association that was to last for over fifty years.

Beauvoir's joy in her academic successes and in having found a soulmate with whom to share her life was mitigated by the untimely death of her friend Zaza, whose romantic attachment to future philosopher Maurice Merleau-Ponty (Jean Pradelle in the memoirs) was aggresively discouraged by her family once they discovered that Merleau-Ponty was an illegitimate child. Zaza, who had remained a devout Catholic and was deeply attached to her mother, agonized over whether she should satisfy her own desires or remain obedient to her mother and to the family's somewhat skewed interpretation of God's will. She suddenly developed a high fever and within three days she was dead, consoling her mother on her deathbed by assuring her that every family must have its black sheep and that she was the black sheep of the Lacoin clan. Undoubtedly experiencing considerable guilt because her attentions were centered on Sartre rather than on Zaza during this final year of her friend's life, Beauvoir remained convinced that Zaza had been "assassinated" by bourgeois morality and spent the rest of her life rebelling against the milieu in which the two classmates had been raised.

Shortly after they had become intimately involved in one another's lives, Beauvoir and Jean-Paul Sartre worked out their famous "pact," distinguishing their own "essential" love from the "contingent loves" that each must retain the freedom to pursue in the interest of exploring all of the possibilities life had to offer them. When Beauvoir, assigned to a *lycée* teaching position in Marseille while Sartre was assigned to Le Havre, was disturbed at the prospect of being separated from him by the whole length of France, Sartre suggested that they marry in order to take advantage of a double assignment. Beauvoir declares that she never for a moment gave serious thought to this proposal, knowing that marriage would be an unwelcome imprisonment for Sartre and convinced by the example of her parents that bourgeois marriage was an "unnatural institution." The only reason for a couple to marry, in her opinion, was a desire to see a reproduction of themselves in the children they might have, a desire neither she nor Sartre experienced, she hastens to assure her readers.

Named to a *lycée* in Rouen after a year of teaching in Marseille, Beauvoir developed a friendship with the bright and capricious Olga Kosakievicz, a student in her philosophy class. Olga's youth and unpredictability attracted both Sartre and Beauvoir, who attempted to form a viable trio with her and to partake of her youthfulness as they both approached the dreaded age of thirty, which signified an unwelcome plunge into adult maturity for them. The convoluted emotions aroused by this experiment in unconventional relationships provided the inspiration for Sartre's character Ivich in his novel series *Les Chemins de la liberté* (*The Roads to Freedom*) and for Beauvoir's Xavière Pagès in *L'Invitée* (*She Came to Stay*), her first published work.

While teaching in Rouen, Simone de Beauvoir incurred the wrath of the local authorities when she pointed out to her students that giving birth should not be considered a woman's sole destiny. Eventually both she and Sartre were named to *lycées* in Paris, she to the Lycée Molière and he to the Lycée Pasteur. They chose to live separately, sometimes in different rooms in the same hotel, and Beauvoir felt that this arrangement gave them all of the benefits of communal life with none of its disadvantages.

In 1939, Beauvoir found herself plunged into the historical drama exploding all around her as Hitler continued his relentless marches and World War II became inevitable. She remained in Paris, teaching and worrying, as Sartre was drafted and then taken prisoner. When in 1943 the mother of her student Nathalie Sorokine (Lise in the memoirs) accused her of corrupting a minor, Beauvoir was temporarily suspended from her teaching position and forced to pursue a brief career in radio. After Sartre's release from prison camp, he and Beauvoir participated in the Parisian Resistance network, collaborating on the writing and distribution of clandestine pamphlets and newspapers. They were advised by Albert Camus, editor of the underground paper *Combat*, to go into hiding in July 1944 after one of the members of their Resistance group had been arrested.

Beauvoir considered Liberation Day in August 1944 one of the most exhilarating moments of her life. Before her lay a world wide open and waiting to be claimed by the group of forward-minded intellectuals of which she was a part. She was now a published novelist and a founding member of the left-wing journal *Les Temps Modernes*, whose title had been inspired by the popular Charlie Chaplin film *Modern Times*. With the war behind her, she was free to travel, first to Portugal to visit her sister and brother-in-law, then on a lecture tour to America, where she began a four-year liaison with Chicago author Nelson Algren. Along with Claude Lanzmann, a Jewish journalist seventeen years younger than she whom she met through *Les Temps Modernes*, Algren was an extremely significant "contingent love" in Beauvoir's life, and even asked her to marry him in 1948. It was as much her conviction that she would totally lack inspiration for her writing in Chicago as her commitment to Sartre that made her turn him down.

"One is not born a woman, one becomes one," proclaims the opening sentence of the fourth section of *Le Deuxième Sexe*. In the late 1940s, Beauvoir was ready to begin writing her autobiography when she realized that she first needed to examine the degree to which having been born female had influenced the course of her life. After months spent in the Bibliothèque Nationale researching the history, biology, mythology, and literature associated with women, she published her seminal work *Le Deuxième Sexe* in 1949. Translated into more than a dozen languages, the text provided the inspiration for such American feminists as Betty Friedan and Kate Millett.

Beauvoir's talent as a writer of fiction was recognized in 1954 when she was awarded the prestigious Prix Goncourt for *Les Mandarins* (*The Mandarins*), a story of the hopes and frustrations of the postwar intellectuals in France. The book is commonly considered, despite the author's protests to the contrary, a roman à clef, with the main characters representing Camus, Sartre, and Beauvoir.

Critical of Beauvoir's attacks on marriage and maternity, the Catholic Church placed both *Le Deuxième Sexe* and *Les Mandarins* on the Index in 1956.

Beginning in 1958 with the publication of *Mémoires d'une jeune fille rangée* (*Memoirs of a Dutiful Daughter*), Simone de Beauvoir produced six autobiographical works. Three more fictional works, *Les Belles Images* (published under the same title in English translation), *La Femme rompue* (*The Woman Destroyed*), and early short stories entitled *Quand prime le spirituel* (*When Things of the Spirit Come First*), as well as a companion piece to *Le Deuxième Sexe* focusing on old age (*La Vieillesse* [*The Coming of Age*]) and numerous prefaces, articles, and interviews all contribute to the long list of publications associated with the name of Simone de Beauvoir at the time of her death on April 14, 1986. Although she did not consider herself a feminist at the time she wrote *Le Deuxième Sexe*, Beauvoir was extremely active in promoting and supporting feminist causes in France and abroad from 1970 until her death. Her decision to adopt Sylvie Le Bon, a *lycée* philosphy teacher whom she had first met in 1960 and who became her companion and confidante during the final decades of her life, meant that she left behind her a member of the younger generation who would keep a conscientious watch over her manuscripts and her intellectual legacy.

MAJOR THEMES

One of the major themes in the works of Simone de Beauvoir is, not surprisingly, the role of woman in twentieth-century society. From her earliest short stories to the interviews granted just a few months before her death, she pointed out through fiction, autobiography, and carefully documented essays the need for women to maintain their autonomy and to make full use of their talents. The adolescent Marguerite in the final story of *Quand prime le spirituel* sees the world as a bright new coin just waiting for her to pick it up. Françoise Miquel chooses herself and her own interests over those of her capricious and self-centered young rival Xavière when she turns on the gas and leaves Xavière to die at the end of *L'Invitée*. Hélène Bertrand emerges from the cocoon she has built around herself to take an active part in the Resistance movement in *Le Sang des autres* (*The Blood of Others*). Despite the close relationships both Françoise and Hélène have to their male companions in Beauvoir's early novels, these two protagonists and Marguerite are fictional forerunners of the liberated woman described by the author in the final section of *Le Deuxième Sexe*.

In *Le Deuxième Sexe*, Simone de Beauvoir articulated themes that have since become the focus of feminist literature and criticism. Presenting woman as myth, woman as the other, she documented her ideas and her theories with extensive references to literary, historical, and scientific sources. Although some of the scientific references are now dated, the sheer weight of her evidence and brilliance of her arguments could not fail to have an enormous influence on generations of readers, both male and female.

Beauvoir had observed the negative results of limiting a woman's life to family and home in her own mother, who resented the chores foisted upon her by the change in family fortunes brought about by World War I and who vented her frustrations by investing herself totally in her growing daughters. Deploring the fact that the bourgeois society of the early twentieth century did not allow married women the option of working outside the home as she looked back on her own embattled adolescence in *Une Mort très douce* (*A Very Easy Death*), Beauvoir was convinced of the importance of careers and paying jobs in facilitating independence and autonomy for women. She encouraged women to take a long, hard look at marriage and motherhood before devoting all of their energies to these traditional roles so likely to drain them of the time and strength to develop other interests in their lives; she participated actively in the battle to make contraception and abortion readily available in France.

Throughout her fictional works Beauvoir championed movement away from the hearth and toward involvement in the world beyond the family. In the 1960s her novels and short stories documented the devastating consequences of cutting oneself off from these larger areas of concern. Laurence, in *Les Belles Images*, is a wife, mother, and successful career woman sensitive to the problems of poverty and hunger. She has nonetheless attempted to insulate herself from the darker side of the world around her by avoiding reading newspapers or listening to news reports on television, leaving it to her husband to interpret current events for her. Forced to face these issues by her impressionable ten-year-old daughter, she retreats into anorexia, yet recuperates sufficiently in the final scene of the novel to promise herself that she will raise her two daughters very differently from the way in which she and her sister were raised. ''L'Age de discrétion'' (The Age of Discretion), the first story of *La Femme rompue*, chronicles a retired professor's disappointment and total loss of perspective when her newly married son decides to abandon the academic life for which she has carefully groomed him for a more lucrative position in the business world. The reader is plunged into the loneliness and neurotic frenzy of the manipulative Murielle in ''Monologue.'' It is gradually revealed that Murielle is psychologically responsible for the suicide of her teenage daughter. She is frantically and unsuccessfully trying to redeem herself in the eyes of society by forcing her ex-husband and son to move back in with her. In the title story, which was dramatized on French television with Malka Ribowska playing Monique, narrator and reader painfully observe the despair of a forty-three-year-old matron hitherto secure in her domestic role who discovers that her husband has taken up with a somewhat younger and more vivacious divorcée. Monique suddenly finds herself with no purpose in life now that her two daughters are grown and have moved away from the Paris apartment that has been the center of her universe.

Closely tied to Beauvoir's analysis of ''the second sex'' is a severely critical analysis of traditional bourgeois society. It seems quite clear that in the author's eyes it is the expectations and limitations imposed by the middle class that have restricted women to repetitive and stultifying roles in life. Convinced by her observation of members of her own family and especially by the tragedy of Zaza

Lacoin's premature death that conformity to social convention can be quite literally fatal to the vitality and development of a mature and autonomous young woman, Beauvoir strove throughout her life to distance herself from the bourgeois milieu in which she had been raised and to highlight its foibles and follies for her readers.

Although at first Beauvoir and Sartre resisted the label "existentialist," which was affixed by the public to everything they said and wrote, both eventually attempted to explain the tenets of this postwar philosophy to the public. In *Pour une morale de l'ambiguïté*, (*The Ethics of Ambiguity*), Beauvoir defines existentialism as a philosophy of ambiguity that forces human beings both to live in the present and to act with an eye to their own mortality. The four essays that make up *L'Existentialisme et la sagesse des nations* (*Existentialism and the Wisdom of the Ages*) defend existentialism from accusations of gratuitousness and frivolity and emphasize the optimism of a philosophy which gives individuals full control of their destinies through the choices they make throughout their lives. In Beauvoir's writings the importance of making one's own choices is emphasized again and again as her characters approach adulthood, the war, the frustrations of the postwar intelligentsia, politics, old age, and death. Acting in bad faith is condemned, and the Other becomes a haunting and omnipresent judgmental eye.

Once her belief in God and in a life after death had been lost, death became an important theme and even what some critics have labeled an obsession in Beauvoir's writing. Her 1947 novel *Tous les hommes sont mortels* (*All Men Are Mortal*) was a valiant attempt to prove to both her readers and herself that human mortality was essentially desirable because life and its challenges would have no meaning without it. Taken along by her mother on a condolence visit to the Beauvoirs' former maid, Louise, when she was still quite young, the adult Simone never forgot the trauma of confronting the reality of the death of Louise's newborn baby. From that tragedy, transposed into fiction in *Le Sang des autres* and recounted again in *Mémoires d'une jeune fille rangée*, to the devastation of Sartre's death in 1980, Beauvoir's works focus again and again on the passage from energetic involvement in this world to the nothingness she and Sartre agreed was all that one could anticipate beyond human mortality. The death of Zaza Lacoin was the motivating force behind many of Beauvoir's early attempts at fiction. Her mother's death prompted what is considered by many critics to be her finest work, *Une Mort très douce*. The loss of Sartre led to the cathartic review of every detail of the last ten years of his life that makes up the pages of *La Cérémonie des adieux* (*Adieux: A Farewell to Sartre*).

Beauvoir's politics were consistently left-wing and inspired by Marxist ideals. Given the choice between the USSR and the United States, she always opted for the former, condemning the latter's capitalist ideology. She strongly supported the war for Algerian independence and was appalled by the tales of torture that came out of it. She never hesitated to defend the freedom of the downtrodden, writing prefaces, speaking out in interviews, and often appearing in court to lend her prestige to causes she considered worthy of her efforts. In *Le Sang des autres*, she explored the theme later taken up by Sartre in his play *Les Mains sales* (*Dirty Hands*), the degree to which one can keep one's hands "clean" and still participate meaningfully in contemporary political life. Her only play, *Les Bouches inutiles* (*Who Shall Die?*), again raised the issue of action and responsibility through Jean-Pierre Gauthier, who, like Jean Blomart in *Le Sang des autres*, hesitates to assume an active role in the political decisions of his community because of his fear of the consequences of his involvement. The whole question of the value of human activity was one which was evidently very much on Beauvoir's mind during the 1940s and which she explored from a philosophical point of view in her 1944 essay *Pyrrhus et Cinéas* (Pyrrhus and Cineas). *Les Temps Modernes* was conceived immediately after World War II as an effective way of publishing immediate reactions to contemporary events and remaining constantly involved in the political activities of the postwar era.

The act of writing was an essential element in Beauvoir's life and a dominant concern in her works. When she was an adolescent, she proclaimed her ambition to become a famous writer. She admits in her autobiography that she always felt guilty if a day passed when she had not written something. Her goal was to share her life and her ideas with her readers, yet she also used her writing as a catharsis, expurgating the frustrations of the trio formed with Sartre and Olga in her first novel, *L'Invitée*, the paradoxes of postwar France for the intellectuals in *Les Mandarins*, the desolation she felt at the loss first of her mother and then of Sartre in *Une Mort très douce* and *La Cérémonie des adieux*.

Beauvoir's travels occupy many pages of her autobiography and are often transposed in her fictional works. As a child, she developed a profound love of nature during the summers spent at Meyrignac and La Grillère, the homes of her father's relatives in the Limousin area. When she was teaching in Marseille, her free time was used to hike through the countryside. Once she had the time and the funds to travel to other countries, she was impressed both by their natural beauty and by the pulsating life of their big cities. She and Sartre pooled their meager funds in order to travel throughout France and to Spain (1931), Morocco (1932), London (1933), Italy (1933), Germany, Austria and Czechoslovakia (1934), Switzerland (1935), Belgium (1936), and Greece (1937). Immediately after the war, she joined her sister and brother-in-law in Portugal (1945). After spending four months in 1947 lecturing on college campuses in the United States, she recorded her sometimes naive impressions through a series of journal entries in *L'Amérique au jour le jour* (*America Day by Day*). *La Longue Marche* (*The Long March*) is a similar account of her impressions of a trip to China in 1955. Once they became well-known writers, she and Sartre received invitations to travel all over the world. During the 1960s, they made official trips to Cuba (1960), Brazil (1960), the USSR (1962–1966), Japan (1966), Egypt (1967), and Israel (1967). Beauvoir's memoirs record in considerable detail reactions to both the cultural and the political atmospheres of these countries.

A dominant theme in Simone de Beauvoir's writing is her long-lasting relationship with Jean-Paul Sartre. Her memoirs provide one of the most complete sources of information on Sartre's life beyond the early years he himself described in his autobiography *Les Mots* (*Words*). From her immediate fascination with his brilliant mind and his intellectual generosity at the Sorbonne to her wrenching observations of his physical and mental decline, Beauvoir followed Sartre's philosophical, political, and personal evolution with empathy and solidarity. Sometimes criticized by contemporary feminists for her total investment in her relationship with Sartre, Beauvoir repeatedly pointed out the extent to which theirs was an intellectual partnership in which each discussed and commented upon the other's ideas, manuscripts, and projects. It was, in fact, Sartre who encouraged her to return to her writing and her professional ambitions when the euphoria of their early years together made her temporarily content to accept a subordinate role in their relationship and to seek fulfillment through his achievements rather than through her own.

SURVEY OF CRITICISM

When *Le Deuxième Sexe* was first published in France in 1949, Simone de Beauvoir was taken aback by the acrimony of some of the impassioned attacks on her ideas and, indeed, on her person. In *La Force des choses*, she catalogues correspondence signed by persons identifying themselves as members of "the first sex" and accusing her of being everything from frigid to a nymphomaniac. At the same time, she was extremely gratified by letters from women indicating that her book had addressed concerns that they themselves had been afraid or unable to articulate.

The first full-length books dealing with Beauvoir's work began to appear in the late 1950s in France. Hélène Nahas included detailed references to Beauvoir's early fiction seen in the light of the theories expounded in Sartre's *L'Étre et le néant (Being and Nothingness)* and in *Le Deuxième Sexe* in her 1957 analysis of the woman in existential literature. In her 1959 study of Beauvoir, Geneviève Gennari treated such themes as responsibility, the temptation of indifference, love, death, and the female characters in the fictional works. Georges Hourdin, a devout Catholic and a close friend of Zaza Lacoin's uncle, chose as the focus of his 1962 book the author's conception of freedom. His final chapter labeled Beauvoir and Sartre "God's orphans."

A number of books dealing with Beauvoir were published in France in 1966. Philosopher Maurice Merleau-Ponty devoted a chapter of *Sens et non-sens* (*Sense and Non-Sense*) to the metaphysical aspects of *L'Invitée*, concentrating on the themes of freedom and alterity. Francis Jeanson began his study by avowing that only Jean-Paul Sartre could really do justice to its subject, Simone de Beauvoir or the enterprise of living. Highlighting Beauvoir's complete involvement in the world around her, Jeanson included in his book two lengthy interviews he conducted in November 1965, which add valuable information to his presentation of Beauvoir and her ideas. Serge Julienne-Caffié's biography of Beauvoir contains dialogues with Madeleine Chapsal and Madeleine Gobeil, the latter focusing on Beauvoir's comments about the influence of English literature on her writing. Suzanne Lilar attacked many of the ideas presented in *Le Deuxième Sexe* in her 1970 analysis entitled *Le Malentendu du "Deuxième Sexe."*

Beauvoir's refusal of indifference is the focal point for Laurent Gagnebin's 1968 study, which contains a preface written by Beauvoir. Annie-Claire Jaccard provides a detailed and highly philosophical textual analysis of Beauvoir's characters in another book that appeared in 1968, while Anne-Marie Lasocki echoes Jeanson's earlier title in her 1971 study of Simone de Beauvoir and the enterprise of writing. A biographical approach to Beauvoir's ideas informed by the four volumes of her memoirs can be found in Madeleine Descubes's 1974 book entitled *Connaître Simone de Beauvoir* (Knowing Simone de Beauvoir).

In 1979, Claude Francis and Fernande Gontier made a significant contribution to Beauvoir scholarship with their careful documentation of the author's life and works, which contains chronological details and unpublished texts not readily available elsewhere. Alice Schwarzer's collection of six interviews held between 1972 and 1982 supplies valuable testimony to the evolution of the author's ideas in this critical period when feminism was becoming a major influence on Western mentality. This evolution is the subject of Jacques J. Zéphir's 1982 study, *Le Néo-Féminisme de Simone de Beauvoir* (Simone de Beauvoir's Neo-Feminism). Shortly before Beauvoir's death, Francis and Gontier published a biography disclaimed by its subject as overly romanticized and inaccurate in an angry interview granted to the newspaper *Le Matin* (Cathy Bernheim and Antoine Spire, "Simone de Beauvoir: le désaveu" [The Disavowal], *Le Matin*, December 5, 1985, 26–27). After the proliferation of articles that followed the author's death on April 14, 1986, two books provided further personal insight into her life: Françoise d'Eaubonne's *Une Femme nommée Castor* (A Woman Named Castor) and Hélène de Beauvoir's *Souvenirs* (Memories).

Although *Le Deuxième Sexe* appeared in English in 1953 and caused a considerable stir in the United States at the time, it was not until the 1970s that interest in Simone de Beauvoir began to result in scholarly works on this side of the Atlantic. In 1973, Elaine Marks published a penetrating analysis of the scandal which death represented in Beauvoir's eyes. Jean Leighton's 1975 book is scathingly critical of Beauvoir's portrayal of women in her fictional works, and Robert Cottrell is equally severe in his interpretation of the author's rebelliousness as an indication of the drive to succeed; he finds this drive characteristic of the bourgeois mentality she denounced so vigorously. Acknowledging her profound debt to Simone de Beauvoir, Betty Friedan is nonetheless outspoken in her criticism of Beauvoir's ideas on motherhood and the family in her book about the feminist movement entitled *It Changed My Life*.

In 1977, Alex Madsen published a romanticized version of information gleaned primarily from Beauvoir's memoirs in *Hearts and Minds: The Common Journey of Simone de Beauvoir and Jean-Paul Sartre*. Konrad Bieber's 1979 book on Beauvoir for the Twayne series provides a valuable introduction to her works and her ideas. British critic Anne Whitmarsh examines the ethical, social, and political implications of Beauvoir's commitment to the leftist cause in *Simone de Beauvoir and the Limits of Commitment*. Carol Ascher's often quite personal analysis of Beauvoir and freedom was an outgrowth of a September 1979 conference, "The Second Sex—Thirty Years Later," held at New York University. Terry Keefe's 1983 study of Beauvoir's works is a comprehensive and well-documented source of information.

Donald L. Hatcher wrote *Understanding "The Second Sex"* in order to help his students comprehend the philosophical premises on which Beauvoir's ideas are based. Mary Evans, in her 1985 book *Simone de Beauvoir: A Feminist Mandarin*, suggests that Beauvoir attempted to solve the dilemmas faced by women by urging them to adopt male habits and values and to reject the traditional ties that have in the past bound them to both men and children. She criticizes the bourgeois mentality that informs Beauvoir's ideas and emphasizes the influence of "the capitalist ethic of individual responsibility" (128) on her values. Judith Okely's 1986 study focuses on a very personal comparison of her own reactions to the reading of *The Second Sex* in 1961 and again more than twenty years later. The year 1988 produced a brief portrait of Beauvoir by Lisa Appignanesi and an analysis of Beauvoir's novels by Elizabeth Fallaize. Yolanda Astarita Patterson's 1989 book, *Simone de Beauvoir and the Demystification of Motherhood*, examines memoirs, fiction, and essays in the light of the author's repeated pronouncements about the enslavement of women represented by family obligations and maternity.

Beginning in 1983, the International Simone de Beauvoir Society has published an annual journal, *Simone de Beauvoir Studies*, with articles analyzing the author's life and works from a biographical, literary, psychological, philosophical, political, and sociological point of view. In 1987, special issue No. 72 of the *Yale French Studies* was devoted to "Simone de Beauvoir: Witness to a Century."

BIBLIOGRAPHY

Works by Simone de Beauvoir

L'Invitée. Paris: Gallimard, 1943.
Pyrrhus et Cinéas. Paris: Gallimard, 1944.
Le Sang des autres. Paris: Gallimard, 1945.
Les Bouches inutiles. Paris: Gallimard, 1945.
Tous les hommes sont mortels. Paris: Gallimard, 1946.
Pour une morale d'ambiguïté. Paris: Gallimard, 1947.
L'Existentialisme et la sagesse des nations. Paris: Nagel, 1948.
L'Amérique au jour le jour. Paris: Morihien, 1948.
Le Deuxième Sexe. 2 vols. Paris: Gallimard, 1949.
Les Mandarins. Paris: Gallimard, 1954.
Privilèges. Paris: Gallimard, 1955.

La Longue Marche. Paris: Gallimard, 1957.
Mémoires d'une jeune fille rangée. Paris: Gallimard, 1958.
La Force de l'âge. Paris: Gallimard, 1960.
La Force des choses. 2 vols. Paris: Gallimard, 1963.
Une Mort très douce. Paris: Gallimard, 1964.
Les Belles Images. Paris: Gallimard, 1966.
La Femme rompue. Paris: Gallimard, 1967.
La Vieillesse. Paris: Gallimard, 1970.
Tout compte fait. Paris: Gallimard, 1972.
Quand prime le spirituel. Paris: Gallimard, 1979.
La Cérémonie des adieux, suivi de Entretiens avec Jean-Paul Sartre, août-septembre 1974. Paris: Gallimard, 1981.
Journal de guerre: septembre 1939-janvier 1941. Paris: Gallimard, 1990.
Lettres à Sartre. 1930–1939, 1940–1963. 2 vols. Paris: Gallimard, 1990.

Translations of Simone de Beauvoir

She Came to Stay. Trans. I. Drummond. New York: World, 1954.
The Blood of Others. Trans. Roger Senhouse and Yvonne Moyse. New York: Alfred A. Knopf, 1948.
Who Shall Die? Trans. Claude Francis and Fernande Gontier. Florisant, Mo.: River Press, 1983.
All Men Are Mortal. Trans. Leonard M. Friedman. New York: World, 1955.
The Ethics of Ambiguity. Trans. Bernard Frechtman. New York: Philosophical Library, 1948.
America Day by Day. Trans. Patrick Dudley. New York: Grove Press, 1953.
The Long March. Trans. Austryn Wainhouse. New York: World, 1958.
The Second Sex. Trans. H. M. Parshley. New York: Alfred A. Knopf, 1953.
The Mandarins. Trans. Leonard M. Friedman. New York: World, 1960.
Memoirs of a Dutiful Daughter. Trans. James Kirkup. New York: World, 1959.
The Prime of Life. Trans. Peter Green. New York: World, 1962.
Force of Circumstance. Trans. Richard Howard. New York: Putnam, 1964.
A Very Easy Death. Trans. Patrick O'Brian. New York: Putnam, 1966.
Les Belles Images. Trans. Patrick O'Brian. New York: Putnam, 1968.
The Woman Destroyed. Trans. Patrick O'Brian. London: Collins, 1968.
The Coming of Age. Trans. Patrick O'Brian. New York: Putnam, 1972.
All Said and Done. Trans. Patrick O'Brian. New York: Putnam, 1974.
When Things of the Spirit Come First. Trans. Patrick O'Brian. New York: Pantheon Books, 1982.
Adieux: A Farewell to Sartre. Trans. Patrick O'Brian. New York: Pantheon, 1984.

Studies of Simone de Beauvoir

Appignanesi, Lisa. *Simone de Beauvoir*. London: Penguin Books, 1988.
Ascher, Carol. *Simone de Beauvoir: A Life of Freedom*. Boston: Beacon Press, 1981.
Audet, Jean-Raymond. *Simone de Beauvoir face à la mort*. Lausanne: L'Age d'homme, 1979.

Bair, Deirdre. *Simone de Beauvoir: A Biography*. New York: Summit Books, 1990.

de Beauvoir, Hélène. *Souvenirs*. Paris: Librairie Séguier, 1987.

Bieber, Konrad. *Simone de Beauvoir*. Boston: Twayne, 1979.

Cayron, Claire. *La Nature chez Simone de Beauvoir*. Paris: Gallimard, 1973.

Cottrell, Robert D. *Simone de Beauvoir*. New York: Frederick Ungar, 1975.

Descubes, Madeleine. *Connaître Simone de Beauvoir*. Paris: Éditions Resma, 1974.

d'Eaubonne, Françoise. *Une Femme nommée Castor*. Paris: Encre, 1986.

Evans, Mary. *Simone de Beauvoir: A Feminist Mandarin*. London and New York: Tavistock Publications, 1985.

Fallaize, Elizabeth. *The Novels of Simone de Beauvoir*. London and New York: Routledge, 1988.

Francis, Claude, and Fernande Gontier. *Les Écrits de Simone de Beauvoir*. Paris: Gallimard, 1979.

———. *Simone de Beauvoir*. Paris: Librairie Académique Perrin, 1985.

Friedan, Betty. *It Changed My Life*. New York: Random House, 1976.

Gagnebin, Laurent. *Simone de Beauvoir ou le refus de l'indifférence*. Paris: Librairie Fischbacher, 1968.

Gennari, Geneviève. *Simone de Beauvoir*. Paris: Témoins du XXe siècle. Éditions Universitaires, 1959.

Hatcher, Donald L. *Understanding "The Second Sex."* New York: Peter Lang, 1984.

Henry, A. M. *Simone de Beauvoir ou l'Échec d'une chrétienté*. Paris: Arthème Fayard, 1961.

Hourdin, Georges. *Simone de Beauvoir et la Liberté*. Paris: Les Éditions du Cerf, 1962.

Jaccard, Annie-Claire. *Simone de Beauvoir*. Zurich: Juris Druck and Verlag Zurich, 1968.

Jeanson, Francis. *Simone de Beauvoir ou l'entreprise de vivre*. Paris: Éditions du Seuil, 1966.

Julienne-Caffié, Serge. *Simone de Beauvoir*. Paris: Gallimard, 1966.

Keefe, Terry. *Simone de Beauvoir: A Study of Her Writings*. London: Harrap, 1983.

Lasocki, Anne-Marie. *Simone de Beauvoir ou l'Entreprise d'écrire*. The Hague: Martinus Nijhoff, 1971.

Leighton, Jean. *Simone de Beauvoir on Woman*. Cranbury, N.J.: Associated University Presses, 1975.

Lilar, Suzanne. *Le Malentendu du "Deuxième Sexe."* Paris: Presses Universitaires de France, 1970.

Madsen, Alex. *Hearts and Minds: The Common Journey of Simone de Beauvoir and Jean-Paul Sartre*. New York: Morrow Quill Paperbacks, 1977.

Marks, Elaine. *Simone de Beauvoir: Encounters with Death*. New Brunswick, N.J.: Rutgers University Press, 1973.

Merleau-Ponty, Maurice. *Sens et Non-Sens*. Paris: Les Éditions Nagel, 1966.

Nahas, Hélène. *La Femme dans la littérature existentielle*. Paris: Presses Universitaires de France, 1957.

Okely, Judith. *Simone de Beauvoir*. New York: Pantheon Books, 1986.

Patterson, Yolanda Astarita. *Simone de Beauvoir and the Demystification of Motherhood*. Ann Arbor, Mich.: UMI Research Press, 1989.

Schwarzer, Alice. *Simone de Beauvoir aujourd'hui. Six entretiens*. Paris: Mercure de France, 1984.

Simone de Beauvoir Studies. Vol. 1-   . Menlo Park, Calif.: Simone de Beauvoir Society, 1983- .

"Simone de Beauvoir: Witness to a Century." *Yale French Studies* No. 72 (1987).
Whitmarsh, Anne. *Simone de Beauvoir and the Limits of Commitment.* Cambridge, Eng.:
     Cambridge University Press, 1981.
Winegarten, Renee. *Simone de Beauvoir: A Critical View.* New York: Berg, 1988.
Zéphir, Jacques J. *Le Néo-Féminisme de Simone de Beauvoir.* Paris: Denoël/Gonthier,
     1982.

ISABELLE DE CHARRIÈRE (1740–1805)

Janet Whatley

BIOGRAPHY

Some of the most subtle and original of eighteenth-century novels in French were written by a woman whose native language was Dutch and who spent most of her adult life in Switzerland. Mme de Charrière was born Isabella-Agneta-Elisabeth Van Tuyll Van Serooskerken, at the chateau of Zuylen near Utrecht. Her family was of the old Dutch Protestant nobility; Belle grew up in a familial atmosphere of patrician reserve, strict probity, and affectionate loyalty. She learned French early and well, and developed a lucid and supple French style.

As she entered her twenties, she became known throughout a good part of Europe as a highly eligible young woman: charming, but of a disconcerting intelligence. Her first work, *Le Noble* (*The Nobleman,*) (1763), was a high-spirited satire of the pretentions of the nobility, in which the rebellious aristocratic heroine elopes with her lover by leaping onto a platform built of the family portraits.

Belle's family managed to get *Le Noble* withdrawn from further publication, but the damage was done. Suitors (among them James Boswell) came—and left, daunted. Meanwhile, she was drawing sustenance from a rather curious clandestine relationship. At the age of twenty she had met at a ball the Swiss officer Constant d'Hermenches, a man of considerable wit and a married philanderer. D'Hermenches quickly learned that this was no easy prey. She kept him at a safe epistolary distance, and made of him her admiring confidant, pouring into letters of astonishing frankness all her reflections on the possibilities and constraints of the condition of young womanhood.

As Belle approached thirty, she began to take notice of her brother's mathematics tutor, a Swiss of the minor nobility, Charles-Emmanuel de Charrière. She recognized in him great intelligence and integrity; if she also recognized the temperamental gulf between them—between her impetuosity and his deliberate-ness—she paid no heed. They were married in 1771 and went to live at his home in Colombier, in the principality of Neuchâtel.

While it may not have been the happiest marriage imaginable, it was probably not the living death that a certain biographical tradition has presented. Belle desired children, but there were none. She had friendships, and abundant correspondence, books, newspapers, and the quiet comradeship of her husband, who supported all her endeavors. Then suddenly in the 1780s she published three epistolary novels of provincial life and domestic relationships: *Lettres neuchâteloises* (Letters from Neuchâtel, 1784), *Mistress Henley* (1784), and *Lettres écrites de Lausanne* (*Letters from Lausanne*, 1785–1787).

This last novel contained a section published separately in 1787 as *Caliste*, which was to become the most popular of her works. Mme de Charrière was in Paris at the time, and there she met the nephew of her old admirer Constant d'Hermenches. Benjamin Constant was nineteen: gifted, lonely, half-orphaned, and at loose ends. They took to each other instantly, developed an immense mutual affection, and were for several years each other's preferred intellectual companion and correspondent. Their friendship eventually cooled when Constant began his liaison with Mme de *Staël, but they never completely lost contact: her last letter is to him.

That year and a half in Paris (1786–1787) also put her in touch with the political and philosophical circles of a society on the verge of revolution. When she returned to Colombier to stay, she had become acquainted with both the future makers and the future victims. When the Revolution broke out she followed its development with intense involvement. She came to know a number of aristocratic exiles (émigrés); their situation inspired in her a whole new wave of writing—political essays, plays, novels, and philosophical tales—which constitute a sustained and complex reflection on the significance of the Revolution; on education and its place in a society which is dismantling its structure of privilege and trying to find a new equilibrium.

Despite bouts of depression and chronic ill health, Mme de Charrière continued to write important works until late in her life. Her immense correspondence is in itself a masterpiece; it documents the evolution of her sensibility and her thought, her close relations with her family, her friendships with old colleagues and young protégés (she readily took on the role of mentor) that kept her in contact both with European political and intellectual life and with her own community. She died in 1805, at the age of sixty-five.

MAJOR THEMES

The three epistolary novels of the 1780s form the cornerstone of her reputation as a novelist. Fine-grained, unsentimental, and penetrating, they record the evolution of human relationships through the myriad details of everyday existence; the ordinary is transfigured, shimmering with revelations and laden with consequences. In her precisely delineated milieux (Protestant and provincial) characters collide with each other—or just miss each other—because of the tensions and balances, the specific economy, of each society.

In the *Lettres neuchâteloises* (1784), several voices contrapuntally develop a story that is simple in plot but complex in interaction. In the first letter, an uneducated young seamstress tells, in breathless, unshaped cadences, how a certain young gentleman came to her rescue when she dropped a client's dress in the muddy street. The next voice is that of the young man, Henry Meyer. A merchant's son recently arrived in Neuchâtel as an office apprentice, Meyer is trying to hold onto his hopes for himself in the midst of his numbingly tedious office work. A young man of broad and generous sympathies, he is aware of the laborious lives—especially women's lives—that provide the economic base for even the very modest ease that he enjoys. The third voice is that of Marianne de la Prise (the owner of the mudstained dress), a young girl of an impoverished noble French family, as lonely in her way as Meyer is in the narrow and insular society of Neuchâtel.

The young seamstress (already sexually experienced) becomes pregnant by Meyer in a brief unpremeditated involvement. Julianne goes to Marianne for help; the revelation that might have destroyed Meyer's chances with Marianne in fact brings them closer together and quickens their maturing. Marianne has shown throughout the novel an unfussy practicality, a sure and frank grasp of realities. Now she performs what is, for her class and time, a remarkable act of generous involvement; she tells Meyer, using no euphemisms, that Julianne is pregnant, and sets in motion the arrangements that will provide for the child's welfare. Meyer, who is by no means a casual or callous seducer, is compelled to recognize yet more immediately something he already knew: "Nothing happens merely to us alone" (translations mine).

Within the suggested if not definitive happy ending, there is a hard little nugget of socioeconomic fact. The characters whose "destiny" everyone is concerned with are Meyer and Marianne; in this Charrière has followed novelistic convention. But she makes it unconventionally and uncomfortably clear that the lovers' happiness has come at a cost paid by others. Julianne is not destroyed, but she is isolated and neutralized: sent off to the country to have her baby, which Meyer's uncle will take charge of and which will be irrevocably separated from its mother. "Have the girl leave," orders the uncle, who pays Meyer's bills and now clears from his path a tired, slovenly, barely literate working-class girl who is possibly the most unforgettable figure of the novel, and for whose creation Charrière was just barely forgiven by her contemporaries.

Lettres neuchâteloises deals in revelations and resolutions, *Mistress Henley* in impasse. The young heroine begins a series of letters to a friend by trying to describe an obscure malaise. It is an unhappiness without a name, without an obvious cause rooted in some prior folly. She had made an irreproachable choice of a spouse, rejecting a worldly man of great wealth in favor of a handsome, reasonable widower who promises her a tranquil life in the country and the worthy mission of being a mother to his little girl.

Yet from the beginning it seems to be someone else's happiness that she is trying to adopt. She is an impassioned young woman of urban tastes, married to an utterly complacent country gentleman who, with the best will in the world, instinctively rejects all of his wife's gifts, material and temperamental (the flowered hats, the poetry of La Fontaine that she would bring to his daughter); she, in turn, is so vulnerable and impatient that she throws away her gifts just at the point when her husband might begin to accept them and allow them to leaven his stolidness.

The tensions engendered by this incompatibility are felt down through the social hierarchy. A local farmer is smitten with Mrs. Henley's elegant chambermaid Fanny, with disastrous consequences to other relationships. Mrs. Henley, frantic to repair the damage, sends Fanny away. But she discovers that her sacrifice is not admired by her husband, who had not requested such drastic and self-punishing measures, and who marvels at the impetuosity of "you passionate people." Yet Mr. Henley cannot impart his tranquillity to his wife, any more than she can communicate her enthusiasms to him. His complacency keeps him from reaching out to her in time; her low self-esteem, her panicky sense of guilt—underlined by the repeated and obsessive expression "I was wrong"—keep her from seeing what her responsibility and her choices really are.

Her insecurity deepens, as does her husband's bland impenetrability. The question of breastfeeding her expected child is yet another locus of humiliation; a doctor will decide, says Mr. Henley, whether her "extreme vivacity and frequent impatience" should "make a stranger preferable." But she is resilient; one day, she "unfolds her fantasies" about her child's brilliant future to Mr. Henley, who informs her that he has ordered their life differently. He has just turned down a seat in Parliament and a place at court in favor of domestic and rural occupations. An impeccable choice, it would seem; but it is a life that Mr. Henley will control utterly, chosen without the slightest consultation with his wife. Mrs. Henley is dumbfounded; she is torn between her admiration of her husband's "reason and probity" and "the horror of seeing myself so foreign to his feelings, so thoroughly excluded from his thoughts, so useless, so isolated, that I was unable to speak."

Mrs. Henley faints, but does not die; a miscarriage seems imminent, but is averted. "In a year, in two years, you will learn, I hope, that I am reasonable and happy, or that I am no more." Does the last sentence suggest that Mrs. Henley will in fact come to some happy terms with her life, or that to be "reasonable and happy" in ways that would content Mr. Henley would be tantamount to death? Charrière refuses to resolve the ambiguities, but rather asks us to confront the forms of pain produced in part by the wear and tear of daily life on incompatible personalities yoked together, and in part by social and domestic expectations and definitions that inhibit the development of self-confidence in women, encourage a patronizing complacency in men, and severely limit the happiness each can give the other.

The epistolary voice of the narrator in *Lettres écrites de Lausanne* is a more robust and self-confident one, that of a mind (much like that of her creator) that ranges imaginatively and critically over her situation. A widow in her late thirties, she is writing to a friend about the pleasures and pains of raising a daughter and securing for her a reasonably happy marriage even with a scanty dowry. How can she protect Cécile, strengthen her, preserve her options—do all this in a society permeated by self-contradictory pedagogical conventions that "fabricate characters, legislations, educations, and ideas of domestic bliss that are impossible"?

The society of Lausanne is more cosmopolitan than that of Neuchâtel; wealthy foreigners stream through it, complicating the courtship expectations; among them is a young English lord, with whom Cécile falls in love under the watchful and anxious eye of her mother. One quiet afternoon, over a long chess game, a muffled explosion of feeling between the two leads Cécile's mother to tell her what she regards as the essential social and emotional facts of life: that women care more about men than men care about them as individuals; that men may desire hints of passion in a potential mistress, but are suspicious of them in a potential wife. (There are also, adds the mother, inexorable social constraints on men; they too may pay a higher price for an imprudence than for a hidden vice.)

Yet for all the emphasis she lays on chastity (ambiguously called *sagesse*: wisdom or prudence?), she would not have her daughter believe that chastity is synonymous with virtue, or that its loss would vitiate all other virtues—that she would no longer be a loving daughter, a good friend, a faithful lover. But those very qualities would make any sexual imprudence all the more unfortunate: where an unchaste hypocrite could rule the roost, the modest and equitable Cécile would feel that by such imprudence she would have abrogated her rights in her own household and any just limits to her indulgence toward others.

But neither does Cécile believe that marriage is synonymous with life, and she makes to her mother the astonishing (and unaccepted) proposal that they *work*: that they open a shop in Holland or England, and live without high society, novels, envy, or boredom. For the courtship is going nowhere; the young lord remains an amiable puppy.

This protracted not-quite-courtship has had another concerned witness: William, tutor to the young lord, who writes to Cécile's mother an account of his own life. In his youth he had suffered a great loss in the death of his brother, a devastation that leaves him incapable of any emotional attachment until he meets Caliste. She is beautiful, kind, generous, marvellously talented in the arts—but she is damaged goods. She had been an actress; her mother had sold her to a nobleman who had cared for her and to whom she had been strictly faithful until his death. William falls in love with her, and she with him; in vain he asks his father's blessing to marry her. The warnings of Cécile's mother are borne out here; Caliste's "unchaste" relationship with her protector has, in the eyes of society, invalidated all her other virtues; at the same time, her profound psychological chastity and her sensitive respect for decorum condemn her to a state of painful humility. And something keeps William from investing the energy to persuade his father, or to marry Caliste in spite of his father. The secret of that inner obstacle is not explicit; hints are planted throughout the text that the unhealed wound of his brother's death makes it impossible for him to commit himself to the "otherness" of a woman, and that he will keep gravitating to young men who resemble that brother. William and Caliste (both of whom have made unhappy marriages of convenience) meet in a final wrenching scene, which does not alter their fates, and she goes home to die.

In its time, this story had a great success quite independent of the inconclusive Cécile plot (Benjamin Constant's *Adolphe* and Mme de Staël's *Corinne* owe much to it). It had a lyrical intensity and a narrative shape much more satisfying to the taste of the period; Caliste's death was a more recognizably appropriate ending than Cécile's sturdy persistence in finding other reasons for living. But the stories are thematically interrelated. In both narratives, the obstacle to a marriage seems first to be a social prejudice (against a girl of small dowry, against a woman with a past); but in fact the more insuperable obstacle is in an insufficiency of available desire on the part of the man. William's narrative in his letter to Cécile's mother is both an examination of his conscience and a warning against men like him and against the indecisiveness that wastes opportunities for happiness. For his and Caliste's story is a romance version of Cécile's and the young lord's; it has a conventionally dramatic conclusion, while with a more everyday sanity, Cécile gets on with her life.

These novels of the 1780s depict relatively closed and static societies of the Ancien Régime. Severely limited in their external choices, Charrière's characters achieve different kinds and degrees of internal liberty. By reaching out beyond the bounds of feminine prudery, Marianne escapes her isolation; Mrs. Henley internalizes her resentment and anxiety to the point of sickness; Cécile and her mother are alone, but possessed of their love for each other and their freedom of mind and movement. And while power would seem to reside with men, it is often they who are the most frustrated; they are restricted in their capacity to give or receive love by a patriarchal ethos that is in fact less absolute than they imagine it to be.

It might appear that there is a great watershed between Charrière's novels of the 1780s and the post-Revolutionary works. By the 1790s, Charrière was writing less about subtle ramifications than about cataclysmic upheavals. But there is also a continuity. In the domestic dramas of the earlier novels, Charrière's heroines respect the social rules that they do not completely internalize or endorse: rather than overtly rebelling, they keep seeking the inner and authentic essence of these rules, redefining women's virtue not as an accidental chastity but as a profound integrity. The later novels move the problem to other terrain, to analogous inquiries into the sources of cultural energy, which are to be found neither in blind adherence to religious doctrine nor in the militancy of the dogmatic atheist; neither with the revolutionary sloganeer nor with the nostalgic reactionary. All these texts suggest that when one dismantles a structure—of social or sexual behavior, of religious faith, of noblesse oblige—one is responsible for the consequences; one should weigh what its absence will cost and have some idea of what will replace it as a bulwark against chaos—if not for oneself, then for those less privileged and more vulnerable.

This later body of work is less well known than the novels of the 1780s, but in fact it is an invaluable documentation for a certain vision of the post-Revolutionary world that escapes easy classification. Charrière witnessed the abolition of feudal privilege without regret; but she feared the disappearance of a certain moral style, an ethos of courtesy and generosity. She was repelled not only by the violence of the Terror but by the dogmatism of the Revolutionary regimes, and yet she had little sympathy for those aristocrats who bogged down in nostalgia and who refused to try to understand what had happened or to learn anything new. She admired those émigrés who responded with lucidity, flexibility, and courage to their situation and seems to have set herself the task of keeping the dialogue open among classes and factions. Several plays (*L'Emigré* is one) and an epistolary novel, *Lettres trouvées dans des porte-feuilles d'émigrés* (Letters Found in Emigrants' Portfolios, 1793), are built on communications among royalists and revolutionaries, with admirable and unsympathetic characters on all sides of the various ideological divides.

Her long-standing concern with education became the overriding preoccupation of her later works. In a series of odd, enigmatic narratives (of which, she said, Rousseau was the godfather) she inquired into the transformations brought about by the Revolution: What had been swept away? What remained of old values and cultural traits? Whom does one now educate, and how, and for what?

"For whom does one write, from now on?" begins *Trois Femmes* (Three Women, 1796). Ostensibly a debate on the Kantian idea of duty, this novel is really a study in experience: the virtuous heroine Emilie, an orphaned émigrée, learns that her naïveté has blinded her to the predatory nature of her own class and family and prevented her from intervening to protect her maid Josephine. (Charrière's sense of mutual obligation within a hierarchy outlasted all the social turmoil of her lifetime.) Emilie is "educated," her intransigence modulated, in part by the vicarious sexual experience of Josephine's pregnancy (one thinks again of Julianne's role), in part by a worldly friend, Constance, who uses an unethically acquired fortune to do good in the world. More directly, Emilie learns from her condition of exile in Germany that she cannot recreate around her a little enclave of Ancien Régime France. When she falls in love with a German, their cultural differences seem to threaten a repetition of the Henley fiasco. But Revolutionary exile has opened doors and minds, aired out stifling enclosures: the lovers come to happy terms with each other's Frenchness or Germanness.

Trois Femmes treats the dogmatism of certain concepts of duty and virtue;

Honorine d'Userche (1798) deals with dogmatic atheism. Intelligent, passionate, and tyrannical, Honorine learns early how to exploit the vices and weakness of those around her. While still a child, she falls in love with a boy, Florentin, who is, unbeknownst to everyone, her illegitimate brother. Honorine shares the lessons of her tutors with him; unfortunately, he also shares his with her. The Marquis de la Touche, without revealing his paternity, communicates to his son a kind of systematic incredulity which, for Charrière, amounts to bigotry, annulling not only the idea of God but also that of any other hope or faith. The effect on Honorine is devastating. By the time her relationship to Florentin is revealed, the incest taboo has no meaning for her (although it does for him). Florentin disappears into the abyss of the Revolutionary Wars; Honorine lives on utterly bereft, not only of Florentin himself, but of all other sources of consolation.

Les Ruines d'Yedburg (The Ruins of Yedburg, 1799) displaces the émigré concerns onto a Scottish family of Stuart loyalists; like *Honorine d'Userche*, it treats the interplay between education and the vulnerable young consciousness. *Sir Walter Finch et son fils William* (Sir Walter Finch and His Son William, published posthumously in 1806) is a letter from father to son, beginning with the latter's birth and continued until his adolescence. Watching the developing faculties of his own boy and that of a working-class child, noticing the consequences of early expectations and pedagogical choices with their dissimilar but comparably valuable results, Sir Walter is Charrière's educational experimentalist.

In a remarkable letter to her nephew in 1799, which is a sort of summing-up of her post-Revolutionary reflections, Charrière tries to explain her own contradictory advice: ''In turn, I make you read *Sainte-Anne* and I recommend learning to you; I speak of society as rapidly destroying itself and I advise for you a use of your faculties which is only appropriate in an ordered, well established society.'' Her story *Sainte-Anne* (1799) is a particularly suggestive and teasing parable. Its hero is a Breton nobleman freshly returned from Revolutionary exile. Attractive young women crowd around him; but he is drawn only to Mlle d'Estival, who (as everyone exclaims) does not know how to read. But she knows everything else: how to treat a wound, foretell the weather, quiet an angry dog. Sainte-Anne is looking for a partner with whom to rebuild his life. In Mlle d'Estival he chooses the person who has the most direct and vigorous contact with the natural world; she is possessed by all the local superstitions, but also possesses all the legends and songs. Through his marriage to her he makes a healing bond with the Revolutionary peasant community and goes off to repair his ancestral home.

In that letter of clarification to her nephew, Charrière provides the complementary perspective. Illiteracy is a conceptual tool, not a recommendation. Only by ''learning to learn'' may you hope to earn a place of distinction, for such is no longer guaranteed by your noble origins. Amidst the upheavals, do not throw away your Homer and Virgil, your Pascal and Newton. Cultivate them, cherish them, let them be a resource within yourself—even if hidden and unrecognized, ready to nourish your children for whatever new world they must live in.

Many of these rich and dense texts are only recently available; the publication of the complete works is making us aware for the first time of the coherence and acuity of the whole body of the work and of the luminous mind of the skeptical and compassionate, detached and committed Isabelle de Charrière.

SURVEY OF CRITICISM

The numerous editions of Charrière's work in her own lifetime, the translations into English, German, and Dutch, testify to the interest of her work to her contemporaries. Approbation was often mixed with blame: for audacities of thought, for excessive attention to the "vulgar" details of life, and for her apparent reluctance to provide dramatic plots and conclusions.

Sainte-Beuve wrote two essays on her: one an admiring appreciation of her novels, and one on her relationship with Benjamin Constant. The first full-length biography, the massive and detailed work of Philippe Godet, has never been superseded. Geoffrey Scott's *Portrait of Zélide* is an interpretation based on Godet's information. It is elegantly written, but misleading: Charrière's whole life would seem to be centered on her relationship with Benjamin Constant. Scott deals with only a handful of her works, and those chiefly for their biographical implications. The later writing is dismissed as empty wheel-spinning, and her later years as a wasteland of sterile boredom.

The critical and editorial work of the last two decades has altered these interpretations. Critics have been looking at Mme de Charrière's work not as a reflection of her biography, but as a highly crafted literary creation. Christabel Braunrot's thesis explicates her virtuosity in the technique of the epistolary novel. Jean Starobinski analyzes the problematics of her profoundly structured fictional world. He sees her female characters as condemned to immobility in a rigid caste system, living out a peculiar, sacrificial heroism: they are "divided between their opposition to an unjust order of prejudices, and their effort to give full meaning to values which prejudice posits in a purely formal fashion. They criticize accepted notions of nobility, of wealth, of honorability, so as to give all the better the example of true nobility, veritable wealth, authentic honorability"(139).

A number of critics have recently addressed Charrière's work as specifically feminine writing. Béatrice Didier treats Charrière's skill in the recreation of both feminine and masculine perspectives; apart from a mistaken attribution to Charrière of Samuel Constant's *Le Mari sentimental*, her study is valuable. Elizabeth MacArthur and Susan Jackson have both discussed the absence of closure in her novels: they see it as a positive and significant trait—a challenge to the inevitable fictional solutions of death or marriage—rather than as a failure of creative energy. Jackson presents Mme de Charrière's fictional world as "open-ended, subject to change for better or worse, perhaps tedious, even trivial, but at least not necessarily or uniformly tragic . . . the female novelist's work has been made to consist, not so much in doing, as in *un*doing, stitch by careful stitch, the ever-so-tightly woven tapestry of novelistic convention'' (303).

Monique Moser-Verrey looks at the three early epistolary novels as a triptych of the successive phases of feminine existence—the young girl, the wife, the mother. Through their practical optimism, their dejection, or their utopian speculations, these characters are Charrière's instruments for "rethinking the management of sexuality, marriage, and the state" (76). Marie-Paule Laden's article explores the ambiguitie of *Mistress Henley*, and particularly the anxiety of a masked rebellion, "a kind of guerilla maneuver" (297) on the part of the female protagonist, a "disguised rejection" (295) of her social role. Susan Lanser's article on "courting death" speaks of "marriage *as* death" in *Mistress Henley*; in Lanser's view, by making minute domestic detail serve as the vehicle for the most intense and profound aspects of a woman's life, Charrière performs a "radical narrative act," which is diminished in the more conventional Romantic despair of *Caliste*. Joan Hinde Stewart's essays situate Mme de Charrière's work in the whole enterprise of women's writing in the eighteenth century. Stewart studies the subversive undercurrents of her seemingly conformist plots; she also analyzes the economic and social specificity of her settings and their linkage with the destinies of the characters, the particular currency of an uninflated rhetoric, the mutual mirroring of sexual and textual transactions.

Alix Deguise's book-length study of *Trois Femmes* acquaints us with Charrière's involvement in the concerns of the post-Revolutionary era; the situation of the émigrés; the cultural relationship between France and Germany; the influence of the philosophy of Kant; and the pervasive notion of duty in Charrière's life and work. Isabelle Vissière accompanies her selections of Charrière's writings concerning the Revolution with a vehement assertion of the value of her political thought and her importance in the web of communications among émigrés, writers, editors, and political thinkers. New interpretative work on Charrière is continually appearing, fueled by the availability of the whole body of her writing and its increasingly apparent relevance, scope, and import.

BIBLIOGRAPHY

Major Works by Isabelle de Charrière

Le Noble. Amsterdam: van Harrevelt, 1763.
Lettres neuchâteloises. Lausanne, 1784.
Lettres de Mistress Henley publiées par son amie. Geneva, 1784.
Lettres écrites de Lausanne. Geneva: Bonnant, 1785.
Caliste, ou suite des Lettres écrites de Lausanne. Geneva and Paris: Prault, 1787.
Observations et conjectures politiques, 1787–1788. Verrières: Witel, 1787–1788.
Henriette et Richard. 1792 (uncompleted novel).
Lettres trouvées dans des porte-feuilles d'émigrés. Lausanne: Durand, 1793.
L'Emigré. Neuchâtel: Spineux, 1793.

Lettres trouvées dans la neige. Neuchâtel: Fauche-Borel, 1793.

Trois Femmes. London: Baylis, 1796.

Honorine d'Userche, Nouvelle de L'Abbé de la Tour, suivie de Trois Dialogues. Leipzig: Wolf, 1798.

Sainte-Anne et *Les Ruines d'Yedburg*. Zurich: Orell-Fussli, 1799.

Sir Walter Finch et son fils William. Geneva: Paschoud, 1806.

Oeuvres complètes. Ed. Jean-Daniel Candaux, et al. 10 vols. Amsterdam: Van Oorschot, 1979–1984.

Translation of Isabelle de Charrière

Four Tales by Zélide. Trans. S[ybil] M. S[cott]. New York: Scribner's, 1926. Reissued Freeport, N.Y.: Books for Libraries Press, 1970. (Includes *The Nobleman, Mistress Henley, Letters from Lausanne*, and *Caliste*.)

Studies of Isabelle de Charrière

Braunrot, Christabel. "Madame de Charrière and the Eighteenth-Century Novel: Experiments in Epistolary Techniques." Diss., Yale University, 1973.

Courtney, C. P. *Isabelle de Charrière (Belle de Zuylen): A Secondary Bibliography*. Oxford: Voltaire Foundation, 1982.

Deguise, Alix. *Trois Femmes: Le Monde de Madame de Charrière*. Geneva: Slatkine, 1981.

Didier, Béatrice. *L'Ecriture-femme*. Paris: PUF, 1981.

Godet, Philippe. *Madame de Charrière et ses amis, d'après de nombreux documents inédits (1740–1805)*. Geneva: Jullien, 1906.

Jackson, Susan. "The Novels of Isabelle de Charrière, or, A Woman's Work Is Never Done." *Studies in Eighteenth-Century French Culture* 14 (1985): 299–306.

Laden, Marie-Paule. " 'Quel aimable et cruel petit livre': Madame de Charrière's *Mistress Henley*." *French Forum* 11 (September 1986): 289–99.

Lanser, Susan. "Courting Death: *Roman, romantisme* and *Mistress Henley*'s Narrative Practices." *Eighteenth-Century Life* 13, n.s. 1 (February 1989): 49–59.

MacArthur, Elizabeth J. "Devious Narratives: Refusal of Closure in Two Eighteenth-Century Epistolary Novels." *Eighteenth-Century Studies* 21 (Fall 1987): 1–20.

Moser-Verrey, Monique. "Isabelle de Charrière en quête d'une meilleure entente." *Stanford French Review* 11, no. 1 (Spring 1987): 63–76.

Sainte-Beuve, C.-A. "Benjamin Constant et Mme de Charrière." In *Portraits littéraires*. Vol. 3. Paris: Garnier, 1862. 184–280.

———. "Madame de Charrière." In *Portraits de femmes*. Paris: Garnier, 1886. 411–57.

Scott, Geoffrey. *The Portrait of Zélide*. London: Constable, 1925.

Starobinski, Jean. "Les *Lettres écrites de Lausanne* de Madame de Charrière: inhibition psychique et interdit social." In *Roman et lumières au XVIIIe siècle*. Paris: Editions sociales, 1970. 130–51.

Stewart, Joan Hinde. "Designing Women." In *A New History of French Literature*. Ed. Denis Hollier. Cambridge, Mass.: Harvard University Press, 1989. 553–58.

————. "Sex, Text and Exchange: *Lettres neuchâteloises* and *Lettres de Milady Juliette Catesby*." *Eighteenth-Century Life* 13, n.s. 1 (February 1989): 60–68.

Vissière, Isabelle, ed. *Isabelle de Charrière, une aristocrate révolutionnaire: Ecrits 1788–1794.* Paris: des femmes, 1988.

ANDRÉE CHEDID
(1920–   )

Bettina L. Knapp

BIOGRAPHY

Andrée Chedid was born in Cairo on March 20, 1920, of Egypto-Lebanese origin. Chedid's parents separated when she was very young, and she was sent to boarding schools in Cairo and in Paris. Although she had little family life, she always maintained a warm and loving relationship with both her father and mother. Chedid received her B.A. degree specializing in journalism from the American University in her native city. In June 1988 she was awarded the degree of doctor *honoris causa* from the same university. Married at the age of twenty-one to Louis Chedid, a medical student, she spent the next three years (1942–1945) in Lebanon. In 1946 the couple moved to Paris, where Louis earned his degree in medicine. After a number of years the author's husband became associated with the Pasteur Institute. A prominent scientist, he now heads a research laboratory in Florida. The Chedids have two children and six grandchildren.

Chedid has repeatedly said that she is the product of two civilizations, two ways of life, two psyches. These dichotomies are fused, however, in the works of art that are her novels, plays, and poetry. Her childhood days and her early memories, particularly those associated with Egypt, played an important role in her formation as a writer, as evidenced in her novels, *Le Sommeil délivré* (*From Sleep Unbound*, 1952), *Jonathan* (1955), *Le Sixième Jour* (*The Sixth Day*, 1960), *Le Survivant* (The Survivor, 1963), *L'Autre* (The Other, 1969), *La Cité fertile* (The Fertile City, 1972), *Néfertiti et le rêve d'Akhnaton* (Nefertiti and Akhnaton's Dream, 1974), *Les Marches de sable* (Steps into the Sand, 1981), *L'Enfant multiple* (The Multiple Child, 1989), and others. The emotional colorations and images that mark her writings bear the impress of a dry, parched land, its sun-drenched tonalities ranging from deep ocher to sandy-brown whiteness and its seemingly endless skies depicted in nuanced tones of incandescent blue set against a blazing sun or juxtaposed to the sinuous, easy-flowing, but sometimes turbid waters of the Nile. "It is less a matter of nostalgic return to the past, of a concerted search for memories," Chedid remarked in an interview I had with her, "than it is a need to experience the permanent presence of an inner sentiment—pulsations, movements, chants, misery and joy, sun and serenity, which are inherent in the Middle East. I seem to feel all these emotions pulsating within." Her novels, poems, and plays are a complex of endlessly shifting emotional climates, disclosing and secreting shapes and hues—energy patterns—that are then transmuted into human beings or landscapes.

Because Chedid's writings for the most part are situated in Egypt, the land of her birth, they all bear the veneer of the Middle East as well as the modernism of her adopted land, France. Ancient and modern civilizations fascinate Chedid—the known and the unknown. In her novels, plays, and poems, the past is ushered into being; creatures are enticed to spin their webs, to evolve, to act; and as they do, each in his or her own way reveals a tarnished or unblemished inner world. Chedid's characters are endowed with a sense of proximity and distance, rootedness and rootlessness. They are paradigms of a personal quest and a collective search: the need to communicate not only with one's own multileveled self but also with those organic and inorganic forces that surround each being. Her works, then, are stamped with universal feelings as well as with personal yearnings, each set apart or opposed to the other. The tension that results from this dynamic is frequently evoked in muffled and muted tones, sometimes in blazing cacophonies that feed on and then dilate the imagery that abounds in her writings.

MAJOR THEMES

Chedid's themes—fusing ancient and modern ways; European and Middle Eastern concepts; creating a harmony between warring religious groups; equality between men and women; raising the standard of living in backward areas via self-help—are implicit in her fiction. An anecdote, be it about the spread of disease or the inferior status of women in Islamic countries, can readily be understood and assimilated at one level; on another, however, it involves a symbolistic approach and requires on the part of the reader not merely a functioning intellect but also active participation by the senses and feelings.

Premonitions, intuitions, forebodings—a world of mystery is also aroused by Chedid from the very outset of her novels. Like fine wine decanted and passing through the reader's physical being, her prose sweetens or embitters every fiber, pore, nerve ending of those exposed to it. Only after the work's completion does the full impact of her literary experience bear down upon the reader.

Chedid's novels, both thematically and stylistically, bear no resemblance to the writings of such contemporaries as Michel Butor and Alain Robbe-Grillet, who consider the novel to be a type of "puzzle," a "mythology difficult to unravel," whose works are divested of plot and characters and whose beings are perpetually following the same repetitive patterns. Nor are they like the novels or short stories of Nathalie *Sarraute, which stem directly from the interplay of tropisms, those hidden forces within each individual that are at the root of gestures, words, and feelings. If any comparison were to be made, one might say that Chedid's novels resemble to a certain degree Marguerite *Duras's early fugal works, such as *Le Ravissement de Lol V. Stein* or *Le Vice-Consul*, in which sequences of evanescent shadowy forms and shapes flow forth in the prose on the page, and in so doing capture and enclose ephemeral thoughts and feelings in dazzling poetic images.

Le Sommeil délivré, Chedid's first novel, is the story of a woman, Samya, the product of a certain type of contemporary Middle Eastern upbringing with its harsh and brutal customs, particularly in regard to women, whose earthly existence is wholly devoted to serving certain specific purposes—to service man and to procreate. Why learn to read and write? Women need not and should not be educated. Samya is paralyzed as the novel opens. She had not been so at the time of her marriage. From the day she became the wife of Boutros, an unfeeling and detached man, completely uninterested in her, she felt her life eroding, slowly crumbling and slipping away. Only after the birth of her daughter, Mia, was the void that was her life filled. Not for long, however, since Boutros looked upon Mia as just another useless mouth to feed. When Mia developed a fever and Boutros refused to call the doctor even though Samya begged him to do so, the child died. Two years elapsed. Rage seethed in Samya until it burst and she shot her husband in the heart. *Le Sommeil délivré* captures not only one woman's world but that of many women, whether living cloistered in a Middle Eastern land or liberated to all intents and purposes in a modern metropolis yet still imprisoned within their own psychological worlds.

Jonathan deals with the choice that many young Christians make in the Middle East between religion and revolution, a choice that often occurs today in many lands where the church is still very traditional and conservative. Envisaged symbolically, however, *Jonathan* may be considered an aborted rite of passage. It reveals the difficulties that arise when a young person attempts to take on the world and is unprepared to do so. That the protagonist dies indicates his inability to assume the active role of revolutionary: his inner vision is still too undeveloped, not strong enough to carry out his ideations.

Like a classically constructed tragedy, *Le Sixième Jour* can be seen as a death and resurrection myth, like that of Osiris, Dionysus, or Christ. A cholera epidemic raged in Egypt in 1948, Chedid tells us, and this simple fact inspired the novel, which revolves around an archetypal mother principle, a collective image representing good, and not evil, restorative and not destructive in its power. Om Hassan, whose only daughter has died some years before the incidents related in the novel, is devoting her life to bringing up her grandson, Hassan. *Le Sixième Jour* narrates her struggle to save her grandson's life after he is infected with cholera: she countermands the laws of the land by refusing to inform the authorities of Hassan's illness, by taking him to another area where she lives with him in hiding. Although she fails in her endeavor, the child dying in the end, her devotion and love for him is so great as to encompass all of human existence, as does Mother Nature in her eternal death and rebirth cycle.

In *Le Survivant*, the reader is plunged into a world where the protagonist, Lana, attempts to discover whether or not she is capable of living and functioning independently. The novel begins as she emerges from sleep. It is morning. Her husband, Pierre, left yesterday on a business trip. The phone rings, jarring the peaceful calm that inhabits the atmosphere. An official at the airport tells her that a plane has crashed. Lana refuses to listen. The voice is insistent. Lana's mind turns back to Pierre's departure. The voice is adamant. The dialogue is now lived out in two modalities, yesterday's and today's: life and death. Each tone and the emotional equivalents of the harrowing feelings aroused when confronting the possibility of a finale are superimposed upon one another. From the very outset, the reader knows that a dual time scheme will be experienced: linear, as Lana deals with the unfolding empirical situation, the developing crisis; and cyclical, as it is experienced by the unconscious. Such layering allows her to come into contact with past, present, and future events, all of which are integrated into the text and make for its intense drama.

Chedid's writings are marked by their intermingling of tragedy and hope, and *L'Autre* is no exception. Unlike *Le Survivant*, which concentrates on death, *L'Autre* is a canticle, a hymn to life. It is also an exploration of the complex problem of human relationships in general. An earthquake has leveled a hotel and surrounding buildings; a young man, a stranger to the town, is buried alive. Just moments earlier, he has been talking to an old peasant named Simm. The novel centers around the efforts of Simm to save ''the other''—the unknown lad, and in so doing to halt the powers that destroy and hurl the living into oblivion.

The most important image in *La Cité fertile*, as in *Le Sixième Jour*, is that of the archetypal mother figure who sweeps into the story, arrests the reader's attention, then vanishes, only to return moments later, energizing feeling, act, and word. This figure is universalized in the person of Aléfa the dancer, who could be a hundred thousand years old, Chedid suggests. A practitioner of one of the most ancient arts, dancing, an elemental form of expressing human emotion, she moves about like a deity or queen, mistress of all she surveys. When she walks, she oscillates, when she moves her limbs, she concretizes them in a series of hieratic gestures, transforming them at times into natural forces: a tree, a stone, silence, air, a city, tears. Aléfa is the universe.

La Cité fertile is the work of a consummate artist/stylist. The images imprinted on Chedid's verbal canvas are alchemical in quality; primary colors merge there in sequences of stark blendings. A city, for example, is depicted in terms of multiple molten metals, as though exposed to intense heat. Flowing outward through a maze of intricate verbal patterns, the elements of earth, water, and air are transformed into rows of concrete houses, vast landscapes, clumps of sandscapes, flowers of pastel shadings.

Néfertiti et le rêve d'Akhnaton differs from Chedid's earlier novels in that it combines history and fiction. It plunges the reader back into a remote period, 1388–1344 B.C.—the eighteenth dynasty in Egypt—when the pharoah, Akhnaton, rebelled against polytheism in favor of monotheism, favoring the concept of one God as manifested in the visible Sun. Nevertheless, *Néfertiti et le rêve d'Akhnaton*, like the preceding novels, deals with woman, this time an Egyptian queen who worked behind the scenes, directing both her land's government and religious practices in secret, her husband, a sickly man, being incapable of assuming such functions.

In *Les Marches de sables* Chedid introduces her readers to a world coming to its end. The characters, three women, have shed whatever specificity they once may have had. Now they are people of all seasons. Rather than a city room, or a grotto or region under the earth, or a remote historical setting—the background for Chedid's previous novels—she underscores the desert experience. Unlike *Le Survivant*, in which the protagonist goes into the desert to discover her husband's whereabouts, in *Les Marches de sable* the three main characters exile themselves amid the infinite desert sand, withdrawing from the world, from life itself. In this barren and desolate environment, they begin to search for their own center of gravity, their own absolute, longing to discover an answer to their unfulfilled life experience.

La Maison sans racines (*Return to Beyrouth*) gravitates around the theme of war: specifically, the Lebanese tragedy so close to Chedid's heart. The plot revolves around the excoriating killing of a little girl during a gun battle between political and religious factions tearing the country apart.

Mondes Miroirs Magies (Worlds Mirrors Magic) comprises twenty-one short stories divided into three sections. The first, *Mondes*, relates to the parts of the globe in which the actions and situations take place: France, the United States, and the Middle East. The second, *Miroirs*, focuses on reflections, images, and memories so tenuous as to be barely discernible in the shadow of memory. *Magies* revolves around the fantasy world: the irrational to which the artist clings with such fidelity and strength, since it is this sphere that allows one to glimpse otherwise unknown dimensions and then return with the new poetic message.

A poet but also a humanitarian, Chedid in her novel *L'Enfant multiple* deals with the Lebanese war, a paradigm of all wars, through the feeling world of an eleven-year-old orphan boy who must leave his native land and live in Paris. That two lands, France and Lebanon, and two religions, Islam and Christianity, are focused upon is not surprising in view of Chedid's own multinational origins. Convinced that the worship of Deity should help bring people together rather than destroy them, the very idea of creating war to proseletyze or dominate others, she contends, defeats the basic purpose and principle of religion.

Poetry is humanity's common language. For Chedid poems are, to a great extent, plainchants in honor of life, hymns to the earth and the heavens, to the vastness of the cosmic experiences.

Chedid the poet belongs to no group, no school. Her poetry is her own, a unique distillation of what she has experienced and felt most deeply. Whether in *Textes pour une figure* (Texts for a Face), *Textes pour un poème* (Texts for a Poem), *Textes pour le vivant* (Texts for the Living), *Terre et poésie* (Earth and Poetry), *Cavernes et soleils* (Caverns and Suns), or *Epreuves du vivant* (Ordeals of the Living) or other collections of poems, Chedid's stanzas contain all sorts of aromatic flavors, collages of sensual arabesques, and disquieting abstractions. Hers is poetry divested of all sentimentality and any taint of romanticism. Solidly structured, like blocks of granite or marble, each word, line, and verse is hewn from her inner being, anchored to her psyche, while its meanings, rhythms, and sensations impact through pleromatic spheres.

Egypt, Lebanon, and France are focused upon in her verse, as they are in her novels. Chedid endows these lands with soul and psyche, form and flesh. Their different mores and topographies are underscored by tracing out their lifelines through imagery, their currents, crosscurrents, and undercurrents via cumulative rhythmic devices. Distinct in their own ways, under her aegis these disparate lands form a cohesive whole. Frontiers, for Chedid, whether spiritual, political, philosophical, or literary, are artificial obstructions, barriers that prevent human beings from communicating freely with one another; impediments erected by those whose vision is stunted, short-sighted, whose cares are mundane, even retrograde, whose desires are petty and conventional. Such forms and formalities do not exist for Chedid. Humanity, she believes, possesses a common meeting ground, an area that exists within each person and which she continually probes in her writings—the collective unconscious, the deepest layer of the psyche.

Chedid came to playwriting late in life. While still in Egypt, she worked closely with a number of amateur groups, but only as actress and not as dramatist. Everything onstage emerges directly from the body of the written text. Her protagonists are flesh-and-blood beings, but they also are atemporal, archetypal, arising from the deepest layers of the unconscious. Chedid's characters do not develop psychologically as in conventional theater. When they move about on stage weaving intricate patterns in space, each becomes an energy center, diffusing its own aura, which either attracts or repels the others. Her frequently statically paced dialogue injects her plays with a sense of timelessness, capturing thereby the stillness and terror of eternity. Suspense is accentuated not by exaggerated rhythmic effects, not by plot, but rather by the juxtaposition of images and/or emanations. Actions and gestures are studied, restrained, rarely flamboyant. Silences and breathing, both spasmodic and in long protracted intervals, heighten the feelings of apprehension implicit in her dramas.

Bérénice d'Egypte (Berenice of Egypt, 1968) deals again with woman's power. Set in Alexandria (58–55 B.C.) under the rulership of Ptolemy XI, the illegitimate son of Ptolemy VIII of the Macedonian dynasty, it is innovative in its use of lighting, masks, puppets, and dialogue. Each of these elements is orchestrated into the body of the play, infusing it with complexity, variety, and emotional impact.

Les Nombres (Numbers, 1968) is based on the story of Deborah, recounted in the Old Testament (Judges 4:4–9). Unlike other twentieth-century biblically inspired dramas, such as Gide's bombastic *Saul* or Giraudoux's lifeless *Sodom et Gomorrhe*, Chedid's two-act play is wholly free of pseudoerudition and maudlin sentimentality. The philosophical and thematic import of *Les Nombres* is relevant to today's problems: issues such as large-scale war, pollution, and the like, but with respect to one's own private, personal existence. Questions of identity and fulfillment, of the significance of one's relationships with others, are broached—all in an effort to determine at what point one is most truly oneself.

Le Montreur (The Puppeteer, 1969), with musical accompaniment, is a blend of whimsy and banter; it consists of passionate tirades and sequences of dancing and mime in a *commedia dell' arte* atmosphere. The Puppeteer, the prime instigator of the activities, represents consciousness. Ageless and emotionless, his face bears the immobility and the fixity—even the pallor—of those ancient masters of ceremonies, those divine seers, and prophets, who precipitate action, encourage divisiveness, and empower the play to go on.

Echec à la Reine (Queen's Checkmate, 1984), played out in nine sequences, dramatizes the story of a Queen and her Buffoon, their adventures, and the tensions arising between laughter and sorrow, love and power during the course of the events. On another level, a second couple plays out its views of the farce, which is their life and life in general, with its anguishes and moments of tenderness and violence.

Chedid's novels, poems, and plays speak to audiences today. Her writings are direct, unvitiated, and divested of all preciosity and rococo elaboration. Unsparing in the authenticity of the feelings or sensations she seeks to convey, she inoculates her readers with pain and torment, if these are deemed necessary, in order to disclose the acute nature of the protagonist's struggle. Language for Chedid is *being*: a catalyst that acts and reacts on the reader visually, spiritually, totally.

SURVEY OF CRITICISM

Two full-length works, both entitled *Andrée Chedid*, have appeared on Chedid's writings: a study of her poetry by Jacques Izoard (1977) and an analysis of her novels, poetry, and theater by Bettina L. Knapp (1984). An interview with Chedid has also been published: in *French Novelists Speak Out* (1976), edited by Knapp. Magazine and newspaper articles have been plentiful, including those by Patric Rosbo in *Lettres françaises* (October 4, 1971); Robert Abirached (*L'Avant-scène*, April 1–15, 1971); Michel Bourgeois (*La Quinzaine littéraire*, October 16, 1972); Michel Cournot (*Le Nouvel Observateur*, October 2, 1972); Tahar ben Jelloun (*Le Monde des livres*, May 5, 1988); Claude Margat (*La Quinzaine littéraire*, June 1, 1988); and in reference works (*Contemporary Literary Criticism*, vol. 47, 1988).

The critical articles and volumes on Chedid's work have been highly favorable, underscoring her originality and the thoughtful and profound nature of her works.

NOTE

Portions of this chapter appeared in Bettina Knapp's *Andrée Chedid* (Amsterdam: Editions Rodopi, 1984). Reprinted with permission of the publisher.

BIBLIOGRAPHY

Works by Andrée Chedid

Novels

Le Sommeil délivré. Paris: Flammarion, 1952.
Jonathan. Paris: Le Seuil, 1955.
Le Sixième Jour. Paris: Flammarion, 1960.
Le Survivant. Paris: Juillard, 1963.
L'Autre. Paris: Flammarion, 1969.
La Cité fertile. Paris: Flammarion, 1972.
Néfertiti et le rêve d'Akhnaton. Paris: Flammarion, 1974.
Les Marches de sable. Paris: Flammarion, 1981.
La Maison sans racines. Paris: Flammarion, 1985.

Poetry

Textes pour une figure. Paris: Pré aux Clercs, 1949.
Textes pour un poème. Paris: G.L.M., 1950.
Textes pour le vivant. Paris: G.L.M., 1953.
Textes pour la terre aimée. Paris: G.L.M., 1955.
Terre et poésie. Paris: G.L.M., 1956.
Terre regardée. Paris: G.L.M., 1960.
Double-pays. Paris: G.L.M., 1965.
Contre-Chant. Paris: Flammarion, 1969.
Visage premier. Paris: Flammarion, 1972.
Fêtes et lubies. Paris: Flammarion, 1973.
Prendre corps. Paris: G.L.M., 1973.
Fraternité de la parole. Paris: Flammarion, 1975.
Cérémonial de la violence. Paris: Flammarion, 1976.
Le Coeur et le temps. Paris: L'Ecole, 1977.
Cavernes et soleils. Paris: Flammarion, 1979.
L'Enfant multiple. Paris: Flammarion, 1989.

Short Stories

Le Corps et le temps suivi de l'Etroite Peau. Paris: Flammarion, 1979.
Mondes Miroirs Magies. Paris: Flammarion, 1988.

Theater

Théâtre I. Paris: Flammarion, 1981.
Echec à la Reine. Paris: Flammarion, 1984.

Essays

Le Liban. Paris: Le Seuil, 1974.
Guy Levis-Mano. Paris: Seghers, 1974.

Books for Children

Grandes Oreilles, toutes oreilles. Paris: Laffont, 1976.
Le Coeur et le temps. Paris: L'Ecole, 1976.
Lubies. Paris: L'Ecole, 1976.
Le Coeur suspendu. Tournai: Castermann, 1981.
L'Etrange Mariée. Paris: Editions du Sorbier, 1983.
Grammaire en fête. Romille: Folle Avoine, 1984.

Translations of Andrée Chedid

From Sleep Unbound. Trans. Sharon Spencer. Athens: Ohio University Press/Swallow Press, 1983.
Return to Beyrouth. Trans. Roz Schwartz. London: Serpent's Tail/Grove, 1989.
Translation of seventeen of Chedid's poems in *Contemporary French Women Poets*. Ed. and trans. Carl Hermey. Van Nuys, Calif.: Perivale Press, 1977.
The Sixth Day. Trans. Isobel Strachey. London: Serpent's Tail/Grove, 1988.

Studies of Andrée Chedid

Izoard, Jacques. *Andrée Chedid*. Paris: Seghers, 1977.
Knapp, Bettina L. *Andrée Chedid*. Amsterdam: Rodopi, 1984.
————, ed. *French Novelists Speak Out*. Troy, N.Y.: Whitson, 1976.

CHRISTINE DE PIZAN
(c. 1365–c. 1430)

Charity Cannon Willard

BIOGRAPHY

Christine de Pizan was not the first woman writer in France, but she was the first to leave behind her information about her life or intellectual formation. Although this is not as complete as one might wish, it is still possible to follow her progress from her birth in Venice around 1365 to her death, probably in the Abbey of Poissy, soon after 1430.

In spite of having spent most of her life in Paris, she was, indeed, Italian by birth. Her father was a native of Bologna, although the family had originated in Pizzano, south of the city. Tommaso de Pizzano earned a medical degree at the University of Bologna and for a short time was a lecturer there in astrology, then considered a science related to medicine, before entering the service of the Venetian Republic. The Venice that he knew was a prosperous city, frequented at that same time by Petrarch and Boccaccio. He had been urged to go there by a friend of university days, Tommaso Mondino of Forlì, whose daughter he subsequently married. He did not, however, remain in Venice long after Christine's birth, for in that day astrology flourished at royal courts, and he was given the opportunity to go to the court of Charles V in Paris, as royal astrologer and scientific advisor. He went at first for a trial period, but soon decided to establish himself there at the court ruled by an unusually capable king, whose intellectual curiosity and respect for learning were remarkable for the period. The Italian family flourished under the king's patronage.

As Christine grew up in that favorable atmosphere, she gave evidence of a distinct taste for learning, a quality encouraged by her father. Little is known of the actual details of her early education, although it seems possible that she studied with her two younger brothers. In any case, her studies were interrupted when she was sixteen by her marriage to a promising young notary, a university graduate, from Picardy. The year of the marriage, her husband, Etienne du Castel, was given a promising appointment as a secretary in the Royal Chancellery. His future seemed very bright indeed.

The marriage turned out to be a very happy one, enhanced by the birth of three children, a daughter and two sons. Their happiness was somewhat dimmed, to be sure, by the death of the benevolent king, followed by that of Christine's father. True disaster struck, however, with Etienne's sudden death, after only ten years of marriage. He was on a mission away from Paris with the young king, Charles VI. One suspects that he may have been the victim of one of the plague epidemics that swept over Europe repeatedly at this period. Thus at twenty-five, Christine found herself the sole support of three children, not to mention a niece who had been left in Paris when her brothers returned to Italy to claim family property there. Christine soon found herself in a world that had little respect for women, where she was cheated at every turn and involved in endless lawsuits when she attempted to claim money that was due her from her husband's estate. A woman of weaker will would certainly have been daunted, but not Christine. In order to provide herself with some comfort in this hostile world, she returned to studying on her own and to writing poetry in order to give expression to her grief. She soon discovered in herself a talent for writing verse in the fixed forms popular in her day: the ballade, the rondeau, and the virelay. It was undoubtedly this skill that provided her with a point of contact with the court of the king's brother, Louis of Orleans, whose wife, Valentina Visconti, was, like Christine, an Italian by birth. Furthermore, the head of this noblewoman's household was Giles Malet, who had been in charge of Charles V's library and was also a longtime friend of Etienne du Castel's family.

The character of the Orleans court inevitably influenced the nature of Christine's poetry beyond the earliest verses devoted to her widowhood. In contrast to Charles V's admiration for learning, his sons encouraged a revival of traditional chivalric values, thus inspiring poetry celebrating so-called *fin'amors* and delighting in discussions and debates centering on love. Christine adapted herself to these ideals, admitting that love was the matter most pleasing to everyone, but also complaining that she was obliged to write about love with quite another sentiment in her heart.

It was to the Duke of Orleans that Christine dedicated several early works, and it was undoubtedly at his court that she met noblemen who would later play a role in her life, notably the Earl of Salisbury, a close friend of the English king, Richard II, who offered a place in his household to Christine's son Jean, now thirteen years old. Unfortunately, Jean had not been long in England when Salisbury was killed by a mob while defending his king, and although the usurper of the English throne, Henry IV, offered Christine, as well as Jean, a place at his court, she was determined to bring the boy back to France. It was probably her unsuccessful effort to have the Duke of Orleans find a place for Jean in his household that encouraged Christine to change her alliance to the Duke of Burgundy, who not only found employment for the young man but also commissioned Christine to write an account of the life and reign of his brother, the late King Charles V. This was her first major work in prose.

Slightly earlier, however, her views on Jean de Meun's continuation of the *Roman de la rose* (*Romance of the Rose*), some forty years after the original poem had been composed by Guillaume de Lorris, involved Christine in a debate with former colleagues of her husband's at the Royal Chancellery, notably Jean de Monstreuil and Jean and Pierre Col. These early humanists admired the erudition of the poem, which was extremely popular at the end of the fourteenth century, whereas Christine deplored the bad influence on young men of the poem's misogynistic attitude toward women. She was seconded in her disapproval by the Chancellor of the University of Paris, Jean Gerson, although he was more disturbed by the poem's possible influence on public morality than by its misogyny. Christine did not initiate the debate or the resulting exchange of letters, as was formerly believed, but she brought it to public attention by giving copies of the letters to the queen, Isabeau of Bavaria, early in 1402. The publicity Christine gained from this gesture, as well as from the letters themselves, undoubtedly played an important part in establishing her reputation as a writer. It also established her as a defender of women against traditional literary slander and inspired her to write further works in their defense.

The year 1405, when she wrote her autobiographical *Avision-Christine* (Christine's Vision), marked not only a high point in her career, but a low point in the affairs of France. In the course of the summer there was a showdown between two rival princes, the dukes of Orleans and Burgundy, for John the Fearless had recently inherited Burgundy from his father, Philip the Bold. The resulting crisis was the inspiration for a letter written by Christine to the queen on October 5, begging her to follow the traditional role of queens as peacemakers, and by mediating this quarrel to become the savior of France.

It may also have been this crisis that focused Christine's attention on the importance of a suitable education for the heir to the French throne, Louis of Guyenne, to whom she subsequently dedicated several works dealing with the popular humanistic theme of the Perfect Prince. At the same time, however, the political situation in France was constantly deteriorating, and to internal problems there was added the threat of invasion by the English. These problems inspired Christine, in 1410, to address a letter to the king's uncle, the elderly Duke of Berry, begging him to take the lead in saving the country. Soon after this, a civil uprising, the so-called Cabochien revolt, broke out, protesting abuses in the government. This led her to appeal again, this time to the Duke of Guyenne, the dauphin, as this prince, now sixteen, appeared to be developing much-needed qualities of leadership. Unfortunately, his untimely death, shortly after the French defeat at Agincourt (November 1415), merely added to the country's misfortunes.

The Agincourt disaster inspired Christine's *Epistre de la prison de vie humaine* (*The Epistle of the Prison of Human Life*), addressed to the Duke of Berry's daughter Marie, Duchess of Bourbon, but attempting to console all the women who had suffered losses at Agincourt. The grieving young widow of earlier years had now learned to address herself to the sorrows of other women.

As the violence in Paris continued to grow, Christine sought refuge in a convent away from the troubled city, probably the Abbey of Poissy, where her daughter, Marie, had been a nun for many years. It was there, eleven years later, that her hopes for the salvation of France were renewed by the appearance of Joan of Arc, who not only raised the lengthy siege of the city of Orleans, but made possible the coronation of Charles VII at Rheims. It was this event that inspired Christine to write one more poem, the first inspired by this unexpected heroine, the *Ditié de Jeanne d'Arc* (*The Poem of Joan of Arc*). Thus her career as a writer ended on a note of triumph. The date of her death is unknown, but Guillebert de Mets, recording in 1434 his memories of Paris, refers to her in the past tense, and Martin LeFranc wrote of her in 1441, ''Though death may draw a curtain around her body, her name shall still endure.''

MAJOR THEMES

The variety represented by Christine's writings is, in a certain sense, astonishing, but a detailed examination makes it evident that they represent a coherent evolution in Christine as an intelligent, reflective human being following, as she herself put it, the ''long road of study.'' Beginning with the short lyric poems in the popular fixed forms of her day, she wrote first on courtly themes, eventually putting these short poems together into cycles representing conversations between lovers, sometimes from a lady's point of view, and even sometimes from a man's. She did not believe that the traditional courtly customs concerning love were admirable, nor indeed did they bring happiness, for taking place outside marriage, they had no possible outcome but deception and even death. She also wrote poems of circumstance and apparently some for the sort of poetic contests popular for celebrating St. Valentine's Day or May Day. From these she progressed to longer poems on more serious subjects. The first of these was the *Epistre au Dieu d'Amour* (*The Letter to the God of Love*, 1399), in which she made fun of the pretenses of young noblemen to honor women when they really mocked them and held traditional misogynistic views. Although it has been shown that this poem was not the origin of the debate over the *Roman de la rose*, undoubtedly it prepared the way for her participation in the exchange of letters that took place between 1401 and 1403. The publicity that resulted was important in establishing her literary reputation. It also turned her attention to writing prose, although not before she had written poems of increasing length, from the *Dit de la pastoure* (The Tale of the Shepherdess), a pastoral poem along traditional lines, but told from the point of view of a shepherdess, to the *Livre du duc des Vrais Amants* (*The Book of the Duke of True Lovers*), in which she undertook to demonstrate the folly of a love affair between two cousins, one of them married, for which there could be no possible happy ending. Between these two she wrote a long narrative poem, *Le Débat de deux amants* (The Debate of Two Lovers), in which she introduced an independent young lady, the forerunner of the ''Belle Dame sans Merci,'' who was not impressed by the theories of love expressed by either an old knight or an idealistic young squire. Along with these, she wrote, in a mixture of poetry and prose, an allegorical *Epitre de la déesse Othéa à Hector* (*The Letter of Othea to Hector*), in which she made use of such classics as Ovid and the story of the Trojan War to inculcate a suitable standard of behavior in a young knight. This was one of her most popular works, although its appeal to modern readers is limited.

Of greater interest is her semi-autobiographical *Chemin de long estude* (The Long Road of Learning) in which, guided by the Cumean sibyl, she travels across the world into the celestial realm, where she finds herself at the court of Reason. There she is given a message to take back to Earth to the French princes, reminding them of how the world should be governed. Thus, there is not only an interesting revelation of Christine's ambitions for study, but also her justification, because of her learning, to speak out on public issues. The following year (1404), she devoted her efforts to an even longer allegory, which also had some autobiographical elements, *La Mutacion de fortune* (The Mutation of Fortune), examining the role of the fickle goddess Fortuna in human affairs, describing not only the demands made on her because of her widowhood, but her personal problems seen in the context of universal history. It was undoubtedly this lengthy poem that brought about the Duke of Burgundy's commission for the biography of Charles V.

The year 1405 saw the completion of several of Christine's most important works: the *Livre de la Cité des Dames* (*The Book of the City of Ladies*), a reworking of Boccaccio's *De Claris mulieribus* (*Concerning Famous Women*) in terms more favorable to women in history, along with its sequel, the *Livre des trois vertus* (*The Book of the Three Virtues*), dedicated to the old Duke of Burgundy's granddaughter, recently married to Louis of Guyenne, heir to the French throne, a book of advice to princesses, but also to women of all sectors of society, from queens to prostitutes. It was, perhaps, her final word on the Rose debate. In the course of the same year, she completed her semi-autobiographical commentary on the state of France, *L'Avision-Christine*, and in October, in the midst of the threat of civil war, she addressed to Isabeau de Bavière the letter on the duty of queens as peacemakers mentioned earlier.

This letter launched Christine on the final stage of her career as commentator on the public scene and also as educational advisor to Louis of Guyenne. It was for him that she wrote the *Livre du corps de policie* (The Body of Policy), based on the image of the state as a body with the ruler as the head, inspired by John of Salisbury's *Policraticus*. It is probably also for this prince that Christine wrote the *Livre des fais d'armes et de chevalerie* (*The Book of Fayttes of Arms and of Chivalry*), an adaptation and modernization of the *De Re Militari* by the Roman writer Vegetius. This was intended to call the attention of the pleasure-loving prince to the need for a ruler to be a military leader. If contemporary military leaders had paid more attention to the Roman examples cited by Christine, the disaster of Agincourt might have been avoided, or at least mitigated. It was, however, read by a later generation of military men in the second half of the fifteenth century and was translated into English and printed by Caxton.

It was certainly to Louis of Guyenne that she dedicated her *Livre de la paix* (Book of Peace, 1413), which grew out of her hope that the young prince, who by now had begun to show some qualities of leadership, would be able to save France from the increasingly serious threat of both civil war and English invasion. Unfortunately, he did not long survive the disaster of Agincourt. He died in December 1415.

In the course of these years, she also wrote the *Sept Psaumes allegorisés* (Seven Allegorized Psalms) at the request of the king's cousin, Charles, King of Navarre. He was one of several noblemen who tried repeatedly to reconcile the quarreling French factions. The following year she addressed to the king's only surviving uncle, the elderly Duke of Berry, one more letter, the *Lamentacion sur les maulx de France* (Lament on the Evils of Civil War), in which she begged the frivolous old man to take more seriously his responsibilities as peacemaker.

Unfortunately, neither Christine's pleas nor those of any of her contemporaries prevailed. The lines for the civil war between the Burgundian and the Orleans (or Armagnac) factions were sharpening, and all was brought to a crisis by a popular uprising in Paris headed by the butchers' guild. This was known as the Cabochien revolt after Simon Caboche, the leader. Although the Armagnacs gained the upper hand, the situation was soon complicated by the English invasion led by Henry V and the French defeat at Agincourt, in which many French leaders were slaughtered on the battlefield and many others were taken prisoner. The plight of the women who were left behind was the inspiration for Christine's *Epistre de la prison de vie humaine* (The Epistle of the Prison of Human Life). By the time she had finished it at the beginning of 1418, the Armagnacs had instituted such a reign of terror in Paris that Christine was fortunate to have a place of retreat available. It is true that Poissy was soon occupied by the English, but they respected the protecting walls of the royal abbey.

At some point during the eleven years between her retreat and the appearance of Joan of Arc, Christine wrote her *Heures de contemplation de la passion* (The Hours of Contemplation of the Passion). It is tempting to see in this meditation on Mary at the foot of the Cross a reflection of Christine's own sorrow at the news of her son's death in 1425. And, of course, the triumph of Joan of Arc crowned her long insistence on the capabilities of women. Not every writer ends a career on such a triumphant note.

SURVEY OF CRITICISM

The popularity of Christine de Pizan's writings has fluctuated according to interest in the writings of women. Although she herself thought that she would be more appreciated after her lifetime, the number of manuscripts containing her works which still exist indicates that she was appreciated throughout the fifteenth century, not least of all in the final decades, when several of her works were printed by Antoine Vérard, William Caxton, and other early printers. In the sixteenth century she was praised by both Jean and Clément Marot and mentioned by Jean Bouchet in his *Tabernacle des illustres dames*. She was undoubtedly read by Marguerite de *Navarre.

Even in the seventeenth century, when there was scant regard for medieval writers, Gabriel Naudé expressed a desire to publish the *Livre des trois vertus* and the *Livre de la paix*, although they remained in manuscript until the twentieth century. In 1653 Denys Godefroy undertook to make the *Livre des fais et bonnes meurs de Charles V* better known. The eighteenth century, however, marked a more significant revival of interest. Jean Boivin de Villeneuve published a biographical sketch of Christine in the *Mémoires de l'Académie des inscriptions et belles lettres* (1751), and Prosper Marchand included her in his *Dictionnaire historique* (1758–1759). Her first recognition as a feminist writer, however, occurred in Mlle de Kéralio's *Collection des meilleurs ouvrages français composés par des femmes* (1787).

The increasing interest in the Middle Ages of the early nineteenth century turned attention to Christine's political writings, producing Raimond Thomassy's *Essai sur les écrits politiques de Christine de Pisan* (1838), although in 1880, when the subject "Etude critique sur la vie et les oeuvres de Christine de Pisan" was proposed for a literary contest, none of the entries was considered worthy of the prize. The last decade of the century, however, saw the publication of Maurice Roy's monumental three-volume work, *Oeuvres poétiques de Christine de Pisan* (1886–1896), finally making available the text of a good portion of her writings.

It remained for the women's movement of the twentieth century to direct serious attention to the interpretation of Christine's writings, from Alice Hentsch's *De la littérature didactique du moyen âge s'adressant spécialement aux femmes* (1903), Rose Rigaud's *Les Idées féministes de Christine de Pisan* (1911), and Lula McDowell Richardson's *Forerunners of Feminism in French Literature of the Renaissance. Part I: From Christine de Pisan to Marie de Gournay* (1929) to the landmark biography of Marie-Josèphe Pinet (1927) and Suzanne Solente's valuable contributions.

Modern feminists are not entirely correct in seeing the 1970s as the beginning of women's studies, but it is true that contemporary interests have brought about a veritable deluge of new studies. In general these have centered around Christine's role in the debate over the *Roman de la rose*, her history of women adapted from Boccaccio in the *Cité des Dames*, and recently, her poem inspired by Joan of Arc. Mention must also be made of Millard Meiss's important studies of the early manuscripts containing Christine's works, especially his *French Painting in the Time of Jean de Berry: The Limburgs and Their Contemporaries* (1974), as well as the studies of her Italian sources encouraged by Franco Simone and his students. A detailed guide to these and other modern studies can be found in Angus Kennedy's admirable *Christine de Pizan: A Bibliographical Guide* (1984), of which a second edition is in preparation.

BIBLIOGRAPHY

Modern Editions of Christine de Pizan

Individual Works

Le Débat sur le Roman de la Rose. Critical Edition, with introduction, translation, and notes by Eric Hicks. Paris: Champion, 1977.
Le Livre des Fais et Bonnes Meurs du Sage Roy Charles V. Ed. Suzanne Solente. 2 volumes. Paris: Champion, 1936–1940.
Le Livre du Chemin de Long Estude. Ed. Robert Püschel. Berlin: Hettler, 1887; Rpt. Geneva: Slatkine, 1974.
Le Livre de la Mutacion de Fortune. Ed. Suzanne Solente. 4 volumes. Paris: Picard, 1958–1966.
Le Livre des Trois Vertus. Ed. Charity Cannon Willard. Paris: Champion, 1989.
L'Avision-Christine. Ed. Sister Mary Louise Towner. Washington, D.C.: The Catholic University of America Press, 1932.
"Epistre à la Reine." Ed. Angus J. Kennedy in *Revue des Langues Romanes* 91 (1988): 253–264.
Le Livre du Corps de Policie. Ed. Robert H. Lucas. Geneva: Droz, 1967.
Le Livre de la Paix. Ed. Charity Cannon Willard. The Hague: Mouton, 1958.
Les Sept Psaumes Allegorisés. Ed. Ruth Ringland Rains. Washington, D.C.: The Catholic University of America Press, 1965.
"La Lamentacion sur les Maux de la France." Ed. Angus J. Kennedy in *Mélanges de Langue et Littérature françaises du Moyen Age et de la Renaissance offerts à Charles Foulon.* I. Rennes: Institut de Français, Université de Haute-Bretagne, 1980. 177–185.
Epistre de la Prison de Vie Humaine. Ed. Angus J. Kennedy. Glasgow: At the French Department, 1984.
La Ditié de Jeanne d'Arc. Eds. Angus J. Kennedy and Kenneth Varty. Oxford: Society for the Study of Medieval Languages and Literature, 1977.

Collected Works

Christine de Pisan: introduction, choix et adaptation. Ed. Jeanine Moulin. Paris: Seghers, 1962.
Ballades, Rondeaux and Virelais: an Anthology. Ed. Kenneth Varty. Leicester: University Press, 1965.
Oeuvres Poétiques. Ed. Maurice Roy. 3 volumes. Paris: Firmin Didot, 1886–1896; Rpt. New York: Johnson, 1965.
La Querelle de la Rose: Letters and Documents. Eds. Joseph L. Baird and John R. Kane. Chapel Hill: University of North Carolina, 1978.
Cent Ballades d'Amant et de Dame. Ed. Jacqueline Cerquilini. Paris: Union Générale d'Editions, 1982.

Translations of Christine de Pizan

Individual Works

The Book of the Duke of True Lovers. Trans. Alice Kemp-Welch. London: Chatto and
  Windus, 1908.
The Epistle of Othea to Hector. Trans. Anthony Babington. Ed. James D. Gordon. Diss.,
  University of Pennsylvania, 1942.
The Epistle of Othea. Trans. Sir Stephen Scrope. Ed. Curt F. Bühler. London: Oxford
  University Press, 1970.
Christine de Pizan's *Letter of Othea to Hector*. Ed. and trans. Jane Chance. Newburyport,
  Massachusetts: Focus Library of Medieval Women, 1990.
The Boke of the Cyte of Ladyes. Trans. Brian Anslay (London, 1521). Rpt. in *Distaves
  and Dames: Renaissance Treatises for and About Women*. Delmar, New York:
  Scholars' Facsimiles and Reprints, 1978.
The Book of the City of Ladies. Trans. Earl Jeffrey Richards. New York: Persea Books,
  1982.
The Treasure of the City of Ladies. Trans. Sara Lawson. London: Penguin Books, 1985.
A Medieval Woman's Mirror of Honor: the Treasury of the City of Ladies. Trans. Charity
  Cannon Willard. Ed. Madeleine Pelner Cosman. New York: Persea Books, 1989.
The Middle English Translation of Christine de Pisan's Livre du Corps de Policie. Ed.
  Diane Bornstein. Heidelberg: Carl Winter, 1977.
Caxton, William. *The Book of Fayttes of Arms and Chyvalrye*. Ed. A.F.P. Byles. London:
  Oxford University Press, 1932.
*The Epistle of the Prison of Human Life with an Epistle to the Queen of France and
  Lament on the Evils of Civil War*. Ed. and trans. Josette A. Wisman. New York:
  Garland Library of Medieval Literature, 1984.

Collected Works

The Selected Writings of Christine de Pizan. Ed. Charity C. Willard. New York: Persea
  Books, 1991.
Poems of Cupid, God of Love: Christine de Pizan's *Epistre au Dieu d'Amours* and *Dit
  de la Rose*; Thomas Hoccleve's *The Letter of Cupid*. Ed. and trans. Thelma S.
  Fenster and Mary C. Erler. Leiden: E. J. Brill, 1990.

Studies of Christine de Pizan

Bornstein, Diane, ed. *Ideals for Women in the Works of Christine de Pizan*. Michigan
  Consortium for Medieval and Early Modern Studies I, 1981.
Hentsch, Alice. *De la littérature didactique du moyen âge s'adressant spécialement aux
  femmes*. Cahors: Coueslant, 1903. Rpt. Geneva: Slatkine, 1975.
Hindman, Sandra. *Christine de Pizan's "Epistre Othea": Painting and Politics at the
  Court of Charles VI*. Toronto: Pontifical Institute of Medieval Studies, 1986.
Kelly, Joan. *Women, History and Theory: The Essays of Joan Kelly*. Chicago: University
  of Chicago Press, 1984.
Kennedy, Angus J. *Christine de Pizan: A Bibliographical Guide*. London: Grant and
  Cutler, 1984.

McLeod, Enid. *The Order of the Rose: The Life and Ideals of Christine de Pizan*. London: Chatto and Windus, 1976.

Meiss, Millard. *French Painting in the Time of Jean de Berry: The Limburgs and Their Contemporaries*. New York: Braziller, 1974.

Pinet, Marie-Josephe. *Christine de Pisan (1364–1430). Etude biographique et littéraire*. Paris: Pierre Champion, 1927. Rpt. Geneva: Slatkine, 1974.

Rigaud, Rose. *Les Idées féministes de Christine de Pisan*. Neuchâtel: Attinger frères, 1911. Rpt. Geneva: Slatkine, 1973.

Richardson, Lula McDowell. *The Forerunners of Feminism in French Literature of the Renaissance from Christine of Pisa to Marie de Gournay*. Baltimore, Md.: Johns Hopkins Press, 1929. Rpt. Johnson Reprint Corp., 1973.

Solente, Suzanne. "Christine de Pisan." In *Histoire littéraire de la France*, vol. 40. Paris: Imprimerie Nationale and G. Klincksieck, 1969. 1–81.

Willard, Charity Cannon. *Christine de Pizan: Her Life and Works*. New York: Persea Books, 1984.

Yenal, Edith. *Christine de Pisan: A Bibliography of Writings*. 2nd ed. Metuchen, N.J.: Scarecrow Press, 1989.

HÉLÈNE CIXOUS
(1937-   )

Verena Andermatt Conley

BIOGRAPHY

Hélène Cixous was born on June 5, 1937, in Oran, Algeria. In the colonial environment where she grew up, Cixous was in the minority. Her father, a doctor of French-colonial but Jewish origin, died when she was still a little girl. This event marked all of her writing. Her mother, Eve, now living in Paris, was of Austro-German origin, and German, rather than French, is Cixous's native tongue. Cixous continues to insist that for her, German is a richer, more guttural language than the more abstract idiom of French. Members of her family were Sephardic Jews, and she lived through the persecutions of World War II. Subsequently, Cixous never lost her desire to fight the encroachment of power in all of its forms upon the human body and the human mind. She felt the need to break out of the world in which she was born and look for other worlds or realities less marked by the horrors of the political events of her childhood. She found these worlds in fiction. Sensitive to power at institutional levels—familial, academic, political—she has striven to find out where, historically, such repression occurs and how exclusions are articulated. In addition to reading myths and the German romantics, such as Heinrich von Kleist, Cixous began to study English literature, especially Shakespeare, whose passionate and diverse writings held much attraction. *Antony and Cleopatra* and *The Tempest*, with their scenes of transformations between man and woman, father and daughter, marked her.

Cixous went to study in France and began her career as an academic. In 1959, at the age of twenty-two, she passed the prestigious *agrégation* in English. She married and had two children, a daughter and a son, born in 1959 and 1962. In 1962 she became *assistante* at the Université de Bordeaux. In 1965 she and her husband were divorced and Cixous moved from Bordeaux to Paris. She was *maître assistante* at the Sorbonne from 1965 to 1967 and was appointed *maître de conférences* at Nanterre in 1967. Also in 1967 she published her first text, *Le Prénom de Dieu* (God's First Name). In 1968 she became *docteur ès lettres*. She was appointed *chargé de mission* to found the experimental Université de Paris VIII-Vincennes, now at Saint Denis, in the aftermath of the student riots of May 1968. An alternative to the traditional and, in the view of many, repressive French academic environment, Paris VIII was to be a center of learning where power structures and hierarchies would be kept to a minimum. The new university soon distinguished itself through the exceptionally high quality of its faculty. Since 1968 Cixous has been professor of English literature at Paris VIII. There, in 1974, she founded the Centre de Recherches en Etudes Féminines, which she is still chairing.

In 1969, Cixous founded with Tzvetan Todorov and Gérard Genette the experimental review *Poétique*, which soon became a forum for new ways of reading texts on both sides of the Atlantic. As a university professor, Cixous published her thesis, *L'Exil de James Joyce ou l'art du remplacement* (1968; translated as *The Exile of James Joyce*, 1972). Also in 1969, Cixous published her novel *Dedans* (*Inside*, 1986), for which she was awarded the prestigious Prix Médicis. Since then she has published close to fifty novels and plays and some more theoretical essays like *La Jeune Née* (1975; translated as *The Newly Born Woman*, 1986), the best known of Cixous's texts to date in the United States. Cixous continues to be the champion of freedom in her writings. The causes she espouses vary. From a need for personal liberation through a reading of psychoanalysis, she moves on to more collective struggles, the woman's cause, an interest in the Third World (expressed in her interest in Clarice Lispector and Nelson Mandela and in her plays on Cambodia or India), the German and Russian death camps (through Paul Celan, Ossip Mandelstam, Marina Tsvetayeva, Anna Akhmatova). Her involvement in these causes is parallelled by other textual and personal encounters: the philosophical texts of Jacques Derrida help her develop her own textual readings; her encounters with Antoinette Fouque, one of the most prominent figures in the women's movement in France, a psychoanalyst and founder of the French publishing house Des Femmes, who, for political reasons, never wrote a work of her own; Ariane Mnouchkine, the director of the experimental Théâtre du Soleil with whom Cixous has been collaborating for the past decade. Cixous conceives of her life as a constant search for new ways of emancipating the self and others, along with an ongoing discovery of the "mystery of life." The "themes" of her work are therefore intricately linked to her meditations and cannot simply be abstracted. What sets Cixous apart from many of her contemporaries is her insistence on, and celebration of, life rather than death.

MAJOR THEMES

Cixous's work does not deal with "themes" in any standard sense of the term. "Theme," for her always between quotation marks, deals with ways of inscribing life or death and with articulating the two. Her privileging of life is accompanied by a growing insistence on the fictional and the poetic. The poetic for her, though distinct from the fictional or from theater is not limited to verse. It deals with deliverance from social stigmas through a freeing of language, through invention of new ways of speaking and writing, as well as other ways of seeing, hearing, touching, and tasting. It is always her relationship with the other, with otherness, that allows for an opening. A transformation of the dynamics of self and other constitutes the political dimension underlying all of her writing. That transformation follows a general shift, in her words, from "the scene of the unconscious to that of history," or from the autobiographical "write yourself!" to theater dealing with history. This shift in Cixous's work is similar to that taking place on the French intellectual scene over the last twenty years or so. Cixous's trajectory, a combination of a fight for life and a meditation on writing, leads her through various causes: the freeing of the self under the impact of psychoanalysis, the freeing of women, legal injustice in France around the trial of the Jewish immigrant Pierre Goldman, the cause of the Third World, the exposure of torture in the death camps.

As a young professor of English, Hélène Cixous published articles on English literature in *Tel Quel* and wrote her thesis on James Joyce. Cixous never hid her ambivalence toward Joyce. On the one hand, she was interested in his techniques, his belief that transformations of linguistic structures would alter mental structures, and his awareness of ideological and political manipulations through language. On the other, she always marked her distance from a writing caught up in guilt and the anguish of paradox. Though Joyce influenced her work through his insistence on the necessity to create new languages, on musicalizing literature and joining body and spirit, she criticized him for his creative paradox: for Joyce, one must lose in order to have. In other words, one must kill in order to live, and the movement to life starts with a killing of the other, with death and with guilt. This concept differs significantly from Cixous's recognition that even though loss and death are inevitable and indeed necessary for life, the emphasis must be on life.

Cixous's first fictional texts, *Dedans* (1969), and especially her trilogy, *Le Troisième Corps, Les Commencements,* and *Neutre* (The Third Body, Beginnings, and Neuter), published from 1970 to 1972, mark a period of great hope. In the aftermath of May 1968, everything seemed possible. Writing under the sign of Marx and Freud or of political and libidinal economies, Cixous questions power structures and advocates a freeing of self and—or through—writing. Written at a time when the euphoria of new discoveries outweighed theoretical divergences, these texts combine many incompatible theories. The freeing of the subject and the undoing of repression go along with a reevaluation of what has been repressed: body, woman, writing.

Dialogue among different voices, and, in the form of intertextual references, with other writings, replaces the monologue of authorial control to keep the text open. In *Le Troisième Corps,* for example, the voice of the lover echoes that of other fictional lovers, especially those of Kleist's Jeronimo and the count F.

from "Das Erdbeben in Chili" (The Earthquake in Chile) and "Die Marquise von O" (The Marquise of O), respectively. Freud's rewriting of Wilhelm Jensen's *Gradiva*, a love story dealing with fetishism, entombment, entrapment, and life and death in the archeological setting of Pompeii, examining passion in its relation to life and death, also haunts Cixous's text.

Cixous's political and ideological commitments made her take a stand in the 1970s on a trial that polarized the French, that of Pierre Goldman, accused, without sufficient evidence, of murder. Cixous, like Foucault and others, wrote in his defense. *Un K. incompréhensible: Pierre Goldman* (An Incomprehensible Kase: Pierre Goldman, 1975), the letter *K* playing on echoes from Kafka's *Der Prozess* (*The Trial*) and "Vor dem Gesetz" (Before the Law), is a violent outcry against prejudice in the French legal system.

Her stance against repression and social injustice, which she sees as one with the death drive, led Cixous to espouse the cause of women. In her theoretical *Prénoms de personne* (Nobody's Name, 1974), a collection of essays on Freud, Hoffmann, Kleist, Poe, and Joyce, she deals with the association of the unified (phallic) subject, narcissism and death. She denounces in her readings of Poe and Joyce the attempt to put woman on the side of death. She shows how these writers' dialectical structures enclose women in a "limited economy" and an exchange dominated by a desire for death. To this, she opposes a general economy, a term that Georges Bataille, the contemporary French writer and philosopher, popularized via his works on anthropology and psychoanalysis. Cixous proposes an economy of the gift, related to spending and loss. Because for Cixous and other contemporary theoreticians the subject exists only in a differential relationship with other subjects, the insistence is on modes of exchange. Exchange, thought of in terms of giving and receiving, plays a crucial role in the woman question. How does one give, how does one receive? What, in such an exchange, is the relationship to alterity and the other? How does exchange affect language and writing? Like many contemporary writers and thinkers, Cixous believes that there is no possible social change—one with new ways of exchanging—without linguistic change.

Emphasis on new ways of exchanging and an affirmation of life function as the most important concerns of *La Jeune Née* (1975), by Cixous and Catherine Clément. The title *La Jeune Née* plays on *Là-je-nais*, there I am being born, and *La Genet*, a reference to the writer Jean Genet, whose poetic writings insist on the general equality of all human beings. In *La Jeune Née*, Cixous insists on the necessity of displacing the desire for recognition, always based on sexual war, which ends, symbolically, with the succumbing of one of the partners. To this, she opposes a desire for alterity, by which, through a journeying toward the other, through a process of identification without fusion, the self goes as far as possible toward the other, lets herself be altered by the other, yet does not become the other. This desire keeps the other alive. To bring about change, Cixous urges women to break their silence, to "write themselves." They must write their bodies, their desires, which heretofore have only been talked about by men. Freud's Dora is a central concern in *La Jeune Née*. Dora's "no," which terminates prematurely and on her own volition her sessions with Freud, leaves the latter despondent and defensive. Dora's "no" stops momentarily the familial merry-go-round of lies and adultery. It also strips Freud of his authority. Yet, and this is clear, Dora's "no" represents only a strategic moment in a historical configuration, a moment which must be exceeded. Dora is a major preoccupation in *Portrait du soleil* (Portrait of the Sun, 1974) and in a play, *Portrait de Dora*, performed at the Théâtre d'Orsay in 1975, published in 1976, and translated in 1977. It puts Freud on stage to show the analyst's own projections in his treatment of Dora and his writings on her.

Feminine pleasure, which has been denied to women and confiscated by men, is a preoccupation of such texts as "La Missexualité, où jouis-je?" (The Missexual, Where Am I Having Pleasure?), published in *Poétique* in 1976, and *La Venue à l'écriture* (*Her Arrival in Writing*, 1977; translated 1990), written in collaboration with Annie Leclerc and Madeleine Gagnon. In the latter, playing on *la venue*, she who has come, and *l'avenue*, the path, Cixous traces the origin of women's writing to the mother's voice and body.

In *Souffles* (Breath, 1975)—the title evokes breath, inspiration, rhythm—Cixous proposes to analyze the origin of writing in terms of a mother/daughter relationship. Men have made women into hysterics; they have vitiated the relationships between women, especially between mother and daughter. Cixous insists on the origin of writing as song, as something that comes from the body. *Souffles* insists on the necessity of rewriting mythology, the Bible, and literary history from a feminine point of view.

Cixous's personal difficulties contributed to the 1977 text *Angst*, which deals with the breakdown of a love relationship. The pain and anguish are not expressed in existential, representational terms, but in a metaphoric exchange of letters. The text, as always one of transformation, led Cixous to another phase in her consideration of women's issues. For the next few years Cixous espoused the cause of women in a more militant language, and her work appeared almost exclusively under the imprint of the publishing house Des Femmes, where Cixous enjoyed a close association with Antoinette Fouque, founder of a controversial but influential political group within the women's movement called Politique et Psychanalyse ("Psych et po"). She explained her decision to espouse the woman's cause in more militant fashion in an interview (published in Verena Andermatt Conley, *Hélène Cixous: Writing the Feminine*, 1984 and 1990) as reflecting her having attained an intellectual limit which, she felt, had to be surpassed. Consequently she developed a more marked interest in relationships among women, because, as she says, any liberation of women has to come from women, though men are never completely absent in her writing.

Cixous's work from this period intersects with both Derrida's essay on Kant, "Economimesis," in *Mimesis désarticulation* (1975) and Jean-François Lyotard's *Economie libidinale* (1974). The attributes masculine and feminine will eventually be replaced by other descriptive terms which make no reference to sexual difference, she believes. In this time of transition, Cixous clearly privileges women, capable, in her terms, of giving. She redefines the maternal. The daughter is always in tune with the mother. The woman gives because she nourishes the child. Because she is able to contain the child, the mother is both container and contained; her relationship to otherness is different from that of men, to whom things happen from the outside.

In her works from the late 1970s and early 1980s, influenced by her reading of Heidegger on poetry and language, Cixous asks and works through questions of knowledge, innocence, the law, life, and death in *Préparatifs de noces au-delà de l'abîme* (Wedding Preparations Beyond the Abyss, 1978), *Anankè* (1979), *Illa* (1980), *With ou l'art de l'innocence* (With or the Art of Innocence, 1981), and *Limonade tout était si infini* (Lemonade All Was So Infinite, 1982). Her militancy has taken a different turn. Less concerned with flight, flow, and abundance, she now meditates on the sublime and develops the notion of the infinitely small.

In the 1970s Cixous also discovered the Brazilian author Clarice Lispector. Meditating on the relationship between life and writing, Lispector put emphasis on the flowing quality of the word and on the origin of—or, as Cixous says, the arrival in—language and writing. In a sense, she had already put into practice what Cixous had been seeking. Cixous's article in *Poétique*, "L'Approche de Clarice Lispector," appeared in 1979, the same year as the bilingual text *Vivre l'orange/To Live the Orange*, which insists on sweet nourishing juices and on the necessity of keeping the other alive. In this work, the orange is closely related to the child and birth, to life, as well as to that other paradisiacal fruit, the apple, read simultaneously in English and French as fruit and calling, as apple and *appel*. Orange, as noun and adjective, as fruit and color, functions as a locus of correspondences of sight, touch, smell, taste, affecting reading and writing.

A break with Antoinette Fouque in the early 1980s prompted Cixous to leave Des Femmes temporarily. Her relationship with the publishing house had been increasingly strained. Cixous claims that she resented the limits a certain militancy imposed on her freedom. Another text, *Le Livre de Promethea* (*The Book of Promethea* or *Promethea's Book*, 1983; translated 1990), written after her encounter with Ariane Mnouchkine, the director of the experimental Théâtre du Soleil, marks a turn. The book is a celebration of their encounter and a feminine rewriting of the Promethean myth, which, along with the myths of Orpheus and Ulysses, has figured prominently in literature. *Le Livre de Promethea* marks the culmination of a search for a positive passion, for a positive love and a language that touches lightly, intermittently, without seizing or appropriating, but infusing with life. The Promethean myth, from its epic dimensions of freeing the world and mankind, is transposed to quotidian passion, to detail, to a market scene, to fruits and flowers.

Cixous's encounter with Mnouchkine proved decisive. Mnouchkine was known for her innovative productions of Shakespeare, linking the Elizabethan stage with Far Eastern techniques. The collaboration also marks in Cixous's production a shift toward what she calls the "scene of history." With Mnouch-kine, Cixous traveled to Cambodia to study a group of people that had been disinherited by their neighbors. Cixous's and Mnouchkine's play *L'histoire ter-rible mais inachevée de Norodom Sihanouk roi du Cambodge* (The Terrible but Unfinished Story of Norodom Sihanouk, King of Cambodia), performed in 1984, is the story of a people that had lived in happiness and who paid for their innocence with their lives. Always haunted by the notion of paradise, Cixous found in Cambodia the remnants of a people who had lived according to these ethics. Such an overtly political play is a continuation of Cixous's fight against all forms of bodily and spiritual repression. The play is infused with a contem-porary reading of the concept of freedom which, for Cixous, is linked to poetry and writing. *L'Indiade ou l'Inde de leurs rêves* (The Indiad or India of Their Dreams), a play produced in 1986, deals with problems of colonialism, the liberation of India, and nonviolence.

Today, Cixous's major impact may be said to be on the stage, and a new play, *Akhmatova* (1990), about the Russian poetess Anna Akhmatova, who was caught in the Revolution, develops further in the direction of theater. A script written for a televised film directed by Mnouchkine, *La Nuit miraculeuse* (The Miraculous Night, 1989), about the heritage of 1789, adds a new twist, that is, an opening to the world of cinema and television. Cixous's historical and political contributions, possibly under the influence of Ariane Mnouchkine, are now her most compelling. Yet, she herself is more at ease in, and derives more pleasure from, the writing of fiction. *La Bataille d'Arcachon* (The Battle of Arcachon, 1987) extends her experiments with new ways of writing about love, of linking absence and presence, self and other. She also produced *Entre l'écriture* (Be-tween Writing, or Enter Writing, 1986), a collection of new and previously published meditations on writing and painting. She has also focused on the relationship between writing and history in her lyrical account *Manne* (Manna, 1988), a tribute to Ossip Mandelstam, the Jewish Russian poet who died under the Stalinist regime, and the poet and fighter against apartheid, Nelson Mandela. A recently published work, *Jours de l'an* (Days of the Year, 1990), returns to a meditation on authorship, on the relation between author and writing, something dear to Cixous but that seems less pressing today than other more political issues raised in her plays.

SURVEY OF CRITICISM

In French, Claudine Fisher's *La Cosmogonie d'Hélène Cixous* is a painstaking and possibly the most complete explication to date of many of Cixous's writings. Another volume entirely devoted to Cixous consists of the proceedings of a conference organized in her name at the Utrecht Summer School of Critical Theory, entitled *Hélène Cixous, chemins d'une écriture*. Articles have appeared in many reviews, such as *Critique* and *Poétique*. Among the best is Lucette Finas's "Le Pourpre du neutre," reprinted in her *Le Bruit d'Iris*. Christiane

Makward, in "Structures du silence ou délire: Marguerite Duras, Hélène Cixous," performs a Lacanian reading in an analysis of the two women writers.

It appears that it is in Great Britain and in the United States that Cixous's work has attracted the most critical attention, especially around issues of feminism. In Great Britain, the chapter in Toril Moi's *Sexual/Textual Politics* entitled "Cixous: An Imaginary Utopia" tries to take Cixous to task for being essentialist and for not tying her writing to a precise political and social context. A recent article by Morag Sihach, "Their 'Symbolic' exists, it holds power—we, the sowers of disorder, know it only too well," in *Between Feminism and Psychoanalysis*, rehabilitates Cixous. Though Sihach mainly concentrates on *La Jeune Née*, she extends her article to Cixous's more recent plays. *Writing Differences*, edited by Susan Sellers, consists of articles by Cixous and her students. It illustrates how students can read in Cixous's way. The proceedings of a British conference organized around Hélène Cixous in Liverpool in 1989 have been published under the title *The Body and the Text: Hélène Cixous Reading and Teaching* (1990). The volume includes many sympathetic articles on and around Cixous.

In the United States, chapters have appeared in works such as Jane Gallop's *The Daughter's Seduction*; Dina Sherzer's "Postmodernist Feminist Fiction," in her *Representation in Contemporary French Fiction*; and Domna C. Stanton's, "Language and Revolution: The Franco-American Disconnection," in *The Future of Difference*. My own study, *Hélène Cixous: Writing the Feminine*, presents Cixous to American readers. For a more critical overview that historicizes Cixous without being antagonistic, see my introductions to Cixous's *Reading with Clarice Lispector* and *Readings*.

BIBLIOGRAPHY

Published Works of Hélène Cixous

Le Prénom de Dieu. Paris: Grasset, 1967.
L'Exil de James Joyce ou l'art du remplacement. Paris: Grasset, 1968.
Dedans. Paris: Grasset, 1969.
Le Troisème Corps. Paris: Grasset, 1970.
Les Commencements. Paris: Grasset, 1970.
Un Vrai Jardin. Paris: Editions de l'Herne, 1971.
Neutre. Paris: Grasset, 1972.
La Pupille. Paris: Gallimard, 1972.
Tombe. Paris: Seuil, 1973.
Portrait du soleil. Paris: Denoël, Collection Lettres Nouvelles, 1974.
Prénoms de personne. Paris: Seuil, Collection Poétique, 1974.
La Jeune Née (in collaboration with Catherine Clément). Paris: Union Générale d'Editions, 1975.
Un K. incompréhensible: Pierre Goldman. Paris: Christian Bourgois, 1975.
Révolutions pour plus d'un Faust. Paris: Seuil, 1975.

"Le Rire de la Méduse." *L'Arc* (1975): 39–54.
Souffles. Paris: Des Femmes, 1975.
LA. Paris: Gallimard, 1976.
"La Missexualité, où jouis-je?" *Poétique* 26 (1976): 240–49.
Partie. Paris: Des Femmes, 1976.
Portrait de Dora. Paris: Des Femmes, 1976.
Angst. Paris: Des Femmes, 1977.
La Venue à l'écriture (in collaboration with Annie Leclerc and Madeleine Gagnon). Paris: Union Générale d'Editions, 1977.
Chant du corps interdit, le nom d'Oedipe. Paris: Des Femmes, 1978.
Préparatifs de noces au-delà de l'abîme. Paris: Des Femmes, 1978.
Anankè. Paris: Des Femmes, 1979.
"Quant à la pomme du texte." *Etudes Littéraires* 12 (December 1979): 408–19.
"L'Approche de Clarice Lispector." *Poétique* 40 (1979): 408–19.
Vivre l'orange/To Live the Orange. Bilingual ed. Trans. Ann Liddle and Sarah Cornell. Paris: Des Femmes, 1979.
Illa. Paris: Des Femmes, 1980.
With ou l'art de l'innocence. Paris: Des Femmes, 1981.
Limonade tout était si infini. Paris: Des Femmes, 1982.
"Cahier de métamorphoses." *Corps écrit* 6 (1983): 65–75.
"Tancrède continue." *Etudes freudiennes* 21, 22 (1983): 115–31.
Le Livre de Promethea. Paris: Gallimard, 1983.
"12 Août 1980." Bilingual ed., trans. Betsy Wing. *Boundary 2* 12 (Summer 1984): 8–39.
La Prise de l'école de Madhubaï. Paris: Avant-Scène, 1984.
L'Histoire terrible mais inachevée de Norodom Sihanouk roi du Cambodge. Paris: Théâtre du Soleil, 1985.
La Bataille d'Arcachon. Quebec: Editions Trois, 1986.
Entre l'écriture. Paris: Des Femmes, 1986.
Théâtre. Paris: Des Femmes, 1986.
L'Indiade ou l'Inde de leurs rêves. Paris: Théâtre du Soleil, 1987.
Manne. Paris: Des Femmes, 1988.
La Nuit miraculeuse. Téléfilm. (Film Script by Ariane Mnouchkine and Hélène Cixous.) F.R. III, La Sept, December 1989.
Jours de l'an. Paris: Des Femmes, 1990.
"Clarice Lispector, Marina Tsvetayeva. Autoportraits," in "Femmes, Women, Frauen." *Avant-garde* 4 (1990).
"De la scène de l'inconscient à la scène de l'Histoire. Chemins d'une écriture." In *Hélène Cixous, chemins d'une écriture*. Amsterdam: Rodopi; Paris: P.U.V., 1990.
Akhmatova. Paris: Théâtre du Soleil, 1990.

Play Productions

Portrait de Dora. Paris, Théâtre d'Orsay, 1975.
La Prise de l'école de Madhubaï. Paris, Théâtre de l'Odéon, 1984.
L'Histoire terrible mais inachevée de Norodom Sihanouk roi du Cambodge. Paris, Théâtre du Soleil, 1984.

L'Indiade ou l'Inde de leurs rêves. Paris, Théâtre du Soleil, 1986.
Akhmatova. Paris, Théâtre du Soleil, 1990.

Film Productions

La Nuit miraculeuse (in collaboration with Ariane Mnouchkine). Paris: F.R. III, La Sept, December 1989.

Translations of Hélène Cixous

The Exile of James Joyce or the Art of Replacement. Trans. Sally Purcell. New York: David Lewis, 1972; London: Calder, 1976; New York: Riverrun, 1980.

"The Character of 'Character.' " Trans. Keith Cohen. *New Literary History* 5 (Winter 1974): 384–402.

"At Circe's or the Self-Opener." Trans. Carol Bové. *Boundary 2* 3 (Winter 1975): 387–97.

Interview with Christiane Makward. *SubStance* 13 (1976): 19–37.

"Fiction and Its Phantoms: A Reading of Freud's 'Das Unheimliche' ('The Uncanny')." Trans. R. Dennomé. *New Literary History* 7 (Spring 1976): 525–48.

"The Laugh of the Medusa." Trans. Keith Cohen and Paula Cohen. *Signs* 1 (Summer 1976): 875–99.

"Introduction to Lewis Carroll's *Through the Looking-glass* and *The Hunting of the Snark.*" Trans. M. Maclean. *New Literary History* 13 (Winter 1982): 231–51.

The Newly Born Woman. Trans. Betsy Wing. Minneapolis: University of Minnesota Press, 1986.

Inside. Trans. Carol Barko. New York: Schocken, 1986.

"Joyce: The Ruse of Writing." Trans. Judith Still. In *Post Structuralist Joyce.* Cambridge, Eng.: Cambridge University Press, 1984.

"Extreme Fidelity." Trans. Ann Liddle and Susan Sellers. In *Writing Differences.* Milton Keynes: Open University Press, 1987. 9–36.

"Tancrede Continues." Trans. Ann Liddle and Susan Sellers. In *Writing Differences.* 37–53.

"Reaching the Point of Wheat, or a Portrait of the Artist as a Maturing Woman." *New Literary History* 19 (Autumn 1987): 1–21.

"Writings on the Theater." Trans. Catherine Franke. *Qui Parle* (Spring 1989): 133–52.

"Foreword." Trans. Verena Andermatt Conley. In Clarice Lispector, *The Stream of Life.* Minneapolis: University of Minnesota Press, 1989. ix–xxxv.

"Difficult Joys." In *The Body and the Text: Hélène Cixous, Reading and Teaching.* Ed. Helen Wilcox, Keith McWatters, Ann Thompson, and Linda Williams. Hemel Hempstead: Harvester-Wheatsheaf, 1990.

Reading with Clarice Lispector. Ed., trans., and intro. Verena Andermatt Conley. Minneapolis: University of Minnesota Press, 1990.

Readings: The Poetics of Blanchot, Joyce, Kleist, Kafka, Lispector and Tsvetayeva. Ed., trans., and intro. Verena Andermatt Conley. Minneapolis: University of Minnesota Press (forthcoming).

Studies of Hélène Cixous

Armbruster, Carol. "Hélène-Clarice: nouvelle voix." *Contemporary Literature* 25 (Summer 1983): 145–57.

Boundary 2 12 (Winter 1984). Special issue on Cixous edited by Verena Andermatt Conley.

Camelin, Colette. "La Scène de la fille dans *Illa*." *Littérature* 67 (October 1987): 84–101.

Cameron, Beatrice. "Letter to Hélène Cixous." *SubStance* 17 (1977): 159–65.

Conley, Verena Andermatt. "Le Goût du nu." *Lendemains* 51 (1988): 120–28.

———. *Hélène Cixous: Writing the Feminine*. Lincoln: University of Nebraska Press, 1984, 1990.

———. Introduction to Hélène Cixous, *Reading with Clarice Lispector*. Minneapolis: University of Minnesota Press, 1990; Hemel Hempstead: Harvester-Wheatsheaf, 1990.

———. Introduction to Hélène Cixous, *Readings*. Minneapolis: University of Minnesota Press, 1990 (forthcoming).

Crowder, Diane Griffin. "Amazons and Mothers? Monique Wittig, Hélène Cixous and Theories of Women's Writing." *Contemporary Literature* 24 (Summer 1983): 117–44.

Defromont, Françoise. "Faire la femme, différence sexuelle et énonciation." *Fabula* 5 (1985): 95–112.

Duren, Brian. "Cixous' Exorbitant Texts." *SubStance* 10 (1981): 39–51.

Evans, Martha Noel. "Portrait of Dora: Freud's Case History as Reviewed by Hélène Cixous." In *SubStance* 11 (1982): 64–71.

Finas, Lucette. "Le Pourpre du neutre." In *Le Bruit d'Iris*. Paris: Flammarion, 1981.

Fisher, Claudine. *La Cosmogonie d'Hélène Cixous*. Amsterdam: Rodopi, 1988.

———. "Le Vivant de la mort chez Hélène Cixous." *Bérénice: Letteratura Francese Contemporanea* 10 (March 1984): 345–51.

Gallop, Jane. *The Daughter's Seduction*. Ithaca: Cornell University Press, 1984.

Gibbs, Anna. "Cixous and Gertrude Stein." *Meanjin* 38 (September 1979): 281–93.

Jardine, Alice, and Anne M. Menke. "Exploding the Issue: 'French' 'Women' 'Writers' and 'the Canon'?" *Yale French Studies* 75 (1988): 235–38.

Jones, Ann Rosalind. "Inscribing Femininity: French Theories and the Feminine." In *Making a Difference: Feminist Literary Criticism*. Ed. Gayle Greene and Coppélia Kahn. London: Methuen, 1985. 80–112.

———. "Writing and Body: Toward an Understanding of L'Ecriture féminine." *French Studies* 7 (Summer 1981): 247–63.

Kogan, Vivian. "I Want Vulva! Cixous and the Poetics of the Body." *Esprit Créateur* 25 (Summer 1985): 73–85.

Kuhn, Annette. "Introduction to Hélène Cixous's 'Castration or Decapitation?' " *Signs* 7 (Autumn 1981): 36–40.

Le Clézio, Marguerite. "Psychanalyse-poésie. Le Rite de Cixous la Méduse." *Bonnes Feuilles* 9 (Fall 1980): 92–103.

Makward, Christiane. Interview with Cixous. *SubStance* 5 (Autumn 1976): 19–37.

———. "Structures du silence ou délire: Marguerite Duras, Hélène Cixous." *Poétique* 9 (September 1978): 314–24.

Marks, Elaine, and Isabelle de Courtivron, eds. *New French Feminisms.* Amherst: University of Massachusetts Press, 1980.

Micha, René. "La Tête de Dora sous Cixous." *Critique* 33 (February 1977): 114–21.

Miller, Judith G. "Jean Cocteau and Hélène Cixous." In *Drama, Sex and Politics.* Ed. James Redmond. Cambridge, Eng.: Cambridge University Press, 1985. 203–11.

Moi, Toril. "Cixous: An Imaginary Utopia." *Sexual/Textual Politics.* New York: Methuen, 1985.

Richman, Michèle. "Sex and Signs: The Language of French Feminist Criticism." *Language and Style* 13 (Autumn 1980): 62–80.

Salesne, Pierre. "Ou l'art de l'innocence: The Path to You." In *Writing Differences.* Ed. Susan Sellers. Milton Keynes: Open University Press, 1988. 113–26.

Sandré, Marguerite, and Christa Stevens. "A Bibliography of the Works of Hélène Cixous." In *Hélène Cixous: chemins d'une écriture.* Ed. Françoise Van Rossum-Guyon and Myriam Diaz-Diocaretz. Amsterdam: Rodopi; Paris: P.U.V., 1990. 235–42.

Sherzer, Dina. "Postmodernist Feminist Fiction." In *Representation in Contemporary French Fiction.* Lincoln: University of Nebraska Press, 1986.

Sihach, Morag. "Their 'Symbolic' exists, it holds power—we, the sowers of disorder, know it only too well." In *Between Feminism and Psychoanalysis.* Ed. Teresa Brennan. New York: Routledge, 1989.

Stanton, Domna C. "Language and Revolution: The Franco-American Disconnection." In *The Future of Difference.* Ed. Hester Eisenstein and Alice Jardine. Boston: G. K. Hall, 1980. 73–87.

Van Rossum-Guyon, Françoise, and Myriam Diaz-Diocaretz, eds. *Hélène Cixous: chemins d'une écriture.* Amsterdam: Rodopi; Paris: P.U.V., 1990.

Wilcox, Helen, Keith McWatters, Ann Thompson, and Linda Williams, eds. *The Body and the Text: Hélène Cixous, Reading and Teaching.* Hemel Hempstead: Harvester-Wheatsheaf, 1990.

Willis, Sharon. "Hélène Cixous's *Portrait de Dora*: The Unseen and the Un-Scene." *Theater Journal* 37 (October 1985): 287–301.

———. "Mis-translation: Vivre l'orange." *SubStance* 16 (1987): 76–83.

COLETTE
(1873–1954)

Catherine Portuges and Nicole Ward Jouve

Like the pen name she chose to be known by, the writer who was born Sidonie-Gabrielle Colette is unclassifiable. Colette was her father's surname: it is also a French girl's first name. First and last, female and male, familiar and official, combine in that name, which refuses to be any one thing. It took her more than thirty years to establish it.

Her being was protean. She occupied and eluded all categories: serious writer, popular writer, vaudeville artist, trapeze then theater artist, makeup artist; *enfant terrible*, and at the end, *grande dame* of French letters; cook, gardener, cyclist, journalist, traveler, hostess, pin-up girl, three times wife; lesbian, mistress, lover; a daughter, a mother; secretive, a lover of solitude. And throughout it all, writing.

BIOGRAPHY

As with everything else about Colette, it is difficult to separate the life from the works. All her writing was in a sense drawn from, or shadowed forth, her life. Never autobiography in the normal sense, it also stretched the boundaries of fiction. Colette has written so much about her life that all biographies have had to be based on her own self-narrations. Untrustworthy narrator that she is, one never gets to the bottom of her life, and when the biographer gets hold of evidence or documentation she never used, it never makes as good a story as she would have told. Yet she has attracted more biographers than most other writers, and some excellent ones.

Her life thus comes to us mediated by an incredible number of personae, of careers, of self-narrations. It is also mediated by an incredible number of images. Throughout those many careers, Colette posed for hundreds of photographs, which most biographers, especially those who insist on her love-life, her taste for life, have used plentifully. She was extremely beautiful. The temptation is to dream in front of these pictures. The temptation is to naturalize those images, take them as the thing itself. But she posed for every one of them, for self-publicizing or theatrical purposes. She was in charge, even in the nude performances. The "real" Colette that is supposed to be behind the photographs, as behind the self-narrations, it is the purpose of the photographs, the narrations, to keep hidden, like her own *La Femme cachée (The Other Woman)*. The act is what there is to see, what there is to read.

The master-wizard with whom she served her apprenticeship to the art of manipulating images, of handling words, was her entrepreneurial first husband, Henri Gauthier-Villars, alias Willy. Sidonie-Gabrielle Colette (Gabri, as her parents called her) had been born January 28, 1873, in the Burgundy village of Saint-Sauveur-en-Puisaye, the last of four children, the daughter of retired captain Jules-Joseph Colette, who had lost a leg in Napoleon III's Italian campaign, and of Adèle-Eugénie Landoy, "Sido," whose second marriage this was. She had spent her childhood in the country and gone to the village school. The family, through bad financial transactions, had lost everything and had to sell the family house. Willy, a Parisian man-about-town, was fourteen years older than his country wife. He must have appeared as something of a godsend to the relatives of dowryless though pretty twenty-year-old Gabri.

Despite his resourcefulness as a reviewer, music critic, and editor, Willy had trouble making ends meet. He used hacks of all kinds, whose books he signed. It occurred to him that he could make something by using his young wife as a hack too: she had such good stories to tell about her village school, and was pining away. Dutifully, Gabri complied. The result was *Claudine à l'école (Claudine at School*, 1900), which Willy signed.

Colette was to claim that had it not been for Willy she would never have written, and that ever after her taskmaster would be financial necessity. Be that as it may, *Claudine à l'école* was a great success, all the more so as Willy deployed all his advertising genius to promote the book. He made Colette pose as schoolgirl Claudine for photographs; he encouraged her to put in spicy bits, developing the peasant nymphette, compliant pupil, and budding lesbian act. He made her play the Claudine part, dressed up as Claudine, on stage and in town. He made her follow suit. Three sequels came: *Claudine à Paris (Claudine in Paris*, 1901), *Claudine en ménage (Claudine Married*, 1902), and *Claudine s'en va (Claudine and Annie*, 1903); then *Minne* (1904) and *Les Egarements de Minne (The Innocent Libertine*, 1905). All were signed "Willy."

In 1906 Colette separated from Willy. Her father had died on September 17, 1905. She had been studying mime with George Wague. Willy, a consistent philanderer and lover of very young women, had a new, young mistress. It was he who told Colette to leave, but some sort of link endured, which included Colette now signing her books "Colette Willy." The divorce was not signed until 1910. Colette began acting in mimodramas. She created a scandal at the Moulin-Rouge by playing opposite the Marquis de Belboeuf, alias Missy, her

friend and lover between 1906 and 1912. She went on tours with fellow enter-
tainers, moving in and out of the world of music-hall theater, the so-called
demimonde, the elegant circles of *belle époque* lesbian Paris, strong friendships
with women friends such as Annie de Pène, and one half-hearted affair with
Auguste Hériot. *Les Vrilles de la vigne (The Tendrils of the Vine*, 1908), *La
Vagabonde (The Vagabond*, 1911), *L'Entrave (The Shackle*, 1913), and *L'Envers
du Music-Hall (Music-Hall Sidelights*, 1913) were the products of those years.
She also wrote about animals, cats and dogs in particular, whom she loved and
kept, and would continue to write about them for the rest of her life.

Colette's life underwent another dramatic change when she met Henri de
Jouvenel, the editor-in-chief of the paper *Le Matin*, for which she had begun to
write. They fell in love. Though both had prior attachments and the association
created more than a few ripples, they ran away together and eventually married
on December 19, 1912. Sido had died on September 25. Daughter Colette de
Jouvenel, "Bel-Gazou," was born on July 3, 1913. Six months later, on December 31 of the same year, Colette's half-brother Achille died. Her half-sister,
Juliette, had committed suicide in earlier years. Only brother Leo was left. In
the 1920s, Colette began to write about her childhood.

Colette worked as a journalist during the war, going up in a balloon, sometimes
reporting from the front, and visiting Jouvenel at Verdun. The years that followed
the war saw Colette's reputation as a writer grow: she published *Chéri (Cheri*,
1920), which she dramatized for the stage, playing the lead part of the aging
courtesan Lea. *Le Blé en herbe (The Ripening Seed)* came out in 1923, signed
just "Colette." Both books are concerned with the love between an aging woman
and a very young man: and this is precisely what had begun to concern Colette
in life, as between the books, at the Brittany seaside house where she vacationed
with her daughter, relatives, and friends, she began an affair with her sixteen-
year-old stepson, Bertrand de Jouvenel. This was, together with Jouvenel's own
infidelities, to lead to the breakup of the marriage, divorce being pronounced in
1924.

Yet another, crucial love relationship was to blossom. In 1925 Colette met
Maurice Goudeket, sixteen years younger than herself. They lived passionate
days at La Treille Muscate, the house at Saint-Tropez, on the Mediterranean,
that Colette had bought in 1926. They stayed together till Colette's death in
1954. Colette was the main breadwinner, an increasingly famous writer who
traveled to many places—Austria, Rumania, North Africa, New York. She was
made a member of the Académie royale de langue et de littérature françaises de
Belgique (1935), elected to the Académie Goncourt (1945), and named grand
officer of the Légion d'Honneur (1953). She made further attempts at earning
her living by other means than her pen, including, on the advice of her friend
Maginot, opening a beauty institute, which foundered some years ahead of the
celebrated line.

Goudeket, who was of Dutch Jewish extraction, was arrested by the Germans
in 1940 but was released thanks to the intervention of Colette's influential friends.

He was hidden during the rest of the Occupation years by a network of neighbors and shopkeepers from the Palais-Royal where, in a second-floor apartment, 9 rue de Beaujolais, Colette now had the last of her many homes. In the postwar years Goudeket in his turn looked after Colette, whose mobility and health had steadily declined after the shock of Goudeket's arrest. He supervised the edition of her *Oeuvres complètes* (Flammarion, 1948–1950). To the last Colette remained faithful to her many female friends. In the midst of Paris, and though she was now a literary celebrity, a formidable wise old woman giving interviews and around whom new generations flocked, she still kept her provincial Burgundy accent. Stranded as she was on her raft, as she called the couch on which she spent her last years half-paralyzed by arthritis, waking by the light of her *fanal bleu*, her blue lantern, over sleeping Paris, she retained her endless taste for life. She died on August 3, 1954, the first French woman of letters to be granted a secular state funeral. She is buried in Père-Lachaise cemetery.

MAJOR THEMES

Like everything else about Colette, her themes are inflowing. One cannot neatly separate them, nor can one nail them down. She eludes all isms. Colette the writer, narrator, and sometimes protagonist of her own fictions is no more bound by genre than her pen name is bound by gender.

She touched all genres, from the diary, as in *Journal à rebours (Looking Backwards,* 1941), to the essay, the memoir, the libretto of *L'Enfant et les sortilèges (The Boy and the Magic,* 1925), which she wrote for Ravel to put to music, the short story, the novella, animal plays such as *Dialogues de bêtes (Creature Conversations,* 1904) in the tradition of animal fables but also grandly predating Disney, prose poems of the love between women, a blend of the meditative and the elegiac: *Les Vrilles de la vigne.* Yet none of the categories just mentioned totally fits any of the works one might want to describe them by. There is in all she did an intrapenetrability of genre boundaries, so that, for instance, *Mitsou* (1919) is both theater and epistolary novel; novels like *Chéri* were made into plays; and family memoirs or apparent autobiographies are fictions: the doubleness shows in the mere fact that the English title *My Mother's House* (announcing autobiography) can be the translation of the French *La Maison de Claudine,* literally, "Claudine's House" (suggesting a return to the youthful fictions). Crafting everything she wrote with the most painstaking and professional care, always engaging and attractive and creating the illusion of effortlessness, Colette is also elusive. What she shows is in order to hide. She is always elsewhere.

Yet there is a wonderful clarity, sensuousness, and presence to her prose. From first to last, she wrote about childhood, the country she said she had lost but inhabited forever: the house and two gardens and the neighboring woods, countryside, and springs found in the Claudine novels as in *Sido* (1929), *La Naissance du jour (Break of Day,* 1928), or *L'Etoile Vesper (The Evening Star,*

1946). Her lore about plants and animals, her mouthwatering writing about food, her endlessly evocative sensuousness have tended at times to relegate her to a marginalized reputation. But her attention to the individuality and quiddity of every leaf, bird, and beast, to the the particularity and fullness of smell, sound, and touch redresses the balance in the hierarchy of values. Life is made by writing into a thing to be relished and wondered at; it is never anthropomorphized. A cat can play its full part in a love triangle with two humans, as Saha does in *La Chatte (The Cat*, 1933).

That Colette should at times have been regarded as a writer of the lesser aspects of life makes it important to stress that she was throughout the brilliant chronicler of successive eras: from the Belle Epoque to post-Occupation France through two world wars, the unsteady or fashionable thirties, changing sexual mores and fashions. She never seems to set out to write deliberately about big things like history. What she picked up as a reporter was never classifiable as ordinary journalism. But she was a witness of transition. She had her own political commentary, though it was not couched in political terms. Her writing is unerring and of amazing profundity. From her renderings of the Wagnerian jamborees at Bayreuth, which elegant Europe flocked to, from remarks about how Proust misrepresented "Gomorrhe"—though he was so accurate about "Sodome"— in *Le Pur et l'impur (The Pure and the Impure*, 1932), to the portrayal, through Chéri, of a generation of young men blasted and unmanned by World War I, in *La Fin de Chéri (The Last of Cheri*, 1926), to the exodus of June 1940 in *Journal à rebours*, she captured every time something essential and elusive about sixty years of modern history.

Almost all her works are concerned with love, even those she called her *blancs*, her whites, corresponding to the blank periods when a woman is not in love: bisexual love; desire and tenderness and passionate attachment between women; desire and jealousy and passion between men and women of all ages, from the very young girl's fascination for older men to the husband's suicide from insufferable jealousy in *Duo* (1934) to the aging woman's affair with a very young man. She has captured sexual awakening in male and female adolescents in quite extraordinary ways, from *Le Blé en herbe* to *Gigi* (1944). She has also movingly captured the tenacity and wisdom of older women's loves, the agonies and pleasures of aging, the growth in stature that comes with renunciation, letting go, opening out the hands toward what may be the birth of a new day rather than the end of a life in *La Naissance du jour*. And she has embodied the vagaries of the passions of so-called demimonde women, the actresses, music-hall comediennes, grisettes, and good-time girls, naive, generous, big-hearted, their solidarity, their vulnerability, their prodigality and splendor. Colette's writing about love is also deeply erotic in the best sense of the word, in that it imparts the thrill of pleasure, the feel of desire, but not, with the arguable exception of the Claudine and Minne novels, from a voyeuristic point of view: from the inside, as something shared and communicated and somehow known, even when it sweeps one away.

Again, throughout her work, Colette wrote about female friendships, from Claudine's worship of Mademoiselle Aimée and ambiguous bullying of Luce, to the equal, fun-loving, lifelong relationships with Marguerite Moréno, Annie de Pène, Germaine Beaumont, Renée Harmon, and others, the stage complicities and supportiveness of music-hall artistes, the unpredictable genderdance of the three sisters in *Le Toutounier* (*The Toutounier*, 1939), the deep feeling that relates the wife and mistress in *La Seconde* (*The Other One*, 1929) below the surface of the classical triangle.

The figure of the mother, on the other hand, was absent from all the early works: as long, in fact, as Colette's mother Sido was alive. The mother appears indirectly at first, partly through the figure of Lea, whose feeling for Cheri grows maternal through renunciation; also, through Colette's ambiguous writing about herself becoming a mother. But then, through the figure of Sido, the motif of the mother becomes prominent. The writer Colette writes about above and below, as it were, from the inside and from the outside: about being a mother's daughter, about being a daughter's mother. Creatively brooding over all is the figure of Sido, loving, possessive, large-hearted, hospitable, deeply original Sido, the giver of water chestnuts and hot chocolate, the heart of the home, open to garden and weather and the world at large as if she were the center of the four cardinal points, a mariner's compass to navigate by. The mother is a model, the horizon, something subtle and nobler toward which to travel in old age.

Like the figure of the father, also present in more discreet but crucial ways, the figure of the mother is connected with writing. The father gives the blank books, the name that until now has not become an inscription. The mother is the one who wrote. Her letters, remodeled by Colette, give the pattern and impulse of *La Naissance du jour*.

Above all, perhaps, Colette wrote about writing. She is a much more self-reflective writer than most, though the reflection is so deft, so pleasurable, with so little theorizing, that the self-awareness, the figures in the mirror, the relation to the model and to self-portraiture, the return of former fictional characters like Claudine as lovable or dangerous doubles, the temptation to let the power of memory, of nostalgia, sink you, the power of words to kill, never draw attention to themselves.

SURVEY OF CRITICISM

The critical literature on Colette is massive and filled with controversy, suggesting the range and vitality of the debates that continue to engage scholars across disciplinary and theoretical boundaries. Colette's work has enjoyed the attention of gifted scholars and translators whose fascination with the interrelationships between the persona of the author and her narrational personae is unabating. New editions and literary discoveries will no doubt give rise to still other debates, as a new generation of scholars resituates the writer in light of contemporary concerns.

In this constantly shifting critical terrain, readers will have the benefit of previously unpublished biographical material and primary texts. Colette's insufficiently recognized importance as a witness to her historical epoch is certain to be revealed by the extensive publication of her journalism, now in preparation by the Editions de la Pléiade, and a reissue of her work in paperback by Robert Laffont testifies to the sustained attraction of her texts.

The titles of articles on Colette indicate the diversity of current critical, more theoretical tendencies when compared with earlier, primarily biographical studies. Some, such as Sherry Dranch's "Reading Through the Veiled Text" and Diana Holmes's "The Hidden Woman," speak from a psychoanalytic standpoint in order to address persistent constructions of "hiddenness," while others take up the contradictory role of Willy in the writer's project as thief of her authorship or indispensable initiator.

The disputes are, if anything, even more passionate with regard to the blurred boundaries between autobiography and fiction: Nancy K. Miller's "Woman of Letters: The Return of Writing in Colette's *The Vagabond*" and "D'Une Solitude à l'autre: vers un intertexte féminin" are important interventions in the discourse of Colette in the context of autobiographical theory of the narrating self, as is Danielle Deltel's "Journal manqué, autobiographie masquée." Elaine Marks's unsurpassed volume, *Colette*, remains an indispensable point of reference for contemporary interpretations, while Eisinger and McCarthy's *Colette, the Woman, the Writer* offers a carefully balanced collection of critical perspectives.

The pre-oedipal dimension of Colette's texts has been a frequent critical subject privileged by feminist critics considering the textual body in light of "l'écriture féminine" in works such as Mary Lydon's "Myself and M/others" and Mary McCarthy's "Possessing Female Space: The Tender Shoot." The extent to which Colette may be read as "feminist" or as a more traditional "feminine" writer is a focus of Michèle Sarde's *Colette: Free and Fettered*, Nicole Ward Jouve's *Colette*, and Geneviève Dormann's *Amoureuse Colette*.

Finally, discourses of difference and otherness, particularly in French studies, point toward more focused interpretations of sexuality and the erotic than the critical literature—often evasive or silent on the subject—has yet offered. As these debates evolve, and as the resistance of Colette to gender categorization addresses post-modern and feminist critics, the issue of the self in writing is likely to remain central, reconceptualizing previous notions of autobiography as fiction and widening still further the horizons of Colette studies.

BIBLIOGRAPHY

Works by Colette

Claudine à l'école. Paris: Ollendorff, 1900.
Claudine à Paris. Paris: Ollendorff, 1901.
Claudine Amoureuse. Paris: Ollendorff, 1902.

Claudine en ménage. Paris: Mercure de France, 1902.

Dialogues de bêtes. Paris: Mercure de France, 1904.

Minne. Paris: Ollendorff, 1904.

Les Egarements de Minne. Paris: Ollendorff, 1905.

Sept Dialogues de bêtes. Preface by Francis Jammes. Paris: Mercure de France, 1905, 1943.

La Retraite Sentimentale. Paris: Mercure de France, 1907.

Les Vrilles de la vigne. Paris: Editions de la vie parisienne, 1908.

L'Ingénue libertine. Paris: Ollendorff, 1909.

La Vagabonde. Paris: Ollendorff, 1911.

L'Entrave. Paris: Librairie des Lettres, 1913.

L'Envers du music-hall. Paris: Flammarion, 1913, 1948.

Prrou, Poucette et quelques autres. Paris: Librairie des Lettres, 1913.

La Paix chez les bêtes. Paris: Georges Crès et Cie., 1916.

Mitsou ou Comment l'esprit vient aux filles. Paris: A. Fayard, 1919.

Chéri. Paris: A. Fayard, 1920.

La Chambre éclairée. Paris: Eduard Joseph, 1920.

Chéri, comédie en quatre actes. With Léopold Marchand. Paris: Librairie théâtrale, 1922.

La Maison de Claudine. Paris: J. Ferenczi et Fils, 1922.

Le Voyage égoiste. Paris: Editions d'art Edouard Pelletan, 1922; Paris: Fayard, 1986.

Le Blé en herbe. Paris: Flammarion, 1923.

Rêverie du nouvel an. Paris: Stock, 1923.

La Vagabonde, comédie en quatre actes. With Leópold Marchand. Paris: Imp. de L'Illustration A. Chatenet, 1923.

La Femme cachée. Paris: Flammarion, 1924; Paris: Gallimard, 1974.

Quatre Saisons. Paris: Philippe Ortiz, 1925.

L'Enfant et les sortilèges. Music by Maurice Ravel. Paris: Durand et Cie., 1925; video-recording: Home Vision, 1987.

La Fin de Chéri. Paris: Flammarion, 1926.

Renée Vivien. Abbeville: F. Paillart, 1928.

La Naissance du jour. Paris: Flammarion, 1928, 1984 (Preface by Claude Pichois).

La Seconde. Paris: Ferenczi et fils, 1929; Paris: Hachette, 1970.

Sido. Paris: Editions Kra, 1929.

Douze Dialogues de bêtes. Paris: Mercure de France, 1930.

Ces Plaisirs. Paris: Ferenczi et fils, 1932; title changed to *Le Pur et L'impur*, 1941.

Paradis terrestres. Lausanne: Gonin et Cie., 1932.

La Treille muscate. Paris: Aimé Jourde, 1932.

Prisons et paradis. Paris: Ferenczi et fils, 1932; Paris: Fayard, 1986.

La Chatte. Paris: Grasset, 1933.

Duo. Paris: Ferenczi et fils, 1934.

Cahiers de Colette. Paris: Les Amis de Colette, 1935/36.

La Jumelle noire. Paris: Ferenczi et fils, 1935/36.

Mes Apprentissages. Paris: Ferenczi et fils, 1936.

Bella-Vista. Paris: Ferenczi et fils, 1937; Paris: Fayard, 1986.

Le Képi. Paris: Fayard, 1939.

Le Toutounier. Paris: Ferenczi et fils, 1939.

Chambre d'hôtel. Paris: A. Fayard, 1940.

Journal à rebours. Paris: A. Fayard, 1941.

Julie de Carneilhan. Paris: A. Fayard, 1941.
Gigi et autres nouvelles. Lausanne: La Guilde du Livre, 1944.
L'Etoile vesper. Geneva: Editions du Milieu du Monde, 1946; Paris: Hachette, 1979.
Pour un herbier. Lausanne: Mermod, 1948.
Le Fanal bleu. Paris: Ferenczi et fils, 1949.
Gigi, adapté pour la scène par Colette et Anita Loos. Paris: France-Illustration, 1954.
Lettres à Hélène Picard. Paris: Flammarion, 1958.
Paysages et portraits. Paris: Flammarion, 1958.
Lettres à Marguerite Moréno. Paris: Flammarion, 1959.
Lettres de la vagabonde. Paris: Flammarion, 1961.
Paris de ma fenêtre. Preface by Francis Carco. Paris: Hachette, 1976.
Le Fanal bleu; En Pays connu, journal intermittent. Paris: Hachette, 1979.
Lettres à sa fille/Sido. Précédé de lettres inédites de Colette. Preface by Bertrand de
    Jouvenel, Jeannie Malige, and Michèle Sarde. Paris: Des Femmes, 1984.
Oeuvres complètes. Ed. Claude Pichois. Paris: Gallimard, 1984.
Belles Saisons; Nudités; Mes Cahiers; Paysages et portraits; Aventures quotidiennes.
    Paris: Flammarion, 1985.
Trois . . . six . . . neuf. Paris: Buchet-Chastel, 1988.
Théâtre, Chéri, La Vagabonde, La Décapitée, L'Enfant et les sortilèges. Paris: Fayard,
    1989.

Translations of Colette

The Complete Claudine. Trans. Antonia White. New York: Farrar, Straus and Giroux,
    1976; London: Secker and Warburg, 1976.
Creatures Great and Small; Creature Conversations; Other Creatures; Creature Comfort.
    Trans. Enid McLeod. New York: British Book Service, 1951; London: Secker
    and Warburg, 1951; New York: Farrar, Straus and Cudahy, 1957; New York:
    Farrar, Straus and Giroux, 1978.
Retreat from Love. Trans. and intro. Margaret Crosland. New York: Harcourt Brace
    Jovanovich, 1974; London: Peter Owen, 1974.
The Innocent Libertine. Trans. Antonia White. London: Secker and Warburg, 1968;
    Harmondsworth: Penguin, 1972; New York: Farrar, Straus and Giroux, 1978.
The Vagabond. Trans. Enid McLeod. London: Secker and Warburg, 1954; New York:
    Farrar, Straus and Young, 1955; Harmondsworth: Penguin, 1972; Westport,
    Conn.: Greenwood Press, 1973; New York: Farrar, Straus and Giroux, 1974;
    London: Penguin, 1972.
Captive. West Dayton: Penguin, 1986.
Recaptured. Trans. Viola Garvin. Garden City, N.Y.: Doubleday, 1932.
The Shackle. Trans. Antonia White. London: Secker and Warburg, 1970; Harmondsworth:
    Penguin, 1970; New York: Farrar, Straus and Giroux, 1976.
Music-Hall Sidelights and *My Apprenticeships*. London: Secker and Warburg, 1957.
Mitsou: or, The Education of Young Women; Music-Hall Sidelights. Trans. Raymond
    Postgate and Anne-Marie Callimachi. New York: Avon, 1958; New York: Farrar,
    Straus and Cudahy, 1958; London: Trans World, 1967; New York: Farrar, Straus
    and Giroux, 1976.
Cheri and *The Last of Cheri*. Trans. Roger Senhouse. New York: Farrar, Straus and

Young, 1951; London: Secker and Warburg, 1951; New York: Farrar, Straus and Giroux, 1953; New York: New American Library, 1955.

My Mother's House and *Sido*. Trans. Enid McLeod and Una Troubridge. New York: Farrar, Straus and Young, 1953; London: Secker and Warburg, 1953; Westport, Conn.: Greenwood Press, 1972; New York: Farrar and Straus, 1975.

Journey for Myself; Selfish Memories. Trans. David LeVay. London: Peter Owen, 1971.

The Ripening Seed. Trans. Roger Senhouse and Herma Briffault. London: Secker and Warburg, 1955; New York: Farrar, Straus and Cudahy, 1956; Harmondsworth: Penguin, 1959; London: Secker and Warburg, 1959; Westport, Conn.: Greenwood Press, 1972; New York: Farrar, Straus and Giroux, 1975; West Dayton: Penguin, 1986.

The Other Woman. Trans. and intro. Margaret Crosland. London: Peter Owen, 1971; Indianapolis: Bobbs-Merrill, 1972; New York: New American Library, 1975.

The Boy and the Magic. Trans. Christopher Fry. New York: Putnam, 1965.

The Last of Cheri. Trans. Roger Senhouse. New York: Putnam, 1932; London: Secker and Warburg, 1951.

The Break of Day. Trans. Enid McLeod. Intro. Glenway Westcott. New York: Farrar, Straus and Cudahy, 1961; London: Secker and Warburg, 1961; London: The Women's Press, 1979.

A Lesson in Love. Trans. Rosemary Benet. New York: Farrar and Reinhart, 1932.

The Other One. Trans. Elizabeth Tait and Roger Senhouse. New York: Farrar, Straus and Cudahy, 1960; London: Secker and Warburg, 1960; New York: New American Library, 1962; Westport, Conn.: Greenwood Press, 1972.

The Pure and the Impure. London: Secker and Warburg, 1968.

Earthly Paradise. Ed. Robert Phelps. Trans. Herma Briffault, Derek Coltman, Helen Beauclerk, et al. New York: Farrar, Straus and Giroux, 1966; London: Secker and Warburg, 1966; London: Sphere, 1970; London: Penguin, 1974.

The Cat. Trans. Morris Bentinek. New York: Farrar and Reinhart, 1936.

Duo and *The Toutounier*. Trans. and intro. Margaret Crosland. Indianapolis: Bobbs-Merrill, 1974; London: Peter Owen, 1974; New York: Dell, 1977.

Gigi; The Cat. Trans. Roger Senhouse and Antonia White. London: Secker and Warburg, 1953; Harmondsworth: Penguin, 1958.

Gigi; Julie Carneilhan, Chance Acquaintances. Trans. Roger Senhouse (*Gigi*) and Patrick Leigh Fermor (*Julie* and *Chance Acquaintances*). New York: Farrar, Straus and Giroux, 1952; New York: New American Library, 1958; New York: Farrar, Straus and Giroux, 1975.

Looking Backwards. Trans. David LeVay. Intro. Maurice Goudeket. Bloomington: Indiana University Press, 1975; London: Peter Owen, 1975.

The Evening Star: Recollections. Trans. David LeVay. London: Peter Owen, 1973; Indianapolis: Bobbs-Merrill, 1974.

The Thousand and One Mornings. Trans. Margaret Crosland and David LeVay. Intro. Margaret Crosland. London: Peter Owen, 1973; Indianapolis: Bobbs-Merrill, 1973.

For a Flower Album. Trans. Roger Senhouse. New York: D. McKay, 1959; London: Weidenfeld and Nicolson, 1959.

The Blue Lantern. Trans. Roger Senhouse. London: Secker and Warburg, 1963; New York: Farrar, Straus, 1963; New York: Farrar, Straus and Giroux, 1966; Westport, Conn.: Greenwood Press, 1972.

Collections of Colette's Writings

The Collected Stories of Colette. Ed. Robert Phelps. Trans. Matthew Ward. New York: Farrar, Straus and Giroux, 1983.
The Collected Stories. London: Secker and Warburg, 1984.
Collected Stories. London: Penguin Books, 1985.
Flowers and Fruit. West Dayton: Penguin, 1986.
Letters from Colette. Selected and trans. by Robert Phelps. New York: Farrar, Straus and Giroux, 1980.
Places. Trans. David LeVay. London: Peter Owen, 1970.
Short Novels of Colette. Intro. Glenway Wescott. Various trans. including Janet Flanner. New York: Dial Press, 1951.
The Tender Shoot and Other Stories. Trans. Antonia White. New York: Farrar, Straus and Cudahy, 1959; New York: New American Library, 1961; New York: Farrar, Straus and Giroux, 1975.

Studies of Colette

Beaumont, Germaine, and André Parinaud. *Colette par elle-même*. Paris: Le Seuil, 1951.
Biolley-Godino, Marcelle. *L'Homme-objet chez Colette*. Paris: Klincksieck, 1972.
Bray, Bernard, ed. *Colette: Nouvelles Approches critiques. actes du colloque de Sarrebruck, 22–23 juin 1984*. Paris: Librairie A. G. Nizet, 1986.
Carco, Francis. *Colette, mon ami*. Paris: Rive Gauche, 1965.
Colette. *Autobiographie tirée des oeuvres de Colette* par Robert Phelps. Paris: Le Club Français du Livre, 1968.
"Colette." *Europe* (November-December) 1981. Special issue.
Cottrell, Robert D. *Colette*. New York: Ungar, 1974.
Crosland, Margaret. *Colette: The Difficulty of Loving*. London: Peter Owen, 1973.
Deltel, Danielle. "Journal manqué, autobiographie masquée: Claudine à l'école de Colette." *Revue des Sciences Humaines* 192 (1983): 47–71.
D'Hollander, Paul. *Colette: ses apprentissages*. Montreal: Presses universitaires de Montréal; Paris: Klincksieck, 1978.
Dormann, Geneviève. *Amoureuse Colette*. Paris: Herscher, 1984. Trans. as *Colette: A Passion for Life*. London: Thames and Hudson, 1985.
Dranch, Sherry A. "Reading Through the Veiled Text: Colette's *The Pure and the Impure*." *Contemporary Literature* 24, no. 2 (1983): 176–89.
Eisinger, Erica Mendelson, and Mari Ward McCarthy, eds. *Colette, the Woman, the Writer*. University Park: Pennsylvania State University Press, 1981.
Fraiman, Susan D. "Shadow in the Garden: The Double Aspect of Motherhood in Colette." *Perspectives on Contemporary Literature* 11 (1985): 46–53.
Giry, Jacqueline. *Colette et l'art du discours intérieur*. Paris: La Pensée universelle, 1981.
Goudeket, Maurice. *Près de Colette*. Paris: Flammarion, 1956.
Harris, Elaine. *L'Approfondissement de la sensualité dans l'oeuvre romanesque de Colette*. Paris: Nizet, 1973.
Holmes, Diana. "The Hidden Woman: Disguise and Paradox in Colette's *La Femme cachée*." *Essays in French Literature* 23 (1986): 29–37.

Houssa, Nicole. *Le Souci de l'expression chez Colette*. Brussels: Palais des Académies, 1958.

Ketchum, Anne Duhamel. "Defining an Ethics from a Later Short Story by Colette." In *Continental Latin-American and Francophone Women Writers*. Ed. Eunice Myers and Ginette Adamson. Lanham, Md.: University Presses of America, 1987. 71–77.

Larnac, Jean. *Colette, sa vie, son oeuvre*. Paris: Kra, 1927.

Lastinger, Valerie C. "*La Naissance du jour*: La Désintégration de 'moi' dans un roman de Colette." *French Review* 61, no. 4 (1988): 542–51.

LeClercq, Pierre-Robert. "Le Moi-je de Colette, ou l'affirmation d'une écriture femme." *Etudes Littéraires* 364, no. 6 (1986): 785–92.

Lydon, Mary. "Myself and M/others." *SubStance* 32 (1981): 6–14.

Malige, Jeannie. *Colette*. Lyon: La Manufacture, 1987.

Marks, Elaine. *Colette*. New Brunswick, N.J.: Rutgers University Press, 1960.

Massie, Allen. *Colette*. Harmondsworth: Penguin, 1986.

McCarty, Mari. "Possessing Female Space: *The Tender Shoot*." *Women's Studies: An Interdisciplinary Journal* 8, no. 3 (1981): 367–374.

Miller, Nancy K. "Woman of Letters: The Return of Writing in Colette's *The Vagabond*." In *Subject to Change: Reading Feminist Writing*. New York: Columbia University Press, 1988.

Miller, Nancy K. "D'Une Solitude à l'autre: Vers un intertexte féminin." *The French Review* 54, no. 6 (1981): 797–803.

Millot, Catherine. "La Vocation de Colette." *Infini* 21 (1988): 60–75.

Mitchell, Yvonne. *Colette: A Taste for Life*. New York: Harcourt Brace Jovanovich, 1975.

Pichois, Claude. *Album Colette*. Paris: Gallimard, 1984.

Pujade-Renaud, Claude. "La Chimère maternelle et le sceau paternel." *Europe* (November-December 1981): 86–95.

Raaphort-Rousseau, Madeleine. *Colette, sa vie et son art*. Paris: Nizet, 1964.

Reboux, Paul. *Colette ou le génie du style*. Paris: Rasmussen, 1925.

Resch, Yannick. *Corps féminin, corps textuel*. Paris: Klincksieck, 1973.

Richardson, Joanna. *Colette*. London: Methuen, 1983.

Sarde, Michèle. *Colette libre et entravée*. Paris: Stock, 1978. Trans. as *Colette: Free and Fettered*. New York: Morrow, 1980.

Stewart, Joan Hinde. *Colette*. Boston: Twayne, 1983.

Tinter, Sylvie. *Colette et le temps surmonté*. Geneva: Slatkine, 1980.

Viel, Marie-Jeanne. *Colette au temps des Claudine, récit*. Paris: Les Publications Essentielles, 1978.

Virmaux, Alain, and Odette Virmaux. *Colette au cinéma*. Paris: Flammarion, 1975. Trans. as *Colette at the Movies: Criticism and Screenplays*. New York: Ungar, 1985.

Ward Jouve, Nicole. *Colette*. Brighton: Harvester, 1987.

SOPHIE COTTIN
(1770–1807)

Samia I. Spencer

BIOGRAPHY

Sophie Cottin was a famous and celebrated author in the early part of the nineteenth century. She was considered not only one of the foremost female novelists of that time—with Mmes Souza, *Genlis, and *Staël (Arnelle, 16)—but also "the prime writer of the era," at least according to Victor Hugo (quoted in Gaulmier, *Roman et société*, 9). Long after her death, her novels continued to enjoy widespread popularity in Europe and the United States. They were available in Danish, English, German, Italian, Portuguese, and Spanish.

Biographical information on Sophie Cottin is both scarce and controversial. Simple details such as name, date, and place of birth and death are uncertain. Was her maiden name Ristau (Boileau, viii), Restaud (Rossard, 15), Ristaud (*The Bibliophile Library*, n.p.; Michaud, 7), Ristand (*The National Union Catalog* 124: 459), or Risteau (*The National Union Catalog* 124: 454)? Was she born in Bordeaux (Boileau, viii), Tourne, Tonneins (Marquiset, 15; Michaud, 7), or Paris (Marquiset, 16)? Was her death the result of an illness or a gun wound, and did it occur in April or August 1807 (Marquiset, 57)? We cannot be certain.

According to Marquiset, who based his biographical information on the study of family documents, Marie Risteau was born into a family of wealthy Protestant merchants, in Paris, on March 22, 1770. The second forename, Sophie, was given to her by her paternal grandmother, who was also her godmother. The proper computer and library entry is, thus, Cottin, Marie Risteau (called Sophie). Shortly after her birth, the family moved to Bordeaux, where she lived until her marriage in 1789. Her childhood appears to have been uneventful, except for frequent lengthy sojourns in her uncle's country estate in Tonneins, near Bordeaux. She was educated at home, by her mother and a Protestant minister who probably became the model for the young pastors in her novels. The child was also cherished by her father, who poured all his affection onto this daughter, especially after the premature death of her older sister in 1785. This bond may have inspired the privileged father-daughter relationships that are often described in her fiction.

As M. Risteau's health and business began to decline, he sought a suitable husband for his only daughter. Paul Cottin, a handsome, wealthy, and successful twenty-six-year-old banker from Paris, was introduced to the attractive nineteen-year-old Marie Sophie Risteau by his partners' relatives in Bordeaux. The young couple was married in Paris, on May 16, 1789. Their happiness, however, was short-lived, not only because of the political unrest that was to follow, but also because of Paul's ill health. In 1791, the Cottins fled to England to escape the dangers of the Revolution; they returned to the French capital shortly thereafter, for fear that their possessions might be totally confiscated. A few days after the arrest and incarceration of his business associates, Paul Cottin died in his home, in the autumn of 1793. At age twenty-three, Mme Cottin had lost her father (1792) and her loving husband, and was in near financial ruin. She sought refuge in Champlan, in the country home that her husband had purchased only three months before his death. Tragedy and financial difficulties, however, continued to plague her life. Mme Risteau, who joined her daughter in this retreat, died four months after her son-in-law. Eventually, the young widow had to sell her cherished property and return to Paris, to settle in a modest apartment.

These losses exacerbated her feelings of grief, solitude, and depression, and led her to implore death for relief: "When the darkest night surrounds me with gloom, it is less somber than my soul. . . . the world in its vastness is nothing but a sterile solitude. I feel that I live in a strange land where nothing suits me . . . there is not an instant in the day when I would not welcome death voluptuously" (quoted in Gaulmier, "Sophie et ses malheurs," 12; this translation and all subsequent ones are my own). Her health was seriously affected by this misery and distress, to the extent that relatives feared for her life.

In spite of these feelings of sadness and sorrow, Mme Cottin found consolation in her love of nature and her warm and affectionate bonds with relatives and friends. The most intimate among them were cousins Marie Laforgue and Julie Verdier (whose youngest daughter she had briefly considered adopting), sister-in-law Sophie Girardot, and close friends Fanny Soubise and Adélaïde de Pastoret. Mmes Lafargue and Verdier went often to Champlan for extended visits and maintained a regular correspondence with their cousin. It is in these letters that Sophie Cottin's talent as a writer first became evident. Mme Verdier gave a private reading of a letter from her cousin to an assembly of intimate friends, who were struck by the quality of the prose and suggested that the author exercise her pen on longer pieces.

Among male friends, Joseph Michaud, a member of the French Academy, was undoubtedly the closest and most faithful. In later years he also became a valuable literary advisor, her editor, collaborator, and biographer. Romantic relationships, however, were not nearly as satisfying. The first man to enter her life after Paul Cottin's death was Etienne Gramagnac, one of her late husband's business associates and a widower himself. This elderly gentleman took it upon himself to advise the young widow on the management of her estate and her declining resources. With time, their correspondence took on a more personal tone, and M. Gramagnac's admiration and love for his protégée prompted him to propose. She did not share his feelings and gently declined the offer, preferring instead to maintain their friendship as such.

Jacques Lafargue, the twenty-one-year-old son of her cousin Marie Lafargue, who accompanied his mother on her frequent trips to Champlan, was another admirer. He fell passionately in love with the twenty-six-year-old widow, and also proposed. When she refused to entertain the offer, he shot himself in the head, dying of his wound on her property (Marquiset, 27).

Mme Cottin's most tumultuous liaison was with Pierre-Hyacinthe Azaïs, a pretentious individual and a second-rate philosopher whom she met in the Pyrénées in 1803. Fascinated by his knowledge and captivated by their intellectual discussions, Mme Cottin idealized Azaïs and saw in him the incarnation of the romantic heroes of her novels. She herself identified with her heroines, so that life became an imitation of art and reality a mirror of fiction. Against everyone's advice, she wanted to marry him; however, when the recalcitrant bachelor agreed to the idea of marriage, it was for the purpose of having children—a dream she knew she could not fulfill. Gradually the illusion wore off, and she began to see the man for what he clearly was.

During the three-month illness that preceded her death, Sophie Cottin was surrounded by friends and relatives, especially Julie Verdier and her three daughters. Faith, which had provided strength and guidance throughout her life, continued to ease her pain in these final moments. She died on August 25, 1807, in her Paris home; she was only thirty-seven.

MAJOR THEMES

Like most female writers of her time, Sophie Cottin did not intend to become an author; in fact, she firmly believed that women should not write. According to her close friend and biographer, Joseph Michaud, she vehemently condemned female authors—a group in which she naturally included herself—in the first edition of *Amélie Mansfield*. After considerable pressure from her friends, she reluctantly agreed to eliminate this judgment from later editions. She continued, however, to be critical of her own works and uncomfortable with her literary success. She was also embarrassed by the exposure to the public of her innermost thoughts and private feelings, which she would have preferred instead to share with only a small circle of friends. In order to counter the guilt that resulted from acting against her own convictions, she donated the profits from her books to charity (Michaud, 9–14).

Sophie Cottin's literary career was due to a casual incident. In 1798, a friend who feared for his life asked her to lend him fifty louis so that he could flee the country. Because of her dwindling resources, she was unable to respond to his request. It then occurred to her to write a novel, whose royalties could be used to help her friend. She set to work immediately and within two weeks had completed *Claire d'Albe (Dangerous Friendship)*. An instant success, the book was followed by four other popular novels within a period of seven years: *Malvina* (1801), *Amélie Mansfield* (*Amelia Mansfield*, 1802), *Mathilde* (*Matilda*, 1805), and *Elisabeth ou les exilés de Sibérie* (*Elizabeth, or The Exiles of Siberia*, 1806). The specific details of the publication of a short piece she authored, *La Prise de Jéricho ou la pécheresse convertie* (The Fall of Jericho, or The Converted Sinner), inspired by the Bible and often referred to as a poem—although not in verse—are not known. The work is usually printed in the same volume as *Elisabeth*; however, it will not be included in the discussion of Mme Cottin's novels.

Despite notable differences between these works in setting, chronology, situation, plot, and geography—for example, *Claire d'Albe* takes place in Touraine, *Malvina* in Scotland, *Amélie* in Germany and Switzerland, *Mathilde* in Egypt and Palestine, and *Elisabeth* in Russia—there are also striking parallels. The heroines, whether named Claire, Malvina, Amélie, Mathilde, or Elisabeth, bear a remarkable resemblance to each other and to their author. They are young, romantic, attractive, intelligent, discreet, charming, respected, and virtuous. Like Sophie Cottin herself, they prefer a quiet and retired life, are sensitive to the beauty of nature and prone to experience acute sadness, and find great comfort in friendship and religion. Their sweet, delicate, and fragile beauty, however, does not reflect inner weakness or lameness of character: these are strong-minded, determined, confident, and passionate "women of fire" (Gaulmier, "Sophie et ses Malheurs," 9).

The heroines' families are small—with one or at most two children. They belong to the upper middle class or the nobility and live comfortably. Present or absent, the mother is a minor figure who has little influence on her daughter. Her death, as her life, is mentioned in passing; it occurs in the absence of the children and appears to be of little consequence (*Oeuvres complètes* [hereafter OC] 3: 42–43). While daughters may inherit some of their mothers' physical characteristics or demeanor, they clearly favor their fathers—the role model. For example, the Count of Lunéville, Amélie's father, was "passionately interested in arts and letters. He sought and welcomed the company of famous scientists and artists and, thus, his residence was the refuge of talented and enlightened people" (OC 3: 27). His daughter shares his tastes and inclinations and falls in love with an artist whose talent is much admired by the Count. M. de Lunéville's death, which occurs shortly after his wife's, is described in more detail and has a devastating impact on the children: "How can one describe the terror and affliction of the two young orphans at the loss of their father, the best father in the world, and their sole support in life?" (OC 3: 39).

Pierre Springer, Elisabeth's father in *Elisabeth ou les exilés de Sibérie*, is a more typical male character, endowed with "extraordinary energy" (OC 1: 27). He too passes his values on to his admiring daughter: pride, nobility, heroism, glory, and honor. At an early age, Elisabeth shows a marked preference for active roles and finds inspiration in historical books, not children's literature or fiction. It is thus natural that she grows up to be a "female hero" herself. Her determination and courage enable her to defy the harshness of the Siberian elements in order to meet the Emperor, explain her parents' situation, and free them from exile.

The heroines' fathers are not only supporting and understanding, they are also concerned about their daughters' happiness and well-being. M. de Lunéville's last words and thoughts on his deathbed relate to Amélie's happiness (OC 3: 49). M. and Mme d'Albe fondly and gratefully remember her late father, to whom they owe their bliss, their marriage having been concluded at his initiative. These strong and untainted relationships between fathers and daughters strengthen considerably the heroines' characters and enrich their personalities. These extraordinary women take charge of their lives and dominate Mme Cottin's fiction, where they occupy center stage.

Male characters, while important players in the novels, do not possess the depth, fullness, and texture of their female counterparts. Outwardly, they are handsome, distinguished, well-educated, intelligent, and sensitive, forming, with the heroines, most attractive couples. Inwardly, however, these couples are uneven and not equally matched. At twenty-six, Claire d'Albe is a mature and sensible woman; her lover, at nineteen, is naive and inexperienced. Their relationship at first is almost that of a mother and son. Sir Edmond Seymour, Malvina's admirer, is gullible, flighty, and easily manipulated by astute enemies. Unlike her cousin Ernest, Amélie is endowed with a strong personality. Malek Adhel's religious convictions and heroic aspirations are less firm than Mathilde's. Smoloff, Elisabeth's husband-to-be, is clearly weaker, less energetic, and less courageous than his partner. Not only do women have the leading roles in the novels, they are also the leaders in the couples.

Unlike the female characters, who gain from their privileged relationships with older men—be they fathers or protectors—the male characters are adversely affected by their bonds to older female relatives. Mothers or pseudo-mothers are overshadowing, domineering, merciless, ruthless, and tyrannical, of a cruelty that has no limits. Their determination to achieve their goals blinds them to any other consideration and leads them to cause the death (Ernest) or virtual death (Sir Edmond) of their less powerful and less willful young adversaries.

For the heroine, the pursuit of love and happiness is generally linked to a higher and more noble goal: to be a perfect wife and mother (Claire), to please her family and protector (Amélie), to help virtue triumph (Malvina), to better serve God and Christianity (Mathilde), or to restore justice (Elisabeth). The heroes appear to have no particular purpose or mission in life—the novels are generally presented from the heroine's perspective. Only when they fall in love do they seem to acquire a heightened sense of identity and begin to share the values and convictions of their female partners.

For four of the five heroines, love creates intense inner conflicts between their feelings, on one hand, and their virtue and moral values, on the other. The insurmountable difficulties and obstacles love faces doom it from the very beginning to a tragic end. Claire is married to another. Malvina promised her dying friend to devote her life to raising her orphaned daughter, and never to marry. Because of Amélie's first marriage, Mme de Woldemar fiercely opposes her niece's marriage to her son. Not only has Mathilde vowed her life to God, but she and her lover are also separated by a bloody religious war.

However, the sense of accomplishing an important mission, intensified by the exalted blessings of glorious and awesome natural surroundings, leads to the triumph of love over other considerations. The couples experience perfect physical and spiritual harmony and ecstasy, and escape, temporarily, the power of time and space. But the world's order is implacable, and soon it defeats nature's voice and command. Lovers are forced to part not only with each other, but also with life—literally or figuratively. Claire d'Albe dies, and her lover disappears from the face of the earth. Amélie and Ernest die within hours of each other and are buried together. Malvina joins her predecessors, and her lover, too, might as well be dead: "Nothing could make him lose sight of his wife's tomb" (OC 8: 235). After Malek Adhel's majestic funeral, Mathilde returns to the convent where, in essence, she ceases to exist: she does not utter "a single murmur," remaining "alone in the East, without family, and without ties" (OC 12: 287). The tragic destinies of these characters are reminiscent of the inevitable sense of fatality that dominates Racine's plays (Gaulmier, "Sophie et ses malheurs," 9).

Only the last heroine, Elisabeth, achieves her mission and survives: she restores justice, frees her parents, and will, presumably, marry Smoloff and be happy ever after. Or will she? Before concluding the novel, the author sheds serious doubt on the outcome: "If I added one more page to this story, it would certainly include a calamity" (OC 1: 208). In fact, we know that in Mme Cottin's fiction marriage and happiness do not go hand in hand; they appear to be mutually exclusive. Shortly after Amélie's first marriage, M. Mansfield loses interest in his wife and their son, and looks for pleasure in the company of other women. Lady Sheridan, Malvina's best friend, finds marriage unfulfilling; her husband, too, is a womanizer who cannot be entrusted with his daughter's upbringing. Mme Simmeren, Amélie's older friend, shares troubling thoughts with her younger confidante: "I will tell you in private (because these thoughts cannot be stated openly) that love can only grow in freedom; it cannot flourish in marriage. If I were young again, the man that I would want most to love me would be the one I would want least to marry" (OC 3: 101).

Although love is doomed to die in marriage, or live and cause the death of the protagonists, it also brings a sense of achievement and victory. On her deathbed, Claire asserts her love for Frédéric, assumes full responsibility for her actions, continues to inspire respect and admiration, and reflects upon her life with remarkable clarity of vision. Her maturity has been communicated to her teenage lover, who becomes a "free man" (OC 1: 219). After Malvina's death, Sir Edmond overcomes his weaknesses, is loyal to the memory of his wife, loses interest in women, and thus lives up to Malvina's ideal of virtue. Ernest and Amélie are vanquished in life but triumph in death. They have a magnificent funeral procession and, each year, on the anniversary of their death, six couples are married in celebration of their love: the grandfather's will—that his grandchildren Ernest and Amélie marry—is indeed executed. The cause of God and Christianity is well served by Mathilde's love for Malek Adhel. A majority of Moslems rally behind the funeral procession of the martyr, who is buried atop Mount Carmel. When the heroine returns to conventual life, she, too, appears triumphant, as she experiences the "beginning of eternity" (OC 12: 284): thus "love and death blend into a boundless apotheosis" (Gaulmier, "Sophie et ses malheurs," 10).

Claire, Amélie, Malvina, and Mathilde, like many of their eighteenth-century predecessors, find that happiness can only be achieved in the afterlife. The revolutionary winds of the late eighteenth century, however, have not gone unnoticed, and their impact on Mme Cottin's heroines is not negligible. Before they are overcome by pain and destroyed by life, these women fight long and arduous battles, cross entire continents, challenge authority, and defy the social order in their attempt to change the world. In the process, they suffer tremendous agony and pain. Before giving in to death, these heroines dare, during their brief but intense passage in this world, to be their own persons and experience the fullness of earthly existence.

SURVEY OF CRITICISM

For nearly thirty years after Sophie Cottin's death, her books continued to be popular with French readers, as evidenced by the frequency of their printing. Toward the middle of the century, however, interest in her works began to wane, although her name continued to be mentioned in all dictionaries of literature (Arnelle, 1).

It is particularly through English translations that Mme Cottin's works lived on in the nineteenth century after they had fallen into obscurity in France. The Anglo-Saxon public seemed to have an insatiable interest in them. *Claire d'Albe*, *Malvina*, *Amélie*, *Mathilde*, and *Elisabeth* were available to British readers only a few years after their publication in France. Of all the novels, however, *Elisabeth* stands out for the remarkable popularity it enjoyed in England, which led to its adaptation to the stage as a play by the same title and also as a "musico-dramatic work" entitled *The Exile* by Joseph Mazzinghi.

Even more extraordinary was the public's fascination with this novel in the United States, where, year after year, publishers continued to print the book, producing more than fifty-five editions in the late nineteenth century and the early twentieth. It seems that at least one publisher was confused about the national origin of the book: he presented *Elisabeth* as a "British Pocket Classic," together with Goldsmith's *The Vicar of Wakefield*! The novel appears also to have been used as a textbook in French classes. The many identical editions that appeared in a twenty-five-year span (1856–1880) would indicate the popularity of the book as a pedagogical tool. Gradually, however, Sophie Cottin's name and novels fell into obscurity, then near oblivion. The nineteenth-century editions of her complete works are difficult to find, and only *Claire d'Albe* seems to have survived in print into our century.

While there seems to be no doubt about the readers' enthusiasm for Mme Cottin's literary production and their appreciation for her remarkable skill— especially in describing the range, intensity, and effect of feelings and emotions— critical reaction appears to be more ambivalent. Chateaubriand, Lamartine, and Hugo were great admirers of her prose; Napoleon read *Claire d'Albe* during his exile; and Stendhal preferred her novels to those of Mme de *Staël. Others, however, like Mme de *Genlis, deplored the "revolting immorality" of her books. Few critics, beyond those of her own generation, seem to have focused attention on Sophie Cottin's works, and those who mention them do so only tangentially, while discussing other authors.

To this day, there is no full-length study of Mme Cottin's novels. In recent years, however, Sophie Cottin has aroused some attention. A number of documents, including manuscripts, correspondence, drafts, and book reviews, were donated to the Bibliothèque Nationale by a family descendant. Furthermore, a few critics are rediscovering the importance of her novels, especially Jean Gaulmier, who has authored well-researched articles on her works and offered a new edition of *Claire d'Albe* in 1976—the first novel by Sophie Cottin to be published in France since 1856. Gaulmier attributes to Sophie Cottin the place she rightly deserves among her contemporaries, notes her influence on many Romantic authors and poets, assesses the strengths and weaknesses of her works, and agrees with Ferdinand Brunetière that an accurate study of sensibilities in nineteenth-century France must include Mme Cottin's novels.

A thorough scholarly study of French fiction during the first decades of the nineteenth century has yet to be written. Such a project would focus welcome attention on the literary achievements of Sophie Cottin and those of many other female writers; it would also greatly contribute to our understanding of French life, literature, and "mentalités" during the Romantic era.

BIBLIOGRAPHY

Works by Sophie Cottin

Claire d'Albe. Paris: Maradan, 1799.
Malvina. Paris: Maradan, 1801.

Amélie Mansfield. Paris: Giguet et Michaud, 1802.
Mathilde. Paris: Giguet et Michaud, 1805.
Elisabeth ou les exilés de Sibérie. Paris: Giguet et Michaud, 1806.
Oeuvres complètes. Ed. J. Michaud. Paris: Corbet, 1820.
Claire d'Albe. Paris: Régine Desforges, 1976.

Translations of Sophie Cottin

Dangerous Friendship; or The Letters of Clara d'Albe. Baltimore: Joseph Robinson, 1807.
Malvina. London: C. Chapple, 1810.
Amelia Mansfield. London: Cox and Baylis, 1803.
Matilda and Malek Adhel, the Saracen: A Crusade Romance. London: R. Dutton, 1809.
Elizabeth or The Exiles of Siberia. London: Lane, Newman and Co., 1807.

Studies of Sophie Cottin

Arnelle. *Une Oubliée: Madame Cottin d'après sa correspondance*. Paris: Plon, 1914.
The Bibliophile Library of Literature, Art, and Rare Manuscripts, S.V. "Sophie Cottin." Rpt. Detroit: Gale Research, 1966.
Boileau, D. "Notice de la vie et des ouvrages de Mme Cottin." In *Oeuvres complètes de Mme Cottin*. Paris and London: Colburn, 1811. v-xxiv.
Castel-Cagarriga, G. "Le Roman de Mme Cottin." *Revue des Deux Mondes* (May-June 1960): 120–37.
Gaulmier, Jean. "Roman et connotations sociales: *Mathilde* de Mme Cottin." In *Roman et société*. Ed. Michel Raimond. Paris: Colin, 1973. 7–17.
———. "Sophie et ses malheurs ou le romantisme du pathétique." *Romantisme* 3 (1972): 3–16.
Gorsse, Pierre de. "Sophie, romancière oubliée." *Historia* 353 (April 1976): 107–13.
Lacy, Kluenster W. "An Essay on Feminine Fiction 1757–1803." Diss., University of Wisconsin, 1972.
Marquiset, Alfred. "Madame Cottin." In *Les Bas-Bleus du Premier Empire*. Paris: Champion, 1914. 15–61.
Michaud, J. "Notice historique sur l'auteur." In *Oeuvres complètes de Mme Cottin*. Paris: Corbet, 1820. 1: 8–15.
Pratt, T. M. "The Widow and the Crown: Mme Cottin and the Limits of Neoclassical Epic." *British Journal for Eighteenth-Century Studies* 9 (1986): 197–203.
Rossard, J. "Passion et tensions pudiques dans *Claire d'Albe*." In *Pudeur et romantisme*. Paris: Nizet, 1982. 15–23.
Sainte-Beuve, Charles-Augustin. *Oeuvres complètes*. Vol. 2. Paris: Gallimard, 1960.

HÉLISENNE DE CRENNE
(c. 1510–c. 1560)

Paul J. Archambault
and Marianna Mustacchi Archambault

BIOGRAPHY

Born in Abbeville, in Picardy, around 1510, Hélisenne (whose real name was Marguerite de Briet) was the daughter of a municipal magistrate named Daniel Briet. Hélisenne, her pen name, is perhaps derived from a female character in a popular contemporary romance, the *Amadis*. She acquired the surname de Crenne after her marriage to a country squire named Philippe Fournel, lord of Crasnes (which is today called Craonne), near Coucy in the vicinity of Compiègne. Of this marriage, which must have occurred some time around 1530, was born a son named Pierre who, incidentally, is never mentioned in Hélisenne's works. A document dated August 9, 1548—one of the few that serve as a source for the reconstruction of Hélisenne's life—states that Pierre Fournel, a student at the University of Paris and lodging at the Collège de la Marche, was receiving from his father, Philippe Fournel, an annual allowance of fifty livres *tournois*— a term used for money that was struck in Tours—for his studies. Another document, dated 1550, mentions a debt of forty livres *tournois* that Philippe Fournel and "demoiselle Marguerite" were forced to pay a baker of the Faubourg Saint Marcel. The size of the debt indicates that Hélisenne resided, at least occasionally, with her husband, for some time in that section of Paris.

By 1552, Hélisenne seems to have obtained a legal separation from Philippe, if we are to believe a document dated August 25 of that year and issued at the Châtelet in Paris. The document mentions a donation made by "demoiselle Marguerite de Briet, wife of Philippe Fournel, esquire, lord of Crasnes, and separated from him as to possessions, residing at Saint Germain des Prés, near Paris." The donation, made out to a certain Christophe Le Manyer, residing in Paris, is couched in the form of a will and provides Le Manyer with an annual income of 213 livres *tournois*, to which is added the possession of one-half of

Hélisenne's two houses, located at Rue des Postes, in the Faubourg Saint Marcel. The donation is intended to reward Le Manyer for "good and pleasant services" as well as "salaries and sessions" received from him. We know nothing else about the identity of this young equerry or about the nature of the "good and pleasant services" for which Hélisenne felt bound to reward him.

Might Le Manyer be the model for the secret lover of Hélisenne's two major works, *Les Angoysses douloureuses qui procèdent d'amours* (The Painful Anxieties Which Proceed from Love, 1538) and *Les Epistres familieres et invectives* (1539; translated as *A Renaissance Woman: Helisenne's Personal and Invective Letters*, 1986)? Commentators of these two works have usually assumed that they have a broad autobiographical base. The *Angoysses douloureuses* tells a three-part story of a young woman named Hélisenne, given in marriage at age eleven to a cantankerous, jealous, and presumably unexciting husband, who is so infuriated when a young man named Guénélic enters Hélisenne's heretofore uneventful life that he locks her in her room, violates her privacy only to beat her at will, and consequently secludes her in one of his several other castles. This first work contains so many elements that are directly lifted out of medieval romance—particularly Guénélic's adventurous search for Hélisenne in parts two and three—that only the most naive or romantic of commentators could assume that it is more than minimally autobiographical.

Hélisenne's second work, the *Personal and Invective Letters*, appears somewhat more likely to record a lived experience in suggesting, as do several of the letters, that the hottest subject of disagreement between Hélisenne and her husband may not have been her alleged marital infidelity—the writer of the letters constantly protests her fidelity and argues that she is being maligned and slandered—but her desire to be an independent writer and to reside in Paris, which she describes in her fourth invective letter as "this great city which is filled with innumerable crowds of people who love science, elegance, leisure and culture—the graces that flow from conversing with Minerva." And in her fifth invective letter, she flays the citizens of the small provincial town of Icvoc (presumably an anagram for "Couci") for their idleness and their pettiness of spirit and concludes, apostrophizing what appears to be the most wicked of her enemies in that remote settlement: "Believe me, if you, the most wicked inhabitant of this town, had spent a long time in Paris, the noble citizens of that great city would have had sure evidence of your detestable life because of their subtle and splendid minds. I know, without a doubt, that like the good laborer, who is used to pulling out the weeds from his garden, they would have expelled you from such a place of which you are unworthy." Only a cultured despiser of petty provincial life who had found her liberation in the intellectual circles of Paris could have written lines like these.

There is no documented information about Hélisenne's education. For a provincial lady to have read widely in classical and patristic literature, to have resided in Paris for a number of years, to have obtained a legal separation from her husband, and to have had Parisian properties of her own seems uncommonly "liberated" in the early sixteenth century, even for a Picardian lady of the lower nobility. Hélisenne may have been taught by tutors, as were many young women of her class. She may have been essentially self-taught. In any case she unquestionably received much practical and, no doubt, intellectual assistance from Denys Janot, the Parisian book dealer and printer, who published her major works between September 1538 and March 1541, and who seems to have played the role of mentor, patron, and promoter as well. Active in the Parisian publishing world between 1529 (when he inherited his father's business) and 1544 (the year of his death), Janot printed a variety of texts, including anatomical treatises by Galen; but he concentrated on literary works representing the major intellectual currents of his time. A perusal of the catalogue of Janot's published books (to be found at the Bibliothèque Nationale) makes it clear that Hélisenne's own works are part of a larger publishing scheme that includes epistolary novels as well as French translations of Ovid, Cicero, and Boccaccio. Besides the *Angoysses* of 1538 and the *Epistres* of 1539, Janot also published the first editions of two other, minor, works by Hélisenne, *Le Songe* (The Dream, (1540; reprinted 1541) and a French translation of the first four books of Virgil's *Aeneid* (1541), which is dedicated to King Francis I.

Hélisenne's collected works—excluding the translation of Virgil—were printed seven times between 1543 and 1560. Since nothing of Hélisenne's was ever printed after 1560, we have arbitrarily chosen that year as the year of her death. Her name is not mentioned in any civil document known to us. We have no record of her death.

MAJOR THEMES

Modern commentators might be tempted retrospectively to consider Hélisenne as a "feminist" writer whose major works deal with themes such as a woman's right to a sexual and emotional life of her own, to love, to extrication from an unhappy marriage, to education, to a writing career. In point of fact nothing seems more anachronistic than to suppose that Hélisenne, or any woman of the sixteenth century, would have been concerned with women's "rights," in the modern sense, for that would be reading the sixteenth century as if it had experienced the Enlightenment, the French Revolution, and women's political and social struggles of the nineteenth and twentieth centuries. Even sixteenth-century political thinkers did not think of "rights" as we understand them today, that is, as privileges automatically due to a person from birth.

It might be more accurate to describe Hélisenne's major literary themes in terms of the conflicts and struggles that could be experienced by a woman in everyday reality, as well as of the literary themes that were fashionable in the literary corpus of Hélisenne's time. Hélisenne drew upon the same literary canon as male writers—Graeco-Roman literature, Christian patristic literature, medieval theology, romance, epistolary literature, and contemporary treatises on the "Quarrel of Women"—to produce her arguments "for" and "against" the alleged deceitfulness or lasciviousness of women. Her two major works, the *Angoysses* and the *Epistres*, as well as *Le Songe*, might, each in its own way, be considered a dialogue on the condition of women which, while it seems to question the social and ideological tradition in which Hélisenne was raised, remains squarely within the boundaries of that tradition. In this regard, Hélisenne's work is essentially conservative in tone and content.

The two chief interlocking themes of her works are that marriage is constraining, tyrannical, and devoid of physical passion (though not of physical violence); and that sexual attraction is necessarily extramarital and experienced as an inescapable illness. This illness, which might today be clinically described as an anxiety neurosis, proceeds from highly conflicting emotions, which Hélisenne occasionally personifies as allegorical realities (as in *Le Songe*), and which she is occasionally able to describe in movingly precise and simple words: "Where then, does this harsh passion reside? The rest of my body feels no pain; wherefore it must surely be located in my mind . . . my mind is filling my heart with an affliction for which there is no cure" (tenth personal letter, *Epistres*, 62). Like her heroine, Hélisenne is, of course, conditioned by a religious and moral tradition so unbending that any deviation from its norms might be interpreted as a form of pathological behavior. Consequently, while Hélisenne's works record (in part) a woman's experience with illicit and extramarital love, the moral to be drawn from the experience always comes down on the side of tradition. In the introductory pages of her *Angoysses*, for example, Hélisenne offers her "painful" narrative to noble ladies in order to "gain their compassion and deter them from illicit love." Similarly, any reader of Hélisenne's philosophical allegory, *Le Songe*, which depicts a psychological combat between sexual desire and rational restraint, will be disappointed if he/she assumes from the opening sections of the dialogue that the work pleads for a pagan liberation of the senses, for the Christian and Pauline orientation of the work has already been clearly proclaimed in the full title, which, translated, reads: "The Dream of Lady Hélisenne composed by the said Lady, the consideration of which is apt to instigate all persons to alienate themselves from a vice and approach virtue."

Of her three major works, Hélisenne's *Epistres* contain some of her least conventional and most readable writing. As in the *Angoysses*—but in epistolary rather than fictional form—marriage is depicted as tyrannical, constraining, and withering; and extramarital passion is presented as something exciting, but beset with so many social obstacles as to produce illness in the woman who experiences it. The sweep of Hélisenne's argument, especially in the thirteen personal letters, does not take the reader from unconventionality back to convention, but leads one outward from a smug, bookish wisdom to a slow-but-sure assertion of mature personality, after traversing the tunnel of depression and emerging into the sunshine of maturity. Whereas the first eight personal letters contain many of the themes and tropes familiar to readers of Cicero's *Letters to his Friends* and abound with Hélisenne's exhortations to female friends to resist sexual passion, letters nine to thirteen bear vibrant, vivacious witness to Hélisenne's newly discovered conviction that passion and reason might, in some cases, end up strengthening each other, that passion need not be couched merely as a struggle between the "higher" and the "lower" orders of the soul, and that a higher wisdom can emerge from a socially disapproved experience.

The five invective letters, which follow the personal ones, introduce and vary what appears to be the most passionately "feminist" theme of Hélisenne's oeuvre, which is that the most liberating of all acts for a woman, and the one worthiest of her combat, is the act of writing itself. When she defends woman's right of access to the house of intellect—whether its rooms be called "poetry," "rhetoric," or "philosophy"—Hélisenne argues with a passion that is all the more vehement because it has precedents within a literary canon and tradition that men have created. In her fourth invective letter, Hélisenne dedicates a full page of names of illustrious women who, in the past, have demonstrated the arrogance and presumptuousness of men who would "deny women the privilege of pursuing literature." She adds: "I am convinced that whoever would accept to sail over the sea of great women of science and to list and talk about their works would spend more time navigating than Ulysses ever did in his painful wanderings."

In the first, second, and third invective letters, Hélisenne creates an imaginary exchange of missives with her "husband," wherein other traditional literary themes dealing with the condition of women are discussed and argued: whether or not a woman's writing about an illicit love is necessarily the recording of personal experience; whether or not women are faithless; whether or not a man should engage in marriage with a woman (in the traditional literature about marriage, the question was rarely posed from the woman's point of view); whether or not women's use of ornaments and makeup is proof that they are lustful; whether or not women are to blame if men succumb to their charms. There are precedents, of course, for the tone and content of these "invectives," for example, the long complaints by Ovid's mythological women, in the *Heroides*, intended for lovers both absent and unfaithful.

Hélisenne's letters must be considered within the context of the "Quarrel of Women" literature, which had become a live issue once again since the early sixteenth century. This quarrel had emerged as early as 1277, when Jean de Meung, the continuator of Guillaume de Lorris's *Romance of the Rose*, had attacked the courtly love conception proposed by his predecessor and argued—perhaps tongue-in-cheek, in any case provocatively—that women are notoriously lascivious, deceitful, and conniving creatures. During the fourteenth century, the Quarrel of Women was pursued by such male adversaries as Jean de Montreuil and the humanists Gontier and Pierre Col, and by such passionate defenders of womanhood as *Christine de Pizan (1365–1430), who, in her *Book of the City of Ladies* in particular, countered traditional accusations (which must have animated many a medieval court and many a church council) that women are more lascivious than men, lead men to perdition, and are the sole cause of unhappy marriages. While the Quarrel of Women was to all intents and purposes discontinued during much of the fifteenth century, owing to French political instability and French wars with England, it gathered new momentum during the decades immediately preceding the publication of Hélisenne's works. As in the two previous centuries, women were not without male defenders. As early as 1503, the Lyonnais physician Symphorien Champier published a profeminist *Nef des dames vertueuses* (The Ship of Virtuous Ladies) in terms largely borrowed from Italian Neoplatonism. Cornelius Agrippa's *De nobilitate et praecellentia feminei sexus* (On the Nobility and the Excellence of the Female Sex), written in 1509 but published only in 1529, was a book that Hélisenne unquestionably read and borrowed from, to judge by certain similarities of phrasing; and if Agrippa's assertion that "woman's body is the most admirable and best arranged thing in all Creation" can hardly be considered a lusty predecessor of the "rhetoric of the body" criticism flourishing in academe today, it nevertheless may have made Hélisenne somewhat more conscious of having a body than Champier's all-too-ethereal *Ship of Virtuous Ladies*. Other treatises perhaps read by Hélisenne were Jean Tixier's profeminist manual entitled *De memorabilibus et claris mulieribus* (On Memorable and Famous Women, 1521) and Gratien Du Pont's violently antifeminist diatribe, *Controverses des sexes masculin et féminin* (Controversies about the Male and Female Sexes), first published (anonymously) in Toulouse in 1534.

Hélisenne's writings, particularly her invective letters, stand, then, at the center of the Quarrel of Women literature as it appeared to her around 1540. One senses in these letters, above all, an expression of deep conviction and intensely felt emotions and frustrations stemming from the constraints and pains of her marriage, and from her intense struggle to gain access to the world of literature. It was a struggle in which she never compromised, and from which she emerged victorious, if one is to judge by the results. There is in her letters a ring of life that is hardly present in most of the didactic Quarrel of Women manuals.

This being said, one should add a caveat about the ring of "passion" and "conviction" in literature. That ring, it should be remembered, is part of a game whose rules Hélisenne appears, in her invective letters at least, to have mastered. One might do well to remember Hélisenne's own assertion in the first invective letter: to write passionately about love does not mean that one is recording a lived experience. Many an intensely lived experience has been badly recorded; many an imaginary experience has been vividly recorded, as if it were lived. It matters little, finally, whether Hélisenne literally experienced what she recorded. Perhaps the best tribute one could pay her literary talent is to imagine that even in writing her invective letters she was merely enjoying the game of literature.

SURVEY OF CRITICISM

Hélisenne seems to have been very popular in her lifetime. Ten editions of *Les Angoysses* appeared between 1538 and 1560, and seven editions of collected works—excluding her translation of Virgil—were published between 1543 and 1560. Then Hélisenne fell into oblivion for nearly three centuries, only to be rescued by J. M. Guichard's sympathetic general article, "Hélisenne de Crenne," in 1840, which Guichard intended as a reintroduction, or resurrection, of Hélisenne's name in French letters. In *Le Roman sentimental avant l'Astrée* (1908), Gustave Reynier claimed for Hélisenne's *Les Angoysses* the distinction of being the first "sentimental novel" in France; but he dismissed parts two and three as insignificant, medieval, and didactic, recommending that future critical editions of the novel restrict themselves to part one only.

His recommendation was perhaps followed too literally. Harry Secor's doctoral dissertation (1957), which was never published, was a critical edition of *Les Angoysses douloureuses*, limiting itself to part one. Jérôme Vercruysse's edition of the same work (Lettres Modernes, 1968) also omits parts two and three, but contains an excellent introduction, with perhaps the most complete biographical information about Hélisenne. Paule Demats's edition, which appeared the same year (Les Belles Lettres, 1968), also limits itself to part one. One wonders whether these critics were being finicky out of deference to Reynier; or had they, perhaps, found parts two and three of *Les Angoysses* too strung-out for their tastes? Or might they be respectfully imitating Hélisenne, who, after all, limited her translation of the *Aeneid* to the first four books?

Critical commentary on Hélisenne between 1950 and 1980 was largely focused on *Les Angoysses*. Besides the three critical editions just mentioned, studies of Hélisenne paid little attention to her other works. Irene Bergal's doctoral dissertation, "Helisenne de Crenne: A Sixteenth-Century Novelist" (1968), contains an excellent general introduction on Hélisenne, but it is essentially a structural and technical study of *Les Angoysses*. Helen Waldstein's earlier, shorter dissertation (1964) presents itself as a general study but gives little evidence of its author's having carefully read any other of Hélisenne's work except the first. Two articles on Hélisenne appeared jointly in the Winter 1973 issue of *Symposium*, both dealing exclusively with *Les Angoysses*. M. J. Baker's "Fiammetta and the *Angoysses douloureuses qui procèdent d'amours*" dealt with the influence of Boccaccio's epistolary novel on Hélisenne's *Angoysses*, while Tom Conley's "Feminism, *Ecriture*, and the Closed Room" was a study of the woman writer constrained to write as an escape from an even more constraining marriage. It seems futile, in retrospect, to remark that both Baker's and Conley's articles would have been considerably richer had they included Hélisenne's *Epistres* within their purview: indeed, Boccaccio's *Fiammetta* has more in common with the *Epistres* than with the *Angoysses*; and the issues of feminism, *écriture*, and the closed room are discussed even more pointedly in Hélisenne's second work than in the first.

Until 1985 or so, the only academic critic to study Hélisenne's letters had been the German critic Fritz Neubert, who in a series of three articles written between 1965 and 1970 paid tribute to Hélisenne de Crenne as one of the first *französischen Briefschreiber* (French letter-writers) of the Renaissance. It was largely in reaction to this relative critical indifference to the letters that Marianna M. Mustacchi and Paul J. Archambault published, in 1986, their English translation of Hélisenne's *Epistres familieres et invectives*. Their critical introduction concentrates on some literary facts and hypotheses that were stressed insufficiently, if at all, in previous biographical commentaries on Hélisenne: the importance of classical and patristic sources on her personal and invective letters, and the availability, to her, of contemporary French translations of these sources at Denys Janot's publishing house in Paris. In a section of their introduction entitled "Hélisenne and Her Time," Mustacchi and Archambault argue with textual collations that Hélisenne's letters are to be inserted into the larger context of the Quarrel of Women literature of the sixteenth century.

Thus far Hélisenne scholarship has focused on the *Angoysses* and, only more recently, on the *Epistres*. There is as yet no published criticism of Hélisenne's *Le Songe* or of her translation of Virgil. Hélisenne scholarship would be the richer for a critical edition/translation of *Le Songe* in particular. This text is often dismissed as a secondary work by commentators of Hélisenne, some of whom give little evidence of having read it closely. As an allegorical *psychomachia* (mental combat) which prolongs a medieval tradition extending from Prudentius to the *Roman de la rose* and beyond, *Le Songe* is a rich illustration of the manner in which the conflict between sexual desire and rational restraint (or repression) was being given literary expression by a woman of the 1540s.

BIBLIOGRAPHY

Works by Hélisenne de Crenne

Sixteenth-Century Editions

Les Angoysses douloureuses qui procedent d'amours. Paris: Denys Janot, 1538.
Les Epistres familieres et invectives. Paris: Denys Janot, 1539.
Les quatre premiers livres des Eneydes du treselegant poete Virgile, traduictz de latin en prose Francoyse par ma dame Helisenne, à la traduction desquelz y a pluralite de propos qui par maniere de phrase y son adjoustez: ce que beaucoup sert a l'elucidation et decoration desdictz livres, dirigez à tresillustre et tresauguste Prince Françoys, premier de ce nom invictissime Roy de France. Paris: Denys Janot, 1541?
Les Oeuvres de Ma Dame Helisenne de Crenne, A Sçavoir, Les angoisses douloureuses qui procedent d'amours. Les Epistres familieres & invectives. Le Songe de ladicte Dame, Le tout reueu & corrigé de nouveau par elle. Paris: Estienne Grouleau, 1560.

Modern Editions

Les Angoysses douloureuses qui procedent d'amours, Première partie. Ed. Paule Demats. Paris: Les Belles Lettres, 1968.

Les Angoysses douloureuses qui procedent d'amours. Jérôme Vercruysse. Paris: Lettres Modernes, 1968.

Translations of Hélisenne de Crenne

Mustacchi, Marianna M., and Paul J. Archambault. ed. and trans. *A Renaissance Woman: Helisenne's Personal and Invective Letters*. Syracuse, N.Y.: Syracuse University Press, 1986.

Studies of Hélisenne de Crenne

Baker, M. J. "Fiammetta and the *Angoysses douloureuses qui procèdent d'amours*." *Symposium* 27, no. 4 (Winter 1973): 303–8.

Bergal, Irene. "Hélisenne de Crenne: A Sixteenth-Century Novelist." Diss., University of Minnesota, 1968.

Conley, Tom. "Feminism, *Ecriture*, and the Closed Room: The *Angoysses douloureuses qui procedent d'amours*." *Symposium* 27, no. 4 (Winter 1973): 322–31.

Guichard, J. M. "Hélisenne de Crenne." *Revue du XIXe siècle* (August 1840): 276–84.

Neubert, Fritz. "Antike und Christentum bei den ersten französischen Epistoliers der Renaissance, Hélisenne de Crenne und Estienne du Tronchet (1539 und 1569)." *Romanische Forschungen* 77 (1965): 1–41.

———. "Hélisenne de Crenne (ca. 1500-ca. 1560) und ihr Werk. Nach den neuesten Forschungen." *Zeitschrift für Französische Sprache und Literatur* 80 (1970): 291–322.

Possenti, Antonio. "Hélisenne de Crenne nel secolo dei romantici e la prima conquista della critica." *Francia* 13 (January-March 1975): 27–40.

Reynier, Gustave. *Le Roman sentimental avant l'Astrée*. Paris: Armand Colin, 1908.

Saulnier, V. L. "Quelques nouveautés sur Hélisenne de Crenne." *Bulletin de l'Association G. Budé*, 4th Series, 4 (December 1964): 459–63.

Secor, Harry. "Hélisenne de Crenne: *Les Angoysses douloureuses* (Part One)." Diss., Yale University, 1957.

Vercruysse, Jérôme. "Hélisenne de Crenne: notes biographiques." *Studi Francesi* 31 (January-April 1967): 77–81.

Waldstein, Helen. "Hélisenne de Crenne: A Woman of the Renaissance." Diss., Wayne State University, 1964.

LUCIE DELARUE-MARDRUS
(1874–1945)

Pauline Newman-Gordon

BIOGRAPHY

As a child, Lucie Delarue-Mardrus had many advantages. Her father was a successful lawyer and her mother a descendant of talented Parisian artists. She studied English and music at an early age and enjoyed playing with her five older sisters in the family's country homes in the Paris suburbs and Normandy. The last of these, Vasouy, serves as a backdrop for the semi-autobiographical novel *Le Roman de six petites filles* ("The Novel of Six Girls"). All her life, Mardrus[1] remained attached to her native Honfleur and was intrigued with the character of the Norman peasants and with the dialects and customs of the region, which are vividly depicted in such novels as *Graine au vent* ("Seed in the Wind") and *L'Ex-voto* ("The Ex-Voto"). Her most often quoted line of poetry captures her wistful nostalgia for her native province, in a striking synesthesia: "I held my homeland in the smell of an apple" ("L'odeur de mon pays était dans une pomme"; *Ferveur* [Fervor]).

Mardrus's memoirs tell of her early fascination with poetry, which she looked upon as a vehicle for the total expression of the self. When she was twenty, she summoned the courage to show her work to the older poet François Coppée, who advised her to take up sewing and housework instead. Not easily discouraged, she turned to Théodore de Banville's well-known treatise on versification, ascribing to the view that craftsmanship is essential to the poet. Little by little, she gained enough self-confidence to recite her poems in social gatherings and was soon surrounded by a circle of admirers, including the well-known translator of the *Arabian Nights*, Dr. J. C. Mardrus, who proposed to her at a dinner party. Despite the eccentricity of his ways, he proved to be her most avid reader and promoted her career through his connections with the *Revue Blanche*.

The Mardruses spent a total of seven years in the Near and Far East. During her travels, Lucie mastered Arabic, an accomplishment she attributed to her ear for music and gift of mimicry. In Cairo, she was able to converse with Princess Nazli in her native tongue and charmed all of her hosts with her sketches, piano playing, and horsemanship. She took an obvious pleasure in being seductive and gave her recitals clad in lavish costumes and jewels. In Cairo, she was compared to Athena and Apollo for her beauty.

Back in Paris, the Mardruses entertained celebrated writers and artists, including Henri de Régnier, Gide, and Debussy. Lucie became a close friend of Natalie Clifford Barney, whose mansion on rue Jacob was open to a select circle of friends. Natalie did nothing to conceal her lesbian tendencies, and her daily rides on horseback with Lucie in the Bois de Boulogne were the subject of much gossip. In her memoirs, Mardrus records discovering, as a child, her own sexual attraction to an older woman. Her brief, passionate friendship with Natalie Clifford Barney is depicted in a volume of poems entitled *Nos Secrètes Amours* (Our Secret Loves), which Natalie published after her friend's death.

After her divorce in 1913, Mardrus moved to an apartment on Quai Voltaire next to a doctor and his companion, nicknamed "Chattie." A close friendship developed between the two women, which was interrupted by Chattie's resentment when Mardrus left for America to visit a friend and, later on, when she invited the singer Victoria Gomez, otherwise known as Germaine de Castro, to her home in Honfleur. She hoped to capture the stage for Gomez, whose voice she admired, and did not hesitate to accompany her on the piano at recitals, much to the dismay of her admirers, who deemed such a role unworthy of the well-known writer.

During World War I, Mardrus drove an ambulance for the Red Cross. Her last years were marked by depression and loneliness. Crippling rheumatism and financial problems forced her to move into smaller quarters in Paris and to sell her house in Honfleur. Finally, she settled in another section of Normandy, Château-Gontier in Mayenne, in order to be close to Victoria Gomez. Three of her novels were rejected by the publishers, which shocked her into the realization that hard times were ahead. However, the year 1944 brought a resurgence of publications suspended during the war, and the corpus of Mardrus's writing awaits fresh evaluation.

Lucie Delarue-Mardrus was at home in many forms of expression. She was the author of at least forty novels, nine volumes of poetry, essays, plays, biographies, and short stories. As a journalist, she was a contributor to important reviews such as *Les Annales* and *Le Figaro*. Although she considered herself primarily a poet, she reached millions of readers through her serial novels in *L'Illustration* and other journals. She also painted watercolors that were exhibited in the Galerie Drouot in Paris, sculpted a statue of Sainte Thérèse de Lisieux that stands in a church in Le Havre, and molded wax figures that were displayed in the Carnavalet Museum. Her flamboyant personality and many-faceted talents were legendary. Her wide array of friends and admirers included *Colette, Sarah Bernhardt, and Rodin, and she was the heroine of a novel by Félicien Champsaur entitled *La Caravane en folie* (The Mad Caravan). Yet, celebrated in appearance, she often felt deserted in reality. Her nomadic tendencies were held in check by her attachment to her native province and a fast disappearing way of life. There is a wistful nostalgia in her writing for the *belle époque* (turn-of-the-century) society she knew so well, and she could never adjust to the realization, as she said in *Up to Date*, that "France remained aristocratic under three republics, and is now like a great lady of the manor who remarried a wine merchant" (17). She was apprehensive of modern technology with its impersonality, and fearful of the threat of war. She was sensitive to the plight of the orphan, the poor, and the homeless, and to the anxieties of the modern mind, torn between the aristocratic and the plebeian, the province and the city, the old and the new.

MAJOR THEMES

In an age of post-modernism, the determination to present the lives of men and women in their natural habitat may arouse some suspicion. Mardrus is the all-knowing narrator, slipping into the minds of her characters and never disdainful of rhetorical effect. In *Graine au vent*, her moralizing stance prompts her to intervene in the first person, to draw conclusions and guide the reader through the symbolism of the work. Yet she has the ability to create believable dialogue and to capture the deceptive simplicity of the Norman peasant: tricky, resourceful, never at a loss for words. In *L'Ex-voto*, she manages to draw her observations from several worlds: the violently xenophobic peasantry, the local aristocracy, the Parisian nouveaux riches. She has the gift of making whole towns come alive in their regional specificity, as she depicts boat christenings, processions, and the arrival of the fishing boats in Honfleur.

The children depicted in *L'Ex-voto* and *Graine au vent* are inseparable from Normandy. They have inherited the rebellious spirit of the Vikings, the need to defy, tease, contradict, and fight. Yet they reverse the course of their lives in a moment of great need.

Ludivine in *L'Ex-voto* lives in a hovel. Poverty and alcoholism have decimated her family, and in her idleness and rebellion, she spends most of her time in the streets. On one of her forays into Honfleur, she notices a well-kept house very different from her own and throws a stone in the window. Immediately, the owner emerges and slaps her in front of the other children. Smarting from humiliation, she wishes death on the man who has punished her, and two days later he perishes at sea with his son. His grieving widow soon follows. Secretly haunted by guilt, Ludivine persuades her father to adopt the remaining son, Delphin. She scrubs the hovel, takes control of the household, restrains her drunken father, and assumes the authority over the other children that her mother lacks.

In *Graine au vent*, Alexandra's rebellion is directed against her mother. When she dies in childbirth, Alexandra refuses to mourn and is jealous of her infant sister. But when the deathly sick sibling smiles at her and wants to be held, she responds with the determination to rescue her from an abusive guardian. She will raise her alone and keep house for her father, the award-winning sculptor who has taken to drink.

In a sudden inspiration, she draws sketches of the sister and molds a statue from them. Despite his bitterness at the rejection of his *Winged Victory*, the father is vindicated as he sees in Alexandra the sculptor he wanted to have been.

Forest and farm are pervasive presences in *Graine au vent*, as in many of Mardrus's novels. Other examples are *L'Enfant au coq* (The Rooster Boy), so named because of the boy's attachment to his rooster, and *Fleurette*, the story of Dédé Clairval, inseparable from his horse, who is even called by the animal's name. In *L'Enfant au coq*, Alexandre decides that the land has more value than the cities and opts for tilling the soil rather than following his amorous twelve-year-old neighbor to Paris, even though she writes fairy tales and her mother is a writer. His choice between "literature" and the "real" is set against a backdrop of seasonal chores—sowing, welding, harrowing, and hoeing—which are described with minute tenderness.

Graine au vent also illustrates the ever-present tribulations of the artist. Alexandra's father, Bruno Horp, has not produced a statue since his *Winged Victory* was rejected by the members of the City Council, who preferred to have a more pragmatic symbol of the war erected on the public square. Victoria Gomez in *Une Femme mûre et l'amour* (A Mature Woman and Love) electrifies her audience with the beauty of her voice but fails an audition because of the bias and corruption of the judges. Narcisse in *L'Ame aux trois visages* (The Soul with Three Faces) is the great-granddaughter of the genial composer Babalt. While her father is at war, her mother drives an ambulance and elopes with a wounded soldier. Soon left an orphan, she is entrusted to her paternal grandmother, who discovers her musical talent and gives her Babalt's violin. After the grandmother dies, Narcisse is sent to live with a greedy aunt who forces her to take a job in a cinema where she will have to play pop music on the Amati she inherited.

Mardrus depicts many an artist who struggles against her own temperament as well as physical loss and aging. In *La Cigale* (The Cicada), Marion Laurella captivates all her listeners, from the timid bureaucrat she has married to the rich Englishman who offers to sponsor her career. But the petulant "cicada" sacrifices wealth and recognition for an auto worker who lives in a garret and treats her with brutality. In *Verteil et ses amours* (Verteil and Its Loves), Amelia has lost her voice. The soprano captivates four men during her stay in the Verteil castle where a group of Parisians have taken refuge from the war. Among them is her former lover, the Count de Chambord, who left her when she could no longer sing.

The plight of the musician is seen in the broader context of class consciousness in *L'Amour attend* (Love Is Waiting), where the wife and the mistress of the same man are drawn together at his funeral. Torn by loneliness, the two aging women agree to live under the same roof. Louis's mistress, Gabrielle, has been a first-rate concert pianist; his widow, Armide, has been prominent socially. The women work through spite and anger, and as Armide takes delight in Gabrielle's playing, she realizes that music is their greater bond. But the arrival of Rafael Servin with his good looks and award-winning talent revives the flirtatious instincts of Gabrielle. He comes as a piano tuner but stays to perform on the violin. He is a brilliant musician, but his manners are less than perfect at tea. All becomes clear when he elopes with the kitchen maid, thereby reviving Armide's resentment as a woman of rank.

L'Amour attend offers glimpses of a privileged but fast-disappearing society when influential patrons built their salons around a presiding figure and maids addressed their employers in the third person. The author's aristocratic nature aligns itself with Armide and with the countess in *Verteil et ses amours*, shocked by the abrasive manners of the Parisians who have come to stay in her castle. But changing manners are symptomatic of greater social ills. Many tales contain evidence of the general mobilization and families trying to survive in the aftermath of war—orphans like Narcisse suddenly uprooted from her home, or the Parisians who fled in panic to Verteil. Others contain pathetic testimony of those who are displaced by modern technology, like Dédé Clairval in *Fleurette*, whose horse is his constant companion as he plies his haberdasher's trade on the long trek from Mayenne to Brittany. On the other hand, Alexandre, the "rooster boy," clings to his old ways by choice, never forgetting his excitement at setting a train in motion or his suffering at the death of his rooster. Others remain attached to local dialects, to language as a source of identity. For Narcisse's grandmother, speech is the last bastion of Frenchness, and it is a duty to speak it correctly while soldiers are fighting to save the country. The innocent French of an American heiress stands in stark contrast to Henriette de Villenval's distinguished speech, which reveals her noble birth after she is mistaken for a milkmaid (*Hortensia dégénéré* [The Withered Hydrangea]).

The dying nobility is depicted in its own period of transition. Count Ernoult de Beauvaisnes is a scion of an aristocratic family (*Hortensia dégénéré*). He is attracted simultaneously to Geraldine Oswald, an American heiress, and to Henriette de Villenval, the daughter of a ruined nobleman, who forces her to tend the pastures. After a brief, passionate love affair with Henriette, he marries the heiress. When he returns to the Villenval castle two years later, he learns that Henriette drowned in the pond shortly after his departure and suspects that her father had fired pistol shots just before the suicide. In his guilt at having deserted her, Beauvaisnes jumps into the same pond. It was there that he first plucked a hydrangea and let it wither like the title and fortune of the Villenval family, so similar to his own.

Like Beauvaisnes, Georges Antoine de Surville in *Un Cancre* (A Dull Schoolboy) is at the crossroads of the old and the new. An aristocrat by birth, he is a semi-orphan who vegetates in a Parisian lycée. In reality, he lives in the dream world of a Norman castle, where he spent seven years listening to tales about his ancestors. In the absence of parental supervision, his guardian decides to send him back to Normandy for hard labor on a farm. Thereupon the young count finds himself sleeping in stables, tending cows, and ploughing the earth, and is even beaten by his master, who is a peasant. But he remains attached to the land and is a man of valor. One day he acquires some land of his own and becomes known as "the gentleman farmer," the last survivor of the Counts de Surville. But he cannot forget the peasants' life. If he marries his attractive cousin, Hermine, he will be able to restore the castle of his dreams. If he chooses the wily peasant, Mathilde, he will remain close to his other self. His conflict is in his inability to choose.

In both novels, the aristocrats are consigned to the fringes of insanity. Beauvaisnes considers himself a madman despite his moments of lucidity, and Georges Antoine is divided to the point of incoherence. The woman he rescues from malicious children on the road, Madame De Gravières, is also a vestige of the dying aristocracy. Half madwoman and half madonna, she has returned to the Eden of her youth, and it is in her home that the once recalcitrant schoolboy discovers his love of poetry and music. But she cuts a sad figure on the road in her wig and outrageous makeup, and is considered an eccentric at best.

Mardrus does not hesitate to venture into the suppressed realms of the psyche. Beauvaisnes is writing a novel. He distances himself from people and events in alternate chapters, with the aid of a first-person narrative. Although the two women he loves are finely drawn, they become interchangeable in his mind. He embraces one while thinking of the other, and Geraldine is a composite of many heroines encountered in his reading. He marries Geraldine but is unable to sever himself from Henriette, and dies in the pursuit of her memory. The night, the danger of the father's revenge, the flower that draws Beauvaisnes to the malevolent pond like a talisman, accentuate the obsessive nature of a social conflict in one who sees himself as a madman. The real clash takes place between the decadent aristocracy of which he is a part and the new order that invades his life through an American heiress and the colony that gravitates around her.

Like Beauvaisnes, Georges Antoine is fixated on memories of a manor and a noble name. But he is also rooted to the soil through his peasant past, and can only resort to illusion as a way out of his dilemma. He creates the woman of his dreams from fleeting recollections, transmogrifying the peasant Mathilde into a fairy princess and his cousin Hermine into Beatrice. He adores a dead woman in a portrait when real footsteps are approaching. Indecisive like the Norman peasant ("maybe yes, maybe no"), soliloquizing like Hamlet, he cannot establish his identity.

The plight of women could not fail to be a topic of arresting concern to the chronicler of changing mores. Early in her career, Mardrus produced an article in *La Fronde* entitled "Du Chignon au cerveau" (From the Chignon to the Brain). In it, she pleads for woman's acceptance of her own nature and the unabashed expression of her most intimate reactions.

Since instinct which is more beautiful than intelligence guides you with a leap of its subtle antennae . . . what will you do in the masculine realms . . . we want you to be a different kind of humanity, compared to masculine humanity, rotten with reason, science and [rigorous] method. Express bravely the animal that you are. . . . Capture the inner monster in all the forms of your art. Cast out your devils!

The metaphorical passage just quoted dwells heavily on instinct and seductiveness and makes no attempt to demonstrate equality by minimizing the differences between the sexes. If anything, it reinforces the stereotype of feminine instinct versus masculine intellect. In the rest of the article, Mardrus looks approvingly upon seductive feminine attire, circa 1920, with its cumbersome dress and hairstyles. Her advice on feminine pulchritude generated considerable discussion in the press when her woman's guide to beauty was published in 1926, under the title *Embellissez-vous* (Beautify Yourself). Henriette Sauret was one of the first to react, exclaiming in *La Fronde*: "Mme. Mardrus with her gifts and accomplishments is a living testimony of the capabilities of the feminine mind. Instead of helping other women overcome prejudice, she reinforces the stereotype of the woman whose role is to please." According to Seuret, she played into the hands of the well-known critic Paul Souday, who lauded Mardrus's article in an otherwise misogynous column. To add insult to injury, when Jean Portail of *L'Intransigeant* solicited Mardrus's views on the suffrage of women, she declared that she was not interested in politics and that "the harm [had] already been done. Now that women gave up the protection of men, . . . now that they have killed chivalry, . . . they must have something instead! . . . We cannot go back" (*Le Moniteur du Calvados*, May 6, 1932).

Mardrus took great pleasure in displaying her own physical beauty, sometimes on the covers of magazines or in self-portraits, and in accepting male tributes. Her initiatives in advocating the art of seduction are not unrelated to such concerns. Yet, the advocacy was by no means mindless. She had seen too much suffering to be unaware of woman's vulnerabilities and had called attention to the plight of the unwed mother in her novel *Marie, fille-mère* (Marie, the Unwed Mother), the story of a pregnant servant deserted by a rich farmer. In her poems also, Mardrus shows great sympathy for prostitutes and battered women. For her, the answer did not lie in subordinating femininity, but in accepting the responsibility it entailed through the uninhibited expression of feeling, intellect, and sensuality. In this sense, the accusation of antifeminism loses its relevance. "Your work must wear a skirt," as she said in the same article, is not a cry of resignation, but a call to action.

Despite appearances, Mardrus was ahead of her time in many ways: her open nonconformity in sexual life, her determination as a poet to express the feminine body, and her tendency to look upon maternity with suspicion. Time and time again, her poems articulate pity for women, the "complex flesh offered to virility" ("Femmes," in *Ferveur*), and her refusal to add tomorrows to her life through reproduction ("Refus," in *Horizons*). The frailties of the feminine species are seen as a threat to survival, particularly in the case of aging, and her frescoes of prostitutes and homeless women testify to a deep social concern.

Mardrus is ahead of her time also in her depiction of sexual marginality, as in her play, *Sapho désespérée* (Sappho in Despair), and in her treatment of lesbians, homosexuals, and hermaphrodites. To be sure, hermaphrodites are present in nineteenth-century French writing, but in *L'Ange et les pervers* (The Angel and The Debased) an entire milieu comes alive to which Mardrus had been introduced by Natalie Clifford Barney, a way of life which for a short time she had adopted (*Mes Mémoires*, 144). In this work, Marion Valdeclare frequents two worlds, the lesbian circle that gravitates around Laurette Wells and the homosexuals who frequent Ginette Lobrée's basement. She has two Paris apartments, two names (Marion and Mario), and uses both masculine and feminine attire. Marion is an amused by-stander in the episode of an unwanted birth, but little by little, she gets caught up in the human side of the story and adopts the child in whose embrace she finds the affection she had never known. Her spiritual odyssey extends from her early suffering over her parents' hatred and embarrassment to her later attraction to a convent and search for spiritual redemption.

Like the bisexual Marion, the lesbian Laurette Wells is sympathetically drawn. The American expatriate modeled after Natalie Clifford Barney is impractical, stubborn, impulsive, but also brilliant and generous. The same is true of Victoria Gomez in *Une Femme mûre et l'amour*, who, when her impoverished and estranged in-laws appear at her doorstep, takes them in, although she is unable to earn her living as a singer. When her brother-in-law gets an important job in the provinces, he offers to marry her, but the prospect of small-town gossip and the prejudice against artists and Jews that had alienated him before are too frightening. Victoria is a triple target for discrimination, as Jew, artist, and woman of many love affairs.

Mardrus is ahead of her times in the example she sets as a self-supporting writer of professional status. One of her novels, *L'Autre enfant* (The Other Child), elucidates the stark opposition of two stepsisters: Gizelle, who personifies the old-fashioned virtues of nurturer and teacher, and Marinette, the liberated woman of post–World War I, who smokes, drives an automobile, and gets engaged without seeking consent. As a law student, she pleads the cause of liberated women. Now that they are admitted to the university, she argues, they are prepared to accept risks and responsibility. Changes wrought by the war have made independence a necessity. Parenthood is more a biological fact than a deliberate choice. Ironically, her arguments alienate her parents and make them realize their greater affinity to Gizelle, whom they resented while she was growing up. Of the two, she is the more sympathetically drawn, and it is she who goads her father on to artistic achievement when his faith in his ability fails. There can be no doubt that the choice was not clear-cut in the author's mind. She was a feminist by example, but not allegiance.

Amanit presents another view of women, afforded by Princess Antinidès. She is none other than the eternal woman, perpetually young and beautiful. The Egyptian goddess Isis punished her for killing a priest who had attempted to seduce her. She is condemned to live as others are condemned to die, and for

3,000 years has roamed the earth in various guises—as a fisherman's wife in the Delta, a priest in Persia, a nun in the Italian Renaissance—and her beauty has always awakened hatred, jealousy, and fatal love. Only the spectacle of true love can constitute her deliverance, and when she becomes the not-so-disinterested spectactor of Charles-Etienne's love for Geneviève in France, she is finally free to die.

The seductress so beautiful that she must die or cause death is a timeworn cliché of the *femme fatale*. It is not unfitting to Mardrus's depiction of woman's tribulations.

SURVEY OF CRITICISM

Until the close of her life, Lucie Delarue-Mardrus lamented the fact that her poetry did not enjoy the recognition it deserved. On the other hand, her well-established reputation as a novelist increased with a long succession of crisp, entertaining novels that she published as serials in journals.

Renée Vivien was the first to hail her as the great poetess of the times. But her poetry was discovered by a broader audience when Count Robert de Montesquiou asked her to give a reading in his "Pavilion of Muses." Unfortunately, he did so with the ulterior motive of slighting her rival, Anna de *Noailles, who came to the event believing that it was held in her honor. She promptly retaliated in a derogatory review of Mardrus's poetry in *Le Journal*, written by her friend, Jean Lorrain. It did not help matters when the renowned critic Emile Faguet exclaimed that he had never read anything "more frankly comical" than Mardrus's poetry (*Mes Mémoires*, 130). On a more positive note, other critics tended to applaud her originality, her ardor, the sensual quality of her poetry, her "healthy animality, frankness and precision" (Maury, *Figures*, 303), her "feline languor" and "romantic ardor" (Ernest-Charles, *Samedis*, 233). Sometimes reviewers were quite contradictory. Walch sees the poet "thirsting for eternal human truths" (quoted by Sirieyx de Villers, *Bibliographie*, 34), whereas Sirieyx de Villers finds that she ignores important questions, like death. Some critics are too rhetorical to be taken seriously. Bonnefon exclaims, for instance, "In her veins, the flame of her soul shines forth" (*Corbeille*, 94), and Spalikowski dubs her "the fairy of the pen and paint brush" (*Honfleur*, 9). Predictably, the more scholarly sort of criticism emphasized her romantic and symbolist affiliations and her attachment to Normandy as a source of imagery.

Among the negative comments, Jean de Gourmont muses that Mardrus's accumulation of metaphors sometimes becomes a technique overshadowing inspiration, and Jean Charpentier points out the declamatory character of her lyricism. Charles Maurras detects a penchant for the bizarre in her style, which he calls "the caprices of [a] little girl wanting to seem original," but concedes that her incongruous metaphors are "tempered by the orderly instinct of the housewife" (*L'Avenir*, 211). Most of the male critics evaluate her poetry along gender-related lines. The most sexist overtones are heard in the commentary of

Paul Flat, who admires Mardrus's ability to elucidate intimate recesses of feeling and express women's suffering, but at the same time maintains that when she enters the realm of the metaphysical, she steps out of her role as a woman. Like Paul Flat, Charles Maurras sees her greatest originality in her personal, direct confession, but is alarmed at the "perversity" of *Horizons* and its sapphic implications. On the other hand, Jean de Gourmont sees her "ostentatious display of virginity" in the early works as a source of poetic strength and muses that "no one has ever spoken with such naïve, unblushing shamelessness of the mysteries of women" (*Muses d'aujourd'hui*, 76–77).

The novels enjoyed almost unequivocal acclaim and were compared to the writing of George *Sand and *Colette. Albéric Cahuet admired the undisciplined vigor of *L'Ex-voto* and its delicate balance between lyricism and realism and José Vincent appreciated its mix of local dialects and French, reminiscent of Montaigne. But Jean Charpentier found the thesis of *Graine au vent* too obvious, unconvinced as he was by the story of a woman who discovered her talent as a sculptor. Henri Clouard was puzzled by the choice of Hamlet as a "patron saint" of Normandy in *Un Cancre*, and, more incisively, wondered how Amanit could have roamed the earth for 3,000 years in search of true lovers and yet ignored the famous example of Abélard and Héloïse, among others. Perhaps Aurel summed it up best in her comment that Mardrus wrote too much to avoid a certain negligence. But all in all, her novels constitute an animated fresco of French society at the turn of the century, nostalgic yet surprisingly modern in their expression of the feminine and their concern for social justice.

NOTES

I have used the date of birth recorded by House and Frauschiger, the editors of *L'Enfant au coq* (*Un Garçon Normand*), who interviewed Lucie Delarue-Mardrus in Honfleur. (See bibliography.) All translations are mine. Acknowledgments are due to the Institute for Research on Women and Gender at Stanford University for financing part of this project through the Marilyn Yalom Research Fund, and also to the National Endowment for the Humanities, whose travel grant made it possible to conduct research in Paris.

1. For the sake of concision, I shall refer to the author as Mardrus, a form used by Henriette Seuret in the article quoted in the bibliography.

BIBLIOGRAPHY

All works not otherwise designated are fiction. All publishers, unless otherwise noted, are in Paris.

Major Works by Lucie Delarue-Mardrus

Occident. Revue Blanche, 1901.
Ferveur. Revue Blanche, 1902.
Horizons. E. Fasquelle, 1904.

La Figure de proue. E. Fasquelle, 1908.

Marie, fille-mère. E. Fasquelle, 1908.

La Monnaie de singe. E. Fasquelle, 1912.

Un Cancre. E. Fasquelle, 1914.

Un Roman civil en 1914. E. Fasquelle, 1916.

Deux Amants. E. Fasquelle, 1917.

Souffles de tempête. E. Fasquelle, 1918.

Toutoune et son amour. A. Michel, 1919.

Les Trois Lys. Ferenczi, 1920.

L'Apparition. Ferenczi, 1921.

L'Ex-voto. E. Fasquelle, 1922.

Le Pain blanc. Ferenczi, 1923.

La Mère et le fils. Ferenczi, 1924.

La Cigale. A. Fayard, 1924.

Le Roman de six petites filles. E. Fasquelle, 1924.

A Côté de l'amour. Ferenczi, 1925.

Graine au vent. L'Illustration, 1925.

Sainte Thérèse de Lisieux. E. Fasquelle, 1926.

Embellissez-vous. Illustrated by the author. Les Éditions de France, 1926.

La Petite Fille comme ça. Ferenczi, 1927.

Hédalga. Ferenczi, 1928.

Amanit. L'Illustration, 1929.

Les Amours d'Oscar Wilde. E. Flammarion, 1929.

Hortensia dégénéré. Ferenczi, 1929.

L'Ame aux trois visages. E. Fasquelle, 1929.

Les Sept Douleurs d'octobre. Ferenczi, 1930.

L'Ange et les pervers. Ferenczi, 1930.

Le Cheval. Nouvelle Société d'Édition, 1930.

Guillaume le Conquérant. E. Fasquelle, 1931.

L'Autre enfant. Ferenczi, 1931.

L'Amour à la mer. Lemerre, 1931.

Le Far-West d'aujourd'hui. E. Fasquelle, 1932.

François et la liberté. Ferenczi, 1933.

Passions américaines et autres. Ferenczi, 1934.

L'Enfant au coq. Ferenczi, 1934.

Eve Lavallière. Albin Michel, 1935.

Une Femme mûre et l'amour. Ferenczi, 1935.

Up to Date. R. Allou, 1936.

Chênevieil. Ferenczi, 1936.

L'Amour attend. L'Illustration, 1936.

Roberte. Ferenczi, 1937.

L'Hermine passant. Ferenczi, 1938.

Mes Mémoires. Gallimard, 1938.

Fleurette. Petite Illustration, 1938.

La Girl. Ferenczi, 1939.

L'Homme du rêve. Tallandier, 1939.

Tout l'amour. Tallandier, 1940.

Verteil et ses amours. Editions Self, 1948.
Nos Secrètes Amours. Les Iles, 1957.

Translations of Lucie Delarue-Mardrus

Sainte Thérèse de Lisieux: A Biography. Trans. Helen Younger Chase. New York: Longmans, Green, 1929.

Studies of Lucie Delarue-Mardrus

Aurel. *La Conscience embrasée*. Radot, 1927.

Barney, Natalie Clifford. "Les Mardrus." In *Souvenirs indiscrets*. Flammarion, 1960. 147–85.

Billy, André. "Lucie Delarue-Mardrus." In *L'Epoque 1900*. Tallandier, 1951. 224–27.

Bonnefon, Jean de. *La Corbeille aux roses ou les dames de lettres*. Bouville, 1909.

Cahuet, Albéric. "L'Ex-voto." *L'Illustration*, No. 4125 (March 25, 1922): 224–27.

Charpentier, Jean. "Amanit." *Mercure de France*, October 1, 1929, 156–57.

———. "Graine au vent." *Mercure de France*, July 1, 1926, 160.

Clouard, Henri. "Lucie Delarue-Mardrus." *Romanciers, Revue critique des idées et des livres* (   ): 204.

Descaves, Pierre. "La Ronde de Lucie Delarue-Mardrus." In *Visites à mes fantômes*. Denoël, 1949. 111–29.

Ernest-Charles, J. "Lucie Delarue-Mardrus." In *Les Samedis littéraires*, 4th series. Sansot, 1905. 227–40.

Flat, Paul. "Madame Lucie Delarue-Mardrus." *Nos Femmes de lettres*. Perrin, 1909. 57–97.

Gourmont, Jean de. *Muses d'aujourd'hui, essai de physiologie poétique*. Mercure de France, 1910.

Harry, Miriam. *Mon Amie, Lucie Delarue-Mardrus*. Ariane, 1946.

House, Roy Temple, and Fritz Frauschiger, Eds. Introduction to *Un Garçon normand* (*L'Enfant au coq*). Boston: D.C. Heath, 1946.

Le Roy, Paul. "Colette, Lucie Delarue-Mardrus." In *Nos Femmes de lettres*. Maugard, 1936.

Maurras, Charles. *L'Avenir de l'intelligence; Auguste Comte; Le Romantisme feminin; Mademoiselle Monk*. Paris: Nouvelle Librairie Nationale, 1917.

Maury, Lucien. "Trois poétesses, Lucie Delarue-Mardrus, Hélène Picard, Jeanne Perdriel-Vaissière." In *Figures littéraires*. Perrin, 1911. 297–308.

Montesquiou, Robert de. "Madame Lucie Delarue-Mardrus." In *Professionnelles beautés*. F. Juven, 1905. 51–67.

Néron, Marie-Louise. "Littérature et poudre de riz." *La Fronde*, September 8, 1926.

Réval, Gabrielle. *La Chaine des dames*. Crès, 1924.

Sauret, Henriette. "Politique contre la beauté." *La Fronde*, 1926–1927. (Lucie Delarue Mardrus File, Marguerite Durand Library).

Sirieyx de Villers, Emilie. "Lucie Delarue-Mardrus." In *Bibliographie critique, suivie d'une biographie critique, suivie d'opinions et d'une bibliographie*. Sansot, 1923.

Spalikowski, Edmond. *Honfleur et Madame Lucie Delarue-Mardrus*. Rouen: Imprimerie de A. Lainé, 1931.

Vincent, José. "L'Ex-voto." *La Croix*, February 12–13, 1922.

Walch, Gérard. *Anthologie des poètes français contemporains, 1866–1914*. Vol. 3. Delagrave, [1914?].

MARCELINE DESBORDES-VALMORE (1786–1859)

Michael Danahy

BIOGRAPHY

Marceline Desbordes was born on June 20, 1786, the fifth of six children in a working-class family. Her father was an artisan whose livelihood came from painting family crests, shields, and coats of arms for members of the aristocracy. When this trade became obsolete as a result of the French Revolution, Desbordes-Valmore's father went bankrupt and never recovered from the blow. During the same period, Desbordes-Valmore's mother took a lover, with whom she fled in 1797, leaving behind all but the youngest surviving girl, Marceline, then eleven years old. Family ties, parent-child relations, and the meaning of motherhood, as well as the woes of the dejected and downtrodden, would deeply preoccupy the writer ever after.

Both of Desbordes-Valmore's parents had grown up in Douai, which remains to this day a relatively small and quiet provincial town in the north of France. Prior to the Revolution, it had been the capital of French Flanders, the administrative seat of its Parliament, and the location of a distinguished Catholic university. The brief decade of early childhood that Desbordes-Valmore spent in Douai was the only secure dwelling she ever experienced, and it left a lasting impression on her life and works, her memory, imagination, and writing. Over and over again in her letters, her three novels, her more than fifty stories, and several volumes of poetry, she expresses a strong sense of place and speaks with great longing for the town. Vividly she remembered its inhabitants and surrounding countryside, its fields and wildflowers, and fondly she evokes La Scarpe, the picturesque stream that meanders through town, the ruins of ancient ramparts, medieval stone buildings, the Gate of Valenciennes near her working-class neighborhood, her friends, and the local parish church of Notre Dame. Douai's cool summer climate and rainfall favor the lush green vegetation and flowers that she often evokes in her poetry. Indeed, to this day one may touch the dried flowers that she preserved in her albums and notebooks as a source of inspiration, symbolism, and nostalgia for the past. These are housed in the extensive archives devoted to the native poet in the municipal library of Douai.

To an extent, Desbordes-Valmore sentimentalized or romanticized both family life and nature, these early years in Douai. The fact is that after leaving town with her mother in 1797, the future poet never returned for more than very brief visits. Her purpose on these occasions was usually to transact sorrowful family business that left little time for pleasure or inspiration.

Immediately upon their departure from Douai, mother and daughter embarked upon a series of impulsive escapades that took them all over France and eventually to the Caribbean. Starting in Lille and then in the Bordeaux region of south-western France, the young girl's mother put her to work on the stage. The pair led a hand-to-mouth existence as traveling actresses until 1801, when they set sail for Guadeloupe, where Catherine Desbordes intended to seek help and protection from a wealthy cousin about whom she had heard only stories. Upon arrival, however, the two travelers found that their hopes had already been dashed by a slave rebellion, in the course of which the distant cousin and his wealth had been lost. Worse yet, an epidemic of yellow fever carried off the mother soon after, leaving the young girl a penniless orphan alone in the new world. In a very real sense, from this time on she was a "woman on her own," to borrow a phrase ˚Colette uses in her novel *The Vagabond*.

Desbordes-Valmore's short story "Le Nid d'hirondelles" seems to offer an allegory of the trauma of these early experiences. Although ostensibly intended for children, it makes for a bizarre and gruesome bedtime story, in which a lonely adolescent orphan writes a letter to her sister. In the letter, she recounts a scene that she still remembers from their childhood. A male swallow brutally destroys his brood, wrenching the hatchlings from the nest and hurling them to earth. His mate then takes revenge by killing him. The following day, blood and feathers lie strewn about and the nest has fallen onto rocks. Ominously, the story ends with a sentence about the storyteller: "She stopped writing."[1]

Not without difficulties and dangers, but with some help from strangers, Desbordes-Valmore, now sixteen, managed to return to France in 1802. She continued to pursue a career as an actress and opera singer, moving with great success from Douai to Rouen to Paris. In 1807, while working in Brussels, she published her first verses, "Le Billet," a *romance* that was meant to be set to music. Out of work in 1808, she lived a rather adventuresome life for the next four years, moving about considerably and bearing two illegitimate children. The first died shortly after his birth, but the second, also a son, she raised alone courageously as a single parent, until he too died of an illness in 1816 at the age of five.

The theme of a mysterious lover, Olivier, was to run throughout Desbordes-Valmore's poetry for the next forty years. Legend had it that this poetic figure in her work was based on only one real person, namely, Henri de Latouche, a well-known journalist and poet of the time. So reserved and proud is Desbordes-Valmore about divulging personal information, however, that scholars have only recently concluded that the father of her second child was in fact an otherwise unknown fellow named Eugène Debonne, rather than her more famous lover, who later on probably fathered another of her children, Ondine.

A year after the death of her illegitimate son, while Desbordes-Valmore was acting in Brussels, she met and married, in the space of six months, a fellow actor, Prosper Valmore, seven years her junior. The couple had four children, one of whom died in infancy. During their lifelong marriage, Marceline and Prosper endured extraordinary hardships both personally and as a couple. The emotional and financial burdens included moving constantly from place to place—Lyon in 1821, 1827, and 1834, Bordeaux in 1823, Rouen in 1832, Italy in 1838, and well over a dozen different residences in Paris over the years. Valmore never managed to earn a steady income, and when he did find employment, it was frequently on the road as an actor. This chronic instability left Desbordes-Valmore alone for long periods of time. Not only did she have to raise the children on her own, she also had to eke out a meager subsistence and provide the bare necessities for herself and children. She worked in the theater until 1823 when she became a full-time freelance writer, selling children's stories and other pieces as best she could. These include *Veillées des Antilles* (Evenings in the Antilles, 1820), a series of stories based on her memories of the trip with her mother; lyrics for musical romances; an autobiographical novel evoking the artisanal circles of her father and uncle, *L'Atelier d'un peintre* (A Painter's Atelier, 1833); *Contes en vers* (Verse Tales), *Contes en prose* (Prose Tales), and *Le Livre des mères et des enfants* (The Book of Mothers and Children), all in 1840; *Huit Femmes* (Eight Women, 1845); *Les Anges de la famille* (Angels of the Family, 1849); and *Jeunes Têtes et jeunes coeurs* (Young Heads and Young Hearts, 1855). She had begun selling her poetry by the piece as early as 1813, and her separate volumes include *Poésies* (Poems, 1830), *Les Pleurs* (Tears, 1833), *Pauvres Fleurs* (Poor Flowers, 1839), and *Bouquets et prières* (Bouquets and Prayers, 1843). Not the least of the couple's other burdens also included the marital infidelity of both partners and the loss of both their adult daughters after protracted illnesses. Finally, the couple also had to cope late in life with the death of their only grandchild.

This summary can give no idea of the psychological, social, and professional struggles and obstacles Desbordes-Valmore confronted in becoming a successful, if marginalized, poet. In her letters and elsewhere she writes apologetically that she received no formal schooling and had no opportunity to study great literature or learn how to write well. Had education been available to young women of her class, the turmoil of her existence left no hope for it. Nonetheless, she was able to turn this disadvantage dialectically to her own advantage in two distinct ways.

First, a bookish culture did not cramp her style. Whatever literary training and inspiration she managed to come by did not derive from the stultifying rhetorical tradition of the "masterpieces," whose style and diction were best suited for written argumentation, narration, description, and philosophical analysis. Rather, her training derived from vocal performance, salon concerts that were often improvised, and her working knowledge of eighteenth-century lyric opera, musical elegies and romances, and of course the great tradition of French drama. In point of fact, therefore, she did learn much about literature and style from her experiences both as an actress and singer. Later in life she also studied English and even translated some English verse, notably the ballads and lyrics of the Irish Romantic, Thomas Moore.

The second way in which she turned the liabilities of being denied access to book learning into an asset was by making her marginal situation into an explicit theme. Like many male counterparts during the Romantic movement in France, Desbordes-Valmore exalts emotion and nature over culture and artifice. But she makes this dichotomy and the critique of book learning an element in her uniquely female experience. Several of her poems thus satirize the androcentric values of educational institutions.

Another professional obstacle Desbordes-Valmore had to confront was a cut-throat publishing industry run by men for their own purposes. Publishing was undergoing tremendous changes with the development of technology, improvements in printing presses, and techniques for mass producing books inexpensively. For the first time in history, therefore, it became possible for writers, theoretically either men or women, to make a living by selling their products as entrepreneurs. In practice, of course, the unregulated introduction of laissez-faire capitalist marketing techniques ruled out this theoretical possibility for women in all but the most exceptional of cases. Desbordes-Valmore complains in her letters, quite bitterly at times, of the mistreatment and dishonesty of publishers with whom she was negotiating.

Finally, a lingering battle with cancer during the last two years of her life left Desbordes-Valmore housebound and essentially unable to write new material. Nonetheless, she was still at work at the time of her death, editing what most now agree represents her finest collection, *Poésies inédites* (Unpublished Poems, 1860), for it includes "Les Cloches et les larmes," "Allez en paix," "Les Roses de Saadi," "La Couronne effeuillée," and "Une Nuit de mon âme."

MAJOR THEMES

The poetry of Desbordes-Valmore provides readers today their best access to what women of the nineteenth century had to say on their own behalf about themselves, their bodies, and their inner lives during a period of tremendous changes in all aspects of life. Motherhood, autonomous sexuality, and related forms of sensuousness not accessible to or controlled by men deeply interested her. Her focus on boys and girls as unique individuals endowed with a complex inner life was truly exceptional at the time in France. Seldom, if ever, had childhood been imagined as a separate state of existence intrinsically worthy of attention by serious writers or analysts of human nature. To make children, their behaviors, feelings, and character, a central theme of literature was no more possible for French writers 150 years ago than it was permissible to make them the center of attention in polite society. In fact, concepts of children as autonomous beings with progressive stages of development were basically unthinkable.

Writing outside the dominant cultural patterns, however, Desbordes-Valmore was able to express such concepts. From her writings emerges a composite portrait that depicts mothering as both a libidinal and a conscious moral activity. As an instinct or drive, first of all, mothering is fraught with complex emotional and physical needs for both mother and child. Desbordes-Valmore shows that children are not empty shells or dolls, upon which a set of moral precepts can simply be imposed like clothing. Rather, she shows how children are driven by needs and emotions that are as varied, as complex, and as subtle as those of adults. Satisfying the appetites—for freedom, power, love, and companionship—brings an inextricable mixture of pleasures and pains that are both physical and psychological.

This bonding begins with life in the womb, which Desbordes-Valmore considers as more than a period of physical movement and growth. Her poem ''Un nouveau-né'' reflects a view widely held at the time by homeopathic doctors that a mother's sensory input was organically absorbed by her foetus during pregnancy. Long before modern biology and chemistry understood the uterus and its processes, Desbordes-Valmore intuitively felt that a pregnant woman's choices—sights, colors, tastes, sounds, even musical rhythms—could significantly affect the personality and temperament of the unborn foetus.

In a similar vein, Desbordes-Valmore writes about dreams and the psychosomatic origins and treatment of a condition like stuttering (in ''Le Petit Bègue''). The attention she paid to children's dreams shows that she understood their nature as wish-fulfillments that were structured from the fragments of the preceding day's events and realities. Finally, her works make us aware of the almost compulsive erotic urges that characterize some parent-child bonds.

As a conscious activity, on the other hand, motherhood involves principles and social roles that lead inevitably to conflicting choices and responsibilities. Childhood is a separate and distinctive phase or stage in human development characterized by its own distinctive patterns of behavior, yet the child is mother/father to the woman/man. So children's personalities can be typed on the basis of behavior observed early on. Many of Desbordes-Valmore's prose narratives offer a balanced portrait of the charm, innocence, and pious compliance of children, but others frankly depict their petty brutality, their manipulative egocentrism, and even their wanton, vicious, destructive impulses. One story, aptly named ''Les Petits Sauvages,'' focuses on the sadistic mutilation of animals by children, and the young protagonist of ''Le Petit Incendiaire'' sets his family dwelling on fire, causing his grandfather to die in the ensuing blaze. Boldly and clearly, Desbordes-Valmore depicts the physical and psychological brutality practiced by, as well as against, children.

Based on the intensity with which she experienced motherhood and her single-minded resolve to write about concerns of vital importance to women, Desbordes-Valmore's insights into child psychology come remarkably close to contemporary understandings of children. On the social level as well, descriptions of children's behavior, parties, clothing, games, and interactions with each other and adults are remarkably vivid and detailed. At times, they read like the equivalents of television documentaries about social patterns of the day. No contemporary reporting, video, or photograph is more graphic and unsettling than the five pages of "Le Nain de Beauvoisine," depicting an incident of wife and child abuse. Likewise, at a time when society dismissed her stance against cruelty and corporal punishment as a squeamish womanish piety, Desbordes-Valmore does not cease to condemn, explicitly and by implication, the various forms of child abuse practiced in the name of maintaining masculine authority and discipline. Finally, her tales are interesting in a sociological sense, because they disclose her philosophy of child-rearing. Children are to be treated with kindness in ways that we may take for granted nowadays, but one has the feeling that women of Desbordes-Valmore's day were not always in charge of the principles by which children were actually raised and disciplined.

Desbordes-Valmore saw the child as an individual long before most people of her time did. Yet she does not make motherhood women's sole purpose, and certainly not the justification of women's sexuality. Carnal sensuality exists in its own right. Thus, her nature imagery, far from embodying vague symbols of idealized desire or sentimentalized beauty, can be read as minute expressions of physiological reactions and embodiments of the female anatomy. Descriptions of landscapes covered with bushy vegetation, the hidden recesses of thickets and undergrowth, undulating, dark, and moist knolls, odors, flowers, and valleys, all embody the female anatomy every bit as vividly as do the paintings of Georgia O'Keeffe and Léonor Fini. In "Augure" (Augury), for instance, the poet's love of the sun leads to an image of the earth lustily embodied as a woman, who opens the belted robe she is wearing and exposes hidden lips. These smile with an odor in response to the sun's penetrating rays.

For the most part, Desbordes-Valmore's flower imagery does not transmit the usual cultural symbolism of male-female coitus, although this is not absent from her work. Different from the androcentric tradition of love lyrics, the persona in many of Desbordes-Valmore's poems is not speaking to or about a partner. Many do, of course, but many involve a person of the same sex and speak of the physical intimacies of friendship—touching, breathing, and the like. She does not shrink from inscribing metaphorically what can only be the intimate details, the physical movements, pulsations, and rhythms of orgasm. But the emphasis on the non-genital and non-phallic aspects of sensuality is consistent with modern research findings on sexuality among both heterosexual and homosexual women.

If phallic brutality is not taken for granted in her love lyrics, neither is another theme prevalent among male Romantic poets, the myth of Mother Nature. That is to say, for Desbordes-Valmore Nature is not, as it is in male Romantic poetry, an alien body of fearful external forces that can swallow up the poet in wild vegetation. Thus, Desbordes-Valmore does not depict the earth as the hostile Other, the source of difference in all its destructive fury.

Desbordes-Valmore's physical landscapes are invested with joy, warmth, and freedom at times, but at other times with negative feelings, trepidation, defloration, regret, pain, and sorrow. Often the poet speaks metaphorically of her anxiety and the bitter solitude that follows paternal reprimands. But more often, she speaks with exuberance and vitality of the flowers of female desire.

Desbordes-Valmore's flower accepts her own vulnerability and risks her safety, as she opens gladly to the frictions of Nature and bends to its touch, the sensory stimuli of water, air, and sunlight. Frequently, lush underbrush is the setting for memories of sensory calm and pleasure shared with others. The poet invites her reader to experience, to savor innocent embraces, alive with caresses, kisses, whispered desires, shadowy enclosed gardens bursting with fruit, inundated sometimes with gushing or piercing rays of sun, at others marked with cracks and crevices quietly flowing alone and by themselves.

Gratification in this kind of setting is often oral or olfactory, but also mutual. The ostensible subject of one poem, "Une Ruelle de Flandres" (An Alley in Flanders), is the neighbor's garden that the poet remembers as a young girl. Her reminiscences evolve in an atmosphere of slightly vibrating leafiness and dilation, voicing her delight in the female anatomy. Thus she writes:

> Some indulgent fairy, invisible you might have said,
> Had dilated with a sigh the smothering street.
> Wandering mid the scents of all these green trees,
> Boldly plunging our temples into their half-parted flanks,
> We flirted with odorous roses
> Which returned the favor, happy to be loved.

What makes these sensory images different, over all, is not the exactitude or explicitness of anatomical description, which any nineteenth-century male poet might equally well have undertaken. Rather, what makes them different is the familiarity with the feminine body and the fondness for it which they express, along with the sense of acceptance and enjoyment of its various polymorphous states. It is this polymorphous world of the female imagination, where sexuality is not controlled or authorized by men, not labeled perverse, that Desbordes-Valmore's poetry gives voice to and gives us access to anew.

Underlying these themes is another, more basic theme, that of intersubjectivity. What this concept meant to Desbordes-Valmore is that not all human relations had to be played out in terms of master/slave, active/passive, subject/object dichotomies. Dialogue, communion, love, I-thou, or subject/subject relationships could be achieved through gentleness, mutual dependence, ecological balance. Her poem "Révélation," for instance, blurs various images of husband, lover, woman companions, father, god, mother, and child in a manner reminiscent of the songstress Edith Piaf. All of these objects of desire, or "charmed hearts," as Desbordes-Valmore calls them, are compared to two streams. Silently, they flow together in a warm summer breeze, "quenched by/with one another and content to quiver." Playfulness, as much as work, enters into the formation of such relationships, and to express the theme, Desbordes-Valmore turned primarily to the plant kingdom—buds and blossoms forming flowers and fruits on trees—for images of change, growth, cross-pollination, and symbiosis. Generally speaking, when she introduces animal imagery to depict the processes of metamorphosis at work, she prefers creatures not favored in the long tradition of male poets, predatory four-footed beasts. Rather, she turns to caterpillars, silkworms, butterflies, bees, or domestic, rather than mythological, birds for expressing human relationships, human creativity, the processes of metamorphosis, whereby one creature becomes or gives birth to the other. As with the separate beloved or "charmed hearts," the animal and the vegetal tend to blend, blur, or converge. From its own body, for instance, the silkworm produces a tissue of cloth in the process of becoming a butterfly. Birds hover in between heaven and earth, matter and spirit, freedom and captivity. Desbordes-Valmore's idea of a happy union is one in which male and female likewise hover between the poles of their maleness and femaleness. All boundaries between creatures, physically and mentally, are permeable. Thus her imagery invalidates and undercuts certain of the symmetrical binary oppositions on which sexual tyranny has always rested.

On the physical level, the ideal of intersubjectivity is expressed in the interplay of wind and branches, sunshine and flowers, the natural recycling of rain, the intertwining of the branches and roots of two trees that benefits both organisms or that forms a cycle of completion and ecological balance. A poem like "Les Deux Peupliers" (The Two Poplar Trees), often (mis)read as a conventional love poem, is, in fact, addressed to one or two of the poet's women friends. In it, she addresses the two trees: "The fluid that binds you withdraws to your hearts. / The fluttering of your leaves and branches forms only a murmur; / Married in the earth, through your sacred bonds / You live for each other." In "Les Roseaux," she tells of two reeds who "intertwined their days and nights / In the breezes" and "became as one to be together as two forever . . . / And from this cool wedlock issued a harmony / Which spoke! Which sang! sad, intimate, infinite." Here again the role of heterosexual love is reversed. It no longer functions as the only or ultimate reality signified or symbolized; instead, love is only the signifier or symbol of something more heartfelt. The poem is dedicated to her sister, and its figures and themes apply as well to special female bonds as they do to love or marriage. When images of marriage are thus used as figures of friendship, and images of friendship are used to speak of marriage, male and female cease to be objects of desire or exploitation and become instead interchangeable subjects.

SURVEY OF CRITICISM

Desbordes-Valmore was one of the earliest and most talented Romantic lyric poets in France. For her versatility and originality, she received not only the admiration of most of her contemporary colleagues, men like Hugo, Dumas, and Lamartine; she also received various royal grants and government subsidies in recognition of her literary abilities, accomplishments, and precarious finances.

The noted literary journalist Sainte-Beuve, a lifelong friend, and, for a time, an unsuccessful suitor to Desbordes-Valmore's daughter Ondine, remained her unflagging promoter during her lifetime as well as his own. For over thirty years, he published and republished numerous articles in various journals, books, collections, and editions as he worked tirelessly to make her name known, secure publishing contracts for her, and edit her works. In fact, the only booklength English translation of her poetry was based on Sainte-Beuve's edition and memoirs of the poet. It appeared in Boston over a hundred years ago during the early stage of the women's movement in this country.

Sainte-Beuve's devotion to the cause of Desbordes-Valmore may have turned out to be a mixed blessing, however. He is generally considered the greatest biographical critic ever to write about French literature, so the approach he took proved influential for over a century. Sainte-Beuve praised Desbordes-Valmore's primitive charm, passionate nature, feminine graces, and the like, and saw her as more of a poet than an artist. This meant that the writer was endowed with a soul made deep and beautiful by suffering and that one could read her work as a detailed, direct report or confession not only of her intimate emotions but of her personal life. Thus, while her writing was used as a guide to "reading" her life, in a kind of vicious circle what was known of her life served as a guide to "reading" her poetry. Recently, however, scholars and critics like Christine Planté and many others have come to recognize that reading Desbordes-Valmore's poetry autobiographically has not only led to misleading interpretations of individual poems based on inaccurate biographical information, but has proved to be an unreliable way of sorting out the evidence and documents concerning her life. This change is due primarily to the recent trailblazing research of Marc Bertrand and Francis Ambrière, which is discussed below.

In 1861, the great poet Baudelaire published an essay commemorating Desbordes-Valmore's death. The essay, appearing in "Réflexions sur quelques-uns de mes contemporains" (Reflections on Some of My Contemporaries), laid the foundations for the (male) dominant view of Desbordes-Valmore as a feminine poet par excellence, one who is endowed by birth, that is, with spontaneous, natural sentiment—all heart, no head, and little style, but intensely sensuous. Yet Baudelaire also admired her idealism, her transcendental aspirations for an existence more pure and sublime than that found on earth. Baudelaire's appreciation of Desbordes-Valmore, like that of Sainte-Beuve, is based intrinsically, though not exclusively, on biographical rather than aesthetic considerations.

What makes a good woman writer good is the content of her work, the confessional outpouring of her limited but real-life experiences. In the twentieth century, the German writer Stefan Zweig picked up and amplified this tradition, while the leader of surrealism, André Breton, hailed Desbordes-Valmore as one of his own when it came to the topic of love.

Toward the end of the nineteenth century, a different approach to her work had also begun to emerge, however. The homosexual poet Rimbaud called for an end to the "infinite slavery of women" and for a period when women would live for and by themselves. This liberation, he predicted, will turn women into poets with their own ideas, their own language, and their own unfathomable visions. He had in mind Desbordes-Valmore, whose work he introduced to his lover and fellow poet Verlaine.

Verlaine's famous "Art poétique" seems, in fact, tailor-made to describe or justify Desbordes-Valmore's as well as his own poetry. Although this poem dates from 1874, it was not published until 1885. Yet it was then and still is widely held to be the manifesto of the Symbolist movement. In it, Verlaine called for dislocated verse forms and metric patterns, an uneven number of syllables in lines, the use of musical and singing techniques rather than logical construction, an emphasis not on ideas, persuasion, and teaching, but on shimmering impressions, on what he called nuance rather than color or analysis. All of this we would call impressionism in poetry; Verlaine called it "the drunk or gray song."

When Verlaine published his famous study of the "poètes maudits" of the nineteenth century, Desbordes-Valmore was the only woman on the list. What Verlaine found to admire in her work were the many unexpected contradictions and originalities, her sensuousness yet innocence, primitive forces of the earth yet delicate refinement, Christianity yet a sense of despair. Fundamentally, however, what attracted him was the musicality, the oral qualities of her language, which he prized above all. In fact, Verlaine attributed to Desbordes-Valmore the single most beautiful verse written in French or possibly any human language; it reads: "Je dépends d'un nuage et du vol d'un oiseau / Et j'ai semé ma joie au sommet d'un roseau" (I hang from clouds and a bird on the wing / And sowed my joy on the tip of a reed).

From Verlaine's approach has emerged not only the appreciation, but the debt of gratitude of contemporary poets like Apollinaire and Bonnefoy, who singled out in her writing "the authenticity and intensity of being finite." In retrospect, Desbordes-Valmore's work now appears unique in preserving and transmitting a current of musicality based on the oral qualities, expressive powers, and rhythms of the spoken language. On one level, there are nursery rhymes, bedtime stories, and her children's poems, like "Cher petit oreillet," which continue to be sung and taught by French mothers to their children from one generation to the next. But on another level, according to many critics and writers, the revitalization of French poetry starting at the end of the nineteenth century owes much to this current of musicality. Desbordes-Valmore's work is the primary source for its revival.

There is no need to review much of the criticism written about Desbordes-Valmore through the early twentieth century for two reasons. Most of it is out of print, hard to find, and out of date, and, in any case, Eliane Jasenas has already done the job admirably well in her book, *Marceline Desbordes-Valmore devant la critique*. Jasenas astutely observes that in her evolution from teary-eyed sentimentality to impressionism, Desbordes-Valmore resembles Emily Dickinson more than any other woman poet.

With the appearance of Marc Bertrand's complete critical edition of Desbordes-Valmore's poetry and of Francis Ambrière's exhaustive and superbly documented biography, readers have at their disposal, for the first time in over a century, both a chronology of Desbordes-Valmore's life that is accurate and complete and a version of her texts that is reliable. It is now clear, from the discoveries that Ambrière made in archives throughout France, that the mysterious Olivier of her poems cannot refer exclusively to Latouche or to any one man, for that matter. Regarding her maternity, Desbordes-Valmore had six pregnancies, rather than the five previously known. Regarding her values and lifestyles, Ambrière establishes among other things that Desbordes-Valmore did not leave the theater because of a sudden mysterious voice loss. Her transition to the world of letters was gradual and due to many factors: maternity, financial need, financial success in other areas, disgust with theatrical intrigues, love of literature.

The depth and intensity with which Desbordes-Valmore was politically and socially engaged also emerges in Ambrière's study. She was a liberal in the classic French sense of the word—an advocate of the individual's liberty to pursue happiness despite norms imposed by social institutions like the church and the state. She espoused the cause of militant workers in revolt against the government and the capitalist class; she pleaded for clemency on behalf of political prisoners of war. Because of her politics and despite the resulting economic hardships, she turned down several offers of government pensions, as well as a post for her daughter as tutor to the Duchess of Orléans. Desbordes-Valmore also enjoyed the social whirls of artsy-craftsy Paris. Thus, Ambrière debunks any lingering sentimental romantic image of her as a withering home-body.

Recently, however, some feminist critics have slighted Desbordes-Valmore in their attempts to revise the literary canon and accord to women a greater place in it. Thus, Domna Stanton excludes her from *The Defiant Muse*, a bilingual anthology of French feminist poems from the Middle Ages to the present. And the trend-setting *Histoire du féminisme français*, published by the militant feminist publishing house Des Femmes, tends to confirm this exclusion by judging Desbordes-Valmore rather harshly for what can only be ideological reasons. One has the impression that these and other critics are perhaps turned off by Desbordes-Valmore's reputation among men like Breton and Aragon, who called her "Our Lady of the People," more than by her work as a whole or individually. In any case, they see her as androcentric and unselfassertive.

The content of her work may not be explicitly "feminist" when measured in the context of the twentieth century. One could hardly expect her to take a pro-choice stand on abortion, for instance. But the assertion that she had no political consciousness or gave no voice to issues of gender, as well as class, oppression, is not true. Measuring Desbordes-Valmore's feminism in terms of her time, one can say that her voice was muted but that with this muted voice she spoke of gender, class, and even racial differences and conflicts. I have tried to show that she was systematically excluded from the literary canon for trespassing in a literary genre that was gender-coded masculine. Yet her themes and her art make her poetry the "Flowers of Evil" of difference or otherness, on a par with the other great corpus of the nineteenth century, whose title is similar. For what it means symbolically, Marceline Desbordes-Valmore is one of only six French women writers during the nineteenth century to sign her true name without cover of anonymity, aristocratic pretensions, or pseudonyms.

NOTE

1. The author has supplied all translations.

BIBLIOGRAPHY

Works by Marceline Desbordes-Valmore

First Editions

Poésies. Paris: Boulland, 1830.
Les Pleurs. Paris: Charpentier, 1833.
Une Raillerie de l'amour. Paris: Charpentier, 1833.
L'Atelier d'un peintre. Paris: Charpentier-Dumont, 1833.
Le Salon de Lady Betty. Paris: Charpentier, 1836.
Pauvres Fleurs. Paris: Dumont, 1839.
Violette. Paris: Dumont, 1839.
Le Livre des mères et des enfants. Lyon: L. Boitel, 1840.
Bouquets et prières. Paris: Dumont, 1843.
Huit Femmes. Paris: Chlendowski, 1845.
Les Anges de la famille. Paris: Desesserts, 1849.
Jeunes Têtes et jeunes coeurs. Paris: Bonneville, 1855.
Poésies inédites. Geneva: Fick, 1860.
Contes et scènes de la vie de famille. Paris: Garnier, 1865.

Modern Editions

Les Oeuvres poétiques de Marceline Desbordes-Valmore. Ed. Marc Bertrand. Grenoble: Presses universitaires de Grenoble, 1973.
Poésies de Marceline Desbordes-Valmore. Preface by Yves Bonnefoy. *Poésie* 178. Paris: Gallimard, 1983.
Contes. Ed. Marc Bertrand. Lyon: Presses universitaires de Lyon, 1989.

Translations of Marceline Desbordes-Valmore

Sainte-Beuve, Charles. *Memoirs of Madame Desbordes-Valmore, with a Selection from Her Poems*. Trans. Harriet W. Preston. Boston: Roberts Bros.; 1873.

Studies of Marceline Desbordes-Valmore

Ambrière, Francis. *Le Siècle des Valmore*. Paris: Seuil, 1987.
Baudelaire, Charles. "Réflexions sur quelques-uns de mes contemporains." In *Oeuvres complètes*. Ed. Y.-G. Le Dantec and Claude Pichois. Paris: Gallimard, 1961.
Danahy, Michael. "1859: Marceline Desbordes-Valmore." In *A New History of French Literature*. Cambridge, Mass.: Harvard University Press, 1989. 731–37.
———. "Marceline Desbordes-Valmore and the Engendered Canon." *Yale French Studies* 75 (1989): 129–47.
Jasenas, Eliane. *Marceline Desbordes-Valmore devant la critique*. Geneva: Droz, 1962.
———. *Le Poétique, Desbordes-Valmore et Nerval*. Paris: Delarge, 1975.
Planté, Christine. "Marceline Desbordes-Valmore: ni poésie féminine, ni poésie féministe." *French Literature Series* 16 (1989): 78–93.
Verlaine, Paul. *Les Poètes maudits*. Ed. Michel Décaudin. Paris: SEDES, 1982.

MARIE DE VICHY-CHAMROND, MARQUISE DU DEFFAND (1697–1780)

Caryl L. Lloyd

BIOGRAPHY

Marie de Vichy-Chamrond, later Marquise du Deffand, was born in 1697 to Burgundian aristocrats of modest fortune. Having lost her mother at an early age, du Deffand was sent to a Parisian convent where, by her account, she received a mediocre education and acquired the reputation of being intelligent and gifted in argument. That her lifelong skepticism dates from her childhood is confirmed by an incident in which Father Massillon, the priest sent to convert her, admitted that the girl not only resisted his efforts but charmed him by her good sense. Despite her small fortune, du Deffand was married in 1718 and soon became a leading figure of Regency society. Described by contemporaries as witty and beautiful, du Deffand enjoyed many "seasons of gallantry," which most likely included a brief liaison with the Regent himself. An attempt at reconciliation with the Marquis du Deffand failed for at least two reasons: he grew intolerant of her independence, and she became convinced that her uninspiring spouse would not improve with time.

While du Deffand's literary work consists primarily of her posthumously published correspondence and portraits of prominent contemporaries, she was widely quoted as the author of parodic songs and verses, notably a 1723 satire of the then popular play *Inès de Castro*. In a self-portrait from this period du Deffand describes herself as lively, tender-hearted, intolerant of fools, and subject to bouts of depression. The latter would haunt her all her life and became one of the recurrent themes of her correspondence.

Du Deffand's apprenticeship as a *salonnière* began in the 1730s with her annual stays at the Petite cour de Sceaux, presided over by the Duchesse de Maine until her death in 1753. It was there that she met Louise d'Epinay, the

Marquise de Lambert, and Helvétius as well as her lifelong friends and correspondents, Voltaire and Charles-Jean Hénault. With the latter she embarked upon an "affair of convenience" and soon enlisted him as a regular in her own salon in Paris, first at the Rue de Beaune and, after 1747, at her apartment in Saint Joseph convent. If she was unable to win the loyalty of Diderot, whose atoms, as she put it, were not attracted to hers, she counted among the faithful brilliant representatives of the social and intellectual elite.

Letters exchanged with Jean Baptiste Nicolas Formont, D'Alembert, Voltaire, Montesquieu, Antoine de Pont-de-Veyle, Hénault, and others created a daily extension of salon discussions, brought news of court to those in the provinces, analyzed new literary works and the ideas of the *philosophes*, became the medium in which character was judged and friendships were scrutinized, and, for the insomniac du Deffand, provided a necessary distraction while Paris slept. Seldom a completely private genre, eighteenth-century letters circulated among members of society, were read aloud at gatherings, and were included by quotation or allusion in subsequent correspondence. Well before her letters were published du Deffand was spoken of as the century's Madame de ˚Sévigné.

Completely blind by 1754, du Deffand returned to the family estate in Chamrond, where she met Julie de ˚Lespinasse, the ward, and quite likely the illegitimate daughter, of du Deffand's brother. After delicate negotiations, including a stern warning that Julie was to forget her past and presumably any claims to family property, du Deffand established Lespinasse as her companion at Saint Joseph's. Their ten-year relationship, while mutually beneficial, came to a violent end when du Deffand discovered that her companion had been receiving visitors on her own. Already suspicious of the social program of the Encyclopedists, du Deffand was further cut off from their influence by the subsequent defection of D'Alembert and Anne Robert Jacques Turgot. In her letters to Julie about their break, du Deffand conveyed her deep sense of betrayal by the younger woman. She ultimately replaced Lespinasse with the faithful secretary Jean François Wiart, who remained with her until her death.

In the early correspondence with Hénault, du Deffand had warned him that, while she felt love, she was not moved by sentimental discourse or romantic excesses. In letters to her friend the Duchesse de Choiseul, du Deffand further analyzed the paradox of her emotional life: the inability to feel great passion, coupled with a deep sense of its loss. Writing to Voltaire, she explored the metaphysical anguish brought on by her dark moods. An acute sense of the meaninglessness of existence underlay her observations about love and the shallowness of social life.

In the last fifteen years of her life du Deffand devoted herself to a singular friendship with the English novelist Horace Walpole, to whom she wrote over 800 letters. Although she was sixty-eight when Walpole made the first of five visits to Paris, du Deffand experienced a profound and jealous love despite the twenty years' difference in their ages. Although he remained her close friend, Walpole constantly chided her about the intensity of her passion; he feared that the letters might be intercepted by the Cabinet Noir, the King's postal censorship office, and cause him embarrassment. While she claimed to accept his rules limiting the number of letters and her talk about love, she continually found ways to subvert his epistolary laws. Walpole brought English literature to du Deffand's critical attention, and her appreciation of Shakespeare and Samuel Richardson illustrates an intellectual openness and vitality that was undiminished until her death in 1780.

MAJOR THEMES

When Voltaire suggested writing as a remedy to her chronic ennui, du Deffand responded unequivocally: one must be a Voltaire or nothing at all. Between the conflicting ideals of sociability and dignified retreat that continued to define the aristocratic woman's choices in the eighteenth century, du Deffand chose a mode of expression that bridged the two. Epistolary writing opened the world of intellectual exchange while affirming the relevance of social discourse, specifically of talk animated by women in the self-contained world of the salon. The refusal to be a Voltaire is not simply a refusal of vocation; it is a choice of an alternative site of discourse, one which is neither fully private nor yet completely public.

It is undeniable that this prolific *épistolière* held a prominent position among eighteenth-century stylists. Her letters were circulated and cited as models of neoclassical clarity and insight. The portraits in particular are exemplars of the style and analysis found in La Bruyère and her much admired La Rochefoucauld. Less concerned with physical than psychological detail, du Deffand drew character sketches that, although subtly phrased, never compromised the honesty of her judgment. While the ideal of the *honnête homme*, *honnête femme*, with its emphasis on sociability, naturalness, originality, and moderation, informs her portraits, a second, more personal text can be read.

In the portrait of the Duchesse de Luynes, Mme du Deffand paints a model of reason and moderation, who also professed a profound love of freedom. The Duchesse soon recognized, however, that new chains, the duties required of marriage, were preferable to the uncertainty and terrors of freedom. That du Deffand, who chose the unfettered life, was well acquainted with its darker side is evident in her evocative descriptions of those troubled spirits desperately seeking a point of attachment in the world. In her remarkably modern analysis of the Duchesse de Chaulnes, du Deffand described a consciousness with no fixed point of reference, an overstimulated imagination flitting from one object to another with no real sense of understanding. Her mind, like a magic lantern, cast brilliant but fleeting images into the world. A critic of the Encyclopedists' social program and tedious proselytizing, du Deffand nonetheless shared their suspicion of unrestrained imagination, of an undisciplined mind wandering freely toward the unknown. Her self-portraits of 1728 and 1774 reveal a woman plagued by her own restless intellect. Easily bored, requiring constant social distractions, she was also impatient with pretense and driven to seek the reality beyond appearances. Her finely crafted, well-balanced portraits provide a link with the seventeenth-century genre yet reveal a modern sense of the anguished face behind the social mask.

The terrors of night, her eventual blindness, and an increasingly restricted social life further encapsulated her within the pure negativity of her remarkable vision. Darkness revealed the truth of daily life: "the void present in all that surrounds us" (letter of September 27, 1773, vol. 2, Lescure edition. All du Deffand quotes are from this edition; all translations are mine). The vision of her insomniac nights is a barren landscape, an abyss of uncertainty, a profound pessimism despite her constant activity. Writing to Voltaire, she questioned whether all of life was an illusion, all thoughts pathways to a vast nothingness. "It seemed to me," she explained, "that I have known no one . . . that none have known me, and that perhaps I have not known myself" (letter of October 20, 1766, vol. 1). Throughout her life du Deffand would suffer from the mood she described as "ennui" or "black vapors," yet she was able to transform the personal state into insightful analyses of her society and the metaphysical anxiety circumscribing its progressivism.

Du Deffand's epistolary project was defined in negative reference to existing models. In the stages of her life when the theme of love dominated her writing, she rejected the well-worn path of Héloïse, of the Lettres portugaises and their eighteenth-century descendant, Lettres d'une Péruvienne. That she resisted situating her work at the site of female abandonment made her a challenging, sometimes prickly, correspondent. She disdained the idle revery about the love object, which she called rêvasserie; to the effusions of Hénault she responded that she was unsuited to such lyricism in feeling or in literature. The literature of the lover's absence, a celebration of rejection, never suited the independent du Deffand: "Be Abélard, if you will, but never expect me to be Héloise" (letter of April 21, 1766, vol. 1). She explained to an understandably irritated lover that his absence was "delicious."

The letters to Horace Walpole, from age sixty-eight until her death, however, have been seen by most of her editors and critics as an abject reinscription into the text of the unloved woman. This spirited writer, who never allowed blindness to affect her life, told her reluctant correspondent to treat her like a child, like Magdalen, like a servile animal, but not to ignore her. It is undeniable that these letters are passionate analyses of the feelings of one who waits for letters, who loves more than she is loved. Aware that her current feelings contradicted all she had written about love, she responded defensively to charges that she sounded like other women, notably like the author of Lettres d'une Peruvienne: "I, the avowed enemy of anything that has the slightest trace of it [of romantic excesses], I who have made enemies of all who fell into such foolishness, I now stand accused of such behavior?" (letter of April 21, 1766, vol. 1). Du Deffand once wrote to Voltaire that deathbed conversions do not redefine one's life but represent a reasonable giving in to the inevitability of death. To Madame de Luynes, who praised her courage in accepting blindness, du Deffand protested that there is no courage in such acceptance, only an intelligent refusal of despair. It is perhaps in this philosophical perspective that one might situate the final surrender to passionate love of a blind woman near the end of her life.

Bored by discussions of politics, du Deffand consistently reported on events at court with little analysis. The fall of once favored courtiers, their banishment or death, elicited little personal comment. She was contemptuous of Madame de Choiseul-Stainville, confined to a convent by her husband's *lettre de cachet* for having taken a lover beneath her social caste. A similar respect for the established order underlay her hostility to the *philosophes*. Her friend Formont was not "one of those in-folio *philosophes* who preach contempt for the public and hatred of those in power" (undated letter, November 1758, vol. 1). Jean-Jacques Rousseau, on the other hand, would lead the world into chaos. It was the dogmatic certainty, the intolerance for those who disagreed with them, that made the *philosophes* seem cold and hypocritical to du Deffand. She was convinced that they only preached equality in order to dominate others. Sainte-Beuve believed that Lespinasse's "betrayal" was the cause of du Deffand's antagonism, but while Julie's D'Alembert is a frequent object of criticism, it is as much due to a profound conservatism as personal pique.

As much as she despised the *Lettres portugaises* and their imitators, du Deffand was much less negative in her judgments of the English female protagonists Clarissa and Pamela. She was entertained by such "endless stories" and argued with Voltaire that these works made one desire virtue and believe it was attainable. While *Richard III* and *King Lear* were repulsive to her, the power and beauty in *Othello* and *Henry VI* convinced her that the French respect for dramatic rules was overrated. She preferred the breadth and poetic truth of Corneille over Racine's more limited focus on the passions of love. Shunning the vulgarity of the old fabliaux and the prolongation of that Gallic tradition in Rabelais, du Deffand was equally intolerant of her contemporaries who composed pedantic treatises rather than uplifting entertainments. *Emile* and *La Nouvelle Héloïse* were both immoral and tedious. Aware of her own literary antecedents, du Deffand read and admired the letters of Bussy de Rabutin, Madame de Maintenon, Madame de *Lafayette, and Madame de Sévigné. Realizing that Horace Walpole also admired the seventeenth-century *épistolière*, du Deffand began to imitate Sévigné in letters to him. She gave up the experiment when Walpole protested that her own style was as worthy of admiration.

Although regretting her shallow education, she had no desire to return to the days of her youth unless it could be under the tutelage of a Horace. Two authors who would most certainly have figured in her revised course of studies are Voltaire, whose letters revived her in times of depression, and Montaigne. While critical of a certain "puerility" in Voltaire's historical writing and censorious of his lapses into informal discourse, she consistently praised him as a stylist. Essentially neoclassical in her tastes, du Deffand insisted that works be entertaining models of clarity. She found these qualities in the 109 volumes of Voltaire's work that she claimed to possess. She further recognized her affinity with

Montaigne, the philosopher of skepticism, calling him the best metaphysician, the only good philosopher there has ever been. His acceptance of life's perpetual contradictions, his rejection of dogmatic systematizing and, finally, his insistence on deflating the presumptuous certainties of his contemporaries made him an apt mentor for the energetic mind of du Deffand.

SURVEY OF CRITICISM

The letters and portraits of Madame du Deffand were seen by her contemporaries as exemplary yet somewhat unsettling additions to the neoclassical canon. D'Alembert frequently quoted her letters as models of the balanced, classical style. Voltaire further urged her to write since she, unlike most women, was a true philosopher, a free-thinker liberated from superstition and the prejudices of religion. He encouraged her to suppress the darker side of her thoughts, which kept her from realizing her potential as a writer and thinker. Forcalquier, a frequent guest in her salon, praised her rigorous mind but found the portraits cruel in their honesty. Her faults were those of her age, however, of a time when compassion was subordinated to intellect. Chatel, making explicit the gender text embedded in the other assessments, considered du Deffand's solid judgment and quick mind to be manly attributes. The "problem" posed for Chatel was the form containing this manly substance: that of the weak, impressionable female body. Her fluctuating moods and inconsistent judgment were due to weaknesses of the vessel, which led to frequent states of despair. Her faithful Hénault, perhaps the first to make the comparison with Sévigné, joined Voltaire in the wish that her works be preserved (see Appendix, Lescure edition, for portraits by contemporaries). When Walpole began writing to and about the witty Marquise, he took the comparison with Sévigné as given, a conventional coupling of names in the history of French letters. Irritated by her emotional demands, Walpole was nonetheless appreciative of the quality of her mind. He enjoyed her clever songs and epigrams and admired the tenacity of her arguments with Voltaire and the "charming" friendships she created through her lifelong correspondence.

When the Berry edition was published in 1810, containing 338 letters to Walpole, nearly a hundred to Voltaire, and many of the portraits, it created an immediate sensation. To a contemporary observer the letters were an important condensation of the previous century's ideas. Written by a former mistress of the Regent who was also a friend of Voltaire, the letters were clues to both the ideas and the social life of the time (Remusat, 1–2). Napoleon took the letters on his Russian campaign and insisted that no more than two words be censored. The du Deffand presented to the French public in the preface of this edition was a *bel-esprit* of an affectionate nature whose letters to Walpole were tender but not foolish. Berry criticized Walpole's excessive fear of ridicule, which led him to rebuff his old friend's effusions.

Reading this edition at mid-century, Sainte-Beuve calls for a new, more complete treatment of the letters. Du Deffand deserves a place among the classics for her style and for her ideas. He places her on the continuum from Sévigné to *Sand. Not only was she the only woman writer of substance in her century, she wrote prose that equals Voltaire in its classic purity. A tolerant free-thinker, she was able to face reality without illusions. Although explaining the du Deffand–Lespinasse break as generational, du Deffand representing the period before Rousseau, he nonetheless observes elements of pre-romanticism in her famous ennui. The relationship with Walpole, he further suggests, is incestuous, the repressed side of a late-blooming maternal love (*Causeries Sainte-Beuve*, 1: 413–31). The 1865 Lescure edition is the most complete of the nineteenth-century editions and includes not only the previously published Walpole letters but those to and from Voltaire, d'Alembert, Hénault, Choiseul, Montesquieu, d'Aissé, and many others as well as an extensive biographical essay. Like Sévigné, du Deffand is the most perfect literary and moral type of her century. Her letters reflect the dual currents of the end of the Old Regime: social decadence and the anguish of an intelligence deprived of faith. The fiercely partisan introduction is placed in the perspective of post-Revolutionary France. After a denunciation of the *philosophes* and praise for du Deffand's independence from their ideas, Lescure observes that this essentially apolitical writer can best be appreciated by nineteenth-century readers tired of political writing.

Gustave Lanson, writing just before publication of the Paget Toynbee edition, returns to the view of du Deffand as both representative and victim of the skeptical century in which she lived. The moral sterility of her times, coupled with her own critical intelligence, led to the acute metaphysical crisis she called ennui. Like her century, du Deffand abandoned cynicism in her declining years and gave in to the comforts of sentimentality. Lanson admires the mordant wit of her portraits, the originality of her literary criticism, and the psychological depth of her self-analysis. Although she never claimed the vocation, du Deffand is recognized nonetheless as a serious writer for her precision and the "energetic sobriety" of her prose. With Chatel, Lanson ascribes these qualities to the author's masculine side, more precisely to the suppression of "essentially feminine qualities" (Lanson, 370–73).

Following the 1912 publication of the best edition to date of du Deffand's letters, there was a slow but steady revival of interest in the author. Paget Toynbee's work, with its careful restitution of previously published material and the inclusion of nearly 500 unpublished letters, marks an important stage in du Deffand scholarship. Subsequent scholarship can be divided into two categories: studies of the theme of ennui and those concerned with the epistolary genre itself.

For Wilhelm Klerks, du Deffand offers the purest example of the ennui that would become a major theme in Romantic literature. In a work devoted entirely to this one aspect, Klerks draws the detailed psychological portrait of a woman living in a state of moral isolation. The decline of the monarchy and the subsequent decentralization of social life created a world of relative values which led to an identity crisis among the elite. The further subordination of the instinctive part of the human personality and a valorization of analytical reason contributed to the moral void of du Deffand's world. Her indifference to religion and the shallowness of her emotional life made it impossible for du Deffand to find a way out of the impasse. Klerks sees her as an unusually lucid subject whose illness reveals the weaknesses of her society. The most recent study of this theme emphasizes the fear behind the brilliant facade of the salons. For Savater, du Deffand's letters reveal the "secret terror" behind the preciosity and flirtations of the dominant social discourse (Savater, 93).

Kurt Kloocke, on the other hand, describes du Deffand's negativity as a personal vision. Her letters are the agonizing testimony of a precursor to existential nihilism in France. Presented at a conference on Benjamin Constant, the thesis was criticized by one of the discussants for whom eighteenth-century malaise has little in common with modern nihilism.

Perhaps the most fruitful area for future du Deffand scholarship will be that of research into the epistolary genre itself. In 1963 Lionel Duisit studied the formal aspects of du Deffand's letters: their antecedents and relationship to other genres, their art of portraiture and use of irony, parody, and allusion. He answers affirmatively the question of whether "one can legitimately speak of an epistolary art" (Duisit, 13). Roland Barthes, in his *Fragments d'un discours amoureux*, influenced future scholars to reevaluate the genre, specifically the tradition of the discourse to an absent lover. Susan Lee Carrel's *Le Soliloque de la passion feminine* and Linda S. Kauffman's *Discourses of Desire* reasess the role of private writing within the canon. Susan Curtis, in her essay "The Epistolières," challenges the notion that "the letter is a negligible genre" suited to women who lacked the discipline required of "real authorship." For du Deffand, as for other women in the eighteenth century, "the letter is quite simply the only logical form" and satisfied a need "to involve others in continuous social discourse" (Curtis, 232). These works, along with such studies as Janet Altman's *Epistolarity: Approaches to a Form*, suggest that du Deffand may ultimately benefit from new critical scrutiny.

BIBLIOGRAPHY

Major Works by Mme du Deffand

Letters of the Marquise du Deffand to Horace Walpole. 4 vols. Ed. Mary Berry. London: Longman, 1810.

Correspondance complète de la Marquise du Deffand avec ses amis, le Président Hénault, Montesquieu, d'Alembert, Voltaire, Horace Walpole. 2 vols. Ed. M. de Lescure. Paris: Henri Plon, 1865.

Correspondance de Mme du Deffand avec la Duchesse de Choiseul, l'Abbé Barthélémy et M. Craufurt. Intro. M. le Marquis de Sainte-Aulaire. 3 vols. Paris: Michel Levy, 1866.

Lettres de la Marquise du Deffand à Horace Walpole. 3 vols. Ed. Mrs. Paget Toynbee. London: Methuen, 1912.

Madame du Deffand: Lettres à Voltaire. Intro. Joseph Trabucco. Paris: Bossard, 1922.

Letters to and from Madame du Deffand and Julie de Lespinasse. Ed. Warren Hunting Smith. New Haven: Yale University Press, 1938.

Studies of Mme du Deffand

Bohmer, Ursula. "Konversation und Literatur: Zur Rolle der Frau im französichen Zalon des 18, Jahrhunderts." In *Die Französische Autorin: Vom Mittelalter bis zur Gegenwart.* Ed. Renate Baader et al. Wiesbaden: Athenaion, 1979. 109–29.

Craveri, Benedetta. *Mme du Deffand et son monde.* Trans. Sibylle Zavriew. Paris: Le Seuil, 1987.

Curtis, Judith. "The Epistolières." In *French Women and the Age of Enlightenment.* Ed. Samia I. Spencer. Bloomington: Indiana University Press, 1984. 226–41.

Doscot, Gerard. *Madame du Deffand.* Lausanne: Editions Rencontres, 1966.

Duisit, Lionel. *Madame du Deffand, Epistolière.* Geneva: Droz, 1963.

Giraud, Victor. "La Sensibilité de Madame du Deffand." *Revue des Deux Mondes* 8 (August 1, 1933): 688–703.

Goncourt, Edmond, and Jules de Goncourt. *La Femme au dix-huitième siècle.* Paris: Flammarion, 1938.

Klerks, Wilhelm. *Madame du Deffand, Essai sur l'ennui.* Leiden: Universitaire Pers Leiden, 1961.

Kloocke, Kurt. "Benjamin Constant et les débuts de la pensée nihiliste en Europe." In *Benjamin Constant, Madame de Stäel et le Groupe de Coppet.* Ed. Etienne Hofman. Oxford: Voltaire Foundation, 1982. 189–220.

Lanson, Gustave. *Choix de Lettres du XVIIIe Siècle.* Paris: Hachette, 1908.

Maurois, André. "Madame du Deffand et Horacle Walpole." In *Etudes anglaises.* Paris: Grasset, 1927. 171–208.

Naughton, A. E. "Some Literary Opinions of Madame du Deffand." *Stanford Studies in Language and Literature* (1964): 157–274.

Remusat, Charles de. "Horace Walpole." In *L'Angleterre au dix-huitième siècle.* Vol. 2. Paris: Didier, 1856.

Sainte-Beuve. *Causeries du lundi.* Vols. 2, 6, 14. Paris: Garnier, 1850–1857.

———. *Les Nouveaux Lundis.* Vol. 1. Paris: Garnier, 1863–1873.

———. *Quelques portraits féminins.* Vol. 11. Paris: Garnier, 1927.

Savater, Fernando. "Madame du Deffand: Frivolidad y agonia." *Revista de Occidente* (July-August 1987): Vol. 74–75, 88–102.

Scherer, Edmond. "Le Roman de Madame du Deffand." In *Etudes sur la littérature contemporaine.* Vol. 3. Paris: Calmann Lévy, 1885. 191–218.

Sienkewicz, Anne Waterman. "Two Women of Letters: Mme de Sévigné and Mme du Deffand." Diss., Johns Hopkins University, 1978.

Strachey, Lytton. *Biographical Essays.* New York: Harcourt, Brace, and World, 1966. 165–86.

———. *Books and Characters.* New York: Harcourt and Brace, 1922. 81–111.

PERNETTE DU GUILLET (1520?–1545)

Marian Rothstein

BIOGRAPHY

Pernette du Guillet lived her short life in Lyons at a very lively time in that city's intellectual history. Few details of her life have been preserved: the date of her birth is uncertain, her maiden name unknown. She died very young, on July 7, 1545, possibly of the plague, of which there was an epidemic in Lyons in 1544. The limited biographical information we do have is derived from Antoine du Moulin's preface to the first edition of her *Rymes* (Rhymes), collected and published in mid-August 1545, and from conjectures that may be made based on her own poems, or on the four poems (two by Maurice Scève, two by Jean de Vauzelles) that appear at the end of the volume of her *Rymes* as poetic epitaphs. We can draw inferences about her appearance from Scève's epitaphs, which imply that she was beautiful. She played the lute and other musical instruments. Du Moulin tells us that she knew Italian, Spanish, and the rudiments of Latin and was working on Greek at the time of her death. Claims of learning are sometimes lightly made for women in the Renaissance, but in this case, although there is no specific evidence of her command of Spanish, we do know that she wrote poems in Italian (Epigrams 51 and 52); she clearly knew Italian sources; twice she makes puns using Greek words (Epigrams 40 and 41).

Following Joseph Buche's article in 1904, du Guillet has been taken to be the model for the Délie of Maurice Scève's *Délie, object de plus haulte vertu* (Delia, Object of the Greatest Power/Virtue, 1544). A collection of 449 *dizains* (poems of ten lines) centered on his love for the eponymous lady, *Délie* is a major poetic achievement of the French Renaissance. Du Guillet's *Rymes* are therefore understood today as being addressed to Scève, whom she met when she was about sixteen and he a rather ugly man (to judge from his portraits) of about thirty-five. Some critics, overlooking the force of literary conventions, have regarded the *Délie* as a source of additional biographical information about Pernette. Délie is more likely described as blond because heroines always are than because that was the real color of Pernette's hair.

In a preface addressed to the ladies of Lyons, du Moulin explains that he is bringing together the slim volume of her extant works at the request of her bereaved husband (*affectionné mari*), whom she must have married in about 1538. Her poems, especially Epigram 35 (lines 1–10), cast some doubt on the happiness of this marriage.

> Si j'ayme cil, que je debvrois hayr,
> Et hays celuy, que je debrois aymer,
> L'on ne s'en doit autrement esbayr,
> Et ne m'en deust aucun en rien blasmer.
>   Car de celuy le bien dois estimer,
> Et si me fuict, comme sa non semblable;
> Mais de cestuy le plaisir trop damnable
> M'ost le droict par la Loy maintenu.
> Voila pourquoy je me sens redevable,
> A celuy là, qui m'est le moins tenu. (lines 1–10)

> (If I love him whom I ought to hate
> and hate him whom I ought to love,
> This should startle no one,
> nor should any blame me for it.
> For I esteem the qualities of the one,
> and yet he flees, and treats me as though I were not like him.
> But the too damnable pleasure of the other
> takes from me the rights maintained by law.
> That is why I feel beholden to him who is the least held to me.)

(All translations of du Guillet are my own.) Her husband is generally taken to be the one whose damnable pleasures she does not wish to share, legal though they may be. This does not suggest conjugal bliss.

The double standard glowers over a woman writing poems to her lover. There were accusations that du Guillet was not chaste and, in her Chanson 7, what seems to be a direct denial: "Qui dira ma robe fourée / De la belle puye dorée..." (Who will say my dress is lined with a fine golden shower...). The image is, of course, a play on the story of Danaë, whom Jove visited disguised as a fine shower of gold, at once lucre and illicit love. Elsewhere in her poetry she proclaims her virtue and her chastity, as does the full title of the *Rymes de gentile, et vertueuse dame D. Pernette du Guillet, Lyonnoise* (Rhymes of the Gentle and Vertuous Lady, Dame Pernette du Guillet of Lyons). So too do the poetic epitaphs, especially in the punning plays of Jean de Vauzelles on Pernette/*perle nette* (unblemished pearl), and in Scève's reference to her *vertue vive* (lively virtue) and *corps chaste* (chaste body). The ladies of Lyons may take her as a model of virtue and also as a role model, says du Moulin, so that French women may be admired in all countries for their literary achievements, as Italian women are.

Much of the text of the *Rymes* as well as du Moulin's introduction praising the young woman's virtue suggest that the love shared by Scève and du Guillet was a highly intellectualized one, influenced by the theories of the fifteenth-century Florentine Neoplatonist Marsilio Ficino, and even more directly by Leone Ebreo's *Dialoghi d'amore*, of which du Guillet left several verse paraphrases (e.g., Epigrams 19, 21, 27, 45, 46).

Scève was at the center of what is now called the Ecole Lyonnaise (School of Lyons), with which one also associates Antoine Héroët, Pontus de Tyard, Olivier de Magny, and two women: du Guillet and Louise 'Labé. There were other women poets in Lyons at the time whose work has not come down to us: Jeanne Gaillard, Jeanne and Claudine Scève, Marguerite de Bourg. They all had the good fortune to live during the most intellectually exciting period in the history of Lyons. In the second quarter of the sixteenth century it was a prosperous commercial center with great trade fairs and frequent contact with both Germany and Italy. The richness of its intellectual life is attested to by a flourishing printing and publishing trade, second only to that of Paris. Ideas in Lyons could develop freely, spared the pressures of the capital, the influence of the theologians of the Sorbonne, and the implicit presence of the court. Du Guillet clearly had a place in the intellectual circles of Lyons, where humanistic learning was highly valued and the influence of Italian Neoplatonism was keenly felt.

This is the world that marked her short life, preserved for us in her poems, which, as du Moulin tells the ladies of Lyons in his introduction to her works, "privately in many social gatherings she recited when they were appropriate, as most of them were suited to an occasion" (3). Nothing suggests that she herself intended to publish these poems as we have them, although some of them are finely polished. Du Moulin speaks of copying drafts that she had left in rather poor order for his edition. However, two of her epigrams (43 and 44) appeared in collections of songs published during her lifetime (*Second Livre contenant vingt-sept chansons nouvelles*, Paris, 1540; *La Fleur de Poésie*, Paris, 1543). Perhaps they were included with her permission, perhaps even, as was the case for the works of Labé, by her own efforts.

MAJOR THEMES

The *Rymes de gentile, et vertueuse dame D. Pernette du Guillet, Lyonnoise* form a single slim volume of poems written where she was in her mid-twenties. The major theme of the collection may be called love, understood in its broadest sense, that is, relations between two people, between speaking subject and beloved/object (coexisting in the poems probably addressed to Scève with the relations between pupil and master). In form, the poems are epigrams, chansons, elegies, and verse epistles. More than half of her lines are decasyllables, and she experiments with a wide range of rhyme schemes, including *terza rima* (not very felicitously, in her third elegy). What most marks the collection is the fact that the nature of the love expressed in these poems has been understood by most readers to be spiritual rather than sexual. Du Guillet often takes mischievous pleasure in the similarities between sexual love and the ennobling, virtuous Platonic exchange of souls in the joint pursuit of the Good (Epigram 13). Unlike the yearning lover of the Petrarchan tradition, from which du Guillet borrows certain conceits, love here tends to be reciprocal and fulfilling, resulting in lovers who are *content*, an important word in the *Rymes*. The idea of contentment—a state beyond desire—occurs elsewhere in Neoplatonist and mystical expressions of love, in the works of du Guillet's contemporary, Marguerite de *Navarre, for example. The poems use a narrow palette of generally abstract vocabulary, with few images, few adjectives. Neither lover nor beloved is in any way described. Antitheses of dark and light/day, knowledge and ignorance, joy and suffering, body and soul play a considerable role. The epigrams in particular frequently end in a *pointe*, a witty and unexpected turn, as is the case in Epigram 21:

> Si le servir merit recompense,
> Et recompense est la fin du desir
> Tousjours vouldrois servir plus qu'on ne pense,
> Pour non venir au bout de mon plaisir.

> (If serving merits recompense,
> and recompense is the end of desire,
> I should like to serve always, more than one would think,
> so as not to come to the end of my pleasure.)

The poem uses an intentionally limited vocabulary, typical of its writer; its wit derives from suddenly reversing the lover's goal—the end/goal of desire—so as not to come to the end/finish of it. Epigram 35, cited earlier, also repeats *aimer*, *haïr*, *devoir* (love, hate, ought/must), a small choice of abstract verbs, and presents similarly carefully wrought reasoning.

Du Guillet's poetry is marked by various poetic influences, among them, of course, that of Maurice Scève, whose hermetism she sometimes reflects (e.g., Epigrams 4, 5, 17). The influence of Clément Marot and the *Rhétoriqueur* tradition of the first part of the century makes itself felt in puns (Epigrams 40, 43), in rhyme schemes restricted to two or three rhymes (Chanson 2), internal rhyming (Epigram 1), and a tone of light banter specifically reminiscent of Marot. Occasionally, poems are clear imitations of Marot (Epître 2). Her generic categories— epigrams, elegies, epistles—are notably those of that poet. The presence of Jean Lemaire de Belges can be felt in a poem comparing the virtues of Italian and French (Epigram 50), a subject Lemaire treated in the *Concorde des deux langages* (1513) as well as elsewhere. There are poems that reflect the influence of Mellin de Saint Gelais (Epigram 18, Chanson 4). Italian sources are to be noted for several of the epigrams (Epigram 4, Chanson 4), and du Guillet's paraphrases of Leone Ebreo have already been alluded to. In sum, these verses show a sensitive appreciation of the poetic trends of the earlier sixteenth century in France and a close acquaintance with Italian materials as well.

The many technical debts du Guillet owes her contemporaries and those of the generations preceding her own help us understand the tone and intent of some of her verse. Some poems, because they have unknown and probably unknowable referents, remain at best subjects of conjecture to us (e.g., Epigram 7). Other poems suggest enough of the occasion that prompted them—a meeting promised and not kept (Epigram 19), the harvest (Epigram 22)—so that the specific event in the poet's daily life can be reconstructed from the poems.

What may well be her best-known poem, her second Elegy, lies halfway between these two extremes, in part because of the imaginary nature of the scene presented (although one suspects a real incident in her life among its generative stimuli). In the second Elegy she imagines herself on a hot summer's day by a clear pool "Où mon desir avec cil se pourmaine / Qui exercite en sa philosophie / Son gent esprit" (where my desire accompanies him who exercises his noble spirit in philosophy). From the first few lines, in which the heat of summer could be expected to suggest the heat of passion, she makes elegant use of the traditional postures of erotic poetry to express her own kind of love. Most of the elegy stages one of the poet's fantasies: "Combien de fois ay-je en moi souhaicté . . ." (How many times have I within myself wished . . .); the imaginary enactment of that wish is the subject of the poem. The aspect of fantasy is marked by the use of the conditional tense.

Although they would be alone together, she would not be indecorously alone with a man, since this one, given only to holy works, would bring his constant companions Apollo, the Muses, and many nymphs. In the heat of the summer she would throw herself naked into the cool water (a typical antithesis of hot and cold) and play a song on her lute. (It is quite possible that this nakedness is intended to be an arresting symbolization of her baring of her soul before her master.) If he attempted to touch her (i.e., to extend his mastery beyond the point deemed suitable), she would splash his eyes with the pure water in which she stands. The elegy teases the reader with the possibility of physical contact between the naked young woman and her beloved master. The woman's control is extended, for she now imagines herself to be like the chaste goddess Diana, and that the water might have the power to change her beloved, as Actaeon was changed into a stag and devoured by his own hunting dogs as punishment for coming upon Diana in her bath. Here du Guillet, building on the *Rhétoriqueur* tradition, constructs her poem on a pun, cerf/serf (stag/servant), which may have been the generative point of the fantasy. In the end, she rejects the fantasy, deciding that her powers ought not to go so far as to make a servant of her beloved, since he is properly a servant of Apollo. What he writes brings her contentment (a word whose importance we noted earlier), as—she tells us—it will some day to the world: "le monde / Lequel un jour ses escriptz s'attend / D'estre avec moi et heureux et content" (the world / which awaits his writings one day, / to be with me both happy and fulfilled; lines 52–54). Du Guillet bows before the power of Apollo and the Muses, representing the power of poetry itself. And poetry, the power of words, becomes for du Guillet the means of shaping relations between people.

SURVEY OF CRITICISM

Interest in du Guillet, strong during the sixteenth century, revived in the nineteenth, which produced three editions of her work. Her status was forever changed by Joseph Buche's 1904 article identifying her convincingly with the eponymous beloved of Maurice Scève's *Délie*. The risk of such fame is that, like the moon with which Délie is associated, du Guillet sometimes seems to shine largely by Scève's reflected light.

In 1944 V. L. Saulnier produced the first thorough study of the poet. He identified four major influences, poetic and philosophical, on du Guillet: (1) the chivalric, (2) Marot, (3) the Petrarchan, and (4) the Platonic/Neoplatonic. Each of these valorizes love. Saulnier, rather than placing du Guillet in any of these camps, characterizes her conception of love as a humanist one, in which love is associated with knowledge, poetically figured as light (day, sun) that produces an intellectual, moral, and sentimental transformation in the lovers. Her poetry is marked, says Saulnier, by a "mixture of stern reflection and the enthusiasm of youth" (74). Many of the epigrams seem so closely tied to a specific event that the *Rymes* become a poetic journal of sorts. He notes her limited, abstract vocabulary and demonstrates in some detail the various influences on her work— French, Italian, and the Greek Anthology. In the sixteenth century, he notes, her poems were imitated by Pontus de Tyard and Ronsard and were included in anthologies until the 1580s. Saulnier concludes by classifying the poems generically.

For Robert Griffin, du Guillet's poetry is the expression of moral truths, of a love which is a rational faculty suitably expressed by abstractions; the consummation of such a love is the extinction of physical desire, du Guillet's *contentement*.

Robert Cottrell sees Platonic myths as "suggesting a code of manners" according to which the relationship between du Guillet and Scève was ruled. He takes the *Rymes* as autobiographical, describing moments in the relationship between the two poets, the young woman and the mature man. The theme of love is elaborated in the *Rymes* "within the context of a philosophy of being, becoming, and knowing, that is to say within the context of a philosophy that is both ontological and gnostic" (555). Love is a source of being: before Scève there was only darkness (Epigram 2). Love is also a source of knowledge. From Scève she learned to understand the Platonic sense of "virtue" and "knowledge," as well as gaining insight into poetic creation. Cottrell too remarks on the importance of the contrasts of darkness and light, the shadows of ignorance dissipated by the light of knowledge, emanating in good part from Scève. The most salient features of du Guillet's poetry serve her purposes: in speaking of her love, she excludes any element tending to establish a physical presence, leaving herself at liberty to celebrate a spiritual union. Antitheses in her verse form a structure that demonstrates the emergence of consciousness from previous unawareness. He finds her verse impish, graceful, "subtle in composition and felicitous in expression," recording a "love both ardent and chaste, passionate and idealized" (571).

In Cottrell's estimation, du Guillet may be important because of her relation to Scève, but she also has a serious claim to be read in her own right. Paul Ardouin, who sees in the poet a mixture of sensuality and virtue, is driven to wonder how much attention her poems would receive left entirely to their own merits.

Only two critics characterize du Guillet's love as physical: T. A. Perry, and Gisèle Mathieu-Castellani, to whose interpretation we will return when considering feminist readings of du Guillet. Perry, following Saulnier and Cottrell, sees the poems as a kind of poetic journal. Unlike them, he understands her claims of chastity as merely the declaration of her state of mind. There are many sensitive readings here, but the physical interpretation of du Guillet's eroticism and sensuality has failed to convince other scholars.

Plato's primacy of vision is behind the approach of Lance K. Donaldson-Evans's *Love's Fatal Glance*, although du Guillet's abstraction deprives the topos of the wounding eye-beam of any aggressive quality. Seeing, light, the Sun, the Day, Apollo as Sun god are all essential expressions of her spiritual passion.

The second Elegy (summarized above), du Guillet's most successful longer poem, has been interpreted with a variety of shadings by Griffin, Scollen, Cottrell, Perry, Dellaneva, James, and Jones.

It is only in the last decade that critics have broached the specific problems of du Guillet as a woman writing, and as a woman writing love poetry. Both Ann Rosalind Jones and Colette Winn evoke female silence as being, in a tradition of male-female oppositions, the normative counterpart to male eloquence. To speak in a love poem is, implicitly, to act, and with few exceptions, one has learned to expect women to be passive. Jones notes that although du Guillet clearly makes use of Petrarchan and Neoplatonic traditions, these must be exploited in revisionary and interrogatory ways when spoken in a woman's voice. Du Guillet stresses the reciprocity of the lovers; she presents herself as Scève's *semblable*, his like, his equal, in proactive poetic terms, by writing a poem (Epigram 5) that uses nearly the exact words of Scève's *Délie* 136, changing their order to produce a reply. If Scève is *le jour*, du Guillet is *la journée* (Chanson 9): it is hard to attach a hierarchy to the two words, which conceive day as a unit (*jour*) and as duration (*journée*). If Scève is Apollo, she is Diana, his twin. Jones's study shows that "women's situations and women's voices do more than modify poetic style. They rewrite the rules of the game" (1981, 53).

Françoise Charpentier, in the introduction to her 1983 edition of the works of Louise Labé and Pernette du Guillet, elaborates on the new ground to be cleared before a woman can find an authentic voice to speak love—Eros is masculine. Donaldson-Evans shares this conviction in "The Taming of the Muse." He sees the female voice, coming from the margins of a tradition, as lending a certain ironic distance to du Guillet's poetry, and sees the pairing *jour*, *journée* as being a complementary (rather than antithetical) one, breaking down traditional phallocentric oppositions.

Gisèle Mathieu-Castellani reads du Guillet's collection as a search for identity, and explores her *parole chétive* (weak words). *Chétive* is a word in which Mathieu-Castellani reads both weakness and captivity, each caused by a situation that threatens to reduce a real woman, Pernette, to the status of an echo of the fictional Délie, and thereby to imprison her in Scève's writing. In du Guillet's poems, Mathieu-Castellani, like Winn, whose article appeared at the same time, sees a refusal to remain an object. She proposes replacing the Neoplatonic interpretation of several Epigrams, most notably 35 (cited above) and 45 (*Un seul je hais, qui deux me fait aimer* [One alone I hate who makes me love two]) by a more literalist reading, as a woman's need to tell of her multiple loves, multiple erotic objects. The weak (*chétive*) voice of woman deliberately creates texts with blurred referents, preferring suggestion to description precisely because it is more erotic.

Colette Winn continues this series of new feminist approaches to the problematization of du Guillet's poetic achievement, seeking the voice of both subject and object, torn between these two poles that create the tension by which woman's voice is formed. Winn situates the relationship between Scève and du Guillet textually, as an implicit dialogue between the *Rymes* and *Délie*, but she stresses du Guillet's position as a "resisting reader," unwilling to slip quietly into the role that has been prepared for her, seeking to expose the contradictions of the conventionalized relations between lover and (female) beloved. Du Guillet's love is reciprocal, the joining of two wills that leads to *contentement*, on the one hand, and gives du Guillet a voice, on the other. Her rebirth—in love, in knowledge—is a liberation, enabling her to speak. Her position is paradoxical, or at the least circular, since it is Scève's discourse that enables du Guillet's, his words to which hers are a reply. However, as her master and her model, it is his words, his poetic heights, to which she aspires, creating an authentic woman's voice from which, nonetheless, the masculine Other cannot be excluded.

Recent feminist criticism has encouraged reading of du Guillet on her own merits, and not merely in the shadow of Scève. Her poems, because they are sensual, because they deal primarily with love between a man and a woman, belong to the mainstream of lyric love poetry. They depart from this center in that they seem to most readers to speak of spiritual love, of love ideally shared equally between equals (*semblables*), and that they do so in a woman's voice.

BIBLIOGRAPHY

Works by Pernette du Guillet

Rymes de gentile, et vertueuse dame D. Pernette du Guillet, Lyonnoise. Lyons: Jean de Tournes, 1545.

Modern Editions

Poètes du XVIe siècle. Ed. Albert-Marie Schmidt. Paris: Gallimard, 1953. 227–68.
Rymes. Ed. Victor E. Graham. Geneva: Droz, 1968.
Rymes. Ed. Françoise Charpentier. Paris: Gallimard, 1983. (In the same volume with *Oeuvres poétiques* of Louise Labé.)

Translations of Pernette du Guillet

Epigrams 2, 4, 5, 8, 13, 17, 24, 26, 31, Chansons 5, 7, 9, and Elegy 2. Trans. Ann Rosalind Jones. In *Women Writers of the Renaissance and Reformation.* Ed. Katherina Wilson. Athens: University of Georgia Press, 1987. 224–31.
Epigrams 2, 21, 22, 24, 48, and Chansons 2, 3. Translated into prose. In *Penguin Book of French Verse.* vols. Ed. Geoffrey Brereton. Harmondsworth: Penguin, 1958. 2:20–24.

Studies of Pernette du Guillet

Ardouin, Paul. *Maurice Scève, Pernette du Guillet, Louise Labé: l'amour à Lyon au temps de la Renaissance.* Paris: Nizet, 1981.
Bots, W.J.A. "Maurice Scève, Pernette du Guillet, ou la victoire de deux voix sur les escarpements de la syntaxe." *L'Information Littéraire* 39, no. 3 (1987): 102–6.
Buche, Joseph. "Pernette du Guillet et la 'Délie' de Maurice Scève." In *Mélanges de philologie offerts à Ferdinand Brunot.* Paris, 1904; Geneva: Slatkine, 1972. 33–39.
Cottrell, Robert D. "Pernette du Guillet's *Rymes.*" *Bibliothèque d'Humanisme et Renaissance* 31 (1969): 553–71.
Dellaneva, Joann. "Mutare/mutatus: Pernette du Guillet's Actaeon Myth and the Silencing of the Poetic Voice." In *Women in French Literature.* Ed. Michel Guggenheim. Saratoga, Calif.: Anma Libri, 1988. 47–56.
Donaldson-Evans, Lance K. *Love's Fatal Glance: A Study of Eye Imagery in Poets of the Ecole Lyonnaise.* University, Miss.: Romance Monographs, 1980.
———. "The Taming of the Muse: The Female Poetic Voice in Pernette du Guillet's *Rymes.*" In *Pre-Pléiade Poetry.* Ed. Jerry C. Nash. Lexington, Ky.: French Forum, 1985. 84–96.
Griffin, Robert. "Pernette du Guillet's Response to Scève: A Case for Abstract Love." *L'Esprit Créateur* 5, no. 2 (1965): 110–16.
James, Karen Simroth. "Pernette du Guillet: Spiritual Union and Poetic Distance." *French Literature Series* 16 (1989): 27–37.

Jondorf, Gillian. "Petrarchan Variations in Pernette du Guillet and Louise Labé." *Modern Language Review* 71 (1976): 766–78.

Jones, Ann Rosalind. "Assimilation with a Difference: Renaissance Women Poets and Literary Influence." *Yale French Studies* 62 (1981): 135–53.

———. "Pernette du Guillet: The Lyonnais Neoplatonist." In *Women Writers of the Renaissance and Reformation*. Ed. Katherina Wilson. Athens: University of Georgia Press, 1987. 219–31.

Mathieu-Castellani, Gisèle. "La Parole chétive: les *Rymes* de Pernette du Guillet." *Littérature* 73 (1989): 47–60.

Perry, Theodore Anthony. "Pernette du Guillet's Poetry of Love and Desire." In his *Erotic Spirituality*. University: University of Alabama Press, 1980. 53–67.

Saulnier, Verdun L. "Etude sur Pernette du Guillet et ses *Rymes*." *Bibliothèque d'Humanisme et Renaissance* 4 (1944): 7–119.

Scollen, Christine. *The Birth of the Elegy in France 1500–1550*. Geneva: Droz, 1967. 123–33.

Winn, Colette H. "Le Chant de la nouvelle née: les *Rymes* de Pernette du Guillet." *Poétique* 78 (1989): 208–17.

CLAIRE DE DURAS
(1777–1828)

Lucy M. Schwartz

BIOGRAPHY

Claire-Rose-Louise-Bonne de Coëtnempren de Kersaint was born in Brest in 1777. Her father, the Count de Kersaint, was an admiral in the royal navy. Her mother, Claire d'Eragny, was born in Martinique and was related to the governor of the Windward Islands. An only child, she received constant attention from her parents during her youth. At the age of twelve, she entered the Panthémont Convent in Paris. There she made two friends who were to remain close to her throughout her life, Anna Dillon, who became the Countess de la Tour du Pin, and Josephine Damas, who became the Marquess de Sainte-Maure.

Her innocent and happy youth was swiftly ended by three tragedies. First, her parents were legally separated in 1792, as divorce was illegal. Second, Louis XVI was beheaded by the revolutionary assembly in January 1793. Finally, Claire's father, who had been a part of the assembly but had refused to vote for the death of the king, was guillotined in December of the same year. This must have been very traumatic for Claire and her mother, who heard the news from a newspaper crier on the dock at Bordeaux as they were setting sail for America.

Partly because of these events, Claire's mother was in very ill health and could not make any decisions for the family. After a visit in Philadelphia, the two women sailed to Martinique, where Claire took charge of their financial affairs and managed to salvage much of her mother's fortune. Accompanied by her aunt, Madame d'Ennery, Claire and her mother went to Switzerland for a brief stay before establishing themselves in the emigrant French community in London in 1795.

In 1797 Claire married another French emigrant, Amédée-Bretagne-Malo de Durfort, Duke de Duras. Like Claire, he was from the province of Brittany. Two daughters were born to them in London: Félicie in 1798 and Clara in 1799.

In 1805 Claire again traveled to Switzerland, where she visited Madame de
*Charrière and met Charrière's niece, Rosalie de Constant. Constant was to
become one of Duras's closest friends and her correspondent for the rest of her
life.

Napoleon's imperial government made it possible for some of the emigrants
to return to France. In 1808 the Duke and Duchess de Duras bought the Chateau
of Ussé in the Loire valley and moved there with their daughters and Claire's
mother. Until the restoration of the French monarchy in 1815, Claire devoted
most of her time and efforts to her daughters, of whom she was quite fond.
However, in 1813 Félicie left her to marry the Prince de Talmont.

When Louis XVIII ascended to the French throne, he chose the Duke de Duras
to be his chamberlain. Thus, the family moved into the Louvre Palace to live
with the king. During this period the Duchess de Duras became famous for her
salon, which was frequented by important political, intellectual, and literary
figures like Charles Maurice de Talleyrand, Wilhelm Humboldt, Georges Cuvier,
and Charles de Rémusat. The most famous person in the salon was Chateaubriand. The duchess had met him in 1808, and they remained close friends
throughout her life. She served as his protector and helped his political career by
getting him posts such as ambassador and emissary of the French government.

In 1819 her daughter Clara married Henri, Duke de Rauzan. Her other daughter
Félicie, now a widow, was remarried to Auguste de Vergier, Count de la Roche-
jaquelein. Unfortunately, the Duchess de Duras was too ill to attend the ceremony. For the rest of her life she considered herself too sick to go out into
society; however, she did continue to receive a few intimate friends every evening.

Near the end of 1821 she began to write down the stories she had been telling
to her friends. From that period until the end of 1822 she wrote five novels, of
which only three have been published. *Ourika*, the first to be written, was
published in 1824; *Edouard* was published in 1825; and *Olivier ou le secret* was
not published until 1971. Claire de Duras probably stopped publishing her novels
when Hyacinthe de Latouche published a licentious parody of *Olivier* in 1826
and led the public to believe that it was her novel. In 1827 she published her
Pensées de Louis XIV (Thoughts of Louis XIV).

She died in Nice, where she had gone in hopes of improving her health,
surrounded by her family, in January 1828. Her daughter Clara was given the
manuscripts of the unpublished novels and a contract with a publisher to publish
them after Claire de Duras's death. However, they were never published, and
now the manuscripts are lost. Clara did publish a book of her mother's religious
meditations called *Réflexions et prières inédites* (Unpublished Reflections and
Prayers) in 1839.

MAJOR THEMES

Ourika, *Edouard*, and *Olivier ou le secret* all share the theme of social exclusion. Each protagonist faces a barrier that separates him or her from the person

he or she loves. These barriers are essential factors of the protagonists' lives and totally beyond their control. For Ourika it is the color of her skin that makes her a social outcast. For Edouard it is his inferior social status, and for Olivier it is his impotence, which makes marriage impossible for him. Each protagonist feels alone and isolated because of the rigid attitudes of pre-Revolutionary French society.

Each story has its point of departure in an actual person. *Ourika* is based on the story of a Negress given to the Marquess de Beauvau by her nephew, the Chevalier de Boufflers, and brought up by her as her own daughter. *Edouard* finds its source in the story of a Monsieur Benoist d'Azy, son of a justice of the Supreme Court, who was in love with Clara, the duchess's daughter. *Olivier*, according to an article recently published by Pierre Riberette in the *Bulletin de la Société Chateaubriand*, has for a prototype a Monsieur de Simiane at the court of Louis XVI.

These basic events were elaborated and changed by Claire de Duras. However, the main interest of the stories is not their plot but their modern and detailed psychological analysis. Ourika suffers from an acute inferiority complex and has completely internalized the norms of the aristocratic white society in which she was brought up. Edouard has a better sense of his own worth and feels strongly that nobility lies in the soul and not in useless titles. In spite of this, he is unwilling to destroy the reputation of the Duchess Natalie de Nervers, the woman he loves, by letting her condescend to marry him. Count Olivier de Sancerre is torn between his love for his cousin, Countess Louise de Nangis, and his realization that their love can find no physical expression.

Duras uses powerful metaphors to convey to the reader the isolation of her protagonists. Ourika embarks on an extensive campaign of self-hatred, telling herself that she looks like a monkey. She begins to wear gloves and a hat even inside and has all the mirrors removed from her room. She seems to believe that if she cannot see her black skin, then it ceases to exist.

Two scenes in *Edouard* underline the separation of the lovers. Edouard buys a ticket to a ball given by the English ambassador because he wants to see Natalie dance. His ticket entitles him to sit on some bleachers but not to dance. He feels very uncomfortable with people of his own social class whom he finds on the bleachers; he sees them as grotesque, clumsy, and unmannerly. He is discovered by Natalie, who comes over to talk to him, but they are still separated by a fence, which Edouard calls "the sad symbol of the [barrier] which separates us forever" (Herrmann edition, 73; all translations are mine). This separation seems all the more unjust because, as the ambassador reminds Edouard, in England men of merit can rise in society and government. He dreams that in England he could earn a place that would permit him to marry Natalie.

In the second scene Edouard follows Natalie to Versailles, although he knows he can never enter the royal palace. He wanders on the hills and in the woods, daydreaming about Versailles, and the palace becomes in his mind a "magical castle . . . defended by . . . [a] fierce monster" (Herrmann edition, 106).

Similarly, Olivier feels that he is separated from Louise by "those walls of crystal described in fairy stories; we see each other, we speak, we approach one another; but we cannot touch each other" (Virieux edition, 147).

These images of separation come to symbolize the whole relationship between the lovers and between the lovers and society. They capture the nature of the situation so well that the reader remembers the images long after finishing the novels.

All three heroes find an escape from their dilemmas in a brief moment of happiness in the country away from the omnipotent society that seems to have caused their unhappiness. These happy country gatherings seem to replicate the happiness they had when they were young. Ourika finds this happiness when Madame de B . . . (her protector, modeled on Madame de Beauvau) is exiled from Paris by the Revolution. An intimate society composed of Madame de B . . . , her grandson Charles, who is the man Ourika loves without being conscious of it, and an old abbot makes Ourika perfectly comfortable in the country, where she goes for long walks with Charles, who treats her as his sister. This is very similar to the situation of the child Ourika playing with Charles at Madame de B . . . 's feet before Ourika realized that she was different from other children.

Edouard finds similar peace at Faverange, the country estate where the Marshal d'Olonne, in disfavor with the king, has been exiled. The marshal is Natalie's father and Edouard's adopted father since his natural father's death. At Faverange Edouard and Natalie walk in the garden, appreciate the beautiful flowers, and confess their love to each other. This reminds Edouard of the long walks and solitary meditations he experienced as a boy at his father's property in Forez.

Olivier associates happy memories with the two contiguous country estates, Rouville and Flavy, where he and his cousins played in their youth. After the deaths of the two mothers who had watched their children play together, Louise and Olivier become the owners of the estates. Like the protagonists of the other novels, they share several months of happiness, walking in the country, enjoying the beauties of nature, and reliving the memories of their youth.

Unfortunately for the protagonists, society is still powerful, and these happy moments have to come to an end. Madame de B . . . is permitted to return to Paris, the king recalls the Marshal d'Olonne, and Louise's sister Adèle reminds Olivier that he must not spend any more time with Louise if he does not intend to marry her. These events precipitate the final catastrophe in each novel.

When Ourika returns to Paris, a marriage is arranged for Charles, and she becomes very ill. When the Marquess de . . . , a friend of Madame de B . . . who had first made Ourika aware that she was destined to be alone forever, comes to visit Ourika, she opens Ourika's eyes to her hopeless passion for Charles. Ourika becomes a nun and tries to live to bring happiness to others, but it is too late. Her health is destroyed, and she soon dies. Duras compares her death to the falling of autumn leaves.

When Edouard and Natalie return to Paris, they find that they can no longer spend happy, innocent moments alone together. The Duke de L . . . and the Prince d'Enrichemont, both of whom would like to marry Natalie, become jealous of Edouard and sense Natalie's love for him. The duke spreads a rumor that Edouard is Natalie's lover. As a result, Edouard leaves to join the French army fighting in America, in despair because he has betrayed the marshal, who had been like a father to him, and because he can do nothing to avenge the false rumor that has destroyed Natalie's reputation. Edouard had attempted to challenge the Duke de L. to a duel; however, the duke had refused because he could not fight a commoner. In America Edouard receives a letter announcing Natalie's death. Inspired by this omen, he rushes onto the battlefield and finds the death which he had desired because it would unite him with Natalie.

When Olivier realizes that his days of happiness have ended, he shoots himself beside the Beauval Oak, the tree that had been the meeting place of the lovers and the center of their childhood games. Louise, who witnesses the suicide, becomes insane and wanders to the tree daily for the rest of her life.

Death, then, is the inevitable result of all these impossible love affairs. Love leading to death is a typically Romantic theme. In *Edouard* and *Olivier* death offers the lovers hope of a union that they could not have in life. This hope, even longing, for death, which will bring the desired fusion of the lovers, was a central theme in Madame von *Krüdener's novel *Valérie*, published in 1804 in Paris, which contained many German Romantic themes.

The fourth novel Duras wrote was entitled *Le Moine du Saint-Bernard* (The Monk of Saint Bernard). All we know of it comes from Duras's description in a letter to Rosalie de Constant dated May 15, 1824. It is about a monk who has become very worldly and has lost his natural faith and simplicity of character. He rediscovers what he has lost and is brought back to true faith by love.

Fragments of the fifth novel, *Les Mémoires de Sophie* (Sophie's Memoirs), were published by Agénor Bardoux in his biography of Claire de Duras. These evoked the time Duras spent in London as an emigrant. Duras told Chateaubriand in a letter that the heroine was Breton (as she was). Chateaubriand also mentions a passage where Duras describes Lausanne, which she visited before settling in London. For these reasons Denise Virieux believes that the book was not a novel but real memoirs about her own life.

Duras's book of religious meditations, *Réflexions et prières inédites*, contains her thoughts on topics such as indulgence, passion, piety, the fear of God, and strength. Each meditation ends with a short prayer. Gabriel Pailhès shows that the religious themes treated in this book resemble the themes of the speech of Ourika's confessor in the novel of the same name. Pailhès thinks that some meditations are missing from the book, because four of the meditations belong to the series of the "Seven Gifts of the Holy Spirit," but the other three from the series do not appear.

SURVEY OF CRITICISM

The first critic to deal extensively with Claire de Duras's work was Charles-Augustin Sainte-Beuve, who wrote a critical portrait of her that first appeared in 1834. Sainte-Beuve presented the Duchess de Duras's salon in the historical context of the Restoration. He found it to be the perfect synthesis of the opposing political currents of the period because of the liberal ideas she inherited from her father and the prominent place of her husband in the conservative monarchic government. Sainte-Beuve seemed to feel that this salon was as important as her literary works, which he rated highly. After discussing *Ourika* and *Edouard* and referring briefly to the other novels, he concluded his essay with the entire text of her religious meditation on indulgence. He added a note at the end of the essay quoting Paris gossip that insinuated that Claire de Duras was Chateaubriand's mistress.

Agénor Bardoux searched more deeply into Duras's life. With the aid of her correspondence with Anna de la Tour du Pin, Chateaubriand, and others, and manuscripts provided by the duchess's daughter, Clara de Rauzan, he published a detailed biography in 1898. Unfortunately, he did not treat her entire life.

Joachim Merlant studied the Duras novels in his 1905 book on the personal novel from Rousseau to Fromentin. He saw *Edouard* as an important model for Fromentin's *Dominique*.

In 1910 the Abbot Gabriel Pailhès finished the most complete study to date of the life of the Duchess de Duras. His goal was to disprove the rumors quoted by Sainte-Beuve. His strategy was to use quotations from the correspondence between Claire de Duras and Rosalie de Constant to prove that the loneliness and isolation that all her protagonists feel were not caused by Chateaubriand's rejection of her love but by the desertion of her daughter Félicie. Félicie married at the age of fifteen, becoming part of a family with ultra-royalist political opinions, which her mother rejected. She seemed to be more attached to her mother-in-law than her mother. When her first husband died, she stayed close to her in-laws and remarried in the same political milieu.

While Pailhès was undoubtedly right that Félicie hurt her mother very much, later scholars have rejected this as proof that Claire did not love Chateaubriand. In fact, her letters to him and to La Tour du Pin and Constant and their responses seem to prove how much in love with him she was. However, there is no evidence that she ever became his mistress. Since she called him "dear brother," and he called her "dear sister," it appears that she was deluding herself, as were Ourika and Edouard, by calling her love "friendship." Her letters reveal that she was often hurt by his insensitivity and by his lack of appreciation for her passionnate friendship. It is likely that both Chateaubriand and Félicie were sources of the suffering that Duras portrays in her novels.

In any case, it is clear that Claire de Duras identified with her outcast heroes. She felt their suffering and separation from true love. She seemed to blame the strict social order for this unhappiness, but it is doubtful whether she felt that society was to blame because it made females subservient to males. However, her letters do show that she was conscious of a greater commitment to love by females than by males.

Juliette Decreus-Van Liefland in 1949 studied Duras in light of Sainte-Beuve's portrait of her. She discussed many of the biographical questions on which the scholars disagree, including the issue of Chateaubriand. Her conclusion was that, except for a few minor discrepancies (such as being Chateaubriand's mistress), Sainte-Beuve's portrait of her was quite accurate.

Finally, in the 1970s, critics began to deal with her fiction rather than her life, a trend begun by Merlant over sixty years earlier. Much of the credit for this reexamination must be given to Denise Virieux. In 1971 she published a manuscript of *Olivier ou le secret* with extensive critical apparatus, including a critical introduction that rectified some of the errors of earlier scholars, especially those dealing with the dates of the composition of her works.

After Virieux, Claudine Herrmann published editions of *Ourika* and *Edouard* with critical introductions that show that Stendhal was indebted to Duras, not only for the source of *Armance* in *Olivier* as Virieux had demonstrated, but also for the source of *Le Rouge et le noir* in *Edouard*.

Claire de Duras's novels were widely read by both men and women during her lifetime. In addition to Stendhal and Fromentin, minor novelists like Astolphe de Custine imitated her works. It appears that even the unpublished novels, which she read in her salon, influenced other writers. The best example of this, besides Stendhal, is Hyacinthe de Latouche, whose parody of *Olivier* copied the style and even the format of the original. Duras certainly deserves to be considered an important early Romantic author. It is likely that the significance of her works has been ignored in part because of her sex. Scholars like Virieux and Herrmann are now making the case necessary to reestablish her literary reputation.

BIBLIOGRAPHY

Works by Mme de Duras

Ourika. Paris: Ladvocat, 1824.
Edouard. Paris: Ladvocat, 1825.
Olivier. Paris: U. Canel, 1826.
Pensées de Louis XIV, extraites de ses ouvrages et de ses lettres manuscrites. Paris: Firmin-Didot, 1827.
Réflexions et pièces inédites, par Mme la duchesse de Duras. Paris: Débécourt, 1839.

Modern Editions

Ourika. Ed. Claudine Herrmann. Paris: Editions des femmes, 1979.
Edouard. Paris: Mercure de France, 1983.
Olivier. Ed. Denise Virieux. Paris: J. Corti, 1971.

English Translations of Mme de Duras

Ourika. London: Longman, Hurst, Rees, Orme, Brown, and Green, 1824.

Studies of Mme de Duras

Bardoux, Agénor. *La Duchesse de Duras*. Paris: C. Lévy, 1898.

Bearne, Catherine Mary. *Four Fascinating French Women: Mme de Souza, Mme de Duras, la Duchesse de Berry, Mathilde Buonaparte*. London: T. F. Unwin, 1910.

Crichfield, Grant. *Three Novels of Madame de Duras: "Ourika," "Edouard," "Olivier."* The Hague: Mouton, 1975.

Decreus-Van Liefland, Juliette. *Sainte-Beuve et la critique des auteurs féminins*. Paris: Boivin, 1949.

Giraud, Victor. "Madame de Duras et Chateaubriand." In *Passions et romans d'autrefois*. Paris: Champion, 1925.

Herrmann, Claudine. "Madame de Duras et Ourika." In *Ourika*, by Madame de Duras. Paris: Editions des femmes, 1979.

———. Préface to *Edouard*, by Madame de Duras. Paris: Mercure de France, 1983.

Merlant, Joachim. "Le Roman d'analyse de 1804 à 1830: Mme de Duras." In *Le Roman personnel de Rousseau à Fromentin*. Paris: Hachette, 1905. 301–15.

Pailhès, Gabriel. *Mme de Duras et Chateaubriand, d'après des documents inédits*. Paris: Perrin, 1910.

Riberette, Pierre. "Le Modèle d'*Olivier*." *Bulletin de la Société Chateaubriand* 28 (1985): 93–100.

Sainte-Beuve, Charles-Augustin. "Madame de Duras." In *Oeuvres*. 2 vols. Paris: Gallimard, 1951. 2:1042–58.

MARGUERITE DURAS
(1914-   )

Thomas F. Broden

BIOGRAPHY

Marguerite Donnadieu was born in colonial French Indochina on April 4, 1914, to a family of public school teachers. From the outskirts of Saigon her family moved to Hanoï, then Phnom Penh; after the father's death, the family returned to the Saigon area in 1918. As a child Duras spoke Vietnamese, but at school and at home the language was French. The author has spoken and written much about her early years, portraying a mother of immense but suffocating love, a younger brother who was her constant playmate, and an older brother on whom the mother doted but who terrorized his siblings. When the colonial administration deeded nonarable land to her mother in return for her life's savings, the event burned in the daughter images of a system corrupted by venality and injustice. The writer also remembered the tough woman, her mother, who, with a tenacious desire for land, a home, and financial security, battled bankers and administrators for years.

Having obtained a *baccalauréat* at the distinguished French *lycée* in Saigon, Duras went on to Paris, where she began studies in mathematics, earned a *licence* in law from the Sorbonne (1935), and attended the Ecole Libre des Sciences Politiques. She married in 1939 and two years later quit her job as secretary at the Ministére des Colonies to devote herself to getting a first novel published. *Les Impudents* (The Shameless), under the (toponymic) pen name Duras, was refused by many editors before Plon finally published it in 1943.

Under the Occupation, Duras frequented the salon of Ramon Fernandez, where she mingled with collaborationist writers including Drieu la Rochelle. Active in the Resistance in the same period, she had as one of her leaders "Morland," François Mitterrand. The stories of *La Douleur* (*The War*, 1985), which she presents as autobiographical, recount her Resistance adventures as a driver, as well as her violent interrogation of a prisoner. Her husband, Robert Antelme, was captured and deported to Auschwitz, then Dachau. Duras joined the Communist Party the same year (1944). During the Occupation she lost her younger brother as well as a first baby; after the war she divorced Antelme for Dionys Mascolo, with whom, in 1947, she had her only surviving child, Jean. Her relationship with this second writer, intellectual, and Communist militant, broke up after the mid-fifties. Duras speaks of a tumultuous and violent love affair at that point which proved decisive for her writing. She abandoned her routine— mainstream novels, written with relative facility from nine to five, the proper literary dinner parties in the evening—and entered the realm of "dangerous books" whose production each time became a solitary crisis in which she feared for her sanity. In the tradition of Georges Bataille, the crisis of the writing as event survives in the radical character of the writing as product in the book. The mid-fifties saw her first bout with alcoholism, which lasted until a cure in 1964; a third crisis and treatment came in the eighties.

Duras's narrative oeuvre begins with a period of increasingly well-crafted novels. *Un Barrage contre le Pacifique* (*The Sea Wall*, 1950) was the author's first major success. In the later fifties she began experimenting with blending novelistic and dramatic forms and disrupting narrative movement; with *Moderato cantabile* (1958), one of her finest works, Duras temporarily joined the New Novelists at the Editions de Minuit. She tried out variations in point of view and stream of consciousness narration, for example, *Dix heures et demie du soir en été* (*Ten-thirty on a Summer Night*, 1960) and *L'Après-midi de Monsieur Andesmas* (*The Afternoon of Mr. Andesmas*, 1962); these experiments enabled Duras to use narrative technique effectively for thematic purposes in mature works of the sixties and seventies such as *Le Ravissement de Lol V. Stein* (*The Ravishing of Lol V. Stein*, 1964), *Le Vice-consul* (*The Vice-Consul*, 1965), and *India Song* (1975). With books such as *Détruire, dit-elle* ("*Destroy*," *She Said*, 1969) and *L' Amour* (Love, 1971) the author turned to a radical reworking of language and genre. The *écriture* (writing) of Duras's experimental texts explores regions of the lyrical, the sublime, and the inexpressible, verging on the mystical; vocabulary and grammar are rarefied in ways that recall Samuel Beckett and Maurice Blanchot. The Durassian work questions textuality itself by alternating between superfluity and allusiveness, negating communication by an equally radical surfeit and dearth of words. Such stylistic features, along with thematic and structural considerations, led Hélène *Cixous to single out Duras as a rare modern French practitioner of an *écriture féminine*, a woman's writing. Best-seller success unexpectedly came to Duras with her celebrated *L'Amant* (*The Lover*, 1984), which also garnered the premier prize for fiction in France, the Goncourt.

Although Duras has been the most productive and original in narrative prose, she is well published in every major genre except poetry. Her entry into the theater came when she adapted her 1955 novel *Le Square* (*The Square*) to the stage in 1957; along with Nathalie *Sarraute she represented a return of French women playwrights to the theaters in France. Two years later she made her cinema debut when the director Alain Resnais asked her to script a Franco-Japanese film on "the bomb"; the success of *Hiroshima mon amour* (1960) catapulted Duras into recognition from a broader international public. Having been active in magazine and newspaper journalism since the fifties, Duras acquired a certain renown for her televised interviews with political and intellectual personalities in the following decade. After an unsatisfactory attempt at directing her own plays in 1968, she began making films. Throughout the seventies this cinematic activity, together with some writing for the theater, displaced all interest in nonperformance media; her film *India Song* was a considerable avant-garde and critical success. The eighties saw a return to the written text and to narrative. Duras's work has long enjoyed considerable success in English translation.

Duras has lived the life of a committed intellectual, although only a handful of her works treat historical or socioeconomic issues explicitly and extensively. Expelled from the Communist Party in 1950, she retained an adherence to many of its founding aspirations. Her sympathies grew increasingly radical (*gauchiste*) and anarchistic from the sixties on. She participated in the Writers-Students Committee in May-June 1968, worked actively for Amnesty International and for the rights of foreigners in France throughout the seventies, and supported Solidarity in Poland and the rebels in Afghanistan in the eighties. Although her positions provoke controversy in feminist as well as antifeminist circles, Duras has consistently spoken out on women's issues, particularly in the seventies. She is a signatory of the 1971 Declaration of the 343 in France, in which (mostly famous) women declared having had an abortion and petitioned for its legalization.

MAJOR THEMES

The beginning of Duras's literary career coincides with the blossoming of existentialism in France; her Saint-Germain-des-Prés politics and apartment were both close to those of Jean-Paul Sartre and Simone de *Beauvoir. Many of her themes echo familiar existential preoccupations: the problem of freedom, underlying *angst*, and the absence of absolutes grounded in God or in lay metaphysics. The critic Julia *Kristeva places Duras's opus under the sign of the dark existential pessimism experienced by so many writers when faced with Hiroshima and the revelations of the concentration camps at the end of the war. The human body in Duras's fiction, like its Sartrean counterpart, is characterized by nerves and rarely by an appetite, and demonstrates a sexuality tinged with introspection and voyeurism more than with warmth. Her recently published autobiographical texts based on wartime manuscripts (in *La Douleur*) depict a woman of action much in the "virile" tradition of the existentialist action novel (André Malraux, Antoine de Saint-Exupéry). Yet even in *La Douleur* the author refuses any heroic vision, displaying a fundamental irony about the feasibilily of meaningful action in the world.

Among existentialists, Duras resembles Beauvoir and Sartre in envisioning alternative social forms which could alleviate the oppression of modern society and its state. Many of her novels explore contacts among people that rarely come into dialogue, as when the wealthy industrialist's wife Anne Desbaresdes has a series of rendezvous with the unemployed laborer Chauvin in *Moderato cantabile*. Some of her works investigate attempts at utopias or experiment with sites of refuge from society, for example, *La Douleur*, *Le Marin de Gibraltar* (*The Sailor from Gibraltar*, 1952), and *Nathalie Granger* (1972 film). Her works never contest the social status quo through an exaltation of nature, however, which sets her apart from Camus, Malraux, and Saint-Exupéry.

No theme appears more central to the works of Marguerite Duras than that of desire, developed particularly with reference to female characters. Durassian desire needs multiple objects and variation. In *Détruire, dit-elle* desire circulates freely among individuals unfettered by monogamy and homophobia. Most of Duras's texts offer all too realistic and tragic counterparts to that utopian and comedic depiction, however. External and internal obstacles oppose the circulation of desire: the father figures of *Hiroshima mon amour* and *L'Amant* uphold narrow traditional class or ethnic views, and the social structure of *Agatha* (1981) censors incest. The entropy of habit and the lure of new adventures compromise deeper relationships in *Les Petits Chevaux de Tarquinia* (The Little Horses of Tarquinia, 1953) and *Dix heures et demie du soir en été*.

Alterity stimulates Durassian desire. Her characters are attracted to partners of a different color or nationality: the white French heroine of *Hiroshima mon amour* breaks a strong racial taboo by sleeping with the Japanese architect, as does the young Duras persona of *L'Amant* by taking a Chinese lover. The class barriers violated in *Moderato cantabile* can be compared to the social boundaries crossed in *India Song* when the suave Europeans make contact with the two outsiders of the text, the Vice-Consul and the beggarwoman. Criminality bestows a pedigree of rebellion and possesses a similar appeal for the characters of *Dix heures et demie du soir en été* and *Le Marin de Gibraltar*.

Numerous triangular situations set up studies of jealousy, exclusion, and emotional crises. Already in the recurrent "family romance" of her autobiographical novels Duras presents the daughter as the unsuccessful rival of her brother for the mother's affection. As an adolescent, the title character of *Le Ravissement de Lol V. Stein* experiences severe emotional trauma after finding herself at the wrong corner of a love triangle; later in life voyeurism and the triangular structure reassert themselves as the privileged frameworks in which she seeks transcendence. Durassian desire can ultimately appear narcissistic; the critic Carol Murphy has emphasized that no relationship insulates a character from loneliness and alienation. In *Moderato cantabile* the protagonist, Anne Desbaresdes, is alienated from her affluent milieu and her husband; at the same time she is attracted to alcohol and violent states of passion. Surrounded by a harem of lovers, Anne-Marie Stretter (*India Song*) appears distant, listless, even empty.

Durassian *eros* is intertwined with *thanatos*. If *Le Navire Night* (The Ship Night, 1979) is essentially a symbolist telling of a romantic tale, the original and disturbing *La Maladie de la mort* (*The Malady of Death*, 1982) sets death alongside love to question the limits of communication and the very commitment to life. *Moderato cantabile*, *Hiroshima mon amour*, and *Le Vice-consul* affirm that the paroxysm of desire is matched only by the absolute character of death; they also depict desire kindled by violence. *L'homme assis dans le couloir* (The Seated Man in the Passageway, 1980) points to a manner in which desire can lead directly to death, via sadomasochism, while the initial section of *Le Marin de Gibraltar* exemplifies the spiritual death that can result from this link between attraction and destruction, via debasement and loss of self-esteem.

In Duras's works the desire to see (cf. voyeurism and scopophilia), but also to *recount*, is linked to the desire for a person. This desire for another subject is itself tied up with the problematics of self and other as suggested above. The very construction of Duras's texts explores seeing and telling in relation to power, desire, and the other. In *Le Ravissement de Lol V. Stein* the doctor-narrator tells the story of his lover, Lol; the narrator's desire to possess the woman translates into the need to appropriate her as a known entity by telling her story. He converts fragments of hearsay and invention into a seamless and univocal account of Lol's past which presents her difficult situation as a natural result of adolescent traumas. The story confronts a fascination for the other with the drive to deny the other by reducing it to reassuring images of the habitual and the familiar. The form of the text is developed from confessional novel, detective story, and narratives of analysis (with Lol as analysand).

Duras investigates an ethnic and racial dialectic of alterity and specularity in *Le Vice-consul* when a member of the European colonial community in the novel takes to observing a Southeast Asian beggarwoman and inquiring about her. In a novel he is writing, he sews together bits of her situation and anecdotes about other Asians to come up with a narrative which he presents as *her* history. The text explains the scandal of the beggarwoman's condition in the midst of the affluent milieu in a seductive account combining moral tale and adventure story. The film version of the same story, *India Song*, stages the seduction of watching and telling in a text-within-a-text structure. Off-screen voices function as viewers and narrators positioned between the spectator and the spectacle. The unidentified and unseen off-screen voices are caught between desiring each other and desiring to lose themselves in the on-screen story of love. Capturing the anachronistic character of the colonial empire, Duras's film presents the whole story it tells as a legend or a ritual reenactment, acted out by silent, ghostlike figures on screen. The themes of watching and telling come together with those of violence and desire to form particularly powerful structures in "Albert des Capitales" (from *La Douleur*) and *L'Homme assis dans le couloir*.

The ubiquity of desire in the texts never dissipates the ennui, distractedness, and inaction that weigh on so many of Duras's characters. Social conventions, habit, and destructive forces such as alcohol asphyxiate them. Nostalgia, regret, and alienated contemplation replace planning, deciding, and enjoying in her characters. A number of Duras's protagonists display a peculiar form of passivity. Early novels (through *La Vie tranquille* [The Calm Life, 1944]) portray a heroine whose hypersensitivity and intense mental activity are not matched by powers of will or a spirit of confrontation. Irresolution and lack of clear thinking accompany the disinclination to act. Duras herself links this passivity to feelings of metaphysical and political despair, but also, dialectically, to a form of liberation via silence and refusal. This global pacifism has been connected to a "neo-femininity" entailing a celebration of strengths more typical of women than of men in our societies. The inaction can in any case disquiet and alarm readers; it appears tied to a lack of self-esteem and initiative in the characters that leaves them open to psychological and even physical abuse.

Duras's psychological climate of inertia is matched and sharpened by oppression depicted in the social sphere in connection with such categories as class and gender, religious and sexual preference, and ethnic identity. The exploitation is answered by revolt but not revolution in the texts. In *Un Barrage contre le Pacifique*, the poverty of lower-echelon white society is set alongside the even poorer indigenous population of between-the-wars French Indochina; the greed and graft of the colonial administration perpetuate the inequities. The contrasting sketch of the upper-class white neighborhood in Saigon, resembling an extended country club for the European elite, is found again in the cosmopolitan circle around the French embassy in the India of later texts (e.g., *India Song*). The exploited family of *Un Barrage contre le Pacifique* revolts against the French administration by plotting a peasant resistance to the law, whereas the central male character of *India Song*, the Vice-Consul, effects a desperate inner revolt by shooting at the crowds and at his own image in the mirror. Social oppression within power relations is specified as gender-driven in *Nathalie Granger*, in which the peaceful relationship of two women friends is contrasted with the turbulent violence of two male criminals loose in the area. Duras has depicted the victimization of the Jews in the Holocaust, manifesting her solidarity with them in the face of that specific horror and violence in history (e.g., *Abahn, Sabana, David*, 1970; the Aurélia Steiner texts of the late seventies). She has indicated that the Jews in her texts also point beyond themselves to all those victims who refuse power and the state. The same injustices encountered at the levels of state, economic system, and society may be found again within the individual family (cf. the older brother in *L'Amant*).

Many of Duras's works critique the oppression of women in society. Her strategy often works through counterexample, provoking the reader to draw the appropriate conclusions. The empty life of Anne Desbaresdes (*Moderato cantabile*), for example, invites a dialectical approach to the character and the novel. Relations among women in the texts are generally problematic, secondary, or altogether absent. The mother's rejection of the daughter looms as a recurrent fear when it is not explicitly enacted in the text (*Le Vice-consul, India Song*). Men replace women in the slots privileged for interaction: male lovers take the place of female friends (*Le Marin de Gibraltar, Le Ravissement de Lol V. Stein, Le Vice-consul* and *India Song, La Douleur*), mothers dote on a son and not a daughter (*Un Barrage contre le Pacifique, L'Amant*), and brothers replace sisters and girlfriends for adolescent heroines (*Un Barrage contre le Pacifique, L'A-mant*). When a fellow schoolgirl appears as a friend for the young protagonist of *L'Amant*, the relationship is tinged with sensual attraction; rare are the dynamics among peers in Duras where sexuality does not play a role.

Nathalie Granger provides an important exception to the theme of difficult relationships among women in Duras's opus. The film presents an alternative domestic economy founded on the friendship between two women. Reminders of violence in society maintain the utopian scene as an island retreat from history, while isolated victories won by the women against the patriarchal market society assert the possibility of local and particular advances for the oppressed. The value of relations among women and the timeliness of women's new avenues of creativity today are stressed in the Xavière Gauthier interviews with Duras in *Les Parleuses* (*Woman to Woman*, 1974).

SURVEY OF CRITICISM

A number of studies done in the eighties embrace the whole of Duras's oeuvre. With a careful eye and ear for the movement of Duras's language, Bajomée distills the essentials of the author's fictional universe; her study makes use of the postwar critical methods of phenomenology and psychoanalysis. Guers-Villate reads Duras with great insight; her book highlights the internal parallels within the opus and sketches contrasts among the different genres, (for example, between *Le Vice-consul* (novel) and *India Song* (film). Borgomano provides an astute analysis relying on continental psychoanalytical models; the comparative work with the various "primal scenes" is particularly compelling. Pierrot's survey makes intelligent use of biographical information to interpret the texts, grouped in eight (largely) chronological segments. Ames's collective work contains valuable pieces by many contemporary scholars (Andermatt Conley, Cismaru, Cohen, Lydon, etc.). Recent periodical issues devoted to the writer include *L'Arc, L'Esprit Créateur*, and *Magazine Littéraire*.

For the novels, Carol Murphy's limpid study examines each work in sequence with a focus on how the characters face two of the most fundamental concerns in Duras's fiction, alienation and absence. Papin's *L'Autre Scène* is the first book-length study of Duras's theater; in addition to its analysis, it contains valuable interviews with the author and her theater associates. The *Cahiers Renaud-Barrault* have devoted parts of three issues to theatrical presentations. A considerable number of studies have been done on Duras's cinema. The collective *Marguerite Duras* is anchored by reflections on the filmic portion of the India Cycle; Bernheim's *Marguerite Duras tourne un film* provides interviews with almost the entire crew from *India Song*.

Other sources can be found in the bibliographies included in *Magazine Littéraire* (good on audiovisual and journalistic sources), in Murphy's and Guers-Villate's studies, and in the first issue of the *Journal of Durassian Studies*. Significant articles devoted to Duras have been written by such well-known figures as Kristeva, Blanchot, Foucault, Cixous, and Sollers.

BIBLIOGRAPHY

Major Works by Marguerite Duras

Les Impudents. Paris: Plon, 1943.
La Vie tranquille. Paris: Plon, 1944.
Un Barrage contre le Pacifique. Paris: Gallimard, 1950.
Le Marin de Gibraltar. Paris: Gallimard, 1952.
Le Square. Paris: Gallimard, 1955.
Moderato cantabile. Paris: Minuit, 1958.
Dix heures et demie du soir en été. Paris: Gallimard, 1960.
Hiroshima mon amour. Paris: Gallimard, 1960.
L'Après-midi de Monsieur Andesmas. Paris: Gallimard, 1962.
Les Petits Chevaux de Tarquinia. Paris: Gallimard, 1963.
Le Ravissement de Lol V. Stein. Paris: Gallimard, 1964.
Théâtre I, II, III. Paris: Gallimard, 1965, 1968, 1984.
Le Vice-consul. Paris: Gallimard, 1965.
Détruire, dit-elle. Paris: Minuit, 1969.
Abahn, Sabana, David. Paris: Gallimard, 1970.
L'Amour. Paris: Gallimard, 1971.
Nathalie Granger and *La Femme du Gange*. Paris: Gallimard, 1973.
Les Parleuses. Interviews with Xavière Gauthier. Paris: Minuit, 1974.
India Song. Paris: Gallimard NRF; Film, Paris: Armorial, 1975.
Le Navire Night, Césarée, Les Mains négatives, Aurélia Steiner, Aurélia Steiner, and
       Aurélia Steiner. Paris: Mercure de France, 1979.
L'Homme assis dans le couloir. Paris: Minuit, 1980.
Agatha. Paris: Minuit, 1981.
La Maladie de la mort. Paris: Minuit, 1982.
L'Amant. Paris: Minuit, 1984.
La Douleur. Paris: P.O.L., 1985.

Translations of Marguerite Duras

The Sea Wall. Trans. Herma Briffault. New York: Farrar, Straus and Giroux, 1985.
The Sailor from Gibraltar. Trans. Barbara Bray. New York: Riverrun, 1980.
Ten-thirty on a Summer Night. Trans. Anne Borchardt. London: Calder, 1962.
Hiroshima mon amour. Trans. Richard Seaver. New York: Grove Press, 1966.
The Afternoon of Monsieur Andesmas; and Rivers and Forests. Trans. Anne Borchardt
       and Barbara Bray. London: Calder, 1965.

Four Novels by Marguerite Duras. Trans. Richard Seaver et al. Intro. Germaine Brée. New York: Grove Press, 1965.

Three Plays. London: Calder and Boyars, 1967.

The Ravishing of Lol V. Stein. Trans. Richard Seaver. New York: Grove Press, 1966.

The Vice-Consul. Trans. Eileen Ellenbogen. London: Hamish Hamilton, 1968.

Suzanna Andler, La Musica, L'Amante anglaise. London: Calder, 1975.

"Destroy," She Said. Trans. Barbara Bray. New York: Grove Press, 1970.

Woman to Woman. Trans. Katharine A. Jensen. Lincoln: University of Nebraska Press, 1987.

India Song. Trans. Barbara Bray. New York: Grove Press, 1976.

The Malady of Death: Five Novels. New York: Grove Press, 1985.

The Lover. Trans. Barbara Bray. New York: Pantheon, 1985.

The War: A Memoir. Trans. Barbara Bray. New York: Pantheon, 1986.

Studies of Marguerite Duras

Ames, Sanford Scribner, ed. *Remains to Be Seen: Essays on Marguerite Duras*. New York: Peter Lang, 1989.

Armel, Aliette, ed. *Marguerite Duras*. Special issue of *Magazine littéraire* 278 (June 1990).

Bajomée, Danielle. *Duras ou la douleur*. Brussels: De Boeck, 1989.

Bernheim, Nicole Louise. *Marguerite Duras tourne un film*. Paris: Albatros, 1974.

Blanchot, Maurice. *La Communauté inavouable*. Paris: Minuit, 1983.

Borgomano, Madeleine. *Duras: une lecture des fantasmes*. Petit Roeulx, Belgium: Cistre, 1985.

Cahiers Renaud-Barrault 52 (1965), 89 (1975), 106 (1983). Special issues on the theater of Marguerite Duras.

Cohen, Susan D., ed. *Marguerite Duras*. Special issue of *L'Esprit créateur* 30, no. 1 (Spring 1990).

Duras, Marguerite, et al. *Marguerite Duras*. Paris: Albatros, 1977. Trans. Edith Cohen and Peter Connor. San Francisco: City Lights, 1987.

Foucault, Michel, and Hélène Cixous. "A propos de Marguerite Duras." *Cahiers Renaud-Barrault* 89 (1975): 8–22.

Guers-Villate, Yvonne. *Continuité/Discontinuité de l'oeuvre durassienne*. Brussels: Eds. de l'Université de Bruxelles, 1985.

Journal of Durassian Studies (1989-).

Kristeva, Julia. "The Pain of Sorrow in the Modern World: The Works of Marguerite Duras." Trans. Katharine A. Jensen. *PMLA* 102, no. 2 (March 1987): 138–52.

Murphy, Carol J. *Exile and Alienation in the Novels of Marguerite Duras*. Lexington, Ky.: French Forum, 1983.

Papin, Liliane. *L'Autre Scène: le théâtre de Marguerite Duras*. Saratoga, Calif.: Anma Libri, 1988.

Pierrot, Jean. *Marguerite Duras*. Paris: José Corti, 1986.

Saporta, Marc, ed. *M. Duras*. Special issue of *L'Arc* 98 (1985)

Sollers, Phillipe. "Détruire, dit-elle." *Ça Cinéma* 1 (1970): 9–14.

JUDITH GAUTIER
(1845–1917)

Danielle Mihram

BIOGRAPHY

Judith Gautier was the elder daughter of Théophile Gautier (1811–1872), a leading writer of the Romantic period, and of the singer Ernesta Grisi. Théophile Gautier was an enormously prolific writer of novels and short stories, a poet, playwright, and journalist, and was known for his credo, "art for art's sake." Judith's mother belonged to the Grisi family of Milan, famous in the world of music and theater. Ernesta Grisi, a singer at the Théâtre des Italiens in Paris, became Gautier's mistress in 1844, and their liaison endured for over twenty years. Their daughter Judith was born on August 25, 1845, and a second daughter, Estelle, three years later.

When Gautier, who already had a son, Théophile, by another mistress, Eugénie Fort, found himself with two mistresses and two children to support, he undertook to fulfill his commitments by writing on a regular basis for *La Presse*. He became a critic of art, music, theater, and literature, and traveled abroad quite often. These voyages inspired many articles as well as a number of his novels and short stories. As for Ernesta, she continued to perform at the Théâtre des Italiens: within a few weeks of Judith's birth, a wet-nurse, Damon, was entrusted with the baby.

We find fond reminiscences of Judith's childhood in her autobiographical work, *Le Collier des jours* (The Necklace of Days, 1902), and it is certain that as an infant she developed a very strong bond with Damon, whose affection for the child was boundless. Indeed, many tears were shed when Judith outgrew the need to nurse and was sent to live with her grandfather, Pierre Gautier, a retired tax collector, who resided with his two unmarried daughters at Montrouge on the outskirts of Paris. In *Le Collier des jours*, Judith recalls the days spent with a rather severe and authoritarian man and two aunts totally inexperienced in the art of child-rearing. During that period, the little girl developed an independence of spirit that she exhibited throughout her life.

In 1852, at age seven, Judith was still free to roam on her grandfather's property, and, in contrast with other girls of her age and means, she was receiving no formal education. Her Aunt Carlotta took matters into her own hands and sent her niece to board at the Soeurs de Notre-Dame de Miséricorde. Undaunted by the disciplinary efforts of the sisters, Judith continued to maintain an independent demeanor during the two years she spent there. By 1854, however, her father, resenting the suggestion that he was unfit to undertake his daughter's education, removed her from the convent. Judith spent her adolescent years in her parental home, in the company of her younger sister and a succession of governesses. Her father was a very indulgent parent (Gautier fondly referred to her as "his last hope"), while Ernesta was, to a large extent, a mother *in absentia* because her career required frequent trips abroad. "We were free," wrote Judith, "to do anything that we wanted, and even, to do nothing at all" (*SRC*, 193).[1]

Judith's intellectual growth was influenced by the visits of well-known literary men who were friends of her father, among them Hugo, Baudelaire, Flaubert, and Dumas. Théophile Gautier, who believed that "reading is the key to everything" (*SRC*, 39), quickly recognized his daughter's talents, and at the age of nine she was permitted free access to his library, wherein the Romantics were well represented.

When Théophile Gautier wrote *Le Roman de la Momie* in 1857, he enlisted Judith as his assistant, and later she provided him with details of her convent life which he used in *Spirite* (1865). Théophile also transmitted to his daughter his interest in the Orient, an interest he shared with many of his contemporaries and which provided him with exotic place names and a poetic vocabulary evocative of gods and plants as well as unusual settings. The Orient, particularly the Far East, became one of Judith's major interests, which continued throughout her life.

A chance encounter with Tin-Tun-Ling, an unemployed Chinese translator in need of financial support, led to lessons in Chinese for Judith when she was still in her teens, and later she learned to read Japanese. Charles Clermont-Ganneau, who was to become a professor at the Collège de France, taught her Persian. For Judith, such mental immersion into what was considered at the time "exotic literature" led her to write *Le Livre de jade* (The Book of Jade) in 1867 and *Le Dragon impérial* (The Imperial Dragon) in 1869.

Her personal life, however, was not so idyllic. As a young woman she was renowned for her beauty, which was compared to that of the ancient Greeks, and many men fell deeply in love with her. Rémy de Gourmont describes her as tall and statuesque, with a profile like those engraved on medals, and with a "luminous smile" (16). In 1865, the Persian general Mohsin-Khan asked for her hand in marriage, but Judith had fallen in love with Catulle Mendès, whom she married against her father's wishes when she turned twenty-one. The rift between father and daughter created by this marriage took years to heal.

Catulle Mendès was a poet and novelist and also wrote musical and theatrical criticism. For a third of a century he managed to associate himself with literary celebrities such as Théophile Gautier, Leconte de Lisle, Paul Verlaine, and Stéphane Mallarmé, but he was himself a literary dilettante, and his personal life was certainly not above reproach.

Judith was soon to discover Mendès's real character, and, after tolerating a series of affairs, she separated from him in May 1874. Since divorce was still not legal at the time, she obtained a judicial separation four years later. Hurt and disillusioned, she remained deeply suspicious of men and extremely wary of deep, lasting emotional commitments. Although she had an affair with Victor Hugo, she did not encourage Richard Wagner's passionate advances.

For the rest of her life Judith remained single and self-supporting. In 1904, she found emotional solace with the twenty-two-year-old Suzanne Meyer-Zundel, thirty-seven years her junior, and they lived together until Judith's death in 1917. According to Joanna Richardson, Gautier's biographer, who interviewed Meyer-Zundel, the bond between the two women was very close and loving, but "whether that relationship was maternal or Lesbian one cannot ever know" (xvi).

Judith Gautier, like her father, was a prolific freelance writer, and she succeeded in maintaining a rather comfortable existence: a maid, an apartment in Paris, and a summer villa in Brittany at Saint-Enogat, which became her residence for the last forty years of her life. In 1911 she was the first woman to be elected a member of the Académie Goncourt. She led a very active social life and opened doors for many aspiring young men in the world of music and letters.

MAJOR THEMES

Art, music, and the literature of Asia and India (China, Japan, Siam, and Persia, in particular) were Judith Gautier's lifelong interests. Her debut in the world of letters came in 1864 at the age of nineteen when, under the pseudonym Judith Walter, she reviewed an art exhibition for the March issue of L'Artiste. The following month, under the same pseudonym, she contributed another article to the same magazine, enthusiastically describing an exhibit of a Chinese collection: "I think," she wrote, "that it has been given to few people to contemplate such a profusion of marvels: it is a confusion of porcelain, a mountain of jade, a cascade of precious stones; you emerge from it dazzled" (188).

Impressed by her descriptive talents, editors asked her to review art exhibitions, and she contributed articles on well-known artists such as Moreau, Courbet, Gérome, Monet, and Doré. In 1867 she published five articles dealing with the China-Japan-Siam exhibits at the Exposition Universelle. Inspired by Chinese poetry, she also composed eight prose poems, "Variations sur des thèmes chinois" (Variations on Chinese Themes), which were published by Arsène Houssaye in L'Artiste in June 1865.

Judith's interest in literature was not confined to the Far East. In 1864, at the suggestion of her father, she reviewed Baudelaire's translation of *Eureka*, again using the pseudonym Judith Walter. Baudelaire was immensely pleased by the accuracy of her analysis and communicated to her his pleasure at being "so well understood" (*SRC*, 67).

During her marriage, she wrote largely out of necessity, to support herself and Catulle, who was often in financial difficulties. One interest she shared with her husband was Richard Wagner's music, whose epic dimensions appealed to her. While still in her teens, she had often attended the Concerts Populaires de Musique Classique at which Wagner's music was performed. When she married Mendès, the couple traveled to Germany to attend performances of Wagner's work, which she reviewed enthusiastically. In 1869, Judith Gautier was chosen by the Wagners to be the godmother of their son Siegfried and, for the next five years, letters and presents were exchanged between her and the Wagners.

When Wagner met her again after her separation from Mendès, he fell in love with her, but the courtship was to be short-lived and purely epistolary. Nevertheless, Judith became his inspiration for *Parsifal*, which she translated into French.

Judith Gautier wrote prolifically all her life and in a variety of genres: novels, plays, short stories, reports about interesting cultural events. In all her works, the Orient remains an important element, whether as subject or as setting. In France, interest in the Orient had evolved in two phases. In the seventeenth and eighteenth centuries, it grew as a result of French commercial and colonial interests, first in China, then in India and the Levant (now called the Middle East). Toward the end of the seventeenth and the beginning of the eighteenth centuries, foreign embassies opened in Versailles and religious missions to the East were undertaken, primarily by the Jesuits. The publications of these missionaries influenced the writings of Montesquieu, Voltaire, and Diderot. In the nineteenth century interest in the Orient focused mainly on the Levant, primarily as a result of Bonaparte's Egyptian expedition (1798–1801). French writers began to travel there and to report on their voyages, but it was Chateaubriand, in his *Itinéraire de Paris à Jerusalem*, who established a route that many aspiring young writers were to retrace enthusiastically: around the Mediterranean, to Greece, Turkey, Lebanon, Jerusalem, Tunis, and home through Spain. Works by Nerval and Flaubert, and Delacroix's enormous dossier of drawings from Morocco are but a few examples of the extraordinary influence that orientalism had on France in the nineteenth century.[2]

Judith Gautier's interest in the Far East thus ran contrary to her contemporaries' prevalent interest in the Middle East. Aside from translations of Chinese and Japanese poems (*Le Livre de jade* [1867] and *Poèmes de la libellule* [Poems of the Dragonfly, 1885], she wrote at least sixteen plays, with subjects as varied as Chinese courtesans (*Princesses d'Amour* [The Love Princesses], performed in 1908), a Russian drama, *La Barynia* (based on her short story, *Les Cruautés de l'amour* [Love's Cruelties, 1879] and written in collaboration with Joseph Gayda), and a ballet-pantomime in collaboration with Armand Tonnery (1893).

In 1911 Judith collaborated with Pierre Loti on a Chinese play for Sarah
Bernhardt, *La Fille du ciel* (The Daughter of Heaven). It was never performed
in France, and the success of an English adaptation in New York City in 1912
was probably due more to the innovative sets and magic illusions on stage than
to the plot. It is based on historical facts (the reign of the emperor Kwang-Su),
but the dialogue is quaint and almost childlike: "Stay! . . . I have said all that I
am empowered to say . . . I await your decision . . . I have finished" (act 4, scene
9). The imagery, like Chinese screens and tapestries, is drawn from the world
of plants: "The flowers grow pale with envy at the approach of our sovereign";
"In truth she is as beautiful as the pink peony" (act 2, scene 8).

Judith also "specialized" in documentary articles about the Far East. Her
articles about China in *Le Journal Officiel* dealt with a great many subjects: the
theater (comedy in particular), painting, poetry (especially the poems of Li-Tai-
Pei), and music. She also wrote about Chinese medicine, stressing Chinese
preferences for cures and simples, and about ceremonial rites such as marriages
and funerals. A large number of those writings were reprinted in *Les Peuples
etranges* (Foreign Peoples, 1879) and later in a book for children and the general
reader: *En Chine* (In China, 1911). Japan provided the setting for a chapter titled
"Tokyo" in *Les Capitales du monde* (The Capitals of the World).

Her works of fiction are also given exotic locales. Several of her novels, *Le
Dragon impérial* (The Imperial Dragon, 1869) and *L'Usurpateur* (The Usurper,
1875; reissued as *La Soeur du soleil* [Sister of the Sun] in 1941), were set in
China; another novel, *Iskender* (1886) in Persia; and *La Conquête du paradis*
(The Conquest of Paradise, 1887) in eighteenth-century India. She covered an
even greater geographic area in her collection of short stories, *Fleurs d'Orient*
(Flowers of the Orient, 1893), which take the reader from Arabia to China.
Mémoires d'un éléphant (Memories of an Elephant), a children's book published
in 1893, takes place in Siam. What is remarkable about Judith's works is the
descriptive, childlike, evocative quality of her prose as well as her memory for
details. She never traveled to the Orient. Her knowledge of the East owed much
to books (she had been consulting the Bibliothèque Nationale's Oriental collection since her teens), pictorial representations, and conversations with travelers
who had visited those lands. She was able to recreate these places not only
accurately but also vividly, as attested by contemporaries who were natives of
these countries.

The quality of Judith Gautier's writing is not uniformly high. Many of her
publications were commissioned and written hurriedly to meet deadlines or to
oblige friends. In 1913, for instance, she wrote a series of fictitious letters
published as *Lettres inédites de Madame de Sévigné* (The Unpublished Letters
of Madame de Sévigné). Twelve hundred copies of this work were distributed
to favored customers of the chocolatier "La Marquise de Sévigné," located on
the Boulevard de la Madeleine. In this whimsical work of publicity the "marquise" writes to her daughter about the irresistible sweets available in that shop

and reports on the latest technological advances of the day: telephones, trains, aeroplanes.

Judith Gautier lived in a world in which everyone wrote and published, and she did the same. Much still remains to be done to sort through her voluminous writings to evaluate the quality and significance of her literary contributions.

SURVEY OF CRITICISM

Almost no critical studies have been written about Judith Gautier. Except for very short entries in a few literary histories (two or three paragraphs at most), her work has provoked no comment. One possible reason for this neglect is the sheer volume of her publications. Like her father's, her literary output was enormous. For almost forty years she contributed to newspapers and periodicals under various pseudonyms. She also published a large number of books (translations, novels, short stories, plays, poetry). Toward the end of her life, she reproduced large parts of her earlier published work almost verbatim under new titles. Her biographer, Joanna Richardson, suggests that a comprehensive bibliography of all her writings is now impossible. For instance, we may never know what other works of publicity she wrote besides the one for the chocolatier.

An early attempt at a scholarly evaluation of her work was undertaken by Mathilde Camacho in a doctoral dissertation published in Paris in 1939. Despite its numerous errors and incompleteness, this remained the only substantial study of Gautier until Joanna Richardson's excellent biography in 1987.

Anyone undertaking a serious study of her autobiographical work, *Le Collier des jours*, and its two sequels, written more than thirty years after the event, would need to highlight the inevitable errors, inaccuracies, and lacunae in Gautier's texts. Such a work of verification has already been started by Margaret Lyons in her 1980 article on Gautier's recollections of her convent days. The reminiscences of Suzanne Meyer-Zundel also need serious examination, since her recollections are not always accurate or complete. A few of Gautier's letters have been published by Claudine Lacoste, but a comprehensive inventory of her correspondence still needs to be made.

Because Gautier's work is based on information derived from her readings at the Bibliothèque Impériale (now the Bibliothèque Nationale), it should be regarded largely as an imaginative transposition of Asia. A study of her works would probably show that her view of the Orient was a mixture of facts culled from her readings and abstract interpretations of Oriental culture. In a manner comparable to that of the narrator of the Arabian *A Thousand and One Nights*, she delighted in recreating in her imagination the deeds of Asiatic princesses, mighty warriors, beautiful courtesans, and breathtaking "exotic" landscapes. Her fertile imagination was her "magic carpet": how successful were her creations remains to be shown.

NOTES

1. Quotations are from *Le Second Rang du collier: souvenirs littéraires*, abbreviated in the text as *SRC*. All translations from the French are my own.

2. See Edward Said's study, *Orientalism* (New York: Pantheon, 1978), for an evaluation of the nineteenth century's interpretations of the cultures of the Orient.

BIBLIOGRAPHY

Major Works by Judith Gautier

Le Livre de jade. Paris: Lemerre, 1867. (Published under the name of Judith Walter.)
Le Dragon impérial. Paris: Lemerre, 1869. (Published under the name of Judith Mendès.)
L'Usurpateur. Paris: Librairie Internationale, Albert Lacroix, 1875. (Published under the name of Judith Mendès.)
Les Cruautés de l'amour. Paris: Dentu, 1879.
Richard Wagner et son oeuvre poétique depuis "Rienzi" jusqu'à "Parsifal." Paris: Charavay frères, 1882.
Iskender. Histoire persane. Paris: Frinzine et Cie, 1886.
Parsifal. Poème de Richard Wagner. Traduction littérale de Judith Gautier. Paris: Armand Colin, 1893.
Le Collier des jours: souvenirs de ma vie. Paris: Félix Juven, 1902.
Le Second Rang du collier: souvenirs littéraires. Paris: Félix Juven, 1903.
Le Troisième Rang du collier. Paris: Félix Juven, 1909.
Poésies. Paris: Eugène Fasquelle, 1911.
La Fille du ciel. Paris: Calmann-Lévy, 1911. Written with Pierre Loti.
Auprès de Richard Wagner. Souvenirs (1861–1882). Paris: Mercure de France, 1943.
Lacoste, Claudine. "Six lettres inédites de Judith Gautier." *Bulletin de la Société Théophile Gautier* 3 (1981): 131–37.
———. "Lettres inédites d'Ernest Legouvé, de Jehan Duseigneur, de Lamartine, d'Arthur Stevens, de Judith Gautier." *Bulletin de la Société Théophile Gautier* 7 (1985): 73–79.

Translations of Judith Gautier

Richard Wagner and His Poetical Work from "Rienzi" to "Parsifal." Translated with the author's special permission by L.S.J. Boston: A. Williams, 1883.
Wagner at Home. Trans. Effie Dunreith Massie. London: Mills and Boon, 1910.
The Daughter of Heaven. Trans. Ruth Helen Davis. New York: Duffield and Co., 1912.
Chinese Lyrics from the Book of Jade. Trans. James Whitall. New York: B. W. Huebsch, 1918.

Studies of Judith Gautier

Camacho, Mathilde Dita. *Judith Gautier, sa vie et son oeuvre*. Geneva: Droz, 1939.
Gourmont, Rémy de. *Judith Gautier*. Paris: Bibliothèque Internationale d'Edition, 1904.
Lyons, Margaret. "Judith Gautier and the Soeurs de Notre-Dame de Miséricorde: A

Comment on *Spirite*." In *Literature and Society*. Ed. C. A. Burns. Birmingham: Published for the University of Birmingham by J. Goodman, 1980. 56–65.

Meyer-Zundel, Suzanne. *Quinze ans auprès de Judith Gautier*. [Porto: Numes], 1969.

Noblet, Agnès de. "Une Collaboratrice de Pierre Loti: Judith Gautier." *Revue Pierre Loti* 6, no. 24 (1985): 173–75.

———. "*La Fille du ciel*, de Pierre Loti et Judith Gautier—New York, 1912." *Revue Pierre Loti* 8, no. 29 (January-March 1987): 103–10.

Richardson, Joanna. *Judith Gautier: A Biography*. New York: Franklin Watts, 1987.

Said, Edward. *Orientalism*. New York: Pantheon, 1978.

Schwab, Raymond. *Oriental Renaissance: Europe's Rediscovery of India and the East 1680–1880*. New York: Columbia University Press, 1984.

STÉPHANIE-FÉLICITÉ, COMTESSE DE GENLIS (1746–1830)

Marie Naudin

BIOGRAPHY

Stéphanie-Félicité Ducrest de Saint-Aubin, the future comtesse Bruslart de Genlis and marquise de Sillery, was born at Champcéry in Burgundy on January 21, 1746. Most of her youth was spent in the company of her mother, a frivolous lady, while her father, although a member of the oldest nobility, was often away looking for money. Her formal education was limited to training in acting, dancing, and playing music, and she became a virtuoso of the harp. On November 8, 1763, she secretly married Charles Alexis, comte Bruslart de Genlis, who was nine years older and who allegedly fell in love upon seeing her portrait. Her husband's uncle, the prominent marquis de Puisieux, then minister of foreign affairs, did not approve of the marriage, and it was not until two years later that he accepted her as a member of the family and had her introduced at court. Meanwhile she spent her time in her brother-in-law's residence at Genlis, reading and educating herself. Her first daughter, Caroline, was born in 1765.

Under the protection of the Puisieux and Montesson families, she began to have great success in the most exclusive circles with her talent as a musician, her gift for acting, and her vivacity and charm. She bore a second daughter, Pulchérie, in 1766, and a son, Casimir, in 1768 (he died in 1773). In 1769 at Villers-Cotterêts, the duc d'Orléans's summer residence, she met his son, the duc de Chartres (the future Philippe-Egalité), who fell in love with her at first sight. She was twenty-two and married; he was a year younger and about to be married.

In 1772, the woman who was to become Philippe de Chartres's Egeria entered the Palais-Royal and would spend nineteen years in the service of the Chartres family. She was first a lady-in-waiting to the duchess Marie-Adélaïde, and her husband, the comte de Genlis, became captain of the duke's guard. In 1779 she left her husband and her apartment in the Palais-Royal and settled in a pavilion which she had designed and planned on the grounds of the convent of Bellechasse, rue Saint-Dominique in Paris. There she began her work as the tutor of the five Chartres children and, for the first time in history, the "governor" of royal princes was a woman. In addition to her Chartres pupils and her own daughters, she took on the education of many other children, including Paméla Seymour and Hermine Compton, rumored to be her children by Philippe; a nephew, César Ducrest; a niece, Henriette de Sarcey; two English boys; and some sons and daughters of Parisian families. She acquired a reputation as an excellent teacher. Friederich Melchior Grimm and d'Alembert admired her and even proposed her for membership in the French Academy. She wrote several books based on her experience as a teacher and on education in general: *Thèâtre à l'usage des jeunes personnes* (Theater of Education) in 1779, *Adèle et Théodore ou Lettres sur l'éducation* (Adélaide and Théodore or Letters on Education) in 1782, *Les Veillées du château ou cours de morale à l'usage des enfants* (Tales of the Castle: or, Stories of Instruction and Delight) in 1784.

In 1785 she went to England, where Oxford University granted her an honorary degree based on the quality of her books, which had been translated into English. There she met Fanny Burney, Horace Walpole, Edmund Burke, Richard Sheridan, Charles Fox, and other prominent personalities. The same year was marked by the deaths of her oldest daughter and the duc d'Orléans. The young Louis-Philippe (Genlis's pupil and future king of France) became duc de Chartres, and his father became the new duc d'Orléans. Meanwhile the Genlises inherited the Puisieux's land at Sillery and the titles of marquis and marquise.

As the Revolution drew near, Genlis's influence on Philippe d'Orléans was rivaled by that of the novelist Choderlos de Laclos. Laclos was the duke's private secretary and influential in the Orleanist political party, which wanted a constitutional monarchy with Philippe at its head. While Laclos tried to create disturbances and to induce Philippe to spend money on a large scale for bribes and charity, Genlis held a salon at Bellechasse every Sunday attended by reformists such as Stanislas de Clermont-Tonnerre, Jacques Pierre Brissot, Bertrand Barère, Antoie Barnave, Emmanuel Sieyès, and Joseph Jérôme Pétion. Thrilled by the events occurring around her, she was present at the destruction of the Bastille, attended some sessions at the National Assembly, and watched the return of the royal family to Paris.

In 1790–1791 she published three interesting discourses dedicated to the National Assembly: *Discours sur l'éducation de M. le Dauphin et sur l'adoption* (Essay on the Education of the Dauphin and on Adoption), *Discours sur la suppression des couvens de religieuses et l'éducation publique des femmes* (Essay on the Suppression of Religious Convents for Nuns and Public Education of Women), the *Discours sur l'éducation publique du peuple* (Essay on the Public Education of the People). One should also add a vindication of the education she gave the Chartres children: *Leçons d'une gouvernante à ses elèves* (Lessons of a Governess to Her Pupils). The duchess, who suspected Genlis's affair with her husband and who did not like her support for the Revolution, ordered Genlis to resign. But she was soon recalled, and the Orléans couple separated.

In October 1791 she was sent to England by Philippe, probably with a secret mission to arrange a marriage between her pupil Adélaïde and the duke of York. She was accompanied by Paméla, Adélaide, Henriette, her granddaughter Eglantine, and Voidel and Pétion. Genlis, Adélaïde, and Henriette were placed on the list of émigrés and remained in exile for nine years. Then began a long period of travel and extended sojourns in northern Europe. From 1794 on Genlis was on her own, Adélaïde having been taken in by the princess of Conti and Paméla and Henriette having married. She suffered not only from lack of money but also from rejection by most royalist émigrés because she had formerly supported Philippe-Egalité and his party, which had voted for the death of Louis XVI.

She learned of the execution of both her lover and her husband in 1793. In order to survive, she gave lessons and published feverishly: *Les Chevaliers du cygne* (*The Knights of the Swan*) in 1795, *Les Petits Emigrés* (*The Young Exiles*) and *Les Voeux téméraires* (*Rash Vows*) in 1798, *Les Mères rivales* (*The Rival Mothers*) in 1800, three educational works and a short but famous letter to Louis-Philippe called *Lettre de Sielk* in 1796. In 1798 she adopted an eight-year-old German boy, Casimir Daeker, whom she would treat as her real son until her death.

Once removed from the list of émigrés, she returned to Paris and signed a contract with Maradan for the re-edition of some of her books and for her future collaboration on a collection of novels and short stories. In 1802, thanks to Napoleon, she settled in the Arsenal in Paris with Casimir and two other protégés and reopened her salon. From 1805 to 1814 she received an annuity from the Emperor. In exchange she had to write him on different topics every two weeks or so.

During her stay in the Arsenal (1802–1811) she continued to be a prolific writer, publishing novels with historical backgrounds, such as *Mademoiselle de Clermont* (1802), *La Duchesse de La Vallière* (1804), *Madame de Maintenon* (1806), *Le Siège de la Rochelle* (1807); fictions, *Alphonsine ou la tendresse maternelle* (*Alphonsine: or Maternal Affection*) in 1806, *Alphonse ou le fils naturel* (*Alphonso: or the Natural Son*) in 1809; and partial memoirs in 1804. In 1811 she published *De l'influence des femmes sur la littérature française comme protectrices des lettres et comme auteurs* (On Women's Influence upon French Literature as Patrons and as Authors), followed by three polemical essays against detractors of this book. In 1812 she was nominated inspector of the elementary schools of her district. Unfortunately the premonitory symptoms of the fall of the empire prevented her from fulfilling her task.

Meanwhile she began the comprehensive writing of her *Mémoires* and continued to publish: *Mademoiselle de La Fayette* (1813) and *Histoire de Henri le grand* (1815), *Les Battuécas* (*Placide, A Spanish Tale*) in 1816, *Les Parvenus ou les aventures de Julien Delmours* (*The New Era: or Adventures of Julien Delmours*) in 1819; two short-lived newspapers, short stories, manuals, and almanacs; and she edited works such as Rousseau's *Emile* and Voltaire's *Le Siècle de Louis XIV* in 1820. She even intended to rewrite the *Encyclopédie* from a religious point of view. Her best attacks against the Encyclopedists came out in 1822 with *Les Dîners du baron d'Holbach* (The Suppers of the Baron d'Holbach). The years 1825–1826 saw the publication of ten volumes of her *Mémoires*. She wrote her last historical novel, *Athénais ou le château de Coppet*, in 1807 describing Mmes Récamier and de *Staël.

She had become reconciled with the Orléans family during the second Restoration and received an annuity as well as generous gifts from them. She rejoiced when her former pupil Louis-Philippe came to the throne. Her last residence was in a Parisian boarding house in the rue du faubourg du Roule. During the last two years of her life she was to publish two manuals and a novel, *Le Dernier Voyage de Nelgis* (Nelgis's Last Trip), Nelgis being an anagram for Genlis. She died in her sleep on December 31, 1830. She had a splendid funeral ordered and paid for by the king. Her body was first buried on Mont-Valérien, then transferred to Père-Lachaise.

MAJOR THEMES

Throughout her life Mme de Genlis's leading preoccupation was education. She was very proud of her *Théâtre à l'usage des jeunes personnes* and her *Veillées du château*, which today seem old-fashioned. The *Veillées* tales are written to illustrate moral truths, with emphasis on resisting laziness and selfishness. In these stories charity always pays. But it is the *Lettres sur l'éducation* that constitute a kind of survey of Genlis's thought. Often quoting Rousseau, she departs from him on the question of teaching, which, according to her, is the parents' responsibility; in addition, she opposed his belief in natural human kindness.

The *Lettres* point out that for the dauphin, a "governor" seems necessary. The emphasis in his education is placed on history, military and naval techniques, a thorough knowledge of administrative duties, and the needs and strengths of the kingdom. Theory is complemented by practical experience: several months' travel incognito in foreign countries and a few tests given to male and female friends to learn how to detect seduction and flattery.

On the other hand, young aristocrats are to be taught mainly by the parents, with the help of private tutors. Genlis insists that both boys and girls learn the catechism, history, mythology, geography, and foreign languages, that both boys and girls make a trip of eighteen months to Italy accompanied by parents for the study of men and laws, to get rid of superfluous delicacy, to develop a taste for grandeur and appreciation of the arts, and to benefit from further training in drawing and singing. Until the age of twelve and the trip to Italy, knowledge is to be acquired mostly through games, conversation, pictures on the walls, and memorizing. After, the child begins reading serious books, starting in literature with second-rate works in order to be able later to appreciate masterpieces. She also recommends physical exercise and practical training in matters ranging from crafts to managing money and, for girls, raising a younger child. Latin is not mandatory for boys, mathematics is emphasized, and girls are encouraged to study literature and art.

Two essays written during the Revolution that deal respectively with the education of girls and the education of the masses are of particular interest. In her *Discours sur la suppression des couvens* she proposes replacing convent education by ''cloistered schools,'' a type of public boarding school for girls directed by secular women. The schools would follow a detailed plan of study prepared by the National Assembly and would emphasize knowledge of the state's laws and institutions. This education would not include the study of Greek and Latin but would include religion, geography, mythology, domestic duties, elements of medicine, drawing, vocal music, gardening, and physical exercise. In her *Discours sur l'éducation du peuple* she advocates the establishment of secular schools free of charge for everybody until the age of sixteen or seventeen. The program would include books on the new constitution and debates on the Old Regime, a survey of French history, an anthology of French poetry, patriotic plays, and physical exercise.

On the whole, Genlis's programs of studies may be considered discriminatory with respect to sex and social class, but they can also be considered truly modern in their practical orientation, the simultaneous attention to mind and body, the emphasis on foreign languages and mathematics, and their civic awareness in offering education to all citizens without exception.

Adoption and the care of poor children are among her principal concerns. In her *Discours sur l'adoption* she sees adoption as replacing child care in convents and contributing to social equality since adoption would not be based on social class. She recommends that every family adopt an extra daughter. Paradoxically, however, she wants the adopted to be able to prove a legitimate birth.

In her novels, she dramatizes the suffering of children who cannot be adopted. In *Le Siège de La Rochelle*, a daughter born of a secret marriage is separated from her parents at birth and placed in a convent, where she becomes the victim of her father's trusted friend. In *Les Mères rivales* and in *Alphonsine* and *Alphonse*, she portrays on the one hand the situation of single mothers trying to raise by themselves children born out of wedlock, and on the other hand the problems encountered by illegitimate youths who want to have a career and/or marry. Those novels, set in the context of the Old Regime, stress the heartlessness of the powerful and society in general toward marginal love.

Genlis's practical orientation is also evident in her views on marriage. She is sympathetic to love, but it must be ratified by reason; according to her, the best type of marriage is the one foreseen and wisely prepared by the parents, with the couple living for the most part in the bride's mother's house. Genlis is adamantly opposed to passion, which she considers to be based on illusion, a product of the imagination resulting from the reading of novels. In her historical novels, which deal with the birth and development of a passion rather than with history itself, she emphasizes the problems that arise when the protagonists are swayed by emotion rather than reason, and she counsels the *juste milieu*, the classical golden mean.

Her ideal of society is based on the notion of humanistic improvement of human nature. For instance, in *Les Battuécas*, the natives live happily in a self-sufficient economy around a church and a monastery. They receive instruction in religion and an appreciation for the religious arts. Genlis believed in the compatibility of church and reason and despised what she perceived to be the laxity of those philosophers of the Enlightenment who chose deism over the church establishment.

Her political ideology also remained primarily traditionalist. Although enthusiastic at first about the Revolution, she soon changed her mind and could not bear the Convention and the king's execution. In her novel *Les Chevaliers du cygne*, she depicts Charlemagne's reign as a model of constitutional monarchy as opposed to the popular government, the independent republic of the Saxons. Fundamentally an aristocrat, she advocated all the types of government that favor elitism. If for many years she backed the Orléans branch, the *Lettre de Sielk à M. de Chartres*, dated March 8, 1796, expressed her repugnance at the possible replacement of the Bourbons by the Orléans branch. Although she had been deferential toward Napoleon, who protected her, she was pleased with the Bourbon Restoration.

The *Mémoires*, which are not as truthful as one would wish, express the need to please, which is a Genlis constant, as well as her ability to adjust to any circumstance. They also portray a strong woman who, without any serious formal education, became an excellent pedagogue through sheer willpower and intelligence. The reputation she acquired through the quality of her teaching and the excellent education she gave to students of royal blood gave her a degree of prestige and power that, in her time, belonged exclusively to men.

She was so confident of the advantages of learning and knowledge that in her *De l'influence des femmes sur la littérature française* she states quite clearly that any educated woman can aspire to a position of influence as long as she does not wish to occupy any important political office or to participate in wars, since her children must be cared for. With such an assertion, Genlis takes her place among the feminine and feminist writers of the eighteenth and early nineteenth centuries—Mesdames de Lambert, du Châtelet, d'Epinay, and de Staël—who insist on the benefits of education to women. Nevertheless, her main claim to fame remains the promotion of secular education for the masses and her intelligent review of the curriculum for boys and girls at the primary and secondary levels.

SURVEY OF CRITICISM

The memoirs of the time (those of Charles Maurice de François-René de Talleyrand, Chateaubriand, Charles de Rémusat, the countess Victorine de Chastenay, Laure Junot, duchess of Abrantès, and *L'Histoire des Girondins* by Alphonse de Lamartine) express mixed opinions on Genlis's personality, which they consider with more curiosity than reverence. The worst attacks are in *Genlisiana* (1820) by Cousin d'Avallon, who underlines her pretentiousness, her hypocrisy, and her "easy morals." The first objective biography, Jean Harmand's *Madame de Genlis, sa vie intime et politique 1746–1830*, did not appear until 1912. This book takes into account the letters exchanged between Genlis and her lover Philippe-Egalité, disclosed for the first time by Gaston Maugras in *L'Idylle d'un gouverneur* (1904). It also contains a good bibliography and a pertinent summary of the three roles played by Genlis as moralist, playwright, and educator. Two other biographies are important for different reasons. Violet Leverson Wyndham, in her *Madame de Genlis, a Biography* (1958), views with sympathy an author who has often been judged sarcastically by male critics. Wyndham also has the merit of making profitable and extensive use of Genlis's correspondence with Casimir Baecker and Antoine de Montesquiou, which reveals a naturalness and warmth that had seemed lacking in the last period of the *Mémoires*.

The bibliography of Gabriel de Broglie's *Madame de Genlis* (1985) provides a survey of unpublished sources in private, royal, national, and Orléans archives, although the critical part of this bibliography is incomplete and outdated.

Most of the nineteenth-century critics commented on Genlis's production in their works (Friederich Melchior Grimm's *Correspondance*, Jean-François de La Harpe's *Correspondance littéraire*, *L'Année littéraire*, *Le Journal de l'Empire*), but the first extensive analysis came from Charles-Augustin Sainte-Beuve, who discussed her work in his *Causeries du lundi* (1852). He reproached her for being pedantic, romantic, and mundane. In his *Educational Ideas and Activities of Mme de Genlis, with Special Reference to Her Work "Adèle et Théodore"* (1926), William M. Kerby did little more than summarize the contents of each chapter of this novel.

It is only in 1963 that a real feminist perception of Genlis's activities emerges. In her *Literary Women* Ellen Moers devotes to Genlis a good part of a chapter entitled "Educating Heroinism: Governess to Governor." Moers views her as the prototype of those women who gained power as governesses and who, in the last quarter of the eighteenth century, began to write "courtesy books" for the training of their own sex. Two works with the same title, "L'Oeuvre de Madame de Genlis," published, respectively, in 1966 and 1969, provide solid analyses of Genlis's works. The better one is by Alice Laborde, who had the advantage of having at her disposal a rare edition of the so-called *Oeuvres complètes* and who did not hesitate to examine in depth quite "dull" moralistic books. However, the review of the novels is brief and incomplete. The second work, by Anna Nikloborc, is particularly good for the study of the theater.

There are interesting analyses of individual books beginning with George *Sand's comments on *Les Battuécas*. In *Histoire de ma vie*, Sand describes the novel's opposition between natural and civilized life and declares that she owes her democratic initiation to this novel. Madeleine Raaphorst provides an excellent comparison of Rousseau and Genlis in "Adèle Versus Sophie: The Well Educated Woman of Mme de Genlis" (1978). In "Une Avocate des mères célibataires et des enfants naturels: Mme de Genlis," published in 1983, Marie Naudin shows the sociological side of the three novels that deal with the problem of illegitimate birth, *Les Mères rivales, Alphonsine*, and *Alphonse*. In her "Madame de Genlis et le roman troubadour," published in 1982, Huguette Krief gives a very valuable political interpretation of *Les Chevaliers du cygne*. And, finally, there are the illuminating prefaces to the re-editions of *La Duchesse de La Vallière* (1983) and *Mademoiselle de Clermont* (1977). In the first introduction, Gabriel Balin discusses the mysticism of the heroine, and in the second, Béatrice Didier examines Genlis's development as a writer of fiction from classical short story to poetic romantic narrative. It is unfortunate that a thorough study of the novels has not yet been done, and also unfortunate that a complete edition of Genlis's works does not exist.

BIBLIOGRAPHY

Major Works by Mme de Genlis

First Editions

Théâtre à l'usage des jeunes personnes. Vol. 1. Paris: Panckouke, 1779; Vols. 2, 3, 4. Paris: Lambert and Baudoin, 1780; 7 vols. Paris: Lambert, 1785. New complete ed. *Théâtre d'éducation*. 5 vols. Paris: Maradan, 1813.

Adèle et Théodore ou Lettres sur l'éducation. 3 vols. Paris: Lambert, 1782.

Les Veillées du château ou cours de morale à l'usage des enfants. 2 vols. Paris: Lambert, 1784.

Discours sur l'éducation de M. le Dauphin et sur l'adoption. Paris: Onfroy, 1790.

Discours sur la suppression des couvens de religieuses et l'éducation publique des femmes. Paris: Onfroy, 1790.

Discours sur l'éducation publique du peuple. Paris: Onfroy, 1791.

Leçons d'une gouvernante à ses élèves ou fragment d'un journal qui a été fait pour l'éducation des enfants de M. d'Orléans. 2 vols. Paris: Onfroy, 1791.

Les Chevaliers du cygne ou la cour de Charlemagne. 3 vols. Hamburg: Hoffmann, 1795.

Précis de la conduite de Madame de Genlis depuis la Révolution suivi d'une lettre à M. de Chartres et de réflexions sur la critique. Hamburg: Hoffman, 1796.

Les Mères rivales ou la calomnie. 3 vols. Berlin: La Garde, 1800.

Mademoiselle de Clermont. Nouvelle historique. Paris: Maradan, 1802.

La Duchesse de La Vallière. 2 vols. Paris: Maradan, 1804.

Madame de Maintenon pour servir de suite à l'histoire de Madame de La Vallière. 2 vols. Paris: Maradan, 1806.

Alphonsine ou la tendresse maternelle. 2 vols. Paris: Nicolle, 1806.

Le Siège de La Rochelle ou le malheur de la conscience. 2 vols. Paris: Nicolle, 1807.

Alphonse ou le fils naturel. Paris: Maradan, 1809.

De l'influence des femmes sur la littérature française comme protectrices des lettres et comme auteurs. Paris: Maradan, 1811.

Histoire de Henri le grand. 2 vols. Paris: Maradan, 1815.
Les Battuécas. 2 vols. Paris: Maradan, 1816.
Les Parvenus ou les aventures de Julien Delmours. 3 vols. Paris: Baecker, 1819.
Les Dîners du baron d'Holbach. Paris: Trouvé, 1822.
Mémoires inédits sur le 18e siècle et la Révolution française. 10 vols. Paris: Ladvocat,
    1825–1828.
Oeuvres. 84 vols. Paris: Lecointe and Duray, 1825–1826.

Modern Editions

Lettres inédites de Mme de Genlis à son fils adoptif Casimir Baecker, 1802–1830. Ed.
    Henri Lapauze. Paris: Plon, 1902.
*Dernières Lettres d'amour. Correspondance inédite de la comtesse de Genlis avec le
    comte Anatole de Montesquiou.* Ed. André Castelot. Paris: Grasset, 1954.
"Lettres inédites de Mme de Genlis à Bernardin de Saint-Pierre, 1786–1791." Ed.
    Monique Stern. *Studies in Voltaire and the Eighteenth Century,* No. 169 (1977):
    187–275.
Mademoiselle de Clermont. Preface by Béatrice Didier. Paris: Régine Deforges, 1977.
*Mademoiselle de Clermont suivie de L'Histoire intéressante de Madame la Duchesse de
    C***.* Intro. Alix S. Deguise. Geneva-Paris: Slatkine, 1982.
La Duchesse de La Vallière suivi de Deux Lettres de Mademoiselle de La Vallière. Intro.
    Gabriel Balin. Paris: Fontaine, 1983.

Translations of Mme de Genlis

Theater of Education. 4 vols. London: Cadell, 1781.
Adelaide and Theodore: or Letters on Education. 3 vols. London: Bathurst, 1783.
Tales of the Castle; or, Stories of Instruction and Delight. Trans. Thomas Holcroft. 4
    vols. Dublin: Price, etc.; London: Robinson, 1785.
Lessons of a Governess to Her Pupils. 3 vols. London: G.G.H and J. Robinson, 1792;
    2 vols. Dublin: Wogan, Byrne, 1793.
The Knights of the Swan; or, The Court of Charlemagne. Trans. Rev. Mr. Beresford. 3
    vols. Edinburgh: Bell and Bradfute; London: Vernor and Wood, 1796; Dublin:
    Wogan, 1797.
*Short Accounts of the Conduct of Mme de Genlis, since the Revolution. To which is
    subjoined, a Letter to M. de Chartres, and the Shepherds of the Pyrénées, a
    fragment.* Perth: Morison, 1798.
The Rival Mothers or Calumny. 4 vols. London: Longman and Rees, 1800.
The Duchess de La Vallière and Madame de Maintenon. 2 vols. London: Colburn, 1837.
Alphonsine; or, Maternal Affection. 4 vols. London: J. F. Hughes, 1807.
The Siege of Rochelle; or, The Christian Heroine. Trans. R. C. Dallas. 3 vols. London:
    Cox and Baylis, 1808.
Alphonso; or, The Natural Son. 3 vols. London: Colburn, 1809.
Placide, a Spanish Tale. Trans. Alexander Jamieson. 2 vols. London: Simpkin and
    Marshall, 1817.
The New Era; or, Adventures of Julien Delmours: Related by Himself. 4 vols. London:
    Colburn, 1819.
*Memoirs of the Countess of Genlis, Illustrative of the History of the Eighteenth and
    Nineteenth Centuries.* 8 vols. London: Colburn, 1825–1826.

Studies of Mme de Genlis

Avallon, Cousin d'. *Genlisiana*. Paris: Librairie politique, 1820.

Badinter, Elisabeth. "L'Émancipation de Louise." In *Emile, Emilie*. Paris: Flammarion, 1983.

Balin, Gabriel. "Avant-propos," in *La Duchesse de la Vallière*, by Madame de Genlis. Paris: Fontaine, 1983.

Broglie, Gabriel de. *Madame de Genlis*. Paris: Perrin, 1985.

Didier, Béatrice. "Preface," in *Mademoiselle de Clermont*, by Madame de Genlis. Paris: Régine Deforges, 1977.

Harmand, Jean. *Madame de Genlis, sa vie intime et politique 1746–1830 d'après des documents inédits*. Paris: Perrin, 1912.

Kerby, William M. *The Educational Ideas and Activities of Mme de Genlis, with Special Reference to Her Work "Adèle et Théodore."* Paris: PUF, 1926.

Krief, Huguette. "Madame de Genlis et le roman troubadour." *La Licorne*, no. 6 (1982): 313–33.

Laborde, Alice. *L'Oeuvre de Madame de Genlis*. Paris: Nizet, 1966.

Maugras, Gaston. *L'Idylle d'un gouverneur: la comtesse de Genlis et le duc de Chartres*. Paris: Plon, 1904.

Moers, Ellen. "Educating Heroinism: Governess to Governor." In *Literary Women*. Garden City, N.Y.: Doubleday, 1976. 213–31.

Naudin, Marie. "Une Avocate des mères célibataires et des enfants naturels: Mme de Genlis." *Romance Quarterly* 30, no. 4 (1983): 349–58.

Nikliborc, Anna. "L'Oeuvre de Madame de Genlis." *Acta Universitatis Wratislaviensis*, no. 96 (1969).

Raaphorst, Madeleine. "Adèle Versus Sophie: The Well Educated Woman of Mme de Genlis." *Rice University Studies* 64, no. 1 (1978): 41–50.

Sainte-Beuve, Charles-Augustin. "L'Oeuvre de Madame de Genlis." In *Causeries du lundi*. 15 vols. Paris: Garnier, 1852. 3:16–30.

Sand, George. *Oeuvres autobiographiques*. 2 vols. Paris: Gallimard-Pléiade, 1970. 1:627–30.

Wyndham, Violet Leverson. *Madame de Genlis, a Biography*. London: Deutsch, 1958.

DELPHINE GAY DE GIRARDIN (1804–1855)

Dorothy Kelly

BIOGRAPHY

Delphine Gay de Girardin came from an exceptional family that destined its female members for fame. Her grandfather claimed to have given her mother, Sophie Gay, née La Vallette, to the aged Voltaire to be kissed when she was a child; legend has it that Delphine's father had her baptized on the tomb of Charlemagne; and Delphine was named not only after her godmother but also after the heroine of a novel written by one of Sophie Gay's famous acquaintances, Germaine de *Staël, who later died in Sophie Gay's house (she had rented some rooms from Sophie Gay in order to rest).

It was Sophie Gay in particular who encouraged her daughter and set a literary example. Known as a witty conversationalist, Sophie Gay was acquainted with the most renowned figures of the time: Chateaubriand, Talma, Mme Récamier, Lamartine, Constant, Mme de Staël. Indeed, Sophie Gay's quick tongue was responsible for her husband's dismissal as the Receiver-General in the Rhenish provinces, and soon after, when her husband died, she turned to writing novels to earn a living. It was she who encouraged her daughter at age fourteen to read poetry in her salon, and later arranged for Delphine to read her own poems; who, with the aid of her other daughters, helped Delphine to gather information for her columns, which appeared in the daily newspaper *La Presse*; and who advised Delphine to be "a woman in dress and a man in grammar." It was she who brought Delphine into contact with the great writers of the time.

Delphine became somewhat of a legend in those literary circles. Known as a beautiful, graceful, modest genius, later called the "Muse of the nation," she won her first acclaim at age eighteen when awarded a special prize from the French Academy for her poem "Le Dévouement des médecins français et des soeurs de Sainte-Camille dans la peste de Barcelone" (The Devotion of the

French Doctors and of the Sisters of Sainte-Camille During the Barcelona Plague). She brought legend to life when she, like the heroine of another novel by Staël, *Corinne*, was crowned with laurels by the Tiber Academy of Rome and conducted in public triumph to the Capitol. She became a legend, also, because of the admiration she inspired in the literary and political giants of the time: Alphonse de Lamartine called her a goddess and remained a close friend until her death; Alfred de Vigny wanted to marry her (but his mother opposed the marriage because Delphine was not wealthy); the future Charles X was rumored to have an interest in a morganatic marriage; Théophile Gautier described in the most flattering terms her applauded entrance at the first presentation of *Hernani*; George *Sand sent her cheese and compliments and wrote a touching piece after her death; Balzac first met Lamartine at her home; Hugo turned tables with her in his exile. Hugo, Lamartine, and Balzac either wrote pieces for her or dedicated them to her. She prevented Hugo from quarrelling with Lamartine, encouraged Gautier, consoled Sand, recited poetry before Hugo, Dumas, and Musset, contributed to the Romantic journal *La Muse française*, and attended meetings of its Cénacle.

In 1831 she married Emile de Girardin, who first wrote novels and later turned to journalism, founding the first inexpensive popular newspaper of the time, *La Presse*. To Delphine's sorrow, they had no children, and when her husband presented his illegitimate child to her, she accepted it as her own. It was for her husband's newspaper that she wrote her best-known work, the letters written under the pen name of the Vicomte de Launay and called *Les Lettres parisiennes* (*Parisian Letters*), dating from 1836 to 1848. When she turned her talents to drama she realized that dream of so many of the great nineteenth-century novelists: she became a successful playwright. Her plays debuted in Paris, were translated into English, Italian, Spanish, and German, and were produced in London, New York, Boston, and Philadelphia, among other places. It seems that she had no problem remaining a respectable woman even though she was associated with the theater, because almost all of her biographers, writing of her while she was living or after her death, emphasize her fine character and her fidelity to her husband. She died of stomach cancer at the peak of her literary production in 1855.

MAJOR THEMES

In her poem "Le Dernier Jour de Pompéi" (The Last Day of Pompeii) Girardin sings the praises of a beautiful young priestess, Théora, who remains at her place by the altar and perishes in *la cendre*, the ash of the volcano, *la cendre* being also a commonplace for death in French poetry. However, if Girardin ends her poem by describing how, 2,000 years later, Théora's lyre was unearthed from the ash, we must unfortunately say that Girardin's poems have not been unearthed and remain for the most part entombed in the more mundane dust of old libraries. Like Théora, Delphine Gay de Girardin was a legend, a legend in her own time, and it is that very legendary nature that seems to have buried her works in oblivion. Her beauty was so great that its parallel with the beauty of her works became the subject of praise in the writings of those great authors who knew her. Once her physical beauty was erased by death, the renown of her works faded, and they were, ultimately, excluded from the canons of literature. Of the six volumes of her complete works, only recently have a few been reissued, among them *La Croix de Berny* (*The Cross of Berny; or, Irene's Lovers*), an epistolary novel written by four different people (one being Gautier), each of whom wrote the letters of one character, and *Lettres Parisiennes: 1836–1848*, a collection of her chronicles written for the newspapers. The one adjective that best describes the works of Girardin is heterogeneous: in roughly chronological order, she began by writing poetry (most of the poems were written in the 1820s, the rest in the thirties, and very few after that); began to write prose in the early thirties and continued through the forties; popularized the new genre of newspaper chronicles in the mid-thirties through the forties; and wrote successful plays in the forties, continuing until just before her death.

Another possible reason for the oblivion into which the works of Girardin have fallen is that one of the recurrent topics of her poems is woman—consider simply the titles of the following selection: "Magdeleine," "La Confession d'Amélie" (Amélie's Confession), "Napoline," "La Noce d'Elvire" (Elvire's Wedding), "La Druidesse" (The Druidess), "La Folle des Champs-Elysées" (The Madwoman of the Champs-Elysées), "Corinne aimée" (Corinne Loved), "Mathilde," "Sainte Cécile," "La Jeune Fille enterrée aux Invalides" (The Girl Buried in the Invalides). Indeed, her poems often sing the praises of exceptional women, such as her famous poem about the anonymous nuns of Sainte-Camille who risked their lives to save others during the plague, and her poem about an innocent girl who was struck down by a bullet destined for the king, a girl so young and innocent that she had not yet had the chance even to dream of the honors paid to her after her death.

In this often feminocentric poetry, Girardin constructs a network of metaphors that converge in the figure of women's tears: the opening poem of the volume of poetry traces the beginning of Girardin's desire to be a writer to her father's death and to her mother's tears, and thus, instead of the image of the seminal power of ink, she establishes a feminine symbol as the origin for her writing. As this image of tears appears in almost every poem, it establishes a link between them and the women who are often the subjects of that poetry. For them, the image of the tears represents an unusual kind of strength: not the common, straightforward notion of physical strength or stoic fortitude in a world of disease, war, and betrayal, but rather the more complicated, ironic notion of the shared well of tears from which they can tap strength from their very weakness: "Leur puissance est dans leur faiblesse" (Their power is in their weakness, line 24; all translations from the French are mine), as we read in "La Druidesse."

The tears of the poem are linked to woman's writing, not simply in the sense of the origin of woman's writing in the mother's tears, but also in the tears and pain that are the fate of the woman because she writes. Of Théora, the priestess in "Le Dernier Jour de Pompéi," who sings her tales accompanied by her lyre, it is said that inspiration is one of the sources of her pain because it and her status as priestess separate her from the common fate of others; they make her live and die in difference and solitude:

> Sais-tu que d'Apollon la faveur est cruelle?
> Il nous défend l'amour que son feu nous révèle;
> Pour celle qu'il inspire il n'est point de secret:
> Sa gloire est un exil, sa vie un long regret.
> Malheur à qui reçut la science divine!
> L'espoir est inconnu de l'âme qui devine;
> Aimer est son remords, savoir est son tourment,
> Et l'inspiration devient son châtiment. (Lines 101–108)

> (Do you know that Apollo's favor is cruel?
> He forbids us the love that his flame reveals;
> For the woman he inspires there is not one secret:
> Her glory is an exile, her life a long regret.
> Woe to the one who received divine knowledge:
> Hope is unknown to the soul that divines;
> To love is her remorse, to know is her torment,
> And inspiration becomes her punishment.)

For her, death, in the form of the ash, dries her tears in the end. In the poem "Sainte Cécile," the martyr/songstress is decapitated in a Cixousian image of the silencing of woman, but, uncannily, the blade cannot stop her song, which continues in a kind of undoing of law and authority. The thematic thread of women writers extends to a network of historical figures to whom she refers: her mother, *Desbordes-Valmore, *Sévigné, Récamier, Madame de *Duras; Girardin will often quote a line from a woman writer in the beginning of her poems.

As the ocular image of the tears shows the negative and painful side of the condition of "seers" such as Théora and other women who are inspired, so the gaze functions as a constant threat from the eyes of the other in Girardin's poems. As a result another feminine image makes an appearance in almost every poem, the image of the veil and the techniques of irony and reversal:

> . . . sous le voile ingénieux
> D'un trait comique et d'un refrain joyeux,
> La sévère raison se cache avec adresse.
> "Le Retour" (The Return, lines 6–8)

> (. . . under the ingenious veil
> Of a flash of wit and a joyous refrain,
> Severe reason hides itself with skill.)

This reversal can be thematic, as in the conversion of Magdeleine in the poem of that name, the description of woman's condition as one in which she must suffer but make pleasantries, of tragedy that kills and makes one laugh, and of woman's condition as one of a "paradise of snow." But it is often the reversal of a more subtle form of irony, which critics of Girardin's time labeled her *esprit*. For instance, in the poem about the nuns of Sainte-Camille, the poet/narrator admits that by singing their praises she is betraying them, because to praise virtue is to disobey it, and the nuns must ask God's pardon for their glory. Sometimes this irony takes the form of a small twist in an idea: Napoline dies not because her lover has betrayed her but because she herself no longer loves. Or it can take the form of a juxtaposition of ideas, the most interesting being in the poem "Le Bonheur d'être belle" (The Good Fortune of Being Beautiful). This is one of the most cited of Girardin's poems, and it is usually read as a literal autobiography of the author, who was, of course, quite beautiful. Commentators praise the innocence of young beauty expressing itself, but fail to notice the ironic punctuation provided by the initial citation from *Corinne*: "Pourquoi me dire que j'étais charmante, si je ne devais pas être aimée?" (Why tell me that I was charming, if I was not to be loved?). If this is not enough to mitigate the literal, naive innocence of the poem, then the mere presence later in the volume of the poem entitled "Le Malheur d'être laide" (The Misfortune of Being Ugly) should do so, as should the content of the poem written with Lamartine, "Le Rêve d'une jeune fille" (The Dream of a Young Woman), in which a beautiful girl would prefer to be old and out of danger. Veiling, irony, and reversal appear to be defenses against the penetrating gaze of the other, and often a kind of response to the power of language and society to dissimulate.

In another kind of reversal, we often find that at the same time that the poems tell of woman's adherence to the law, they also suggest, even revel in, the details of that law's transgression. For instance, in the poem "Ourika" the heroine dies a Christian while lamenting this fate, and in the poem "Magdeleine" the heroine is converted, although much of the poem is a kind of fascinated description of her beauty and evil. There is furthermore often a kind of fascination with horror, such as in the image of the volcanic death of the Pompeii poem and the plague faced by the nuns of Sainte-Camille.

Several of these themes and structures are carried over into Girardin's prose and theatrical works. Her *esprit* and her art of turning something into its opposite can be seen in many novelistic ploys: one woman is unhappy because she is going to marry the man she really loves (*La Croix de Berny*); a Don Juan type feels that he has been unfaithful in good faith (*Monsieur le Marquis de Pontanges*); and in the cleverest of twists, the heroine of one novel must hide not the predictable case of her loss of virginity, but rather the fact that she is still a virgin (*Le Lorgnon* [The Lorgnon]). Perhaps the most common theme in Girardin's prose and drama is the ambiguity of love; a good person (good in the universe set up in the novel) can love two people at once, a good person is sometimes unable to disentangle feelings about those loved, a good person can experience a combination of conflicting, opposing feelings, and a woman who is not a fallen woman can doubt her love.

The name of one play, *La Joie fait peur* (literally, *Joy Frightens*, but translated into English variously as *Kerry; or, Night and Morning* and *Sunshine Follows Rain*), exemplifies the clever twist in theatrical form, and again in another play, an innocent girl makes a terrible moral blunder while attempting to save a man's life. Girardin makes explicit reference to this play of opposites in her work in the preface to her censored play *L'Ecole des journalistes* (The School for Journalist). In this preface she talks of the themes of her works as products of modernity: classes are mixed together; ranks are inverted; it is a century of sublime reason combined with incurable madness. She speaks of this play itself, in which a newspaper named *The Truth* excels in propagating lies, as exemplifying what she describes as the "modern" characteristic that what once made us laugh (an allusion to Molière's *L'Ecole des femmes* perhaps) now makes us cry in this tragedy. In her plays she often takes classical plays or themes, twists them slightly, sometimes writes them in prose, and places them often in a modern setting: witness *L'Ecole des journalistes* and *Lady Tartuffe*. Or she can take a classical theme, *Cléopatre*, and write it in classical tragic form, complete with some beautiful couplets that often present in poetic form her characteristic clever twists:

> Tu ne t'attendais pas, en venant aujourd'hui,
> A trouver tant d'amour entre ta haine et lui.
> (*Judith*, Act 2, scene 4)

> (You were not expecting, in coming today,
> To find so much love between your hate and him.)

Her verse in these plays sometimes seems to prefigure poetic images that are associated only with the latter half of the nineteenth and the beginning of the twentieth centuries:

> Pas une larme d'eau dans l'implacable azur! . . .
> Toujours ce soleil rouge à l'horizon désert,
> Comme un grand oeil sanglant sur vous toujours ouvert.
> (*Cléopatre*, Act 2, scene 2)

> (Not one teardrop of water in the implacable azure sky! . . .
> Always that red sun on the desert horizon,
> Like a large bloody eye always looking at you.)

This image of the ever-open eye and the lack of tears/water evidently continues the themes of the gaze prevalent in Girardin's poetry. In the novels and stories various characters fight against the power of language and society to dissimulate as they attempt to find true love and real forthrightness. In *Le Lorgnon*, the main character possesses a magic lorgnon that permits him to see beneath the false

surface of others to their real thoughts. He does not succeed in finding anyone
who is totally candid, but does find and fall in love with a woman who, ironically,
hides not her falsity but her candor. In two of the novels, the power to see
beyond surfaces is related to male "props," linking the power of the gaze, not
surprisingly, to the male: there is the aforementioned lorgnon and, in *La Canne
de Monsieur de Balzac* (Monsieur de Balzac's Cane), a magic cane belonging
to the novelist Balzac that permits the one who holds it to become invisible. In
the light of history it is ironic that Girardin, who was so attuned to the problems
of visibility and invisibility, and to the novel's relation to voyeurism (seeing
without being seen), should have become invisible to posterity, perhaps because
of her very visible beauty.

Finally, the prose and theater continue to weave the network between women
artists and feminocentric texts in their portrayal of a feminine strength in weakness
in *Judith* and in *Cléopatre* (furthermore, Rachel, a renowned actress of the time,
was repeatedly cast in her plays). They continue to weave the feminine network
in the use of citations from other women writers, and even of the self-citation
of Girardin in her own works, an auto-quotation that never takes itself too
seriously and always continues the ironic twist so characteristic of her oeuvre:
on the first page of *La Canne de Monsieur de Balzac* we find the title of her
well-known poem, "Le Bonheur d'être belle," immediately followed by a new
twist, "Le Malheur d'être beau" (The Misfortune of Being Handsome).

The crossover in genders seen in the previous example is evident in the nom
de plume, Le Vicomte de Launay, which she used in her best-known work, *Les
Lettres parisiennes*. The epistolary genre and the importance of everyday life,
usually associated with women in French letters, further complicate this gender-
crossing in these pieces written in a male narrator's voice. These letters are most
valuable for that recording of everyday life in France at the time: the daily life
of Paris, the fads and irritations of life there, the disappearance of a certain city
life and the birth of the modern metropolis (there are no more people who stroll
in Paris, and it takes longer to get to the train station than to one's destination).
Her biting wit concentrates on political life, on the attempt to record the truth,
on Parisians, and of course, on the author's own self.

SURVEY OF CRITICISM

Most of the critical work done on Girardin addresses itself to her life and to
the legendary nature of her beauty and talent. Relating her to the well-known,
now canonical, figures of her time, it has mainly anecdotal value, for it rarely,
if ever, discusses her writing. Léon Séché's *Delphine Gay*, one of the most
thorough of the biographical works done on her, has the telling subtitle, *Mme
de Girardin in Her Relations with Lamartine, Victor Hugo, Balzac, Rachel,
Jules Sandeau, Dumas, Eugène Sue, and George Sand*.

Sainte-Beuve's 1851 essay actually comments on this type of criticism, which
is, as he says, necessary in Girardin's case because one must "draw a circle"

around the discussion of any "beautiful and brilliant woman" (*Causeries du lundi*, 297), and he concludes that "the woman, Mme de Girardin, particularly when she shows herself in person, appears to be much superior, until now, to what she was as a writer" (313). Although Sainte-Beuve does discuss the evolution of her works and their relation to their literary predecessors, the main thrust of his analysis is historical anecdote. The fact that Girardin popularized a new genre with her *Lettres parisiennes* does not seem to matter, for Sainte-Beuve accuses her of not finding her own voice, of imitating other styles. Finally, he finds in her writing, not surprisingly, a strange heterogeneous blend—those ironic twists—that he cannot assimilate and synthesize, so he must end by saying that her writing is caught up in a circle of artifice; it is imperfect because it is not *natural* (that highly charged word of praise and damnation used for women).

Lamartine, too, finds her style "artificial," with the "solidity and shine of marble." Gautier's essay concentrates mostly on her life but does analyze her works, and is thus the most interesting of the pieces written by her contemporaries. Barbey d'Aurevilly, who perceives those ironical twists of *esprit* in her poetry, in which he especially appreciates the image of the young woman who is proud but who keeps her eyes lowered, says that she, like all women writers, can be but an imitator.

Some of the better of the few modern biographical essays on Girardin are by Joanna Richardson and Jean-Louis Vissière. Anne Martin-Fugier's notes and index to the *Lettres parisiennes* are excellent and thorough. Although there appears to be an effort to reissue some of her works, very little has been written on them recently. Certainly, the quality of her writing is uneven: in its best moments it is striking in its images, beautiful in its lyric quality, brilliant in its irony; at its worst it is overly melodramatic, mediocre in its adherence to the Romantic code, uninteresting in its plots. Yet, however uneven the quality, the very good works merit review and reevaluation in the light of the fresh perspectives of the critical concerns of today, and they certainly merit more attention than they have received and are receiving.

BIBLIOGRAPHY

Major Works by Delphine Gay de Girardin

Oeuvres complètes de Madame Emile de Girardin, née Delphine Gay. 6 vols. Paris: H. Plon, 1860–1861. Vol. 1: Poèmes, Poésies, Improvisations. Vol. 2: Romans: *Le Lorgnon, La Canne de M. de Balzac, Monsieur le Marquis de Pontanges.* Vol. 3: Nouvelles et contes: *Marguerite, ou deux amours; Il ne faut pas jouer avec la douleur; Contes d'une vieille fille à ses neveux.* Vols. 4, 5: *Lettres parisiennes,* années 1836–1840, 1840–1848. Vol. 6: Théâtre *L'Ecole des journalistes, Judith, Cléopatre, C'est la faute du mari, Lady Tartuffe, La Joie fait peur, Le Chapeau d'un horloger, Une femme qui déteste son mari (A Woman Who Detests Her Husband).*

Modern editions

Lettres parisiennes du Vicomte de Launay. 2 vols. Ed. Anne Martin-Fugier. Paris: Mercure
    de France, 1986.
Chroniques parisiennes: 1836–1848. Ed. Jean-Louis Vissière. Paris: Editions des femmes,
    1986. (Selected letters from *Lettres parisiennes.*)
La Croix de Berny. Paris: Editions France-Empire, 1980.
Nouvelles. Paris: Slatkine, 1979.
La Croix de Berny; roman steeple-chase [by] Charles de Launay, Théophile Gautier,
    Jules Sandeau [and] Méry. Brussels: Société Typographique Belge, 1845.

Translations of Delphine Gay de Girardin

The Clockmaker's Hat. Trans. William Robertson. New York: S. French, n.d.
The Cross of Berny; or, Irene's Lovers. Trans. Florence Fendall and Florence Holcomb.
    Philadelphia: Porter and Coates, 1873.
Kerry; or Night and Morning. (*La Joie fait peur*). Adapted to the English stage by Dion
    Boucicault. New York: De Witt, [c. 1892].
Lady Tartuffe. New York: Darcie and Corbyn, 1855.
Parisian Letters; in *Celebrated Saloons*, by Madame Gay; and *Parisian Letters*, by
    Madame Girardin. Trans. L. Willard. Boston: W. Crosby and H. P. Nichols,
    1851.
Stories of an Old Maid, Related to Her Nephews and Nieces. Trans. A. Elwes. New
    York: Appleton and Co., 1856.

Selected Studies of Delphine Gay de Girardin

Barbey d'Aurevilly, Jules Amédée. *Les Bas-bleus.* Paris: V. Palmé, 1878. 33–43.
———. *Les Oeuvres et les hommes.* Third part, *Les Poètes.* Paris: Amyot, 1862. 291–
    304.
Bertaut, Jules. "Muse Fille de Muse." *Le Figaro Littéraire*, May 4, 1957, 1–9.
Challice, Annie Emma. *French Authors at Home.* 2 vols. London: L. Booth, 1864. 1:
    105–45.
Corriere, Alex. "Madame de Girardin as a Dramatist." *Romance Notes* 9, no. 1 (Autumn
    1967): 68–74.
Gautier, Théophile. "Madame Emile de Girardin." Introduction to vol. 1, *Oeuvres
    complètes de Madame Emile de Girardin.* i-xx.
Hamlet-Metz, Mario. "Note sur une digression: Lamartine et Madame de Girardin."
    Romance Notes, 16, no. 2 (Winter 1975): 305–11.
Saint-Amand, Imbert de. *Madame de Girardin, avec des lettres inédites de Lamartine,
    Chateaubriand, Mlle Rachel.* Paris: Plon, 1875.
Lamartine, Alphonse de. *Cours familier de littérature.* Entretien II. Paris: Privately
    printed, 1856. 98–159. (This essay also appears in different form in *Souvenirs et
    portraits.* 2 vols. Paris: Hachette, 1871. 1: 370–402.)
Malo, Henri. *La Gloire du vicomte de Launay, Delphine Gay de Girardin.* Paris: Emile
    Paul Frères, 1925.
———. *Une Muse et sa mère: Delphine Gay de Girardin.* Paris: Emile Paul Frères,
    1924.

Marsan, Jules. "Une Muse romantique: Delphine Gay." *Bulletin de l'Université et de l'Académie de Toulouse*, 46th year new series, no. 8 (June-July 1938).

Martin-Fugier, Anne. Preface to *Lettres parisiennes du vicomte de Launay*. 2 vols. Paris: Mercure de France, 1986. 1: ii-xxi.

Michel, Arlette. Introduction to *Nouvelles*, by Delphine Gay de Girardin. Geneva: Slatkine Reprints, 1979. i-xxi.

Mirecourt, Eugène de. *Madame de Girardin (Delphine Gay)*. Paris: Havard, 1855.

Richardson, Joanna. "Madame de Girardin: The Tenth Muse." In *Genius in the Drawing-Room*. Ed. Peter Quennell. London: Weidenfeld and Nicolson, 1980. 71–83.

Sainte-Beuve, C.-A. *Causeries du lundi*. 16 vols. Paris: Garnier Frères, 1851. 3: 297–314.

Séché, Léon. *Le Cénacle de la Muse française 1823–1827*. Paris: Mercure de France, 1909.

———. *Delphine Gay, Mme de Girardin*. Paris: Mercure de France, 1910.

Vissière, Jean Louis. Preface to *Chroniques parisiennes: 1836–1848*, by Delphine Gay de Girardin. Paris: Editions des femmes, 1986. 7–43.

MARIE LE JARS DE GOURNAY (1565–1645)

Elyane Dezon-Jones

BIOGRAPHY

As she writes in her 1616 autobiographical *Copie de la Vie de la Damoiselle de Gournay* (Imitation of the Life of the Damoiselle de Gournay), Marie de Gournay was "born in Paris, to Guillaume de Jars and Jeanne d'Hacqueville, the eldest of all their children." She lived to be eighty, during the reigns of five kings, and spent most of her adult life in the capital of France as an independent and productive woman of letters. Three years after her birth into a Catholic family, on October 6, 1565, her father, who was then Secrétaire Ordinaire de la Chambre du Roi, acquired the feudal rights to the castle of Gournay-sur-Aronde, in Picardy. When he died suddenly in 1577, his widow took their six children to this estate because it was a cheaper and safer place than Paris; unfortunately, it was also "remote from any facilities for studying." That did not deter Marie de Gournay from reading every book in sight or from learning Latin by comparing the French and the original versions of the same texts, in spite of her mother's opposition to any kind of formal education for girls.

When she was eighteen or so, Marie de Gournay accidentally opened a copy of Montaigne's recently published *Essais*. The book had such an impact on her that she had to be given a sedative and "started wishing to know the author more than anything in the world" (*Copie de la Vie*). In the spring of 1588, Marie de Gournay was taken to the capital by her mother to be presented at court. For personal and political reasons, Montaigne happened to be in Paris at the same time and answered the enthusiastic letter Marie de Gournay sent to his hotel by coming to see her the very next day and asking her to become his *fille d'alliance* (adopted daughter). In the summer and the fall of the same year, Montaigne spent several weeks at Gournay-sur-Aronde, discussing revisions and additions to his book, as well as literature in general, during his daily walks with Marie de Gournay. Out of these conversations grew her first work, *Le Proumenoir de M. de Montaigne* (M. de Montaigne's Walkway), which consists of a short novel followed by a few poems and selected passages translated from the *Aeneid*. Before it was published by Abel L'Angelier in 1594, two unfortunate events affected Marie de Gournay's life and career: her mother died in 1591 and left her with no choice but to take care of the family and to deal with severe financial difficulties. Then, in the spring of 1593, she was informed by a letter from Justius Lipsius of Montaigne's death, which had actually happened on September 13, 1592, without her knowing it.

In spite of her grief, Marie de Gournay started working on a posthumous edition of the *Essais* in order to establish a text based on the "papers" sent to her by Madame de Montaigne and Pierre de Brach. She also wrote a long preface to this 1595 edition, which was a defense of Montaigne's style and had to be retracted the following year because it was perceived as being biased and self-serving. Invited by Madame de Montaigne to come and spend some time in Montaigne's library so that she might prepare a more accurate edition of the *Essais* based on Montaigne's manuscripts, Marie de Gournay worked on the project for several months and produced the well-known 1598 edition. She then traveled to the Netherlands to promote the book and the new edition of her *Proumenoir* as well.

In 1599, Marie de Gournay decided to settle permanently in Paris, where she intended to obtain the protection of "noble ladies" and to live by her writings. Her first opportunity came with the birth of the son of King Henri IV and Marie de Medici: in 1600, Marie de Gournay wrote a treatise, *De l'education des enfans de France* (On Educating the Children of France), which was favorably received. During the first years of the seventeenth century, she became familiar with the intellectual life of the capital thanks to Marguerite de Valois, who gave her a small pension to take care of her library and allowed her to mingle with the distinguished guests of her famous salon: not only poets and writers like François Maynard, Philippe Desportes, Honoré d'Urfé, Pierre de Bourdeilles de Brantôme, the cardinal Jacques du Perron, and Joseph Justus Scaliger, but all sorts of influential people who later became Marie de Gournay's benefactors and regular visitors. In 1608, she celebrated the birth of Gaston d'Orléans by publishing *Bienvenue de Monseigneur le Duc d'Anjou* (Welcome to My Lord the Duke of Anjou). Still living on the rue des Haudriettes with her servant and friend Nicole Jamin, she practiced alchemy in the hope of alleviating the financial difficulties she describes at length in her *Apologie pour celle qui escrit* (Apology for the One Who Writes) in 1634.

The year 1610 is a turning point in French history and in Marie de Gournay's life as a writer. After the assassination of King Henri IV by Ravaillac, she composed a dialogue, *Adieu de l'Ame du Roy de France et de Navarre, Henry le Grand à la Royne, avec la Defence des pères Jesuites* (Farewell of the Soul of Henry the Great, King of France and Navarre, to the Queen, with the Defense of the Jesuit Fathers). Her personal stance provoked violent reactions on the part of those who believed that the Jesuits were partly responsible for the king's death and that Marie de Gournay herself was somehow implicated in the plot, through her connection with Jacqueline Le Voyer, demoiselle d'Escoman, who had allegedly warned her of the conspiracy. An insulting pamphlet, *L'Anti-Gournay ou le Remerciement des Beurrières de Paris au Sieur de Courbouzon-Montgomery* (Against Gournay or Thanks Given by the Paris Buttermaids to Sir Courbouzon-Montgomery), was the first in a long list of vicious attacks against Marie de Gournay's name, person, and reputation.

Having moved to rue de l'Arbre-Sec, she received many literary and political figures of the time in her modest apartment—her "garret," as Richelieu later put it. While working on another edition of the *Essais*, for which she identified and translated the Greek and Latin quotations, Marie de Gournay became more and more interested in the evolution of the French language, poetic theory, and philological questions in general. In 1616, she became the victim of a prank, which led her to write her first autobiographical text: three men from Malherbe's circle pretended that King James I of England wanted her portrait and her biography as part of a collective work on famous men and women of the time. She consequently drafted her *Copie de la Vie de la Damoiselle de Gournay* and sent it along with her portrait, as Tallémant des Réaux relates in his *Historiettes*. After discovering that it was a hoax, she went to court and later included the text, preceded by an explanatory letter to M. le Trésorier Thévenin, in the 1641 edition of her collected works: *Les Advis ou les Presens de la Demoiselle de Gournay* (The Demoiselle of Gournay's Presents and Offerings). The sketchy autobiographical document covers Marie de Gournay's life from her birth to her return from Montaigne at the end of the sixteenth century. She completed it with a poem entitled *Peincture de moeurs* (A Moral Portrait), which is alluded to at the end of the *Copie de la Vie* and later appeared in her collected works. The clever use she makes of a text that was supposed to discredit her as a writer is typical of Marie de Gournay's art of recuperation and of the oblique way in which she states again and again that "it is a woman who speaks," in spite of the male efforts to silence her through verbal and written intimidation.

In 1619, Marie de Gournay published her *Versions de quelques pièces de Virgile, Tacite et Saluste, avec l'Institution de Monseigneur, frère unique du Roy* (Some Fragments Translated from Virgil, Tacitus and Sallust, with the Institution of My Lord, the Only Brother of the King) in collaboration with Monseigneur Bertaut, the Bishop of Seez. It was accompanied by a treatise on poetry, in which Marie de Gournay praised Ronsard and the Pléiade conception of poetry as "inspired language" while sharply criticizing Malherbe's new ideas concerning the strict ruling of poetic production and the need to purge the French language of its obsolete forms. Her position started a polemical discussion of the issue. Her stand, which was in fact a cry for freedom in art and a defense of baroque style, as Peggy Holmes pointed out in a very perceptive article in 1954, was interpreted as a proof of her anti-classical tastes and a sign of old age.

In 1622, the publication of *Egalité des hommes et des femmes (Of the Equality of Men and Women)*, dedicated to Queen Anne d'Autriche, did not help to correct Marie de Gournay's image as a troublemaker. Seen as a feminist in a time when a famous male writer like Guez de Balzac could seriously write in a letter to a friend that if he "were a police officer, [he] would drive back to domesticality all the women who wanted to write books," Marie de Gournay got into even greater trouble when she tried to assert herself as a scholar by publishing her *Remerciement au Roy* (Thanksgiving to the King). Because she had revised a poem written by Ronsard, *Harangue du Tres-Illustre et Tres-magnanime Prince François, Duc de Guise, aux Soldats de Mets, le jour de l'assault*, and used challenging editorial principles, she was accused of literary fraud and violently attacked in 1624, whereas she had merely intended to show the superiority of the sixteenth-century "Prince of Poets" by restoring his text. The controversy did not prevent her from having the first volume of her collected works published by Jean Libert in 1626. Because nobody understood the reference to Pindarus's eighth *Pythic*, line 95, which she had chosen as her title, *L'Ombre de la Damoiselle de Gournay* (The Shadow of the Damoiselle of Gournay), she changed it to *Les Advis ou les Presens de la Demoiselle de Gournay* in 1634. It contained everything she had written so far and a new autobiographical text, *Apologie pour celle qui escrit*, which shed light on her family history, personal choices, and the social circles in which she moved.

In 1629, she rented an apartment in the rue Saint-Honoré, not far from Conrart's building, where the first meetings to discuss the foundation of the French Academy took place. Marie de Gournay had an active role in the subsequent proceedings and, through the Abbé de Boisrobert, was introduced to Richelieu. Thanks to his recommendation and the small pension he granted her, she was able to publish her last edition of Montaigne's *Essais* in 1635. Although she appeared as a ridiculous figure in many of the plays satirizing the French Academy, which caricatured her ideas and bordered on character assassination, she spent the last years of her life working on a new edition of her collected works, *Les Advis ou les Presens de la Demoiselle de Gournay*, which was published in 1641. When she died, on July 13, 1645, she had indeed become "that extreme rarity in her time, a professional writer, not a princess or a great lady dabbling in literature" (Boase, 55).

MAJOR THEMES

Until recently, Marie de Gournay was mainly remembered and assessed as an editor of Montaigne's *Essais*, and it is true that she devoted much time and skill to make sure that the work of her "adopted father" was properly printed, understood, and promoted. Her association with Montaigne certainly helped her find a publisher for her first book, misleadingly entitled *Le Proumenoir de M. de Montaigne* and signed by his "adopted daughter." But it has also overshadowed the importance of her own contributions to French literature and criticism:

thousands of pages on education, poetry, philosophical issues as well as reflections on the art of translation, feminist pamphlets, and autobiographical texts, which have not been reprinted since 1641. Therefore one tends to forget that the "adopted daughter" is also "the mother of modern feminism," as Théodore Joran aptly stated in *La Trouée féministe*. Marie de Gournay's concern with "the ladies oppressed by the tyranny of men" appears as early as 1594, in the first edition of her *Proumenoir*. Considered by Paul Bonnefon as the "embryonic form of the psychological genre" (*Montaigne et ses amis*, 325), this short novel, based on the *Accidents of Love* in Plutarch and a sixteenth-century story by Claude de Taillemont, *Discours des Champs Faez, à l'honneur et exaltation des Dames* (1553), demonstrates "the pestilent disaster of depending on someone else," through the adventures of Alinda—the one who wanders—who betrays her father and her country to follow her lover, only to be abandoned and driven to suicide. The author portrays the heroine's tragic fate as the direct consequence of her lack of formal education and vibrantly defends the right of women to be taught the same intellectual skills as men. Again and again, in the long preface to the 1595 edition of the *Essais*, in her *Egalité des hommes et des femmes* (1622) and in *Grief des dames* (*The Complaint of the Ladies*, 1626), Marie de Gournay insists on education as the key to women's liberation. Herself a victim of prejudices against female scholars, she examines the roots and manifestations of sexism in society and literature and, manipulating the traditional arguments and rhetorical devices used to "prove" the inferiority of women, she counterattacks, makes her point, and wins her case. Her theories on the equality of men and women precede Poulain de la Barre's *De l'égalité des deux sexes* (Of the Equality of Both Sexes) by half a century, and her position on confession and repentance, as expressed in her *Advis à quelques gens d'Eglise* (Advice to Some Clerics), anticipates Pascal's thoughts on the subject in his *Lettres à un Provincial* by thirty years. The negative image of Marie de Gournay as a thinker lagging behind her time has to be replaced by that of a fighter for women's rights and a pioneer in the field of translation, linguistics, and poetic theory. She was aware of how bold she was to compete with the literary men of the beginning of the seventeenth century and cleverly protected herself by addressing the king on the subject of her translation of the *Aeneid* in 1619: "What temerity, Sir, a distaff battling a crosier and the illustrious crosier of a Bertaut, no less? . . . although it was reasonable to think that under such a brave and magnanimous King as Louis XIII, ladies would dare to act like Amazons."

At a time when an excess of classical rules threatened to clip the wings of creative expression, Marie de Gournay stood for the poetic value of metaphors and diminutives and the right for old words to live on. As a linguist, she understood the necessity of codifying certain aspects of the French language, and she gave her full support to the founding of the French Academy. But, as a literary critic, she made no secret of her preference for Ronsard's "true poetry" over Malherbe's "clear broth." In many ways, her own writings reflect her genuine love for words—for all words, as she humorously explains in her *Defence de la Poesie* (In Defense of Poetry), dedicated to Mme des Loges: "These doctors may very well try to show me that they will give me twelve words in which to say such or such a thing, without the one they pretend to condemn in order to take it away from me: I want fifteen of them and not to lose any. I feel very much like the little girl who cried out loud because she had lost her doll and who, when her mother came running to comfort her with another one, just as jolly, took it with both hands but started to cry again even more loudly, alleging that, had she not lost the first doll she would now have two." Marie de Gournay's style was profoundly affected by the fact that she learned how to read and write by comparing two languages, then fell in love with Montaigne's prose. Her own voice slowly emerged out of her unconditional admiration and early imitation of the Renaissance writers, as well as out of the scholarly rendering of ancient authors, which she practiced all her life through her numerous translations. "Vigor and exactness of expression" remained her first priorities, immediately followed by "grace and skill," as is clear in her autobiographical texts.

Marie de Gournay's major contribution to French literature may very well be the subtle art of self-portrait, which she undoubtedly learned from working so closely on and with Montaigne's *Essais*. She left us with three partial portraits of the artist as a woman. *La Copie de la Vie de la Damoiselle de Gournay, Peincture de moeurs*, and *Apologie pour celle qui escrit* are valuable historical documents on the condition of literary women in an era of transition between the Renaissance and the classical age. Experimenting with form, writing in defense of herself as a woman writer, confronting her own words with the words of others—including the *père d'alliance* on the question of the education of women—Marie de Gournay finally became "the subject of her book" and an inspiration for many more. At the very outset of her literary career, in her *Proumenoir*, she expressed her indignation against "whoever forbade women learning" and ironically added: "The common man says that in order for a woman to be chaste, she must not be that clever: truly, it is giving chastity too little credit to believe that only the blind can find it beautiful." Her plea in favor of the recognition of intellectual women by the society of her time became even more vehement in *L'Ombre*. In the 1641 edition of *Les Advis*, she still deplores the prevailing sexism she had previously denounced in her feminist pamphlets: "Is there today a more specific target for slanderers than the condition of those who love learning if they do not belong to the church or the law? In our epoch nothing is more stupid or ridiculous, next to poverty, than being an enlightened and learned man: except, of course, being an enlightened and learned *woman*, or simply aspiring, like me, to become one."

SURVEY OF CRITICISM

During her lifetime, Marie de Gournay was as highly praised for her writings by some of her contemporaries as she was severely criticized by others for her way of life and literary positions. She personally met or corresponded with numerous scholars of France, Holland, and Italy. Besides Montaigne, who wrote that "if youth can give promise, this soul will one day be capable of the noblest things," the Belgian humanist Justus Lipsius predicted that she would be "the real Thano," and Dominique Baudius, a sharp critic of Montaigne's work, called her "the tenth Muse." Her name is mentioned with admiration by Heinsius, the well-known philologer, by Julio Cesar Capacio in his *Illustrium mulierum et illustrium virorum elogia*, and by Anne Marie de Schurman in her correspondence. It appears in most of the biographical works and memoirs of the second half of the seventeenth century, such as Baudeau de Somaize's *Dictionnaire des Précieuses* (1660), Jean de la Forge's *Cercle des Femmes savantes* (1664), or Louis Moréri's *Grand Dictionnaire critique*. Episodes of her life are reported in Tallémant des Réaux's *Historiettes* and Abbé de Marolles's *Mémoires* (1657), among others. The first long article dealing with *la fille de Montaigne* (Montaigne's daughter) is part of Pierre Bayle's *Dictionnaire historique et critique* (1697). It suggests that "this lady was not so far wrong . . . and it would have been desirable that the most illustrious writers of that time had vigorously opposed the suppression of several words."

On the other hand, eighteenth-century critics generally misjudged the *littérarité* of Marie de Gournay's works. It started with Niceron, who stated in his *Mémoires* (1733) that "nothing can equal the praise she received during her lifetime . . . but her works are no longer read by anyone and have fallen into an oblivion from which they will never emerge." The abbé Goujet failed to understand the originality of Marie de Gournay's critical approaches and dismissed her as a "boring, detestable" poetess in his *Bibliothèque française* (1744). At the end of the century, M. L. Coupé simply repeated the clichés about her "idolatry of old words," although he came to the conclusion that "she had not only a wide range of knowledge but also a rare understanding" in his *Soirées littéraires* (1797).

In 1828, after a long eclipse, Marie de Gournay's theories on poetry attracted the attention of Sainte-Beuve, who profusely quoted her *Traité des Rimes* and deplored that her works were "too little known," when they should have been "read by every Academician." During the second half of the nineteenth century, a revived interest in biographical data prompted Paul de Musset to consecrate a long article to Marie de Gournay's life and autobiographical writings in his *Extravagants et Originaux* (1863). In 1859, Charles-Louis Livet had included Marie de Gournay in his *Précieux et Précieuses* and recognized that "her whole merit lay in her well-thought and well-expressed phrases." The following year, Léon Feugère's *Femmes poètes au XVIᵉ siècle* gave an accurate view of Marie de Gournay's "undeniable literary qualities" and remarkable achievement as a translator. At the same time, she benefited from the multiplication of studies on Montaigne, which could not ignore her role as the first editor of the *Essais*. Paul Stapfer devoted fifty pages of *La Famille et les amis de Montaigne* (1896) to studying the relationship between adopted father and daughter, and two years later Paul Bonnefon wrote two chapters on Marie de Gournay as an editor and a polemicist in *Montaigne et ses amis*. The main contribution to Marie de Gournay studies, however, was the publication of some of her letters to Justus Lipsius, Henri Dupuy, and Richelieu by J. F. Payen in the *Bulletin du Bibliophile* of 1860 and 1862.

In 1910, Mario Schiff published the first separate monograph on Marie de Gournay, entitled *La Fille d'alliance de Moutaige, Marie de Gournay* (The Adopted Daughter of Montaigne Marie de Gournay). Although flawed and biased because the author constantly uses derogatory vocabulary to refer to his subject and is convinced that "she owes her little immortality to Montaigne," it cannot be overlooked, since three major texts of Marie de Gournay are reprinted in the appendixes following the biographical essay. Apart from *Des diminutifs françois* (Of French Diminutives), which K. Nyrop included in his *Grammaire historique de la langue française*, first published in 1899, no other text by Marie de Gournay had been reprinted since 1641.

Joseph Dappen published a scholarly biography in 1927, *Marie de Jars de Gournay (1565–1645), die "Wahltochter" Montaignes*, but one had to wait until 1963 to have a reliable, well-documented, and ground-breaking study of Marie de Gournay's life and work: Marjorie Ilsley's *A Daughter of the Renaissance, Marie Le Jars de Gournay, her Life and Works*. Another important landmark is the publication by Anne Uildricks of *Les Idées littéraires de Mlle de Gournay* in 1962, because the author presents and comments on most of the philological treatises included in *Les Advis* with their variants, as well as the 1635 preface to Montaigne's *Essais* with the variants of 1595 and 1598.

The main problem with Marie de Gournay studies today is the lack of a complete and available edition of her works. Recently, partial efforts have been made by scholars such as Patricia Cholakian, who published a facsimile of the 1594 edition of the *Proumenoir* in 1985, or Elayne Dezon-Jones, who edited the feminist and autobiographical texts in *Marie de Gournay: Fragments d'un discours féminin* (1988). Eva Sartori's English translations of *De l'égalité* and *Grief des dames* have been published in *Allegorica*, and François Rigolot presents Marie de Gournay's preface to the 1595 edition of the *Essais* in the first issue of *Montaigne Studies* (1989). Of course, feminist critics are particularly interested in Marie de Gournay, as is any critic concerned with poetic theory, linguistics applied to literature, the philosophy of education, the art of translation, auto-biographical forms, and editorial practices. But no global interpretation can be risked until every reader is given access to the whole corpus of Marie de Gournay's work, now kept in the reserve room of the Bibliothèque Nationale in Paris. Because of the palimpsestic quality of her writing, Marie de Gournay, who revised every work of hers several times, is the perfect example of a writer to whom the principles of textual criticism can be successfully applied—successfully and carefully, since she herself warned her future editors in a note added at the end of her *Advis*: "If this book lives after me, I forbid anyone, whoever

he or she may be, to add or cut or change anything to its wording or its matter—
for fear of being considered by honorable people as violators of an innocent
tomb.''

BIBLIOGRAPHY

Works by Marie de Gournay

Le Proumenoir de M. de Montaigne, par sa fille d'alliance. Paris: Abel L'Angelier,
    1594.
Bienvenue de Monseigneur le Duc d'Anjou. Paris: Fleury Bourriquant, 1608.
*Adieu de l'Ame du Roy de France et de Navarre, Henry le Grand a la Royne, avec la
    Defence des pères Jesuites.* Paris: Fleury Bourriquant, 1610.
*Versions de quelques pièces de Virgile, Tacite et Saluste, avec l'Institution de Monseig-
    neur, frère unique du Roy*, par la Damoiselle de Gournay et M. Bertaut, éveque
    de Seez. Paris: Fleury Bourriquant, 1619.
Egalité des hommes et des femmes. A la Reyne, 1622.
Remerciement au Roy. 1624.

Collected Works

L'Ombre de la Damoiselle de Gournay. Oeuvre composée de Meslanges. Paris: Jean
    Libert, 1626.
Les Advis ou les Presens de la Demoiselle de Gournay. Paris: Toussainct Du-Bray, 1634.
Les Advis ou les Presens de la Demoiselle de Gournay. Paris: Jean Du-Bray, 1641.
    (Includes *Apologie pour celle qui escrit*).
Preface to Montaigne's *Essais.* Paris: Abel L'Angelier, 1595. Reprinted with revisions
    in the 1598, 1600, 1604, 1611, 1617, 1625, and 1635 editions of the *Essais.*

Modern Editions

Le Proumenoir de M. de Montaigne, par sa fille d'alliance. Preface by Patricia Cholakian.
    Scholar's Facsimile Reprints. New York: Delmar, 1985.
Preface to the 1595 edition of Montaigne's *Essais*, with an introduction by François
    Rigolot. *Montaigne Studies* 1 (1989).

Translations of Marie de Gournay

''Of the Equality of Men and Women'' and ''The Complaint of the Ladies.'' Trans. Eva
    M. Sartori. *Allegorica* 9 (Winter 1987): 135–64.

Studies of Marie de Gournay

Boase, Alan. *The Fortunes of Montaigne: A History of the Essay in France (1580–1669).*
    London: Methuen, 1935 (chapters 4–5).

Bonnefon, Paul. *Montaigne et ses amis*. Paris: Armand Colin. 1898 (Vol. 2, chapters 1–2).

———. "Une Supercherie de Mlle de Gournay." *Revue d'Histoire littéraire de la France* 3 (1896): 71–89.

Cauchie, Maurice. "Nicole Jamin est-elle la fille d'Amadis Jamin?" *Revue des Bibliothèques* (1922): 289–93.

Dappen, Joseph. *Marie le Jars de Gournay (1565–1645), die "Wahltochter" Montaignes*. Düsseldorf: J. Schwann, 1927.

Dezon-Jones, Elayne. *Marie de Gournay: Fragments d'un discours féminin*. Paris: Corti, 1988.

———. "Marie de Gournay: le je/u/ palimpseste." *L'Esprit Créateur* 23 (Summer 1983): 26–36.

Feugère, Léon. *Les Femmes poètes au XVIᵉ siècle*. Paris: Didier, 1853.

Holmes, Peggy P. "Marie de Gournay's Defense of Baroque Imagery." *French Studies* (April 1954): 122–31.

Ilsley, Marjorie. *A Daughter of the Renaissance, Marie le Jars de Gournay, her Life and Works*. The Hague: Mouton, 1963.

Joran, Théodore. *Les Féministes avant le féminisme*. Paris: A. Savaète, 1910.

Livet, Charles. *Précieux et précieuses, caractères et moeurs littéraires au XVIIIᵉ siècle*. Paris, 1859.

Nicolai, Alexandre. *Les Belles Amies de Montaigne*. Paris: Editions Dumas, 1950.

Payen, Dr. J. F. "Note bibliographique sur les diverses éditions du *Proumenoir de M. de Montaigne*." *Bulletin du Bibliophile* (1860): 1285–87.

———. "Recherches sur Michel de Montaigne: correspondence relative à sa mort." *Bulletin du Bibliophile* (1862): 1291–1311.

Schiff, Mario. *La Fille d'alliance de Montaigne, Marie de Gournay*. Paris: Champion, 1910.

Séché, Léon. *Les Muses françaises*. Paris: Mercure de France, 1908.

Stanton, Domna. "Women as Object and Subject of Exchange: Marie de Gournay's *Le Proumenoir*." *L'Esprit Créateur* 23 (Summer 1983): 9–25.

Stapfer, Paul. *La Famille et les amis de Montaigne*. Paris: Hachette, 1896 (chapter 6).

Uildricks, Anne. *Les Idées littéraires de Mlle de Gournay*. Groningen, 1962.

FRANÇOISE D'ISSEMBOURG D'HAPPONCOURT DE GRAFFIGNY (1695–1758)

Judith Curtis

BIOGRAPHY

Françoise d'Issembourg Du Buisson d'Happoncourt was born in 1695 into a family of modest but respectable nobility in what was then the independent duchy of Lorraine. In 1712 she married François Huguet de Graffigny, a minor figure at the ducal court. The marriage was plagued by money problems and by episodes of violence so frightening that on one occasion the young husband was arrested and confined. At the time of his death in 1725 the couple had been separated for seven years; their three children had died in infancy. By the early 1730s, under the protection of Madame, duchess then regent of Lorraine, Françoise de Graffigny was seeing happier days at the court in Lunéville. During this time she made her first attempts at writing, mostly in play or dialogue forms, in collaboration with a group of poets that included Jean-François de Saint-Lambert and François-Antoine Devaux. Presumably this was when, reading and discussing the great authors and thinkers of the day, she began to make up for the inadequacies of the education then commonly given to girls, a topic she would later develop in her novel. She was also engaged in a liaison with a young cavalry officer, Léopold Desmarest, who was probably the only man she ever deeply loved.

Upon the conclusion of the Treaty of Vienna in 1736, the ducal court began to break up. This was the turning point in Graffigny's life. For some time she was forced to depend on the hospitality of various acquaintances, not all of them congenial. The experience left a little more iron in the soul and produced the first major set of letters, addressed to the loyal Devaux back in Lunéville. In the winter of 1738–1739 she was delighted to be the guest of Voltaire and Mme Du Châtelet at Cirey; however, the letters sent from there (prized by later generations for what they reveal of the great man's private life) were the cause of distressing scenes. Accused by Du Châtelet of literary espionage, Graffigny fled to Paris, where she would spend her remaining twenty years.

The Paris years, chronicled in minute detail in the continuing exchange with Devaux, began badly in a succession of temporary lodgings and not very suitable arrangements. Lonely and uprooted, Graffigny also had to contend with unending financial difficulties. Desmarest was more and more erratic in his attentions, and the affair was finally broken off. But by 1743, the year of the break, she had her own house and a wide circle of friends, including the particular intimates of the comte de Caylus, elegant man of letters, and Jeanne-Françoise Quinault, a retired actress. She rubbed shoulders with popular authors and developed contacts with influential men, such as Caylus and the novelist-historian Charles Duclos, whose aid would be invaluable when it later came to getting her own works published or staged. She completed the period of her literary apprenticeship by revising a play-text of Devaux's and by working up two short tales, from outlines provided for her, for inclusion in collections put together by the Caylus group. "La Nouvelle espagnole" (The Spanish Novella, subtitled "A Bad Example Produces as Many Virtues as Vices) appeared in the *Recueil de ces messieurs* (The Gentlemen's Collection), and "La Princesse Azerolle," a fairy story, was published in *Cinq Contes de fées* (Five Fairy Tales, attributed to Caylus), both in 1745.

The experience of writing fiction was to lead to a new project. Over the next two years she created the *Lettres d'une Péruvienne* (*Letters Written by a Peruvian Princess*), demonstrating the breadth of her awareness of contemporary thought, and writing Desmarest out of her life in the character of the faithless lover. The work appeared anonymously, but the author was soon known and widely praised. This kind of venture was unusual enough for a woman of her position, but Graffigny liked the idea of "being a man right under people's noses" (see Showalter, "A Woman of Letters," 97) and went on to the harder but more lucrative enterprise of getting a play produced. In 1750 *Cénie* had a phenomenal first run of twenty-five performances at the Théâtre Français and made Graffigny one of the most admired writers of the age. In her parlor, which had always been open to an assortment of authors, "artistes," and expatriate Lorrainers, she received such philosophers and public figures as Helvétius, Choiseul, and Turgot.

Fame, while gratifying, did not solve all the money problems, and robbed her of time. She did win a pension from the Austrian imperial family and wrote morally improving plays for the children of Maria Theresa. Her final eight years were creative (she added important new material for a second edition of the novel—material that has apparently not found its way into any English translation), but they were largely taken up with the needs of friends, relatives, and the many who solicited her aid or influence in a variety of enterprises. Her last play, *La Fille d'Aristide* (The Daughter of Aristides), was a decided failure; it was spoiled, reportedly, by the bad judgment of her many advisors. The already precarious state of her health—much affected, she always said, by her nerves—was not improved by critical jibes. She died in December 1758.

MAJOR THEMES

This study will concentrate on Mme de Graffigny's main fictional and dramatic works. Her vast correspondence, now being edited for the first time, is an invaluable but as yet only partially explored mine of supporting material. Her two society pieces, "La Nouvelle espagnole" and the fairy tale "Azerolle," are interesting chiefly as examples of the story teller's tentative first steps. We may note, before examining the *Lettres d'une Péruvienne*, that the "Nouvelle espagnole" already contains a heroine who has developed "that strength of character (*fermeté d'âme*) which is as neglected in women's upbringing as it is essential to their conduct" as well as "a liking for the accomplishments of the mind (*les belles connaissances*), which women acquire only rarely, and always too late."

In outline, the *Lettres d'une Péruvienne* seem to offer a standard sentimental letter-plot with some exotic overtones. Zilia, destined for marriage with the young Inca ruler, is abducted from the Temple of the Sun during the conquest of Peru. Rescued from her Spanish captors by a Frenchman of impeccable gallantry, she ends her journey in eighteenth-century France (an anachronism of which the author was fully aware). Thus separated from her beloved Aza, almost from the moment of her capture she composes a series of impassioned letters, using first her *quipus* (knotted cords used by the Incas as a device for keeping records), then pen and ink, once she has acquired a knowledge both of French and of writing. When Aza is finally located, he is about to marry another. Zilia, brought close to death by this betrayal, recovers; but in a surprise ending she refuses to marry the Frenchman who has been her mentor. The love story is the novel's framework and its heart: even at the end, Zilia makes it clear that to renounce her devotion to Aza would be to abandon her own integrity. However, the use Graffigny makes of this framework is not conventional.

Zilia is of course also that familiar device of Enlightenment literature, the naive observer. Her discovery of an unfamiliar world reflects the Sensationalist thought of the period, with its emphasis on the senses as our primary stimulus and source of knowledge; and her introduction to French society permits the author to point up its inconsistencies, intolerance, and shallowness. In particular, Graffigny denounces a legal and social system that lets men exercise abusive power with impunity and that, in part through convent education, relegates women to an institutionalized state of moral and intellectual inferiority. (Janet Altman, in her article on Graffigny's epistemology, has shown how Europe's conquest and appropriation of Peruvian culture may be seen as a metaphor for female experience, just as the relativistic point of view that shapes Zilia's commentary challenges "patriarchal Europe's ethnocentric perspective" [175]). But Graffigny's juxtaposition of a European and a "native" culture is more subtle and balanced than that of many of her contemporaries. Zilia is not simply a child of nature, a "noble savage": her Inca heritage and education have given her a fortitude, an awakened appetite for learning, and, above all, a sense of self-respect beyond the understanding of the Frenchwomen she meets. On the other hand, French culture is not to be dismissed as the merely vile and corrupting counterpoint to New World civilization. For example, it is thanks to European technology—coach travel—that Zilia, liberated from her temple, first appreciates the beauties of nature; and upon mastering her new language, this Enlightenment heroine discovers with delight the wealth of ideas waiting to be explored in her private library.

To use traditional critical categories, the novel is on the one hand "sentimental," on the other "philosophical," a mingling of genres that has made some readers uneasy. However, the two strands are seen to be tightly and logically interwoven in the more recent interpretation of the work as a kind of *bildungsroman*, which places the heroine, not the contrast of cultures, securely at its center, and highlights the themes of learning, experience, and change. Even more interesting is the story's emphasis on communication and self-expression—in fact, as Nancy K. Miller argues (in "The Knot, the Letter and the Book"), on the whole question of female authorship, of a woman "coming to writing." Deprived of her voice when she exhausts the resources of her *quipus*, and surrounded by speakers of an unknown tongue, Zilia reaches the outer limits of despair. Learning the language of her new country and the technique of recording her thoughts on paper releases in her an explosion of energy and joy that is a reminder of Graffigny's own more modest remarks to Devaux about the satisfactions to be had from shaping a paragraph or finding the words for a deeply felt experience.

Seen in this light, the structure of the novel is not dysphoric, and the ending, with its refusal of the predictable, ceases to be a puzzle. Passing through the pain of exile and loss, as well as through the finishing school of European culture, Zilia emerges with the strength and knowledge needed to adopt an unconventional course. Nor should it come as a surprise, if we are aware of the author's own circumstances, that she endows her heroine not only with wealth, independence, and a splendid country house, but also with a preference for the life of the mind and the tranquil pleasures of friendship. Graffigny's is not the only example in the period of a plot that sidesteps the possibilities both of death and of marriage for the heroine, but it is one of the first and most striking. It can comfortably be termed, on several grounds, feminist in its conception.

Less accessible to us today, more marked by the tastes of the time, are the situations elaborated in *Cénie*, a play strongly reminiscent of Philippe Destouches and Pierre Claude Nivelle de La Chaussée. Graffigny had learned some practical lessons from her attempts to get Devaux's comedy performed and was inclined to rely on expert advice when it came to refining her tactics. *Cénie* is in one respect at least a "woman's work": unlike most "serious" comedies of the period, it was written in prose, the choice of verse being regarded as pretentious in a woman writer, as Mlle Quinault pointed out. Like the *Lettres* and even more like *La Fille d'Aristide*, it is the story of a virtuous young woman who suffers tribulations so cruel and undeserved that only her exceptional purity of soul enables her to endure until circumstances, which she does not control, change for the better. Cénie, raised by a loving and well-to-do father, is shown to be merely the daughter of her own governess. Her pain and humiliation finally end with the return of her true father; both women are restored to their proper rank, and Cénie is able to marry her heart's choice. The plot turns on a stunning series of coincidences and creates effects both larger and more subtle than those that appeal to modern audiences. At the same time, it is hard to imagine a more tidy parable about the situation of both men and women within the complex system of economic, social, and moral constraints that informed behavior in Graffigny's France: from Cénie's dead "mother," who is found to have faked motherhood in order to fix the affections of a wealthy husband, to the real parents, stripped of fortune and social standing by a disastrous "affair of honor." The heroine herself is first bound to silence by the code relentlessly enjoined on her by her governess-mother, then forced by events into speech which painfully violates her sense of modesty and duty. The insistence in *Cénie* on silence and flight makes an interesting point of comparison with Zilia's urgent need to communicate, and the playwright clearly maneuvers the spectator into wanting Cénie to find her voice, in defiance of the code.

In *La Fille d'Aristide* the main character is similarly the victim of deceit and misrepresentation and even more obviously sacrifices herself to the interests of an amiable but weak surrogate father (selling herself into bondage in order to pay off a fine). This not very Attic comedy of sentiment, set in ancient Greece, is weighed down by a sententious text in which money matters—squandered estates, the agony of debt, the horror of fiscal irresponsibility—are the only element likely to wring the heart. "Poor!" cries the heroine, "what a word!" (II, 4). As in Graffigny's other works, the central figures tend to be simplified so as to exemplify some salient virtue or vice, while the supporting characters are more realistically shaded; and there is an ironic suggestion that, in the way of the world, people of apparently sound moral fiber cause as much heartache and disorder as do the "bad." The play has its value for those interested in reconstructing Graffigny's literary career, as it hints at the character of some of the unknown texts she composed in Lorraine or for the court in Vienna, texts with such titles as *L'Honnête Homme* (The Honest Man or The Gentleman) and *Le Temple de la Vertu* (The Temple of Virtue).

SURVEY OF CRITICISM

If *La Fille d'Aristide* was judged to be a failure, eighteenth-century critics were warm in their overall assessment of the *Lettres d'une Péruvienne* and *Cénie*. Fréron and La Porte, the *Mercure* and the *Mémoires de Trévoux* praised Graffigny's elegant style, delicacy of feeling, and deft portrayal of manners. With *Cénie* in particular they could find no fault, and it came to be seen as a worthy forerunner of the new type of drama promoted by Diderot. *Cénie* was revived and performed a further forty times by 1762.

In the case of the novel, some reservations were expressed about the verisimilitude of certain important details, but what chiefly troubled the otherwise enchanted readers of the *Lettres d'une Péruvienne* was its ending. Turgot, Graffigny's friend, wrote a long commentary (reproduced in Nicoletti's edition of the novel) in which he took exception to the heroine's "female" preeminence in loyalty and called upon the author to write in not only a marriage between Zilia and Aza but a sequel offering examples of civic and domestic virtue. Sequels were readily supplied by other writers. Hugary de Lamarche-Courmont came up with Aza's "missing" letters (*Lettres d'Aza*, 1749). Mme Morel de Vindé in 1797 provided a continuation in which Zilia marries not Aza but her French suitor. The "corrected" ending became the rule in translations of the text as well; but the sheer number of repeat editions and translations (well over seventy by 1835) demonstrates the novel's sturdy popularity. The nature of the response makes it clear, however, that the book was being read purely as sentimental fiction, its philosophical or feminist content becoming ever less comprehensible with the passage of time.

Graffigny's reputation held up and Zilia's story continued to be read well into the nineteenth century. Puymaigre in 1848 ("Mme de Graffigny" in *Poètes et romanciers de la Lorraine* [Metz], 97–112) was still able to write a sympathetic evaluation of the novel's somewhat faded charm, despite the "clumsiness" of its conclusion. But in 1850 Sainte-Beuve indicated the decline in her fortunes and legitimized a century of condescension and neglect by his much-quoted "reassurance" to his readers that he was not about to discuss either the novel or the play (*Causeries de lundi*, June 17, 1850). He established as Graffigny's only claim to our attention her links with men like Turgot and Voltaire. This shift in emphasis had been under way since the appearance in 1820, in the *Vie privée de Voltaire et de Mme du Châtelet* (Paris: Treuttel et Wurtz), of the letters written at Cirey in 1738–1739.

In the second half of the century only the Cirey letters and, in Lorraine, a certain interest in homegrown celebrities kept Graffigny's name alive. In 1871 the anti-republican Louis Etienne launched a surprising attack on the so-called socialist content of the *Lettres d'une Péruvienne* and fostered, by his comparisons with Rousseau, the tendency to define Graffigny as a pre-Romantic, possessed of abundant sensibility but very little understanding of the ideas in which she dabbled. This was essentially the tack taken by Noël in 1913, in the first major study of her life and works. Noël attempted a full-length portrait, but his account contains many errors. He did not have access to the full correspondence, and he was unable to escape either the prevailing view of his subject or his own dismay at her flouting of strict religious and moral principles. The title he chose is a summary of his attitude: Graffigny was "a forgotten primitive of the tenderhearted school," a "poor" creature who wrote superficial and second-rate literature. Noël's tone set that of other studies, an example being the article by Gabriel Aubray, who found in Graffigny's works only "insipid nonsense" (*fadaises*), "dreary pleasure" (*plaisir grisâtre*), and "gentle boredom" (*doux en-*

nui). In 1965 Vivienne Mylne observed that if the *Peruvian Letters* are barely mentioned in histories of literature, it is "with good reason" (*The Eighteenth-Century French Novel* [Manchester University Press], 148). Two years later it was still possible to read that Graffigny's claim to fame was the fact that Voltaire found her charming (Fleuriot de Langle, "Une Amie de Voltaire . . . ," *Revue générale belge* 4 [April 1967]: 67–76). Even Susan Lee Carrell, in 1982, declares that the main if not the only interest in Graffigny's "highly undistinguished" novel must be for the historian (*Le Soliloque de la passion féminine* . . . [Tübingen: Gunter Narr], 92).

In the meantime, academic criticism had begun to take an objective look at the place of the *Lettres* in the pattern of their time. At widely spaced intervals such articles as those by Delchef (1910), Arciniegas (1964), and Cipriani (1985) compared the work with others in the currents of exoticism, primitivism, or the literature of exile. In 1964 English Showalter devoted his doctoral thesis to the *Lettres* ("An Eighteenth-Century Bestseller . . . ," Yale University). This would be followed by Pascale Dewey's on Mme de *Tencin and Mme de Graffigny (Rice University, 1976); and throughout the sixties and seventies there was a steady revival of interest. Gianni Nicoletti prepared a critical edition. Bray and Landy-Houillon included the work in their 1983 collection of epistolary novels. (Interestingly, while response has become more sympathetic and more informed, male critics have tended to see the story's conclusion as dark or at best ambiguous, whereas most female readers offer a more positive interpretation.)

In the mid- and late 1980s, all accepted wisdom about the *Lettres* was cogently challenged. A work so decidedly excluded from the canon, judged unreadable because it did not conform to accepted models (see Nancy K. Miller's "Men's Reading . . . "), with the application not only of feminist and deconstructionist approaches but of new attitudes in a broader sense has quite dramatically found a new audience. Clifton Cherpack's remarks, for instance, invite us to focus on the observing, awakening mind of the narrator and to look beyond the traditional comparisons of the work with the *Lettres persanes* (Montesquieu's *Persian Letters*) and the *Lettres portugaises* (Guilleragues's *Letters of a Portuguese Nun*), or the repeated attempts to define its genre, which have largely proved to be critical dead ends. As Janet Whatley points out, Graffigny, by her title and by her text, asked to be placed alongside "mainstream Enlightenment discourse," but the realization was long overdue that, rather than trying to say the same things in a less successful way, she might have been presenting an original, specifically a woman's, point of view.

Three contributors to the recent movement in Graffigny criticism call for particular mention. English Showalter has shed light on every aspect of her literary career, laying the groundwork for an edition of her complete correspondence and for the current reassessment. Janet Altman's studies integrate the "ethnic" and feminist aspects of the novel and complement Nancy Miller's analysis of it as protest literature, the reflection of "a woman intellectual [writing] in a man's Enlightenment" (see "The Knot . . . ," 131). If there is a risk in the tendency of the late 1980s to see in the *Lettres* some rather complex and perhaps anachronistic narrative strategies, the appearance of the correspondence should enable criticism to strike a balance between the weight that should be given to literary models (whether imitated or subverted) and the writer's own experience and aspirations.

The novel has thus regained a good deal of its lost prestige and is making its way as a textbook in at least a few college courses on eighteenth-century fiction (see Gelfand and Switten). Graffigny's dramatic works, on the other hand, have not yet been accorded more than a few lines in the literary histories. It remains to be seen whether a revival of interest in the author will prompt a rereading of her plays, or indeed an examination of the smaller works to which we still have access.

BIBLIOGRAPHY

Works by Mme de Graffigny

Héraclite, prétendu sage. MS. Yale University, Graffigny Papers, LXXIX.
La Réunion du bon sens et de l'esprit. MS. Yale University, Graffigny Papers, LXXIX.
"La Nouvelle espagnole." *Recueil de ces messieurs.* [Caylus, Anne-Claude-Philippe, comte de, et al.] Amsterdam [Paris], 1745.
"La Princesse Azerolle." *Cinq Contes de fées.* [Caylus, Anne-Claude-Philippe, comte de.] N.p., 1745.
Lettres d'une Péruvienne. A Peine [Paris, 1747].
Cénie. Paris, 1750.
Lettres d'une Péruvienne. Nouvelle Edition, Augmentée de plusieurs Lettres. . . 2 vols. Paris, 1752.
La Fille d'Aristide. Paris, 1759.
Oeuvres posthumes de Mme de Grafigny contenant Ziman et Zenise suivi de Phaza, comédies en un acte en prose. Amsterdam and Paris, 1770.
Lettres de Madame de Graffigny, suivies de celles de Mmes de Staal. . . Ed. E. Asse. Paris, 1879.
Les Saturnales. See English Showalter, "Madame de Graffigny and Rousseau: Between the Two Discours." *Studies on Voltaire and the Eighteenth Century* 175 (1978): 1–191.

Modern Editions

Correspondance de Madame de Graffigny. Ed. J. A. Dainard, English Showalter, et al. 2 vols. to date. Oxford: Voltaire Foundation, 1985-

Translations of Mme de Graffigny

Letters Written by a Peruvian Princess. London, 1748. New York: Garland, 1974.
Cenia or, The Suppos'd Daughter. London, 1752.

Studies of Mme de Graffigny

Altman, Janet Gurkin. "Graffigny's Epistemology and the Emergence of Third-World Ideology." In *Writing the Female Voice: Essays on Epistolary Literature*. Ed. Elizabeth C. Goldsmith. Boston: Northeastern University Press, 1989. 172–202.

————. "Making Room for 'Peru': Graffigny's Novel Reconsidered." In *Dilemmes du roman*. Ed. Joan DeJean, Catherine Lafarge, Philip R. Stewart, et al. Stanford, Calif.: Anma Libri, 1989.

Arciniegas, German. "Le Bon Sauvage." *Revue de Paris* 71 (December 1964): 85–90.

Aubray, G. "Mme de Grafigny." *Le Correspondant* 253 (1913): 958–76.

Bray, Bernard, and Isabelle Landy-Houillon, eds. *"Lettres portugaises," "Lettres d'une Péruvienne" et autres romans d'amour par lettres*. Paris: Garnier-Flammarion, 1983.

Cameron, C. Bruce. "Love: The Lightning Passion in *Les Lettres Péruviennes* of Madame de Graffigny." *Encyclia* 56 (1979): 39–45.

Carrell, Susan Lee. *Le Soliloque de la passion féminine*. Tübingen: Gunter Narr, 1982.

Cherpack, Clifton. *Logos in Mythos: Ideas in Early French Narrative*. Lexington, Ky.: French Forum, 1983. 147–51.

Cipriani, Fernando. "Mme de Grafigny: Dalle *Lettres de Cirey* alle *Lettres d'une Péruvienne*." *Rivista di Letteratura moderne e comparate* 33 (1980): 165–86.

————. "Primitivismo e civiltà nelle *Lettres d'une Péruvienne* di Mme de Grafigny e nei *Mémoires* di Jamerey-Duval." *Esperienze letterarie* 10 (1985): 163–80.

Delchef, Marguerite. "Les Oeuvres de Mme de Graffigny." In *Mélanges de philologie romane et d'histoire offerts à M. Maurice Wilmotte*. 2 vols. Paris: Champion, 1910. 1: 153–64.

Dewey, Pascale. *Mesdames de Tencin et de Graffigny, deux romancières oubliées des coeurs sensibles*. Diss. Rice University, 1976.

Etienne, Louis. "Un Roman socialiste d'autrefois." *Revue des Deux Mondes* 94 (July 15, 1871): 454–64.

Fréron, Elie-Catherine. *Lettres sur quelques écrits de ce tems*. 13 vols. Paris, 1749–54. (See 1: 80–102 on *Lettres d'une Péruvienne* and 4: 99–112 on *Cénie*.)

Gelfand, Elissa, and Margaret Switten. "Gender and the Rise of the Novel." *French Review* 61 (February 1988): 443–53.

Grimm, Frédéric-Melchior, et al. *Correspondence littéraire, philosophique et critique*. 16 vols. Paris, 1877–82. (See 3: 501–8 on *La Fille d'Aristide*.)

Hogsett, Alice Charlotte. "Graffigny and Riccoboni on the Language of the Woman Writer." In *Eighteenth-Century Women and the Arts*. Ed. Frederick M. Keener and Susan E. Lorsch. Westport, Conn.: Greenwood Press, 1988. 119–27.

[Lafond de Saint-Yenne.] "Lettre sur Cénie." *Le Mercure*, January 1751, 134–49.

La Porte, Joseph de. *Observations sur la littérature moderne*. 9 vols. Paris, 1749–52. (See 1: 33–54 on *Lettres d'une Péruvienne* and 3: 145–80 on *Cénie*.)

"Lettre au P.B.J. sur la Pièce en cinq Actes intitulée *Cénie*." *Mémoires de Trévoux*, January 1751, 161–76.

MacArthur, Elizabeth J. "Devious Narratives: Refusal of Closure in Two Eighteenth-Century Epistolary Novels." *Eighteenth-Century Studies* 21 (Fall 1987): 1–20.

Mangeot, G. "Une Biographie de Mme de Graffigny." *Le Pays Lorrain* 11 (1914–1919): 65–77, 145–53.

Miller, Nancy K. "The Knot, the Letter, and the Book: Graffigny's *Peruvian Letters*." In *Subject to Change: Reading Feminist Writing*. New York: Columbia University Press, 1988. 125–61.

———. "Men's Reading, Women's Writing: Gender and the Rise of the Novel." *Yale French Studies* 75 (September 1988): 40–55.

Mylne, Vivienne. *The Eighteenth-Century French Novel*. Manchester: Manchester University Press, 1965.

Nicoletti, Gianni, ed. *Lettres d'une Péruvienne*, by Mme de Graffigny. Bari: Adriatica, 1967.

Noël, Georges. *Une Primitive oubliée de l'école des coeurs sensibles: Mme de Graffigny (1695–1758)*. Paris: Plon-Nourrit, 1913.

Showalter, English. *An Eighteenth-Century Bestseller*. Diss. Yale University, 1964.

———. "Authorial Self-Consciousness in the Familiar Letter: The Case of Madame de Graffigny." *Yale French Studies* 71 (1986): 113–30.

———. "The Beginnings of Madame de Graffigny's Literary Career: A Study in the Social History of Literature." In *Essays on the Age of Enlightenment in Honor of Ira O. Wade*. Ed. Jean Macary. Geneva: Droz, 1977. 293–304.

———. "Les *Lettres d'une Péruvienne*: composition, publication, suites." *Archives et Bibliothèques de Belgique* 54, no. 1–4 (1983): 14–28.

———. "A Woman of Letters in the French Enlightenment: Madame de Graffigny." *British Journal for Eighteenth-Century Studies* 1 (1978): 89–104.

———. "Writing Off the Stage: Women Authors and Eighteenth-Century Theater." *Yale French Studies* 75 (September 1988): 95–111.

Smith, D. W. "Les Correspondances d'Helvetius et de Madame de Graffigny." *Studies in Voltaire and the Eighteenth-Century* 265 (1989): 1767–71.

Undank, Jack. "Grafigny's Room of Her Own." *French Forum* 13 (September 1988): 297–318.

Vierge du soleil/Fille des Lumières: La Péruvienne de Mme de Graffigny et ses suites. Travaux du Groupe d'Etude du XVIIIᵉ siècle, Université de Strasbourg II 5. Presses Universitaires de Strasbourg, 1989.

Whatley, Janet. "The Eighteenth-Century Canon: Works Lost and Found." *French Review* 61 (February 1988): 414–20.

BENOÎTE GROULT
(1920–   )

Nicole Fouletier-Smith

BIOGRAPHY

Benoîte Groult was born in Paris in 1920 to André and Nicole Groult. Her father was a successful interior designer. Her mother was a fashion designer who created her own fashion house and was recognized along with her celebrated brother, the designer Jean Poiret, as a master of the Art Deco fashion. The Groult family was prominent in Paris and entertained such famous contemporaries as Jean Cocteau, Marcel Jouhandeau, and Marie Laurencin. Of all the guests, Benoîte Groult and her younger sister Flora knew Marie Laurencin best. Benoîte Groult often speaks of the great friendship her mother had for Marie Laurencin, a relationship she even refers to at times as a "love affair."

Nicole Groult took a strong interest in her daughters' education, wanting them to become all they could be and more particularly what she wanted them to be: accomplished wives of successful men. To this end she spared no effort and monitored closely her daughters' clothes and social life. She required her daughters to keep journals, even during vacation trips, and to read them aloud every night to both parents, who acted as critics. Such an exercise was later to bear fruit, but at the time Benoîte resented her mother's tight control and constant prodding.

The two sisters had a long and protected adolescence, as did many daughters of the Parisian bourgeoisie of this era. Summer vacation was spent at their grandmother's estate in Brittany, where Benoîte first fell in love with the world of nature, both the land and the sea. As a student Benoîte, who was the more intellectual of the two sisters, did well at the Institution Sainte-Clotilde and the Lycée Victor Duruy. Flora was more of a visual artist, and she went on to art school while Benoîte studied Latin and Greek at the Sorbonne during World War II. It is interesting to note that during this troubled period both Benoîte and her mother exhibited the same kind of courageous stubbornness: Nicole Groult kept her fashion house going and Benoîte kept preparing for her exams despite delays and changes in schedule imposed by the war and the German occupation. She also found a job teaching English in a Catholic private school, the Cours Bossuet, where, in addition, she tutored students in Latin.

So life went on pretty much as normal for the Groult household in occupied Paris, in spite of the lack of heat and difficulties in obtaining food. Nicole Groult's efforts were still directed toward helping her daughters find husbands, since she believed that a woman became a worthy human being only through marriage. However, Benoîte surprised her mother by choosing her husband herself: at the age of twenty-four she married a medical student. When her husband died eight months later from tuberculosis, she was totally grief-stricken and went into seclusion in her beloved Brittany. Upon her return to Paris, she refused to move back home. By then the war was almost over; the Americans had landed in Normandy, and many were stationed in Paris. She volunteered to help the American Red Cross. Her knowledge of English landed her a hostess job at the Rainbow Club, one of the many organizations designed to help the American servicemen during their stay in the capital.

Although her American friends were generous with gifts, mostly gifts of food, Benoîte experienced some serious financial difficulties. She was relieved to find a better-paying job than teaching, and she became a journalist for the French national radio, where her duties included reporting and conducting interviews. She also remarried, too hastily, she concedes, and had two daughters, Blandine and Lison de Caunes. Her journalist husband expected her to produce a son, which she did not succeed in doing, and he forbade her to keep a journal because he did not consider writing a worthwhile activity for a mother. She recalls that he even tore up her notebooks. This marriage was short-lived, ending in divorce after four years.

While preparing a news program for the French national radio, Benôite met and in 1951 married Paul Guimard, a journalist and novelist, with whom she had another daughter, Constance, and to whom she is still married.

In 1959 she published a French translation of several of Dorothy Parker's short stories (selected from *Laments for the Living* and *After Such Pleasures*) with the title *Comme ils sont*, the first work to appear under her own name. Her husband encouraged her to start writing seriously and offered to collaborate with her on a book for which he suggested the title *Le Journal à quatre mains* (Journal Written with Four Hands). After a few unsuccessful tries, Benoîte turned to her sister Flora and together they produced *Le Journal à quatre mains*, which was published in 1962.

In collaborating on their works, each author was completely responsible for the chapters she contributed. In order to write the *Journal à quatre mains* each sister used pages of her own personal journals, written many years earlier at the request of their mother. Often the same events are seen from different perspectives; at times one journal explains the events mentioned by the other. The structure of alternating chapters, first Benoîte's, then Flora's, is one that allows each author much freedom. For Benoîte, writing the *Journal à quatre mains* was an exhilarating experience. The book was written with much ease and enthusiasm, and its success inspired the sisters to publish two more novels together, *Le Féminin pluriel* (The Feminine Plural) in 1965 and *Il était deux fois* (Twice upon a Time) in 1968. In *Il était deux fois*, phone conversations and letters written by the two friends become part of the novel. However, no matter how successfully this technique of alternating chapters is used, it tends to become repetitive. This must be why in their children's book, *Histoire de Fidèle* (Story of Fidèle), published in 1976, Benoîte wrote the text while Flora did the illustrations, in what is therefore a completely different form of collaboration.

In 1980, however, they tried another collaborative venture with a collection of short stories, *Des Nouvelles de la famille* (News from the Family), a title containing a pun on *nouvelles*, which means "news" and "short stories." The collection also includes pieces by both husbands, Paul Guimard and Bernard Ledwidge, and Benoîte's two older daughters, Blandine and Lison de Caunes.

When Flora married a diplomat and moved away, the sisters decided that it was time to pursue separate writing careers. In 1972, Benoîte published the first novel she had written alone, *La Part des choses* (Making Allowances), which was moderately successful. But for her second solo venture she wanted to be involved with something other than a novel, something that she calls *un je-ne-sais-quoi* (an I don't know what), *un fourre-tout* (a catch-all) that would reflect her many concerns, which she believed were shared by other women. They included the family, marriage, relationships, the environment, and women's newly acquired right to speak up. The result was the 1975 *Ainsi soit-elle*, part essay and part pamphlet, which was an instant success. The title is a feminist parody of the formula *ainsi soit-il* (French for "amen" or "so be it") and could be loosely translated as "let her be." Sometimes hyperbolically called the "Bible" of the French feminists, the book appealed in fact to a much wider spectrum of people. Its author became a celebrity. She gave interviews, traveled abroad to lecture, prefaced other women's books, and became a member of the jury for the coveted literary prize, the Prix Fémina. In January 1978 Groult and Claude Servan-Schreiber cofounded their own magazine, *F-Magazine*.

Groult, who has never been a member of the French Women's Liberation Movement (MLF), considers herself a true feminist, but is not and refuses to be called a "man hater." In fact, she believes that some men have played an important role in the rise of feminism. In 1978, she published an essay, *Le Féminisme au masculin* (Feminism in the Masculine Mode), which highlights the few men from the past who refused to share the misogynous feelings of their time and spoke out forcefully against them.

In 1981, the year of the election of socialist François Mitterrand to the presidency, Groult published a collection of her editorials written for *F-Magazine* and other women's magazines and weeklies entitled *La Moitié de la terre* (Half of the Earth). In 1983 she published her second novel, *Les Trois Quarts du temps* (Three Quarters of the Time), which was largely autobiographical.

Politically, Groult is a registered socialist, but she never campaigned very actively for the party. She did, however, accept François Mitterrand's invitation to head the national Commission de terminologie pour la féminisation des titres, charged with finding ways to "feminize" titles and professions.

In 1986, President Mitterrand awarded Groult the title of Chevalier de la Légion d'honneur et du Mérite français, one of France's highest distinctions, in recognition of her literary production and involvement in women's issues. That same year, Groult wrote a sixty-page introduction to an anthology of texts written by Olympe de Gouges, a writer who in 1793 was guillotined for expressing her liberal ideas.

Groult's last novel to date, *Les Vaisseaux du coeur* (Vessels of the Heart), published in 1988, was the subject of some controversy. It was called pornographic because it revolves around the theme of feminine sexual pleasure. At the present time, Benoîte Groult divides her life between the South of France and Paris, where she participates actively in the intellectual life.

MAJOR THEMES

Benoîte Groult's works deal with one general topic, the experience of being a woman. Groult feels that for too long the female condition has been described by men to women, a fact that can be seen as both the cause and the result of the conditioning of women as second-class citizens. However, Groult is encouraged by the fact that during her lifetime more and more women around the world have started to speak up for themselves, relating their personal experiences in their own words.

Inspired by the natural beauty of Brittany, Groult gives nature an important role in her work. Gardening, sailing, and fishing are activities in which she herself and many of her heroines lose themselves in order to heal. Nature offers women peace even at the price of physical effort: gardening is made more difficult by the humidity in Brittany, but the rewards of camelias blooming in February justify the work. The sea is a friend, though not always friendly. It is in battling the sea together that many of Groult's torn couples discover how strongly their life together has bonded them.

A second theme in Groult's writings is the relationship of women with other women. In particular the bond between mother and daughter is always seen as very powerful. In the *Journal à quatre mains* Groult describes how she, her mother, and her sister Flora "played troika" during cold evenings in occupied Paris by sitting on a couch, covered by the warmth of the same blanket, and talking late into the night. In *Les Trois Quarts du temps* Louise and her two daughters experience the same closeness in their big old bathtub. The bond created by sharing such intimacy will survive throughout life.

The complexity of the rapport between mother and daughter can take several forms. The first is based on her own relationship with her mother and depicts the mother's effort to shape her daughter according to her own understanding of a woman's place in society. Both *Le Journal à quatre mains* and *Les Trois Quarts du temps* show us Nicole Groult and Hermine (the narrator's mother in the novel) raising their daughters for the purpose of attracting and keeping a man. However, when the daughters (Benoîte and Louise) show some independence and decide to pursue their own interests, conflicts arise. Both works describe a daughter's struggle to reach independence and make a life for herself.

The other form of mother-daughter relations is more contemporary. The mother considers a daughter to be a person in her own right, not someone else's wife and mother-to-be. Both in *Il était deux fois* and in *Les Trois Quarts du temps*, the heroines Anne Hascoët and Louise give their daughters a good deal of freedom, which also involves control over their reproductive systems. When birth control fails for Clarisse in *Il était deux fois*, her mother arranges an illegal but safe abortion, because she is convinced that the respect for life begins with respect for the person giving it. The novel was published in 1968, one year after France's legalization of birth control for women but seven years before legalized abortion.

Groult consistently maintains that motherhood should be a free choice and not a trap or a burden. Becoming a mother must be more than an accident of nature due to erratic spermatozoa; many of Groult's heroines share this belief and practice it with absolutely no regard for the 1920 law that outlawed female contraceptives and forbade abortions. Benoîte, in *Le Journal à quatre mains* (1962), has an abortion just three weeks before her marriage; Juliette, in the part of *Le Féminin pluriel* written by sister Flora, is told by her doctor that she miscarried when, in fact, she too obtained the illegal services of an abortionist; Louise in *Les Trois Quarts du temps* learns how to perform an abortion on herself and is then able to perform one for her friend Agnès, who has started her sixth pregnancy. For Groult, being a mother is not only giving life to a child but also raising that child, and she knows that this formidable task is still too often left entirely to women. In her opinion, the so-called maternal instinct is only a myth, created by men to justify their conspicuous absence from the child-raising process.

Sisterhood is another important theme of *Le Journal à quatre mains*. Life in Paris under the German occupation and during the Liberation serves as a background to the relationship between the two sisters. Their total honesty with each other, their involvement in each other's lives and even their rivalries, create a very strong bond between them. The book ends with Flora's marriage to an Englishman. The recently widowed Benoîte remarks that although she appears to be losing her sister, their ties will not be severed because the love they share will serve as a permanent background against which all other loves will be played.

Friendship between women is also of great concern to Groult. In *Il était deux fois* the heroines are women who had been best friends at the Institution Sainte-Clotilde and whose paths happen to cross again several years later. Or the friends are two women in love with each other throughout their lifetime, as is the case of the narrator's mother and Lou in *Les Trois Quarts du temps*. In *Le Féminin pluriel* Juliette is Marianne's husband's childhood friend (and also his lover). In spite of the differences in status and lifestyle, women who become friends share a great closeness and a great willingness to help each other in all situations, from the most trivial (choosing cosmetics, Sunday afternoon parties in the country) to the most desperate (unwanted pregnancies, runaway children).

Men are not absent from Groult's novels, editorials, and essays. In her novels, women's relationships with men are examined in the context of both marriage and adultery. Many women marry the "wrong men." Except for Benoîte and Flora's father in *Le Journal à quatre mains* and Louise's father in *Les Trois Quarts du temps*, all the men not only openly engage in adultery but at the same time demand understanding and support from their spouses. Jean is both Marianne's husband and her friend Juliette's lover in *Le Féminin pluriel*. The handsome Gauvain in *Les Vaisseaux du coeur* manages to maintain a lifelong affair with the heroine, George, begun before his marriage. The reason for all these philanderings is best expressed by Arnaud's cynical reply to Louise in *Les Trois Quarts du temps*: having been told by his wife that she prefers his company to any other, he explains that for him love creates a kind of prison and that it is healthy for him to be interested in the rest of the world.

Such a remark, which could have been made by several of Groult's male figures, triggers very complex feelings in his partner. Louise (*Les Trois Quarts du temps*), Marianne (*Le Féminin pluriel*), and Marion (*La Part des choses*), betrayed by their husbands, all have similar reactions: shock, feelings of inadequacy, understanding mixed with guilt and jealousy. *Le Féminin pluriel*, composed of the journals of two former friends who are now wife and mistress to the same man, is built around the theme of jealousy. However, with the help of friends, Groult's various women succeed in rebuilding lives for themselves in which they realize their own potential: Louise becomes a successful novelist, Marion and Marianne stay in their marriages not only because their husbands came back to them, but because they discover that they themselves want to.

In Groult's last novel to date, *Les Vaisseaux du coeur*, the lover, Gauvain, takes center stage. The novel retraces the lifelong affair of a woman writer called George and a handsome sailor, each married to someone else, who are bound by sexual pleasure. In fact, the theme of this novel, labeled pornographic by certain critics, is the "sins of the flesh" and the many joys these "sins" can bring to a woman's body. With this novel, Groult attacks squarely the old myth that for a woman it is better to give than to receive. In making love and in admitting loving to make love to Gauvain, George experiences a feeling of real honesty, which benefits her soul as much as an orgasm benefits her body.

If the female body plays such an important and triumphant role in *Les Vaisseaux du coeur*, this glorification may be interpreted as a sort of revenge. In

Groult's preceding novels, the heroines were acutely aware that their bodies were slowly betraying them and becoming unattractive to men. Cosmetics and cosmetic surgery offered Iris (*La Part des choses*) and Louise (*Les Trois Quarts du temps*) a way to regain a youthful appearance. But Groult, the journalist, was always more radical than her characters. For years she denounced a sort of "terrorism of youth" in Western society, where being and staying young is a must. In 1988, through the character of George, who remains overtly sexual and continues to enjoy her body even as she advances in age, Groult may have wanted to show that changes are finally taking place in our society. She, of course, credits women who have started to speak up but also, in *Le Féminisme au masculin, utopie d'hier, réalité d'aujourd'hui*, those few men who early on in history embraced women's causes, among them Poulain de la Barre, Condorcet, Stuart Mill, Saint-Simon, Prosper Enfantin, and Fourier.

In *Ainsi soit-elle* Groult found words equal in boldness to Olympe de Gouges's in her denunciation of misogyny and sexism. She repeats relentlessly that the term "woman" does not equal "wife" or "whore," and that women are not weak of mind. She denies eloquently that women are frustrated beings longing for a penis. Their sexual organs are neither ugly nor shameful, and are not to be "rectified" by men. Clitoridectomy, which continues to be practiced in so many parts of the world, is an act of violence against women and cannot be tolerated. Groult has expressed this point of view in several editorials and in several emotional prefaces to books written by women authors against rape, clitoridectomy and infibulation, and prostitution.

Groult is convinced that mentalities will not change if words stay the same. Paraphrasing Victor Hugo, she believes that all revolutions have to start in the dictionary. That is why she considers her work on Mitterrand's national committee to "feminize" titles to be a very useful exercise. Language is not neutral; it mirrors a society's structures and prejudices. It is therefore of the utmost importance for women to create and use an *écriture féminine*.

Although Groult is not a theoretician of *écriture féminine*, she has spoken out many times on this topic. In her preface to *La Moitié de la terre* she notes that during the past thirty years women have gradually taken over the right to address any issue relevant to their fate. Finally, she says, women are able to translate in women's terms experiences that for centuries had been presented only through men's eyes, pens, culture, and desires: love, children, families, marriage, and work. As a novelist, that is just what Groult does. She chooses her words carefully and exactly, never afraid to shock, crafting many formulas that strike the reader with both their appropriateness and blunt frankness.

Besides her realism and a keen sense of irony, Groult is also recognized for her solid sense of humor. For Groult, humor is a very effective tool to distance oneself from one's condition, a luxury that the drudgery of daily chores seldom affords women.

Many examples of Groult's humor can be found both in her editorials and in her novels. About France's politics of encouraging its citizens to produce more children, she writes: "Faudra-t-il remplacer sur les tombes l'inscription 'mort pour la France' par la mention 'né pour la retraite des vieux'? . . . On s'est avisé que les ventres féminins étaient des instruments de production irremplaçables" (Will it be necessary to replace the words found on grave markers "killed in action" with those "born to support the social security system"? . . . They realized that women's wombs were irreplaceable production tools; *La Moitié de la terre*, 40).

Benoîte Groult, who now calls herself *une écrivaine* (a woman writer), remains a popular novelist, a moderate feminist, and a woman whose example has encouraged other women to speak out. In the last pages of *Ainsi soit-elle* she urges women to scream, not in anger but in order to be heard. Women deserve their share of power, not in order to strip men of what they have considered theirs for so long, but because they now know that they have something valuable to contribute to society. Groult has contributed her talent to weave her stories around such contemporary women's issues as education, reproductive and sexual rights, friendships, marriage and adultery, and love and jealousy. Her frankness and seriousness are all the more effective because they are laced with humor.

SURVEY OF CRITICISM

In spite of her popularity, Benoîte Groult has not yet been the subject of many studies. Fernande Gonthier wrote a biography entitled *Benoîte Groult*, which includes a long interview with Groult (joined briefly by her sister Flora). The book, written in 1978 just after the publication of *Ainsi soit-elle*, is informative and lively, but does not cover later works.

A file containing press clippings about Benoîte Groult can be consulted at the Bibliothèque Marguerite Durand in Paris, which specializes in women's history and the history of feminist movements. The file was started in 1975, and the press clippings it contains consist mainly of interviews granted to journalists by Benoîte Groult and of book reviews that have appeared in newspapers and magazines.

It is difficult to pass judgment on Benoîte Groult's work because it is so diverse. Literary critics generally praise the style of the two essays *Ainsi soit-elle* and *Le Féminisme au masculin*. Part pamphlet, part testimony, their hard-hitting formulas, which purposely shock the reader, are thought very effective, and Groult's biting sense of humor is also noted and appreciated. As a piece of feminist writing, there is no doubt that *Ainsi soit-elle* contributed to raising the consciousness of a very large number of French women.

Le Féminisme au masculin is hailed by Philippe Bourdrel in *L'Express* as "une anthologie de l'antiféminisme" (an anthologie of antifeminism). Dominique Desanti in *Le Monde* calls the book a beautiful proof of women's struggles and of their success, and the reviewer in *L'Express*, announcing its publication in paperback, finds it "always brillant, often amusing, never prejudiced."

As a novelist, Groult remains popular and widely read. *Le Journal à quatre mains* was hailed as a success, both because of its original structure and for the personal and candid touches faithfully depicting a Parisian family's daily life during a troubled period of France's history. André Maurois confessed, in the weekly *Elle*, to be very touched by the charm of this book and admits to having read it several times. François Nourrissier was struck by the journal's authenticity, and saw in it a celebration of youth which supersedes the most tragic historical circumstances.

Les Trois Quarts du temps, her long semi-autobiographical novel, not only sold very well but was also well received by critics such as Pierre de Boisdeffre. He exclaims: "I have had it with feminism . . . however, I read—it's a critic's duty—feminist studies, pamphlets and novels . . . Mme Groult has an excess of talent. . . . This is a masterpiece, and I weigh my words carefully, not because of its feminism, but in spite of its feminism . . . a great way to document how much French women have changed."

With her latest novel, *Les Vaiseaux du coeur*, Groult showed just how much French women have changed. As mentioned earlier, this novel treats frankly the topic of female sexuality and, as a result, reviews were mixed. Renaud Matignon in *Le Figaro Littéraire* considered the novel only a partial success, but Claire Gallois in *Le Magazine Littéraire* was frankly enthusiastic, calling it "the most fantastic love story . . . the apotheosis of feminism. Benoîte Groult's plea for free love is bold enough to make jealous Lady Chatterley's Lover himself."

What conclusion can one draw from such a slight body of criticism? The fact that, to this day, no serious book-length study of Groult has been written is not to be construed as diminishing her place and influence in the feminist discourse. Benoîte Groult deserves a very special place in the recent history of French feminism. She is popular as a novelist, journalist, and media personality. She represents a middle-of-the-road feminism with which many French women can identify.

Groult is more widely read than some of her more famous yet more philosophical and avant-garde contemporaries, such as Hélène *Cixous and Monique *Wittig. Groult's work remains more traditional and therefore accessible to many; realistic and concise, it communicates the author's enormous energy and *joie de vivre*. Its bantering tone becomes, at times, quite bawdy. Her work provides a concrete and popular illustration of women's newly won right to discuss all aspects of their condition and to do so in both a serious and a humorous manner which touches a large and diverse public.

BIBLIOGRAPHY

Works by Benoîte Groult

[Trans.] *Comme ils sont* by Dorothy Parker. Paris: Denoël, 1959. (Reissued in 1984 under the new title *La Vie à deux*).
[with Flora Groult], *Le Journal à quatre mains*. Paris: Denoël, 1962.

[with Flora Groult], *Le Féminin pluriel*. Paris: Denoël, 1965.
[with Flora Groult], *Il était deux fois*. Paris: Denoël, 1968.
La Part des choses. Paris: Grasset, 1972.
Ainsi soit-elle. Paris: Grasset, 1975.
[with Flora Groult], *Histoire de Fidèle*. Paris: Des Femmes, 1976.
Preface to *La Dérobade* by Jeanne Cordelier. Paris: Hachette, 1976.
Preface to *Le Viol* by Susan Brownmiller. Paris: Stock, 1976.
Le Féminisme au masculin. Paris: Denoël-Gonthier, 1978.
Preface to *La Parole aux négresses* by Awa Thiam. Paris: Denoël, 1978.
Preface to *Les Nouvelles Femmes*. F-Magazine. Paris: Mazarine, 1979.
[with Flora Groult, Paul Guimard, Blandine and Lison de Caunes, Bernard Ledwidge],
    Des Nouvelles de la famille. Paris, Editions Mazarine: 1980
La Moitié de la terre. Paris: Editions Alain Moreau, 1981.
Preface to *Des Couteaux contre les femmes; de l'excision* by Séverine Auffret. Paris: Des
    Femmes, 1982.
Les Trois Quarts du temps. Paris: Grasset, 1983.
"La Langue française au fémimin, la féminisation des titres." *Médias et Language* 19–
    20 (April 1984).
Preface to *Oeuvres* by Marie Olympe Gouze, about Olympe de Gouges. Paris: Mercure
    de France, 1986.
Les Vaisseaux du coeur. Paris: Grasset, 1988.

Translation of Benoîte Groult

Gelfand, Elissa, trans. in Elaine Marks and Isabelle de Courtivron. *New French Feminism,
    An Anthology*. Brighton: The Harvester Press, 1980. 68–75.

Reviews of Benoîte Groult

"Ainsi dit Benoîte Groult." *L'Express*, March 10–16, 1975: 90.
Ardvison, Barbero. "Benoîte Groult - romanförfattare, journalist, feminist." *Horisont*
    31 (1984): 45–46.
Bona, Dominique. "Benoîte Groult: l'aurore de la soixantaine." *Quotidien de Paris* 1092
    (May 31, 1983): 30.
Boisdeffre, Pierre de. "Benoîte Groult: Les Trois Quarts du temps." *Nouvelle Revue des
    Deux Mondes* (October-December 1983): 152–160.
Bourdrel, Philippe. "Anthologie de l'antiféminisme." *L'Express* (October 3–8, 1977):
    83–84.
"Cherchez la femme." *Le Monde*, February 28, 1975.
Cesbron, Georges. "Ecritures au féminin: II. Une certaine conception de la parole et de
    l'écriture." *L'Ecole* 13 (1979/80): 27–33.
Collins-Weitz, M. "Les Dilemmes de la femme-écrivain: entretien avec Benoîte Groult."
    Contemporary French Civilization 4–3 (1980): 353–60.
Desanti, Dominique. "Les Féministes au masculin." *Le Monde*, October 14, 1977.
Gallois, Claire. "Célébration du plaisir." *Magazine Littéraire* 252/253 (April 1988): 131.
Gonthier, Fernande. *Benoîte Groult*. Paris: Kliensienck, 1978.
"Le Féminisme au masculin, *Poche*." *L'Express*, November 29, 1980.

Matignon, Renaud. "Un Amour fou trop raisonnable." *Le Figaro Littéraire*, March 21, 1988.

Nourrissier, François. "La Femme, région mal connue." *Figaro Magazine* 212 (July-August 1983): 40.

Pessis, Jacques. "Benoîte Groult au rapport." *Figaro* Magazine 12859 (January 3, 1986): 22.

Rivière, Anne, and Xavière Gauthier. "Des Femmes et leurs oeuvres." *Magazine Littéraire* 180 (January 1982): 36–41.

Savigneau, Josyane. "Histoires de couples." *Le Monde*, February 12, 1988.

Slawy-Sutton, Catherine. "Benoîte Groult: Les Vaisseaux du Coeur." *French Review* 64 (March 1991): 721–22.

Vilaine, Anne-Marie de. "Le corps de la théorie." *Magazine Littéraire* 180 (January 1982): 25–28.

"Le Sexe des âmes, par Benoîte Groult." *Le Point* 128 (March 3, 1975): 78.

Wolfromm, Jean-Didier. "Les Soeurs Groult: deux pour une." *Magazine Littéraire* 16 (March 1968): 30.

———. "Une Femme vers le bonheur." *Magazine Littéraire* 197 (July-August 1983): 44–45.

LUCE IRIGARAY
(193?–   )

Katherine Stephenson

BIOGRAPHY

Born and raised in Belgium, Luce Irigaray moved to France in the early 1960s after receiving a master's degree in philosophy and literature (*Maîtrise en philosophie et lettres*) from the University of Louvain in 1955. Her thesis on the French writer Paul Valéry—*La Notion de pureté chez Paul Valéry, le mot pur, la pensée pure, la poésie pure* (The Concept of Purity in Paul Valéry: The Pure Word, Pure Thought, Pure Poetry)—documents her early interest in philosophical investigations on the nature of language. After passing the rigorous exam for teaching in secondary schools in 1956, she taught high school in Brussels until 1959.

Her university studies in Paris over the next fifteen years were devoted to preparing degrees in philosophy, linguistics, and psychoanalysis. From 1959 to 1962 she worked on a master's degree in psychology (*Licence de Psychologie*, University of Paris, 1961) and a diploma in psychopathology (Institut de Psychologie de Paris, 1962). She worked for the Fondation Nationale de la Recherche Scientifique (F.N.R.S.) in Belgium from 1962 to 1964, then obtained a position at the Centre National de la Recherche Scientifique (C.N.R.S.) in Paris. She began as an assistant researcher in a multidisciplinary team composed of linguists, neurologists, logicians, psychiatrists, and philosophers. She worked her way through the ranks, advancing to the highest position, that of Director of Research. In 1986 she transferred from the Psychology Commission to the Philosophy Commission to pursue research in her preferred discipline.

Upon returning to Paris in 1964 she began ten years of work on doctoral degrees in linguistics (*Doctorat de 3ième cycle en linguistique*, University of Paris X at Nanterre, 1968) and philosophy (*Doctorat d'Etat ès Lettres*, University of Paris VIII, 1974), and her psychoanalytic training at the Freudian School

(Ecole freudienne) directed by Jacques Lacan. Although often loosely described as a member of the Lacanian group at the Freudian School, Irigaray disclaims such notions of a specific or unified group concerning Lacanian psychoanalysis during her years there. She opted for a course of studies less exclusively oriented toward medicine, attending seminars that incorporated philosophy, science, literature, and the arts. As was common for members of the Freudian School, she also taught at the University of Paris VIII at Vincennes from 1970 to 1974, during which time she prepared her second doctorate. Her first dissertation—*Le Langage des déments* (The Language of the Demented), defended in 1968 and published by Mouton in 1973—documented a clinical study of patients with senile dementia from which Irigaray was able to define a grammar of pathological language use. Her second dissertation—*Speculum de l'autre femme* (*Speculum of the Other Woman*)—was the cause of considerable controversy. Its critique of the patriarchal and phallocentric discourse of Freudian—and, implicitly, Lacanian—psychoanalytic theory was considered irreverently heretical by members of the Freudian School. Though she obtained her doctorate with highest honors, the substitution of *Speculum* for her original, more traditional dissertation and its near simultaneous publication by the prestigious publishing house Editions de Minuit led to the refusal of her course proposal for the following year at the University of Paris VIII, and she became persona non grata at the Freudian School. The damage to her academic career and to her reputation in the insular world of Parisian academic institutions was substantial. She had to give up her plans to teach in Parisian universities, from which she was effectively blackballed, and she has never enjoyed the scholarly recognition in France that she has earned on the international scene.

Though marginalized by the Parisian intellectual establishment, Irigaray's ground-breaking work found a receptive audience in more traditional as well as feminist circles, in and outside of France. While working at C.N.R.S., developing her psychoanalytic practice, and writing numerous articles and manuscripts, she was also very active in the growing women's liberation movement of the seventies in France. She helped organize and conduct several important demonstrations for the legalization of contraceptives and abortion and spoke regularly at women's groups and conferences throughout Europe, while never allying herself with a specific organization. During this time of intense political activity she made many international contacts that led to conferences and university seminars in Europe, the United States, and Canada. The publication of *Ce Sexe qui n'en est pas un* (*This Sex Which Is Not One*), *Et l'une ne bouge pas sans l'autre* (*And the One Doesn't Stir Without the Other*), and *Amante Marine* (Seafaring Lover) confirmed her stature as a leading philosopher of the twentieth century.

Not until the 1980s did Irigaray begin to achieve recognition of her talents within academic communities. In 1982 she was named to the prestigious Chaire Internationale de Philosophie at Erasmus University in Rotterdam for a semester-long seminar in philosophy. The texts of the seminar were published in 1984 as

Ethique de la différence sexuelle (Ethics of Sexual Difference). In 1985 she gave
a seminar at the University of Bologna where she introduced her empirical
research on the sexual order of language. Material from this seminar was published in the article "L'Ordre sexuel du discours" (The Sexual Order of Discourse) in the March 1987 issue of the journal *Langages*, edited by Irigaray,
and in *Sexes et parentés*, both of which served as the basis for a month-long
seminar at the International Summer Institute of Semiotic and Structuralist Studies in Toronto in June 1987. The year 1985 also marked the occasion of Irigaray's
reentry into the Parisian academic scene as a teacher at the Ecole des Hautes
Etudes en Sciences Sociales, though she was given only half of a seminar to
teach for that and the following year. This was followed by two years (1988–
1990) at the Collège International de Philosophie in Paris, where she gave
seminars on her empirical research on language and its epistemological elaboration. In 1989–1990 she also taught a seminar at the Centre Américain d'Etudes
Critiques. Irigaray's latest work, *Sexes et genres à travers les langues* (Sex and
Gender in Language), presents the first results of her international project on
theoretical and empirical research on language and includes a collection of texts
by international collaborators and students involved in the Bologna, Toronto,
and Paris seminars. She is presently organizing international research groups,
composed of several teams in Italy, Germany, Canada, and the United States,
to study the sexual order of language and culture.

MAJOR THEMES

The scope of this introduction to Irigaray's oeuvre does not allow a description
of individual texts. For such a description of her works published up to 1982,
see the annotated bibliography in Gelfand and Hules (1985). I shall instead offer
an overview of the principal concerns reflected throughout her corpus. Such an
approach is particularly appropriate with Irigaray, given the seemingly disparate
nature of her works, as concerns both subject matter and style. Like many women
writers, she refuses the limits of traditional genres. Though the essay is her
favored form, she rejects the standard logic of linear argumentation for a style
of presentation that calls into question the phallocentrism of Western philosophical discourse. To enumerate just a few characteristics of her style: there is
rarely any contextualizing introduction to the subject being treated; the reader
is assumed to have substantive knowledge of the classic texts of Western philosophy; the ambiguity, irony, and playfulness of style require active participation
on the part of the reader in interpretation; plays on words, metaphors, analogies,
neologisms, direct authorial intervention from explicit interjections to implicit
commentary (e.g., question and exclamation marks in brackets, ellipses, un-
derlining, quotes around key or problematic words, etc.), ambiguous use of
pronouns, the pulling-apart of words with parentheses and hyphens (e.g., "project," "specula(riza)tion," "hom(m)osexuality") to un-cover lost meanings or
dis-cover hidden ones, and numerous other techniques result in a style requiring

not only careful reading but a certain familiarity with the author's theories and projects.

Such an original style, which evolves and changes from one work to another, is disconcertingly elusive to the neophyte, challenging to the initiate, and has been the cause of a series of misreadings, especially of her early works, which represent the most elaborate stylistic complexity. The forms her writing takes, however, cannot be separated from content since, with the exception of her works on the pathology of language, her primary subject matter is the deconstruction of patriarchal thought and discourse as having excluded any representation of female subjectivity. Her style, then, works both to "disrupt" philosophical discourse and to posit a nonprescriptive model of a discourse in which female subjectivity is not reduced to objectification or to a relationship with male subjectivity (of sameness, dependency, or opposition), but is allowed representation in the gaps and spaces her subversive style opens up.

To fully appreciate Irigaray's individual texts one must read them in the context of her overall agenda: the acknowledgment and recuperation of sexual difference in hopes of establishing a more just and sane social order. For Irigaray, the destructive forces of modern technological society threatening the earth and our very existence are rooted in the structures of patriarchal culture, which have caused us to distance ourselves from, and thus devalue, our material origins. Her entire corpus works toward a reconceptualization of our relationship with our own corporeality and the material basis of all production (of language, texts, knowledges, subjectivity, bodies, etc.). Often criticized for her theoretical rather than pragmatic approach, Irigaray maintains that only through a radical reorganization of society, that is, one which addresses the root problems of patriarchal social (dis)order, can enduring solutions to social injustice be found. This entails reevaluating the systems of representation underpinning the cultural models of human thought, behavior, and interaction which constitute the foundation of social order. Inasmuch as these systems of representation mediate our lived experience of the self and the world and allow us to understand and make sense of the brute facts of existence, they must also be seen as constitutive of reality. Irigaray elaborates a critique of the reductivist conceptualization of reality offered by phallocentric modes and models of representation and looks to more natural regulatory principles for guidance in establishing new cultural models, starting by recognizing sexual difference as the most fundamental, irreducible characteristic of lived human existence and subjectivity. She demonstrates how phallocentric thought actually denies sexual difference, and that this denial operates as the basis for its metaphysics of transcendental being and meaning, which establishes hierarchical social relations. Her vision of a social organization based on respecting the difference between the sexes offers seductive models of revitalized subjective and intersubjective relations which would replace hierarchical structures of domination with ones of reciprocity, based on respect for the other. Indeed, for Irigaray the reworking of the relations between the sexes is *the* ethical question of our time, for until both sexes can be defined and represented autonomously, social relations will remain embedded in an economy of domination and oppression.

Irigaray's is thus a preeminently sociocultural critique composed of complementary deconstructive and reconstructive projects centered on exploring the way language and discourse, the most fundamental systems of representation, constitute our knowledge of self and the world. Her deconstruction of phallocentric structures and processes of signification as founding representation solely on masculine models clears a space for the reconstructive project of examining possibilities for representation of the feminine. Her critique of the phallocentrism of Western thought, which comprises the focus of her works through the early 1980s, is carried out through interpretive rereadings of major texts of Western philosophy and psychoanalysis. In these interrogative analyses, which she has called "having a fling with the philosophers," Irigaray takes up the irreverent position of (amorous) mimic to tease out of (male) philosophical discourses the "blind spots" or areas of repressed terms, concepts, and materiality which serve as their hidden, unavowed support. What her strategy of "mimicry" (*mimétisme*) uncovers is a consistently misogynist tradition from Plato onward in which the feminine has been excluded from representation as a (speaking) subject while serving as the unrecognized material support for phallocentric systems of signification.

As she describes it in *Speculum*, philosophical and psychoanalytic discourses have only given the illusion of recognizing sexual difference, for they have always (mis)represented woman as the mirror image or inversion of man: she has never been described in autonomous terms, only as that which lacks all that man has—a penis, phallus, power, identity, soul, and so on. Governed by a "specular" economy which privileges the visible (penis at the expense of the "invisible" vagina), they claim to reflect the world in their speculations when they reflect only views of the male subject. First the philosophical "I" validated its claims to authority by positing itself as a unified, centered identity which professed to speak from a universal position in a language that supposedly translated directly the truths of which it spoke. Then psychoanalysis posited as universal an account of sexuality and subjectivity-formation based on a uniquely masculine model. These discourses recognize neither the (male) sexualized position from which they are produced nor their "blind spot of an old dream of symmetry" between women and men which conceptualizes woman as a (failed) copy of man, and both phenomena may be seen as primarily (unconsciously?) operating to construct male identity through repression of female subjectivity. The metaphoric and linguistic structures composing these discourses reflect a "logic of the same" privileging unity, identity, and singularity of meaning which attempts to exclude ambiguity, multiplicity, excess, undecidability—all those characteristics traditionally relegated to the feminine. Irigaray recuperates these very same features in her stylistic strategies of "masquerade" and "mimicry," disrupting discursive coherence by deliberately taking on the role of the feminine to seduce these discourses into un-covering her repressed presence. Her excessive style seeks to represent the feminine that exceeds patriarchal representation, the remains or residue of repressed materiality/female sexuality that operates, like the unconscious, as a site of subversion within the system. She plays the hysteric, articulating her resistance by giving voice to her body. In terms of her "specular" pun, Irigaray reverses the positions in the specular economy by introducing the curved mirror of the speculum—the gynecological tool for dilating and inspecting the vagina—to reflect back what the phallocentric flat mirror, which only reflects man's own image back on to himself, fails to apprehend—the specificity of female sexuality and subjectivity.

Irigaray develops this analogy between female sexuality and a feminine language as a strategic response to the "isomorphism" of Western discourse and the masculine sex, that is, the correspondence between phallic male sexuality—which is reduced to one organ, one (orgasmic) pleasure—and phallocentric discourse—which privileges the oneness of (male) identity, meaning, representational models, and so on. Irigaray's giving voice to the feminine through exploring her sexual specificity is the starting point for exploring images that are adequate in representing an autonomous female subjectivity. The most famous of these are the two (genital) lips of "Quand nos lèvres se parlent" (*When Our Lips Speak Together*) in *Ce Sexe*, which portray female sexuality as multiple, simultaneously not (limited to) one, as is the phallic male model, and more than one (for there are always *two* lips, and there are genital and oral lips). This image owes no relation to male sexuality and desire—the lips are autoerotic, continually touching and needing no intermediary to access their pleasure—and subverts phallic hierarchical organization by positing an economy of circularity and reciprocity—simultaneously open and closed, without boundaries or barriers between them, they allow interaction without loss (of fluids, of identity . . .). Their imagery enacts a *parler-femme* ("speaking [as] woman") by which woman at last speaks (of) her desires, needs, and interests rather than those (of men) which phallocentric representation imputes to her.

Irigaray's works after *Speculum* and *Ce Sexe* have received much less critical attention, though they comprise the bulk of her corpus. While her oeuvre resists efforts at categorization, one could broadly characterize her works of the 1980s as an investigation of the ethical dimensions of recognizing sexual difference in which two concerns predominate: the necessity of assuming one's sexualized position in discourse and the possibilities of (representing) reciprocal relations with the other, the latter operating as a definition of ethics itself.

What Irigaray's critiques of Western discourse and her linguistic analyses (*Le Langage des déments*, *Parler n'est jamais neutre*, "L'Ordre sexuel du discours," certain essays in *Ethique de la différence sexuelle* and *Sexes et parentés*, and the forthcoming *Sexes et genres à travers les langues*) have in common is a focus on the speaking subject as a sexed being. All forms of knowledge articulated through a discourse, the subject of which claims universality, must be seen as incomplete, to a certain extent suspect, and fundamentally unethical in the sense that they do not admit or recognize the influence of the sexualized position from which the subject speaks. Beginning from a psychoanalytic understanding of subjectivity as constituted through one's entry into language by taking up a sexualized position in the Symbolic, Irigaray concentrates her analysis of specific discourses on the enunciation. In the act of enunciation, that is, of producing an utterance, the enunciator actualizes her or his vision of the world, traces of which remain in the utterance. By focusing on these traces of subjectivity located within, and operating as the very condition of, every act of communication, Irigaray reveals that what is at stake in a continued denial and repression of the sexual marking of discourse is the very possibility of an ethical social order. In her empirical research on everyday language-use—derived from her initial linguistic analyses of pathological language in *Le Langage des déments*—she demonstrates that women and men privilege distinctively different patterns of communication (see "L'Ordre sexuel du discours" and *Sexes et genres*). The differences in morphologic, syntactic, and semantic structures reveal sexually marked patterns of viewing the self, the world, others of the same sex and of the opposite sex. Results to date seem to suggest that, in general, men's language-use reflects their "self-affection" or ability to represent relations to the self and others of the same sex, while women's language-use does not, privileging instead intersubjective relations between the two sexes. This research uncovers in everyday language-use the same pattern of repression of women's relations to the self and the other revealed in Irigaray's deconstruction of scientific, philosophical, and other "truthful" discourses, the (masculine) subject of which is constituted as universal or objective by repression of the feminine. Irigaray does not contend that this repression is an inherent characteristic of language or subjectivity, rather that discourse reflects the social inscription of the subject, that is, her or his integration of social values and structures, in and by language. Thus language itself must be addressed in any reorganization of the social order, for until the major systems of representation reintegrate an avowed relation to materiality—of language, of bodies—so that both sexes can articulate their difference, the "economy of the same" will dominate social relations.

To read Irigaray's elaborate detailing of the conditions necessary for female autonomy as an attempt to "theorize woman" would be to ignore the context within which it is developed, for it serves as the critical component in establishing an ethical social order. Within patriarchy, ethics—the field that conceptualizes the subject's relations with the other—has been tainted by the "logic of the same," resulting in an ethics of identity, of the one, of the same. The ethics of sexual difference, founded on recognition of the opposite sex as the other most different from oneself, operates, then, to reintegrate a respect for alterity as the basis for intersubjective and social relations. Having moved from (deconstruction of) the universal subject to (reveal) the masculine one and (recuperate) the female subject, Irigaray has more recently focused on the couple, the paradigm for investigating relations between autonomous subjects. To explore the possibilities of ethical relations between the sexes she looks to representational models that are not (necessarily) implicated in phallocentric modes of organization. Beginning from a conceptual framework of the cosmic, wherein intersubjective relations operate in microcosmic relation to the macrocosm of nature and social order, she utilizes the language of the elements—earth, fire, air, water—and, surprisingly, the divine to represent the possibilities for productive, creative relationships based on reciprocity and mutual respect.

The language of the elements is most effective in that it provides a model of productive interaction between material elements rather than one of destructive subordination. Like the image of the female's two lips, it subverts the phallocentric model of oneness and singular being shored up by binary oppositions—male/female, inside/outside, presence/absence, and so on—which set up boundaries between elements and lead to hierarchical and transcendental ordering patterns. The four elements represent the possibility of combining without loss of original identity, of coming together creatively to produce something new, of constant change and interchange. They enact a dynamic "logic of becoming" which, unlike the static "logic of being" (the same) which centers order and the universe around the (male) subject, situates them primarily in relation to each other and to the natural regulatory principles of the cosmos. Herein lies also the key to Irigaray's concept of the divine. In perhaps one of her most controversial moves, she retains the concept of god(s) because the sacred has historically played such a constitutive role in culture: "There has never been any constitution of subjectivity, or of any human society, which has been worked through without the help of the divine" ("Divine Women," 4). The divine functions as a "horizon" against which to envisage our progress in becoming the most we can be as women or as men, situating the "trajectory" of our becoming as sexed beings. Unlike the God of patriarchy, the god(s) Irigaray describes would be female and male representations of the "plenitude" of femininity and masculinity, and of the productivity of the relations between the sexes. This productivity would no longer be ultimately, and reductively, defined as reproduction, whereby the child operates as the horizon or goal of their coming together, but rather as creativity or love. Thus the sacred would no longer be based on sacrifice (of the relation to the mother, of women, of nature) but would honor and celebrate the creativity of reciprocal relations among sexed beings.

SURVEY OF CRITICISM

Irigaray's critical reception among her English-speaking audiences—primarily in North America, England, and Australia—has been phenomenal. In the ten years since the publication of the first English translations of her work, she has been cited and evaluated in hundreds of critical works. Her critique of the phallocentrism of Western thought, as well as many of her terms, concepts, and stylistic devices, has become a mainstay of feminist literary, psychoanalytic, and social criticism. Considered by many to be the preeminent French feminist theorist of this century, rivaled in influence only by Julia *Kristeva, Irigaray has nonetheless been the object of considerable controversy and misrepresentation.

While the complexity of Irigaray's style and thought has always posed considerable difficulties for critics, another principal cause of confusion has been the limited diffusion of her texts (though most are now in the process of being translated). The first translated essays available in the early 1980s—three articles from *Ce Sexe* published separately in 1980 and "And the One Doesn't Stir Without the Other" in 1981—provided a misleadingly limited view of Irigaray's work. When *Speculum* and *This Sex* were translated in 1985, eleven and eight years after their original publications in French, these works, too, were most often evaluated outside the context of her increasingly large corpus, of which most critics remained ignorant. Many tended to concentrate on those elements of her work that could be incorporated into the debate on *l'écriture féminine* (a feminine form of writing)—most notably the analogies between female sexuality and a feminine form of language and writing—and to group her with Julia Kristeva and Hélène *Cixous—with whom she has only the most superficial of affinities—either as a proponent/practitioner of *l'écriture féminine* or as an essentialist feminist critic (e.g., Bowlby, Dallery, Jacobus, Peel).

The essentialist critique (e.g., Jones, Moi, Plaza, Sayers), which charges theorists with reducing the sexed subject to an ahistorical, fixed essence, has been the most damaging element of the criticism of Irigaray, indeed of feminist criticism in general, delaying until recently a more accurate assessment of her work (see Fuss for a detailed examination of the essentialist debate on Irigaray, and Grosz's *Sexual Subversions* for the only comprehensive evaluation to date of Irigaray's oeuvre). This charge of essentialism stems from a variety of factors, from the Marxist and pragmatic commitments of certain critics (e.g., Gates, Papke) to a literal reading of her work, outside the context of the European theoretical background which serves both as the origins and object of its critique. Many critics (especially Anglo-American ones) have been resistant to embracing any theorizing that does not more or less directly translate into praxis, that is, have a practical application to the struggle for social justice. They conceive of this struggle primarily in economic terms of winning equality for women—equal pay, equal rights—and are suspicious of theories that focus on "woman" rather than women, seeing them as almost inherently essentialist or biologist in that they base their analysis of difference on anatomy. Since women's bodies have been the privileged site of their oppression, they fear that feminist criticism advocating sexual difference will only impede efforts to win equality. They also deny the validity of (speculating on) a female or male essence, of isolating characteristics inherent to either sex that could be found in all women or men. Such a conception risks obscuring the differences within the sexes and the social and historical influences that constitute the subject differently in various cultures throughout the ages.

Irigaray's works, more than most, need to be read in the context of her corpus. In addition to her playful style, her predilection for dialogic narrative which disrupts discursive coherence or enacts scenarios evocative of (sexually) different (discursive, subjective, social) orders requires critics to extrapolate much of her meaning. This, coupled with the desire/need on the part of critics to look for unity in assessing a work, causes many to try to overly fix or systematize Irigaray's thought into *a* theory. Others, in frustration, dismiss her work as riven with contradictions, caught up in deconstructive acrobatics at the expense of offering viable alternatives, misrepresenting the theories she critiques, and so on.

Some critics (e.g., Burke, Féral, Fuss, Gallop, Grosz, Schor, Whitford) have resisted (most of) these pitfalls by attempting to play along with her thought, seeing where it leads from one work to the next, concentrating as much on the effects her discourse produces as on interpreting it. These critics offer readings that make sense of the difficulties of her work without imposing restrictive systematization or preconceived notions of "'proper'' forms of theorizing on it; they listen to the many voices Irigaray puts into play without feeling the need to prioritize or choose among them; and, most significantly, they analyze her work within the context of her overall project. The most important insight to come out of these interpretations, outside of the aforementioned reading strategies, is an understanding of the strategic function of Irigaray's style and metaphoric/analogical representational models. They demonstrate that Irigaray's elaboration of feminine specifity is not anatomically but morphologically based. She understands the body as a product of social inscription, that systems of representation constitute the body and mediate our relationship to it, just as they play a formative role in the constitution of subjectivity. Thus her representational models of autonomous female sexuality function to subvert existing phallocentric ones and to provide not a truthful definition of that sexuality, but new ways of representing and conceptualizing our relation to corporeality, and to materiality in general. To read Irigaray "strategically," then, is not to presume that she defines (masculine or feminine sexuality, essence, language, or what a new social order would be), but to see her as opening the door to the possibilities offered by alternative conceptualizations (of the self, the other, and the relations between them).

BIBLIOGRAPHY

Major Works by Luce Irigaray

Le Language des déments. The Hague: Mouton, 1973.
Speculum de l'autre femme. Paris: Minuit, 1974.
Ce Sexe qui n'en est pas un. Paris: Minuit, 1977.
Et l'une ne bouge pas sans l'autre. Paris: Minuit, 1979.
Amante marine: De Friedrich Nietzsche. Paris: Minuit, 1980.
Le Corps-à-corps avec la mère. Ottawa: La Pleine Lune, 1981.
Passions élémentaires. Paris: Minuit, 1982.
La Croyance même. Paris: Galilée, 1983.
L'Oubli de l'air: Chez Martin Heidegger. Paris: Minuit, 1983.
Ethique de la différence sexuelle. Paris: Minuit, 1984.
Parler n'est jamais neutre. Paris: Minuit, 1985.
"L'Ordre sexuel du discours." *Langages* 85 (March 1987): 81–123.
Sexes et parentés. Paris: Minuit, 1987.

"Corps, sexes et genres linguistiques." *Bulletin du Centre de Recherches sur les Arts et le Langage* 4 N.S. 3 (1988): 229–42.

"Sujet de la science, sujet sexué?" In *Sens et place des connaissances dans la société.* Paris: Editions du CNRS, 1988. 95–121.

Le Temps de la différence. Paris: Livre de Poche, 1989.

Sexes et genres à travers les langues. Paris: Grasset, forthcoming.

Translations of Luce Irigaray

Speculum of the Other Woman. Trans. Gillian C. Gill. Ithaca: Cornell University Press, 1985. Trans. of *Speculum de l'autre femme.*

"That Sex Which Is Not One." Trans. Randall Albury and Paul Foss. In *Language, Sexuality and Subversion.* Ed. Paul Foss and Meaghan Morris. Darlington, Australia: Feral, 1978. 161–71. Trans. of "Ce sexe qui n'en est pas un." *Cahiers du GRIF* 5 (1975). Also appears in *This Sex Which Is Not One.*

"This Sex Which Is Not One." Trans. Claudia Reeder. In *New French Feminisms.* Ed. Elaine Marks and Isabelle de Courtivron. Amherst: University of Massachusetts Press, 1980. 99–106.

"When the Goods Get Together." Trans. Claudia Reeder. In *New French Feminisms.* Ed. Elaine Marks and Isabelle de Courtivron. Amherst: University of Massachusetts Press, 1980. 107–10. Trans. of "Des marchandises entre elles." *La Quinzaine Littéraire* 215 (August 1975). Also appears in *This Sex Which Is Not One.*

"When Our Lips Speak Together." Trans. Carolyn Burke. *Signs: Journal of Women in Culture and Society* 6, no. 1 (Fall 1980): 69–79. Trans. of "Quand nos lèvres se parlent." *Cahiers du GRIF* 12 (1976): 23–28. Also appears in *This Sex Which Is Not One.*

This Sex Which Is Not One. Trans. Catherine Porter with Carolyn Burke. Ithaca: Cornell University Press, 1985. Trans. of *Ce Sexe qui n'en est pas un.*

"And the One Doesn't Stir Without the Other." Trans. Hélène V. Wenzel. *Signs: Journal of Women in Culture and Society* 7, no. 1 (1981): 60–67. Trans. of *Et l'une ne bouge pas sans l'autre.*

"Veiled Lips." Trans. Sara Speidel. *Mississippi Review* 11, no. 3 (1983): 98–119. Partial translation of *Amante marine: De Friedrich Nietzsche.*

"Is the Subject of Science Sexed?" Trans. Edith Oberle. *Cultural Critique* 1 (Fall 1985): 73–88. Trans. of "Le Sujet de la science est-il sexué?" *Les Temps Modernes* 436 (November 1982): 960–74. Also appears in *Parler n'est jamais neutre.*

"The Fecundity of the Caress." Trans. Carolyn Burke. In *Face to Face with Levinas.* Ed. Richard A. Cohen. Albany: SUNY Press, 1986. 231–56. Trans. of "Fécondité de la Caresse." *Exercises de la patience* 5 (1983): 119–37. Also appears in *Ethique de la différence sexuelle.*

"Sexual Difference." Trans. Sean Hand. In *French Feminist Thought.* Ed. Toril Moi. Oxford: Basil Blackwell, 1987. 118–30. Trans. of "La Différence sexuelle," in *Ethique de la différence sexuelle.*

"Divine Women." Trans. Stephen Muecke. *Local Consumption Occasional Papers* 8 (1986): 1–14. Trans. of "Femmes divines." *Critique* 454 (March 1985): 294–308. Also appears in *Sexes et parentés.*

"Women, the Sacred and Money." Trans. Diana Knight and Margaret Whitford. *Par-

agraph 8 (1986): 6–18. Trans. of "Les Femmes, le sacré, l 'argent." *Critique* (April 1986): 372–83. Also appears in *Sexes et parentés.*
"Equal to Whom?" *Differences* 1 (1989). Trans. of "Egales à qui?" *Critique* (May 1987): 420–37.

Interviews with Luce Irigaray

Amsberg, Kiki, and Aafke Steenhuis. Trans. Robert van Krieken. "An Interview with Luce Irigaray." *Hecate* 9, no. 1/2 (1983): 198.
Clédat, Françoise, Xavière Gauthier, and Anne-Marie de Vilaine. "L'Autre de la nature." *Sorcières* 20 (1980): 14–25.
Clément, Catherine. "La Femme, son sexe, et le langage." *La Nouvelle critique* 82 (March 1975): 36–39.
Dumouchel, Thérèse, and Marie-Madeleine Raoult. "Les Femmes-mères: ce sous-sol muet de l'ordre social." In *Le Corps-à-corps avec la mère.* Ottawa: La Pleine Lune, 1981. 75–89.
Hans, Marie-Françoise, and Gilles Lapouge. "Luce Irigaray (1)" and "Luce Irigaray (2)." In *Les femmes, la pornographie, l'érotisme.* Paris: Seuil, 1978. 43–58; 302–4.
Henry, Carole, and Francine Pelletier. "Luce Irigaray: un message amoureux." *La Vie en rose* (Summer 1982): 63–64.
Jardine, Alice A., and Anne M. Menke. "Luce Irigaray" in "Exploding the Issue: 'French' 'Women' 'Writers' and 'The Canon'?" Trans. Margaret Whitford. *Yale French Studies* 75 (1988): 244–46.
Lamy, Suzanne, and André Roy. "Nietzsche, Freud et les femmes." In *Le Corps-à-corps avec la mère.* Ottawa: La Pleine Lune, 1981. 35–72.
Maroney, Heather Jon. "Language, Persephone and Sacrifice: An Interview with Luce Irigaray." *Borderlines* 4 (Winter 1985/1986): 30–32.
Serrano, Lucienne, and Elaine Hoffman Baruch. "Luce Irigaray." In *Women Writers Talking.* Ed. Janet Todd. New York: Holmes and Meier, 1983. 230–45.
Storti, Martine, and Marie-Odile Delacour. "Mères et filles vues par Luce Irigaray." *Libération,* May 21, 1979.
"Women's Exile: Interview with Luce Irigaray." Trans. Venn Couze. *Ideology and Consciousness* 1 (1977): 62–76. Trans. of "Kvinner i eksil." In *Seks Samtaler om Psykiatri.* Ed. Svein Haugsgjerd and Fredrik Engelstad. Oslo: Pax, 1976.

Studies of Luce Irigaray

Berg, Elizabeth L. "The Third Woman." *Diacritics* 12, no. 2 (Summer 1982): 11–20.
Berg, Maggie. "Escaping the Cave: Luce Irigaray and Her Feminist Critics." In *Literature and Ethics: Essays Presented to A. E. Malloch.* Ed. Gary Wihl and David Williams. Kingston: McGill, 1988. 62–76.
Bowlby, Rachel. "The Feminine Female." *Social Text* 7 (1983): 54–68.
Burke, Carolyn. "Introduction to Luce Irigaray's 'When Our Lips Speak Together.'" *Signs: Journal of Women in Culture and Society* 6, no. 1 (Autumn 1980): 66–68.
———. "Irigaray Through the Looking Glass." *Feminist Studies* 7, no. 2 (Summer 1981): 288–306.

————. "Romancing the Philosophers: Luce Irigaray." *Minnesota Review* 29 (Fall 1987): 103–14. Rpt. in *Seduction and Theory: Readings of Gender, Representation, and Rhetoric.* Ed. Dianne Hunter. Urbana: University of Illinois Press, 1989. 226–40.

Dallery, Arleen. "The Politics of Writing (the) Body: *Ecriture Féminine.*" In *Gender/ Body/Knowledge: Feminist Reconstructions of Being and Knowing.* Ed. Alison M. Jaggar and Susan R. Bordo. New Brunswick, N.J.: Rutgers University Press, 1989. 52–67.

Felman, Shoshana. "Women and Madness: The Critical Phallacy." *Diacritics* 5, no. 4 (Winter 1975): 2–10.

Féral, Josette. "Antigone or the Irony of the Tribe." *Diacritics* 8, no. 2 (Fall 1978): 2–14.

————. "Towards a Theory of Displacement." *SubStance* (1981): 52–64.

Foss, Paul. "On the Value of That Text Which Is Not One: Inspection and the Disciplinary Society." In *Language, Sexuality and Subversion.* Ed. Paul Foss and Meaghan Morris. Darlington, Australia: Feral, 1978. 173–91.

Freeman, Barbara. "Irigaray at *The Symposium*: Speaking Otherwise." *Oxford Literary Review* 8, no. 1–2 (1986): 170–77.

Fuss, Diana. *Essentially Speaking: Feminism, Nature and Difference.* New York: Routledge, 1989.

Gallop, Jane, *The Daughter's Seduction: Feminism and Psychoanalysis.* Ithaca: Cornell University Press, 1982.

————. "*Quand nos lèvres s'écrivent*: Irigaray's Body Politic." *Romanic Review* 74, no. 1 (January 1983): 77–83.

Gates, Henry Louis, Jr. "Significant Others." *Contemporary Literature* 29 (1988): 606–23.

Gelfand, Elissa D., and Virginia Thorndike Hules. *French Feminist Criticism: Women, Language, and Literature: An Annotated Bibliography.* New York: Garland, 1985.

Gillman, Linda. "The Looking-Glass Through Alice." In *Gender and Literary Voice.* Ed. Janet Todd. New York: Holmes and Meier, 1980. 12–23.

Gross, Elizabeth. "Irigaray and Sexual Difference." *Australian Feminist Studies* 2 (1986): 63–77.

————. "Philosophy, Subjectivity and the Body: Kristeva and Irigaray." In *Feminist Challenges: Social and Political Theory.* Ed. Carole Pateman and Elizabeth Gross. Boston: Northeastern University Press, 1986. 125–43.

Grosz, E. A., and Marie de Lepervanche. "Feminism and Science." In *Crossing Boundaries: Feminisms and the Critique of Knowledges.* Ed. Barbara Caine, E. A. Grosz, and Marie de Lepervanche. Sydney: Allen and Unwin, 1988. 5–27.

Grosz, Elizabeth. *Sexual Subversions: Three French Feminists.* Sydney: Allen and Unwin, 1989.

Holmlund, Christine. "I Love Luce: The Lesbian, Mimesis and Masquerade in Irigaray, Freud, and Mainstream Film." *New Formations* 8 (Fall 1989): 105–23.

Homans, Margaret. "Reconstructing the Feminine." *Women's Review of Books* 3 (1986): 12–13.

————. "The Woman in the Cave: Recent Feminist Fictions and the Classical Underworld." *Contemporary Literature* 29 (1988): 369–402.

Jacobus, Mary. "The Question of Language: Men of Maxims and *The Mill on the Floss.*" *Critical Inquiry* 8 (1981): 207–22. Rpt. in *Writing and Sexual Difference.* Ed.

Elizabeth Abel. Chicago: University of Chicago Press, 1982. 37–52; and in *Reading Woman: Essays in Feminist Criticism*. New York: Columbia University Press, 1986. 62–79.

———. "Reading Correspondences." In *Reading Woman: Essays in Feminist Criticism*. New York: Columbia University Press, 1986.

Jones, Ann Rosalind. "Inscribing Femininity: French Theories of the Feminine." In *Making a Difference: Feminist Literary Criticism*. Ed. Gayle Greene and Coppélia Kahn. London: Routledge, 1985. 80–112.

———. "Writing the Body: Toward an Understanding of *Ecriture féminine*." *Feminist Studies* 7, no. 2 (Summer 1981): 247–63.

Kuykendall, Eléanor. "Toward an Ethic of Nurturance: Luce Irigaray on Mothering and Power." In *Mothering: Essays in Feminist Theory*. Ed. Joyce Trebilcot. Totowa, N.J.: Rowman and Allanheld, 1984. 263–74.

Lecercle, Jean-Jacques. *Philosophy Through the Looking-Glass: Language, Nonsense, Desire*. La Salle, Ill.: Open Court, 1985.

Marini, Marcelle. "Scandaleusement autre." *Critique: Revue générale des publications françaises et étrangères* 373–374 (June-July 1978): 603–21.

Millard, Elaine. "French Feminisms." In *Feminist Readings/Feminists Reading*. Ed. Sara Mills, Lynne Pearce, et al. Charlottesville: University Press of Virginia, 1989. 154–86.

Moi, Toril. *Sexual/Textual Politics: Feminist Literary Theory*. New York: Methuen, 1985.

Munster, Anna. "Playing with a Different Sex: Between the Covers of Irigaray and Gallop." *Futur*Fall: Excursions into Post-Modernity*. Ed. E. A. Grosz, Terry Threadgold, et al. Sydney: Pathfinder Press and Power Institute of Fine Arts, 1986. 118–27.

Papke, Mary E. "The Absent Text: Luce Irigaray's Foray into the Dark Continent of Femininity." *Literature and Psychology* 32, no. 1 (1986): 53–56.

Peel, Ellen. "The Irony of Women: Reflections of Irigaray." *Cincinnati Romance Review* 5 (1986): 109–20.

Plaza, Monique. " 'Phallomorphic Power' and the Psychology of 'Woman': A Patriarchal Chain." Trans. Miriam David and Jill Hodges. *Ideology and Consciousness* 4 (1978): 4–36. Rpt. in *Human Sexual Relations: A Reader*. Ed. Mike Brake. London: Penguin Books, 1982. 323–59. Trans. of "Pouvoir 'phallomorphique' et psychologie de 'la Femme.' " *Questions féministes* 1 (November 1977): 91–119.

Sayers, Janet. *Sexual Contradictions: Psychology, Psychoanalysis, and Feminism*. London: Tavistock, 1986.

Schor, Naomi. "Introducing Feminism." *Paragraph: The Journal of the Modern Critical Theory Group* 8 (October 1986): 94–101.

———. "This Essentialism Which Is Not One: Coming to Grips with Irigaray." *Differences* 1 (1989): 38–58.

Schwab, Gail. "Irigarayan Dialogism: Play and Powerplay." In *Feminism and the Dialogic*. Ed. Dale Bauer and Susan Janet McKinsky. New York: SUNY Press, forthcoming.

Silverman, Kaja. "Disembodying the Female Voice: Irigaray, Experimental Feminist Cinema, and Femininity." In *The Acoustic Mirror: The Female Voice in Psychoanalysis and Cinema*. Bloomington: Indiana University Press, 1988. 141–86.

Stanton, Domna C. "Difference on Trial: A Critique of the Maternal Metaphor in Cixous,

Irigaray, and Kristeva." In *The Poetics of Gender*. Ed. Nancy K. Miller and Carolyn G. Heilbrun. New York: Columbia University Press, 1986. 157–82.

Stephenson, Katherine. "Luce Irigaray: Theoretical and Empirical Approaches to the Representation of Subjectivity and Sexual Difference in Language Use." *Semiotics 1988*. Proceedings of the Thirteenth Annual Conference of the Semiotic Society of America, October 1988. Ed. Terry Prewitt. New York: University Press of America, 1989.

Terzian, Debra. "Luce Irigaray: discours de l'homme ou de la femme?" *Constructions* (1985): 119–25.

Wenzel, Hélène Vivienne. "Introduction to Luce Irigaray's 'And the One Doesn't Stir Without the Other.' " *Signs: Journal of Women in Culture and Society* 7, no. 1 (Autumn 1981): 56–59.

Whitford, Margaret. "Luce Irigaray and the Female Imaginary: Speaking as a Woman." *Radical Philosophy* 43 (1986): 3–8.

———. "Luce Irigaray's Critique of Rationality." In *Feminist Perspectives in Philosophy*. Ed. Morwenna Griffiths and Margaret Whitford. Bloomington: Indiana University Press, 1988. 109–30.

———. "Luce Irigaray: The Problem of Feminist Theory." *Paragraph: The Journal of the Modern Critical Theory Group* 8 (October 1986): 102–5.

JULIA KRISTEVA
(1941–   )

Lynne Huffer

BIOGRAPHY

Since her arrival in Paris from Bulgaria in 1966, Julia Kristeva has become one of the leading intellectual figures in France of the latter half of this century. Trained as a linguist, Kristeva came to France at the age of twenty-five on a doctoral research fellowship; by 1967 she had already published articles in major Parisian journals such as *Critique* and, more important, *Tel Quel*. Kristeva's early association with *Tel Quel* marks a decisive moment in her intellectual development. Self-identified as a movement of the avant-garde, the *Tel Quel* group provided a public forum for the ideas of such theorists as Roland Barthes, Jacques Derrida, Philippe Sollers (whom Kristeva eventually married), and Michel Foucault; their collective work explicitly linked the processes of text-production with social and political change. Not surprisingly, then, *Tel Quel*'s distinctive privileging of writing as a subversive force has become, since the late 1960s, a distinguishing feature of Kristeva's thought.

The traces that map the contours of Kristeva's life are most easily reconstituted by examining the terrain of her immense written production, from the linguistic study *Séméiotikè: Recherches pour une sémanalyse* (Studies in Semanalysis) in 1969, to her latest work, a novel whose title, *Les Samouraïs* (The Samourais), echoes Simone de *Beauvoir's *Les Mandarins* of a generation earlier. Perhaps Kristeva's most famous and influential work is her doctoral thesis, published in 1974 as *La Révolution du langage poétique* (*The Revolution in Poetic Language*), where she first introduces the notion of *le sémiotique* ("the semiotic," to be distinguished from *la sémiotique* ["semiotics"], the science of signs). That year also marks the publication by Des Femmes of Kristeva's observations on Chinese women, *Des Chinoises* (*About Chinese Women*), a book that reflects the Maoist obsession of the *Tel Quel* group during that period as well as Kristeva's own interest in women and, more generally, the "feminine." A more decisive influence during this period was Kristeva's discovery of Freudian and Lacanian psychoanalysis. In 1979 she became a practicing psychoanalyst while retaining her chair in linguistics at the University of Paris VII. Kristeva's written production throughout the 1970s displays her increasing interest in psychoanalysis and, correspondingly, a concern for questions of identity, language, and sexual difference; many of her earliest and, to many, most compelling ideas regarding gender and psychic structures in their relation to artistic production are found in *Polylogue* (*Desire in Language*).

Kristeva's writings of the late seventies and 1980s are less "political" than her earlier work of the *Tel Quel* period (the journal became defunct in 1983). Concomitantly, her focus has shifted geographically from China to the United States, where she holds a position as a regular visiting professor at Columbia University. Her interest in American culture as both naïve and liberatory is manifested in articles such as "D'Ithaca à New York" (From Ithaca to New York) and "Pourquoi les Etats-Unis?" (Why the United States?). The later works also display a heightened commitment to psychoanalytic theory and an increasing focus on the Freudian text, manifested, for example, in her study of abjection in *Pouvoirs de l'horreur* (*Powers of Horror*) or her analysis of depression and melancholy in *Soleil noir* (*Black Sun*). Her influential *Histoires d'amour* (*Tales of Love*) examines love as the constitutive element of every "story" from Plato to *E.T.*, just as it forms the basis for the transference between the psychoanalyst and her patient. In *Etrangers à nous-mêmes* (Strangers to Ourselves), Kristeva responds to the contemporary problem of French racism and xenophobia through an exploration of the social, political, and legal history of the foreigner. Finally, her most recent work, *Les Samouraïs*, a roman à clef, narrates the story of a leftist Parisian intellectual milieu from 1968 to the 1990s primarily through the character of Olga, whose trajectory closely parallels that of Kristeva herself.

MAJOR THEMES

Although the entirety of Kristeva's oeuvre comprises a diverse and complex array of theoretical preoccupations impossible to summarize, a focus on some central Kristevan themes does serve to elucidate important strands of her thought. Not the least of these is the Kristevan notion of *textuality*, first introduced in her earliest work of the late 1960s. Like many of her contemporaries, Kristeva has systematically redefined and pushed open the limits of traditional understandings of written production; the Kristevan text is conceived as a kind of process where "meaning" (*signifiance*) is produced not through the intentionality of a coherent subject, the author, but rather as a result of the forces, drives, and modalities that bring writing into existence. The text thus becomes its own process or production rather than a container for self-expression or a mimetic tool of referential reflection.

Within that general understanding of the workings of the text, Kristeva has introduced a number of theoretical constructs that have become central to post-structuralist discourse. To describe the activity of textual and artistic production, Kristeva employs the concept of the *sujet-en-procès* ("subject in process/on trial"), the speaking subject who, as the text's producer, is neither coherent nor empirically verifiable. Rather, the subject/author is the result of the process of a textual production that is shifting, unstable, and constantly moving beyond itself. Throughout much of her early work, particularly *Séméiotikè*, *La Révolution du langage poétique*, and *Polylogue*, Kristeva explores what she calls the text's *negativity*, indebted in large part to the concept of negation in the Hegelian dialectic, but which for Kristeva becomes a localizable textual effect that manifests itself in certain avant-garde writings as ruptures in syntax, rhythm, and semantic coherence. By the same token, the *sujet-en-procès* is constituted through that negativity; the textual construction of the subject is thus also the subject's own continual disruption.

In her later work, Kristeva expands the concept of negativity within a psychoanalytic frame to examine the *abject* (*Pouvoirs de l'horreur*) and *melancholy* (*Soleil noir*) in their relation to artistic production. Both the abject and melancholy, as forms of negativity associated with the death-drive, are predicated on an oedipal structure where the subject's entry into language parallels a separation from the maternal figure. While an unmediated return to the mother after separation would be tantamount to death or psychosis, in the literary text the repressed maternal element emerges metaphorically through images of impurity like excrement and menstrual blood (the abject) or as the lucid sublimation of the lost object by the depressive poetic subject (melancholy).

Kristeva's most influential thought, particularly in the United States, centers precisely on this notion of the irruption of a latent "feminine" or "maternal" element within paternal discourse. In *La Révolution du langage poétique* Kristeva coined the term *le sémiotique* ("the semiotic") to describe the unsayable, untheorizable space that interrupts and displaces the order of language based on the paternal phallus, which Kristeva (following Lacan) calls *le symbolique* ("the symbolic"). While the "symbolic" is marked by paternal interdiction as the Lacanian *nom/non du père* ("name/no of the father"), the maternal "semiotic" is associated with the pre-oedipal phase of human development; linked with the Platonic *chora*, it precedes the formation of the subject through an entry into language. As such, the pre-linguistic, rhythmic, gestural "semiotic" emerges as a textual force in the work of certain avant-garde writers to disrupt traditional, linear writing. Paradoxically, the "semiotic" exists both as a locus prior to the "symbolic" (as that which precedes language) and as a concept that can only define itself in opposition to the "symbolic," as that which, understood synchronically, emerges and breaks open an already established linguistic system. Kristeva's valorization of the "semiotic" in the work of such authors as Mallarmé, Lautréamont, and Artaud is less a return to the mother than an attempt to expose the traces that remain of the repressed maternal element after the subject enters into the domain of paternal language. The "semiotic" is thus a primary force in the dissolution of the Kristevan subject, the "mobile-receptacle space of process, which takes the place of the singular subject" (*Polylogue*, 57).

Kristeva's attention to the "feminine" in its various guises—whether as the hysteric (*Polylogue*), the virgin mother ("Maternité selon Giovanni Bellini" [Maternity According to Giovanni Bellini], "Stabat Mater"), the mystic (*Histoires d'amour*), or the Chinese woman (*Des Chinoises*)—stems from a concern for that which exceeds rational discursive structures; the feminine is the element of heterogeneity or corporality that is repressed by a system of signification based on the phallus. Her position on the "feminine" has been of considerable interest to American feminist theorists who read in Kristeva's work a radical approach to questions of gender and sexuality. And while Kristeva herself has repeatedly declared her objections to feminism per se as yet another product of an oppressively rationalistic, capitalist culture ("La Femme, ce n'est jamais ça" [Woman Is Never That]), she has become known in this country, along with her contemporaries Hélène *Cixous and Luce *Irigaray, as one of the most notable of the "French feminists." Kristeva has in fact engaged feminism as a theoretical question in her influential "Le Temps des femmes" (Women's Time); here she situates the question of women within an opposition between cyclical, monumental time on the one hand, and the linear time of progress and history on the other. Kristeva argues that in order to change society at its core, to ultimately undo the opposition between man and woman as "two rival entities" (*Kristeva Reader*, 209), women must situate themselves elsewhere, in a new "signifying space, a both corporeal and desiring mental space" (209).

A final theme that emerges both in Kristeva's theoretical writings and in her novel, *Les Samouraïs*, is that of the *intellectual* as dissident. The concept of the intellectual as a fundamental agent of social change is consistent with Kristeva's ideas about the revolutionary potential of experimental writing. Kristeva's work has progressively shifted, however, away from issues concerning the political dimensions of such a revolution to focus instead on the possibilities for a radical new system of *ethics*. This shift is manifested both in *Histoires d'amour* and *Au commencement était l'amour* (*In the Beginning Was Love*) through her emphasis on an ethics of desire and love based on the experience of psychoanalytic transference; similarly, in "Women's Time" Kristeva bypasses the impasses of feminist politics to explore feminism as an ethical question. Correspondingly, the activities of a Parisian group of leftist intellectuals in *Les Samouraïs* represent a radically new ethics of living; like the Japanese Samurai who, excelling in the art of war, also transformed living into an aesthetic project, so the characters of Kristeva's novel—whether traveling in China, making love, playing tennis, or writing poetry—engage in an intellectual search that pushes them beyond the limits of a bourgeois culture; implicitly, the Oriental "Other" of the title represents that "otherness" within themselves that ultimately leads to the transformation of society.

SURVEY OF CRITICISM

Kristeva's work, which has been translated into nine languages, has been the object of sustained critical interest for over two decades, particularly in Europe, Canada, and the United States. Her teacher and mentor, Roland Barthes, recognized the potential force of her work as early as 1970, in a review of *Séméiotikè*: "Julia Kristeva," Barthes writes, "changes the place of things . . . what she displaces is the *already-said*" ("L'Etrangère," 19). Indeed, the profuse and often heated response to Kristeva's work suggests both a recognition of that force and a discomfort with that radically "foreign" ("L'Etrangère," 20) displacement. From *Séméiotikè* to *Les Samouraïs*, Kristeva has forced her readers into an uncompromising and unsettling self-critique that Barthes has called learning "to work within difference" ("L'Etrangère," 20).

In semiotic circles, Kristeva attained early notoriety for her unique approach to linguistic study (*la sémanalyse*) and for her role in introducing the work of the great Russian linguist Mikhail Bakhtin to Western intellectuals. Because of her training as a linguist and her knowledge of Russian Formalism, Kristeva played a key role in providing literary scholars with theoretical and terminological tools, one of the most important of these being the Bakhtinian concept of *intertextuality*. Perhaps most important is Kristeva's landmark status as a theorist of post-structuralist thought. Although she participated in the structuralist project in the 1960s, Kristeva was instrumental in pushing structuralism beyond itself by questioning, from a semiotic and Marxist perspective, some of its basic premises. From the start, her project has been to expose the incompleteness and inadequacy of a kind of thinking that, like structuralism, defines itself as closed and self-sufficient.

Kristeva's theoretical concepts have had a formative influence on an entire generation of literary scholars. Although influential, however, she has been criticized on a number of fronts for the gap between her theories and their practical application. Some have argued, for example, that the "semiotic"—which Kristeva finds to be operational in particular "avant-garde" texts of the late nineteenth and early twentieth centuries (Mallarmé, Lautréamont, Artaud, Bataille, Céline, Joyce, Kafka, among others)—is a concept that in fact works too well; rather than being limited to specific modern texts, the "semiotic" could be shown to function in virtually any text. Further, textual features such as the rigorous and controlled manipulation of syntactic structures (characteristic of Mallarmé, for example) could reflect a reinforcement of syntax itself rather than its disruption.

The most prolonged and well-developed critique of Kristeva's work has come from feminist scholars, who variously read her *oeuvre*, on the one hand, as a radically subversive departure from the status quo or, on the other, as an anti-feminist reinforcement of masculinist thought. Toril Moi's influential *Sexual/Textual Politics* argues, for example, that despite some of the shortcomings of Kristeva's politics, her exploration of marginality, subversion, and subjectivity is both anti-humanist and anti-essentialist, and thus merits sustained feminist attention. In the same vein, Alice Jardine proposes a "politics" or "ethics" of reading Kristeva that allows for her "difference" from Anglo-American feminists; in Jardine's view, Kristeva's "female" voice is "strangely subversive" ("Opaque Texts," 109). Other writers criticize Kristeva for her "post-feminist" (Russo) position; in Jennifer Stone's view, for example, "Kristeva's work is no longer in women's interests" (42).

A number of American critics have attempted to mediate what Domna Stanton calls the "dis-connection" between French and American feminist thought. Kristeva's focus on the symbolic, on the world as text or Logos, has provided American feminists with new possibilities for understanding and ultimately dismantling patriarchal oppression. More recently, however, Kristeva has been increasingly criticized not only for her indifference to feminism as a movement, but also for reinforcing traditional definitions of femininity. Kristeva's thought, so the argument goes, is inherently essentialist, and simply recuperates a binarism based on biological notions of sexual difference, rather than on gender as a social construction. The maternal element so prominent in Kristeva's work has been particularly problematic for a number of critics; Stanton argues, for example, that Kristeva's description of the "semiotic" relies on traditional images of maternity. "By emphasizing the subject's desire to destroy the father and to (re)possess the mother," Stanton writes, "Kristeva's model for engendering the poetic does not then deviate fundamentally from the patriarchal oedipal script" ("Difference," 166).

Even more troubling to other readers are aspects of Kristeva's work that can be interpreted as elitist and ethnocentric. In "Pourquoi les Etats-Unis?," for example, Kristeva describes Americans as non-verbal and naïve, implying that only her intervention as a European intellectual can transform this unrefined culture into something of value. Further, Kristeva's book on China (*Des Chinoises*) has been faulted for its imperialism, both in its homologization of the "Other" through the image of the Chinese woman, and in its generalization of the Western position from which Kristeva speaks. Most notable in this context is Gayatri Chakravorty Spivak's article, "French Feminism in an International Frame," which exposes the problems of ethnocentrism in *Des Chinoises* in order to explore the limitations of speaking about an absolute opposition between "Anglo-American" and "French" feminisms. As Spivak remarks: "The difference between 'French' and 'Anglo-American' feminism is superficial. . . . I see no way to avoid insisting that there has to be a simultaneous other focus: not merely who am I? but who is the other woman?" ("French Feminism," 179).

That concern with the "other woman"—the woman who becomes the silent "other," not only of man, but also of those women whose economic and racial privilege accords them the possibility of speech—has become central to contemporary feminist debates. Correspondingly, Spivak's question—"who is the other woman?"—perhaps most crucially exposes the "difference" (to echo Jardine and Barthes) of Kristeva's text. For Kristeva, "woman" constitutes an unstable concept that is, as Margaret Atack puts it, "always in danger of degenerating into its other" ("The Other," 36). Kristeva's resistance to that degeneration explains in large part those aspects of her thought that are, for many of her readers, most politically problematic. And no doubt the debates around the object "Kristeva" will continue to rage between feminist and anti-feminist, essentialist and anti-essentialist, imperialist and anti-imperialist arguments. It is also inevitable that those oppositions will eventually dismantle themselves, in a typically Kristevan fashion, as yet another displacement of the *already-said*.

BIBLIOGRAPHY

Major Works by Julia Kristeva

Séméiotikè: Recherches pour une sémanalyse. Paris: Seuil, 1969.
Le Langage, cet inconnu: Une Initiation à la linguistique. Paris: Seuil, 1969. (Originally published under the name Julia Joyaux; rpt. 1981.)
Le Texte du roman: Approche sémiologique d'une structure discursive transformationnelle. The Hague: Mouton, 1970. (Rpt. 1976).
Des Chinoises. Paris: Editions des Femmes, 1974.
La Révolution du langage poétique: L'Avant-garde à la fin du XIXe siècle. Lautréamont et Mallarmé. Paris: Seuil, 1974.
"D'Ithaca à New York." *Promesse* 36–37 (1974): 123–40. (Rpt. in *Polylogue*, 495–515.)
"La Femme, ce n'est jamais ça." *Tel Quel* 59 (1974): 19–26. (Rpt. in *Polylogue*, 517–24.)
"Maternité selon Giovanni Bellini." *Peinture* 10/11 (1975): 409–36. (Rpt. in *Polylogue*, 409–35.)
"Pourquoi les Etats-Unis?" (with Marcelin Playnet and Philippe Sollers). *Tel Quel* 71/73 (1977): 3–19.
Polylogue. Paris: Seuil, 1977.
"Héréthique de l'amour." *Tel Quel* 74 (1977): 30–49. (Rpt. as "Stabat Mater" in *Histoires d'amour*, 295–327.)
"Le Vréel." In *Folle vérite et vraisemblance du texte psychotique*. Ed. Julia Kristeva and Jean-Marc Ribettes. Paris: Seuil, 1979.
"Le Temps des femmes." *33/44: Cahiers de recherche de sciences des textes et documents* 5 (1979): 5–19.
Pouvoirs de l'horreur: Essai sur l'abjection. Paris: Seuil, 1980.
Histoires d'amour. Paris: Denoël, 1983.
Au commencement était l'amour: Psychanalyse et foi. Paris: Hachette, 1985.
Soleil noir: Dépression et mélancolie. Paris: Gallimard, 1987.
Etrangers à nous-mêmes. Paris: Fayard, 1988.
Les Samouraïs. Paris: Fayard, 1990.

Translations of Julia Kristeva

About Chinese Women. Trans. Anita Barrows. New York: Urizen Books, 1977.
"The U.S. Now: A Conversation." *October* (1978): 3–17. (Rpt. as "Why the United States?" in *The Kristeva Reader*, 272–91.)

Desire in Language: A Semiotic Approach to Literature and Art. Ed. Léon S. Roudiez. Trans. Alice Jardine, Thomas A. Gora, and Léon S. Roudiez. New York: Columbia University Press, 1980.

"Women's Time." Trans. Alice Jardine and Harry Blake. *Signs: Journal of Women in Culture and Society* 7 (1981): 13–35. (Rpt. in *The Kristeva Reader*, 188–213.)

Powers of Horror: An Essay on Abjection. Trans. Léon S. Roudiez. New York: Columbia University Press, 1982.

The Revolution in Poetic Language. Trans. Margaret Waller. New York: Columbia University Press, 1984.

The Kristeva Reader. Ed. Toril Moi. New York: Columbia University Press, 1986.

Tales of Love. Trans. Léon S. Roudiez. New York: Columbia University Press, 1987.

In the Beginning Was Love: Psychoanalysis and Faith. Trans. Arthur Goldhammer. New York: Columbia University Press, 1988.

Language: The Unknown. An Initiation into Linguistics. Trans. Anne M. Menke. New York: Columbia University Press, 1989.

Black Sun: Depression and Melancholia. Trans. Léon S. Roudiez. New York: Columbia University Press, 1989.

Studies of Julia Kristeva

Adriaens, Mark. "Ideology and Literary Production: Kristeva's Poetics." In *Semiotics and Dialectics: Ideology and the Text.* Ed. Peter Zima. Amsterdam: Benjamins, 1981. 179–220.

Atack, Margaret. "The Other: Feminist." *Paragraph: The Journal of the Modern Critical Theory Group* 8 (1986): 25–39.

Barthes, Roland. "L'Etrangère." *La Quinzaine littéraire* (May 1–15, 1970): 19–20.

Bové, Carol Mastrangelo. "The Politics of Desire in Julia Kristeva." *Boundary 2* 12 (1984): 217–28.

Conley, Verena Andermatt. "Julia Kristeva and the Traversal of Modern Poetic Space." *Enclitic* 1 (1977): 65–77.

———. "Kristeva's China." *Diacritics* (1975): 25–30.

Cornell, Drucilla, and Adam Thurschwell. "Feminism, Negativity, Intersubjectivity." In *Feminism as Critique: On the Politics of Gender.* Ed. Seyla Benhabib and Drucilla Cornell. Minneapolis: University of Minnesota Press, 1987. 143–62.

Féral, Josette. "China, Women and the Symbolic: An Interview with Julia Kristeva." *SubStance* 13 (1976): 9–18.

Fletcher, John, and Andrew Benjamin, eds. *Abjection, Melancholia and Love: The Work of Julia Kristeva.* London: Routledge, 1990.

Gallop, Jane. "The Phallic Mother: Fraudian Analysis." In *The Daughter's Seduction: Feminism and Psychoanalysis.* Ithaca: Cornell University Press, 1982. 113–31.

Jacobus, Mary. "Madonna: Like a Virgin, or, Freud, Kristeva, and the Case of the Missing Mother." *Oxford Literary Review* 8 (1986): 35–50.

Jardine, Alice. "Introduction to Julia Kristeva's 'Women's Time.' " *Signs: Journal of Women in Culture and Society* 7 (1981): 5–12.

———. "Opaque Texts and Transparent Contexts: The Political Difference of Julia Kristeva." In *The Poetics of Gender.* Ed. Nancy K. Miller. New York: Columbia University Press, 1986. 96–116.

———. "Theories of the Feminine: Kristeva." *Enclitic* 4, no. 2 (1980): 5–15.

Jones, Ann Rosalind. "Inscribing Femininity: French Theories of the Feminine." In *Making a Difference: Feminist Literary Criticism*. Ed. Gayle Greene and Coppelia Kahn. London: Methuen, 1985. 80–112.

———. "Writing the Body: Toward an Understanding of L'Ecriture Feminine." *Feminist Studies* 7 (1981): 247–63.

Klein, Richard. "In the Body of the Mother." *Enclitic* 7 (1983): 66–75.

Kuykendall, Eléanor H. "Questions for Julia Kristeva's Ethics of Linguistics." In *The Thinking Muse: Feminism and Modern French Philosophy*. Ed. Jeffner Allen and Iris Marion Young. Bloomington: Indiana University Press, 1989. 180–94.

Lechte, John. *Julia Kristeva*. New York: Routledge, 1990.

Lewis, Phillip. "Revolutionary Semiotics." *Diacritics* 4 (1974): 28–32.

Moi, Toril. Introduction to *The Kristeva Reader*. Ed. Toril Moi. New York: Columbia University Press, 1986. 1–21.

———. "Marginality and Subversion: Julia Kristeva." In *Sexual/Textual Politics: Feminist Literary Theory*. London: Methuen, 1985. 150–73.

Nesselroth, Peter. "Poetic Language and the Revolution." *L'Esprit créateur* 16 (1976): 149–60.

Nye, Andrea. "Woman Clothed with the Sun: Julia Kristeva and the Escape from/to Language." *Signs: Journal of Women in Culture and Society* 12 (1987): 664–86.

Pajaczkowska, Claire. "Introduction to Kristeva." *m/f* 5/6 (1981): 149–57.

Rabine, Leslie. "Julia Kristeva: Semiotics and Women." *Pacific Coast Philology* 12 (1977): 41–49.

Rose, Jacqueline. "Julia Kristeva: Take Two." In *Sexuality in the Field of Vision*. London: Verso, 1986. 141–64.

Russo, Mary. "Notes on 'Post-Feminism.' " In *The Politics of Theory*. Proceedings of the Essex Conference on the Sociology of Literature. Ed. Francis Barker et al. University of Essex, 1983. 27–37.

Spivak, Gayatri Chakravorty. "French Feminism in an International Frame." *Yale French Studies* 62 (1981): 154–84.

Stanton, Domna. "Difference on Trial: A Critique of the Maternal Metaphor in Cixous, Irigaray, and Kristeva." In *The Poetics of Gender*. Ed. Nancy K. Miller. New York: Columbia University Press, 1986. 157–82.

———. "Language and Revolution: The Franco-American Dis-Connection." In *The Future of Difference*. Ed. Hester Eisentein and Alice Jardine. Boston: G. K. Hall, 1980. 73–87.

Stone, Jennifer. "The Horrors of Power: A Critique of 'Kristeva.' " In *The Politics of Theory*. Proceedings of the Essex Conference on the Sociology of Literature. Ed. Francis Barker et al. University of Essex, 1983. 38–48.

Volat-Shapiro, Helene. "Julia Kristeva: A Bibliography of Her Writings." *Bulletin of Bibliography* 45, no. 1 (1988): 51–62.

Zepp, Evelyn. "The Criticism of Julia Kristeva: A New Mode of Critical Thought." *Romanic Review* 73 (1982): 80–97.

JULIANE VON KRÜDENER
(1764–1824)

Lucy M. Schwartz

BIOGRAPHY

Barbara Juliana von Vietinghof was born during the night of November 22–23, 1764, at Riga in the Russian Baltic republic now called Latvia. As the child of a wealthy and highly respected family, she learned both French and German at an early age. When she was thirteen, she traveled with her parents to Paris as well as to Spa (Belgium) and England, accompanied by a French governess.

In 1782 she married Burchhard Alexis Constantine, Baron von Krüdener, who was born in 1744, had been divorced twice, and had a nine-year-old daughter, Sophie. A diplomat by profession, he was Russian minister to Courtland, a Polish province negotiating to be united with Russia. In 1784 their first child, Paul, was born; that same year the baron was named Russian ambassador to Venice.

They were accompanied in Italy by Alexander de Stakiev, a young secretary of the embassy, who fell in love with Mme de Krüdener but kept his passion a secret from her. She was gradually becoming disillusioned with her husband, and after the baron was named ambassador to Denmark, their marital difficulties increased. For diplomatic reasons Baron von Krüdener was required to court a beautiful woman, Mme de Reventlow. His wife did not accept this easily; and when Stakiev decided to confess his love to her, she persuaded him to submit a written confession to her husband. Mme de Krüdener recorded her emotional reactions to these events in a journal written in French.

Finally, in 1789, Mme de Krüdener left her husband to go south, supposedly for reasons of ill health. Accompanied by Paul, her daughter Juliette, born in 1787, the baron's daughter Sophie, and a Swiss governess named Antoinie Piozet, she went to Paris. There she met her first mentor, Bernardin de Saint-Pierre. The group visited Nîmes and settled for the winter of 1789–90 in Montpellier, where she wrote *Geraldine I*, a fictionalized version of her platonic love affair with a French count named Adrien de Lezay-Marnesia.

After trips to Nîmes, Avignon, and Barèges, Mme de Krüdener returned to Montpellier in September 1790, where she fell in love with Charles-Louis de Frégeville. In 1791 they decided to travel together to Copenhagen to obtain the baron's permission to marry. Instead, they separated when Frégeville was called back to France for military service; and she rejoined her parents in Riga. Her father died in June 1792. Soon afterward Julie agreed with her husband to live separately; she would go to Germany, where their son was to study.

Thus, in 1793, Julie settled in Leipzig with the children. There she met Claude Hippolyte Terray, with whom she had a long love affair that she called a "secret marriage" in a letter to her mother. She continued to travel and in 1796 met the German writer Jean-Paul Richter, with whom she carried on a long correspondence that influenced much of her writing.

The period from 1797 to 1803 was very fruitful for her writing. She wrote some of her best prose, including her famous novel, *Valérie*. Many of the other texts of this period have never been published in their entirety. During a stay in Lausanne from 1796 to 1798 she wrote *Alexis ou Histoire d'un soldat russe* (Alexis, or The Story of a Russian Soldier). *La Cabane des lataniers* (The Palm Tree Cabin) was an experiment with an exotic novel imitating Bernardin de Saint-Pierre. The heroine was called Sidonie, a name Mme de Krüdener adopted for herself in letters of this period. *Elisa ou l'Education d'une jeune fille* (Eliza, or The Education of a Young Girl) was a treatise on education mixed with religious meditations and descriptions of the beauty of the Swiss countryside. Finally, *Les Malheurs de l'Helvétie* (The Misfortunes of Switzerland) was written to celebrate the heroism of the Swiss fighting against the French invaders in 1798. In 1801 she sent the manuscript to Jean-Paul Richter.

In 1798 Julie gave birth to the son of Terray. The child, called Philippe Hauger, was secretly raised in Geneva by the governess Antoinie Piozet, now called Mme Armand.

After visiting Mme de *Staël in Switzerland, Julie de Krüdener moved to Paris in 1802. There she lived near her old friend Bernardin de Saint-Pierre and frequented literary salons where she got to know Chateaubriand and Benjamin Constant. The news of the death of the Baron von Krüdener caused her to leave Paris and seek solitude in the country. In August she went to Geneva. From there she wrote letters to friends in France arranging publicity for her "Pensées et Maximes" (Thoughts and Maxims), which appeared in Paris in the journal *Mercure de France* in October with a preface by Chateaubriand.

In December she returned to Lyons, where she finished *La Cabane des lataniers* and worked on *Valérie*. Returning to Paris in May 1803, she devoted much of her time to publicizing *Valérie*, which came out in December. The novel was an instant best-seller, and she was a social success in Paris. However, in January 1804 she fled her celebrity status and retreated to Riga. There she stayed with her mother until 1806 and had a religious conversion that many believe was the turning point in her life. One product of this was an unpublished satirical work, "Les Gens du monde" (Worldly People).

In 1806 she traveled to Wiesbaden and Königsburg, where she met Queen Louise of Prussia. The next few years were spent in Germany. During this time she became acquainted with Johann Heinrich Jung-Stilling, a religious philosopher who strongly influenced her life. Between 1808 and 1809 she wrote *Othilde*, a medieval story with a Christian theme. In 1810 she returned to Riga, where she remained until her mother's death in 1811. After this emotional experience, she went back to Germany, where she preached before the Russian Empress, and the queens of Holland and Sweden, who were together at Karlsruhe. In 1813, in Geneva, Julie met Henri Empaytaz, a young theology student who became a follower of hers.

Mme de Krüdener gradually accumulated a group of faithful disciples who followed her on her travels. After she met the Russian Emperor Alexander in Hielbronn, her band went to Paris with him in 1815. In September Julie stood by Alexander as he reviewed his troops on the Plain of Virtues in France and afterward wrote a pamphlet entitled *Le Camp de Vertus* (The Camp of Virtues), in which she declared that Alexander had been chosen by God to lead sinful Europe out of its sufferings. It seems to some historians that Mme de Krüdener was instrumental in inspiring Alexander to draw up the Treaty of Holy Alliance. This treaty, signed by the rulers of Austria, Prussia, and Russia, bound them to base their conduct on the Christian Gospel, to remain united as brothers, and to admit into the alliance others who would agree to these principles.

When Alexander left Paris, Mme de Krüdener was to follow him to St. Petersburg; but, on the way, she spent two years in Switzerland preaching. She drew large crowds of poor, hungry people. Her revolutionary message and her followers were not often welcomed by municipal authorities. The group was expelled from town after town in Switzerland and Germany and finally settled on her farm at Kosse in Russia. In 1824, despite her bad health brought on by fasts, she accompanied her daughter, her son-in-law, and Princess Galitzin to Crimea, where she died in December of that year.

MAJOR THEMES

Mme de Krüdener's works evolved from the profane to the sacred. Her aspiration was to find love to give meaning to her life. She began with an earthly conception of love, which became a spiritual love for a human being in *Valérie*, and finally an all-embracing love of God and her fellow creatures after her "conversion." It is an oversimplification to divide her life into two periods, before and after conversion, because religious themes were present in her works from the beginning.

In her early diaries and journals she expressed her idealized love for her husband and her disappointment that he did not respond to her in the enthusiastic way she would have liked. Although he was considerate of her, he was not as ''sensitive'' (emotional) as she wished. She felt misunderstood and unappreciated. Thus, although she virtuously spurned the love of Alexander de Stakiev, she hoped to make her husband jealous with it and recapture his attention. She transformed this situation into fiction in *Valérie* years later.

Before writing *Valérie* she had several not-so-chaste love affairs and discovered, thanks to Jean-Paul Richter, an idealized conception of love which endures even after death.

Her Swiss period from 1796 to 1802 was an apprenticeship for *Valérie*. In *Alexis* she dealt with the conflict between military duty and love for family. The Russian soldier is tempted to desert his post because his family is starving in his absence. Luckily, his colonel discovers the situation and returns him to his family. *La Cabane des lataniers*, which was never completed, was written as Mme de Krüdener discovered that life with her husband was no longer possible. In this novel Olivier is in love with Sidonie, who loves love more than her lover. She wishes to move him toward a spiritual love that would transcend their mortal condition. In this way she is like the heroine of *Geraldine I*; both of them have attitudes expressed by the author in her journals.

La Cabane has an exotic setting that the author had never seen, and thus is described in an artificial manner. In *Eliza* she shows that she can capture the beauty of a natural setting—Lake Constance, the peaks of Appenzell, and the Rhine valley. These descriptions were a preparation for *Valérie*, where the beauty of the landscapes contributes to the central theme of hopeless love. In *Eliza*, which was written while she was pregnant with her illegitimate child, she seems to want to redeem herself by losing all thoughts of self in care for the child and others. She declares that happiness is found in faith, good conscience, and the acceptance of one's duty. In contemplation of nature, the author finds a love of God and a resignation to His will. These themes foreshadow her later religious writings.

Some of these themes are also found in her *Pensées et maximes*, published in 1802. In them she treats subjects such as love and friendship, genius and immortality, happiness and virtue, and theater and the arts.

Each of these works in some way prepared her for the writing of *Valérie*, which is considered her masterpiece and is the only one of her novels readily available in the United States. *Valérie* tells the story of Stakiev's unhappy love for her from his point of view. By this time her husband had died, and she felt some remorse for having failed to reconcile her differences with him before his death. Perhaps because of this feeling of guilt, the husband, the Count of B., who lacks an appreciation for Valérie's spontaneous (capricious) nature, is nonetheless portrayed as extremely patient.

Valérie is an epistolary novel composed of letters from a Swede, Gustave de Linar, to his friend Ernest. The story begins when Gustave, who is the secretary and adopted son of the Count of B., accompanies him on a diplomatic mission to Venice. The count is twenty-one years older than his wife, Valérie. A child of sixteen, she considers Gustave as a brother. However, in spite of his admiration for the count and his love for this man who has been a "second father to him," Gustave falls in love with Valérie and constructs an idealized image of her, which he adores. When asked by Valérie why he is sad, Gustave replies that he loves a woman in Sweden whom he can never marry.

Gustave begins to notice that the count does not understand or appreciate his wife as much as he should. How much better Gustave would love her if she were his wife! In one of the most famous scenes of the novel, Valérie performs the shawl dance for a group of admirers while Gustave, who had not been invited to the dance, watches her from the terrace. When she sits down to rest, he kisses the pane of glass close to her arm; but she is unaware of his presence. This glass becomes a symbol of the barriers between them.

When he learns that Valérie is expecting a child, Gustave is insane with worry. The baby, who lives only several hours, is buried at the Lido. Gustave accompanies Valérie regularly to the grave, cares for it, and plants flowers. It seems that he wants to become like the baby Adolphe—a son of Valérie to be reunited with her after death.

The count takes his wife on a trip to cheer her up, and Gustave remains in Venice in hopes of curing his passion. Instead, he creates a shrine to Valérie in her home, having tea every day in front of her portrait. He follows a woman in the street who resembles Valérie. Her name is Bianca. He gets to know her and finally asks her to wear Valérie's shawl and sing a song she used to sing. At first he is captivated by the vision of his beloved; but, when she stops singing, he loses interest and sees her as a useless marionette.

After the return of Valérie, he decides that flight is his only hope of saving his virtue and self-respect. As he is leaving the house, he sees a fire in Valérie's room and rushes in to put it out. He hears her murmur "Gustave" in her sleep, and he cannot leave without kissing her hand. Then he sees the wedding band, another symbol of all that separates him from her.

He retreats to a monastery, where he suffers from his passion. The reports of his health worry Ernest, who writes a letter to the court revealing Gustave's guilty secret. The count rushes to Gustave's bedside to comfort him and assure him that Valérie knows of his love, and they both forgive him. The count describes Gustave's death in a letter to Ernest, and the novel ends with some pages from Gustave's mother's diary that recount his youthful idealism and her hopes and fears for him.

The major themes of the work are Gustave's impossible love and his inevitable death, which is foreshadowed in a cemetery the trio visits on their way to Venice. In addition to these themes, the idea that behavior may be governed by climate, later popularized by Mme de Staël in *Corinne*, is illustrated in *Valérie*. Gustave is a Nordic type who never should have gone to the South. He is destroyed by a passion he cannot fight in the sultry, sensuous climate of Italy. His friend Ernest repeatedly explains this to him and begs him to return home while there is still time. This theme is underlined by detailed descriptions of the Swedish and Italian landscapes, which Mme de Krüdener juxtaposes artistically. She also includes a commentary on the art treasures in Italy and a condemnation of Napoleon for taking some of them from their natural setting to display them in Paris.

Valérie is a typical novel of the pre-Romantic period, owing its structure to Jean-Jacques Rousseau's *La Nouvelle Héloïse*. The second part of *La Nouvelle Héloïse* shows how the heroine, Julie, makes a happy existence for herself with her old husband Wolmar and her former lover Saint-Preux. *Valérie* does not completely replicate this triangle, because Gustave is completely alone, while the count and Valérie form a harmonious couple. Valérie never returns his love, nor is she conscious of it until the end of the novel. This is, of course, a romanticized version of the relationship among Mme de Krüdener, her husband, and Stakiev. The harmonious couple is in her imagination, and most of her biographers reject the legend that Stakiev committed suicide. However, it is difficult to resist seeing the novel also as a vindication of the wife who is pure, innocent, and misunderstood by the husband, who has no appreciation of the overwhelming (if childish) love that his wife gives to him freely.

Mme de Krüdener insists in her preface that the story has a highly moral message because Gustave fights his passion with virtue aided by religion. However, Gustave's lyrico-religious effusions remind us of Chateaubriand's René and other pre-Romantic heroes in their exaltation of passion. This could be the real message of *Valérie*.

Mme de Krüdener's later works are all inspired by her religious mysticism. ''Les Gens du monde,'' which was completed by 1805, was read to social gatherings in Toeplitz. The manuscript has been lost, and all we know of the work is from her letters and comments from people who heard it read. She claimed in a letter to Camille Jordan that it was the opposite of *Valérie* and contributed to morality by showing many rich people who were unhappy (Ley, *Mme de Krüdener et son temps*, 369–70).

Othilde, which was also read aloud to groups, has disappeared except for a fragment published in German in 1818. The novel is said to have as its major theme the redeeming power of Christianity. The story takes place during the Middle Ages; a young girl is imprisoned by her father, and her religious faith helps her face her misfortune (Ley, *Mme de Krüdener*, 369–84).

Her other works are religous pamphlets such as ''Le Camp des vertus'' and sermons. Most of these have disappeared.

SURVEY OF CRITICISM

Charles-Augustin Sainte-Beuve wrote a famous article about Mme de Krüdener in 1837. Entitled ''Madame de Krüdner [*sic*],'' it was later published in his *Portraits de femmes* (*Portraits of Famous Women*, 1844). Sainte-Beuve's critical method was to elucidate the works of authors by referring to events in their lives. His portrait of Mme de Krüdener emphasized the first half of her life as a noblewoman in high society. Against the snowy background of her native

Livonia, he portrayed her as a beautiful lady surrounded by knights in an atmosphere reminiscent of the Middle Ages. What interested him most was her brief time in Paris, where she frequented all the fashionable salons. He saw *Valérie* as a delicate, charming masterpiece appropriately produced by a delicate, charming lady. Her religious writings and her role in the Holy Alliance were passed over rapidly with a little humor.

In his article Sainte-Beuve mentioned the biography of Mme de Krüdener that Charles Eynard was writing and expressed his interest in it. However, when the Swiss scholar's *Vie de Madame de Krüdener* (Life of Madame de Krüdener) came out in 1849, Sainte-Beuve was not enthusiastic. Eynard was convinced that Julie died a saint. Thus, he emphasized all the faults in the first part of her life—her love affairs, her vanity, her publicity-seeking activities. These made her later life and her conversion seem even more saintly.

Sainte-Beuve was angered by this destruction of the image of the elegant lady he had created and replied with "Madame de Krüdner [*sic*] et ce qu'en aurait dit Saint-Evremond" (Madame de Krüdener and What Saint-Evremond Would Have Said about Her), an article later published in his *Portraits littéraires* (*Literary Portraits*, 1864). His thesis was basically that people do not change that much; if Mme de Krüdener was duplicitous in her early life, she was probably a fake saint as well.

Most of the other nineteenth-century biographies of Mme de Krüdener did not add any new facts or discuss her work itself. Many of them simply rehashed the events recorded by Sainte-Beuve or Eynard.

Few early critics studied her novels, a problem that many women writers have had. Often literary critics failed to take their work seriously as literature, preferring to discuss their connections with famous men. There were a few exceptions to this tradition. André Le Breton in *Le Roman français au XIXe siècle* (The French Novel in the Nineteenth Century, 1901) and Joachim Merlant in *Le Roman personnel de Rousseau à Fromentin* (The Personal Novel from Rousseau to Fromentin, 1905) each devoted a chapter to *Valérie*, which they saw as holding an honorable place in the history of the novel. Pierre Kohler in "*Valérie* ou maîtres et imitateurs de Mme de Krüdener" (*Valérie*, or Masters and Imitators of Mme de Krüdener), studied in 1922 the literary sources of *Valérie* and the later works that were inspired by it. *The Lady of the Holy Alliance*, a carefully researched biography of Mme de Krüdener, was written in English by E. J. Knapton in 1939.

In 1961, Francis Ley, a descendant of Mme de Krüdener and heir to many unpublished papers, filled in some gaps in her biography in *Madame de Krüdener et son temps* (Madame de Krüdener and Her Time). He continued to publish articles on her life and revealed in 1965 the existence of her illegitimate son. His second book, *Bernardin de Saint-Pierre, Madame de Staël, Chateaubriand, Benjamin Constant et Madame de Krüdener*, published in 1967, explored her relationship with each of the famous people mentioned.

Finally, in 1972, Michel Mercier published his Sorbonne thesis, "*Valérie*":

Origine et destinée d'un roman, which thoroughly examined all of the Ley documents as well as other manuscripts. He showed how *Valérie* fit into the emotional development of Mme de Krüdener, analyzed in detail her debt to German writers such as Jean-Paul Richter, and compared *Valérie* to other French works such as *La Nouvelle Héloïse* and *La Princesse de Clèves*. In addition, he published in *Les Ecrits de Madame de Krüdener* (The Writings of Madame de Krüdener) some of her unpublished manuscripts. His conclusions were that *Valérie* was quite original in its contribution to Romantic literature and deserved to be respected as an integral part of that tradition.

Valérie has not yet been rediscovered and reexamined by feminist literary critics. If it were, they might find the valorization of the heroine presented through the eyes of the male narrator, Gustave, an interesting strategy when used by a female author for goals other than those of the usual male author who identifies with his male narrator.

Although *Valérie* is rarely studied today, it was widely read during the nineteenth century. It was a best-seller when it came out in 1804, appreciated by both male and female readers. Mme de Krüdener's masterpiece influenced many writers in the Romantic generation of 1830—from lesser-known writers like Maxime Idion and Boulay-Paty to Lamartine, Musset, and especially Sainte-Beuve. Mercier analyzes her influence on these writers and on the Polish writer Adam Mickiewicz. Contemporary interest in her works stems mainly from her importance in the history of romanticism; however, Mercier expresses the hope that his book will inspire new and well-deserved interest in *Valérie* as a novel.

BIBLIOGRAPHY

Major Works by Mme de Krüdener

Valérie ou Lettres de Gustave de Linar à Ernest de G . . . . Paris: Henrichs, 1804.
Le Camp de vertus. Paris: Le Normant, 1815.
Lettre au baron de Berckheim. Karlsruhe: N.p., 1817.
Le Solitaire, fragment of "Othilde," published in German as *Der Einsiedler*. Leipzig: N.p., 1818.
Albert et Clara (Les Malheurs de l'Helvétie). Stuttgart: N.p., 1824.
Ecrits de Mme de Krüdener. Contains *Alexis (Histoire d'un soldat russe)*, *Lettre à Heller*, *Pensées et maximes*, and *Sur l'éducation des princes*. Diss., Michel Mercier, University of Paris IV, 1972.
Ecrits intimes et prophétiques de Madame de Krüdener: 1785–1807. Contains *Après la bataille d'Eylau*, *Geraldine I*, *Geraldine II*, *Le Journal de Venise*, *La Lettre à Hélène*, and *Lettres de voyage de Lyon à Paris*. Paris: CNRS, 1975.

Translations of Mme de Krüdener

There are no English translations of her works.

Studies of Mme de Krüdener

Decreus van Liefland, Juliette. "La Baronne de Krüdener." In *Sainte-Beuve et la critique des auteurs féminins*. Paris: Boivin, 1949. 122–38.

Eynard, Charles. *Vie de Mme de Krüdener*. 2 vols. Paris: Cherbuliez, 1849.

Ford, Clarence. *The Life and Letters of Mme de Krüdener*. London: Adam and Charles Black, 1893.

Knapton, E. J. *The Lady of the Holy Alliance*. New York: Columbia University Press, 1939.

Kohler, Pierre. "*Valérie* ou maîtres et imitateurs de Mme de Krüdener." *Bulletin de l'institut national genevois* 45 (1922–23): 193–222.

Le Breton, André. "*Claire d'Albe—Valérie*." In *Le Roman français au XIXe siècle: Avant Balzac*. Paris: Boivin, 1901. 90–113.

Ley, Francis. *Bernardin de Saint-Pierre, Madame de Staël, Chateaubriand, Benjamin Constant et Madame de Krüdener*. Paris: Aubier-Montaigne, 1967.

———. *Mme de Krüdener et son temps*. Paris: Plon, 1961.

Mercier, Michel. "*Valérie*": *Origine et destinée d'un roman*. Paris: Diss., University of Paris IV, 1972.

Merlant, Joachim. "Mme de Krüdener—*Valérie*." In *Le Roman personnel de Rousseau à Fromentin*. Paris: Hachette, 1905. 167–91.

Sainte-Beuve, Charles-Augustin. "Madame de Krüdner [*sic*]" and "Madame de Krüdner [*sic*] et ce qu'en aurait dit Saint-Evremond." In *Oeuvres*. 2 vols. Paris: Gallimard, 1960. 2:764–84, 1327–52.

LOUISE LABÉ
(c. 1520–1566)

François Rigolot

BIOGRAPHY

Little is known about Louise Labé's life. From a family of ropemakers, barber-surgeons, and butchers, she was the daughter of Pierre Charly (a.k.a. Labé), an industrious ropemaker who, in about 1493, established his own shop, rue de l'Arbre sec, at the foot of Saint Sébastien Hill in Lyons. In 1515, after the death of his first wife, Charly married Etiennette Roybet, whose dowry included a comfortable townhouse, located in the fashionable downtown district. Five children were born from this second wedlock: three sons (Barthélemy, François, and Mathieu) and two daughters (Claudine and Louise). In the absence of more precise dates, one can only conjecture that Louise was born between 1516 (her father's wedding) and 1523 (her mother's death). Some four years later, Pierre Charly married Antoinette Maillard, a master butcher's daughter, who gave him another two children: Jeanne and Pierre II Charly (Labé).

As master craftsman, Louise's father enjoyed a respectable social status. Records tell us, for instance, that in 1534 he was called before the city's governing body, the Assemblée des Consuls, to approve the founding of a relief agency for the poor, the Aumône-Générale (see Natalie Z. Davis, *Society and Culture in Early Modern France*, 17ff.). On Louise's maternal side, several benefactors had endowed a convent school, La Déserte, located near the family townhouse. It is conceivable that after her mother's death, Louise was brought up by the convent nuns, who not only taught her spinning, weaving, and lute playing, but also gave her a full-fledged classical education. This would also explain why, in spite of her relatively low social status, she was later welcomed into Lyons's famous humanist circles. Jean de Vauzelles, a well-known scholar related to the famous poet Maurice Scève, served as chaplain at the Déserte convent. He may have recognized Louise's exceptional talents and introduced her to his fellow scholars of the *sodalitium Lugdunense*. From the 1530s to the 1550s Lyons enjoyed a remarkable intellectual and cultural development. It was a cosmopolitan center with a large Italian population of bankers and lawyers. Away from the Sorbonne's repressive scholastic authority, new intellectual ideas circulated freely. Several hundred printers had set up shops and thrived on best-sellers, which included Greek philosophers, Latin poets, the *Romance of the Rose*, and Italian writers, especially Petrarch. The city was generously hospitable to artists such as the sculptor Philibert Delorme, the painter Corneille de Lyon, or the engraver Bernard Salomon, to mathematicians, scientists, and illustrious writers including Clément Marot and François Rabelais.

In such an open intellectual climate, Louise Labé could familiarize herself with the classics as well as contemporary humanists like Erasmus and B. Castiglione, the author of *Il Cortegiano* (translated into French by J. Colin and published in Lyons in 1537). Between 1543 and 1545 she married Ennemond Perrin, also a Lyons ropemaker. Her nickname, "La Belle Cordière" (the beautiful ropemaker), refers above all to her family's trade, although it may also suggest her skillful use of musical *cordes* (the lute strings) to accompany her poetry (see her sonnet XIV, 1.5: "Tant que ma main pourra les cordes tendre" [So long as my hand can pluck the strings]). Very little is known about Louise's conjugal life, except through Olivier de Magny's rather unreliable account, which portrays Ennemond (Aymon) as a stupid, naïve fool, too busy with his shop and unaware of his beautiful wife's love affairs (see Magny, Ode 40, published in 1559). The rope business must have been rather prosperous since the couple bought, in 1551, a townhouse with a large garden and, in 1557, a country estate at Parcieux-en-Dombes, some fifteen miles from Lyons.

The posthumous publication of Pernette du *Guillet's *Rymes* (Lyons, 1545), a collection of love poems, may have prompted Labé to start writing her own poetry. In any event, she certainly began composing her *Débat*, elegies, and sonnets before she met Olivier de Magny. Magny, a translator and poet, traveled through Lyons in 1554 on his way to Italy, where he was to work as secretary to Jean d'Avanson, the French ambassador. Nothing is clear about the relationship between Labé and Magny except their common passion for love poetry. On the pattern initiated by Scève (*Délie*, 1544) and du Guillet (*Rymes*, 1545), they established a "poetic dialogue," responding to each other with poems often written in similar form (see Labé's *Oeuvres complètes*, ed. F. Rigolot, 223–30).

On March 13, 1555 (new style), Louise Labé formally asked the King for permission to publish her works. They were printed the same year by Jean de Tournes, a respectable Lyons printer specializing in humanist writings. They include a liminary epistle, dated July 24 and dedicated to Clémence de Bourges, an aristocratic young woman of Lyons; the *Débat de Folie et d'Amour* (*Debate Between Folly and Love*), a mythological dialogue in prose; three elegies or fictional love letters in verse; and twenty-four love sonnets. In keeping with the tradition, Labé's own works are followed by another twenty-four poems written anonymously by Labé's friends and all dedicated to her greater glory. Often, in a hyperbolic tone, Labé is compared with Sappho or identified as the tenth Muse. A second edition of Labé's works was published with an *erratum* in 1556.

Labé's fame spread rapidly, but her personal fate, as well as that of her city, took a sadder course. Perrin died in or around 1557 and Magny in 1561. Religious turmoils seized the countryside. On April 30, 1562, Protestant rioters, under the command of Baron des Adrets, took over the city and ushered in a reign of terror. Several members of Louise's family converted, but she remained a Catholic. In 1565, having become seriously ill, Labé moved to the home of her friend Thomas Fortin (or Fortini), a Florentine banker whom she had known intimately for several years. On April 28, she dictated her will and made large donations to the Aumône-Générale and to the children of her brother François. She died early in 1566 and was buried at her country estate at Parcieux-en-Dombes, near Lyons.

MAJOR THEMES

The "dedicatory epistle" to Clémence de Bourges, which prefaces the collected works, is an important document for the history of both humanism and feminism. In a resolute cry of emancipation, Louise Labé rejects the traditional attributes of the woman as object. What is important to her is not a woman's adornment with spectacular jewelry and sumptuous attire, but her equal participation in this new (or renewed) Renaissance culture in which she can forge her own true identity. Her desire constitutes a kind of nascent refusal to be defined by others and a joy of recapturing an *être à soi*, or fundamental being, which is independent of the objectifying desires of men.

At the same time Labé reformulates a typical problematic of the Renaissance: the acute awareness of the inevitable ravages of time and an urgent desire to escape time through fame. Labé willingly recognizes the modesty of her intelligence and the meagerness of means at her disposal. Yet, contrary to her contemporaries, she does not use this standard profession of humility to attain the reader's good will. Out of a sense of mission, she refuses to halt at the societal injunctions that would silence her. Seeing her actions in terms of their communal impact, and herself as performing civic duties, she studies, writes, and appeals to the *dames vertueuses* to "look up from your distaffs and spindles once in a while." Louise Labé understands that a lone woman isolated in a cultural milieu which is at best disdainful cannot hope to change an oppressive mentality. She invites her female audience to help each other along (*s'encourager mutuellement*) in order to publicize their plight and mission. "Do not while away your youth," she says to her friend Clémence, "don't waste your given talents; set yourself this minute to the study of Arts and Letters, for time is fleeting!"

In his famous literary and political manifesto published six years earlier (*La Deffence et illustration de la langue françoyse*), Joachim Du Bellay rallied his French compatriots to "march courageously toward this superb Roman city" and to plunder the rich Latin classical tradition for its laurels of glory. Louise

Labé supplants this patriotic call with an equally fervent yet less military anthem: that of collaboration between the sexes, founded on mutual emulation and respect for the greatest benefit for all. "Our sex will gain in reputation," she remarks, "but will have above all striven for the public good; for men will redouble their efforts in learning out of the fear of seeing themselves shamefully outdistanced by us women to whom they have always believed themselves superior in practically every way." It is not ultimately a question of whether men or women are in the right, but rather of establishing a *dialogue*, or a *debate* which has as its theme precisely the issue of active sharing of power between two rivalrous universal forces: Love and Folly.

The *Débat de Folie et d'Amour* is a mythological story in prose dialogue that illustrates, in allegorical fashion, the conflictual aspects of passion and desire. The "debate" is a well-established literary genre. Numerous examples can be found in the Middle Ages: debates between the Soul and the Body, the Clerk and the Lady, the Clerk and the Knight. All share a common structure of argumentation based on conflict (*conflictus*) wherein the pros and cons are presented in an orderly, systematic fashion. Labé's *Débat* is full of literary references, both ancient and modern, which are at times difficult to discern. From the classics there are allusions to Plato's *Banquet*, Hesiod's *Theogony*, Lucian's *Dialogue of the Gods* (in its 1528 Latin translation), and the works of Ovid, especially the *Metamorphoses*. From the Italian tradition, one senses the presence of Petrarch and Ficino; of Dante, Boccaccio, Bembo, Castiglione, and Leone Ebreo. Finally, among the other sources, Erasmus's *Praise of Folly* is of significant interest for obvious reasons. This work had appeared in several editions from the Gryphe publishers of Lyons beginning in 1511 and was published in translation by Galliot du Pré in 1520.

This weighty arsenal of sources does not, however, impede the extraordinarily lively style of this small masterpiece. The argument is simple. Summoned by Jupiter to the assembly of the Gods, Folly and Love knock elbows at the palace entrance. Love (Cupid) then tries to shoot Folly with his arrow, but Folly dodges it and avenges the assault by blinding his attacker. Jupiter, attached to the case, appoints Apollo to Cupid's defense and Mercury to that of Folly. Their two pleas constitute the body of the work: two juridical discourses that mock the legal jargon and judicial mores of the day. The mythological setting provides the basis for an amusing parody. The gods suffer noticeably, and even Venus does not escape ridicule. Jupiter himself evidences the irony of the Olympian gods, who appear as no better than mortals. Cupid depicts the tragic consequences of his blindness in decidedly burlesque fashion. As for Folly, she cannot resist peppering her opinions with scabrous double-entendres. Obscene jokes, however, so much a part of comical literature of the period, are absent from the *Débat*. Rather, the work can be described as a *facetia*, a literary genre long debated by Renaissance theorists and one that relies heavily on surprise and cunning reversal. Labé sets human beings, men or women, as the target for facetiousness, hinting at satire while delighting in total freedom. No one is spared.

Some twenty years before Labé, Clément Marot had introduced the elegy in France with his *Suite de l'Adolescence Clémentine* (1534). In sixteenth-century poetics, the elegy is an epistle that "speaks of Love and declares one's desire, or pleasure or sadness in a manner both simple and undisguised to the person who is their cause and object" (Thomas Sebillet, *Art poëtique françois*, 1548). The French elegy is written in decasyllabic verse with alternating masculine and feminine rhyme scheme. This is the form adopted by Louise Labé in her three famous elegies. Labé was familiar with Ovid's *Heroides*, which had appeared in several different editions between 1507 and 1552, including a translation in 1552 by Labé's friend and admirer, Charles Fontaine. She had read Tibullus and undoubtedly knew Propertius, perhaps through Petrarch. The dominant theme of her elegies is the destructive passion that leads to folly. Evident here are several Propertian aspects of love's fury, or *furor amoris*: the slow poison which is distilled in the blood and leads to insomnia, anorexia, and, finally, to death. The *Débat*'s protagonists appear no longer as mythological abstractions; they are conflated within the very body of the lover, who endures in her flesh and blood the sufferings of this incurable evil.

Rage and fury do not, however, exhaust the fabric of the elegies. One finds calmer, more peaceful passages that recall by their poignant irony certain quiet yet biting descriptions from the *Débat*. The portrait of the wizened and pathetic Semiramis in the first elegy is an example. In his *Odes* of 1550 Ronsard developed the Horatian theme of *carpe diem*. Labé herself has no taste for fading roses. She prefers to identify herself with Semiramis, the warrior queen who, seized by passion, loses her spirit of combat and pitifully languishes in bed. In spite of her "virile heart" she finds herself suddenly undone by Love: she loses her masculine nature (*virtus, virtù, vertu, virtue*) and reverts to her unwanted femininity, here characterized as a loss.

What is most remarkable in these elegies is the very strong, conscious expression of a poetic identity within the lyric tradition. The first elegy opens with a justification of the choice of genre by refusing epic poetry ("the cruel wars" of Mars) as well as scientific verse ("the roaring thunder" of Jupiter). The appeal to the Petrarchan heritage is obvious in the evocation of Phoebus-Apollo, "friend of the green laurels," the laurel being the vegetal marker of lyrical imitation. Love does not appear only in the guise of Cupid the archer, who targets the heart and opens its uncurable wounds. It is also linked to the fundamental concept of neo-Platonic theory, the driving force of the universe, the key to the harmony of the cosmos. The French translation of Ficino's *De Amore* had appeared in Poitiers in 1546, and Pontus de Tyard had published a new version of Leone Ebreo's *Dialoghi d'amore* in Lyons in 1551.

Despite these male predecessors, Louise Labé turns at the beginning of her elegies to the most illustrious woman poet from the Western tradition to serve as her model. Until approximately 1553–54, Sappho was unknown except for the fictional letter Ovid imagined she might have written to her lover Phaon (*Heroides*, 15) and the adaptation by Catullus in his "Ode to the Lover." This famous poem by Sappho had been rediscovered and published in both Basel and Venice at the time Louise Labé was composing her elegies. The evocation of the loves of Lesbos at the opening of the lyric segment of the text is significant for this poet, whom contemporaries were soon to call the "Sapho lyonnaise." The feminine poetic consciousness expressed by reference to Sappho is reiterated in the address to the famous "Dames Lionnoises" of the opening and closing elegies—the same female audience hailed in the dedicatory epistle. The lack of information concerning their identity is indicative of the role Labé accords them as incarnations of contemporary social censure. The lover sees herself as obliged to forge ahead, regardless of her possibly transgressive conduct, with the contention that they could not judge her without experiencing a similar passion themselves. She pleads with them to sympathize with her case and promises to reciprocate should the tables one day be turned (I, 43–48). We find, therefore, a dialogue that is specific both to a region (Lyons) and to a gender (female).

Taken as a whole, the twenty-four sonnets comprise a harmonious *canzoniere* organized in the following manner: (1) The opening sonnet in Italian serves as a linguistic indicator signalling the traditional Petrarchan mode. (2) The process of the *innamoramento* is then described: the unfaithful lover offers himself initially as the servant-knight; his ardor is readily evident, but as soon as she shows passionate interest, he wants nothing further to do with her. (3) We now witness the turmoils of desire: hopes raised and dashed, the contradictory nature of passion, insomnia, surprises, turn-abouts, accusations followed by excuses, supplications. (4) In the central sonnet (XII) the poet-lover confides to her lute, the ideal substitute for her Lover, "irreproachable witness"; her song triumphs over sentiment ("the true governance"). (5) The fantasies of amorous restraint are further developed: seduction as told through myth (Zephyr, Diana, Mars, Venus, Jupiter, the Sun and Moon); search for the solitary life; reproaches and demands of pardon. (6) The final sonnet emphasizes self-justification and ends with an appeal to sympathy from other women and warnings for future lovers.

An entirely different reading of the collection, however, would lead one from imitation of a purely Petrarchan style (idealized portrait of the Lover, myth of Cupid, hyperbolic description and ornamental stereotypes) to an ironic commentary on the metaphoric language of Petrarchism. The style of Du Bellay's *Olive* (1549–1550), a collection much indebted to Petrarch, had been ironically subverted in his own 1553 poem, "A une Dame"—a poem renamed five years later with the provocative title "Contre les Pétrarquistes." Labé can be seen as both cultivating and abandoning the Petrarchist style in the same collection: a not-so-astonishing stylistical tour de force from the author of the *Débat* which, as we have seen, itself breaks with the polarized mode of the argumentative genre and adopts more ambiguous, discursive structures.

Platonic resonances are pervasive in the final sonnets. Ficino's theory of Love, for example, finds ample expression in the tercets of sonnet XXII: the "powerful harmony" of the cosmos exists only at the hands of Love, the overarching principle governing the universe. A similar thesis had been portrayed by Apollo in the *Débat*. As used in the sonnets, however, this humanist *topos* is but a rather ironic pretext for protesting the unnatural, that is, uncosmic, character of the separation of body and spirit. Suddenly, the beautiful, celestial harmony is threatened by multifarious delusions (*erreurs variables*), turning into a horrible, unwieldy chaos.

Since Petrarch's *Rime sparse*, the notion of "youthful mistakes" (*giovanile errore*) had been a commonplace predicament of love poetry. In the Lyons circles, Maurice Scève used the expression in both his opening *huitain* and the initial *dizain* of his *Délie* (1544), and Pontus de Tyard chose it for the title of his first collection of poetry, the *Erreurs amoureuses* (1549). At the beginning of the third elegy, Louise Labé borrows this same word (*erreur*) to deny that her love could have been a mistake of youth. In the sonnets she goes even further and develops the various connotations of "error" in contrast to the "irrevocable order" of the neo-Platonic cosmos. Thus the tension between Love and Folly continues to impose itself beyond the *Débat* itself and throughout Labé's lyrical work. Like the Renaissance "Dames Lionnoises," twentieth-century readers are invited to live or relive the uncertainties of desire. Such a fate is not the least of the enticements of an oeuvre that speaks to us, women and men of today, with the compelling intensity and fragility of passion.

SURVEY OF CRITICISM

During her lifetime, Labé was either exalted by fellow poets as a new Sappho or the "tenth Muse," or vilified by moralists such as John Calvin as a low-born, licentious courtesan. For a long time her poems were read merely as the diary of her intimate experiences with anonymous male lovers. Nineteenth-century critics tried to identify these lovers. Some thought Olivier de Magny was the villain, while others were convinced that King Henri II, who had apparently paid her a visit in Lyons in 1548, was responsible for her sick passion. Modern readers have given up this identity guessing game and concentrate rather on the problem of literary imitation, searching for possible Latin, Italian, or French models after whom Labé patterned her amorous discourse. The question of sincerity is a most problematic notion in literature, especially in the Renaissance, when poets inherited traditional literary structures through which they had to communicate personal experience. Art and sincerity can hardly be construed as separate poles. As Jerry C. Nash puts it, "Labé's lyrical voice is truly one of the best expressions in literature of *artful simplicity*, of a consistent and masterly synthesis of *fond* and *forme* (content and structure), of passion and poetry" ("Ne veuillez point . . . ," 19).

Today, one is tempted to reject the Romantic interpretation which, starting with Sainte-Beuve, read Labé's sonnets as spontaneous confessions from a deeply hurt feminine heart. Feminist criticism has done much to open the way to fresh interpretative readings of Labé's *Oeuvres*. Whereas Marie-Rose Logan has pointed out the essentially theoretical nature of the *Débat* in terms of Renaissance literary creativity, Ann Jones has shown how Labé entered the terrain of male lyrical poetry and appropriated its rituals for her own ends. Most critics now agree that Renaissance love discourse functions as a system of thematic and linguistic patterns, long-established by the male-oriented theory and practice of medieval *fin'amors'*, and perceived as such by both male and female readers. On what Hans Robert Jauss calls the "trans-subjective horizon" of reading, the Lady ("Donna," "Dame") is viewed as the exclusive object of virtuous love. Sixteenth-century writers were compelled to rewrite these inherited literary models with only a small degree of modification—or, rather, an *apparently* small degree since, as in Labé's case, a slight deviation could be potentially disruptive. These models had been codified by the only idealizing principles that were fully acceptable to the reading public of courtly love and Petrarchist poetry.

Since Renaissance poetry was shared by male and female writers, modern feminist critics have generally looked for unusual or incongruous elements in female-authored texts to see if they could be interpreted in gender-specific ways. For instance, as François Rigolot has shown, grammatical, thematic, or structural deviations encountered by readers in their initial, heuristic readings may point to a creative *misuse* of gender forms as a sexually coded index of self-expression.

In this respect, it is interesting to compare Labé's performance with du Guillet's, the other famous female poet of Renaissance Lyons. As Gillian Jondorf has remarked, du Guillet is obviously uncomfortable with the traditional masculine style of Petrarchist discourse. She writes her poems with a "neutral voice" so that, taken out of context, her readers might assume that they were experienced and written by a male persona. By contrast, Labé manages to work successfully and creatively within the context of a style "overwhelmed and overworked by innumerable male poets." Thus, as recent criticism has shown, Labé's daring "revisionism" asserts, in a devious yet forceful way, her radical reversal of the gender foundations of Renaissance literary authority.

BIBLIOGRAPHY

Works by Louise Labé

Sixteenth-Century Editions

Evvres de Lovize Labé Lionnoize. Lyons: Jean de Tournes, 1555.

Evvres de Louize Labé Lionnoize. ("Revvës et corrigées par la dite Dame.") Lyons: Jean de Tournes, 1556.

Evvres de Louize Labé Lionnoize. Lyons: Jean de Tournes, 1556.

Evvres de Loyse Labé Lionnoise. Rouen: Jean Garou, 1556.

Principal Modern Editions

Evvres de Lovize Labé Lionnoize. Ed. N. F. Cochard and Breghot du Lut. Lyons: Durant and Perrin, 1824.

Oeuvres de Louise Labé. Ed. Prosper Blanchemain. Paris: Librairie des Bibliophiles, 1875.
Oeuvres de Louise Labé. 2 vols. Ed. Charles Boy. Paris: A. Lemerre, 1887. Rpt. Geneva: Slatkine, 1968.
Oeuvres complètes (of Louise Labé). Ed. Enzo Giudici. Geneva: Droz, 1981.
Oeuvres complètes de Louise Labé. Ed. François Rigolot. Paris: Flammarion, 1986.

English Translations of Louise Labé

The Debate Between Follie and Love. Trans. Robert Greene. London: H. Lownes, 1608.
Débat. Ed. and trans. Edwin Marion Cox. London: Williams and Morgata, 1925.
Love Sonnets. Trans. Frederic Prokosch. New York: New Directions, 1947.
Sonnets of Louise Labé "La Belle Cordière." Trans. Alta Lind Cook. Toronto: Toronto University Press, 1950.
Twenty-Four Love Sonnets. Trans. Frances Lobb. London: 1950.
The Sonnets. Ed. and trans. Bettina L. Knapp. Paris: Minard, 1964.

Selected Studies of Louise Labé

Donaldson-Evans, L. K. *Love's Fatal Glance: A Study of Eye Imagery in the Poets of the Ecole Lyonnaise.* University, Miss.: Romance Monographs, 1980.
Giudici, E. *Louise Labé.* Paris: Nizet, 1981.
——. *Louise Labé e l'"Ecole Lyonnaise": Studi e ricerche con documenti inediti.* Intro. Jean Tricou. Naples: Liguori, 1964.
Hanisch, G. S. *Love Elegies of the Renaissance: Marot, Louise Labé and Ronsard.* Saratoga, Calif.: Anma Libri, 1979.
Harvey, L. E. *The Aesthetics of the Renaissance Love Sonnet: An Essay on the Art of the Sonnet in the Poetry of Louise Labé.* Geneva: Droz, 1962.
Jondorf, G. "Petrarchan Variations in Pernette du Guillet and Louise Labé." *Modern Language Review* 71, no. 4 (October 1976): 766–78.
Jones, A. R. "Assimilation with a Difference: Renaissance Women Poets and Literary Influence." *Yale French Studies* 62 (Fall 1981): 135–53.
——. "City Women and Their Audiences: Louise Labé and Veronica Franco." In *Rewriting the Renaissance: The Discourses of Sexual Difference in Early Modern Europe.* Ed. M. W. Ferguson, M. Quilligan, and N. J. Vickers. Chicago: University of Chicago Press, 1986. 299–316.
Larsen, A. "Louise Labé's *Débat de Folie et d'Amour*: Feminism and the Defense of Learning." *Tulsa Studies in Women's Literature* 2, no. 1 (Spring 1983): 43–55.
Logan, M.-R. "La Portée théorique du *Débat de Folie et d'Amour* de Louise Labé." *Saggi e ricerche di letteratura francese* 16 (1977): 9–25.
Nash, J. C. "Louise Labé and Learned Levity." *Romance Notes* 21, no. 2 (1980): 1–7.
——. " 'Ne veuillez point condamner ma simplesse': Louise Labé and Literary Simplicity." *Res Publica Litterarum* 3 (1980): 91–100.
O'Connor, D. *Louise Labé: sa vie et son oeuvre.* Paris: Les Presses Françaises, 1926.
Poliner, S. M. "*Signes d'amante* and the Dispossessed Lover: Louise Labé's Poetics of Inheritance." *Bibliothèque d'Humanisme et Renaissance* 46, no. 2 (1984): 323–42.

Rigolot, F. "Gender vs. Sex Difference in Louise Labé's Grammar of Love." In *Rewriting the Renaissance: The Discourses of Sexual Difference in Early Modern Europe.* Ed. M. W. Ferguson, M. Quilligan, and N. J. Vickers. Chicago: University of Chicago Press, 1986. 287–98.

———. "Louise Labé et la redécouverte de Sappho." *Nouvelle Revue du XVIe siècle* 1 (1983): 19–31.

———. "Signature et signification: les baisers de Louise Labé." *Romanic Review* 75, no. 1 (January 1984): 10–24.

Sainte-Beuve, C.-A. "La Belle Cordière, Louise Labé." *Revue des Deux Mondes*, March 15, 1845 (*Portraits contemporains*, Paris: Didier, 1855, 3: 156–84).

———. "*Oeuvres* de Louise Labé, La Belle Cordière." *Le Constitutionnel*, February 23, 1863 (*Nouveaux Lundis*, Paris: M. Lévy, 1872, 4: 289–317).

Tricou, G. "Louise Labé et sa famille." *Bibliothèque d'Humanisme et Renaissance* 5 (1944): 60–104.

Varty, K. "The Life and Legend of Louise Labé." *Nottingham Medieval Studies* 3 (1959): 78–108.

———. "Louise Labé's Theory of Transformation." *French Studies* 12 no. 1 (January 1958): 5–13.

Woods, C. L. "The Three Faces of Louise Labé." Diss., Syracuse University, 1976.

MARIE-MADELEINE PIOCHE DE LA VERGNE, COMTESSE DE LAFAYETTE (1634–1693)

Faith E. Beasley

BIOGRAPHY

Marie-Madeleine Pioche de la Vergne, comtesse de Lafayette, is one of the best-known figures of the seventeenth-century social and literary scene, and one of the most complex, provocative, and enigmatic. She was born in Paris in 1634, the eldest daughter of Marc Pioche, sieur de la Vergne, and Isabelle Péna. While not among the oldest or highest-ranking French noble families, the Vergnes managed their financial affairs well and succeeded in cultivating a number of important social connections. Isabelle Péna was a lady-in-waiting for Mazarin's niece, the duchesse d'Aiguillon. Lafayette was in fact born in her residence, the Petit Luxembourg Palace, and the duchess was named her godmother at her baptism at St. Sulpice in 1634. Lafayette spent most of her childhood in the *hôtel particulier* (mansion) built by her parents on the rue de Vaugirard, near the Luxembourg Palace. Except for a few years spent in the provinces, she spent her whole life in this quarter of the capital.

Lafayette began to take her place in Parisian society in the late 1640s and early 1650s, a transitional moment that witnessed the decline of the famous salon de Rambouillet and the rise of the tumultuous civil war known as the Fronde (1648–1652). She frequented the marquise de Rambouillet's *chambre bleue* (blue room), where she was joined by a number of people who became her lifelong friends, in particular Gilles Ménage, a celebrated poet and intellectual, and Marie de Rabutin-Chantal, marquise de *Sévigné, whom Lafayette described at the end of her life as "la personne du monde que j'ai le plus véritablement aimée" (the person I've most truly loved; *Correspondance*, January 24, 1692).[1] Lafayette became a fully integrated member of this worldly and intellectual society and earned the reputation of having *beaucoup d'esprit* (a good mind). During this period, she was named a *demoiselle d'honneur* of the Queen. Ménage composed numerous poems for her, and she was frequently mentioned in the newspapers of the time.

Marc de la Vergne died in 1649, and in 1650 Isabelle married Renaud-René de Sévigné (uncle by marriage to the marquise), a wealthy nobleman with some dubious connections during that period of civil unrest. The family was forced to leave Paris after Renaud-René defended the cardinal de Retz, a notable *frondeur* whose party eventually lost to the crown. From her family's chateau of Champiré (in Anjou), Lafayette corresponded with her Parisian friends and kept abreast of social and literary events. Ménage supplied her with books, especially volumes of Madeleine de *Scudéry's immensely popular novel, *Le Grand Cyrus*. She also turned her attention to intellectual pursuits, in particular to learning Italian and Latin. In addition to novels, she read histories, a pastime that would eventually nourish her literary endeavors.

The family returned to Paris in 1655, and Lafayette resumed her active social life. She was recognized as one of the foremost *précieuses* (precious women) before the term possessed the negative connotations bestowed on it by Molière. She married Jean-François Motier, comte de Lafayette, a provincial nobleman from a highly respected family that could trace its roots back to the eleventh century. Both families were pleased with the alliance. Lafayette acquired a prestigious name. In return the Lafayettes obtained crucial financial assistance, for Marie-Madeleine was very wealthy. The Lafayettes left the capital for Auvergne, where Jean-François organized legal proceedings in order to regain his family's many properties lost over the years due to a lack of money. The countess continued her correspondence and self-cultivation. This period also marks the beginning of her migraines and poor health, which were to last until her death. In 1659 the couple returned to Paris in order to settle the legal battles, and Lafayette once again took up residence on the rue de Vaugirard. The years 1659–1663 were occupied by legal proceedings, voyages to and from the Lafayettes' estates in Auvergne (Nades and Espinasse), and the birth of two sons, Louis and Armand. In 1663, Jean-François returned to Auvergne, leaving Lafayette and their sons in Paris. The couple continued to live separate existences until Jean-François's death in 1683.

In Paris, the countess regained the important position she had held in the social and literary circles of the day. Madeleine de Scudéry's salon, her *samedis* (Saturdays), had replaced the hôtel de Rambouillet, and there Lafayette became acquainted with intellectuals such as Pierre-Daniel Huet. In addition, the countess became friends with Mme du Plessis-Guénégaud and frequented her fashionable and influential salon at the hôtel de Nevers. Lafayette could count the most important figures of the court and Parisian society among her acquaintances— La Rochefoucauld, author of the *Maximes*, Mme de Sévigné, Daniel Huet, Jean-Regnauld de Segrais, and Jean Chapelain, among many others. In addition to her activities in Parisian worldly society, Lafayette became a familiar figure at court, due in particular to her friendship with the young Henriette d'Angleterre, who became Louis XIV's sister-in-law in 1661 upon her marriage to Philippe d'Orléans. Lafayette had first met Henriette in 1652 when the princess was only a child at the convent of Chaillot, where Henriette and her mother sought refuge during England's civil war. Lafayette's sister-in-law was the superior there. The countess also knew Anne-Marie-Louise d'Orléans, the duchesse de Montpensier, who was exiled after the Fronde because of rebellious activities directed against her cousin, Louis XIV.

In fact, Lafayette's first literary endeavor was expressly for the princesse de Montpensier. In 1658, the princess became intrigued by the genre of literary portraiture, inspired by the detailed portraits in Madeleine de Scudéry's novels. While in exile at St. Fargeau after the Fronde, Montpensier encouraged her friends to compose self-portraits or portraits of their friends, which she collected and published in 1659 as *Divers Portraits*. The Paris publisher Barbin then republished the volume later in the same year, augmenting it with additional portraits. Lafayette's portrait of her friend Sévigné figures in both the original *Divers Portraits* and in Barbin's *Le Recueil des portraits*. This is the only work Lafayette ever signed explicitly, although she did so obliquely. The portrait bears the curious title: "Portrait de Mme la marquise de Sévigné par Mme la comtesse de Lafayette sous le nom d'un inconnu" (under the name of an unknown person). During approximately the same period, Lafayette began work on her first novel, *La Princesse de Montpensier (The Princess of Montpensier)*, which was published by Barbin in 1662. The work, like all Lafayette's future novels, did not bear the author's name. In letters to Segrais, who read the work before its publication, Lafayette acknowledged her authorship, but urged her friend not to reveal it.

Although Lafayette did not openly publicize her authorship, many of her contemporaries were aware of and valued her writing skills. In 1665, Henriette d'Angleterre requested her friend to compose her biography. In the preface to the work, Lafayette records the genesis of this literary project and reports the princess saying, "You write well. . . . Write, I will furnish you with good memoirs." The *Histoire de Madame Henriette d'Angleterre (The Secret History of Henrietta, Princess of England)* was composed intermittently from 1665 to 1670. The collaborative literary enterprise was abruptly halted in 1670 when the young princess suddenly died. In approximately 1673, Lafayette returned to the manuscript and added an account of the princess's death. Years later, in approximately 1684, she packaged the manuscript for public consumption by composing a preface, but left the main narrative of Madame's adventures incomplete. Both additions contain the author's internal signature, for Lafayette explicitly names herself as the first-person narrator. Although it may have circulated in manuscript form, the *Histoire* was not published until 1720.

During the period when Lafayette was active at court as a member of Madame's entourage, she composed a fiction set in medieval Spain. Correspondences reveal that Huet, Segrais, and La Rochefoucauld were involved in the novel's composition. *Zaïde (Zayde. A Spanish History)* appeared in 1669, accompanied by a lengthy preface by Huet entitled "Sur l'origine des romans" (On the Origin of Novels). The novel itself was attributed to Segrais, although he later stated that Lafayette had actually composed the work (Duchêne, 261). The novel's second volume was published in 1671. In 1672, Huet applied for a *privilège* (permission) for a work entitled "Le Prince de Clèves," most likely the working title for what was to become Lafayette's most celebrated novel, *La Princesse de Clèves (The Princess of Clèves)*. For the next six years the countess was occupied with the historical research for her novel, as well as with establishing her sons in worthy positions. She continued to be plagued by ill health, but managed nonetheless to remain very active. Notably, she served as the agent at court for her friend Jeanne-Baptiste de Nemours, the duchesse de Savoie. *La Princesse de Clèves* finally appeared in 1678 to immediate acclaim and controversy. From its publication, it has been hailed the best example of its genre, the *nouvelle historique* (historical novel), and is now often viewed as the first example of the modern French novel.

Lafayette spent the last decade of her life arranging her elder son's marriage, settling financial affairs, and maintaining an active correspondence, especially with Sévigné. She composed her *Mémoires de la Cour de France* (*Memoirs of the Court of France*) during this period, for which only the years 1688 and 1689 remain. The *Mémoires* was published posthumously in 1731, as was another novel, *La Comtesse de Tende* (The Countess of Tende, 1724), a work most likely composed early in Lafayette's literary career. During the last years of her life, despite illness, Sévigné describes her as extremely active: "See how Mme de La Fayette has many friends on all sides and of all conditions. She has a hundred arms, she reaches everywhere" (Sevigné, *Correspondance*, February 26, 1690). Lafayette died in 1693 and was buried in St. Sulpice.

MAJOR THEMES

Lafayette drew upon her experiences at the center of her century's court and intellectual arenas to nourish her literary works. Her novels and memoirs attest to her keen sense of observation, as they mirror the manners, morals, and general preoccupations of seventeenth-century France. But her works are not only reflections of the shining and magnificent surface of court life. Lafayette explored in depth the theme of *être/paraître* (reality and appearance) so central to the mentality of her time period. In *La Princesses de Clèves*, Mme de Chartres, the heroine's mother, warns her daughter: "If you judge by appearances in this place, . . . you will often be mistaken: for what appears is almost never the truth" (Garnier-Flammarion ed., 56). Lafayette's work unveils this reality—the motivations behind historical events, the various undercurrents and often devious machinations of politics, both personal and public.

In the world Lafayette creates, the primary motivation for both political and personal events is love. With the exception of her *Mémoires de la Cour de France*, each of Lafayette's works is an in-depth exploration of this often tyrannical emotion. Her analyses of the various aspects of the heart can be viewed as extensive narrative commentaries on Madeleine de Scudéry's famous *Carte de Tendre* (Map of Tender) in which the celebrated novelist traced the various steps toward the perfect emotional state of Tendre, where friendship was valued over love and especially over passion. Each of Lafayette's characters travels the various paths of this novelistic and utopian geographical space as the author explores the psychology of love. Her works are not composed to glorify love and its consequences, but rather to ratify Scudéry's valorization of friendship and condemnation of love and passion. Lafayette's portrayal of this emotion is always negative and throws suspicion on love's sincerity. Most often her heroines flee the bonds of love in search of an ideal state of *repos* or individual tranquility. Lafayette's negative conception of love is confirmed by her own correspondence. In an early letter to Ménage, she remarked cynically, ''I am so convinced that love is a bothersome thing that I am happy that my friends and I are exempt from it'' (*Correspondance*, September 18, 1653). Lafayette's literary works indeed convincingly portray love not only as ''bothersome'' but as destructive.

The various amorous plots of Lafayette's works are played out in meticulously constructed historical settings, most frequently of sixteenth-century French society. In Lafayette's novels, history not only provides a backdrop but also constitutes a subtext that is often crucial for the interpretation of the fictional plot. In situating the majority of her fictions—*La Princesse de Montpensier, La Comtesse de Tende*, and *La Princesse de Clèves*—in sixteenth-century French society, Lafayette made a significant departure from preceding novelistic forms. Her works reveal the author's knowledge of conventions of the genre and her desire to experiment and innovate. Scudéry's heroic novels such as *Le Grand Cyrus* and *Clélie* were set in antiquity, and although they are founded on historical fact, she did not hesitate to change history to serve the needs of her fiction. Lafayette, on the other hand, responded to a change in the literary taste of her contemporaries. By approximately 1660, the heroic novel had fallen out of favor and was gradually being replaced by a new genre, the historical novel. *La Princesse de Montpensier* is considered one of the first examples of this new type of fiction. The nascent rules governing the composition of the historical novel stressed that such a work must above all be *vraisemblable*, a complex term with connotations of plausibility and propriety. It was generally agreed that the best method to instill *vraisemblance* was to ally the fictional work intricately with modern French history. Ideally a reader should have the impression that s/he is reading not fiction but history itself. The author's artistry consisted of weaving a fiction between the lines of general well-known history.

Lafayette proved to be a master of this new genre, and in fact theorists often used her works to formulate the rules. She was an avid reader of history and took great pains to ensure the accuracy of her fictions. *La Princesse de Montpensier*, for example, is set in sixteenth-century France, the principal events taking place from 1566 to 1572. The events of *La Comtesse de Tende* occur during the first years of Catherine de Médici's regency, that is, just a few years before the events of *La Princesse de Montpensier*. For *La Princesse de Clèves*,

Lafayette chose the last years of Henri II's reign, more precisely the transitional moment of his death, 1658–1659. Lafayette used a variety of sources to construct the historical foundation of her novels, primarily François Eudes de Mézeray's *Histoire de France* and Pierre de Bourdeille de Brantôme's *Mémoires*. Her creative process consisted of drawing the majority of her characters and the historical framework of her novels from such sources, then weaving a tragic love story among these well-known historical events.

The stories Lafayette imagined between the lines of history, while not historically verifiable in her sources, are plausible, given that history of the time did not record personal, especially amorous, lives. Lafayette's heroines travel Scudéry's map of emotions. They encounter passion in the form of seductive and famous court figures, but are impeded from reaching a state of mutual passion and love. Husbands, or the institution of marriage in general, present an obstacle. The various plots depict similar dilemmas, but offer a variety of solutions. In *La Princesse de Montpensier*, for example, Mlle de Mézières loves the duc de Guise but is married to the prince de Montpensier for political reasons. To escape the dangers of the civil war, she is sent to the chateau of Champigny, where she tries to forget her love for the duke. But chance brings the duke to Champigny, and her emotions are reignited. When the princess returns to the court and is in contact with the duke, she cannot hide her feelings. Her suspicious husband sends her back to Champigny. With the help of her confidant, Chabannes, who is also in love with the princess, she corresponds with the duc de Guise. Aided by Chabannes, the princess arranges a nocturnal rendezvous with the duke. The prince de Montpensier, who happens to be at the chateau, hears noises and goes to his wife's room, where he finds Chabannes, the duke having had time to flee. Chabannes takes the blame and is later killed during the Saint-Barthélemy massacre. The princess dies of sadness when the duc de Guise abandons her for another woman.

Lafayette continues her negative depiction of passion in *La Comtesse de Tende* and offers a more dramatic ending. In this very brief novel, Madeleine de Strozzi marries the comte de Tende. The chevalier de Navarre, the most dashing figure at court, then falls in love with the comtesse de Tende, who reciprocates his passion. In a surprising twist rarely seen in seventeenth-century fiction, the countess becomes pregnant and Navarre is killed at war. Devasted, Mme de Tende tells her husband everything in a letter, hoping he will kill her. The count puts off his vengeance in order to keep the affair secret. Both the countess and her child then die when she gives birth prematurely.

Lafayette proposed yet another ending in *La Princesse de Clèves* and presented a more detailed psychological portrait of love than in any of her other novels. *La Princesse de Clèves* recounts the story of a young ingenue, Mlle de Chartres, who has been raised in the provinces by her mother. Upon her arrival at court, she is immediately hailed the most perfect beauty and is married to the prince de Clèves. The prince loves his new wife passionately, but the princess responds only with conventional feelings of esteem but not love. The most eligible and desirable bachelor at court, the duc de Nemours, falls madly in love with Mme de Clèves, who is herself attracted to the duke, but refuses to give in to her feelings because her mother has taught her that supreme happiness for a woman lies only in virtue and in loving her husband. The novel follows the psychological anguish of this princess as she debates between her duty and her passion. In one of the most famous scenes of the book, the princess asks her husband to allow her to withdraw from court and live at their country estate at Coulommiers, while at the same time stressing that she will always be faithful to him. Nemours overhears this declaration. The prince de Clèves guesses that his wife is in love with someone else and dies of jealousy. Unpredictably, the princess does not marry the man she loves once she is free of her husband. Instead, she admits to Nemours that she loves him, but she refuses to marry him even though she acknowledges that society would have condoned the union. The princess spends the rest of her life in solitude, dividing her time between a convent and her country estate, "et sa vie, qui fut assez courte, laissa des exemples de vertu inimitables" (and her life, which was rather short, offered inimitable examples of virtue; Garnier-Flammarion ed., 180).

While each of Lafayette's three historical *Princesses* explores similar themes of love, marriage, passion, sincerity, societal expectations, duty, individual happiness, and female identity, each work is structured differently and reveals Lafayette's conscientious exploration of narrative technique and experimentation with the new genre. Much of the original character of *La Princesse de Clèves,* for example, resides in Lafayette's depiction of the psychology of love. The lengthy interior monologues are one of her primary innovations to the genre. Lafayette also enriches *La Princesse de Clèves* with four internal narratives, often viewed as disgressions. These narratives, three of which are historically accurate, are reminiscent of Scudéry's techniques in the heroic novel, which in fact consists of a constant succession of such narratives. But in *La Princesse de Clèves,* Lafayette incorporates these "digressions" into the fabric of her main narrative. They can actually be viewed as lessons on love directed to the princess. Lafayette is thus a very self-conscious artist, not simply a good storyteller.

One novel in Lafayette's literary corpus represents a departure from the composition of her other novels, while at the same time echoing their principal themes. *Zaïde* is situated in Spain in approximately 850–900. Although a comparison with her sources attests to Lafayette's accuracy, history plays a more subservient role to the fiction than in her other historical novels, and is reminiscent of Scudéry's use of history more as a framework than as a subtext. Another similarity between *Zaïde* and the heroic novel is the preponderance of internal narratives, many of which bear little relation to the "main" story of Zaïde and Consalve. Lafayette seems to be giving homage to her friend Scudéry and to the tradition of the heroic novel. *Zaïde* is also exceptional in that the principal couple is happily united in a marriage of love at the end, although this one example is not enough to counterbalance the destructive effects of passion described in the internal narratives.

With the exception of *Zaïde*, all Lafayette's works are set during the century preceding her own, although the court ambiance she depicts has many affinities with her own society. Many of her works can be considered portraits of and complex commentaries on seventeenth-century society. Lafayette portrayed this world more overtly, actually adopting the position of historian, in her nonfictional works, the *Histoire de Mme Henriette d'Angleterre* and *Mémoires de la Cour de France*. She profited from her position as a scribe for the princesse Henriette to relate the inner workings of the court of the Sun King. In particular, Lafayette demonstrates that matters traditionally considered as belonging to the domain of "private history," namely, love and interpersonal relationships, not only affect but constitute the events of public history. As the privileged insider to Henriette's experiences, Lafayette focuses on her ability to unveil this other side of history. Her authorial stance in the *Histoire* is very different from the one she chose for her *Mémoires de la Cour de France*. In the *Mémoires*, Lafayette demonstrated that she could be the omniscient historian of the public domain of history, as she recounted well-known events.

All Lafayette's works, fictional and nonfictional, reveal the author's interest in and knowledge of the issues of her day. In particular, the intricate analyses of the human heart were nourished by the debates and conversations about love Lafayette experienced in the salons. In *Zaïde* and *La Princesse de Clèves* especially, Lafayette explored the theme of communication and the importance of language, a topic that reflects the preoccupations of her female contemporaries, as many of them were involved in literary endeavors. Her pessimistic view of marriage also evolves from the countess's contemporary *précieuse* milieu. The *précieuses* viewed marriage as a form of slavery, and their rhetoric frequently expressed repulsion for the institution. Lafayette's heroines often find themselves in arranged marriages, forced to follow the trajectory paved out for the seventeenth-century noblewoman. Lafayette is especially attentive to the female condition and to society's expectations of women. In her final novel, the princesse de Clèves revolts against such constraints, as Lafayette proposes a new, alternative ending for the female plot. Instead of marriage, death, or permanent seclusion in a convent—the conventional endings for both novels and life—the princess rejects societal expectations and chooses to live out the rest of her life on her own terms. Lafayette thus boldly suggests the possibility that women can create their own expectations, their own concept of what is *vraisemblable* within the domain of the novel and perhaps even beyond its boundaries.

SURVEY OF CRITICISM

Lafayette's works have elicited a vast amount of critical response since their publication. One direction this scholarship has taken privileges a biographical component, as commentators analyze not Lafayette's work but the status of her authorship. Despite the fact that Lafayette attempted to preclude such speculation—with the editor of *La Princesse de Clèves* even including an explanation of the author's anonymity in which he stated that the author refused to sign the novel so that it would be received on its own merit—this author's refusal to sign her works has provoked speculation and debate. In this critical vein, critics either refuse Lafayette sole authorship, attributing her novels to a writing collective composed of the countess's male friends Ménage, Huet, Segrais, and La Rochefoucauld, or, in extreme cases, deny Lafayette's authorship altogether, as most recently done by Geneviève Mouligneau (*Mme de Lafayette, romancière?*). Similarly, many biographies have been produced, as historians and literary critics attempt to determine what currents—social, historical, and psychological—combined to produce this seemingly unlikely author of one of the "master"pieces of French literature, *La Princesse de Clèves*.

The nineteenth and early twentieth centuries in particular witnessed the flourishing of this biographical historical criticism, as erudites and critics read Lafayette's historical novels as semi-veiled representations of her own seventeenth-century society. Much effort was spent speculating on who the various characters were meant to represent. Other critics, most notably Chamard and Rudler ("Les Sources historiques de *La Princesse de Clèves*"), identify Lafayette's numerous historical sources in order to reveal her debt to historians or to underscore her occasional infidelity to such sources.

In addition to being considered *à clé* descriptions of seventeenth-century society, Lafayette's works are frequently analyzed as reflections of the literary developments of mid-seventeenth-century France. In French literary histories such as Henri Coulet's *Le Roman jusqu'à la révolution*, both *La Princesse de Montpensier* and *La Princesse de Clèves* are cited as important steps in the development of the novel. Roger Francillon's *L'Oeuvre romanesque de Mme de La Fayette* situates the author's works in the literary context of her day. Much work has focused on the structure of the novels, especially on Lafayette's use of internal narratives in *Zaïde* and *La Princesse de Clèves*. J. W. Scott in "The 'Digressions' of *The Princesse de Clèves*" and John Lyons's illuminating study, "Narration, Interpretation and Paradox: *La Princesse de Clèves*," treat the four "digressions" in the novel and the importance of these internal narratives. In analyzing the composition of Lafayette's works, other critics, such as Ann Moore ("Temporal Structure and Reader Response in *La Princesse de Clèves*"), have centered on the complex notion of temporality. This is especially provocative given Lafayette's meticulous use of history, a narrative strategy that itself has proked much commentary. Most recently, Barbara Guetti (" 'Travesty' and 'Usurpation' in Mme de Lafayette's Historical Fiction") and Pierre Malandain ("Ecriture de l'histoire dans *La Princesse de Clèves*") have suggested various ways that Lafayette rewrote history for a *La Princesse de Clèves*—even feminized it—and her reasons for doing so. These critics and others pay particular attention to Lafayette's highlighting of female historical characters, especially Mary Stuart and Diane de Poitiers, and the relationship of such personages to the princess's fictional narrative.

Most of the criticism and commentary of Lafayette's literary corpus has been

devoted to *La Princesse de Clèves*. From the moment of its publication, it has
been viewed as an exceptional and even unique phenomenon of the classical
period. *La Princesse de Clèves* is in fact the only woman's work of the period,
with the exception of Sévigné's correspondence, to have been granted canonical
status. A virulent quarrel erupted when *La Princesse de Clèves* appeared in 1678.
Jean-Baptiste Trousset de Valincour, in the *Lettres à Madame la Marquise de*
**** *au sujet de la Princesse de Clèves*, denounced the novel, condemning it
as *invraisemblable*, or implausible, and as such a violation of the principal rule
governing literary production. His harshest criticism was directed against the
princess, whom Valincour described as "an incomprehensible woman. . . . She
is the most coquettish prude and the most prudish coquette one has ever seen"
(272–73). Although Valincour attacked Lafayette's use of history and the composition of the novel, in particular her use of internal narratives and the power
of the narrator, he reserved his strongest rhetoric for the princess's comportment.
According to Valincour, the princess's *aveu* (declaration) to her husband in what
is usually referred to as the "confession scene," her solitary reverie of passion
in front of Nemours's portrait, and her final rejection of a union with the duke
are all *invraisemblable*, that is, breaches of plausibility and propriety. His reaction attests to her provocative rescripting of the female plot. These scenes also
elicited the general public's reaction. The newspaper *Le Mercure Galant* asked
its readers to comment in particular on the plausibility of the princess's declaration
to her husband. The literary quarrel continued throughout the year, as the Abbé
de Charnes responded to Valincour's attack in his *Conversations sur la critique
de la Princesse de Clèves*, in which he defended Lafayette's novel and hailed
it as a masterpiece of the new genre. No other seventeenth-century work of
fiction inspired such a response.

Recent studies of *La Princesse de Clèves* often include attempts to account
for this at times excessive response by readers. In *Lectures de Madame de
Lafayette*, Maurice Laugaa provides an excellent overview of the various aspects
of the seventeenth-century quarrel, as he traces the general history of Lafayette
criticism. Joan DeJean has analyzed the complex status of Lafayette's female
authorship and her narrative strategies using the quarrel to establish the expectations of Lafayette's contemporaries and the author's intentional overturning of
those expectations ("Lafayette's Ellipses: The Privileges of Anonymity"). Studies that combine analyses of the quarrel with the novel underscore Lafayette's
originality and her awareness and manipulation of the literary expectations of
her day. The quarrel is also useful for pinpointing the code of societal conventions
at the heart of Lafayette's work, a code that has long attracted critical attention.
Many critics, such as Michael Danahy ("Social, Sexual and Human Spaces in
La Princesse de Clèves") and Laurence Gregorio (*Order in the Court: History
and Society in "La Princesse de Clèves"*), have focused on Lafayette's portrayal
of the court, on its social spaces, morals, and maxims. In a similar vein, the
princesse de Clèves's psychological characteristics and her actions within the
realm of the court have inspired critics to analyze her motivations, leading to

contradictory interpretations of the novel. For some, the overly virtuous princess retreats to solitude in order to escape the tumultuous court, whereas for others she chooses to construct her life outside the reality of the court in order to remain in control of her own plot.

The positive interpretation of the princess has often been advanced in the past ten years by feminist critics. Lafayette's novels, in particular *La Princesse de Clèves*, have greatly benefited from the new visions and reinterpretations by these critics. In fact, Lafayette's corpus as a whole offers numerous avenues for feminist interrogation. Nancy K. Miller was the first to suggest that Lafayette advances an alternative plot for women in *La Princesse de Clèves*, thus challenging the male-defined conception of *vraisemblance* with respect to female behavior ("Emphasis Added: Plots and Plausibilities in Women's Fictions"). Joan DeJean has cast Lafayette's anonymity in a new light, arguing that the author conceived this position as a powerful and liberating one ("Lafayette's Ellipses"). Other feminist critics have been drawn to the role of Mme de Chartres, the princess's mother in *La Princesse de Clèves*. Most notably, Marianne Hirsch discusses the force and implications of this exceptional maternal pedagogy ("A Mother's Discourse: Incorporation and Repetition in *La Princesse de Clèves*"). Inspired by feminist criticism, other critics have reevaluated the female characters in Lafayette's novels. With the growing interest in women's first-person narratives, Lafayette's *Mémoires* is receiving renewed critical attention. Overall, recent critical trends have reaffirmed Lafayette's crucial role in French literary history. Spanning two and one-half centuries, the myriad explorations of the meaning and implications of Lafayette's works convincingly attest to the eternal attraction of her complex and intriguing literary corpus.

NOTE

1. All translations are my own.

BIBLIOGRAPHY

Works by Mme de Lafayette

First Editions

La Princesse de Montpensier. Paris: Jolly, 1662.
Zayde, Histoire espagnole. Vol. 1. Paris: Barbin, 1669.
Zayde, Histoire espagnole. Vol. 2. Paris: Barbin, 1671.
La Princesse de Clèves. Paris: Barbin, 1678.
Histoire de Madame Henriette d'Angleterre. Amsterdam: Le Cène, 1720.
La Comtesse de Tende. Mercure de France (Paris), 1724.
Mémoires de la Cour de France pour les années 1688 et 1689. Amsterdam: Jean-Frédéric
    Bernard, 1731.

Modern Editions

Correspondance. Ed. André Beaunier. 2 vols. Paris: Gallimard, 1942.
Romans et nouvelles. Ed. Alain Niderst. Paris: Bordas-Classiques Garnier, 1989. (Includes all Lafayette's novels.)
La Princesse de Clèves. Ed. Antoine Adam. Paris: Garnier-Flammarion, 1966.
Histoire de Madame Henriette d'Angleterre et Mémoires de la Cour de France pour les années 1688 et 1689. Paris: Mercure de France, 1965.

Translations of Mme de Lafayette

First Editions

The Princess of Montpensier. London, 1666.
Zayde. A Spanish History. Trans. P. Porter. London: Milbourn, 1678.
The Princess of Clèves. London: R. Bentley and H. Magnes, 1679.
Fatal Gallantry, or, The Secret History of Henrietta Princess of England. Trans. Ann Floyd. London: Clay, 1722.

Modern Editions

The Princess of Clèves. Trans. Walter J. Cobb. New York: New American Library, 1989.
The Death of Madame. New York: Minton, Balch and Co., 1931.
The Secret History of Henrietta, Princess of England together with Memoirs of the Court of France for the Years 1688 and 1689. Trans. J. M. Shelmerdine. New York: Dutton, 1929.

Studies of Mme de Lafayette

Beasley, Faith E. *Revising Memory: Women's Fiction and Memoirs in Seventeenth-Century France.* New Brunswick, N.J.: Rutgers University Press, 1990.
Beaunier, André. *L'Amie de La Rochefoucauld.* Paris: Flammarion, 1927.
Chamard, H., and G. Rudler. "Les Sources historiques de *La Princesse de Clèves.*" *Revue du seizième siècle* 2 (1914): 92–131, 289–321; 5 (1917–1918): 1–20, 231–43.
Charnes, Jean-Antoine, abbé de. *Conversations sur la critique de la Princesse de Clèves.* 1679. Ed. François Weil et al. Tours: Université de Tours, 1973.
Coulet, Henri. *Le Roman Jusqu'à la Révolution.* Paris: A. Colin, 1967–1968.
Danahy, Michael. "Social, Sexual and Human Spaces in *La Princesse de Clèves.*" *French Forum* 3 (1981): 212–24.
DeJean, Joan. "Lafayette's Ellipses: The Privileges of Anonymity." *PMLA* 99, no. 5 (1984): 884–900.
Duchêne, Roger. *Madame de La Fayette.* Paris: Fayard, 1988.
Francillon, Roger. *L'Oeuvre romanesque de Mme de La Fayette.* Paris: José Corti, 1973.
Genette, Gérard. "Vraisemblance et motivation." In *Figures II: Essais.* Paris: Seuil, 1969. 71–99.
Gregoria, Laurence A. *Order in the Court: History and Society in "La Princesse de Clèves."* Stanford, Calif.: Stanford French and Italian Studies, 1986.

Guetti, Barbara Jones. " 'Travesty' and 'Usurpation' in Mme de Lafayette's Historical Fiction." *Yale French Studies* 69 (1985): 211–21.

Hirsch, Marianne. "A Mother's Discourse: Incorporation and Repetition in *La Princesse de Clèves*." *Yale French Studies* 62 (1981): 67–87.

Laugaa, Maurice. *Lectures de Mme de Lafayette*. Paris: Armand Colin, 1971.

Lyons, John. "The Dead Center: Desire and Mediation in Lafayette's *Zayde*." *L'Esprit Créateur* (Summer 1983): 58–69.

———. "Narration, Interpretation and Paradox: *La Princesse de Clèves*." *Romanic Review* 72 (1981): 383–400.

Magne, Emile. *Le Coeur et l'esprit de Mme de La Fayette*. Paris: Emile-Paul Frères, 1927.

Malaudain, Pierre. "Ecriture de l'histoire dans *La Princesse de Clèves*." *Littérature* 36 (1979): 19–36.

Miller, Nancy K. "Emphasis Added: Plots and Plausibilities in Women's Fictions." *PMLA* 96, no. 1 (1981): 36–48.

Moore, Ann. "Temporal Structure and Reader Response in *La Princesse de Clèves*." *French Review* 56, no. 4 (1983): 563–71.

Mouligneau, Geneviève. *Madame de Lafayette, romancière?* Brussels: Université de Bruxelles, 1980.

Scott, J. W. "The 'Digressions' of *La Princesse de Clèves*." *French Studies* 11 (1957): 315–22.

Stanton, Domna. "The Ideal of Repose in Seventeenth-Century French Literature." *L'Esprit Créateur* 25, no. 1–2 (Spring-Summer 1975): 79–104.

Stone, Harriet. "Exemplary Teaching in *La Princesse de Clèves*." *French Review* 62, no. 2 (December 1988): 248–58.

———. "Reading the Orient: Lafayette's *Zaïde*." *Romanic Review* 81, no. 2 March 1990: 145–60.

Valincour, Jean-Baptiste Trousset de. *Lettres à Mme la Marquise de **** au sujet de la Princesse de Clèves*. 1678. Ed. Jacques Chupeau. Tours: Université de Tours, 1972.

VIOLETTE LEDUC
(1907–1972)

Isabelle de Courtivron

BIOGRAPHY

Violette Leduc was born in northern France in 1907, the illegitimate daughter of a young servant and the son of the prosperous provincial family for whom she worked. The child was raised in Arras, then Valenciennes, by her mother and her grandmother. Berthe Leduc, the bitter young mother, instilled in the child a strong feeling of guilt for being the source of her disgrace. Berthe was apparently a dutiful parent, vigilant about her daughter's proper upbringing in petit-bourgeois society; nevertheless, Violette suffered from being denied the tenderness of a mother she both feared and adored.

Violette Leduc grew into a plain and sickly young girl. Having been taught by her mother to hate men and fear sex, she was nevertheless sharply reproached by her for her lack of feminine graces. Already perplexed by conflicting signals, Violette Leduc was particularly hurt by what she perceived as the ultimate betrayal when, despite her condemnation of men and pregnancy, her mother eventually married and bore a legitimate son. Thus a childhood that had been marked by marginality and guilt ended in betrayal and rejection. She returned obsessively to early memories, reenacted them in her life patterns, and recreated them in her works. In the end, she found in this tormented past the source of her creativity.

The only positive force in this early period of her life was a crusty middle-aged peasant woman, her grandmother Fidéline, who provided the little girl with the nurture and affection that her mother denied her. Leduc's rare lyrical memories of her childhood years are associated with the "angel" Fidéline and with the loving complicity that existed between the old woman and the little girl. These moments of happiness were short-lived. Her grandmother died, leaving the nine-year-old Violette isolated once again, first in boarding school, then in the household of a stepfather she always disliked.

Dismissed from boarding school because of a lesbian liaison with one of her schoolteachers, the adolescent Violette joined her mother, stepfather, and half-brother, who had moved to Paris. She quickly dropped out of the *lycée* where she was half-heartedly studying for her *baccalauréat*. She then found a small secretarial job with the publisher Plon, where, despite the boredom of her tasks, she was able to observe many of the fashionable authors of the time—Paul Bourget, Henri Bordeaux, Julien Green, Georges Bernanos, Henry de Montherlant—and to follow closely the literary movements of the late 1920s. Struck down by a pulmonary illness, she quit her job to live full time with her lesbian lover. When their relationship ended, Leduc took on a succession of odd jobs. She was earning a meager living writing fashion-magazine articles when the war broke out. Before she left Paris, she entered into a disastrous marriage that was to last only briefly.

During the Occupation, Leduc sought refuge in the Normandy countryside, sharing accommodations with the writer Maurice Sachs, whom she had met when she worked as a receptionist. Sachs was to play a major role in her life. He was already notorious for the scandals associated with his sexual and financial excesses and his stormy relationships with literary personalities, but was not yet known for his literary production, most of which would be published after his death in 1945. Sachs was a familiar figure in the salon society and literary circles of Paris, as well as in the underworld of several big cities. He spent money in an extravagant manner, leaving behind him a trail of creditors, angry acquaintances, and betrayed friends. Yet when Leduc first became acquainted with him, she was charmed by the elegant, refined libertine whose life story may have reminded her of her own excesses, her own misfortune in love, and her worship of literary figures. The luxury with which Sachs surrounded himself and his apparent generosity when he had made a good deal seemed dazzling to Violette Leduc, who was living in the shabbiness of a garret room with her impoverished husband. She gave Maurice Sachs her adoring friendship and he, flattered by her attention, took her under his disreputable wing.

During the war, when his creditors, enemies, and victims, as well as the police, began to close in on him, Sachs fled to the country. Convinced that his chances would be better if he did so as part of a couple, he asked Leduc to join him. In the fall of 1942, the two made their way to the small village of Anceins, in the region of the Orne. There Sachs completed *Witches' Sabbath*, his autobiography, and initiated Leduc into black-marketeering. Eventually, he returned to Paris, then disappeared, only to be heard from again in a German prison. News of his death reached Leduc in 1945.

This forced retreat in Anceins changed the course of Leduc's life. As she compulsively voiced her childhood memories, day after day, to an exasperated Maurice Sachs, he finally ordered her to write them down instead. From this request came the first draft of *L'Asphyxie* (*In the Prison of Her Skin*).

Immediately after the war, Violette Leduc was introduced to Simone de *Beauvoir who, along with Jean-Paul Sartre, was then at the center of the Parisian stage. In her memoirs, Beauvoir writes succinctly about this first encounter with Leduc, whom she describes as a "tall, elegant, blond woman with a face both brutally ugly and radiantly alive" (*Force of Circumstance*, 1:19). Beauvoir was impressed by Leduc's manuscript, made helpful suggestions, and published excerpts of it in the newly created *Les Temps Modernes*. She then drew the attention of the publisher Gallimard to Leduc's volume of childhood reminiscences, and *L'Asphyxie* was published in the newly created series "Espoir," directed by Albert Camus. During the next twenty-seven years Simone de Beauvoir was the driving force behind Violette Leduc's life, the main catalyst of her inspiration as well as of her despair. Beauvoir demanded the hard work, the perseverance, the painful crafting of language that gradually took Leduc from writing down random childhood associations to creating full-fledged literary works. It is clear from her texts that Leduc wrote primarily for Beauvoir and that her entire work is a tribute to this writer. It was Beauvoir who unsuccessfully fought Gallimard when the readers of the publishing house decided to censor 150 pages of *Ravages*, her third text, which they considered too daring. Beauvoir helped support Leduc financially by arranging a small monthly stipend ostensibly paid by Gallimard during the years of extreme poverty. She also took her to a clinic when she judged that Leduc had become too self-destructive. It was Beauvoir who suggested that Leduc start an autobiography, and whose masterful preface to *La Bâtarde* helped to promote it publicly. Finally, it was Beauvoir who edited the last volume Leduc completed just before she died. Although she never became either the lover or the close friend Leduc ardently hoped for, Beauvoir replaced Berthe Leduc as the powerful maternal figure in her protégée's imagination and unwittingly fueled the fantasy life from which some of Leduc's best writing was produced. Most important, she remained her principal literary advisor and her most discerning reader.

Leduc published *L'Asphyxie* in 1946. *L'Affamée* (Ravenous) followed in 1948. *Ravages* appeared, shortened by Gallimard, in 1955. None of these books sold. The indifference of the public, the pressures of poverty, the mutilation of her third text, the growing frustration stemming from her inability to become more intimate with Beauvoir or with a wealthy homosexual businessman with whom she had become obsessed, converged and eventually led to increasing paranoia. This illness intensified to the point where Leduc lost control over her sanity. In 1957 she was taken to a clinic by Beauvoir. There she was subjected to what was considered at the time to be the most effective therapeutic treatment: electroshock and a sleeping cure. Although she left the clinic and a rest home in a state of lessened paranoia, the shadow of madness never completely left her. Leduc nevertheless continued to write and to lead an active though turbulent social life, cultivating uneasy relations with Jean Genet and the aging Jean Cocteau. The relationships of this devotee of literary lights were a mixture of adoration and resentment, characterized by extremes of exaltation, tenderness, and cruelty, which wearied those who became the objects of her attention. Leduc would then retreat to her small studio in a working-class area near the Bastille to continue her lonely writing task. Despite the lack of success of her first works, despite her bouts with mental derangement, she published two more books: *La Vieille Fille et le mort* (*The Old Maid and the Dead Man*) in 1958 and *Trésors à prendre* (Treasures for the Asking) in 1960. Their fate was no different from that of their predecesors.

In 1964 *La Bâtarde* appeared and immediately became the most controversial event of the Paris literary season. It was the uninhibited autobiography of a middle-aged woman who aggressively proclaimed her illegitimate birth, her ugliness, her bisexual passions, her poverty, and her failures. The book became an instant best-seller, eliciting both high praise and strong reprobation. *La Bâtarde* was mentioned by increasing numbers of reviewers as a leading candidate for one of the major literary prizes that ensure their authors momentary celebrity and a surge in sales. Reviewers from major newspapers took sides. "Yes, Simone de Beauvoir is right, *La Bâtarde* is a great book!" exclaimed Jacqueline Piatier in *Le Monde*, and proceeded to draw a comparison with Céline. On the other side of the spectrum, the conservative papers attacked *La Bâtarde* with expressions such as "scandalous immorality," "horrors and perversions," "unparallelled obscenities and pornography." Even the most vituperative of critics admitted, however, that Leduc possessed undeniable talent and that a real work of art hid beneath her "verbal shamelessness." The disputes over *La Bâtarde* intensified, and while press speculation increased, the book sold 125,000 copies. In the end, a safe compromise was devised: since the prizes are to be awarded to works of fiction, the juries of the Goncourt and the Femina concluded that Leduc's work, an autobiography, could not qualify. The prizes were conferred on more acceptable authors, and the vehement disputes died down. One of the consequences of this Parisian brouhaha, however, was to turn critical attention to Violette Leduc and to her overlooked previous literary production.

Encouraged by her success, Leduc continued her long autobiographical project and wrote two additional volumes: *La Folie en tête* (*Mad in Pursuit*) in 1970 and *La Chasse à l'amour* (Hunting for Love) in 1973. She published her most transgressive work, *Le Taxi* (*The Taxi*), a short piece written in the form of a dialogue between two adolescents—a brother and sister—who are making love in a taxi. During the few years that followed the publication of *La Bâtarde*, Violette Leduc was feted by Paris socialites. Her book *Thérèse et Isabelle* (*Thérèse and Isabelle*), consisting of the passages from *Ravages* cut by Gallimard, was published by the latter and was made into a sensationalistic film. Leduc's extravagantly dressed figure was seen in all areas of fashionable Paris for months after she had obtained notoriety. Although this was a situation she had long dreamed about, one that avenged her sense of guilt and anger at being a pariah, she nonetheless had learned to distrust the hypocrisy and superficiality of a world in which she had always felt ill at ease. She gradually found solace in two of the most faithful and fulfilling elements in her life: nature and writing.

She purchased an old house in Faucon, a tiny village at the foot of the Mont Ventoux. There she spent first her summers, then months at a time, and finally the whole year. Although there were still many difficult moments, she was at last taking herself seriously as a writer and as a person. After a lifetime of chaos, "la bâtarde" had given herself a second and legitimate birth through literature, when she died of cancer in May 1972.

MAJOR THEMES

Issues involving the self underlie the corpus of Leduc's autobiographical writing. They create a circular, cumulative, repetitive work that can best be understood by reading the entire corpus as a single text. Themes such as the influence of the mother, the stigma of illegitimacy, the obsession with unattainable love-objects, the mystical quest, and the transformation of body into text recur in Leduc's predominantly autobiographical oeuvre. Thematic elements, patterns, and images that reappear throughout her work place her securely in what is now recognized as a female literary (counter)tradition. The specific context and conditions of female adolescence; the daughter's difficulty in achieving independence from her mother; the victimization by a repressive sexual code, and its concomitant perils for women, including pregnancy, abortion, and rape; the eloquent descriptions of lesbian love and of the pleasures of the female body; the tyranny of the beautification process and of the obligation to please; the self-hatred and impetus to self-destruction engendered by visualization of the self; the recurring patterns of imprisonment, claustrophobia, and narcissism identified by Sandra M. Gilbert and Susan Gubar in *The Madwoman in the Attic*; the lack of power, control, and community that would allow for a meaningful conquest over the absurdity of the human condition—all of these themes and motifs, foregrounded in Leduc's work, place her centrally within the lineage of writers in Western culture who lay claim to the designation "female authorship."

"My mother never held my hand" is the memorable first sentence of *L'Asphyxie*. Whether the portrait of Berthe that reappears in most of Leduc's writings is accurate or whether it is fashioned from the distortions of imagination and neurosis, the image of the mother is undeniably at the source of Violette Leduc's artistic as well as biological birth. The titles of Leduc's first three books, *L'Asphyxie*, *L'Affamée*, and *Ravages*, epitomize the paradox of a character starving for attention and suffocated by it, a character both devastated and relieved by separation from the loved one, longing for a closeness that inevitably ravages her. At the source of this tension is the narrator's ambivalent relationship to the dominant figure in her life, her mother, Berthe. Violette learns to perceive the hostility of the world and to judge her own inadequacies through her mother's "hard blue look" (*L'Asphyxie*, 13). The first mirror in which the little girl seeks her image and from which she will construct her identity reflects mostly the mother's self-absorption. The few times the child sees herself in the mother's eyes, she observes a distorted, negative image of herself that she gradually learns to internalize. Yet despite their tormented rapport, mother and daughter form a couple, united against an unfair world, and Violette dreams of being the protector of the high-strung Berthe. For Violette, the primary bond with her mother will always remain the most influential one: "Let's go backward, open your belly and take me back.... You sometimes say I hate you. Love has innumerable names. You live in me as I lived in you then" (*La Bâtarde*, 33). Not only does Violette not have a father to help break the primary unity with, and dependence on, the mother, but the latter certainly treated her daughter as an extension of herself, impressing on the little girl all of her own fears, concerns, and passions as well as her bitterness about her experience of womanhood. Lifelong issues of merging with and separating from others, which structure the life of Leduc's narrator, can be understood in light of the inability to free herself from this original unity. Violette internalizes its complicated manifestations and turns it into a model for all later love relationships: throughout her life, the mother remains the immutable reference point. Although Violette briefly enjoyed the joys of reciprocity with her beloved grandmother Fidéline, it was always Berthe and the inaccessibility that she represented that Violette was determined to conquer. The craving for presence, the oppressiveness of presence; suffering from distance, feeling relieved by distance; this psychological pull finds its roots in the child Violette, who dreamed of healing her mother's wounds while being fully aware that she *was* her mother's wound. The anxiety generated by the opposition between a mother whose unloving presence strengthened but oppressed her and a grandmother whose love overwhelmed but weakened her also accounts for the narrator's incapacity to balance closeness to and detachment from others. Violette's sexual relationships, with her first love Isabelle, with her lover (Hermine in *La Bâtarde*, Cécile in *Ravages*), with her husband (Gabriel in *La Bâtarde*, Marc in *Ravages*), and her platonic but equally compulsive attachments for Simone de Beauvoir, Jean Genet, or Jacques Guérin, all reenact the primordial tug between the desire to merge and the relief of distance that forms the substance and structure of virtually all of Leduc's texts.

The character Violette, however, controls the mechanisms that lead her to be rejected by her sexual partners, by establishing triangular relationships that can result only in betrayal; later, she adopts the more refined strategy of channeling her desire toward those who cannot respond: the maternal, unapproachable figure of Simone de Beauvoir and the homosexual men Maurice Sachs, Jean Genet, and Jacques Guérin. Despite the pain this process entails, it frees her from a passion that she fears will annihilate her and creates the space she needs to write. With Beauvoir, however, Violette reaches the turning point in the transformation of desire into mystical fervor. The presence of Simone de Beauvoir permeates Violette's adult years and dominates most of her works. When Leduc first saw Beauvoir's name on the cover of a book, "I was breathing in incense" (*Folie*, 42): Beauvoir has become Violette's religion. *L'Affamée* chronicles the narrator's awakening to the consciousness of a divine reality in the person of the ubiquitous Madame who reads peacefully in a café. *Trésors à prendre* chronicles the narrator's entry into the order of literature by appealing directly to the allegory of the pilgrimage. Struggling to accept the fact that she will never mean anything to Madame except in their common enterprise, literature, she gradually succeeds in transforming desire into writing. One can read Leduc's corpus as a single text organized by a central theme—the painful but redemptive act of writing—and this quest is mediated by Violette's sanctification of Beauvoir. Beauvoir is the primary catalyst, the marker who figuratively (and literally in the case of *Trésors à prendre*) traces the road that leads the sinner-bastard from mortification to the discipline and purity of the writing novice.

Haunted by what she perceived as her ugliness, her monstrosity, Leduc's character Violette assumed this burden and made it into the defiant symbol of her destiny as a bastard: "My ugliness will set me apart until I die" (*L'Affamée*, 192). Violette is always locked up, whether it be in the prison of her skin, in the prison of her garret, or in the prison of her solitary writing task. In order to overcome a physical appearance symbolic of her exclusion from humanity, Violette is led to devise certain strategies. By flaunting her alleged ugliness, for example, she draws attention to herself through a form of negative narcissism; such insistence is an act of defiance that stems not merely from self-pity but from provocation. Since Violette cannot be considered traditionally attractive, then she will make her face a unique and striking one. She will make it the focus of the narrative, the central element to which the reader is drawn. Thus the face and the body, which can be sources of agony, also function to protect the self from this agony. They allow the narrator to draw attention to herself when she feels ignored; they also enable her to deflect the onslaught of direct pain. Leduc assumes fully the role of monster, of willing transgressor of the laws of nature and society. She constructs a grotesque autobiographical character, and from it derives the parodic dimension of her work. In what she calls her "circus act," she casts herself in the roles of clown, buffoon, jester, of self-proclaimed "priestess of homosexuality" heading for "sweet immolation." She lingers on moments of embarrassment and ridicule. Her repeated failures at suicide, at elegance, at love affairs and literary accomplishments—even plastic surgery, which leaves her nose practically unchanged—form the basis of Violette's self-mockery. Leduc asserts the uniqueness of her heroine, even if this means emphasizing her most offensive aspects. This emphasis becomes her access to dignity. It also enables her to turn chaos into writing.

Stylistically, Leduc turns quotidian events into uncontrolled hallucinations, of which the most extreme are found in *L'Affamée* and in *La Folie en tête*, in which she relives her bouts with mental illness. Leduc, in surrealist fashion, intermingles planes of reality and fantasy in her writing, abolishing boundaries between interior and exterior, reason and madness, past and present, the visible and the invisible. The subconscious forces that impose themselves on her perceptions dictate her mental associations and closely guide her writing. Passages in Leduc's work would certainly qualify as surrealistic, given the subversive quality of unexpected images, the hallucinatory visions, and the disorder of the text. However, the risks taken by Leduc are not contrived ones, nor does she simulate irrational states of mind or mental disorder. Her lifelong maladjustment to her environment became exacerbated by self-hate and loneliness to the point where, periodically, she lost touch with rationality. What Leduc experienced during this imprisonment in the darkness of the self was not simulated for literary reasons—although, to be sure, she exploited the grotesque, the exaggerated, and the irrational as strategies to create her own personage both in her life and in her work. Leduc's texts read like a stream of violent and richly imaged self-accusations interrupted by occasional moments of tenderness and joyful lyricism. A long line of male French writers known as *poètes-maudits* fashioned their extraordinary literary visions from lived experiences that violated bourgeois norms. Until Violette Leduc, however, virtually no woman had channeled her own mental and social disorder into the substance of an equally disordered work. She broke the code of silence by revealing truths that, up to that point, had been off limits to women. Leduc was the first woman writer in France whose works were published precisely because their originality lay in honest, brutal self-confessions, and in the transformation of psychological desire, shame, and hallucinatory visions into literature.

SURVEY OF CRITICISM

Although Leduc's early works had won her the esteem of a small, prestigious group of writers, including Simone de Beauvoir, Jean-Paul Sartre, Albert Camus, Marcel Jouhandeau, Jean Cocteau, Jean Genet, and Nathalie *Sarraute, it was not until the success of *La Bâtarde* that this writer began to garner critical as well as commercial attention. In the United States, Henri Peyre concluded that Leduc's prose was "rich, sensuous, at times sumptuous with images worthy of Rimbaud, and perhaps the closest counterpart of Jean Genet at his best" (*Saturday Review*, October 30, 1965). Germaine Brée, in *Narcissus Absconditus: The Problematic Art of Autobiography in Contemporary France*, asserted that "probably the best autobiography since the mid-century is Violette Leduc's *La Bâtarde*, the powerful account of a tragic life that bends the traditional narrative form to her own passionate needs" (23). But it is scholars of the homosexual imagination and of women's writings who have made the most vigorous attempts to secure Leduc's place in the history of French literature.

Interestingly, the only full-length critical texts devoted entirely to Leduc's corpus (except for my own *Violette Leduc*) are unpublished dissertations. Jacob Stockinger in "Violette Leduc: The Legitimations of *La Bâtarde*" (1979) and René de Ceccatty in "Evidences de Violette Leduc" (1980) offered comprehensive studies whose originality—which perhaps explains why they were never published—reflects the difficulty of treating this author's work in traditional scholarly manner. In 1981, Ceccatty devoted a section of the French review *Masques: Revue des homosexualités* to Violette Leduc, as an homage to a writer he feared was being forgotten less than ten years after her death. Ceccatty, whose thesis intended, in part, to demonstrate Leduc's exceptional sensitivity to the eroticization of the male body, defended her extraordinary talent as a writer against charges that she had owed her brief fame to either the *Temps Modernes* support or to lesbian or homosexual themes.

In the late 1970s and in the 1980s, critical articles tended to focus on specific aspects of Leduc's work, especially on her relationship to the mother and to Simone de Beauvoir, on lesbian textuality and, occasionally, on autobiography. Elaine Marks, in "Lesbian Intertextuality," identified Leduc's works as a moment in the radical transformation of the Sappho model in lesbian literature, a transition between *Colette and Monique *Wittig, and concluded that "within the context of intertextuality Violette Leduc is indeed the first French writer to take us beyond the Sappho model to Sappho's own texts—the lesbian writer writing as lesbian" (375).

One book and several articles have been devoted to the enigmatic Beauvoir-Leduc relationship. Michèle Respaut in "Femme/ange, femme/monstre: *L'Affamée* de Violette Leduc" demonstrated that while women writers have generally been led to create fantasies in which they project their rebellious impulses onto "maddened doubles," Leduc reverses this process and projects her "angelic double" onto "Madame"—thereby fully assuming the role of monster. Leduc's mystical pilgrimage from the miraculous moment when she meets "Madame" to her "conversion" and entry into the orders of literature was analyzed in my "From Bastard to Pilgrim: Rites and Writing for Madame." Violette Leduc's work lends itself particularly well to psychoanalytic approaches. In France, Pièr Girard published a book entitled *Oedipe masqué, une lecture psychanalytique de "L'Affamée" de Violette Leduc*, a clinical psychoanalytic treatment of Violette Leduc through a close reading of *L'Affamée*. Finally, and perhaps most important, Martha Noel Evans legitimized Violette Leduc critically by including her in *Masks of Tradition: Women and the Politics of Writing in Twentieth-Century France*, along with Colette, Simone de Beauvoir, Marguerite *Duras, Hélène *Cixous, and Monique Wittig. Evans brought together what arguably can be considered the most recognized French women writers of the twentieth century. She examined common patterns that led them to transform the male literary tradition, both by assuming and reshaping the particular mask that this literary tradition had imposed upon each writer—in the case of Leduc, that of the bastard. Evans's analysis of the continuities in twentieth-century French women's texts placed Violette Leduc in the company of five major French writers in a single coherent study and, in doing so, contributed substantially to securing her place, if not in a canonical literary tradition, then in a redefined version of this tradition.

BIBLIOGRAPHY

Works by Violette Leduc

L'Asphyxie. Paris: Gallimard, 1946.
L'Affamée. Paris: Gallimard, 1948.

Ravages. Paris: Gallimard, 1955.

La Vieille Fille et le mort. Paris: Gallimard, 1958. (Includes *Les Boutons dorés*.)

Trésors à prendre. Paris: Gallimard, 1960.

La Bâtarde. Preface by Simone de Beauvoir. Paris: Gallimard, 1964.

La Femme au petit Renard. Paris: Gallimard, 1965.

Thérèse et Isabelle. Paris: Gallimard, 1966.

La Folie en tête. Paris: Gallimard, 1971.

Le Taxi. Paris: Gallimard, 1971.

La Chasse à l'amour. Paris: Gallimard, 1973.

Lettres à Simone de Beauvoir. Paris: Les Temps Modernes, no. 495 (October 1987).

Translations of Violette Leduc

The Golden Buttons. Trans. Dorothy Williams. London: Peter Owen, 1961.

La Bâtarde. Foreword by Simone de Beauvoir. Trans. Derek Coltman. New York: Farrar, Straus and Giroux, 1965; London: Peter Owen, 1965; London and St. Albans: Panther Books, 1967.

Ravages. Trans. Derek Coltman. London: Arthur Baker, 1966; London: Panther Books, 1969. Includes *Thérèse and Isabelle*.

The Woman with the Little Fox Fur. *Three Novellas*. Trans. Derek Coltman. New York: Farrar, Straus and Giroux, 1966; London: Peter Owen, 1967 (as *The Lady with the Little Fox Fur*). Includes *The Old Maid and the Dead Man* and *The Golden Buttons*.

Thérèse and Isabelle. Trans. Derek Coltman. New York: Farrar, Straus and Giroux, 1967; New York, Dell, 1967. Also included in *Ravages*.

In the Prison of her Skin. Trans. Derek Coltman. London: Rupert Hart-Davis, 1970.

Mad in Pursuit. Trans. Derek Coltman. New York: Farrar, Straus and Giroux, 1971; London: Rupert Hart-Davis, 1971.

The Taxi. Trans. Helen Weaver. New York: Farrar, Straus and Giroux, 1972; Toronto: Doubleday Canada, 1972.

Studies of Violette Leduc

Beauvoir, Simone de. Préface de *La Bâtarde*. Paris: Gallimard, 1964.

Beauvoir, Simone de. *Tout compte fait*. Paris: Gallimard, 1972. 57–63.

Brée, Germaine. *Narcissus Absconditus: The Problematic Art of Autobiography In Contemporary France*. Oxford: Clarendon Press, 1978.

Broc-Lapeyre, Monique. "Du traffic à la littérature." *Critique*, no. 282 (November 1970): 935–43.

Ceccatty, René. "Evidences de Violette Leduc." Thèse du 3e Cycle, Philosophie, Université de Paris I, 1980.

Courtivron, Isabelle de. "From Bastard to Pilgrim: Rites and Writing for Madame." In *Simone de Beauvoir: Witness to a Century*. Yale French Studies, no. 72 (1986): 133–48.

———. *Violette Leduc*. Boston: Twayne, 1985.

———. "Violette Leduc's *L'Affamée*: The Courage to Displease." *L'Esprit Créateur* 19, no. 2 (Summer 1979): 95–106.

Crosland, Margaret. "The Search for Love." In *Women of Iron and Velvet: French Women Writers After George Sand*. London: Constable, 1976; New York: Taplinger, 1976. 201–10.

Evans, Martha Noel. "Violette Leduc: *The Bastard*." In Martha Noel Evans, *Masks of Tradition: Women and the Politics of Writing in Twentieth-Century France*. Ithaca: Cornell University Press, 1987. 102–22.

———. "Writing as Difference in Violette Leduc's Autobiography, *La Bâtarde*." In Shirley Nelson Garner, Claire Kahane, and Madelou Sprengnether, *The (M)other Tongue: Essays in Feminist Psychoanalytic Interpretation*. Ithaca: Cornell University Press, 1985. 306–17.

Girard, Pièr. *Oedipe masqué, une lecture psychanalytique de "L'Affamée" de Violette Leduc*. Paris: Des Femmes, 1986.

Hall, Collette. "*L'écriture féminine* and the Search for the Mother in the Works of Violette Leduc and Marie Cardinal." In *Women in French Literature*. Ed. Michel Guggenheim. Saratoga, Calif.: Anma Libri, 1988. 231–38.

Marchessault, Jovette. *La Terre est trop courte, Violette Leduc: A Play*. Montreal: Editions de la Pleine Lune, 1982.

Marks, Elaine. " 'I Am My Own Heroine': Some Thoughts About Women and Autobiography in France." In *Female Studies IX: Teaching About Women in the Foreign Languages*. Ed. Sidonie Cassirer. Old Westbury, N.Y.: Feminist Press, 1975.

———. "Lesbian Intertextuality." In *Homosexualities and French Literature*. Ed. George Stambolian and Elaine Marks. Ithaca: Cornell University Press, 1979. 353–77.

Respaut, Michèle. "Femme/ange, femme/monstre: *L'Affamée* de Violette Leduc." *Stanford French Review* 7, no. 3 (Winter 1983): 365–74.

Rule, Jane. "Violette Leduc." In *Lesbian Images*. Garden City, N.Y.: Doubleday, 1975. 140–46.

Stockinger, Jacob. "Violette Leduc: The Legitimations of *La Batârde*." Diss., University of Wisconsin-Madison, 1979.

JULIE DE LESPINASSE (1732–1776)

Gita May

Until women's studies undertook to review gender relations, social, political, and cultural history, as well as literary canons, certain long-standing myths stressed the female predominance in eighteenth-century France. Contemporary authors, social observers, and chroniclers of the Parisian cultural scene (both French and foreign) were the first to foster the notion that French women enjoyed great personal freedom and exerted considerable political and cultural influence, primarily in their role as salon hostesses. In the *Lettres persanes* (*Persian Letters*), Montesquieu underscored the belief in humorous and satirical terms (notably in Letter 34), but others, including Rousseau, sounded the alarm about what they considered the disruptive role played by women in French society and saw in this female ascendency a threat to the civic and moral fiber of proper family and civic structure.

The Goncourt brothers, for their part, played a key role in perpetuating this myth regarding the role of women in eighteenth-century society, politics, letters, and the arts in their widely read and influential book, *La Femme au dix-huitième siècle*, first published in 1862. While acknowledging the obstacles and disadvantages attending the education, marriage, and family position of women in eighteenth-century France, the Goncourt brothers nevertheless reached the conclusion that women in eighteenth-century France benefited from enormous prestige and great influence through their pervasive presence in all spheres of culture and politics.

The compelling case of Julie de Lespinasse's rise from poverty and illegitimacy to a position of not inconsiderable importance as salon hostess and friend of the *philosophes* is, perhaps, a perfect illustration of the ambiguity and fragility of women's position even in the leading intellectual circles of eighteenth-century France. That she is one of the main protagonists in one of Diderot's boldest works of scientific speculation, the *Rêve de d'Alembert* (*D'Alembert's Dream*, written in 1769 and first published in 1830), is a clear indication of her close association with the prime movers of the *Encyclopédie*. Moreover, she can be considered one of the great *épistolières* (letter-writers) of her century, for the correspondence she bequeathed to posterity affords us an unusually revealing insight into the rich inner life and emotional turmoils of one who has frequently been identified as the Muse of the Encyclopedists.

BIOGRAPHY

Julie-Jeanne-Eléonore de Lespinasse was born in 1732, the illegitimate daughter of the Countess Julie-Claude-Hilaire d'Albon, sole heiress to an old and illustrious family. At the age of sixteen, Countess d'Albon had been married off to Count Claude d'Albon, the last offspring of the family's elder branch, and a distant cousin. She separated from her husband at the time of her daughter's birth. The little girl was baptized as the child of Claude Lespinasse, bourgeois of Lyons, and dame Julie Navarre, his wife, both wholly fictitious characters. A great deal of mystery surrounded the identity of Julie de Lespinasse's father. She was brought up in a convent as the child of Claude Lespinasse of Lyons. It was even rumored that she was the daughter of the notorious Cardinal de Tencin. For a long time the matter remained an enigma, until it was established by Julie de Lespinasse's first serious biographer, the Marquis de Ségur, that her father was Gaspard de Vichy-Chamrond, brother of Madame *du Deffand, one of the most famous *salonnières* of the eighteenth century.

Julie de Lespinasse's early years were joyless, for her illegitimacy and poverty exposed her to constant humiliations and deprivations, even by relatives. She later attributed her excessive emotional vulnerability and perpetual bouts of depression to the effect of her unhappy youth on her sensibility. There was little in her rudimentary convent schooling to account for her solid cultural baggage; but in that she hardly differed from other women through the centuries. An avid reader endowed with a keen, inquisitive mind, she was largely an autodidact.

Julie de Lespinasse was languishing in her convent in Lyons when Madame du Deffand looked her up in order to invite her to become her companion. Since Mademoiselle de Lespinasse's fate became inextricably bound up with that of Madame du Deffand, a few words about du Deffand are in order. Separated from a husband much older than herself, Madame du Deffand had set up her own household in Paris in 1730. In her younger days she had acquired a reputation as a woman of beauty and intellect and had played a not insignificant role in the wicked high society of the Regency as the mistress of the Regent himself, among others. It was in her salon that the spirit of the Enlightenment began to manifest itself more openly, with its daring criticism of political and judiciary abuses as well as religious intolerance. It was there that some of the most notable *philosophes* and Encyclopedists gathered, and her extensive correspondence with such famous contemporaries as Voltaire constitutes a natural extension of the witty conversations held in her salon. Eventually and at various times she was hostess to all the celebrities of the aristocratic and intellectual world of the day, notably the duchesses du Maine and du Luxembourg, the dukes de Choiseul and de Lauzun, the marquises de Boufflers and du Châtelet, as well as Fontenelle, Voltaire, Montesquieu, Marivaux, d'Alembert, Marmontel, La Harpe, Turgot, Condorcet, and others. Madame du Deffand herself, however, was not in tune with the younger generation of *philosophes*. Diderot obviously failed to make an impression on her, for after one visit he never turned up again in her salon. She also disliked Rousseau, who felt the same way about her, as his acid comments about her in his *Confessions* testify.

As old age crept upon her, with all its attending infirmities, Madame du Deffand felt increasingly desolate and lonely. She thought that a younger person with a good education but without any means of her own might be an ideal companion. Her eyesight grew progressively weaker, and in 1754 she decided to call to her side her niece, Julie de Lespinasse, to keep her company, be her reader, and help her run her salon. For ten years, from 1754 to 1764, Julie de Lespinasse was the faithful, uncomplaining, as well as unpaid, companion to the increasingly demanding and crotchety Madame du Deffand, whose day hardly ever began before 6 p.m. and who spent her sleepless night with Julie at her side as her tireless reader, secretary, and gossip partner. Eventually totally sightless and largely invalid, consumed with ill-humor and boredom, the Marquise ended up relying almost exclusively on her long-suffering companion to make life tolerable for herself.

Little by little, however, the habitués of Madame du Deffand's salon, especially the *philosophes*, tended to gravitate around the younger woman, finding in her a kindred spirit, one with whom they felt at ease and free to express their boldest ideas. No wonder, therefore, that they should make it a point to arrive an hour or so before the mistress of the house's own appearance in order to enjoy Julie de Lespinasse's company fully and exclusively. With Mademoiselle de Lespinasse the Encyclopedists did not feel intellectually inhibited, as they did with the more stodgy Madame du Deffand. The latter, however, could not long remain unaware of this competition, and relations between the two women grew more strained when the Marquise once found Turgot, Marmontel, and d'Alembert happily conversing with Julie as she entered her salon. Such a situation soon became intolerable to the egocentric Marquise, who was accustomed to total and unquestioning adulation and who bitterly accused her protégée unexpectedly turned rival of monopolizing her guests. A rupture was inevitable, and it took place in 1764. Lonely and embittered, Madame du Deffand carried her grudge against the one she looked upon as an ingrate and intriguer into her grave.

Public opinion sided with Julie de Lespinasse, and the latter set up her own modest salon. As a result, most of Madame du Deffand's longtime guests switched allegiance to the younger woman, generally considered the victim of a tyrannical old woman. D'Alembert even came to live by her side as a devoted friend rather than lover. As a distinguished mathematician, co-editor of the *Encyclopédie*, friend of Voltaire and of Frederick II, king of Prussia, d'Alembert could only lend prestige to Mademoiselle de Lespinasse's otherwise austere salon. For twelve years, from 1764 to 1776, the luminaries of the day regularly gathered in Julie de Lespinasse's modest salon, notably Turgot, Condorcet, Helvétius, Grimm, Malesherbes, Marmontel, Saint-Lambert, Condillac, Mably, Diderot, Chamfort, Bernardin de Saint-Pierre, and many others. Such distinguished foreigners as the Scottish philosopher and historian David Hume and the Italian economist Ferdinando Galiani also became familiar fixtures in her salon.

Of all the eighteenth-century *salonnières*, Julie de Lespinasse, who did not benefit from wealth, beauty, personal influence, talent as a social or political intriguer, or even good health, was the most remarkable because of her ability to attract the most forward-looking minds of her age and to foster lively conversation and debate. This should hardly be surprising in light of Mademoiselle de Lespinasse's own solid cultural background as well as intellectual and literary predilections. Tacitus, Plutarch, and Montaigne were among her favorite authors. While she had thoroughly read such seventeenth-century classics as Racine, La Fontaine, and others and was conversant with Montesquieu and Voltaire, her own preference was for the younger generation of French and English writers, notably Diderot, Rousseau, Helvétius, Richardson, and Sterne.

Julie de Lespinasse's emotional balance and physical health, however, had been greatly affected by the deprivations and tribulations of her illegitimate childhood and adolescence, as well as by her ten years of subservience to the willful, domineering Madame du Deffand. As her correspondence attests, even during her stormy relationship with the Marquise she had already exhibited depressive, even suicidal, tendencies and a growing dependency on opium, which only aggravated her bouts of nervous prostration and physical exhaustion. Her hard-won success as a *salonnière* did not fill the sense of void in her heart. She desperately yearned for a great, all-pervasive passion that would give meaning to her life. In this she was doubly thwarted.

Julie's first great love was for Don José y Gonzaga, Marqués de Mora, son of the Spanish ambassador. Proud of carriage and with handsome features, Mora was also a serious-minded young man eager to establish contact with the leading intellectual and philosophical circles in Paris. Julie de Lespinasse met him toward the end of 1766. He was twelve years her junior, a Spanish grandee, wealthy and influential, and a passing visitor to Paris. No wonder, therefore, that his disapproving relatives did everything to separate him from her. They nevertheless managed to see each other now and then and to exchange inflamed letters, for he fully returned her love. It turned out, however, that Mora was a consumptive, and repeated cures at various spas did not prevent his premature death in 1774, at the age of thirty.

Mademoiselle de Lespinasse's other all-consuming passion was for a young colonel with literary and philosophical aspirations named Jacques-Antoine-

Hippolyte, Comte de Guibert. In his twelve years in the army Guibert had served with distinction in the last campaigns of the Seven Years' War and in the 1768 military expedition to Corsica. He had also authored several tragedies, notably the well-received historical drama, *Le Connétable de Bourbon*, set during the Italian campaigns of the early sixteenth century, and an essay on tactical warfare, the *Essai général de tactique*, printed in Holland in 1770 and not distributed in Paris until 1773, which was highly regarded (Frederick II of Prussia and even Napoleon are reputed to have read it with profit). Guibert was also looked upon with favor by the *philosophes* because of his belief in social reforms and the political theories set forth in the first half of his book on tactics. Born in 1743, he, like Mora, was considerably younger than Julie de Lespinasse (by eleven years), and he could charm through his wit and intellectual verve.

Even before Mora's death, Julie de Lespinasse had already fallen hopelessly in love with the dashing, brilliant Guibert. Her letters of that period attest to an extraordinary mixture of love and guilt, pleasure and remorse. Unlike Mora, however, Guibert was not a faithful lover, and even married in June 1775. After this, Julie seems to have lost all desire to live, as her letters amply attest. She expired on May 22, 1776, but not before having made the supreme effort of penning a loving farewell note to Guibert. At the time of her death, Julie de Lespinasse was only forty-four years old. D'Alembert, her ever-loyal friend (and perhaps would-be lover), who shared with her a common burden of illegitimacy, was left disconsolate by this loss.

Successive generations of editors and readers of Julie de Lespinasse's letters have perpetuated the image of one who died of love. Tuberculosis was probably the more direct medical cause of her early demise. The fact remains, however, that she is perhaps the most vibrant and tragic figure among the *salonnières* and *épistolières* of the eighteenth century.

MAJOR THEMES

Julie de Lespinasse's correspondence differs from that of other famous letter-writers of her age, notably Madame du Châtelet, Madame de *Graffigny, and of course Madame du Deffand, in that it is more revealing of the inner anguish and torment of an unusually sensitive, emotionally vulnerable, and passionate woman. But it almost exclusively offers us an exceptionally vivid literary expression of Julie de Lespinasse as the tragic heroine and lover whose destiny was to die of grief, leaving out the learned, vivacious, and forward-looking woman who came to be known as the Muse and friend of the Encyclopedists. In that we may consider her correspondence as the deliberate construction and creation of a self that found its raison d'être solely in loving and suffering. Nowhere in the correspondence do we find a significant trace of what inspired Diderot in making her one of the main protagonists of his masterfully visionary *Rêve de d'Alembert*, in other words, a woman capable of comprehending and discussing the most advanced scientific, medical, psychological, physiological, and philosophical ideas of her time with the renowned physician Théophile de Bordeu.

To be sure, Mademoiselle de Lespinasse was none too pleased when she became aware of the existence of this controversial work and felt that she had been dealt with rather cavalierly by her friend Diderot. And d'Alembert, always her loyal spokesman, demanded (fortunately in vain) that Diderot destroy the manuscript. Both Diderot's boldly speculative *Rêve de d'Alembert* and Julie's own correspondence, with its unfolding of an intimate and painful drama of passion, illness, and suffering, as well as constant preoccupation with the thought of impending death, offer us the compelling portrait of an unusually intelligent, cultured eighteenth-century French woman who finally succumbed to irresistible inner forces of self-destruction, but not before having given literary expression to her own lived experience in letters that rival the novels of Prévost or Rousseau's *Julie, ou La Nouvelle Héloïse* in their gripping descriptions of tragic love.

The letters of Julie de Lespinasse have long been regarded as the natural, spontaneous effusions of an exceptionally sensitive, passionate soul. This view, however, tends to simplify matters. As a highly literate person, Julie de Lespinasse could not fail, as her numerous references make clear, to see herself as a tragic heroine comparable to Racine's Phèdre or Rousseau's Julie (with whom she shared the same first name). At the same time, she was thoroughly familiar with a literary tradition of women letter-writers going back to Madame de Sévigné. Neither was she unaware that the epistolary form had been used to excellent effect in novels of unhappy love, from Guilleragues' *Lettres d'une religieuse portugaise* to Madame de Graffigny's *Lettres d'une Péruvienne*. That she combined those elements—the dramatic, fictional, autobiographical, and epistolary—in her own letters should hardly surprise us. She must have derived great emotional gratification from the fact that she saw herself as a tragic figure worthy of the greatest dramas and novels she had read, and her letters are as creatively selective in their representation of lived experience as would be works of drama or fiction. In this respect, it might be noted that eighteenth-century readers had only the vaguest notion of what separates fact and fiction. The deliberate efforts constantly made, especially by novelists, to pass off their imaginary tales as real letters or memoirs only added to the general confusion.

Julie de Lespinasse ultimately made the choice that the only life worth living is one dedicated to passion. In this she may have—consciously or subconsciously—patterned her life after those literary works that exalt intensity of feeling and emotion, and thus managed to transform her own experience into the stuff of which novels are made. If she did not sublimate her own very real suffering into a literary work of the first magnitude, the letters she left behind have earned her a secure place in French literature because they offer us a stunning example of how life and literature can intersect and commingle.

SURVEY OF CRITICISM

The letters of Julie de Lespinasse to the Comte de Guibert were first published in 1806 by Guibert's widow. Subsequent nineteenth-century editions of her letters largely reproduced this first edition. In 1906, a new edition was published by a descendant of the Comte de Guibert, the Comte de Villeneuve-Guibert.

Nineteenth-century critics viewed Julie de Lespinasse's letters as the natural, impulsive outpourings of a passionate soul and a quivering sensibility. Her first biographer, the Marquis de Ségur, whose study (which appeared in 1906) is still considered an authoritative source of information, shared this prevalent notion with Sainte-Beuve and others. For them, Julie de Lespinasse exemplified the woman of feeling, the touching victim of self-consuming passion. Such a reductive interpretation of Julie de Lespinasse's letters as artless, ingenuous, and "sincere" fitted only too well with a traditional view of women writers as excelling in the unselfconscious depiction of intimate sentiments, lived and volatile emotions, and spontaneous self-revelations.

Recently, however, we have come to a fuller, more sophisticated understanding of the mechanisms whereby Julie de Lespinasse transformed and transmuted her tragic personal experience into literary art. Robert Mauzi, the astute analyst of *les maladies de l'âme* (sicknesses of the soul) and *"l'idée du bonheur"* (the idea of happiness) in the eighteenth century, was one of the first modern critics to point out, in 1960, that Julie de Lespinasse's view of herself as a tragic heroine is at once authentic and suffused with literary models and that she valorized her very real suffering through an exalted picture of herself largely inspired and shaped by the novels and plays that fed and fired her imagination.

It should hardly be surprising that feminist studies, which have immeasurably enriched and deepened our understanding of women writers, have also reassessed *épistolières* like Julie de Lespinasse and have suggested that their letters need to be analyzed within the context of the conventions of classical and post-classical French drama and of the widely read and influential contemporary epistolary novels. Among critics who have pondered these questions with special reference to Julie de Lespinasse, mention should be made of Susan Lee Carrell, Judith Curtis, and Dena Goodman.

BIBLIOGRAPHY

Works by Julie de Lespinasse

Lettres de Mademoiselle de Lespinasse, écrites depuis l'année 1773 jusqu'à l'année 1776, suivies de deux chapitres dans le genre du "Voyage sentimental" de Sterne, par le même auteur, augmentées de son "Eloge" sous le nom d' "Eliza" par le comte de Guibert et deux opuscules de l'Alembert. Ed. Madame de Guibert. Paris: Longchamp, 1811.

Nouvelles Lettres de Mademoiselle de Lespinasse, suivies du Portrait de M. de Mora et d'autres opuscules inédits. Paris: Maradan, 1820.

Lettres de Mademoiselle de Lespinasse, avec une notice biographique de Jules Janin. Paris: Amyot, 1847.

Lettres de Mademoiselle de Lespinasse, suivies de ses autres oeuvres et de lettres de

Madame du Deffand, Turgot, Bernardin de Saint-Pierre. Ed. E. Asse. Paris: Charpentier: 1876. Geneva: Slatkine Reprints, 1971.

Lettres inédites de Mademoiselle de Lespinasse à Condorcet, à d'Alembert, à Guibert, au comte de Crillon. Ed. C. Henry. Paris: E. Denty, 1887. Geneva: Slatkine Reprints, 1971.

Lettres de Mademoiselle de Lespinasse, précédées d'une notice de Sainte-Beuve. Paris: Garnier Frères, 1893.

Correspondance entre Mademoiselle de Lespinasse et le comte de Guibert, publiée pour la première fois d'après le texte original par le comte de Villeneuve-Guibert. Paris: Calmann-Lévy, 1906.

Lettres de Mademoiselle de Lespinasse. Paris: Garnier, 1925.

Les Plus Belles Lettres de Mademoiselle de Lespinasse. Ed. Cl. Roy. Paris: Calmann-Lévy, 1962.

Lettres de Mademoiselle de Lespinasse, précédées d'une notice de Sainte-Beuve. Reprint of the 1893 Garnier edition, with a preface by Jean-Noël Pascal. Plan-de-la-Tour: Editions d'Aujourd'hui, 1978.

Translations of Julie de Lespinasse

Letters of Mademoiselle de Lespinasse. Trans. K. P. Wormeley. London: Heinemann, 1903.

Love Letters of Mademoiselle de Lespinasse to and from the Comte de Guibert. Trans. E.H.F. Mills. London: Routledge and Sons, 1929.

Studies of Julie de Lespinasse

Bouissounouse, Janine. *Julie: The Life of Mademoiselle de Lespinasse.* Trans. P. de Fontnouvelle. New York: Appleton-Century-Crofts, 1962.

Carrell, Susan Lee. *Le Soliloque de la passion féminine ou le dialogue illusoire.* Tubingen: Gunter Narr; Paris: Jean-Michel Place, 1982.

Curtis, Judith. "The *Epistolières.*" In *French Women and the Age of Enlightenment.* Ed. S. I. Spencer. Bloomington: Indiana University Press, 1984.

Goncourt, Edmond, et Jules de Goncourt. *La Femme au dix-huitième siècle.* Paris: Charpentier, 1911.

Goodman, Dena. "Julie de Lespinasse: A Mirror for the Enlightenment." In *Eighteenth-Century Women and the Arts.* Ed. F. M. Keener and S. E. Lorsch. Westport, Conn.: Greenwood Press, 1988. 3–10.

Herold, Christopher. *Love in Five Temperaments.* New York: Atheneum, 1961.

Jebb, Camilla. *A Star of the Salons: Julie de Lespinasse.* New York: Putnam's Sons, 1908.

Mauzi, Robert. "Les Maladies de l'âme au XVIIIᵉ siècle." *Revue des Science Humaines* (1960): 460–93.

Pascal, Jean-Noël. "Une Exemplaire mort d'amour: Julie de Lespinasse." In *Actes du Colloque "Aimer en France 1760–1860."* Ed. P. Viallaneix and J. Ehrard. Clermont-Ferrand: Association des Publications de la Faculté des Lettres, 1980.

Royde-Smith, Naomi. *The Double Heart: A Study of Julie de Lespinasse.* New York: Harper and Brothers, 1931.

Sainte-Beuve, Charles-Augustin. Introduction to *Letters of Mademoiselle de Lespinasse*. Trans. K. P. Wormeley. London: Heinemann, 1903.

Ségur, Pierre-Maurice-Henri, Marquis de. *Julie de Lespinasse*. Paris: Calmann-Lévy, 1906.

———. *Julie de Lespinasse*. Trans. P. H. Lee Warner. New York: Henry Holt & Co., 1907.

FRANÇOISE MALLET-JORIS
(1930–   )

Lucille F. Becker

BIOGRAPHY

Françoise-Eugénie-Julienne Lilar (nom de plume Françoise Mallet-Joris) was born in Antwerp on July 6, 1930, to Albert Lilar, lawyer, professor of maritime law, and statesman, and Suzanne Verbist Lilar, writer and member of the Belgian Academy. Her parents were members of the French-speaking upper middle class of Antwerp, a class that figures prominently in Mallet-Joris's first two novels, *Le Rempart des béguines* (*The Illusionist*) and *La Chambre rouge* (*The Red Room*). It was the superficiality of the bourgeoisie among whom she grew up that stimulated the antipathy for hypocrisy and pretentiousness we find throughout her work. Her rebellion against the constraints of her milieu, a rebellion that would motivate the behavior of all of her heroines, took the form of liberation from the sexual taboos of her class; she had a lover at the age of fifteen. The prematurely cynical girl and the older man appear in *La Chambre rouge*, while the revolt against the parental moral code is the framework for *Le Rempart des béguines*.

When her parents found out about her love affair, they shipped her off to study at Bryn Mawr College in the United States. She decided to get married as quickly as possible to free herself of parental authority. Accordingly, she married her professor, Robert Amadou, divorced him, and returned to settle in Paris, pregnant and supported by a new lover, who sent her to study at the Sorbonne, and who continued to support her even after they had grown apart. In 1951, she published her first novel, *Le Rempart des béguines*, under the pseudonym Françoise Mallet, to which she later added Joris to avoid confusion with the writer Robert Mallet. The success of this novel taught her the pleasures of money. It was money, she wrote, that completed her liberation, and that gave her an existence in relation to society. Yet, even while she was living as she chose in complete freedom, she continued to feel a vague malaise, a pull toward something as yet undefined that led finally to her conversion to Catholicism at the age of twenty-four. Her works since then have reflected her religious beliefs, which are based on an acceptance of misery and suffering as part of the order of the world. Her religious conversion, which she describes in an autobiographical work of 1963, *Lettre à moi-même* (*A Letter to Myself*), was accompanied by political and social commitments, and we find in Mallet-Joris's later works great sympathy for the disinherited of the earth.

A brief second marriage to the historian Alain Joxe was followed by a lasting marriage to the artist Jacques Delfau, the father of her second son and two daughters. Her great love for her children is reflected in many of her works, particularly the autobiographical *La Maison de papier* (*The Paper House*) of 1970 and the novel *Allegra* (1976). She is also the author of two books for children, *Le Roi qui aimait trop les fleurs* (The King Who Loved Flowers Too Much, 1972) and *Les Feuilles mortes d'un bel été* (The Dead Leaves of a Beautiful Summer, 1973).

Although Mallet-Joris settled permanently in Paris, where she is a leading member of the literary establishment, vice-president of the Goncourt Academy, television columnist for *Panorama chrétien*, and member of the board of directors of the television station TF–1, her first two novels, as well as *Les Mensonges* (*House of Lies*) and the short stories of *Cordélia* (*Cordelia and Other Stories*), both published in 1956, are permeated with the atmosphere of Antwerp. In these works, she recreates the sensory world of her childhood as she evokes the sounds, sights, and smells of the city: the Flemish-speaking, working-class city, the port of Antwerp with its prostitutes, its bars, and its docks crawling with sailors on leave, the huge village fairs or *kermesses* of the Flemish people. The Flemish influence also explains the unexpected mixture in her work of realism and fantasy. It accounts for the importance she gives to black masses, orgies, and witchcraft, particularly evident in *Trois âges de la nuit* (*The Witches*) of 1968. It took Mallet-Joris five years to free herself sufficiently from the Flemish influence and atmosphere to situate a novel in Paris, *L'Empire céleste* (*Café Céleste*), published in 1958. She returned many years later to the Flemish influence of her first works in two of the stories of the collection *Le Clin d'oeil de l'ange* (In the Twinkling of the Angel's Eye, 1983) and the novel *La Tristesse du cerf-volant* (The Sadness of the Kite, 1988). In 1983, Mallet-Joris made a fifty-minute film on Antwerp for Belgian television.

Since the publication of her first novel in 1951, Mallet-Joris has written an additional twelve novels, three collections of novellas and short stories, and two biographical and three autobiographical works. Her first published work, however, was a collection of twenty poems in free verse, *Poèmes du dimanche* (Sunday Poems), written when she was fifteen years old. These poems, which are for the most part on the lyric themes of love and nature, announce the new career as a songwriter on which Mallet-Joris embarked twenty-five years later. Since 1971, she has been writing lyrics, often in collaboration with Michel

Grisolia, for the popular singer Marie-Paule Belle. She describes this activity as not very different from that of writing a novel, for both must be made up of a symbiotic relationship between words and music. Mallet-Joris also accompanied Marie-Paule Belle on tours made between 1972 and 1979, an experience that provided the background for *Dickie-Roi*, a novel that is rooted in the contemporary mass culture of popular music and religious sects.

MAJOR THEMES

Mallet-Joris's first novel, *Le Rempart des béguines*, is the story of an adolescent who enters into a lesbian relationship with her father's mistress. The protagonist of the novel is the prototype of all of the author's subsequent heroines; she is an independent, brave, and resolute young girl, created in the author's own image, who refuses to play the role assigned to her by society and who revolts against the hypocrisy and constraints of her milieu. Her rebellion is directed solely against family and society, without reference to the human condition. It is only the heroines of the novels written after the author's religious conversion who join a spiritual to a social disquiet. In all cases, however, the heroine's refusal to conform, as well as her lucid, disabused view of society, condemn her to solitude.

The sequel to *Le Rempart des béguines*, *La Chambre rouge*, is also a novel of psychological analysis and a *bildungsroman*. Here the heroine completes her sentimental education as she struggles for dominance in a heterosexual love affair. While the first novel is a remarkable study of the search of a motherless girl for the maternal love that has been denied her, *La Chambre rouge* repeats, with certain variations, the eternal battle between the sexes.

Although the behavior of the heroines of Mallet-Joris's first two novels, as well as of the short stories of *Cordélia*, is motivated by a search for truth, that of the males is characterized by a flight from truth. The men in Mallet-Joris's work are, for the most part, inauthentic beings who have directed their efforts toward creating an image of themselves that will free them from the existentialist imperative to create their own essence. The danger of such behavior is made manifest in the author's next two novels, *Les Mensonges* and *L'Empire céleste*. The protagonists of these two novels would seem to be very different from one another—Klaes van Baarnheim is a successful, violent, domineering man who has made a fortune as a brewer in Antwerp, and Stéphane Morani is a tubercular, third-rate musician who plays the piano in a rundown saloon in Paris. Yet, both find ultimately that the personas they have created have destroyed their authentic being, leaving nothing in its stead. In *Les Mensonges* and *L'Empire céleste*, the author changes from first- to third-person narration. Interior monologues, dialogues, and individual perceptions provide the multiple points of view that were lacking in the preceding works.

Mallet-Joris abandons the weak male and returns to her strong prototypical heroine in two historical fictional works, *Les Personnages* (*The Favorite*) of

1961 and *Trois âges de la nuit*, and two biographical works, *Marie Mancini, le premier amour de Louis XIV* (*The Uncompromising Heart*) of 1964, and *Jeanne Guyon*, 1978. While each of the heroines revolts in a different way against society, all of them are similarly conspired against and attacked on all sides by hostile forces. The plot line of *Les Personnages* corresponds for the most part with historical events: Cardinal Richelieu, concerned with the influence of the mistress of Louis XIII, Louise de la Fayette, enlisted the aid of a Dominican priest to persuade Louise to become a nun. Although the priest's efforts were unsuccessful, Louise did eventually enter a convent. It is within this historical context that Mallet-Joris sets the psychological and spiritual drama of a woman who is led little by little to God. While the novel is inspired by the author's own religious conversion, its classical sobriety and concision mirror the masterpiece based on Louise's story, Madame de *Lafayette's *La Princesse de Clèves*, the prototype for the modern psychological novel.

Les Trois Ages de la nuit consists of three novellas which are fictionalized treatments of case histories Mallet-Joris chose from among the accounts of witchcraft she studied. Here, as in *Les Personnages*, the author did not hesitate to distort or to invent, for she was not seeking historical accuracy. Her aim was rather to re-create as faithfully as possible the climate of the period between 1580 and 1630, a period when persecution for witchcraft was rampant, and to demonstrate that the main stimulus for the persecution of witches was the pervasive misogyny that existed both in village life and in the Church.

Like her historical novels, Mallet-Joris's biography of the seventeenth-century mystic and writer Jeanne Guyon was motivated by what she calls a feminist idée fixe. She was determined to tell the true story about Jeanne Guyon to show how a virtuous woman was vilified and ridiculed because she would not conform to what the Church and the society of her time considered her role as a woman. Jeanne Guyon was persecuted because she broke with all accepted stereotypes. Despite departures from orthodoxy in her work, it was not what she wrote, according to Mallet-Joris, but the fact that she, a woman, had the temerity to write on religious matters that led to Jeanne's persecution.

Mallet-Joris found in Jeanne Guyon's quest for divine grace echoes of her own search for that which gives meaning and value to life. All of her subsequent works are centered around metaphysical disquiet and the search for an absolute. *Les Signes et les prodiges* (*Signs and Wonders*, 1966) is the story of a man, Nicolas Leclusier, who thirsts for God but is unable to reconcile an omnipotent God with the evil he sees everywhere in the world. His spiritual quest, which culminates in suicide, is set in 1962 and is integrated into the political and social life of the time. While the metaphysical disquiet and search for an absolute of Mallet-Joris's later works reappear in *Allegra* (1976), they are accompanied by the search for identity that was characteristic of the heroine of her early novels. In this novel, which deals with the members of a matriarchal Corsican clan who live in Paris, the author returns to the emancipatory, amoral themes of her early novels. Here, however, she goes beyond the revolt of the heroine to show the debasement of all women. *Dickie-Roi* (1979) is the story of the efforts of two groups of young people who dream of beauty, love, and communion to transcend the imperfections and finitude of life. Each group is centered around a charismatic leader: Dickie-Roi, a pop singer, and "Father" Paul, an enigmatic and rather sinister guru of a religious sect.

The protagonist of *Le Rire de Laura* (Laura's Laugh), Laura Jacobi, wife of a successful surgeon, has sublimated her existential angst and taken refuge behind the image of a model bourgeois wife and mother. When the novel opens, Laura is in a hotel room with her son Martin, who is recovering from an aborted suicide attempt, seeking to understand him and the reasons for his action. What she discovers is that Martin, who has inherited her spiritual malaise, has despaired because of the failure of the utopian community he had created in protest against the ugliness and meaninglessness of life. At the end of the novel, Laura finds a key to her own salvation and, by extension, Martin's. She has given up hope of achieving absolute truth, but will continue to struggle and content herself with temporary, partial victories; she has discovered that grace is not a definitive salvation but merely a beginning, that it is not repose but constant effort and choice.

Central, too, to *La Tristesse du cerf-volant* is the search for an absolute. However, many contemporary feminist themes also appear in this novel, which traces the lives of three generations of a family of Flemish mill owners in the town of Kerkhove on the outskirts of Lille. The incestuous brother and sister at the heart of the novel reflect similar couples found in the works of many contemporary female novelists. For these writers, the closely knit, symbiotic union of brother and sister constitutes the perfectly conceived androgynous being in which one sees reflected neither the other nor a mirror image, but rather the other half of oneself. It is a union in which all aspects of love, both homosexual and heterosexual, blend to form the whole which provides a cure for the fragmentation of existence.

SURVEY OF CRITICISM

Mallet-Joris's work has received almost unanimous acclaim since the publication of her first novel, *Le Rempart des béguines*. The noted French critic Pierre-Henri Simon called her "one of the best novelists and one of the most gifted writers of her generation," (9–10) while George Steiner described her as a novelist of great power and a promising candidate for election to the Académie Française. (84) A critical work devoted to Mallet-Joris by Michel Géoris in 1964 discusses the basic themes in the author's first six works. Whether autobiography, short story, essay, historical novel, or psychological novel, all of her works, he writes, express the need for lucidity and revolt. Géoris's text is followed by a critical analysis by Frédéric Kiesel of *Poèmes du dimanche*, entitled "Une Inconnue, Françoise Lilar, poétesse de quinze ans." An article in English by Rima

Drell Reck studies the same works to show how the exercise of the will takes on various forms in these works.

The next complete volume devoted to Mallet-Joris, *Françoise Mallet-Joris: Dossier critique et inédits*, contains a collection of reviews by prominent literary critics of works published through 1976, a selection of unpublished poems, a reprint of *Poèmes du dimanche*, songs, a chronology, and a bibliography. These are followed by a critical essay by Monique Détry on Mallet-Joris's work entitled *Le Miroir, le voyage et la fête*. Détry explains that Mallet-Joris has no gift for abstract expression, and analyzes her works to illustrate the author's use of images and parables to express her ideas.

Several critics have viewed Mallet-Joris's work from the perspective of Catholicism. In *Dieu dans la littérature d'aujourd'hui*, Gérard Mourgue devotes a chapter to the question of God in three of her early works. He explains that the author's preoccupation with death, particularly in the stories of *Cordélia*, disappears in the works that followed her religious conversion. Louis Barjon, in a study in a Catholic journal of *Les Signes et les prodiges*, finds quite logical Mallet-Joris's treatment of a spiritual journey that ends with the suicide of the protagonist. He maintains that her denunciation of the illusions of a faith that depends entirely on external proofs invites the reader to reflect on the nature of true faith. According to Barjon, even the title chosen by the author indicates that this was precisely her intention, for *Les Signes et les prodiges* harks back to a number of biblical texts that speak about the ambiguity of "signs" and warn that an uncritical acceptance of their symbolic nature destroys the true essence of religious faith.

Geneviève Delattre considers Mallet-Joris's work from an existentialist point of view. Like Sartre, she emphasizes the importance of the "look" (*le regard*) of others and the efforts made by characters to elicit a flattering image of themselves in the eyes of others; each one dons a mask and strives to play his or her part in an effort to see in the eyes of others the reflection of the image he or she has chosen.

The only complete work devoted to Mallet-Joris is the critical study in English, *Françoise Mallet-Joris*, by Lucille F. Becker. She analyzes the author's work from traditional, existentialist, Catholic, and feminist points of view. She demonstrates that Mallet-Joris occupies a unique position in contemporary French letters, for she has created a remarkable synthesis between elements of the traditional and modern novel. While her novels remain within the framework of the traditional novel with their emphasis on plot and characterization, they also reflect a modern cinematographic preoccupation with visual detail as well as a twentieth-century note of existential anguish.

In a chapter on Françoise Mallet-Joris in her *Twentieth-Century French Women Novelists*, Lucille Becker analyzes Mallet-Joris's work from a feminist point of view. She points out that Mallet-Joris's portrayal of male and female characters is reminiscent of *Colette's; her females are strong, lucid individuals in search of authenticity, while the males are weak, inauthentic beings who abdicate all responsibility for their lives. Becker notes further that, in her work, Mallet-Joris has given the historical and cultural background for the mistreatment of women. Despite this, her work is generally excluded from all considerations of feminist literature. Becker believes that this may be due in part to her religious beliefs, which postulate an acceptance of misery and suffering as part of the order of the world, despite the imperative to struggle against it.

BIBLIOGRAPHY

Works by Françoise Mallet-Joris

Fiction

Le Rempart des béguines. Paris: Juillard, 1951.
La Chambre rouge. Paris: Juillard, 1955.
Cordélia. Paris: Juillard, 1956.
Les Mensonges. Paris: Juillard, 1956.
L'Empire céleste. Paris: Juillard, 1958.
Les Personnages. Paris: Juillard, 1961.
Les Signes et les prodiges. Paris: Grasset, 1966.
Trois Ages de la nuit. Paris: Grasset, 1968.
Le Jeu du souterrain. Paris: Grasset, 1973.
Allegra. Paris: Grasset, 1976.
Dickie-Roi. Paris: Grasset, 1979.
Un Chagrin d'amour et d'ailleurs. Paris: Grasset, 1981.
Le Clin d'oeil de l'ange. Paris: Gallimard, 1983.
Le Rire de Laura. Paris: Gallimard, 1985.
La Tristesse du cerf-volant. Paris: Flammarion, 1988.
Adriana Sposa. Paris: Flammarion, 1990.

Autobiographical Works

Lettre à moi-même. Paris: Juillard, 1963.
La Maison de papier. Paris: Grasset, 1970.
J'aurais voulu jouer de l'accordéon. Paris: Juillard, 1976.

Biographical Works

Marie Mancini, le premier amour de Louis XIV. Paris: Hachette, 1964.
Jeanne Guyon. Paris: Flammarion, 1978.

Translations of Françoise Mallet-Joris

The Illusionist. New York: Farrar, Straus and Young, 1952.
The Red Room. New York: Farrar, Straus and Cudahy, 1956.
Cordelia and Other Stories. New York: Farrar, Straus and Giroux, 1965.
House of Lies. New York: Farrar, Straus and Cudahy, 1957.
Café Céleste. New York: Farrar, Straus and Cudahy, 1962.

The Favorite. New York: Farrar, Straus and Cudahy, 1962.
A Letter to Myself. New York: Farrar, Straus, 1964.
The Uncompromising Heart. New York: Farrar, Straus and Giroux, 1966.
Signs and Wonders. New York: Farrar, Straus and Giroux, 1967.
The Witches. New York: Farrar, Straus and Giroux, 1967.
The Paper House. New York: Farrar, Straus and Giroux, 1971.
The Underground Game. New York: E. P. Dutton, 1975.

Studies of Françoise Mallet-Joris

Barjon, Louis. "Les Romans." *Etudes* (April 1967): 523–26.
Becker, Lucille F. *Françoise Mallet-Joris.* Boston: Twayne, 1985.
———. *Twentieth Century French Women Novelists.* Boston: Twayne, 1989.
Delattre, Geneviève. "Mirrors and Masks in the World of Françoise Mallet-Joris." *Yale French Studies*, no. 27 (1961): 122–26.
Desnues, R. M. "Etude d'auteur: Françoise Mallet-Joris." *Livres et Lectures* (March 1965): 133–42.
Detry, Monique. *Françoise Mallet-Joris: Dossier critique et inédits* and *Le miroir, le voyage et la fête.* Paris: Grasset, 1976.
Géoris, Michel. *Françoise Mallet-Joris.* Brussels: P. de Méyère, 1964.
Lobet, Marcel. "La Confession féminine d'Héloise à Françoise Mallet-Joris." *Annales 17* (1963–64): 23–28.
Mourgue, Gérard. *Dieu dans la littérature d'aujourd'hui.* Paris: Editions France-Empire, 1961.
Reck, Rima Drell. "Françoise Mallet-Joris and the Anatomy of the Will." *Yale French Studies*, no. 24 (Summer 1959): 74–79.
Simon, Pierre-Henri. *Diagnostic des lettres françaises contemporaines.* Paris, 1966.
Steiner, George. "Books-Ladies' Day." *New Yorker* 17 August 1981: 104.

MARGUERITE DE NAVARRE (1492–1549)

Colette H. Winn

BIOGRAPHY

On April 11, 1492, Louise of Savoie and Charles of Valois, count of Angoulême, learned, not without a certain disappointment, that they had a daughter, whom they named Marguerite. They had wanted a son, who would have been the presumptive heir to the throne of France. Two years later, a son, Francis, was born, who became king when Louis of Orléans, king of France, died in 1515, leaving no male heir. Charles died in 1498 of pleurisy, and Louise moved from Cognac to Chinon, and then on to Amboise. Louise was a dedicated mother and "a firm believer in coeducation of the sexes and in equality of educational opportunity" (Putnam, 44). Thus Marguerite received an education more intensive than that of almost any other young lady of her time.

Louise herself oversaw the children's studies and invited well-known scholars into her home to teach them Greek, Latin, Hebrew, philosophy, theology, and modern languages (Italian, Spanish, and English). Marguerite, early on, manifested a passion for knowledge and exhibited unusual skill in both music and poetry. She spent the impressionable years of her youth reading Arthurian tales, French chronicles, and books of religious devotion. She frequently played with her brother and his friends, all sons of nobility. She knew that Francis would be a man of great destiny and was deeply attached to him throughout her life.

In 1509, Marguerite married Charles, duke of Alençon, and went to live in Argentan. It was a marriage without love, but she kept up with her studies and the intellectual interests of her youth. Although her husband did not care for it, she surrounded herself with some of the best minds of the time: physicians, philosophers, historians, poets, and writers. When Francis became king of France, Marguerite made numerous sojourns at the court, which was then the most scintillating in all of Europe, certainly the most renowned for its elegance, distinction, wit, gallantry, literature, and art. While Claude of France, Francis's wife, settled into obscurity, Marguerite began to play the role traditionally assigned to the queen of France.

The French nation then embarked upon the Italian wars, trying to reconquer the Duchy of Milan and retrieve ancestral claims dating back to Charles VIII. After a memorable victory at Marignano (1515), the French were disastrously defeated at Pavia (1525) by the Holy Roman Emperor, Charles V, and Francis was taken captive to Madrid. Louise assumed the role of regent, and Marguerite was dispatched to negotiate Francis's release. Her heroic mission was successful. Not only was she able to nurse the king back to life, but through her diplomatic skills, she arranged for his release and for a peace treaty on more favorable terms than those under discussion before her arrival. A renewed intimacy was rekindled between brother and sister that was to last until Francis's death some twenty years later.

Marguerite's husband, despised as a "runaway of Pavia," died soon after the Italian wars of wounds received in battle. In 1527, Marguerite married the dashing Henry of Albret, eleven years her junior, to whom she bore a daughter, Jeanne of Albret, the future mother of Henry IV and one of the leaders of the Calvinist party in France. With this marriage she became the queen of Navarre we know today. She turned her new residence in Navarre, Nérac, into a radiant center of humanist cultural activity. She was the great protectress of the cardinal Du Bellay and of poets and writers such as Mellin de Saint-Gelais, Antoine Héroët, and Jacques Amyot. She also favored, and entered into a dialogue with, such controversial figures as Jean Calvin, Clément Marot, Bonaventure des Périers, and Rabelais, who dedicated his *Tiers Livre (Third Book)* to the "transported, ecstatic spirit" of the queen. When Francis founded the Royal Lectors in 1530 (the Collège de France, which still plays a major role in French cultural life), a new learning was launched based upon truth and reason rather than the opinions of men; the teaching of subjects banned by the doctors of the Sorbonne was now encouraged. This "modern university" owed much to the efforts of the queen of Navarre.

While in Argentan, under the influence of her pious mother-in-law, Marguerite of Lorraine, Marguerite focused her energies on devotional and philanthropic activities. She oversaw the reorganization and reform of hospitals and monasteries, including the monastery of Almenesches and the convent of Sainte-Claire at Argentan, which she founded with her mother-in-law. She was, as Putnam puts it, "the prototype of the modern woman in social service" (278). She immersed herself in her Bible readings and in the doctrine of Plato, and was deeply concerned with the nascent reform in the Church. Marguerite carried on a vigorous correspondence from 1521 to 1524 with Briçonnet, the bishop of Meaux, who assisted in the reform of the chapter of Séez, and with Jacques Lefèvre d'Etaples, the great precursor of the Reformation, who had undertaken the translation and publication of the four gospels into French.

Marguerite leaned in the direction of the Reformation, which was headed by some of the most learned men of the century, and yet she died a Roman Catholic. Her footprints are deeply embedded along the path of development of early Protestantism. When Lefèvre d'Etaples was condemned for heresy, she gave him asylum at Nérac, and when Louis de Berquin was on the verge of being burned at the stake, she influenced Francis to intervene on his behalf. In fact, Marguerite's first extended work in verse, *Le Miroir de l'âme pécheresse* (The Mirror of the Sinful Soul), came from her involvement with the Meaux circle. It was printed in Alençon (late 1531) and, soon after, was banned by the theologians of the Sorbonne for containing heretical material. Under Francis's influence the censure was officially revoked, but the matter provoked much controversy and animosity against the queen. In 1534, the Reformationists so antagonized the king with their rebellious posters against the Roman Church and doctrine, an event later to be known as the Affaire des Placards, that his attitude toward the Reformation was forever altered. The major leaders were tried, expelled, or driven into silence, and Marguerite was no longer able to appeal to Francis for clemency on behalf of her protégés.

From 1540 on, Francis's health deteriorated. His death in 1547 was a blow from which Marguerite never totally recovered. Disheartened by the prevailing intolerance and religious hatred, she turned inward for spiritual comfort, pursuing, more wholeheartedly than ever before, her search for moral perfection. As French Platonism attained its peak between 1540 and 1550, she devoted herself to the study of Greek. Living in almost utter solitude at the monastery of Tusson (in Poitou) or in the castle of Andos, near Tarbes, she exchanged letters with Pope Paul III and his nephew, Alessandro Farnese, and the Italian poetess and mystic Vittoria Colonna. Above all, she spent the remaining years of her life writing lyrics and plays of deep religious devotion and trying to complete the *Heptaméron* (Heptameron), a collection of tales which, historians claim, she invented as a means of amusing Francis in his declining days.

MAJOR THEMES

The body of works that Marguerite produced is astonishing in size and range. She began writing in the 1520s and eventually worked in a wide variety of forms in both verse and prose: *rondeaux*, *épîtres*, *oraisons*, songs, spiritual meditations, dialogues, plays, and an unfinished collection of novellas, the *Heptaméron*. Her first collection of poetry was published in 1531 under the title *Le Miroir de l'âme pécheresse*, and some sixteen years later, a definitive collection was to appear, the *Marguerites de la Marguerite des Princesses* (Pearls by the Pearl of Princesses) and *Suyte des marguerites de la Marguerite des Princesses* (Continuation of the Pearls). Marguerite's most significant achievements can be highlighted according to the ways in which she has contributed to literary history: the controversial writer; the dialogist; the mystic; the taleteller; the playwright.

The Controversial Writer

Often dismissed today for its difficulty, Marguerite's first major work to be published, *Le Miroir de l'âme pécheresse*, reveals the queen's courageous spirit and her deep Evangelical convictions. The violent reaction of the conservative Sorbonnists and religious fanatics comes as no surprise when one considers the poem's subject matter (the reading of the Bible, which is done in the vernacular and without clerical supervision), the large percentage of direct quotations and close paraphrases of Lefèvre d'Etaples's translation (for which Marguerite was largely responsible), the transferred application of certain hymns (from the Virgin Mary to Christ), and Marguerite's deliberate silence on saints and merits. Curiously, the work survived, serving some years later as a translation exercise for the eleven-year-old Elizabeth of England.

The Dialogist

Marguerite's three dialogues (only two of which bear the name of dialogue) show the important part she played in what has come to be known as one of the great moments in the history of dialogue. Not only did dialogue come naturally to her, it also suited her epistemological needs. While the *Discord estant en l'homme par la contrarieté de l'Esprit et de la Chair, et paix par vie spirituelle* (Discord that Exists in Man Because of the Opposition of Spirit and Flesh, and Peace Through Spiritual Life) is modeled after the medieval *conflictus*, the *Dialogue en forme de vision nocturne* (Dialogue in the Form of a Nocturnal Vision) marks a shift from the medieval tradition of debate poetry to an autonomous genre which developed during the Renaissance in multiple ways. The death of Marguerite's eight-year-old niece, Charlotte, inspired the *Dialogue* as an examination of conscience. Critics claim that Marguerite drew heavily upon Briçonnet's letter of August 31, 1524, in which he consoles her after the death of Charlotte's mother. In the form of a nocturnal conversation between her departed niece and herself that takes place in Marguerite's troubled dream, the poem focuses on a most controversial point in theology (original sin and redemption) and a key aspect of Evangelical doctrine, the question of free will. It is believed to be among the very first attempts (after Jean Lemaire des Belges but prior to Saint-Gelais's *Hécatomphile*, which appeared in 1534) to use the *terza rima*, a form that had heretofore been unknown in the French language and to which Marguerite returned in later poems such as the *Coche* (Coach) and the *Navire* (Ship). The tripartite nature of the rhyme scheme is particularly well suited to evoking the Christian's journey from *purgatio* through *perfectio* toward *unio*. The use of this form, associated with the *Divina Commedia*, has often led critics to exaggerate the influence of Dante on the *Dialogue*.

Among Marguerite's most famous poems, the *Navire* was written in 1547 when the death of Francis I forced her to confront once again her own mortality and reflect upon her experience as a Christian. The poem's allegorical dimension and its lack of nuance still recall the rigid antagonism of medieval debates between Flesh and Spirit. Yet, the dialogue evolves along two main lines never clearly defined in the text: (1) the self's search for a rational position in the face of death, and (2) the self's effort to silence reason altogether, which will enable it to approach God. The self's gradual progress toward illumination culminates in its acknowledgment that truth is and ever will be beyond its reach. In this sense, the *Navire* can be read as a lesson in humility, as it demonstrates the mind's limitations and forces the self to renounce its illusion of independence. The personal tone of the poem conveys a sense of genuineness that combines the power both to move and to persuade (*movere et docere*). In the course of her lament, Marguerite suggests a therapeutics for the soul in danger and introduces the reader to her own views on humility, faith, and grace. Critics deplore the *Navire*'s lack of consistency and structural rigor. However, they fail to take into account the queen's insight in reproducing both the complexity of the divided mind and the obliqueness of the self-examination process.

The Mystic

Marguerite is sometimes celebrated as "the first mystical poet in our literature," as one to whom we owe "a scrupulous attention . . . to the movements of consciousness, the appearance of the 'moi' (self), in literature" (Girard and Jung, 242). Yet, her poems seldom allude to precise events in her life. Rather, they refer to the history of mankind, its fall through Adam's disobedience, and its redemption through Christ's suffering on the cross. Recounting the Christian's long pursuit of union with Christ, they trace the ways by which he overcomes fear and distress. The Evangelicals of Meaux with whom the queen came into contact in the 1520s exercised a profound influence on her thought and art; her correspondence with Briçonnet, in particular, was to be a lasting source of inspiration throughout her later life. Henry Heller notes that "over the two decades following the collapse of the experiment at Meaux, the religious thought of Marguerite was affected successively to some degree by the influence of Luther, Calvin, and the Spiritual Libertines" (281).

The *Prisons*, Marguerite's longest poem, probably composed after Francis's death, reads like a confession recounting the queen's moral, intellectual, and spiritual evolution. It concerns a third-person male poet who moves successively from a prison of stone (the prison of earthly love) to, paradoxically, one of freedom (that of worldly ambition) to a magnificent white-walled temple (the prison of human knowledge), and finally, by divine revelation through the Scriptures, to union with God. In each instance, it is love that leads to the poet's incarceration, and it is love of a higher form that leads to a conversion, setting him free to pursue his journey upward. This poem reflects Marguerite's philosophic fervor and her renewed interest in Platonic doctrines, which she finds consonant with Christian teachings. But it also exposes her inner contradictions, her enthusiasm for knowledge and beauty (the promises of a new age), and her determination to renounce everything detrimental to contemplative life.

The Taleteller

The *Heptaméron* was the most illustrious prose work in the short story genre to appear during the Renaissance. Like most Renaissance writers, Marguerite situates her work within a tradition, one that draws upon Boccaccio's *Decameron*, whose translation into French Marguerite herself commissioned. And, of course, she is indebted to medieval French writers—such as those who produced moral tales, or *exempla*, and *fabliaux*—as well as to the celebrated Italian moralists Baldesar Castiglione and Pietro Bembo.

The subject matter of the *Heptaméron* tales varies greatly, from greed, deception, thievery, adultery, incest, rape, and sadism to the wickedness of clerics. Nevertheless, the theme of love predominates. It assumes many forms, from the self-denying adoration reminiscent of *fin'amors* to the most brutal and sordid lust. Marguerite pays tribute to a love that is pure and spiritualized rather than carnal; she especially lauds women, whom she regards as the moral guardians of society and the preservers of the holy institution of marriage. She more clearly defines her concept of love, a blend of Platonism and Christianity, later in her life (1546), after reading the French translation of Marsilio Ficino's *Commentaries*.

The collection's lasting fame is due partly to Marguerite's original handling of Boccaccio's *cornice*. In addition to the general prologue, which establishes the particular occasion for the discussants' gathering at the abbey of Sarrance and the why and how of their pastime, she includes, at the beginning of each day, shorter prologues chronicling the discussants' spiritual evolution and, following the tales, long, inconclusive conversations highlighting the author's constant concern with the problem of language and truth. This sort of expanded frame was to become a trademark of Renaissance novella collections.

Marguerite's success in giving the traditional novella a new depth and significance is commonly recognized. The *Heptaméron* is no longer viewed simply as a collection of courtly and bawdy stories. It has been argued that Marguerite was consciously using the tales as *exempla* that illustrate or support various Evangelical teachings. Indeed, a great number of the tales and the discussions center on Pauline folly, the vanity of good works, God's free gift of grace, and the danger of trusting ecclesiastical authorities in matters of salvation. It soon becomes obvious that, as much by their storytelling as by the daily Bible readings, the discussants seek a truth from within, and after adequate spiritual preparation, they are ready for a mystical, rather than an intellectual, experience.

The Playwright

Marguerite wrote a dozen plays, biblical and secular, that were performed in the convent she founded. Her characters tend to be one-dimensional, and her theatrical technique remains awkward. What makes the plays appealing is that Marguerite, rather than imitating an established author, uses the medium to convey and debate her philosophical and religious ideas, many of which are found in the *Heptaméron* and her verse works.

SURVEY OF CRITICISM

Marguerite of Navarre was known to her contemporaries as a skilled diplomat and negotiator, a brilliant conversationalist, a most generous patroness of the arts, and a true Renaissance woman. She was viewed, as Charles of Sainte-Marthe expresses it in the funeral oration he pronounced in her honor, as "one who surpassed others of her sex in intelligence," one who "had a manly heart in her woman's body" (Richardson, 112).

Although Marguerite of Navarre was held in high literary esteem as a writer, nineteenth- and early twentieth-century anthologies such as those by André Lagarde and Laurent Michard and by Pierre-Georges Castex and Paul Surer, among others, mention her only briefly, primarily to comment on her relationship to Francis I, Protestant thinkers, and controversial writers such as Clément Marot and Bonaventure des Périers. Generally, they portray her as a somewhat mediocre literary imitator. They acknowledge her desire to discuss serious ideas and to convey her deep religious sensibility, but they regretfully note that she is wanting in an artistic sense of proportion, imagination, technical skill, and careful workmanship, all key ingredients in the definition of a good narrator of short stories and a "real" poet.

The first comprehensive study devoted to Marguerite of Navarre appeared in 1930. Pierre Jourda's impressive *thèse d'état* provides ample material regarding Marguerite's life, the publication and sources of her works, and critical estimations of themes and composition techniques. Jourda celebrates the queen's erudition and rehabilitates the *Heptaméron* (which had often been dismissed for its licentious nature) by highlighting the moral and religious overtones of the work. He also notes the new dimension Marguerite added to the short story genre, specifically the psychological realism of the tales, and the breadth and diversity of their inspiration.

Jourda's study had a great impact on the orientation of future research. The contradictions found in Marguerite's *Heptaméron*, such as the mixture of the pleasant and the useful, and in Marguerite herself, who wrote both mystical meditations and a collection of love stories, were to intrigue critics to come. For example, in his *Autour de l'Heptaméron: Amour sacré, amour profane*, Lucien Febvre, some fifteen years after Jourda's publication, sets out to resolve the fundamental paradox between the light-hearted storyteller and the Christian mystic. He concludes that the *Heptaméron* reflects the queen's deep Evangelical convictions and her aspiration to moral perfection. Emphasizing the social and moral implications of Marguerite's feminism, Emile Telle, in 1937, situated the

Heptaméron at the head of the strong "civilizing movement" that developed in the second half of the sixteenth century.

Until very recently, the *Heptaméron* has been regarded as Marguerite's one crowning achievement. Investigations of the sources and analogues of the tales, as carried out by earlier critics, are not without virtue, but they often fail to address more exciting questions related to intertextuality, such as Marguerite's relations to her source materials and, more particularly, the question of gender and genre. Michel Olsen, one of the most successful critics, examines the intergeneric combinations that characterize the evolution of the short story genre from its medieval origins to its culminant point in the late sixteenth century. Among the many studies devoted to Marguerite's philosophy of love, Jules Gelernt's deserves special mention. He approaches the *Heptaméron* as a Renaissance treatise on love which must be viewed in relation to the vast body of medieval and Renaissance amatory literature. Marguerite's spiritual development has been the focus of Félix Atance, Michel Dassonville, Henry Heller, V.-L. Saulnier, Hans Sckommodau, and André Winandy in their efforts to illustrate the complex religious influences acting on the queen and to clarify labels commonly assigned to her, such as Lutheran, Orthodox Catholic, Spiritual Libertine, or even follower of Thomas à Kempis. In addition to various speculations on the real-life identities of the discussants and the historical accuracy of the tales, careful attention has been given to the work's themes, language, and structure. Marcel Tetel, for example, demonstrates that Marguerite's *Heptaméron* does not betray haste of execution, as Brantôme contended, but reveals "a conscious design" (206) and ingenious techniques that mirror and communicate the major themes: the duplicity in human behavior and the relativism of truth. Nicole Cazauran deals also with stylistic and narrative devices, use of metaphor and imagery, recurring themes, laughter, irony, and paradox, and she emphasizes the religious inspiration of the tales. It should be noted that while the *Heptaméron*'s serious religious purpose continues to generate interest, its "recreational" aspect, an essential component of the genre, has been overlooked until recently. This persistence in examining Marguerite as the mystic, at the expense of Marguerite the court lady who, we are told in the *Heptaméron*, was well known for her ability to tell a good tale, has inspired Colette H. Winn's soon to be published study, *L'Esthétique du jeu dans l'Heptaméron de Marguerite de Navarre*.

Since Sckommodau's penetrating study in 1955, Marguerite's religious lyrics have begun to receive more attention. Various critical editions of the *Navire*, the *Miroir*, the *Prisons*, and other texts have appeared around the world from the 1960s on, as well as two full-length studies likely to remain the definitive works on Marguerite's poetry for some time to come. In his recent *Grammar of Silence*, Robert Cottrell uncovers the ways in which the text, like the self, strives to efface itself in order to transcend human language and return to "the 'Absolute Perfection' of the Word" (312)—silence, the language best suited to grasping the Beyond. Paula Sommers's *Celestial Ladders: Readings in Mar-*

guerite de Navarre's Poetry of Spiritual Ascent traces patterns of spiritual ascent (*purgatio-perfectio*; *fides-caritas*) through the *Petit Oeuvre*, the *Dialogue*, the *Miroir*, the *Navire*, and the *Prisons*, noting relationships between Marguerite's efforts to comprehend her religious experience and more complex forms of textual organization.

However, English translations are needed to make Marguerite's poetry available for the classroom, as are additional literary analyses that will highlight crucial aspects of her life and personality.

In conclusion, one may say that, without challenging the traditional role of European women in her time, the queen set a critically important example for them to follow. Indeed, her restless, brilliant, contradictory intellect won her honor, respect, and fame throughout her life and a significant place in the literary canon today.

BIBLIOGRAPHY

Sixteenth-Century Editions of Major Works by Marguerite of Navarre

Les Marguerites de la Marguerite des Princesses très illustre royne de Navarre. Ed. Jean de Tournes. 2 vols. Lyon, 1547.
Les Marguerites de la Marguerite des Princesses très illustre royne de Navarre. Ed. Pierre de Tours. Lyon, 1549.
Histoires des Amans fortunez. Paris: G. Gilles, 1558. (Mangled edition of the *Heptaméron*.)
L'Heptaméron des Nouvelles. Paris: J. Cavellier, 1559.

Modern Editions

Chansons spirituelles. Ed. Georges Dottin. Geneva: Droz, 1971.
La Coche. Ed. Robert Marichal. Geneva: Droz, 1971.
Guillaume Briçonnet-Marguerite d'Angoulême Correspondance (1521–1524). Ed. Christine Martineau, Michel Veissière, and Henry Heller. 2 vols. Geneva: Droz, 1975, 1979.
Dialogue en forme de vision nocturne. Ed. Pierre Jourda. *Revue du seizième siècle* 13 (1926): 177–204.
L'Heptaméron. Ed. Pierre Jourda. In *Conteurs français du XVIe siècle*. Paris: Gallimard, 1956. 701–1131.
L'Heptaméron. Ed. Michel François. Paris: Garnier, 1967.
L'Heptaméron. Ed. Simone de Reyff. Paris: Flammarion, 1982.
Les Marguerites de la Marguerite des Princesses. Ed. Félix Frank. 4 vols. Paris: Jouaust, 1873. Rpt. Geneva: Slatkine, 1970.
Le Miroir de l'âme pécheresse. Ed. Joseph L. Allaire. Munich: Fink, 1972.
La Navire, ou Consolation du Roi François Ier à sa soeur Marguerite. Ed. Robert Marichal. Paris: Champion, 1956.
Les Prisons. Ed. Simone Glasson. Geneva: Droz, 1978.

Suyte des marguerites de la Marguerite des Princesses, très illustre Royne de Navarre. Lyon: Jean de Tournes, 1547. Facsimile rpt. Ed. Ruth Thomas. The Hague: Johnson Reprint Corp., Mouton, 1970.
Théâtre profane. Ed. V.-L. Saulnier. Geneva: Droz, 1946.

Translations of Marguerite de Navarre

The Fortunate Lovers: Twenty-Seven Novels of the Queen of Navarre. Trans. Arthur Machen. London: George Redway, 1887.
The Heptameron; or, Tales and Novels. Trans. Arthur Machen. London: G. Routledge; New York: Dutton, 1905.
The Heptameron. Trans. P. A. Chilton. New York: Penguin Books, 1984.

Studies of Marguerite of Navarre

Atance, Félix R. "Les Comédies profanes de Marguerite de Navarre. Aspects de la satire religieuse en France au XVIe siècle." *Revue d'histoire et de philosophie religieuse* 66 (1976): 289–313.

———. "Marguerite de Navarre et ses activités en faveur des novateurs." *Neophilologus* 60 (1976): 505–24.

———. "Les Religieux de l'*Heptaméron*: Marguerite de Navarre et les novateurs." *Archiv für Reformations-geschichte* 64 (1974): 185–210.

Cazauran, Nicole. *L'Heptaméron de Marguerite de Navarre.* Paris: CDU and SEDES, 1976.

Cottrell, Robert. *The Grammar of Silence: A Reading of Marguerite de Navarre's Poetry.* Washington, D.C.: Catholic University of America Press, 1986.

Dassonville, Michel. "Le Testament spirituel de Marguerite de Navarre." In *From Marot to Montaigne: Essays on French Renaissance Literature.* Ed. Raymond La Charité. Supplement to *Kentucky Romance Quarterly* 19, no. 1 (1972): 109–24.

Febvre, Lucien. *Autour de l'Heptaméron: Amour sacré, amour profane.* Paris: Gallimard, 1944.

Gelernt, Jules. *World of Many Loves: The Heptameron of Marguerite de Navarre.* Chapel Hill: North Carolina University Press, 1966.

Girard, Yves, and Marc-René Jung. *La Renaissance I, 1480–1548.* Paris: Arthaud, 1972.

Heller, Henry. "Marguerite de Navarre and the Reformers of Meaux." *Bibliothèque d'Humanisme et Renaissance* 33 (1971): 271–310.

Jourda, Pierre. *Marguerite d'Angoulême, duchesse d'Alençon, reine de Navarre (1492–1549): Etude biographique et littéraire.* 2 vols. Paris: Champion, 1930.

Olsen, Michel. *Les Transformations du triangle érotique.* Copenhagen: Akademisk, 1976. 152–82.

Putnam, Samuel. *Marguerite of Navarre.* New York: Coward-McCann, 1935.

Richardson, Lula McDowell. *The Forerunners of Feminism in French Literature of the Renaissance from Christine of Pisan to Marie de Gournay.* Baltimore: Johns Hopkins Press; Paris: Les Presses Universitaires de France, 1929.

Saulnier, V.-L. "Marguerite de Navarre au temps de Briçonnet." *Bibliothèque d'Humanisme et Renaissance* 39 (1977): 437–78.

———. "Marguerite de Navarre au temps de Briçonnet. 2e et 3e parties." *Bibliothèque d'Humanisme et Renaissance* 40 (1978): 7–47; 193–237.

Sckommodau, Hans. *Die religiosen Dichtungen Margaretes von Navarra*. Cologne and Opladen: Westdeutscher Verlag, 1955.

Sommers, Paula. *Celestial Ladders: Readings in Marguerite de Navarre's Poetry of Spiritual Ascent*. Geneva: Droz, 1989.

Telle, Emile. *L'Oeuvre de Marguerite d'Angoulême, reine de Navarre et la querelle des femmes*. Toulouse: Lion, 1937.

Tetel, Marcel. *Marguerite de Navarre's Heptameron: Themes, Language, and Structure*. Durham, N.C.: Duke University Press, 1973.

Winandy, André. "Piety and Humanistic Symbolism in the Works of Marguerite de Navarre." *Yale French Studies* 47 (1972): 145–69.

MARIE DE FRANCE
(fl. 1160–1178)

Matilda Tomaryn Bruckner

BIOGRAPHY

The first woman poet we can identify in the history of French literature and one of the finest writers of the twelfth century Renaissance, Marie de France enjoys today a popularity that recalls what must have been her fame for medieval audiences. According to the testimony of Denis Piramus in his life of St. Edmund, a ''lady Marie'' was much praised for her lays in verse and rhyme, which were often read out loud in courts to the great delight of counts, barons, and knights. Ladies especially took pleasure in listening to her lays, since they accorded with their own desires. Identifying exactly who this Marie was and the number of works we should attribute to her has remained problematic despite intensive scholarly research. Among the works of this period signed ''Marie,'' three are generally considered to be by the same author: the *Lais* (*Lays*), the *Fables*, and the *Espurgatoire seint Patriz* (The Purgatory of Saint Patrick). In the epilogue to the *Fables*, the author tells us she will name herself for the sake of remembrance: ''Marie ai num, si sui de France'' (My name is Marie and I am from/ of France). From this statement, which seems to imply that Marie, a native of continental France, was writing elsewhere, Claude Fauchet coined the name ''Marie de France'' for his *Recueil de l'origine de la langue et poésie françoise* (Collection on the Origin of French Language and Poetry, 1581)—the first modern reference to Marie, who was then known primarily as the author of the *Fables* until critical attention in the nineteenth and twentieth century shifted to her *Lais*.

Any effort to identify Marie begins with an examination of her works, which can be dated only approximately, based on their language and style, as late twelfth century. Three facts point to the likelihood that Marie was writing in England: Harley 978, a manuscript preserved at the British Museum, which contains both the *Fables* and the *Lais*, was probably copied at the Abbey of

Reading; Marie claims to translate the *Fables* from an English version (which she attributes to King Alfred, although no such version is extant); and the *Espurgatoire* is a translation of a Latin text composed in England, the *Tractatus de purgatorio sancti Patricii* by Hugh (or Henry) of Saltrey. Moreover, the geographical references in the *Lais* suggest that her knowledge of England and South Wales was more precise than that of the continent. Probably a native of the Ile-de-France area or nearby Normandy, Marie shows herself to be familiar with aristocratic life and behavior. She is a woman writing for the court who claims among her patrons a *nobles reis* (a noble king)—to whom she dedicates the *Lais*—and a Count William, mentioned in the epilogue to the *Fables*. Most scholars accept Henry II (1133–1189) as Marie's royal patron, though his eldest son, Henry the Young King (crowned in 1170, d. 1183), has also been suggested. There is no general agreement about the many possible Williams, including William Marshall, William Longsword (the natural son of Henry II), William of Warren, William of Gloucester, and Guillaume de Damspierre.

Marie's works themselves suggest some approximate dates in the way they reflect contemporary works. Although it has been impossible to situate her with respect to Chrétien de Troyes (fl. 1165–1181) and Thomas (fl. mid or late twelfth century), she must have known Wace's *Brut* (1155) and the *Eneas* (1160). Dates proposed for the *Lais* are generally between 1160 and 1170, for the *Fables* between 1167 and 1189. The *Espurgatoire* has been placed after 1208 (based on the dedication of the Latin version to Henry, Abbot of Sartis).

Given all the factors mentioned above, a number of suggestions have been made for identifying the historical Marie, but none of them has been generally accepted. She may have been Mary, Abbess of Shaftesbury, the natural daughter of Geoffrey Plantagenet (the father of Henry II). Abbess in 1181 (and probably the same Mary mentioned as abbess in 1215), this Mary was located at an abbey founded by King Alfred, but there is no evidence of her involvement in any literary activity. Other suggestions include Marie de Meulan or Beaumont (the widow of Hugues Talbot and daughter of Waleron de Beaumont) and the Abbess of Reading (the abbey where Harley 978 may have been copied).

Although Marie thus remains more or less anonymous, her unusual level of learning certainly suggests an aristocratic background. Her translation of the *Tractatus*, as well as remarks in the General Prologue to the *Lais*, attest her knowledge of the Latin language; her works demonstrate further a good knowledge of the classics, especially Ovid. Her reference to Priscian in the *Lais* Prologue may indicate firsthand knowledge of his text. The Prologue to the *Fables* indicates Marie's awareness of the Aesopic traditions in Greek and Latin, while her claim to translate them from English suggests her abilities in that language. She occasionally gives English and even Breton translations of words used as titles for her lays. For example, in the Prologue to *Laüstic*, she explains that Breton word for nightingale by translating it into French and English. Whether or not Marie herself knew Breton remains uncertain, though she demonstrates in the *Lais* her acquaintance with oral as well as written traditions. Her knowledge of contemporary works includes, in addition to those mentioned above, Geoffrey of Monmouth's *Historia regum Britanniae* (1135), Gaimar's *Estoire des Engleis*, and some version(s) of the Tristan story (possibly both written and oral). In general, her descriptions of beds, tombs, luxury items, and so on show Marie to be a master of the rhetorical techniques and literary traditions shared by the writers of her time.

MAJOR THEMES

While the Prologues and Epilogues to all three of Marie's works show her consistently as an author concerned with the theme of remembrance and her own identity as a writer, the works themselves are quite diverse and will be discussed here separately in their probable order of composition. The bulk of this chapter will focus on the *Lais*, since they have claimed most of the attention devoted to Marie by modern scholars and general readers. There has been, in particular, much discussion about what constitutes a "lay," as Marie herself uses the term and as her tales seem to offer a new definition of the genre. Marie appears to be the initiator of the lay as narrative or short tale—a genre that flourished alongside other short narrative types (like the *fabliau*) between 1170 and 1250. About forty narrative lays remain extant, many of them anonymous. In Harley 978, Marie presents a collection of twelve lays, introduced by a General Prologue. Four other manuscripts contain one or more of Marie's lays, mixed anonymously with other "Breton lays" or included in miscellanies. Again, much discussion has focused on Marie's authorship: did she write the anonymous lays; did she write all twelve claimed in Harley 978? Although scholars nowadays generally accept her authorship of the twelve lays in the collection and consider the anonymous lays to have been written after Marie's (as those with authors who identify themselves certainly were), there are still critical voices raised here and there who question the authenticity of the collection (e.g., Baum) or the likelihood of a woman writer in this period (e.g., Huchet), as will be discussed in the next section.

Short prologues and epilogues that frame each of Marie's tales refer to the lays performed by Breton storytellers in order to commemorate adventures truly lived in the past. Celtic and English place names and proper names corroborate to a certain extent Marie's claimed sources: four lays take place in continental Brittany, three in Wales, two in both, and one in an undetermined *Bretagne*, which could be in England or on the continent. Despite her claim to do nothing more than write down in verse and rhyme orally circulating tales, Marie's versions offer artfully crafted compositions that combine the written traditions of Latin and vernacular writings with the legendary materials of Celtic and popular tales. Is Marie simply using a literary device in identifying her stories as Breton lays, or is there some historical truth in the process of transmission she describes? It may be impossible (and unnecessary) to unscramble literary topos from historical reference, but we can delineate the stages of transmission and transformation, as indicated by Marie and other writers of the period. The process begins with an adventure heard by Bretons who compose a "lay"—that is, a musical composition, sung with harp accompaniment—to commemorate and preserve the original adventure. Marie has heard both the music and the adventure, the latter perhaps recounted by the performer as a kind of prelude to the song. Marie then writes down the narrative in rhymed octosyllables (the same form she uses in the *Fables* and the *Espurgatoire*), as she elaborates the truth of the adventure. The title, carefully designated in each case, guarantees the authenticity of the process. While Marie herself generally uses the word "lay" to refer to the musical compositions commemorating the adventure, writers subsequently will refer to her written tales as lays. The narrative genre that she thus launches seems to be unrelated to the lyric lay, which flourished from the twelfth to the fifteenth century.

The General Prologue to the *Lais* opens with a traditional exordial topic on the writer's obligation to share his/her talents and then cites the authority of Priscian to describe the relationship between ancient and modern writers: do philosopher poets hide a "surplus" of meaning to be found later in the obscurities of their writing, or do later, more subtle poets add it to their predecessors' works? Different scholars have variously interpreted these verses (9–22): we are thus drawn into the problem of interpretation at the very moment the subject of glossing is introduced by Marie's authorial persona. She then explains the nature of her project: she will not do a translation from the Latin, as many have done, but rather something new, demanding hard labor and sleepless nights—the writing down in rhyme of those adventures commemorated in (musical) lays. Hoping to receive great joy in return, Marie then offers her collection to an unnamed king. She names herself in the following verses, printed by modern editors as the Prologue to *Guigemar* (3–4), but not set off in the manuscript except by a large capital letter indicating a new section (*G*1).

The twelve lays that follow in Harley 978 are *Guigemar* (886 verses), *Equitan* (314), *Le Fresne* (518), *Bisclavret* (318), *Lanval* (646), *Deus Amanz* (254), *Yonec* (558), *Laüstic* (160), *Milun* (534), *Chaitivel* (240), *Chievrefoil* (118), and *Eliduc* (1,184). As indicated by the considerable variations in length, the *Lais* offer great diversity, but they also operate as a collection with respect to the unifying themes of love and adventure. Indeed, they seem to invite exploration as an open-ended set of theme and variations, in which Marie reveals the complexities and varieties of human experience, without trying to contain them within the confines of any single doctrine of love. Heroes and heroines, all noble, beautiful, handsome, and courteous, are individualized not by psychological development, but rather by the specific situations in which they find themselves. Consider, for example, the two short anecdotes that constitute *Laüstic* and *Chievrefoil*. Both involve a love triangle: married couple plus lover. *Chievrefoil* relates an episode in the story of Tristan and Iseut, a secret reunion of the lovers vouchsafed during one of Tristan's returns from exile. Whereas Mark here remains ignorant of the lovers' tryst, the husband of *Laüstic* discovers his wife's nocturnal meetings with her lover. Although their affair remains innocent, limited to their mutual gaze across facing windows, the angry husband puts an end to their meetings by trapping and killing the nightingale the lady claims as the reason for her nightly visits to the window. When the lady sends to her lover the nightingale's body wrapped in an embroidered cloth, along with a messenger to explain the events, he has a golden box made, adorned with precious stones. The nightingale's body is placed in it and the reliquary accompanies him wherever he goes, hence the name of the lay.

The emblem that thus closes the lay figures the end of the lovers' meetings, though it may also suggest the triumph of continued love, however impossible to realize (optimistic and pessimistic readings of the ending are both possible). The emblem of *Chievrefoil*—"honeysuckle," or "gotelef" in Marie's English translation (115)—also testifies to the enduring nature of Tristan and Iseut's love: just as the hazelwood dies (so it was thought) if the honeysuckle growing around it is cut away, so the two lovers would die if separated: " 'Beautiful friend, so it is with us: Neither you without me, nor me without you' " (77–78). But while that phrasing is negative, what we see realized in this episode is the reunion of the lovers thanks to the piece of hazelwood that Tristan prepares as a signal to Iseut, so that the Queen will know he must be hiding in the woods near the route of her cortege. Whereas the emblem of *Laüstic* ends the lovers' meetings, *Chievrefoil*'s emblem initiates Tristan and Iseut's reunion, just as it symbolizes the durability of their love. This pattern of repetition and variation in the interplay between *Laüstic* and *Chievrefoil* creates doubles, echoes, and contrasts at all levels of Marie's text. Throughout the collection, this tendency to present and explore different combinations of the same materials characterizes the links between the lays and invites readers to analyze and comment on their interactions. The arrangement of twelve lays in a collection thus considerably increases the potential for meaning, however elusive that remains in the beautiful obscurities of Marie's own written text. This intertextual density begins to give her *Lais* the kind of weight and proportion we normally associate with romance.

The brevity of most lays limits their plot development to a single anecdote or episode, although in the mid-length and longer ones, especially *Guigemar* and *Eliduc*, there may be a fuller elaboration as the characters' love develops through a series of episodes. The type of adventure that appears in the *Lais* differs somewhat from that of romance: it does not involve a quest; the hero is more passive, and his personal experience leads to a private fulfillment and happiness; there is no special relationship between the hero's destiny and that of his society. While some lays offer marvelous and folktale elements that recall their Celtic sources (e.g., *Guigemar*, *Yonec*, *Lanval*), others remain realistically placed in the courtly world of the twelfth century (e.g., *Equitan*, *Le Fresne*, *Milun*, *Chaitivel*). All explore the intersection of two planes of existence, where otherness may be magically encountered or simply introduced by the new experience of love. Marie's art is as carefully crafted as the precious reliquary she describes in *Laüstic*. The economy and brevity of her style is enriched by the subtlety of her narrating voice. Her use of free indirect discourse, in particular, allows her to merge her voice with that of her characters while maintaining the distinctness of both. Marie's literary art, sustained throughout the collection of twelve tales, joins her work to that of the philosopher poets, described in the General Prologue as worthy of glossing and interpretation.

The twenty-three extant manuscripts of Marie's *Fables* (two of which are complete with Prologue, Epilogue, and 102 fables) attest the popularity they enjoyed. Marie claims to translate from the English of King Alfred's adaptation of a Latin collection. No such translation is known, and Marie may have invented a fictitious source. Her fables derive from the Latin *Romulus* in combination with other traditions: some details bring her collection closer to the Greek fables than to the Latin; evidence of oral tradition is also apparent. Hers is the first known example of Old French *Isopets*. Each short narrative (8–124 vv.) leads to an explicit moral lesson. This framework of moral and social values provides an underlying unity for the diversity of the fables. The political stance is basically conservative and reflects an aristocratic point of view. But Marie also shows concern that justice be available to all classes; social hierarchy should be maintained for the sake of harmony; people should accept their place, as well as their individual responsibilities.

Consider, for example, Fable 15, "De asino adulante" (The Affectionate Ass): jealous of a little dog playing with his master, the ass tries to imitate him by jumping up, pawing his master, and braying loudly. The master shouts for his servants, who rescue him by beating the ass so much it can hardly reach the stable. Marie's lesson addresses those who try to rise higher than their station, often with the same results as the ass. Her general concern for justice in terms of feudal loyalty between lord and vassal is demonstrated in a number of fables; elsewhere appears a more specific regard for mistreatment of the poor, as in Fable 2, "De lupo et agno" (The Wolf and the Lamb), in which the wolf invents a series of false accusations to justify killing the lamb. Marie's moral targets the abuse of rich robber barons, viscounts, and judges who exploit those in their power with trumped up charges.

Extant in a single manuscript, the *Espurgatoire* combines in its 2,000-plus verses a variety of materials—romanesque, hagiographic, and homiletic. In addition to various anecdotes, the principal narrative concerns the prosyletizing efforts of St. Patrick, thanks to whom an entrance to purgatory for those still living has been established in a churchyard, in order to strengthen belief in the afterlife. After suitable prayers and instructions, many have descended to witness the tortures of the damned and the delights of the saved. Not all have returned from the perilous journey. The greater part of the story follows in detail the preparation and descent of the knight Owein. Through a series of diabolical torments, Owein is saved each time when he invokes the name of Jesus. Upon his return, he is confirmed in his knightly career, now purified and dedicated to saintly pursuits. The *Espurgatoire* offers one of the earliest vernacular examples of the same visionary tradition that inspires Dante's *Commedia*.

SURVEY OF CRITICISM

Continued and continually growing interest in Marie de France is reflected not only in the significant number of modern editions and translations of her works, but also in the enormous bibliography of general and specialized studies that focus on a wide variety of topics generated by Marie and her writings. Glyn S. Burgess has provided an invaluable critical tool in his annotated bibliography, published in 1977 and updated in 1986 (its identification as "Supplement No. 1" suggests the intention to publish further updates as needed).[1] Burgess's "Index of Marie de France's Works" will help students and scholars who want to find books and articles on particular texts. It also indicates the extent to which the *Lais* claim the lion's share of critical interest (each lay is listed separately, as well as the collection as a whole and the General Prologue). Several recent translations of the *Fables* suggest that there may be some renewal of interest in Marie's contributions to the fable tradition (see especially Spiegel's rhymed translation and newly edited text). The *Espurgatoire seint Patriz* remains untranslated into English and has very few items among the critical studies, but probably deserves more attention as modern scholars explore the interface between Latin and vernacular cultures, as well as the way medieval writers combined materials from a variety of sources to create hybrid forms.

Readers looking for a general introduction to Marie de France might start with Emanuel J. Mickle's *Marie de France* (331), which includes chapters on the author and twelfth-century background, the *Fables*, the *Espurgatoire*, and four chapters on the *Lais*. Paula Clifford's critical guide to the *Lais* (580) offers a useful, concise introduction to that work, as does Glyn S. Burgess's The "Lais" of Marie de France. An overview of Burgess's list demonstrates the breadth of studies on different aspects of Marie's work, but it also reveals a number of recurrent interests. First among these, at least chronologically, are studies of Marie's identity, especially with respect to identifying her works and defining the narrative lay. See, for example, studies by Bédier (89), Fox (183), and Holmes (233) for arguments for and against specific historical identifications. Articles by Foulet (176), Foulon (182), and Hoepffner (218) situate Marie and her *Lais* with respect to geographical and historical contexts. Useful studies on the lay as genre include articles by Bullock-Davies (110), Foulet (176), Frappier (192), and Payen (356). In his *Recherches sur les oeuvres attribuées à Marie de France* (Research on the Works Attributed to Marie de France), Baum (85) argues against "Marie" as author for all the lays in the Harley collection. "Marie de France," according to Baum, would be the author of the *Fables* alone. Readers may be unpersuaded by his arguments, but will find useful facts about the manuscripts containing Marie's works, as well as information on biographical and historical problems surrounding Marie and her corpus.

Investigations of Marie's sources, whether Celtic, classical, or contemporary vernacular works, remain an important part of her bibliography, including work by Cross (136), Illingworth (240), Brightenback (102), Hanning (611), and many others. Studies of the marvelous in Marie's *Lais* or the role of adventure are offered by Jonin (619), Sienaert (695), and Poirion (672), while authors like Damon (139) have particularly oriented readers toward the psychological in Marie's tales.

The issues raised by Marie's General Prologue have been repeatedly debated by scholars to determine the sense of her classical allusions and their implications for her own work. Hunt's 1974 article (239) is an excellent analysis of the Prologue in the context of twelfth-century humanist thought (and thus a response to earlier scripturally oriented interpretations of Spitzer [426] and Robertson [386]), but it has by no means ended the discussion. See, for example, more recent articles by Foulet/Uitti (601) and Delclos (588). A rival to the General Prologue as the single most glossed passage in the *Lais* may be found in *Chievrefoil*, where Marie describes how Tristan cuts a piece of hazelwood and inscribes a message on it in order to arrange a secret meeting in the woods. Tristan has either inscribed only his name or a long message about their love, depending on how one interprets verses 61–78—and interpretations have not been lacking (e.g., Cagnon [117], or more recently Burgess [578]). The role of the Tristan legend as a kind of leitmotif worked through many of the lays has also frequently been examined (e.g., Foulet [178], Huchet [615], Trindade [443]).

A number of scholars have tried to determine the order of composition for the twelve lays that follow the General Prologue or have tried to classify them in various categories (e.g., realistic and marvelous). Glyn S. Burgess (576) gives a survey of work on chronology and offers his own suggestion. Examples of classifying systems that aim to account for the unity of the collection or the interplay among the different lays include articles by Frey (193), Smithers (420), and McCulloch (645). Since love is clearly one of the key elements that gives Marie's collection a certain unity across the diverse and varied lays, many studies have examined the character of love expressed in her tales (e.g., Mickel [333], Nelson [653], H. S. Robertson [387], DeCaluwé/Wathelet-Willem [143]). Analyses of narrative structure in the lays have become more frequent (e.g., Lawson [634], Lefay-Toury [636], Ollier [658], Rothschild [390], Pickens [666]), as have analyses of her narrative voice (Malvern [646], Ménard Rychner [689]). Marie's *Lais* have, in general, attracted a good share of interest from critics and scholars working from a variety of perspectives in modern and postmodern critical theory and practice (e.g., Bloch and Dragonetti [518], Maddox and Sturges [700], Vitz [707], Pickens [667]).

Feminism has added a powerful stimulant to the already considerable interest in Marie's works. Marie now appears in a large number of anthologies or studies on the role of women and women writers in the Middle Ages (see, for example, Ferrante [598], Lehmann [637], Lucas [642]). Feminist analyses of the *Lais* have come a long way since the rather naive remarks of Woods on "Femininity in the *Lais* of Marie de France" in 1950 (477). Many of the rhetorical traits identified by Woods as characteristic of her feminine style are just as readily found in Chrétien de Troyes, for example, use of repetition and hyperbole (which

Woods labels "exaggeration" in order to equate it with "gushing"). His notion of the feminine, whether in style or psychology, is historically determined but expressed in a priori categories ("One could make the observation that Marie was similar to women of all times in her use of effective and affective speech," 4). Huchet (615) offers a psychoanalytically oriented reading of the *Lais* in relation to what he identifies as the *donnée tristanesque* (the fundamentals of the Tristan story). For reasons he does not explain, the *Lais'* treatment of that material will reveal whether or not we can speak of *écriture féminine* (feminine writing) in the *Lais*. His analysis leads him to conclude that the *Lais* do indeed reveal an *écriture féminine*, since both women and men suffer from the contagion of sexuality, but he then concludes that the attribution of female authorship is probably a mask for a male author who dares not write in such a way under his own name. Feminists will be troubled by Huchet's tendency here, as in his work on Héloïse and the female troubadours, to empty medieval literary tradition of women authors, in favor of the concept of *écriture féminine* or Lacan's discourse of the other. Two articles by Michelle Freeman are of particular interest from a feminist point of view: one, entitled "Marie de France's Poetics of Silence: The Implications for a Feminine *Translatio*" (605), argues for a specifically feminine way of narrating, in which multiple layers of meaning wrap around what is deliberately kept silent in Marie's text. *Laüstic* and *Chevrefoil* are the two lays chosen for close analysis. Freeman opposes this feminine "poetics of silence," involving the lay as gloss of the title, to a masculine poetics of *translatio* practiced by her contemporaries and predecessors. In her analysis of Marie's werewolf tale ("Bisclavret"), Freeman explores the reversal of gender roles between husband and wife, as well as between author and characters, to suggest how Marie argues for a rightful combining of male and female, as illustrated by Bisclavret (but not the wife) and by herself as female and court poet. Freeman sees Marie using the cliché of clerkly misogyny to point out the dangers of such stereotyping and to explore ways to insert a poetic voice freed from rigid gender classifications: "a voice properly qualified as androgynous" (289).

From whatever perspective they are considered, Marie's works are in no danger of sinking into the oblivion from which Marie worked so hard to save them and herself. Along with the fascination exerted by the tales she tells, respect for Marie's art as storyteller and writer has grown enormously among modern scholars and general readers. In addition to the many editions and translations that make Marie's work available to a wide public, we can even find an example of direct fictional rewriting in John Fowles's translation and transformation of *Eliduc* in *The Ebony Tower* (cf. Hieatt's feminist analysis of Fowles vis-à-vis Marie [614]).

Whether in the guise of fiction or literary criticism, Marie's works continue to fulfill their bountiful and fruitful promise, as she herself describes in one of the opening proverbs of her General Prologue:

> Quant uns granz biens est mult oïz,
> Dunc a primes est il fluriz,

E quant loëz est de plusurs,
Dunc ad espandues ses flurs. (lines 5–8)

(When a great good is much heard, then does it first bloom, and when it is
praised by several, then has it scattered abroad its flowers.)

NOTE

1. Items included in the survey of criticism will be identified by their number in Burgess's
two volumes. They will not be included in the bibliography given in this chapter.

BIBLIOGRAPHY

Works by Marie de France

Ewert, Alfred, ed. *Marie de France: Lais*. Oxford: Blackwell, 1944.

Rychner, Jean, ed. *Les Lais de Marie de France*. Paris: Champion, 1966.

Ewert, Alfred, and Ronald C. Johnston, eds. *Marie de France: Fables*. Oxford: Blackwell,
1942.

Spiegel, Harriet, ed. and trans. *Fables. Marie de France*. Toronto: University of Toronto
Press, 1987.

Jenkins, Thomas A., ed. *Marie de France: Espurgatoire Seint Patriz, an Old French
Poem of the Twelfth Century published with an Introduction and a Study of the
Language of the Author*. Philadelphia, 1894. Rpt. Geneva: Slatkine, 1974.

———. *The Espurgatoire Seint Patriz of Marie de France, with a Text of the Latin
Original*. Chicago: University of Chicago Press, 1903.

Translations of Marie de France

Burgess, Glyn S. *The Lais of Marie de France*. New York: Penguin, 1986

Hanning, Robert, and Joan Ferrante. *The Lais of Marie de France, Translated, with an
Introduction and Notes*. Foreword by John Fowles. New York: Dutton; Toronto:
Clarke, Irwin and Co., 1978. Also published without the foreword: Durham,
N.C.: Labyrinth Press, 1982.

Jonin, Pierre. *Les Lais de Marie de France, traduits de l'ancien français*. 2nd ed. Paris:
Champion, 1978.

Martin, Mary Lou. *The Fables of Marie de France: An English Translation*. Birmingham,
Ala.: Summa Publications, 1982.

Studies of Marie de France

Baum, Richard. *Recherches sur les oeuvres attribuées à Marie de France*. Heidelberg:
Winter, 1968.

Bloch, Howard. "The Medieval Text—*Guigemar*—as a Provocation to the Discipline of
Medieval Studies." *Romanic Review* 79 (1988): 63–73.

Bruckner, Matilda Tomaryn. "Strategies of Naming in Marie de France's *Lais*: At the
Crossroads of Gender and Genre." *Neophilologus* 24 (1991): 31–39.

Burgess, Glyn S. *Marie de France: An Analytical Biography*. London: Grant and Cutler, 1977.

———. *Marie de France: An Analytical Biography*. *Supplement No. 1*. London: Grant and Cutler, 1986.

Freeman, Michelle. "Dual Natures and Subverted Glosses: Marie de France's 'Bisclavret.' " *Romance Notes* 25 (1985): 288–301.

Huchet, Jean-Charles. "Nom de femme et écriture féminine au moyen âge." *Poétique* 12 (1981): 407–30.

Maddox, Don. "Triadic Structure in the *Lais* of Marie de France." *Assays: Critical Approaches to Medieval and Renaissance Texts* 3 (1985): 19–40.

Ménard, Philippe. "Le *Je* de Marie de France dans les *Lais*." *Romania* 103 (1982): 170–96.

ANNA DE NOAILLES
(1876–1933)

Tama Lea Engelking

Anna de Noailles was one of the most admired writers of her era. Contemporary readers voted her their favorite woman poet next to Marceline *Desbordes-Valmore, and along with *Colette, her name dominates the pages of French literary history devoted to early twentieth-century women writers.[1] In 1913 the London *Times* declared Anna de Noailles "the greatest poet that the twentieth century has produced in France—perhaps in Europe."

A prolific writer, Anna de Noailles produced over 1,900 pages of verse along with several novels during her thirty-year career. Her work appealed to a wide readership; she was frequently anthologized and included in popular series, and many of her books became best-sellers. The French Academy expressed its appreciation of Noailles's work by crowning her first collection of poetry, *Le Coeur innombrable* (The Innumerable Heart, 1901), with their annual Archon Despérouses Prize, and in 1921 she received the academy's Grand Prize for Literature. The following year she became the first woman ever accepted into the Royal Belgian Academy of French Language and Literature (Colette was accepted in 1923).

Noailles was more than a successful writer; she was also the star literary personality of her day. Typists recognized her in the Tuileries gardens, the President of the Republic requested her presence at major state occasions, and young poets memorized her verses. Among her close friends and admirers were many important writers such as Robert de Montesquiou, Proust, Barrès, Cocteau, and Colette. The press reported daily on the fragile health and glittering social activities of the popular countess whose aristocratic name, exotic beauty, and fashionable friends impressed her readers as much as her passionate poetry. Although proud of her Romanian and Greek ancestry, Noailles was a staunch French patriot and the first woman ever to achieve the rank of Commander of the Legion of Honor. When Anna de Noailles died in 1933, the French government offered her family the honor of a state funeral. She was, in effect, the official muse of the Republic, and over 10,000 mourners came to pay their final tribute.

As a literary personality, Anna de Noailles is not forgotten—there is a recent biography, and the new wing of the Carnavalet Museum in Paris contains her bed and a reproduction of her bedroom—but as a poet, she has been sadly neglected. Her works are now out of print, rarely studied, and then usually examined only as typical examples of "feminine poetry." Fin-de-siècle critics defined feminine poetry as spontaneous and sensual lyricism deriving from woman's feminine nature. This biased, inaccurate, and restrictive categorization is largely responsible for marginalizing Noailles's work, and thus distracting modern readers from recognizing her influence on a whole generation of men and women writers. Noailles is neither typical nor representative; she is an original who dared to challenge convention and breathe new life into an art form that had become increasingly intellectualized by the end of the nineteenth century.

BIOGRAPHY

Anna de Noailles was born Princess Anna-Elisabeth de Brancovan in Paris on November 15, 1876. Her Romanian father, Prince Grégoire de Brancovan, was a rather severe authoritarian who had been a student at Saint-Cyr. Her mother, Rachel Musurus, was a beautiful and cultivated woman from an old and distinguished Greek family of Cretan origin. As Madame de Brancovan, she kept a salon and was well known for her talents as a pianist. Her love of music had a profound influence on her daughter's poetry; Anna, as a little girl, declared that her first poems came out of her mother's piano.

In the Brancovan family home on Avenue Hoche in Paris, music and poetry held a place of honor. The great pianist Paderewski was a frequent visitor there, along with a number of distinguished politicians and writers. In this atmosphere, Anna, her younger sister Hélène (the future Princess Alexandre de Caraman-Chimay), and their older brother Constantin grew to respect the arts, and as adults all three continued to cultivate an active interest in art, music, and especially literature. The Brancovan children spent an idyllic childhood between Paris and the family's country estate of Amphion, near Evian on Lake Geneva. In her autobiography, *Le Livre de ma vie* (The Book of My Life), Anna de Noailles describes the long hours she spent reading poetry aboard her father's yacht, *La Romania*. Alfred de Musset was an early favorite of hers, but she considered Victor Hugo her spiritual father.

The one shadow cast over Anna de Noailles's childhood was the unexpected death of her father when she was nine years old. The sensitive child, whose later poems would reveal her preoccupation with death, was deeply affected by this tragic loss. Prince Brancovan was buried in Romania, and from there the family traveled east to visit their relatives in Constantinople. Although this was Noailles's first and last encounter with the Orient, it became one of her favorite poetic themes.

Anna de Noailles wrote about many places, but the garden at Amphion holds a special place in her life and work. As a mature poet she declared that she "owed everything" to this garden and the view it gave of the lake, "a double azure" of sky and water that had dazzled her since childhood. It was there, she claimed, "that the universe was revealed to me." At Amphion, the delicate dark-haired princess first felt the call to be a poet, and in her introduction to *Poèmes d'enfance* (Childhood Poems), she tells of delightful walks in the Savoie countryside, which inspired her to compose "little verbal pictures to capture and celebrate these places of enchantment." Noailles built her poetic universe around the sensations she gathered there, recording every nuance of color, perfume, and texture in notebooks from the age of six. By 1907 she had filled fifty notebooks with "the thousand sensations that constitute our life."

Anna's early word portraits were in prose, but she soon discovered the delights of versification, using Musset as her model. For her, writing poetry was more a matter of abandonment than constraint, and she refused to allow the restrictions of prosodic rules to interrupt the inspired flow of her verse. She recalls in *Poèmes d'enfance* that by age twelve, "I definitively rejected and condemned all the shackles that I declared useless. I never gave them back the authority that my youthful audacity had denied them." An "inspired" poet, she identified nature as her only model and guide, and claimed never to correct her verses, which came to her whole, "dictated with a perfume of roses." Manuscripts of her poems reveal, however, that Noailles did do some editing, and that she often worked out the end rhymes in advance before composing the verses.

The blossoming poet continued to fill her notebooks, but on her mother's advice did not publish until after her marriage. On August 18, 1897, Anna became the wife of Count Mathieu de Noailles, and six months later she launched her career with the publication of "Litanies" in *La Revue de Paris*. In 1901, following the birth of her son Anne-Jules, Anna de Noailles published her first collection of poems, *Le Coeur innombrable*, which became a success overnight. Marcel Proust celebrated the occasion by hosting a dinner in her honor, decorating the tables with bouquets of wildflowers mentioned by the poet in her verses, and Sarah Bernhardt gave a public reading of poems from the new volume.[2] In short, Anna de Noailles's first book caused quite a sensation in Paris.

Already famous by age twenty-five, the young countess was a much sought-after salon guest. She was a regular visitor to the elite Belle Epoque salons of her close friends Princess Polignac and Mme Arman Caillavet, where even Anatole France was eclipsed by Anna de Noailles's brilliant conversation. "When the countess is here, you no longer exist," his hostess told him. Anna's friends characterized her as a monologist who was intolerant of the slightest interruption, but the countess never failed to leave an impression on those who were fortunate enough to hear her speak. Jean Cocteau describes a dinner party at which the entire domestic staff crowded into the doorways, hoping to hear the countess speaking.

Noailles's first success was soon followed by a second, more mature volume of poetry in 1902, *L'Ombre des jours* (The Shadow of Days). She then turned to prose, publishing her first novel in 1903. *La Nouvelle Espérance* (New Hope) went into over thirty editions and was recommended for a Goncourt Prize. Her second novel, *Le Visage émerveillé* (The Amazed Face, 1904), provoked a scandal by describing a young nun's sensual awakening in the form of her personal diary. Proust read the novel as a *roman à clef* and identified the heroine's lover as the anti-Dreyfusard writer and politician Maurice Barrès. Despite their opposing political views—Noailles was a self-proclaimed socialist and Dreyfus supporter—Barrès and Noailles shared a fascination with the Orient and maintained a lifelong friendship, which Barrès recorded in his *Cahiers*.

Noailles published her third novel in 1905. *La Domination*, a love story narrated from a male perspective, was severely criticized because of inconsistencies of plot and character. Sensitive to critical opinion, Noailles forbade reprintings of the novel and published nothing for the next two years. She returned to fiction at the end of her life and left an unfinished novel entitled *Octave*, which, like *Le Visage émerveillé*, tells the story of a nun's unhappy love affair. Noailles continued to triumph as a poet, and the astounding success of her next collection, *Les Eblouissements* (Amazements, 1907), firmly established her reputation.

In 1913 Noailles's fragile health took a turn for the worse, and she was forced to spend much of her time in bed, where she contemplated her beloved nature from the single window of her room. Though confined, her imagination compensated for what she was unable to experience: "This room and the horizon beyond that window. . . . Nothing prevents me from believing that, under that ardent sky, we're in Constantinople, or any other enchanting city in the orient." Reclining against satin pillows in a Louis XV bed, a telephone always nearby, Anna de Noailles entertained her friends in the style of a seventeenth-century *précieuse*. The year 1913 also saw the publication of *Les Vivants et les morts* (The Living and the Dead), a rather pessimistic collection of poetry that reveals Noailles's increasing preoccupation with death as she seeks and rejects the consolation of an afterlife.

World War I broke out, and Noailles published no new books until after the armistice was signed. Her fourth collection of poetry, *Les Forces éternelles* (Eternal Forces, 1921), contains a section of poems about the war. The years 1921 and 1922 marked the culmination of Noailles's career when she was doubly honored by two coveted literary awards: the French Academy's Grand Prize for Literature, and a seat in the Royal Belgian Academy. Her triumph was soon overshadowed by grief over the deaths of her mother and her dear friend Maurice Barrès. She dedicated her final volume of poetry, *L'Honneur de souffrir* (The

Honor of Suffering, 1927), to "my friends who have left me and whom I leave not at all."

Anna de Noailles published one other collection of poetry, *Poème d'amour* (Poem of Love, 1924), in which she rather uncharacteristically experimented with more concise poetic forms. She also wrote three collections of essays dealing primarily with love: *Les Innocents ou la sagesse des femmes* (The Innocent Ones or the Wisdom of Women, 1923), *Passions et vanités* (1926), and *Exactitudes* (1930). In addition, she prefaced her childhood poems, published in 1928, and the year before her death published her autobiography, which focuses on her youth. Her final poems were published posthumously.

The postwar generation of writers was increasingly critical of Noailles's lyricism, but despite her poor health, Anna de Noailles remained a vital presence in Parisian literary circles and was known and loved throughout France. She died in 1933 following a long illness. Noailles's friends erected a memorial in her honor overlooking the lake at Amphion; her heart lies buried nearby. After a state funeral at La Madeleine attended by thousands, Anna de Noailles's body was laid to rest in the Bibesco-Brancovan family vault at Père-Lachaise cemetery in Paris. Visitors to her tomb will find a photograph of the poet inscribed with this verse: "I was not made to be dead."

MAJOR THEMES

As a young girl, Anna de Noailles's response to her first military parade was to exclaim, "I want to be one hundred men!" Her writing is similarly motivated by a desire to surpass the ordinary limits of existence, to have an "innumerable heart," and like her heroine Sabine in *La Nouvelle Espérance*, to demand not only the total love of her husband, but "the possibility of the love of all others." Although Noailles once described her poetry as being "devoted to reflecting life," we can best understand her writing as "a vital expansion," which Jean Larnac qualifies as "a means of multiplying her joy or despair." In the final poem of *Le Coeur innombrable*, the poet writes: "—Toi, sois innombrable à force de désirs / De frissons et d'extase" (You, be innumerable by sheer force of desires / Shivers and ecstasy; "Temps de vivre"). Passionate and egocentric, she believed that she would leave a poetic legacy so intense that it would be the envy of her future readers, "Car ma cendre sera plus chaude que leur vie" (Because my ashes will be hotter than their life; "Les Regrets," in *L'Ombre des jours*).

Maurice Barrès called Anna de Noailles "the most sensitive point of the universe." Indeed, her fragile health, romantic temperament, and dionysian nature allowed her to cultivate a hypersensitivity that she strove to capture in verse devoted primarily to love, death, and, of course, nature, whose beauty she endlessly embellished: "C'est de moi que monte et que s'élance / Un univers plus beau, plus plein de passion" (It is from me that rises and springs forth / A universe more beautiful and full of passion; "Plénitude," in *Les Éblouissements*). She noted every nuance of the sensations that excited her and was so bound to immediate sensory perceptions that she declared herself incapable of composing a poem about summer during the winter. Her poems are generously padded with strings of descriptive adjectives, so that they seem to overflow with sensual imagery. Touch, taste, sight, smell, and hearing are all exploited to create some surprising but effective synesthetic images. For example, she compares the morning light to "une chaude neige" (a hot snow; "Jour d'été," in *Les Éblouissements*). The poet uses another striking image to express her anguish over growing old: "La bouche pleine d'ombre et les yeux pleins de cris" (My mouth full of shadow and eyes full of cries; "Jeunesse," in *L'Ombre des jours*).

As a child in the garden at Amphion, Noailles began a love affair with nature that would eventually dominate her entire poetic oeuvre. Though some consider her a pantheist, Noailles was looking for herself, not God, in nature, which seems to exist solely for her sensual enjoyment. These verses from "Offrande à la Nature" (*Le Coeur innombrable*) illustrate the poet's sensual rapport with nature: "J'ai tenu l'odeur des saisons dans mes mains. . . . Et j'ai pleuré d'amour aux bras de vos étés" (I have held the seasons' fragrance in my hands. . . . And I have wept with love in the arms of your summers). Their relationship is so close that the poet's life becomes "an open flower where bees live," which spreads perfumes and songs. "Parfumés de trèfle et d'armoise" (*L'Ombre des jours*) expands the flower image: "Je voudrais faire avec une pâte de fleurs, / Des vers de langoureuse et glissante couleur, / Des vers plus odorants qu'un parterre en juin" (I would like to make a paste of flowers, / Verses of slippery and languorous color, / Verses more fragrant than a flowerbed in June).

Noailles does not restrict her comparisons to flowers, but extends them to the entire vegetable kingdom, a practice that some critics ridiculed. Her use of many of its less poetic members earned her the title "Muse of the Kitchen Garden." In "Le Verger" (*Le Coeur innombrable*), for example, she writes: "Mon coeur, indifférent et doux, aura la pente / Du feuillage flexible et plat des haricots" (My heart, indifferent and soft, will have the bend / Of flat and flexible bean leaves). Her prose contains some equally striking comparisons, such as this description of a pansy from *Le Visage émerveillé*: "its petals of a beautiful smooth yellow, bright and shiny, as if, fallen from a tree, a wren's egg had broken there."

Noailles felt that her writing was shaped by two opposing forces, which she called "the bacchante and the nun," but others have variously labeled these contrasts romantic/classic, northern/southern, and dionysian/apollonian. The poet's exuberance for life, for example, is frequently darkened by a melancholic contemplation of her mortality, nostalgic yearnings, and a fervent desire to be remembered. A materialist who rejected the possibility of an afterlife, Noailles believed only in the natural living world of sensation and envisioned death as cold, dark emptiness. One of her earliest poems, "Offrande à la Nature," ends with the poet's anticipation of the day when her eyes "will fill with shadows" and she will go "au pays sans vent et sans verdure / Que ne visitent pas la lumière et l'amour . . . " (to the country without wind and greenery / That love and light never visit). She had sought to develop a spiritual life when she was younger, but eventually came to believe that there was no God. Besides, as she once told Jean Cocteau, wouldn't she be the first to know if he did exist? Her prayer, "Si vous parliez, seigneur" (If you spoke, Lord) from *Les Vivants et les morts*, concludes with this denial: "Mais je ne vous vois pas, o mon Dieu! et je chante / A cause du vide infini!" (But I do not see you, o my God, and I sing / Because of the infinite void!).

Although Noailles believed that "there is nothing but this earth," she counted on her immortal verses to rule men's hearts from beyond the grave. In both "Offrande" and "J'écris pour que le jour" (I Write for the Day), the poet singles out her young male readers and imagines that they will be so moved by her poetry that they will prefer her over their real wives.[3]

Noailles treats the theme of love more negatively in her novels and essays. She opposed poetry, which "always gives joy, never sadness, because of the exaltation it produces," to prose, which she called "the only garment of all of life's sadness." This categorization oversimplifies the complexity of Noailles's work, but it helps explain why all four of her novels depict failed love affairs. *La Nouvelle Espérance* and *La Domination* both end with suicides, and the heroines of *Le Visage émerveillé* and her unfinished novel, *Octave*, both renounce their lovers in favor of the convent. Colette was among those women who criticized Noailles's pessimistic view of passion in which fulfillment was impossible.

From a thematic perspective, Noailles had much in common with the women poets of her generation, who also wrote of childhood, love, nature, and death, but Claude Mignot-Ogliastri, her biographer, notes that the extremely narcissistic nature of Noailles's poetry separates it from the work of other women.[4] Maternal love, for example, is strikingly missing from her work. When Noailles strays from her major themes, she writes lovingly about her country and the French heroes, whom she calls "the affirmers of life." Scattered throughout her volumes of poetry are poems dedicated to men she admired, including Rousseau, Stendhal, Schubert, and especially Napoleon Bonaparte. Noailles was proud of her "drop of Greek blood" and expressed her orientalism in the exotic Eastern decors of many poems. She was an avid reader, and her themes reveal the influence of a number of writers, especially the French Romantics and Nietzsche. But Noailles's work is far from mere imitation; by the sheer power of her passionate lyricism she created an original oeuvre that is at least as impressive as the hundred marching men she once wanted to be.

SURVEY OF CRITICISM

During her lifetime, Anna de Noailles's poetry excited a lively critical discussion among her contemporaries. The bibliography complied by Jean Larnac lists over 300 critical articles and reviews of Noailles's work over her thirty-year career. Larnac's *Comtesse de Noailles: Sa vie, son oeuvre* (1931) provides a comprehensive summary of these various critical opinions and a good overview of Noailles's work. His book also reveals the biases that plagued early twentieth-century literary critics, who believed that a woman poet's "feminine" nature was the source of her creativity. Fin-de-siècle France was particularly favorable to a "feminine" aesthetic, which Noailles's lyricism seemed to epitomize. This, in part, explains the popularity of her poetry, which was compared to "a basket of fresh fruit," a refreshing change from the intellectual diet of Symbolist and Parnassian verse. Critics called her poems instinctive, close to nature, and anti-intellectual, qualities they associated with the feminine. Feminist critics such as Germine Brée and Béatrice Slama argue that the label "feminine" has trivialized women's writing, which Noailles's current status as token (and unread) feminine poet seems to support. Critics avoided any serious consideration of Noailles's innovations and relevance to mainstream literature by creating a separate (and inferior) category for women's literature. Slama traces the "institutionalization of sexual difference as inferiority" to the turn of the century, when "feminine literature" first emerged as a category in literary criticism ("De 'littérature féminine,' " 52).

By virtue of her popularity, Noailles's poetry became synonymous with "feminine poetry." The sexual biases and double standards of early twentieth-century critics are evident in their reactions to Noailles's work. According to Larnac, her enemies included "envious writers and literary purists who only wanted to see the technical mistakes and negligences of the poet." J. Ernest-Charles, for example, attributed Noailles's success to her celebrity and the influence of the press. J. Calvet characterized Noailles's readers as illiterate, fashion-conscious snobs, and M. O. Jacquemaire suggested that her undisciplined verse was the product of an aristocratic disdain for work. However, the majority of critics "let themselves be taken by the flame of Noailles' genius" (Larnac, 78). Even her harshest critics were forced to admit that Noailles made poetry pleasurable again.

Noailles's poetry did not evolve from any established school, and Larnac predicted that her influence on literature would be limited because her work had no other end than "feeling for the pleasure of feeling. . . . A work thus amputated from all intellectualism cannot satisfy those who search literature for a means of knowing more than an occasion to vibrate" (181–82). Sensation is the basis of what Charles Maurras called "feminine romanticism." In his influential 1903 essay, he accused women poets of pushing romanticism to unbalanced excesses because of their narcissistic and frenzied feminine nature. Maurras could not forgive Noailles for "letting the veil fall" by speaking openly about woman's desires in *La Nouvelle Espérance*. *Poème de l'amour* excited similar negative comments from Marcel Coulon, who read the poems as a lover's monologue with the sex roles reversed. However, Jean de Gourmont praised Anna de Noailles's frankness: "For the first time, a woman dares to be sincere and paint herself as she sees herself."

Noailles's writing has inspired surprisingly little critical inquiry since 1933, and many of the more recent studies of the poet concentrate almost exclusively on her life. One of the best written of these newer books is Louis Perche's *Anna de Noailles* (1964), which contains an interesting analysis of Noailles as a love poet. Edmée de la Rochefoucauld's study of Noailles's life and work, published in 1956, was reprinted in 1976 for the centennial of her birth. She provides a comprehensive overview in addition to analyses of several key poems. Jean Cocteau devoted his final work to Noailles. *La Comtesse de Noailles oui et non* (1963) is more a personal portrait of the woman Cocteau calls an idol of his youth than a critical defense of her work. Another of Noailles's admirers was Marcel Proust, whose letters to the countess have been translated and published. Proust's enthusiasm for her work is usually not taken as serious criticism because of their close friendship. Proust's biographer George Painter believes that Anna de Noailles's nostalgic poems directly influenced Proust's portrait of Combray.

Claude Mignot-Ogliastri's biography, *Anna de Noailles* (1986) draws on substantial archival material, including thousands of letters and over sixty of Noailles's personal notebooks. Mignot-Ogliastri has put together a detailed portrait of Anna de Noailles and her milieu. His book traces her development as a writer and especially documents her relationships with writers such as Barrès, Cocteau, and Colette. Although a significant contribution, Mignot-Ogliastri's work focuses on biography to the exclusion of literary analysis and offers no explanation for the current neglect of Noailles's work.

Critics engaged in reshaping our understanding of literary history, and particularly the role of gender, may yet revive interest in Anna de Noailles's poetry. Contemporary reaction to her work, for example, provides a fascinating example of how women writers were read. But Noailles is more than an interesting case history. Although she did not claim to be a feminist, she broke new ground for women writers through the example of her success, and, by defying poetic convention, produced some startlingly fresh images, with a passion for life and language that today's readers will still find moving.

NOTES

1. The vote was among the women readers of the journal *Femina*. In 1924, the journal *Eva* conducted another poll with similar results: Noailles narrowly defeated Colette for the title ''Princess of Letters'' by receiving 2,397 votes over Colette's 2,363.

2. According to Proust's biographer, George Painter, this gesture was wasted on Noailles, who was unable to recognize the flowers. Colette tells of receiving an impromptu visit from the countess while working in her garden. Noailles asked her to identify a particular herb, and then exclaimed, ''So that's the plant I've written so much about!'' Noailles's love of nature was genuine despite her lack of botanical savvy, although, as Colette explained, ''What I learned from Nature, the fragile child of the well-ordered garden at Amphion had powerfully invented'' (qtd. in Cocteau [1963] from Colette's Speech to the Belgian Academy).

3. ''Offrande'' was included in the first issue of the literary journal *Les Essais*. Claude

Mignot-Ogliastri speculates that it was specifically addressed to the young generation of
male poets, including the founders of *Les Essais*, who emulated the countess and sought
her patronage (203–4).

4. p. 339. Fin-de-siècle critics understood narcissism simply as self-love. Noailles's
narcissism is so blatant that Simone de ˚Beauvoir uses her to illustrate the chapter on
female narcissism in *The Second Sex*. Beauvoir quotes a section from *Le Livre de ma
vie* in which Noailles explains how, as a little girl, she named all her dolls after herself,
"lending the animation of my own existence to their immobile forms."

BIBLIOGRAPHY

Major Works by Anna de Noailles

Poetry

Le Coeur innombrable. Paris: Calmann-Lévy, 1901.
L'Ombre des jours. Paris: Calmann-Lévy, 1902.
Les Éblouissements. Paris: Calmann-Lévy, 1907.
Les Vivants et les morts. Paris: A. Fayard, 1913.
Les Forces éternelles. Paris: A. Fayard, 1921.
Poème de l'amour. Paris: A. Fayard, 1924.
L'Honneur de souffrir. Paris: Bernard Grasset, 1927.
Mes Poèmes d'enfance. Paris: Bernard Grasset, 1928.
Choix de poésies. 1930. Intro. Jean Rostand. Paris: Bernard Grasset, 1979.
Derniers Vers. Paris: Bernard Grasset, 1933.
Derniers Vers et poèmes d'enfance. Paris: Bernard Grasset, 1934.

Novels and Prose

La Nouvelle Espérance. Paris: Calmann-Lévy, 1903.
Le Visage émerveillé. Paris: Calmann-Lévy, 1904.
La Domination. Paris: Calmann-Lévy, 1905.
De la rive d'Europe à la rive d'Asie. Paris: Dorbon aîné, 1913.
"Discours de la comtesse de Noailles à l'Académie royale de langue et littérature fran-
    çaises de Belgique." *Le Temps*, January 22, 1922.
Les Innocentes ou la sagesse des femmes. Paris: A. Fayard, 1923.
"Réponse de la comtesse de Noailles à l'enquête du *Figaro* sur la poésie contemporaine."
    Le Figaro, May, 21 1925.
Passions et vanités. Paris: Crès, 1926.
Exactitudes. Paris: Bernard Grasset, 1930.
Le Livre de ma vie. Paris: Hachette, 1932. Paris: Mercure de France, 1976.

Translations

No English translations exist.

Studies of Anna de Noailles

Blum, Léon. "L'Oeuvre poétique de Madame de Noailles." *La Revue de Paris* 15, no. 1 (January 15, 1908): 225–47.

Cocteau, Jean. *La Comtesse de Noailles oui et non*. Paris: Librairie académique Perrin, 1963.

Colette. *Discours de recéption à l'Académie royale de langue et littérature françaises de Belgique*. Paris: Grasset, 1936.

Cooper, Clarissa. *Women Poets of the Twentieth Century in France*. New York: King's Crown, 1943.

Coulon, Marcel. "Anna de Noailles et l'amour de l'homme." *L'Archer* (November 1933): 367–71.

Ernst-Charles, J. "Poétesses." *Les Samedis littéraires*, 1st series (1903): 252–60.

———. "Poétesses." *Les Samedis littéraires*, 2nd series (1904): 408–18.

Fournet, Charles. *Un Grand Poète français moderne: La comtesse de Noailles*. Geneva: Editions Roulet, 1950.

Gourmont, Jean de. *Muses d'aujourd'hui: Essai de physiologie poétique*. Paris: Mercure de France, 1910.

Hommage à la comtesse de Noailles. Special issue of *Les Nouvelles littéraires*, May 6, 1933.

Juin, Hubert. "Le Centenaire d'Anna de Noailles." *Le Monde*, October 22, 1976, 23.

Larnac, Jean. *Comtesse de Noailles: Sa vie, son oeuvre*. Paris: Kra, 1931.

La Rochefoucauld, Edmée de. *Anna de Noailles*. 1956. Paris: Mercure de France, 1976.

Lefèvre, Frédéric. "Une Heure avec la comtesse de Noailles." *Les Nouvelles littéraires*, September 18, 1926, 1–3.

Lièvre, Pierre. "La Comtesse de Noailles." *Les Marges* (October 15, 1921): 101–14.

Maurras, Charles. "Le Romantisme féminin." In *L'Avenir de l'intelligence*. 1903. Paris: Flammarion, 1927. 115–34.

Mignot-Ogliastri, Claude. *Anna de Noailles*. Paris: Meridiens Klincksieck, 1986.

Perche, Louis. *Anna de Noailles*. Paris: Editions Pierre Seghers, 1964.

Slama, Béatrice. "De 'littérature féminine' à 'l'écrire-femme'; Différence et institution." *Littérature* 44 (December 1981): 52–71.

RACHILDE
(1860–1953)

Melanie Hawthorne

BIOGRAPHY

Rachilde was born Marguerite Eymery on February 11, 1860, at the family home of Cros, just outside the town of Périgueux in southwest France. Her life and work are prefigured by her ancestry. She was distantly related to Brantôme, the sixteenth-century author of scandalous memoirs of court life, as well as to Dom Faytos, a Spanish Inquisitor. Because her great-grandfather had renounced the priesthood, popular belief held that the descendants of the family turned into werewolves once a year. This colorful background suggests how passion and death became, in the words of Rachilde's friend and biographer André David, ''the two words essential to the secret of her life'' (18).

Rachilde's father, the illegitimate son of an aristocrat, was raised by a single mother who suffered social ostracism because of her unmarried status. Joseph became a career soldier and distinguished himself, establishing the military context in which Rachilde would be raised. While stationed in Valenciennes, Joseph met Gabrielle Feytaud, the daughter of a newspaper editor, whom he married in 1859. The couple's only child, Marguerite, was born the following year. It was a source of lifelong disappointment to Joseph that his child was not a son; the fact also exercised enormous influence on Rachilde. Raised as a boy, she began riding lessons at age four and later participated in hunts, constantly trying to compensate her father for his disappointment and to earn his approval. She received an informal, unconventional education at home and read freely in her grandfather's library. For most of her childhood she was able to please herself and was seldom confronted by societal expectations about women's roles. Nevertheless, her childhood, while materially secure and comfortable, left psychological scars that did not heal easily.

When Rachilde was fourteen, her parents arranged a marriage with one of her father's officers, but the strong-willed girl, used to independence, resisted fiercely. After she threw herself in the pond in an attempted suicide, her parents did not insist upon the marriage. She then turned to writing seriously as a form of escape and soon was writing regularly for local newspapers. Her first literary efforts were well received, and she was motivated to write to the legendary author Victor Hugo, who responded with a few encouraging words: "Thanks, applause. Courage, Mademoiselle" (*Quand j'étais jeune* [When I Was Young], 9; this and all subsequent translations from French in this text are my own). The words were still remembered decades later, for the response led Rachilde to set her sights on Paris and on a career as a writer, which would make her independent of her family. A cousin who worked for a fashion review provided an opening into the literary world of the capital. Through this contact Rachilde managed to publish some fiction and also met other writers with more established reputations who would prove useful to her career, such as Arsène Houssaye, Catulle Mendès, and Villiers de l'Isle-Adam.

At twenty-one, Rachilde moved permanently to Paris. By this time (the 1880s), Marguerite Eymery had assumed the name she would be known by for the rest of her life: Rachilde. At first she claimed that this was the name of a Swedish gentleman who had contacted her during a seance, but later admitted that this was a story she had invented for the benefit of her gullible parents. During this period, Rachilde began dressing as a man (which still required the written permission of the police). Men's clothes were much cheaper and much more convenient for moving around freely in Paris. With her pseudonym, male appearance, and visiting cards, which read "Rachilde, man of letters," many people mistook her for a man, and both wrote to her and addressed her in person as "Monsieur Rachilde." The alter ego seemed to fit, and not only did she continue to sign the name Rachilde to both books and personal correspondence, she frequently referred to herself in the French masculine form. She also published under a second pseudonym, the anagram Jean de Chilra (or Childra), and clearly the assumption of a masculine authorial persona played a significant role in the development of Rachilde's writing.

In the early 1880s, Rachilde became infatuated with the poet Catulle Mendès. The details remain obscure, but it ended when Rachilde apparently suffered a nervous breakdown. As with the proposed arranged marriage, however, the long-term result of the emotional upheaval was a positive one, since Rachilde once again wrote her way out of depression. The first novel Rachilde published after this period of reclusion brought her instant fame and notoriety: *Monsieur Vénus* was published by Brancart in Brussels in 1884. It remains Rachilde's best-known novel.

Rachilde was now famous in Paris literary circles, and soon her Tuesday salon became a meeting place for everyone who was anyone. In 1885, she met Alfred Vallette, a "serious young man," through a mutual friend at a dance (she was still dressed as a man). The relationship did not develop smoothly, and at one point Rachilde refused to see or even write to Vallette for a year, but in 1889 they were married in a civil ceremony.

Once married, Rachilde's life began to echo her mother's in an uncanny way. Rachilde frequently expressed criticism of her mother, claiming in *Pourquoi je ne suis pas féministe* (Why I Am Not a Feminist, 1928) that she learned her distrust of women from the example of maternal disappointment. Yet the early years of her marriage suggest that she could not help replicating the structure of her mother's life, a more telling (even if unconscious) tribute to the strong, though repressed, ties she maintained with her. If her words speak long and loud about her affection for her father, her actions speak louder than perhaps she ever realized about the maternal bond. To begin with, she stopped dressing as a man, a symbolic return to femininity. Then, like her mother, Rachilde gave birth to a daughter the year following her marriage. The daughter was named Gabrielle, after Rachilde's mother, and remained an only child, as was Rachilde. Like her own mother, Rachilde was not interested in mothering, maintaining that the maternal instinct was a trap. References to her daughter are painfully absent from Rachilde's autobiographical works, which focus instead on the unfinished business of her own childhood. Furthermore, mothers are seldom portrayed in her novels, and when they are, as in the 1887 novel *La Marquise de Sade* (The Marquise de Sade), they are often selfish and negligent. Becoming a mother herself did little to modify Rachilde's attitudes, and in *Dans le puits ou la vie inférieure* (In The Pit or Lower Life, 1918) she wondered if pregnant women love their husbands and if they forgive their "executioners." The little information available suggests that Rachilde's relationship with her daughter remained strained throughout her life, just as Rachilde was never fully reconciled with her mother.

The birth of Gabrielle was paralleled by another, more literary birth, one which Rachilde greeted with much more pride and attention. In 1890, she and Vallette launched the review *Mercure de France*, which became a leading journal for symbolist work. Vallette had the technical expertise to run the journal, but it was Rachilde's reputation, by then considerable, that underwrote the authority of the review and attracted the attention of readers and writers. She made regular contributions, at first offering short stories or serialized novels (the stories later published under the title *Le Démon de l'absurde* [The Demon of the Absurd] 1894, for example). She also covered huge quantities of fiction in her idiosyncratic reviews, which appeared regularly until 1914. She continued to contribute periodically until 1925, when her health began to fail and the review was taken over by John Charpentier. Although honest and quirky, her critical pronouncements have not always been endorsed by subsequent literary history. In evaluating her literary criticism, however, it should be remembered that Rachilde never claimed to be a critic, merely a "passionate reader" (André David, 49).

If her critical judgment erred, Rachilde was nevertheless a loyal and generous friend, and by helping those she believed in, she also made a great indirect impact on literature. Her most outstanding contribution in this respect is her support of Alfred Jarry. Through her connections with the Théâtre de l'Oeuvre, Rachilde was able to persuade the director to take a chance on Jarry's *Ubu roi*.

The performance was a scandal comparable only to the battle over Victor Hugo's play *Hernani*, which had heralded the arrival of romanticism in 1830. After the first night of *Ubu roi*, many—including those at the Théâtre de l'Oeuvre—considered the matter a disaster. The full importance of the event was only appreciated in retrospect, as it is now viewed as the birth of modern absurd drama. Rachilde also helped support Jarry financially and wrote a book about him—her only book devoted to a single author—entitled *Alfred Jarry; ou, Le Surmâle de lettres* (Alfred Jarry; or, The Supermale of Letters, 1928), which is the source of many of the famous anecdotes about Jarry.

After World War I, Rachilde continued to write, but her popularity was eclipsed by movements such as surrealism and dadaism. In addition to a regular offering of novels, both coauthored and her own work, she produced another collection of stories, *Le Théâtre des bêtes* (The Theatre of Animals, 1926). Misanthrope that she undoubtedly was, she had always claimed both to prefer animals to people and to be closer to animal than human herself. She always had animals about her, especially rats, a species she admired for its pride and loyalty.

This was also a period of nonfictional production. In addition to books about Jarry and other writers (*Portraits d'hommes* [Portraits of Men]), she offered her only "political" book during this time, *Pourquoi je ne suis pas féministe*. Despite the title, the book presents mostly autobiographical material, and, as Rachilde herself recognized, it might better have been named "Why I Don't Like Women." Her lack of esteem for women is defended and illustrated by portraits of the women in her family, who are once again presented as dramatic negative forces in her life. The trend toward autobiography and reminiscence continued in her later years, particularly after the death of Alfred Vallette in 1935. (A workaholic, he died at his desk at the *Mercure de France*.) In 1942, Rachilde published his letters to her, written before their marriage. Her only two volumes of poetry also appeared after Vallette's death, in 1937 and 1945, but these did not meet with much critical success. Her last book, the autobiographical *Quand j'étais jeune*, appeared in 1947.

Rachilde led a very active social life, and even in her sixties and seventies she continued to be escorted by a series of young men. Tongues wagged at the hours and the company she kept, but Rachilde maintained that there was no basis to the rumors of adultery. As she wrote in the *Mercure de France* (April 15, 1921): "I do not smoke, I do not drink. I practice neither adultery, nor drugs. I do not play the piano and I do not get involved in politics." It does not strain credulity to accept that these relationships remained platonic given Rachilde's predilection, noted by her contemporaries, for "rascals, hairdressers and homosexuals" (quoted by Dauphiné in *Rachilde, femme de lettres 1900*, 131).

With her husband's death, however, the Tuesday salon ended, and Rachilde was soon alone and poor. She had always lived hand to mouth, spending what she earned from writing and giving generously to friends with no thought to the ure. When her books were no longer in favor and her declining health interfered ith new production, she found herself increasingly unable to support herself. Her daughter Gabrielle paid regular visits, despite the tensions, but Rachilde continued to live alone in the apartment at 26 rue de Condé, home of the *Mercure de France*, which she had occupied for over sixty years. She died the day before Easter, on Saturday, April 4, 1953, at the age of ninety-three.

MAJOR THEMES

Jarry once wrote of Rachilde's work that, like an icosahedron, it is impossible to take in all at once, and it is true that her work incorporates many genres—novels, short stories, plays, memoirs, criticism, poetry—and her themes are equally varied. Her fiction is often linked to the decadent and symbolist movements in literature, but she continued writing for several decades after these movements had waned. Her novels and stories include historical fiction, an early form of science fiction, humorous parody, animal stories, adventures set in Africa, and tales of the strange comparable to the work of Edgar Allan Poe. Almost all her work, however, displays a preoccupation with the nature of love.

As Marcel Coulon has remarked, "[*Monsieur Vénus*] is not Rachilde's first novel, but it is her first novel that counts" (547). Superficially, the novel has many of the characteristics of decadent novels of the late nineteenth century, but also differs from other novels in presenting a female—and perhaps feminist—heroine. Raoule de Vénérande falls in love with a working-class man and makes him her "mistress" (the lack of an equivalent masculine term is significant). She eventually marries him, and when he is killed in a duel, becomes a reclusive necrophile. In the novel, Rachilde claimed to portray a "new perversion," that of love. Whether Rachilde succeeded in making conventional, conjugal, heterosexual love seem like a new vice is debatable. (As her friend, the poet Verlaine, was to remark, had Rachilde really succeeded in inventing a new vice, the whole world would have been indebted to her.) Nevertheless, the attack on morality conveyed by the gender role reversal of the novel did not go unnoticed. Local authorities in Belgium ordered the book to be seized and imposed a fine and a sentence of two years in prison for the author. In France, Rachilde acquired a reputation as a pornographer, and fellow writer Maurice Barrès dubbed her "Mademoiselle Baudelaire."

Her other novels of the 1880s and 1890s also explore questions of sexuality, often presenting a woman's point of view. *La Marquise de Sade* shows how the heroine, Mary Barbe, becomes a sadist, having learned in her childhood that "to love is to suffer," while *Madame Adonis* tells a story of gender ambiguity. Louisa Bartau, married one year and living with her bourgeois in-laws in the provinces, falls in love with a mysterious and romantic hunter who turns out to be a woman. The themes reach their most complete expression, however, in *La Jongleuse* (*The Juggler*), in which the heroine directly addresses the question of sexual expression. She defends her choice of an alabaster Greek vase as her love-object and criticizes men for being too selfish to be good lovers.

The nature of desire preoccupied Rachilde throughout her life. In a chapter on "love" in *Pourquoi je ne suis pas féministe*, she states that "love is not only a feeling for someone, it is the opening up [*épanouissement*] of a brain touched by it and the *object* is no longer in question" (48). As examples of those affected by this "heavenly affliction," she cites Saint Teresa of Avila and the Emperor Hadrian, noting that such "intoxication" can only develop in the best minds and temperaments. She continued to explore these themes in her later novels, several of which depict homosexual relationships, for example the coauthored *Le Prisonnier* (The Prisoner) and *Les Voluptés imprévues* (Unforeseen Pleasures). The former especially, with a first-person male narrator, represents an interesting experiment in the depiction of an emerging gay consciousness.

Rachilde's involvement with the theater was strongest at the turn of the century. She was primarily associated with Paul Fort's symbolist Théâtre d'Art (her daughter Gabrielle married Fort's nephew) and with Aurélien Lugné-Poë's Théâtre de l'Oeuvre (the connection which had enabled her to promote Jarry). Her plays explore somewhat different themes from those of her fiction of this period. *Madame La Mort* (Madam Death), for example, first performed in 1891, presents a young man's suicide as a "cerebral drama" in which death appears personified as a veiled woman rival to the young man's girlfriend. The opposition between poetic aspiration and mundane reality is amplified in *Le Vendeur de soleil* (The Sun Salesman, first performed in 1894), an allegory of poetic vision in which an out-of-work bohemian hits upon the idea of selling the sun. He sets up as a street hawker, calling the attention of the bourgeois passers-by to the beauty of the setting sun before them. Some spectators can appreciate this new vision, but many remain unable to see what he is talking about and blindly continue on their way, insensitive to the beauty around them. The critique of bourgeois complacency is most explicit in *La Voix du sang* (The Voice of Blood), a one-act play first performed in 1890. A smug bourgeois couple are relaxing after dinner in their living room when their peace is interrupted by cries for help outside. Assuming the disturbance to be some disreputable street fight, they do not respond, thinking it a matter for the police. Their complacency is shattered, however, when their eighteen-year-old son staggers in, bleeding from an attack, and expires before their eyes; he had been slipping out at night regularly without their knowledge.

Rachilde's plays had a part in fuelling the literary controversy between the naturalists and the symbolists, but many of the issues she raises contain moral dilemmas every bit as relevant. Is society today any more capable of seeing and appreciating natural beauty when it is not packaged in the discourse of advertising appropriated by the sun salesman? Complacency and self-satisfaction can still prevent some people from offering help to others, thereby indirectly hurting themselves.

Rachilde's keen dramatic sense, which guided her theatrical works, is also

.Jent in her novels of this period, in which strong emotions and violent action are juxtaposed with comic interludes that defuse the dramatic tension until the final climax. She also creates larger-than-life comic characters drawing on stock traditions, and her caricatures are worthy of Molière (Louisa's profligate yet sentimental father in *Madame Adonis*, for example).

The outbreak of World War I had a profound impact on Rachilde, particularly on her fiction. In her prewar novels, her heroines are colorful, strong-willed, and passionate; she explores the connections among passion, desire, pleasure, sex, and love, connections that psychologists of the era were only just beginning to grasp. Her fiction often contained more than a dash of humor, which set it apart from other decadent texts. After World War I, a darker side emerges. Her main characters are more often male, particularly young men profoundly marked by the war, such as Gaston Louveteau in *Madame de Lydone, assassin* (1928), Gilles de Kerao in *L'Homme aux bras de feu* (The Man with Arms of Fire, 1930), and Lucien Girard of *Les Voluptés imprévues* (1931). The latter is described as the kind of man who, "tired (since birth), represented the new, if not the best, world, and he was naturally artificial" (11). Rachilde's humor survives in the punning titles of her novels (already evident in earlier titles such as *La Sanglante Ironie*, Bloody Irony). *Jeux d'artifices* (Games of Artifice), for example, evokes "feux d'artifices," meaning fireworks, while *Le Grand Saigneur* (The Great Bloodletter) is also "le grand seigneur" or "great lord." But the tone shifts from light-hearted playfulness to a dark cynicism. Perhaps it is not coincidental that Rachilde preferred to recapture the past in memoirs, to pay tribute to other writers, and to delegate some of the burden of writing fiction by collaborating with others during this period of her career.

SURVEY OF CRITICISM

Rachilde achieved notoriety during her lifetime, thus books and articles about her work began to appear before her writing career had ended. Many of the authors, however, were personal friends or connected to the *Mercure de France*, and they offered praise and anecdotes rather than critical study. André David's *Rachilde, homme de lettres*, for example, appeared in 1924. While inevitably incomplete (written nearly thirty years before Rachilde's death), the book combines sketchy biography and an outline of Rachilde's works with a collection of opinions and correspondence, and offers a useful bibliography. Noël Santon's *La Poésie de Rachilde* (1928) studies the poetic language in Rachilde's fiction. It focuses on her probings of the human psyche, a subject linking her to Baudelaire, Rimbaud, and Dostoyevsky, and the author claims her as an important precursor of modern intellectual anxiety. Santon is too preoccupied with disproving the lingering charges of immorality to pursue this point, but it remains an important recognition, for Rachilde's modernism has been studied too little.

Because of her strong heroines and themes of sexual politics, gender is a key element in Rachilde's work. The fact did not pass unnoticed by her contemporaries: as early as 1920, Marcel Coulon, analyzing Rachilde's imagination in the *Mercure de France*, suggested that Rachilde did for women what Stendhal had done for men by offering female characters worthy of representing woman. But the recent developments in feminist criticism especially have favored a fuller appreciation of Rachilde. The last two decades have seen a revival of her work, beginning with the republishing of *Monsieur Vénus* by Flammarion in 1977. This and subsequent re-editions have made her work more accessible, although it is not well known outside France. (Several of her novels were translated into Czech, Hungarian, Polish, and Spanish in the early twentieth century, but *Monsieur Vénus*, which has even been translated into Japanese, and *The Juggler* are her only works to have appeared to date in English.)

The most comprehensive biography of Rachilde's life, Claude Dauphiné's *Rachilde, femmes de lettres 1900*, appeared in 1985. This invaluable source of information draws together the anecdotal materials of earlier works such as André David's and information culled from correspondence. It too focuses on the pre-1914 works, however, and adds little to the scanty information Rachilde herself provided about her later life. Dauphiné has also led the way in assessing Rachilde's importance for feminists, suggesting in her introduction to the 1982 edition of *La Jongleuse*, for example, that posterity must recognize, despite Rachilde's reservations about feminism, that through her analysis of sexual politics, she "joins the ranks of those who intend to supply women with the means to attain freedom" (23).

Jennifer Birkett, on the other hand, is much more skeptical than Dauphiné about Rachilde's feminist message. While she devotes an entire chapter to Rachilde in her book about decadence (*The Sins of the Fathers*), she suggests that "Rachilde puts her creative imagination at the service of male masochistic fantasies, acting out the temporary triumph of the vengeful female and the humiliating overthrow of the male—subject to the reinstatement of paternal power in the last act" (161). Birkett justifies this reading by reference to an impressive number of works (including two novels from the 1920s), but the brief, oversimplified plot summaries are reductive and one-dimensional.

For the most part, then, Rachilde's fiction continues to be treated in the context of the nineteenth-century decadent movement. Rachilde was obviously linked in important ways to this movement, but she continued to produce fiction for several decades in the twentieth century, long after the decadent movement had faded. While her later fiction is arguably not her best, a complete study of her work, including her drama and poetry, has yet to be written. In light of the renewed interest in her work, however, it seems likely that this lacuna will soon be addressed.

BIBLIOGRAPHY

Works By Rachilde

Monsieur de la nouveauté. Paris: Dentu, 1880.
La Femme du 199e régiment. Périgueux: Dupont, 1881.

Monsieur Vénus. Brussels: Brancart, 1884.

Histoires bêtes pour amuser les petits enfants d'esprit. Paris: Brissy, 1884.

Queue de poisson. Brussels: Brancart, 1885.

Nono. Paris: Monnier, 1885.

La Virginité de Diane. Paris: Monnier, 1886.

A Mort. Paris: Monnier, 1886.

La Marquise de Sade. Paris: Monnier, 1887.

Le Tiroir de Mimi-Corail. Paris: Monnier, 1887.

Madame Adonis. Paris: Monnier, 1888.

Les Oubliés: L'Homme roux, filles de neige. Paris: Librairie illustrée, 1889.

Minette. Paris: Librairie française et internationale, 1889.

Le Mordu. Paris: Genonceaux, 1889.

Théâtre: Madame la Mort. Le Vendeur de soleil. La Voix du sang. Paris: Savine, 1891.

La Sanglante ironie. Paris: Genonceaux, 1891.

L'Animale. Paris: Simonis Empis, 1893.

Le Démon de l'absurde. Paris: Mercure de France, 1894.

La Princesse des ténèbres. Paris: C. Lévy, 1896.

Les Hors nature. Paris: Mercure de France, 1897.

L'Heure sexuelle. Paris: Mercure de France, 1898.

La Tour d'amour. Paris: Mercure de France, 1899.

La Jongleuse. Paris: Mercure de France, 1900.

Contes et nouvelles, suivis du Théâtre. Paris: Mercure de France, 1900.

L'Imitation de la mort. Paris: Mercure de France, 1903.

Le Dessous. Paris: Mercure de France, 1904.

Le Meneur de louves. Paris: Mercure de France, 1905.

Son Printemps. Paris: Mercure de France, 1912.

La Délivrance. Paris: Mercure de France, 1915.

La Terre qui rit. Paris: Maison du Livre, 1917.

Dans le puits, ou la vie inférieure, 1915–1917. Paris: Mercure de France, 1918.

La Découverte de l'Amérique. Geneva: Kundig, 1919.

La Maison vierge. Paris: Ferenczi, 1920.

Les Rageac. Paris: Flammarion, 1921.

La Souris japonaise. Paris: Flammarion, 1921.

Le Grand Saigneur. Paris: Flammarion, 1922.

L'Hôtel du grand veneur. Paris: Ferenczi, 1922.

[with Homen-Christo] *Le Parc du mystère*. Paris: Flammarion, 1923.

Le Château des deux amants. Paris: Flammarion, 1923.

[with Homen-Christo] *Au seuil de l'enfer*. Paris: Flammarion, 1924.

La Haine amoureuse. Paris: Flammarion, 1924.

Le Théâtre des bêtes. Paris: Les Arts et le Livre, 1926.

Refaire l'amour. Paris: Ferenczi, 1927.

Alfred Jarry; ou, Le Surmâle de lettres. Paris: Grasset, 1928.

Madame de Lydone, assassin. Paris: Ferenczi, 1928.

[with André David] *Le Prisonnier*. Paris: Editions de France, 1928.

Pourquoi je ne suis pas féministe. Paris: Editions de France, 1928.

Portraits d'hommes. Paris: Mornay, 1929.

La Femme aux mains d'ivoire. Paris: Editions des Portiques, 1929.

[with Jean-Joë Lauzach] *Le Val sans retour*. Paris: Fayard, 1929.

L'Homme aux bras de feu. Paris: Ferenczi, 1930.

Les Voluptés imprévues. Paris: Ferenczi, 1931.

Notre-Dame des Rats. Paris: Querelle, 1931.

L'Amazone rouge. Paris: Lemerre, 1932.

Jeux d'artifices. Paris: Ferenczi, 1932.

Mon étrange plaisir. Paris: Baudinière, 1934.

La Femme Dieu. Paris: Ferenczi, 1934.

[with Jean-Joë Lauzach] *L'Aérophage*. Paris: Les Ecrivains Associés, 1935.

L'Autre Crime. Paris: Mercure de France, 1937.

Les Accords perdus. Paris: Editions Corymbes, 1937.

La Fille inconnue. Paris: Imprimerie La Technique de Livre, 1938.

Pour la lumière. Brussels: Edition de le Nouvelle Revue de Belgique, 1938.

L'Anneau de Saturne. Paris: Ferenczi, 1939.

Face à la peur. Paris: Mercure de France, 1942.

Duvet d'ange. Paris: Messein, 1943.

Survie. Paris: Messein, 1945.

Quand j'étais jeune. Paris: Mercure de France, 1947.

Translations of Rachilde

Monsieur Vénus. Trans. Madeleine Boyd. New York: Covici, Friede, 1929.

The Juggler. Trans. Melanie Hawthorne. New Brunswick, N.J.: Rutgers University Press, 1990.

Studies of Rachilde

Barney, Natalie. "Rachilde." In *Aventures de l'esprit*. 1929. Paris: Editions Persona, 1982. 167–68.

Barrès, Maurice. "Mademoiselle Baudelaire." *Les Chroniques* (February 1887): 77–79.

Besnard-Coursodon, Micheline. "Monsieur Vénus, Madame Adonis: Sexe et discours." *Littérature* 54 (May 1984): 121–27.

Birkett, Jennifer. *The Sins of the Fathers: Decadence in France, 1870–1914*. London: Quartet, 1986.

Charasson, Henriette. "Rachilde." *Revue de Hollande* 4 (1917): 977–85.

Coulon, Marcel. "L'Imagination de Rachilde." *Mercure de France* 142 (August 15-September 15, 1920): 545–69.

Dauphiné, Claude. Introduction to *La Jongleuse*, by Rachilde. Paris: Des Femmes, 1982.

———. *Rachilde; femme de lettres 1900*. Périgueux: Pierre Fanlac, 1985.

———. "Sade, Rachilde et Freud: lecture de *La Marquise de Sade*." *Bulletin de l'Association des Professeurs de Lettres* 17 (1981): 55–59.

———. "La Vision médiévale de Rachilde dans 'Le Meneur de louves.' " In *Mélanges Jean Larmat: Regards su le moyen-âge et la Renaissance*. Ed. Mauride Accarie. Paris: Les Belles-Lettres, 1982. 489–92.

David, André. *Rachilde, homme de lettres*. Paris: Editions de la Nouvelle Revue Critique, 1924.

Gaubert, Ernest. *Rachilde*. Paris: Sansot, 1907.

Hawthorne, Melanie. "*Monsieur Vénus*: A Critique of Gender Roles." *Nineteenth Century French Studies* 16, no. 1–2 (Fall-Winter 1987–88): 162–79.

————. "The Social Construction of Sexuality in Three Novels by Rachilde." *Michigan Romance Studies* 9 (1989): 49–59.

Jarry, Alfred. "Ce que c'est que les ténèbres." In *Oeuvres complètes*. 3 vols. Paris: Gallimard (Plèiade), 1987. 2: 432–35.

Kahn, Gustave. "La Littérature des jeunes et son orientation actuelle." *La Revue* 37 (April 1, 1901): 36–51.

Leblond, Marius-Ary. *La Société française sous la 3e République, d'áprès les romanciers contemporains*. Paris: Alcan, 1905.

Lorrain, Jean. "Mademoiselle Salamandre." In *Dans l'oratoire*. Paris: C. Dalou, 1888. 204–15.

Mauclair, Camille. "Eloge de la luxure." *Mercure de France* 8, no. 41 (May 1893): 43–50.

McLendon, Will L. "Autour d'une lettre inédite de Rachilde à Huysmans." *Bulletin de la Société Joris-Karl Huysmans* 75 (1983): 21–24.

————. "Rachilde et le roman de 'moeurs parisiennes.' " *Bulletin de la Société Joris-Karl Huysmans* 77 (1985): 21–24.

Miomandre, Francis de. "Rachilde, Princesse des Ténèbres." *Art Moderne* 13 and 14 (March 29 and April 5, 1903): 117–19, 125–27.

Organographes du Cymbalum Pataphysicum, no. 19–20 (April 4, 1983).

Orliac, Antoine. "Médailles symbolistes: Rachilde." *Mercure de France* 281 (1938): 294–99.

Quillard, Pierre. "Rachilde." *Mercure de France* 9, no. 48 (December 1893): 323–28.

Santon, Noël. *La Poésie de Rachilde*. Paris: Le Rouge et le Noir, 1928.

Vasseur, Nadine. "Rachilde." *Les Nouvelles Littéraires* 2751 (August 28, 1980): 30.

MARIE JEANNE RICCOBONI
(1713–1792)

Ruth P. Thomas

Mme Riccoboni was one of the most popular novelists of the eighteenth century. Her books were best-sellers, well received in France, critically acclaimed, and translated into all of the major European languages. One of them, *Lettres de Milady Juliette Catesby* (*Letters from Juliet, Lady Catesby, to Her Friend, Lady Henrietta Campley*), was second only to *La Nouvelle Héloïse* in the number of editions and printings during a three-year period. So widely read was she that between 1780 and 1790 there were seven editions of her complete works. Yet Mme Riccoboni's star dimmed in the nineteenth century, and in 1924 Emily Crosby called her study of the author *Une Romancière oubliée* (A Forgotten Novelist). This book did not rescue Mme Riccoboni from neglect, and only within the last two decades has her light begun to shine again. Critical studies, the publication of some of her letters, the re-edition of three of her novels, and most especially a heightened interest in both women writers and the epistolary novel, her favorite form, have all drawn new attention to Mme Riccoboni's distinct voice.

BIOGRAPHY

For an author who deals mainly with men's infidelity and inconstancy, Mme Riccoboni's birth seems prophetic. Her father was a bigamist. Eight months after her birth in October 1713, the fraud was discovered, the marriage annulled, and her father excommunicated. Financially and emotionally unable to take care of her daughter, her mother placed her in a convent where, Mme Riccoboni would say later, she learned nothing. She returned home at fourteen to an intolerable life with her mother, who, still young and attractive, saw her pretty daughter as a rival. Anxious to leave home, the young woman did not neglect opportunity. When her neighbor, Antoine-François Riccoboni, an Italian actor and the son of the famous director of the Comédie Italienne, proposed marriage in 1734, she readily accepted. Six weeks later she made her own acting debut at the Comédie Italienne.

Her marriage was not happy. Ten years older than his wife, Antoine-François was hot-headed and violent-tempered, squandered money, and was, according to all accounts, unsavory. Legally separating from him, Mme Riccoboni in 1755 moved into an apartment with a friend and fellow actress, Marie-Thérèse Biancolelli, with whom she lived until her death in 1792. Her warm and lasting relationship with Thérèse would find its echo in her novels with their portrayal of female friendship and the narrator's observation in *Histoire du Marquis de Cressy* (*The History of the Marquis de Cressy*) that ''un amant ne vaut pas une amie'' (a lover is not worth a [female] friend) seems to be personal.[1] Mme Riccoboni did, nevertheless, continue to pay her husband's debts, and she was with him when he died. During the first ten years of her marriage she fell deeply in love with the Comte de Maillebois, an ambitious soldier who left her for a brilliant and reportedly loveless marriage in 1745, and the unhappy affair served her fiction in her portrayal of unfaithful men.

More successful professionally than personally, Mme Riccoboni was a popular if not, as she herself recognized, especially talented actress, and Diderot cites her in his *Paradoxe sur le comédien* to illustrate his thesis that sensitive people are unsuccessful actors since they cannot distance themselves from their art. Her experience in the theater may have determined to some extent, as Joan Stewart has suggested in *The Novels of Mme Riccoboni*, the kind of novel she would write, since the letter-novel (and the *mémoire*-novel also), like the drama, depends on a direct contact between the character and the public and a desire to communicate and reveal oneself. The absence of an external setting, the emphasis on the expression of emotional states, and the frequently highly charged language that characterize Mme Riccoboni's fiction all link her novel to the theater. At the beginning of her theatrical career, she played supporting roles in Marivaux's plays, and she may owe to him the theme that recurs in several of her novels: the vicissitudes and eventual triumph of nascent love. After twenty-six years in the theater she retired, supporting herself from the sale of her novels. Her interest in the theater continued, however; she later published a translation of five English plays, and she discussed theatrical reforms with Diderot.

In 1751 Mme Riccoboni's writing career began, supposedly on a wager. A friend had declared that Marivaux's style in *La Vie de Marianne* was inimitable. Saying nothing, she sat down at her desk and quickly produced a continuation of the novel that impressed and even fooled her contemporaries. It pleased Marivaux himself, who had it published later. Although she dismissed it as a youthful folly, written when she had not developed a style of her own, her success probably prompted her to recreate in her own way the story of Valville's infidelity to Marianne. Six years later she had her own style, and she published her first novel, *Lettres de Mistriss Fanni Butlerd* (Letters of Mistriss Fanni

Butlerd), the monophonic story of the love between a commoner and the lord who would betray her. Presented as a translation of English letters written in 1735, the artifice fooled no one, and many even thought the novel the actual letters of Mme Riccoboni to the Comte de Maillebois. As an analysis of female love, the book was successful. But Mme Riccoboni had also astutely prepared the public for its reception when, a few months earlier, she had published in the *Mercure de France* a public "letter" from Fanni to her lover, Alfred, denouncing his betrayal.

Her *Histoire du Marquis de Cressy* was published a year later. A tragic novel of a man loved by two women who dallies with a third, the book too was a best-seller. In the following year, 1761, Mme Riccoboni returned to the English setting (which the novels of Samuel Richardson had made so popular), and the epistolary convention with *Lettres de Milady Juliette Catesby*. This time the single correspondent wrote to her absent (and silent) friend about the lover who had betrayed her. In a new twist, the lapse from fidelity was momentary; the lover, honorable; the ending, happy; and harmony, restored.

With three successful novels and her acting career behind her, Mme Riccoboni focused her energies on writing. She experimented with forms. Short pieces—letters, tales, moral reflections—all modeled after the *Tatler* and the *Spectator*, were published in 1761. She continued in her English mode with a "translation" of Henry Fielding's *Amelia* (1762), which was considerably shorter, less bawdy, and less funny than its original. Her English, as she readily admitted, was not up to such a project, and her *Amélie* was not especially successful. Two years later appeared her longest and most ambitious novel, *Histoire de Miss Jenny* (*The History of Miss Jenny Salisbury*). In a style reminiscent of Prévost and Diderot, the orphaned and illegitimate Jenny recounts her various misadventures. Disinherited by her cruel grandfather, tricked into a sham marriage by a bigamist with a double identity, denied a true marriage because her would-be husband is killed by her first husband, the hapless Jenny sacrifices her love when she learns that her dearest friend cares for the same man. The next year (1765) there was another novel and another virtuous orphan, this one in a simpler, Marivaudian mode. Love triumphs over social convention in *Histoire d'Ernestine* (*The History of Ernestina* or *Ernestina, a Tale*) when the Marquis de Clémengis, too honorable to seduce the young woman he loves, overcomes his class prejudices and marries her. Love also leads to marriage in Mme Riccoboni's most elaborate monophonic letter-novel, published a year later. The correspondent in *Lettres de la Comtesse de Sancerre* (*Letters from the Countess de Sancerre, to Count de Nancé, Her Friend*), however, is a man (not a lover but a friend), and the action is centered not just on the heroine but on her circle of friends, all spirited and widowed like herself, and all reluctant to give up their liberty for the "yoke" of (re)marriage.

As a best-selling author, Mme Riccoboni was well known, but she did not especially prize public life. At the popular salon of the Baron d'Holbach (where she was nonetheless a regular visitor), she probably met Diderot and did meet the philosopher David Hume and the actor David Garrick, who became friends and correspondents and who helped with the business arrangements for the English translation and publication of her novels. For Garrick's many favors, she dedicated to him *Lettres de la Comtesse de Sancerre*. About the same time (the mid 1760s), she met a young Scotsman who would later become a diplomat, Robert Liston. Some thirty years younger than Mme Riccoboni, he became her friend and regular correspondent. They were probably never lovers, but for Mme Riccoboni at least, the relationship was more than casual. Life imitates art, and, as Joan Stewart has pointed out, the letters Mme Riccoboni wrote to Liston are not unlike those of her own fictional heroines.

Mme Riccoboni's literary career continued. She collaborated with Thérèse Biancolelli, and their translation of five English plays was published in 1768 and 1769. The long, sentimental *Lettres de Sophie de Vallière* (*Letters from Elizabeth Sophia de Valiere to Her Friend Louisa Hortensia de Canteleu*), appearing in 1771, was really two novels: the first, the misfortunes of another virtuous orphan, unwilling to bring dishonor on the suitor she loves by marrying him; the second, narrated by a man, more somber and romanesque. A father's deathbed curse, a secret marriage, a tragic rivalry, misunderstanding, and a fatal duel explain Sophie's mysterious origins, establish her birthright, and enable her to marry.

Awarded an annual pension from Louis XV in 1772 through the help of Mme Du Barry, Mme Riccoboni was now comfortably well off and no longer needed to depend on the sale of her novels for a living. She was, as she confided to Garrick, too old to be writing love stories. Her last novel, published in 1776, was somewhat different. The only one of her epistolary novels to be polyphonic and whose central character was a man, *Lettres de Milord Rivers* (*Letters from Lord Rivers to Sir Charles Cardigan, and to Other English Correspondents, While He Resided in France*), was also a philosophical novel in the tradition of the *Lettres persanes* by Montesquieu. The love interest between Rivers and his pupil was given less space than the hero's ideas on contemporary society. Mme Riccoboni's writing career ended with a number of published short stories. With their medieval settings and romantic themes—enchanted forests, failed abductions, brave heroes, fine women, and love ever constant and rewarded—they are less typical of her than of the Romantic movement to follow.

Shortly after the publication of *Les Liaisons dangereuses* in 1782, Mme Riccoboni strongly objected in writing to Laclos's sympathetic portrayal of vice in Mme de Merteuil. Laclos took the trouble to reply, and his long justification of his novel indicates Mme Riccoboni's importance and the weight of her opinion in contemporary society. Her last work, *Histoire de deux jeunes amies* (The History of Two Young Friends), published in 1786, was a totally conventional story (a clandestine marriage, a child lost and then reunited with her father). With her friend Thérèse at her bedside, Mme Riccoboni died in 1792 and was buried at Saint-Eustache, where she had been baptized and married.

MAJOR THEMES

The virtuous orphans and independent widows, honorable suitors and fickle husbands and lovers who people Mme Riccoboni's novels are commonplace in the writings of her contemporaries. The exploration of love, shared or not, but always thwarted or obstructed—the common denominator of all her fiction—is as old as the novel. She brings to these novels, though, a female perspective and sensibility. Her focus is specifically female: a woman's experience viewed through a woman's eyes. As many of the titles indicate, her fiction is centered around women, and the fictional reader to whom they are often addressed is usually female (the real reader probably as well). Men sometimes relate their tales (Ossery tells his in *Lettres de Juliette Catesby*, Sir James, his, in *Histoire de Miss Jenny*, and Lindsey's account of his experiences takes up almost half of *Lettres de Sophie de Vallière*); Mme de Sancerre's correspondent is a man. But their words are always filtered through a female consciousness. Milord Rivers, to be sure, writes his own letters. But his writing is philosophical, and his is not a solo voice. The forms Mme Riccoboni most often chooses—the epistolary novel or the letter-*mémoire*—while typical of the eighteenth century, are those particularly suited to the revelation of female sensibility, as they personalize female experience and adventure. The genre, moreover, is frequently associated with women: *Lettres d'une religieuse portugaise*, Crébillon's *Lettres de la marquise de M*** au comte de R****, and Mme de *Graffigny's Lettres d'une Péruvienne* all center on a single female writer. Even in Mme Riccoboni's third-person narratives (*Histoire du Marquis de Cressy*, *Histoire d'Ernestine*), a female narrator often intervenes to generalize experience and to associate herself with women. The narrator of *Histoire du Marquis de Cressy*, for example, points out that "men could spare themselves most of the trouble they take to take us in were they able to imagine how much the nobility of our ideas makes it easy for them to deceive us" (42).

However, there is a deliberate attempt to write as a woman. But here Mme Riccoboni is not merely following an established tradition—women write letters, women confess. Some women—Mme de *Tencin, for example, in *Mémoires du comte de Comminge*—use a man's voice just as Marivaux and Diderot choose the perspective of the woman. Mme Riccoboni believes that men and women think and act differently and that their behavior is gender-specific. Their characters differ, their stories are individualized, but men as a species show certain traits. Her narrators, as noted, often point out what is innate to males, and the novels themselves become exemplary. Fundamental to male behavior, and at the source of all their other qualities, is their egotism. Their self-satisfaction, as Mme de Sancerre observes, is the mainspring of all their acts (*Lettres de la Comtesse de Sancerre*, 189). Since they are at the mercy of their senses, unable to resist their sexual impulses or even to reconcile them with their feelings (*Lettres de Juliette Catesby*, 96–97, 167), their relationship with women is always self-serving. They pursue women out of vanity and desire, consider them as playthings and objects to be used and then discarded, and will do just about anything to fulfill their fantasies. They plead and threaten, feign love or despair, lie with impunity, pretend with ease. And while, as Mme de Sancerre points out, they rarely conserve a desire that they cannot satisfy (*Lettres de la Comtesse de Sancerre*, 308), as a corollary, desire that is satisfied is rarely preserved. The story of the Marquis de Cressy is typical. Handsome, rich, talented, but overly ambitious, Cressy is flattered by the love of the sixteen-year-old Adélaïde de Bugei. Although reluctant to wed Adélaïde because of her mediocre fortune, he nonetheless courts her, swears eternal love, and even considers marriage. But when he discovers he is loved by a woman of greater wealth and social status, the beautiful widowed Mme de Raisel, he abandons Adélaïde (not, however, without trying to seduce her first), convinces Mme de Raisel of his love and good faith, and marries her. Inconstant as a lover, Cressy is unfaithful as a husband. Piqued by the resistance of his wife's new protégée, the none too admirable Hortense de Berneil, he sets out to conquer her, and takes her as his mistress under the eyes of his unsuspecting wife (who kills herself when she learns of her husband's duplicity and betrayal). Cressy's behavior, moreover, is so representative that those men who do not deceive or take advantage of women are specifically singled out as different from the rest. Clémengis, for example, who loves Ernestine from a distance, has "a character that is unique and maybe even a little strange" (*Histoire d'Ernestine*, 448). Germeuil, who would marry Sophie in spite of her unknown origins, himself points out that he has qualities that distinguish him from ordinary men (*Lettres de Sophie de Vallière*, 189).

Objects, Mme Riccoboni's heroines write and become subjects. The very act of writing gives them an identity and validates their existence. But whether they narrate their stories or have their stories told by a female narrator, women reclaim those intellectual and moral qualities that men have refused them. The heroines are informed, intelligent, thoughtful women, given to reflection. By reflecting on their feelings, they have all acquired, as Juliette says modestly about herself, at least some knowledge of the human heart (*Lettres de Juliette Catesby*, 108). Whether they write in the classically analytical or highly sentimental mode, the heroines are moralists who extrapolate from their experience and offer universal truths. They intersperse aphorisms about men, as we have seen, but also about society and destiny, and, most of all, about the joys, dangers, and illusions of love. Some, like Fanni Butlerd and Juliette Catesby, are women of wit and humor who view the world and themselves with detachment and irony.

As they write or are written about, Mme Riccoboni's heroines show how diametrically opposed they are to men. Women match almost every male "vice" with a female "virtue" (and their virtues make them especially vulnerable to men). For self-interest, they substitute altruism: Sophie would rather give up Germeuil than cause him unhappiness, and Jenny sacrifices the one man she loves to the friend who loves him also. Even the independent Fanni expressly states that she prefers her lover's happiness to her own (*Lettres de Fanni Butlerd*, 12). For male callousness and indifference, there is female compassion and empathy and an unwillingness to cause pain. Mme de Sancerre loves the married M. de Montalais, but refuses to consider a relationship possible only through the death of his ailing wife. Fanni, pressed by Alfred, will not become his mistress once he marries someone else. She cannot be happy at the expense of his future wife. Female compassion, of course, extends to men as well, and women generally pardon men their foibles and faults. Women, as the above examples make clear, are guided not by vanity and ambition, but by their feelings, their principles, and the dictates of their conscience. The sensuality that dominates in the male is not absent in the female. Yet it is far overshadowed by her sentiment and sensibility. Men are incapable of loving as women do, and, as Fanni tells Alfred, "The attachment of a delicate woman is beyond the comprehension of your sex" (*Lettres de Fanni Butlerd*, 156). Juliette wonders if there is a man in the world worthy of the tenderness of a thinking woman ("une femme qui pense bien"; *Lettres de Juliette Catesby*, 16). Their attitude, moreover, announces Mme de Rosemonde's summary of male-female differences in *Les Liaisons dangereuses*: men enjoy the happiness they receive, women, the happiness they give.

The duplicity and bad faith that characterize the male are replaced in the female by an openness and sincerity, due in part to the woman's habit of introspection, but also basic to the sex. As her friend points out to Jenny, "The attractive ingenuousness which characterizes you is not usually shared by men" (*Histoire de Miss Jenny*, 162). And while men trick and deceive women, women trust and believe men, incapable of supposing in men faults they do not find in themselves (*Lettres de Fanni Butlerd*, 184). Women even glorify and idealize men since, in Corneillian fashion, the vices of the lover would degrade the woman herself (*Histoire du Marquis de Cressy*, 43). And finally, while the self-indulgent man gives in to his passions, unable to resist the force of his desire, the woman is a model of self-control and self-restraint. As Juliette observes, "the difficult art of resisting and dominating one's instincts and controlling nature itself" (*Lettres de Juliette Catesby*, 96) is left to what men scornfully consider the weaker sex and which is then, paradoxically, the stronger one. Mme Riccoboni's heroines have their failings, of course, and some do not share the virtues of their sex. But such women are in the minority, and those who act like men are not prized (*Histoire du Marquis de Cressy*, 9).

The consciousness of sexual differences becomes automatically an awareness of sexual inequality, and Mme Riccoboni's heroines constantly protest men's unjust treatment of women. They recognize the biological component in male behavior—men's sexual drive, the childlike state to which their passions reduce them (*Lettres de Juliette Catesby*, 96)—but also see that it is socially sanctioned. Daughters, to be sure, as the Count de Lipari remarks in "Suite de l'Abeille" (Continuation of the Bee), are always disadvantaged by birth in a society that seeks to perpetuate the family name more than wealth or morality (480). Women's education is neglected; men are "brought up," women "bring themselves up" (476). But men are specifically educated, groomed, and permitted by society to do and say what they please. Judged by a different standard, they have no sense of shame. Nothing stands in their way or is beneath them, for nothing humiliates them. Similarly, they stifle any remorse they may feel for the women they betray. Nor, as Fanni notes in words Mme de Merteuil will later echo, do men run any risks. Rejected, the male looks back with vanity, free from the shame that covers the woman who is scorned (*Lettres de Fanni Butlerd*, 20). Never is the man held accountable for the consequences of his sexual behavior. The unmarried woman who is pregnant, Jenny observes, is stigmatized and dishonored. Her lover continues to enjoy public esteem (*Histoire de Miss Jenny*, 196). Men constantly demand of women what they do not ask of themselves. The older man, it is pointed out in *Lettres de Milord Rivers*, can indulge his passion for a younger woman. Not so the older woman for a younger man (370). Men's privileges are women's deprivations.

Worse, men control women through unjust and arbitrary laws. They set themselves up as the guides and protectors of the "timid and weak" sex. Then, with their customary hypocrisy and inconsistency, they urge women to break the very laws they have formulated and take advantage of their "weakness" and "timidity" (*Histoire d'Ernestine*, 472). Men's language is not neutral. As Juliette observes, when women are strong and spirited, they are labeled "inhuman." When they exceed the limits men set for them, they become "unjust" (*Lettres de Juliette Catesby*, 97). Jenny's friend, Milady Anglesey, remarks that women yield to men out of pity and a desire to satisfy them. Once women no longer make them happy, men call this weakness (*Histoire de Miss Jenny*, 300).

Nevertheless, the protests of Mme Riccoboni's heroines remain just protests. Her characters do not attempt to change the existing order. Mme Riccoboni herself, as critics have often noted, does not challenge the social structure and does not offer her heroines the economic or emotional independence she has achieved for herself. In her novels the women see themselves as products of their conditioning and are resigned to their inferior social status. Sophie's friend, Cécile, points out that women are born with sensibility, but are brought up to moderate their desires (*Lettres de Sophie de Vallière*, 257), and Mme de Sancerre suggests that because women are accustomed to repressing their passions ("'nos mouvemens''), the constant constraint may even weaken their force. (Consequently, M. de Montalais, saddled with a wife and unable to declare his love for her, may—by virtue of his sex—suffer more than she [*Lettres de la Comtesse de Sancerre*, 260–61].) Sophie observes the double standard, but notes that women are not entitled to the same indulgence as men. For while men can plead the violence of their passion, restraint and moderation are the female sex's ordinary lot. She concludes that "it is an unequal battle where the obligation of victory is imposed on the weaker and more timid side" (*Lettres de Sophie de Vallière*, 200). Not surprisingly, the notions of obligation and duty are internalized, and Sophie, for example, speaks of what she, as a woman, owes to her sex—obligations that do not allow her to accept financial help from Germeuil (183). The heroines, then, are aware of the inequities but are content simply to note women's moral superiority and to excuse and justify men. The justification of men's weaknesses and foibles, moreover, is part of a general indulgence and tolerance that Mme Riccoboni's heroines show for humanity as a whole. As Henri Coulet points out, Mme Riccoboni is not a pessimistic moralist and does not ask the impossible of either men or women.

By accepting a "female" destiny, and by explaining and excusing and justifying men, Mme Riccoboni's heroines themselves help perpetuate an oppressive social order. Nor could it be otherwise. For the values shared by the heroines and espoused in the novels themselves are the traditional, classic ones of a bourgeois society. Women define themselves in terms of their relationships with men. Many of the novels record the thorny path from love to marriage. Young and handsome men and women, clearly suited for one another, meet and fall in love, but are reluctant or unable to wed. As in the plays of Marivaux, the obstacles are removed or overcome, marriage is assured, and the curtain falls. But the careful reader wonders if the woman has not sacrificed more than she has gained and knows that the novel's happy endings are possible only in a world bound by the conventions of fiction.

Even in those novels that end unhappily, the heroines are determined by the same set of values. Deceived and betrayed by her husband, Mme de Cressy commits suicide because she sees herself as a failure. Life has no meaning, she tells the Marquis, because she has not made him happy (*Histoire du Marquis de Cressy*, 19). (And Adélaïde, whom she has unknowingly supplanted in her husband's affections, herself retires to a convent to bury her sadness and rejection.) Jenny, having given up the man she loves to her friend, leaves both and goes off into exile. She will live independently but unhappily, busying herself with memories that are "sad, but dear" (*Histoire de Miss Jenny*, 437). Even Fanni, the most autonomous of Mme Riccoboni's heroines, subscribes to a similar social code. She does reject the lover who has betrayed her and, by publishing her letters, refuses the traditional notions of female dishonor and male impunity. Women do not have to suffer in silence the injustices and misdeeds of men. Yet, because the letters are presumably anonymous, the vengeance remains private, not public, and it does not camouflage the scorned woman's hurt and pain. Most important, Fanni would like to preserve her love, "to immortalize a passion" in which she found happiness (*Lettres de Fanni Butlerd*, 3), the unique love of her life.

The ambiguity of Fanni's final gesture is characteristic of Mme Riccoboni's novels: love around which each life centers causes pain. As the narrator of *Histoire du Marquis de Cressy* points out, "there are no pains harder to endure than those which love causes us" (38). Love is doomed to failure because the sexes are radically different and because men are unworthy of women. But love is also doomed because it is an illusion created by the woman herself. As Juliette says, we are dazzled, taken in, and seduced by the "brilliance" we ourselves give to "the idol of our heart," and "we madly adore the work of our imagination" (*Lettres de Juliette Catesby*, 111). Because they "write" and have the power to create illusion, Mme Riccoboni's heroines are in some sense the equals of the author herself. Their voices echo her own.

SURVEY OF CRITICISM

Mme Riccoboni was not just a best-selling author whose work was imitated and copied and whose novels spawned many pirated editions. She was also widely admired by eighteenth-century authors and critics. Diderot, Laclos, and Restif de la Bretonne all praised her work, and her novels were consistently well reviewed in the *Année littéraire* and the *Correspondance littéraire* by such discriminating critics as Elie Catherine Fréron and Friederich Melchior Grimm. Contemporaries insisted on the purity, delicacy, and natural quality of her style, and Grimm, for example, considered her to be far superior to other contemporary women writers. She was not totally eclipsed in the nineteenth century, but interest in her was more biographical than literary. Collections of her works were prefaced by biographical introductions, and biographical dictionaries like August Jal's *Dictionnaire critique de biographie et d'histoire* (1872) treat Mme Riccoboni's life. At the beginning of the twentieth century the emphasis was still primarily biographical, and Emily Crosby tried to correct biographical errors (made prevalent by Mme Riccoboni's reluctance to talk about her private life), as well as to study the French and English traditions that influenced her and that she would influence in her turn.

Contemporary scholars and critics, though, have focused on her works. Coulet and Fauchery have included Mme Riccoboni in their studies of the novel, Coulet praising *Histoire de Miss Jenny*, which many critics have dismissed. Ronald Rosbottom studied Mme Riccoboni's continuation of *La Vie de Marianne* in 1971 and concluded that she understood and appreciated Marivaux's reasons for leaving his novel unfinished and left her version unfinished as well. In 1976 James Nicholls published an edition of Mme Riccoboni's letters to Hume, Garrick, and Liston, with an excellent biographical and critical edition. In 1976 also appeared the first full-length study of the author in more than fifty years. In an indispensable book, Joan Stewart emphasized the epistolary convention and technique, especially their use in *Lettres de Fanni Butlerd*, for Stewart Mme Riccoboni's best novel. Stewart also published a critical edition of *Fanni Butlerd* in 1979. In 1983 *Lettres de Milady Juliette Catesby*, prefaced by Sylvain Menant, was published by Desjonquères, and Olga Cragg's critical edition of *Histoire du Marquis de Cressy* appeared in 1989.

There are, finally, a number of studies of Mme Riccoboni's feminism. Andrée Demay's very brief book (1977) focuses particularly on *Lettres de la Comtesse de Sancerre* (for this author a reflection of Mme Riccoboni's talent at its best) and her treatment of marriage. For her Mme Riccoboni is a feminist who claims for the woman ''rights which she has been denied . . . education, respect, the equitable judgment of society, and, above all, the right to choose her own destiny'' (56). Arlette André (1980) observes that Mme Riccoboni does not wish to change society but simply to change the attitude toward women. She would like to see a kind of "moral contract" between men and women, so that the woman would no longer be treated like an inferior ("une mineure"). Janet Todd (1980) includes two of Mme Riccoboni's novels in her treatment of female friendship and offers a perceptive reading of *Histoire du Marquis de Cressy* as a study of female relationships. Mme Riccoboni is representative of eighteenth-century authors in the types of friendships she portrays. Colette Piau (1984) considers Mme Riccoboni's adaptations of male writers (Marivaux and Fielding) and male authors' versions of her works. She concludes that women's discourse differs from men's not because of a sexual dichotomy (masculine "reason" versus female "sensibility"), but because of women's "individual biological, psychological, cultural and social experience, confronted with the collective history of their sex" (385).

Clearly Mme Riccoboni deserves a place in the literary canon. In her best novels, with their tightly constructed analyses of female passion, she is a worthy successor to Mme de *Lafayette. The proliferation of feminist articles shows also her relevance for our time.

NOTE

1. *Histoire du Marquis de Cressy* in *Oeuvres complètes*, 6 vols. (Paris: Foucault, 1818), 64. I have quoted from this edition for all of the novels except *Lettres de Mistriss Fanni Butlerd* and *Lettres de Milady Juliette Catesby*, where I have used the modern editions. All translations are my own.

BIBLIOGRAPHY

Works by Mme Riccoboni

Oeuvres complètes. 6 vols. Paris: Foucault, 1818.

Modern Editions

Lettres de Mistriss Fanni Butlerd. Ed. Joan Hinde Stewart. Geneva: Droz, 1979.
Lettres de Milady Juliette Catesby à Milady Henriette Campley, son amie. Preface by Sylvain Menant. Paris: Desjonquères, 1983.
"Suite de Marianne." In Pierre Carlet de Marivaux, *La Vie de Marianne*. Ed. Frédéric Deloffre. Paris: Garnier, 1963.
Histoire du Marquis de Cressy. Ed. Olga B. Cragg. *Studies on Voltaire and the Eighteenth Century* 266 (1989): 5–123.

Translations of Mme Riccoboni

The History of the Marquis de Cressy. London: L. Pottinger, 1759.
Letters from Juliet, Lady Catesby, to Her Friend, Lady Henrietta Campley. Trans. Frances Brooke. 2nd ed. London: R. and J. Dodsley, 1760.

The History of Miss Jenny Salisbury. London: T. Becket and P. A. De Hondt, 1764.

The Continuation of the Life of Marianne. To Which Is Added The History of Ernestina, with Letters and Other Miscellaneous Pieces. London: T. Becket and P. A. De Hondt, 1766.

Letters from the Countess de Sancerre, to Count de Nancé, Her Friend. London: T. Becket and P. A. De Hondt, 1767.

Letters from Elizabeth Sophia de Valiere to Her Friend Louisa Hortensia de Canteleu. 2 vols. Trans. Mr. Maceuen. Dublin: J. Potts, J. Williams, T. Walker and C. Jenkins, booksellers, 1772.

Letters from Lord Rivers to Sir Charles Cardigan, and to Other English Correspondents, While He Resided in France. Trans. Percival Stockdale. London: T. Becket, 1778.

The History of Christina, Princess of Swabia; and of Eloisa de Livarot. 2 vols. London: J. Stockdale, 1784.

Studies of Mme Riccoboni

André, Arlette. "Le Féminisme chez Mme Riccoboni." *Studies on Voltaire and the Eighteenth Century* 193 (1980): 1988–95.

Coulet, Henri. *Le Roman jusqu'à la Révolution.* Paris: Armand Colin, 1967.

Crosby, Emily A. *Une Romancière oubliée, Mme Riccoboni.* Paris, 1924. Rpt. Geneva: Slatkine Reprints, 1970.

Demay, Andrée. *Marie-Jeanne Riccoboni ou De la pensée féministe chez une romancière du XVIIIe siècle.* Paris: La Pensée universelle, 1977.

Fauchery, Pierre. *La Destinée féminine dans le roman européen du dix-huitième siècle 1713–1807. Essai de gynécomythie romanesque.* Paris: Armand Colin, 1972.

Nicholls, James C., ed. *Mme Riccoboni's Letters to David Hume, David Garrick and Sir Robert Liston, 1764–1783. Studies on Voltaire and the Eighteenth Century* 149 (1976).

Piau, Colette. "L'Ecriture féminine? A Propos de Marie-Jeanne Riccoboni." *Dix-Huitième Siècle* 16 (1984): 369–85.

Rosbottom, Ronald C. "Parody and Truth in Mme Riccoboni's Continuation of *La Vie de Marianne.*" *Studies on Voltaire and the Eighteenth Century* 81 (1971): 163–75.

Stewart, Joan Hinde. *The Novels of Mme Riccoboni.* Chapel Hill, N.C.: North Carolina Studies in the Romance Languages and Literatures: Essays; vol. no. 8, 1976.

Todd, Janet. *Women's Friendship in Literature.* New York: Columbia University Press, 1980.

CHRISTIANE ROCHEFORT
(1917–   )

Micheline Herz

BIOGRAPHY

Christiane Rochefort was born on July 17, 1917, in a remarkably ambivalent quarter of Paris. The fourteenth arrondissement had a motley population, mostly artisan and working class, with a scattering of aristocrats, plutocrats, and ladies who walked shampooed poodles. It supported the Commune in 1871, Boulanger in the 1880s, Vichy during the last war, and de Gaulle afterwards—a district, in other words, of the right and left; a fertile seedbed for a writer.

Yet the first years of her life she spent in the province of Limousin before she returned to the capital at the age of five. Like most people of her generation, she regarded her childhood as a period of repression rather than growth. Her first school was located on rue Durouchoux; her second was the lycée Fénelon.

She made an "appearance" at the Sorbonne, where one class on psychology provided enough inducement for her never to return. Despite this, she did manage to develop a grounding in ethnology and psychology as well as an acquaintance with psychiatry. She was also apprenticed to a painter, and she tried her hand at sculpture. Music was another area of interest; she became something of an afficionado in the field.

Writing, however, was an early calling. Her need to earn a living prevented her for a long time from publishing, at least fiction. She worked in offices, became a newspaper correspondent, and authored a number of articles on film criticism. She claims to have memorized the telephone number of every director, producer, and actor she dealt with. At the Cannes film festival, she stuffed her head with the names of 800 newsmen, which she promptly forgot the morning after. Her most affectionate memory of this period was working for Henri Lan-glois of the Paris Cinémathèque.

Georges Lambrich of Grasset accepted her first novel, *Le Repos du guerrier*

(*Warrior's Rest*). An instant success, it sold 600,000 copies, putting her on the best-seller list. She received the Nouvelle Vague prize for her efforts.

Her next novel, *Les Petits Enfants du siècle* (Children of Our Century) has become a classic. It also earned her an award, the Roman Populiste prize. The book demonstrates a caustic disdain for modern French architecture, a feeling one finds in most of her works. It is a very funny book, though her jaunts into demography are not the most accurate descriptions of reality.

Since 1958, Christiane Rochefort has produced a steady stream of works. Her last book, *La Porte du fond* (The Door at the End), got her the Medicis prize in 1988. Her parable, *Archaos*, the story of a simple, delightful, sensual life told through a myriad of symbols, is set in a country under the control of women and children. It is lyrical, solid, and earthy. It is also rather long.

She has written three essays: one on writing, *C'est bizarre l'écriture* (The Strange Business of Writing, 1970); one on the condition of children, *Les Enfants d'abord* (Children First, 1976)—a fundamental statement on her interest in this area; and one, *Le Monde est comme deux chevaux* (The World as Two Horses, 1984), on the dark prospects of the human race.

She has also published a somewhat delirious account of her life, *Ma Vie revue et corrigée par l'auteur* (My Life, as Reviewed and Corrected by the Author), based on recorded conversations with Maurice Chavardes, and has translated with Rachel Misrahi John Lennon's *In His Own Write* (*En flagrant délire*) and two works by Amos Kenan, *Holocauste II*, and *La Route d'Ein Harod*.

The list of her literary forbears—at least those she admits—is rather eclectic: Friedrich Nietzsche, Cervantes, William Faulkner, Franz Kafka, Virginia Woolf, James Joyce; in France, Boris Vian, Robert Desnos; Diderot and Laclos from the eighteenth century; *Christine de Pizan from the Middle Ages. Her disdain for the West derives from René Guénon and Frantz Fanon. She admires modern American writers such as Joseph Heller and Norman Mailer. In psychiatry, David Laing is a favorite.

She once spoke Spanish, Italian, German, and Hebrew, which she has apparently forgotten, and she is fluent in English. She loves traveling and has visited many countries. She holds a special place in her heart for Quebec and its rich language. Brittany is one of the corners of France she loves best.

Rochefort is a forthright citizen and has been involved in a number of battles with French administrators and bureaucrats: banks, government authorities, the office for the redevelopment (i.e., demolition) of old buildings. She knows a lot about foreclosure, objects to organ banks, and has little sympathy for institutionalized medicine and the people who represent it, the doctors. She enjoys good food and good company. She was married for four years but gave that up to return to celibacy, pens, and paper. She has appeared many times on television, most notably on Bernard Pivot's *Apostrophes*.

MAJOR THEMES

Christiane Rochefort is an iconoclast. All her works exhibit a common trait, the abhorrence of respected hierarchies and the indiscriminate use of power. Her writing in general is a passionate plea for the right to be different, to deviate from the norm; it is an appeal for respect for those that are oppressed, whether as children, as women, as workers, or as sexual misfits. For her, the consumer society is a monster that goads people into buying useless commodities and prompts needs that can never be satisfied. Her works represent a permanent battle with urban spoliation: the high-rises built of reinforced concrete, the cemetery of cars, the massacre of nature: these are the threads of the Rochefort tweed, thick, rich, and highly colorful, which, seen as a whole, makes such a vivid impression. But in every one of her narratives, an analyst might tear it apart and peer into the heart of the fabric, the fibers laid bare.

Consider what she has to say about children. *Les Enfants d'abord*, a philosophical pamphlet written as a companion to her novel *Encore heureux qu'on va vers l'été* (Luckily Summer Will Come Soon), studies the very young. Children are born in a violent atmosphere, welcomed with a spanking the second they get their first squint of light. Family control turns them into specimens willed by a patriarchal society. Children are deprived of the right to speak on their own behalf until they reach their majority. The law puts children in the position of a minority and, despite a charter adopted by the United Nations, they continue to be subjected to all the violence of the adult world. They are manipulated and reified by those who are bigger and stronger, by those society designates as more important. Children constitute an oppressed class, and the parent-child relationship is rotten from the very beginning. The body of a child is handled, imprisoned in clothes, forced to adopt a subservient demeanor, compulsorily vaccinated, jailed in a classroom where teaching is often nothing more than brainwashing. Children can be abused physically or mentally, and they have no recourse.

Even love is adulterated. Parents and children practice sentimental blackmail on one another. Parents, in the name of love, murder the child's mind. A girl child is doubly alienated. She has to slave not only for her parents but for her male siblings as well. The right to a normal and happy sexuality is also forbidden fruit—not unlike Eve.

The novel that led to this essay, *Encore heureux qu'on va vers l'été*, deals with twenty-five children who have escaped from school. They walk in small groups toward the sea. It is a fable, half realistic, half dream. The children rely on chance circumstance; they steal a little here, a little there; they are protected by "good" adults. They show their ingenuity, their love for and affinity with nature, their common sense—qualities of which those responsible for bringing them up proved sublimely ignorant. The children baffle the police charged with recapturing them. This book is a song to childhood, beauty, to communion with nature, the earth, to a *joie de vivre* unthwarted by the patriarchy from which innocent beings have managed a timely escape.

Childhood as a state of grace if untouched by the powers that be is a recurrent theme in Rochefort's works. Here is Jocelyne, in *Les Petits Enfants du siècle*, fighting against the burden of domestic tasks. She makes her escape through homework, then through friendship with a migrant Italian stonemason. Rochefort's most recent book, *La Porte du fond*, details a father's crafty effort to molest his daughter and the daughter's opposition. It is a war that lasts seven years, unfortunately not an unusual situation. The main protagonist in the novel gradually becomes aware of companions in similar distress. Like her, they are too traumatized to reveal their ordeal all at once and, instead, make only odd references. They are overcome by a sense of powerlessness, a forced silence, bound before their "boss," the patriarchal beast who robbed them of their innocence.

The child becomes an adolescent. In *La Porte du fond*, we find a narrative that shifts from the present back to the past and forward into the future in a seesaw rhythm. *Une Rose pour Morrison* (A Rose for Morrison) is a paean to youth and young love pitted against a death-dealing society. Children and adolescents unite in an odd kind of anticipation of the events of May 1968. *Printemps au parking* (Blossom on the Tarmac), one of Christiane Rochefort's most interesting works, is the story of a runaway. Christophe, not yet eighteen, is the target of a police hunt that places him under the threat of arbitrary detention. He leaves home because his father objected to his sitting in front of the family television—without the set being turned on. Christophe has a number of adventures in Paris, the most significant being his encounter with Thomas and his pals. Thomas hates Western values, a total quagmire in his view. Not that things are better elsewhere; the bourgeoisie might be the equivalent of death, but so are Soviet Russia and China. Modern man and woman are doomed if they do not make an effort to rediscover *la vraie vie*, to refute stifling ideologies and batter down their personal little boxes. A love between Christophe and Thomas develops. It will act as a catalyst, giving both young men a better sense of self. Atomic energy, threatening wars, concrete buildings—such a lot of battles to wage! Christophe now has a purpose; he will return to school, to home. With the help of another friend, Nicolas, he decides to fan the flames of revolt and revolution by developing an intellect that will shake the mercantile order. Rochefort gives each companion a role. Christophe becomes the protagonist for the working class, Thomas is the intellectual, and Benoît, an important character, is made to play the part of the rich. Benoît is nevertheless convinced of the necessity of change; the victims of patriarchy must unite and allow no social division to stand in their way.

Young women provide another theme in Rochefort's novels. She knows their oppression inside out. *Le Repos du guerrier* tells of the quest, or rather fall, of an upper-class do-gooder, Geneviève, who discovers that sex is fun (though she mistakes it for romantic love). She meets Renaud, her partner, while saving his life by accident. The couple is caught up in a process of creeping corruption. From the very start Renaud is an alcoholic. Now, with the aid of Geneviève's money, he drowns in the stuff. Finally Geneviève becomes sick with tuberculosis and has to go to the hospital. It is a serious loss for Renaud, whose habit of tormenting her has become, like his bottles, something he cannot do without. The narrative stops with Geneviève pregnant and married, with her husband in a detoxification clinic.

There really is no end. The reader is left to imagine the rest of the story. It is a bit like atomic warfare. Renaud's character resembles a personality after the bomb attack, faced with the futility of attempting anything creative in the quiet dusk of radioactive glow. There is a hint that his real love was for a man; it is an androgynous young creature who eventually lures him back to art, music, and the appreciation of nature. Geneviève's child, created through no will of his, prompts Renaud to return to the everyday world. But his ideas are unchanged.

Every now and again the voice of the narrator, like a Greek chorus, intervenes to warn the heroine of the dangers of love. Sex is a pleasure, but do not confuse it with anything else. A woman should not be hypocritical; she should not lie to herself and abandon her personality simply because her partner strikes the right notes. Sexual pleasure is sexual pleasure, nothing more, nothing less. Romance has hidden it in lush garlands. Straitlaced education, to which all women have been exposed, has led them to fall prey to their own unsatisfied desires. It has also caused them to submit and deny their own sense of self. Complacency is the trap, and women are constantly falling into it. They have a bitter choice: either swallow their partner, like a praying mantis, or be swallowed.

Le Repos du guerrier, when published, was considered by many to be pornographic. This is no longer the case. It is rather a study of extremes where both protagonists, male and female, retain a textual emblematic value.

Love is also the undoing of Josyane in *Les Petits Enfants du siècle*. It will take her to Sarcelle, a glamourized version of the H.L.M. (low-rent housing project), and to marriage. She is of course pregnant, and her partner, Philippe (which in Greek means "horselover"), would have preferred a virgin filly.

It is another Philippe in *Les Stances à Sophie* who plays the role of temptor, charming his victim into marriage. Philippe, an executive in grey flannels who has something of a Pygmalion complex, rescues the nonconformist Céline from her wandering ways. He criticizes her looks, her hair, her clothes, her behavior. But because he is a good lover—at least before marriage—he manages to persuade Céline to become his wife. Plunged into stifling yuppie surroundings, Céline begins a war with the established order, which daily confronts her own sensibilities and tastes. Fashions dictate consumption, and the manufacturers dictate the fashions. Céline finds herself acting like a robot, catering to her husband's friends and professional acquaintances. She cooks, she arranges the seating, she lights cigars. "Be pretty and silent" is the husband's motto. It gets a little boring. Finally she finds relief in a close friendship with the neighbor's wife, Julia, who has perfected the art of beguilement, exploiting her husband's foibles as a kind of counter to her own exploitation. Both women hate bourgeois values. They also hate the defacing of the earth by highly placed civil servants. Julia, however, is lazy, while Céline makes continual efforts to express her discontent. Philippe ridicules and belittles everything she does. During an escape to Italy she rediscovers physical ecstasy, a long-lost memory with Philippe. She starts writing. Philippe gets involved in right-wing politics, and Céline decides to leave him to his falsehoods. In the end, despite earnest professions of love from Philippe's brothers and sisters, Céline decides to live alone. She will earn her own keep. Men are friends first, lovers second. *Les Stances à Sophie* is an indignant but funny diatribe against technocracy, capitalism, the depletion of nature, bourgeois beliefs, bourgeois order, and the restrictions imposed on freely expressed personality. It presents an even clearer picture than *Le Repos du guerrier* of the misleading nature of words of love. It is also a victory hymn. Céline Rhodes has scattered the ashes of Philippe Aignan's wife; she has won back her name and her identity; the marital nightmare has made her a wiser woman.

So love is a rather hazardous occupation. But Rochefort sees a healthy side to it too. There are blissful images in her work, such as in *Encore heureux qu'on va vers l'été* or *Une Rose pour Morrison*, of children's first explorations of sensuality, of breast-feeding mothers and other uninhibited activities in communal groups. Love cannot be fitted into categories. Homosexuality has got itself an undeserved pejorative label. In *Les Stances à Sophie*, as already noted, Céline finds solace in her relationship with Julia, and Stéphanie is infatuated with Céline.

The relationship between Christophe and Thomas in *Printemps au parking* defies all categorization. To begin with, it is a perfectly "normal" friendship from a social angle, but then it becomes a passionate affair. After some hesitation, and a great deal of guilt, they finally follow through on their feelings: passion, joy, empathy, tenderness. Their emotions press them into political action. There is no homoerotic sex here that, from society's point of view, would lead to division, separation, a classification of their relationship into its parts; this is a total friendship, which frees them, and, they hope, will free others.

Rochefort thus presents us with an ethics of desire that could be contrasted with more conventional, worn-out notions of love. The only form of deviancy for her is the over-expectation of what sensuality can bring (thus destroying joy), the mutual manipulations that take place within a couple, and the cannibalization of relationships. Christiane Rochefort, like those sixteenth-century writers who took pleasure in the instinctive knowledge of the body, rejects the intellectual game that distorts desire into an exercise in subjection.

The point is taken up in one of her most baffling and fascinating novels, *Quand tu vas chez les femmes* (Now It's Time for the Girls). As in *Le Repos du guerrier*, Rochefort borrows her title from Nietzsche. This work is another descent into hell, this time in the company of a teacher and a psychoanalyst. After a year's absence from teaching, spent on a field trip exploring the grounds for a philosophical treatise, Bertrand makes his return to Paris. Here he pays prostitutes to be beaten and humiliated. They find the task a bit wearing, but then they need the money. In the end they stuff a riding whip in his bum and abandon him, tortured, with his colors flying. This proves a source of great inspiration. With his masochistic friends he founds a fellowship of tails, in which each member gets a chance to heap (and poke) abomination upon the others.

But Bertrand makes a poor masochist. He has a low tolerance of real physical pain and, worse, he is racked by a conscience. In the meantime he has met the well-named Petra, the maiden of stone. Bertrand selects her to act as his master; she acquiesces to his wishes, but not according to plan. She tolerates his presence, lets him continue his hideous games, but manages to ignore him entirely. He does not wring an ounce of pity or sympathy from her. He simply serves as a key to a world unknown to her. He is drenched in his own moral despair. His prayers for pain are handsomely rewarded, but the pains are gnawing, stabbing moral pains. Petra destroys his career. She turns up in the amphitheatre where he is expounding on his latest research and publicly refutes him. Tongue-tied, he abandons the idea that knowledge can act as a crutch in life; he stands witness to his own intellectual demise. All he has left is the laughter of his own executioner.

Bertrand's martyrdom is accompanied by the crude and revolting images of his peculiar companions. They are depicted in detail, a little Bosch here, a bit of Breugel there. One cannot help empathizing with this antihero, an unloved doctor's son whose desire has drawn him into a whirlwind of anguish. He is another victim of patriarchy. He has desire, but an apocalyptic desire of dark dimensions.

Two themes emerge from all this. On the one hand, Christiane Rochefort wants to disturb us with an elaborate description of the loathsome events that accompany the fall of the main character, half male, half neuter. In a sense, we stand outside the strict narrative of gender, for Rochefort, like Genet, is forced to transgress the writing of her own sex in the same manner as her leading character is forced into being a traitor to his own kind; it is a victim's treason.

On the other hand, if the narrative is the fable of a "he" who is not quite a "he" (who has accidentally fathered two children), the women characters turn out to be the victors in the text. Petra, unmoved by Bertrand, is interested in another woman, Edwine. She takes up her defense in a Rabelaisian battle of words. The prostitutes, unscathed, come across as rather ordinary women. It is Bertrand's wife, Malaure, who then appropriates the narrative, instead of Bertrand; she starts writing. Bertrand is left without words. To the extent that he is a female character—his odd position within his society and his so-called perversions are responsible for this—Rochefort treats his transgressions with generosity. To the degree that he acts as an exploiter of women, using his wife's lack of selfishness to his own ends, condemning his daughter to lesbianism, associating with people like Kuntz-Lopez (who destroys the landscape and builds rabbit hutches for the poor), and betraying his own liberal beliefs, Rochefort's style becomes harsh and male. Bertrand the cook, an apron tied round his naked bum, has been transformed into a slave, but he is not a woman. It is a textual irony which permits the character to survive.

The pet peeves of Christiane Rochefort are, without doubt, senseless urbanism and urbanization. The modern architect is present in practically all her books. The architect's work is full of illegalities because he feeds upon the needs for shelter of the working class. French modern architecture and urbanization—they go hand in hand—create an order that fragments social life. Nature is defaced. Human communication becomes impossible. People sink into a marsh of sadness. Even the well-to-do suffer in their decorated barracks. Technocratic civilization exacerbates the relationship of dependency between the dominant rich and the dominated poor, the dominant husband and the dominated wife, the dominant Judeo-Christian system and its victimized families and children. Modern French urbanism is the killer of beauty and also the killer of desire. Whether it is low-income housing or richer estates, the result is the same: it destroys the individual and warps the group, creating a dehumanized environment for everybody. It is not surprising that men's fantasies and aggressions concentrate on the car, a machine of escape and of death in a life perverted by phallocrats.

Christiane Rochefort has established herself as a woman writer. But is she a feminist? She can certainly be regarded as a defender of women inasmuch as they can be considered an oppressed collective group. Her work is a constant attack on patriarchy. It is also a continual warning to women to maintain their independence, to free themselves from their own desires and to avoid the dom-inator/dominated polarization that is common throughout society. However, if women as primary protagonists play a major part in her fiction, her males, as part of the narrative configuration, are also a textual success, whether they are exploiters or not. Some of her male characters are presented with sympathy; some of her female characters are not. Any type of relationship, as long as it is not manipulative, has a place in Rochefort's fictional universe. Rochefort hates sectarian theories; the ''ism'' of feminism has, at times, disconcerted her. First and foremost, she is a writer with a ''she'' that lies hidden within her artistic consciousness. Her literature feeds on the symbolical and a unisex imagination.

Christiane Rochefort uses every tool of the writing trade. She tells a tale where, as we have seen, characters are built in action. Even in situations of resistance they are of primary importance. She plays with time and temporality, weighs description and narrative, criss-crosses points of view. She has a com-mand of indirect style and uses the technique to its fullest. Her dialogues are always lively, scintillating with life and humor. Irony, subtle or not, is one of her favorite devices. Although she does not want to present a ''message,'' and even if her surroundings are quite utopian, she offers plural meanings to the reader.

On the surface at least, Christiane Rochefort's written language appears as a spoken language, but it would be more accurate to describe it as a meticulous ''written spoken language,'' with special attention given to rhythm, pauses, crescendo, and the flow of sentences. From a historical point of view one might argue that she borrows from various language "strata." There is an anarchy in her style of writing. In this sense (not of course political) she resembles Léon Daudet or Louis-Ferdinand Céline. But the latter writers were ill at ease with the feminine element in their writing—Céline, for example, was led into a rather disagreeable form of narcissism—while Christiane Rochefort manages to break the mold of the classical and authoritative French by inventing a language play. *Mulier ludens!*

SURVEY OF CRITICISM

There is no major work presenting an overall view of Christiane Rochefort as a writer. Studies dedicated to women often include lengthy discussions of a single book by her or a critical elaboration of one or many of her themes. Anne Offrir, for example, in *Regards féminins*, offers a thorough textual elucidation of *Les Stances à Sophie*. Christiane Rochefort is placed in the company of Simone de *Beauvoir and Claire Etcherelli. As in a lot of modern analysis, the value of the study of women as an instrument to perceive cultural and linguistic contexts is stressed, with special attention devoted to language.

Numerous articles in English and some in French offer interesting, even brilliant, points of view on specific aspects of Christiane Rochefort's work. Or they might revisit a work that is already well known. Isabelle de Courtivron reinterprets characters in *Le Repos du guerrier*. In "L'Amour et le group," a study of seriality, of closed and open groups as opposed to love, I have pointed out possible parallels with the works of Wilhelm Reich and Raoul Vaneigem. Mary Jean Green, Lynn Higgins, and Marianne Hirsch present an imaginative comparison between Godard's film *Deux ou trois choses que je sais d'elle* and *Les Petits Enfants du siècle*. Other articles are really interviews, which are most useful as insights into a writer known for contradictory statements. Green, Hirsch, and Higgins provide, in addition to their interview with Christiane Rochefort, an interpretation of all Rochefort's novels to 1979, including an especially enlightening and skillful questioning of Rochefort's utopias, her attitudes toward French misogyny, and her quest for female scripted identity. Another interview with Cécile Arsène pivots around literature and homosexuality and the part played by homosexual writing in the female text.

Of immense value to anyone interested in understanding Christiane Rochefort's language is Monique Crochet's meticulous study of the novelist's use of diction and lexical inventions. Although limited to *Une Rose Pour Morrison*, Monique Crochet's work is a model for a linguistic study of all Rochefort's oeuvre. It provides a fascinating focus on Rochefort's creativity and tells us much about the link Rochefort establishes between written language and oral words (*langage* and *parole* in the Saussurian sense).

BIBLIOGRAPHY

Works by Christiane Rochefort

Le Démon des pinceaux. Paris: Les Oeuvres Libres, 1953.
Le Fauve et le rouge-gorge. Paris: Les Oeuvres Libres, 1955.
Le Repos du guerrier. Paris: Grasset, 1958.
Les Petits Enfants du siècle. Paris: Grasset, 1961. Trans. with Rachel Misrahi. *En Flagrant Délire.* Paris: Laffout, 1965. Trans. of *In His Own Write* by John Lennon.
Les Stances á Sophie. Paris: Grasset, 1966.
Une Rose pour Morrison. Paris: Grasset, 1966.
Printemps au parking. Paris: Grasset, 1969.
C'est bizarre l'écriture. Paris: Grasset, 1970.
Archaos ou le jardin étincelant. Paris: Grasset, 1972.
Encore heureux qu'on va vers l'été. Paris: Grasset, 1975.
Les Enfants d'abord. Paris: Grasset, 1976.
Ma Vie revue et corrigée par l'auteur. Paris: Stock, 1978.
Quand tu vas chez les femmes. Paris: Grasset, 1982.
Le Monde est comme deux chevaux. Paris: Grasset, 1984.
La Porte du fond. Paris: Grasset, 1988.

Translations of Christiane Rochefort

Warrior's Rest. Trans. Lowell Bair. New York: MacKay, 1959.

Studies of Christiane Rochefort

Arsène, Cècile. Trans. Marilyn Schuster. "The Privilege of Consciousness." In *Homosexualities and French Literature: Cultural Contexts/Critical Texts.* Ed. George Stambolian and Elaine Marks. Ithaca: Cornell University Press, 1979. 101–13.
Cordero, Anne D. "Effects of Urbanization in the Novels of Christiane Rochefort." In *Faith of a (Woman) Writer.* Ed. Alice Kessler-Harris and William McBrien. Westport, Conn.: Greenwood Press, 1988. 83–93.
Courtivron, Isabelle de. "*Le Repos du guerrier*: New Perspectives on Rochefort's Warrior." *L'Esprit Créateur* II (1979): 23–35.
Crochet, Monique Y. "La Création lexicale dans *Une Rose pour Morrison.*" *Modern Philology* 83 (1986): 379–394.
———. "Entretien avec Christiane Rochefort." *French Review* 54 (1981): 428–35.
Garscha-Weir, Brigitte. "*Les Stances à Sophie* von Christiane Rochefort: zur Verknupfung fiktionaler und nicht-fiktionaler Texte im Französischunterricht der Sekundarstufe." *Literatur im Fremdsprachenunterricht. Beiträge zur Theorie des Literaturunterrichts und zur Praxis der Literaturvermittlung im Fremdsprachenunterricht.* Frankfurt: Diesterweg, 1977. 125–41.
Green, Mary Jean, Lynn Higgins, and Marianne Hirsch. "Rochefort and Godard: Two or Three Things about Prostitution." *French Review* 52 (1973): 440–48.
Herz, Micheline. "Le Groupe et l'amour dans l'oeuvre de Christiane Rochefort." *Perspectives on Contemporary Literature* II (1977): 52–57.

Hirsch, Marianne, Mary Jean Green, and Lynn Anthony Higgins. "An Interview with Christiane Rochefort." *L'Esprit Créateur* II (1979): 107–20.

McDermott, Helen Bates. "Christiane Rochefort's *Ma Vie revue et corrigée par l'auteur*: autobiographie à la dérive." *French Literature Series* 12 (1985): 188–92.

Offrir, Anne. *Regards féminins, condition féminine et création littéraire: Simone de Beauvoir, Christiane Rochefort, Claire Etcherelli.* Paris: Denoël, 1976.

Verthuy, Mair. "De la conscience de classe á la conscience de caste." *Atlantis* 9 (1983): 59–67.

MARIE JEANNE PHLIPON (MANON) ROLAND DE LA PLATIÈRE (1754–1793)

Renee Winegarten

BIOGRAPHY

The deeply studious and immensely gifted Marie-Jeanne (Manon) Phlipon who, as Madame Roland, was to become the moving spirit of the Girondins during the French Revolution, deliberately chose not to be "a woman author." This decision was due not to lack of energy and courage, with which she was liberally endowed, but to deference toward social convention instilled in her by her devout mother. She would uphold the traditional view of woman's subordinate place and role as consecrated by Jean-Jacques Rousseau in his depiction of Sophie in *Emile*, while subverting it by her own activities. She might study in private to her heart's content, write for her own pleasure and instruction or, later, in order to assist her husband in his career, but publish under her own name, never! Ironically, it was not until she found herself in prison during the Terror, under imminent threat of death, that she could give vent freely to her joy in writing and devote herself to composing the remarkable *Mémoires* that were to contribute greatly to her posthumous fame.

Manon Phlipon, born in Paris in modest circumstances, described lovingly her early years in the capital. Both her parents doted on their only surviving child. Her father, then a thriving master engraver, taught her drawing and later took her to art exhibitions. A reputable music tutor claimed that Manon could, with further training, follow a career as a musician. However, her mother did not wish her to become a professional artist and insisted that her accomplishments should include more mundane domestic pursuits suitable to her sex. It is no wonder, though, that Manon grew to possess a keen sense of her own importance, talent, rightness, and value.

At eight or nine, so she averred, she was reading Plutarch's *Lives* in translation, a work that gave her a love of high deeds of patriotism and led her to consider herself a republican. At eleven, however, she expressed a desire to be a nun. Her parents tactfully proposed a year of schooling in a convent. Among her fellow pupils were two well-to-do sisters from Amiens, Henriette and Sophie Cannet. Sophie became her special friend, and they were to correspond for many years.

Soon, no more was heard of Manon's religious vocation. On leaving the convent in 1766, the girl went to stay with her grandmother, who had served as governess to scions of the aristocracy and was keen to show off her accomplished granddaughter to her former employer. Manon was outraged at the haughty and humiliating manner in which this indolent lady treated her aged, respectable grandmother. It was apparently her first serious feeling of plebeian resentment at privilege and injustice, to be followed by deep indignation when, on another occasion, she found herself being entertained in the servants' quarters instead of with her hosts.

Meanwhile, Manon was reading everything she could find, including learned works of divinity, philosophy, and history. Gravely, she made summaries and personal observations. Probing intellectuals of the eighteenth-century Enlightenment, like Voltaire or Helvétius, reinforced her growing doubts about the tenets of the Catholic faith (though she continued to attend church, but only for the "good order of society"). For pleasure she read Cervantes's *Don Quixote* and the lofty dramas of Corneille. Among her favorite writers was the Scottish poet James Thomson, melancholy lover of nature, virtue, and liberty. She herself could indulge a melancholy strain that found in rustic nature something like Thomson's "elegant sufficiency" and quiet repose. Later, she would speak of her imaginative sensibility, her "wandering and romantic imagination," her "romantic mind." (She could find the word "romantic" in Thomson.)

The sudden death of her mother in 1775 left Manon utterly distraught. To try to wean her from her grief, a well-wisher presented her with a copy of Jean-Jacques Rousseau's novel *La Nouvelle Héloïse*. It proved a revelation, for there she found the perfect expression of her own innermost feelings. How different was Rousseau's heroine Julie from his Sophie! Passionately in love with her tutor Saint-Preux, Julie is transformed—after marriage to the rationalist Wolmar, older than herself—into the perfect wife and mother. Here was a trio of rare noble souls, and Julie presented Manon (as well as innumerable readers then and later) with a fascinating role model. Indeed, such was Manon's devotion to the great philosopher that she tried to visit him, only to be turned away by Thérèse, his mistress.

With the death of her mother, Manon's position became equivocal. She kept house for her father, who was in the process of ruining himself (and depleting her small dowry) through speculation and gambling. Certain cultivated middle-aged gentlemen of rank who admired her talents took her under their wing. One gave her free access to his library and introduced her to public gatherings of noted literati, including women of letters. Another discussed with her his travels in India and America (in whose struggle for independence she would take a lively interest). Various suitors presented themselves: one even engaged her feelings, but all of them eventually proved to be unsuitable or unworthy. Then, in 1776, her friends in Amiens, the Cannet sisters, gave an acquaintance of theirs a letter of introduction to her. In this way Manon met Jean-Marie Roland, a highly conscientious inspector of industry and commerce appointed to their region.

There followed one of the strangest courtships ever recorded. Roland was a bachelor, some twenty years older than Manon. Though impecunious, he was a man of higher social position than her own: his family belonged to the gentry and owned a house and vineyards near Lyons. Moreover, he had acquired some reputation as an expert in his field and would later publish his important three-volume dictionary of manufactures, arts, and trades—part of the continuation of the famous *Encyclopédie* of Diderot and d'Alembert. A high-handed man of irritable temperament, austere in manner, Roland appealed to Manon for his learning and integrity, in short, as a kind of Wolmar who would—in theory—serve as an ideal husband. Through his odd vacillation their prospective union was on and off during some four years, and it was only by her skillful diplomatic coup of retiring to the convent of her youth that she brought him to his knees and his final declaration.

They were married in 1780. In 1781 their daughter, Eudora, was born. Manon Roland took a very weighty view of woman's role in marriage: she believed that it was the wife's duty to work for the happiness of both partners. She not only ran the household in Amiens and cared for her infant daughter, she also served assiduously as Roland's secretary and unacknowledged collaborator in his writings. Moreover, she engaged in negotiations with publishers for him. In 1784, he sent her to Versailles to try to obtain a patent of nobility: her stay in the palace attics merely exacerbated her loathing for the monarchy, and especially for that unpopular foreigner, Queen Marie-Antoinette. Unsuccessful in her main mission, for Roland was neither prepossessing nor popular, she nonetheless obtained his promotion from Amiens to Lyons.

While Roland proved an authoritarian husband—he put an end to her association with the Cannet sisters (which she missed)—nonetheless he broadened his wife's horizons. He took her on a visit to England (she would remain an anglophile) and to Switzerland. Through him she met and corresponded with some of the leading spirits of the age. The Rolands detested the abuses that prevailed under the absolute monarchy, and by 1789 they were well known in Lyons as advocates of change. They therefore greeted the Revolution with rapture. Manon Roland distrusted the sincerity of Louis XVI's pledges; equally, she had nothing but contempt for reforming ministers like Jacques Necker, or for the moderate, liberal-minded aristocrats eager to renounce their privileges. Blood was needed to water the tree of liberty, she thought. War she regarded as a school of virtue. Her expressions of revolutionary zeal became ever more violent.

Meanwhile, the Rolands had been corresponding with Jacques-Pierre Brissot, a lawyer known as an opponent of slavery, and founder of the paper *Le Patriote Français*. The group of young lawyers who gathered about him would soon be known as the Brissotins or Girondins (since many of them came from the Gironde region in southwest France). Brissot, taken with Manon's letters, published extracts from them in his paper as "Letters from a Roman Lady." However, it was not until early 1791 that Manon was able to return to Paris and the center of affairs, when Roland was entrusted with the mission of trying to settle the debts of the Lyons municipality. Leaving nine-year-old Eudora in a convent, the Rolands were about to step onto the national stage.

Manon lost no time in visiting the sessions of the Constituent Assembly, but she was far from impressed. Matters were moving far too slowly for her, and she suspected treachery. In her apartment on the Left Bank, she welcomed like-minded members of the Assembly, including Robespierre, whom she held in high regard at that period. Four times a week, Brissot and his associates would be frugally entertained. She herself sat sewing or writing letters, but she did not speak, sometimes having to bite her tongue to refrain from doing so.

When Roland's mission was concluded, the couple returned to his home near Lyons. A few months later, however, they were back in Paris. After their absence, they were no longer as much in demand as before. She was even contemplating defeat and departure when, to general surprise, Roland was named Minister of the Interior. An eyewitness has described how Manon was suddenly transformed by this triumph. In the splendid official residence she now gave modest dinners twice a week, attended largely by political allies: no women were ever invited. Many seeking access to Roland approached her first. It was she who, as unofficial secretary (and private advisor) to Roland, wrote the celebrated letter to Louis XVI, where she ventured to tell the King some home truths in her husband's name. Shortly afterwards, Roland was dismissed, to be followed by the rest of the Girondin ministry.

The "second revolution," the popular insurrection of August 10, 1792, brought Danton to power as Minister of Justice, while restoring Roland to the Ministry of the Interior. Manon's unswerving hostility to Danton (who towered over Roland) was visceral, and has been ascribed to physical repulsion with a sexual undertone. She loathed Danton's large appetites and dubious financial and undercover dealings. Moreover, she chose to hold him responsible for the terrible massacres of September 1792—an atrocity that filled her with horror and indignation. Yet some historians have regarded as deplorable her hatred of Danton and her refusal to consider any accommodation with him.

Among the many foreign admirers of the Revolution who had flocked to Paris was Thomas Paine, feted author of *The Rights of Man*. (Manon acidly considered him to be worth less than his works.) She now possibly met also Mary Wollstonecraft, author of *A Vindication of the Rights of Woman*, who moved in Girondin circles. Yet Manon apparently felt no sympathy for French women who were campaigning for equal rights, like Olympe de Gouges. Nonetheless, along with them, Manon fell subject to sexual innuendo and coarse insults at the hands of Marat and other virulent demagogues.

It was Roland who discovered and opened the King's "iron safe," which contained evidence of royal collusion with foreign powers and invaders. For his pains, he was accused of tampering with the documents. Along with her husband, Manon had desired the fall of Louis XVI, not his execution. On January 22, 1793, the very day after the King died by the guillotine, Roland submitted his letter of resignation, actually written by his wife. There was some truth in Danton's sarcastic remark that any proposal made to Roland should be put to Madame Roland as well.

Now the couple's position grew daily more perilous. Robespierre had embarked upon removing all who stood in his way. On the fall of the Girondins on May 31, 1793, Roland fled. Perhaps Manon could have escaped too, but she had private reasons for remaining in Paris. For, toward the end of the previous year, she and a member of her political circle, the Norman-born lawyer François Buzot, had fallen in love. Previously she had flirted with admirers, but this was deep passion for a married man whom she regarded as a noble soul. He shared her melancholy temperament and lofty outlook. This passion, she insisted, never overstepped "the bounds of virtue," yet she had surely betrayed Roland in her heart. Obsessed by literature, guided by "feeling," she decided to follow Madame de ˚Lafayette's heroine, the Princesse de Clèves, together with Rousseau's Julie, and confess all to her husband. It was a major error. Roland did not rise to the occasion like the hero of a novel: he grew bitter. Mindful of their image, she had to persuade him to destroy his vengeful memoirs.

Arrested on May 31, 1793, Manon was to spend some five months in prison where, according to eyewitnesses, she conducted herself with exemplary courage. She cleaned her cell and made it habitable; cared for her fellow prisoners; devoted hours to drawing, music, and reading; and hastily composed the memoirs that were intended to justify her husband and herself in the eyes of posterity. Manon was able to receive visitors, and she entrusted portions of the manuscript to friends for safekeeping. One section was totally destroyed when an associate feared for his life. (She was already enough of an author to be shattered by its loss.) It was through loyal visitors that she was able to correspond secretly with her distant friends, including Buzot, who, with fellow Girondins, was trying to raise an army in Normandy. She was longing for a provincial uprising against the rule of Paris. The failure of this enterprise and her despair on learning that Buzot and his companions had fled to Bordeaux instead of to the United States, as she had urged, led her to contemplate suicide—the ultimate fate of her husband and her lover.

However, she finally decided against this desperate course, choosing rather to follow the example of her Girondin friends who died by the guillotine on October 31, 1793. At her interrogation, she had bravely refused to name names. She was not allowed to speak at her trial, on November 8, 1793, and was hurried to the guillotine the very same day. Her famous last words, "O Liberty! What crimes are committed in your name!," were addressed to a statue of Liberty made of clay. Her execution—together with that of Olympe de Gouges (whom she ignored), which preceded it, and that of Marie-Antoinette (whom she loathed to the end), which followed it—was treated in the press as a lesson to women to remain in their proper sphere, and has been judged by the historian Simon Schama as an egregious example of sexual politics.

MAJOR THEMES

Manon Roland regarded her memoirs as her "moral and political testament," and she was fully conscious of their originality. She intended to tell the whole truth, but there is also considerable role-playing. Paradoxically, imprisonment gave her the freedom to concentrate on her love for Buzot—release would have meant a return to Roland. Paradoxically, too, imprisonment allowed her to exercise her real talent as a writer, with a gift for vivid and dramatic anecdote, lifelike portraiture, prophetic insight, keen judgment of men, and sharp irony. At last she could write as herself, instead of anonymously or in Roland's name.

Much as Manon sought to elevate Roland as a latter-day Cato, with herself as Cato's wife, the true underlying strains of their marriage, and her ongoing dissatisfaction with it, become manifest. She now laughs at her humility in the early days of their union, as she recognizes the superiority of her own literary gift. She recalls how Roland often convinced himself that he had written passages of her own composition. Finally, she perceives her great contribution to his career, though she does not consider that, in pursuing her ambition, she was largely responsible not only for his elevation but for his downfall (and her own).

She modeled her memoirs, with their avowed aim of revealing everything about herself, on Montaigne's idiosyncratic *Essais* and Rousseau's posthumously published *Confessions*. Strikingly, after Rousseau's manner, Manon seeks to convey her own sensuality and sexual experience as a woman. She indicates the liberties taken by her father's young apprentice; she alludes to menstruation; and on two occasions she comments on the shock of her wedding night. There are veiled allusions to the (unnamed) object of her passion, Buzot. Privately, Manon was not entirely happy with woman's accepted role: she once owned that she would have liked to put on men's clothes so as to see and hear more of life. As a mother, Manon proved less perfect than Rousseau's Julie: she sent her only child to a convent in order to be free for her own political activity in upholding Roland. Indeed, she found Eudora disappointing in character and talent. Only at the last did Manon concern herself with the girl's future and shed tears at the thought of their lasting separation.

If the threat of imminent death made Manon a "woman writer," it was one whose best work, as she well knew, would only be published posthumously. Despite her own pressing "need" to write, she had been convinced that published women authors aroused general ridicule and even failed to obtain the respect of their male colleagues, who (as she tartly put it) blamed women writers for faults they themselves shared. Indeed, Manon, who disliked "bad style," was a sharp critic of contemporary men writers. There is tension between her acceptance of the common prejudice against women who display their talent in public and the real urgency of her repressed gift. She even admitted that, if she were spared, she would want to be the historian of her own country, like Catherine Macaulay, whose history of England she much admired.

As regards politics, it is difficult to find any truly consistent policy or ideology in Madame Roland, just as it is with the Girondins as a whole. However, she was a republican before republicanism became the rule in France. Like the Girondins, she favored (and conspired on behalf of) federalism after the American manner, at a time when Robespierre was promoting indivisible unity. Along with many revolutionaries, she held to the religion of the future and of future generations. She maintained that she never infringed the so-called bounds of her sex by taking an active role in politics. That is not strictly true—and her contemporaries would not have been misled, since they were aware of her influence behind the scenes, both over Roland and as the hostess of a political salon.

Frequently, Manon saw through the vanity and pretensions of the leading political figures she encountered. In her view, the Girondins, divided among themselves, were eloquent, high-minded talkers, not political leaders: they lacked the practical ability to govern. The Revolution itself she saw as the supreme human test, which she herself was determined not to fail. Incompetence, lack of character, frivolity, laziness (shared even by Buzot)—these were the faults she uncovered. Moreover, there was universal mediocrity, cowardice, hypocrisy, folly. Where a great leader was required, it was an age of "pygmies"—an awareness that doubtless increased her sense of her own worth and her frustration at not having free rein herself.

Manon Roland, who had begun with such high hopes and ideals in 1789, ended in bitter disillusionment and disgust at the Robespierrist dictatorship. She, who had pitied the sufferings of the poor, now spoke of the mob, the dregs of society, "a degraded people whom we believed we could lead to regeneration through enlightenment "(Mémoires, 1: 300). She could declare that the tyranny of Robespierre and the Reign of Terror were far worse than the absolute monarchy of the Ancien Régime at whose overthrow she had once rejoiced.

Realism and idealism fought within her. She despised 99 percent of the men she met, while remaining attached to humanity in general and in the abstract. Despite her acute criticism of the shortcomings of the Girondins, she maintained that they were "pure." Hers was a noble ideal in the manner of Corneille's dramas, an ideal to which she must adhere whatever the promptings of reason or common sense. The same kind of illusion inspired her confession to Roland. Like many of her contemporaries, she saw herself and events in terms of ancient Rome. That is one reason why she could carefully prepare herself for death and fame, and behave with such stoic heroism in her last hours.

SURVEY OF CRITICISM

Hitherto, Madame Roland has belonged more to the field of history than that of literature. It was in the nineteenth century, though, that she was elevated into something rather more than a political activist or writer.

For the influential critic Sainte-Beuve, who read her in his youth, she was a noble soul, both muse and martyr. He liked to compare her with her great junior, the novelist and libertarian "dissident," Madame de *Staël. While he recognized Manon's political weaknesses, he observed that she not only marked the advent of solid worth and grace in the middle class but also served as the dividing line in feeling between creative women who came before Rousseau or after. Sainte-Beuve was fascinated by her letters and by her "delightful and indispensable *Mémoires*," by her ready wit and ease of expression. However, he declined to see her as a model for the "new" women of his own day: she was an exception, and limited in her field of action by her sex.

One of those "new" free-living women was Louise Colet, whose *Charlotte Corday et Madame Roland* was published in 1842. Colet, an ardent defender of the Girondins, aroused the irritation of George *Sand, who was then at the height of her admiration for Robespierre. French historians of the Revolution may frequently be divided into those who favor the Girondins and those who support Robespierre, and the nature of their allegiance naturally colors their appreciation of Madame Roland. According to bias, she can thus appear either as a noble heroine or as an ambitious and destructive bourgeoise who forgot her proper role as a woman.

As for Thomas Carlyle, in his celebrated work *The French Revolution* (1837), he spoke of the *Mémoires* "which all the world still reads." He waxed lyrical at "that astonishing woman," "the bravest of all Frenchwomen," queenly, serene, "sublime," a noble vision as a martyr on the scaffold. It is as if the craggy Scot had fallen under her spell. He was not alone.

Of the great nineteenth-century French novelists, Stendhal devoted a veritable cult to her. In 1805 he was reading the memoirs of the "divine" Madame Roland, that "sublime woman," a work that reduced him to tears. Yet he was affected less by her literary merit and her political stance than by her sensibility and her noble character as an example of feminine heroism. Both Mathilde de la Mole (in *Le Rouge et le noir*) and Mme Grandet (in *Lucien Leuwen*) are would-be Madame Rolands who are variously found wanting. Manon Roland serves as a kind of touchstone of Stendhal's private feminine ideal. He rightly foresaw that he would be more appreciated by future generations than by his own, and he looked forward to an ideal reader who would be another Madame Roland. It may even be that the strange sense of liberation that comes to Julien Sorel in prison, as well as to Fabrice del Dongo in the tower, is partly derived from Manon Roland's experience as related in her memoirs.

With the rise of modern feminism, there have been a number of biographical studies of Madame Roland, but little query about her literary standing. Concern with autobiography as an equivocal genre in itself is a comparatively recent phenomenon, and so is the probing examination of women's autobiographical writings in particular. Henceforward, Madame Roland's letters and memoirs should receive closer attention. Certainly, Gita May, in her invaluable book on "the Egeria of the Girondins," held that Manon Roland earned a significant place in the history of French literature with her letters and her autobiography, an observation that might now be extended to literature and culture in general.

BIBLIOGRAPHY

Works by Mme Roland

Appel à l'impartiale postérité par la citoyenne Roland. Ed. Louis Bosc. 4 vols. Paris: Louvet, 1795.
Oeuvres de Jeanne-Marie Phlipon Roland. Ed. Luc-Antoine Champagneux. 3 vols. Paris: Baidaut, 1800.
Mémoires. Ed. Claude Perroud. 2 vols. Paris: Imprimerie Nationale, 1900, 1902.
Lettres. Ed. Claude Perroud. 1900, 1902. Paris: Imprimerie Nationale, 2 vols.
Roland et Marie Phlipon. Lettres d'amour (1777–1780). Ed. Claude Perroud. Paris: Picard, 1909.
Lettres. Nouvelle série. Ed. Claude Perroud. 2 vols. Paris: Imprimerie Nationale, 1913, 1915.
Voyage en Suisse 1787. Ed. G. R. de Beer. Neuchâtel: La Baconnière, 1937.
Nouvelles Lettres inédites. Ed. Claude Perroud. Paris: Charavay, n.d.

Translations of Mme Roland

An Appeal to Impartial Posterity by Citizeness Roland. 2 vols. London: Joseph Johnson, 1795.
The Works (never before published) of Jeanne-Marie Phlipon Roland. London: Joseph Johnson, 1800.
The Private Memoirs of Madame Roland. Ed. E. G. Johnson. Chicago: McClurg, 1900.
The Memoirs of Madame Roland, a Heroine of the French Revolution. Trans. and ed. Evelyn Shuckburgh. Mt. Kisco, N.Y.: Meyer Bell, 1990.

Studies of Mme Roland

Blind, Mathilde. *Madame Roland*. London: W. H. Allen, 1886.
Calemard, J. *Manon Roland chez elle*. Paris: Giraud Badin, 1929.
Chaussinand-Nogaret, Guy. *Madame Roland, une femme en Révolution*. Paris: Seuil, 1985.
Cisar, Mary Ann. *The Image of the Self: Autobiographical Space in the Works of Madame Roland*. Diss., Brown University, 1979.
Cornevin, Marianne. *La Véritable Madame Roland*. Paris: Watelet, 1989.
Dauban, C.-A. *Etude sur Madame Roland et son temps*. Paris: Plon, 1864.

François-Primo, J. *Manon Roland, sa vie passionnée, son secret.* Paris: Argo, 1929.

Huisman, Georges. *La Vie privée de Madame Roland.* Paris: Hachette, 1955.

Kadane, Kathryn Ann. "The Real Difference Between Manon Phlipon and Madame Roland." *French Historical Studies* 3, no. 4 (1964): 542–49.

Kelly, Linda. *Women of the French Revolution.* London: Hamish Hamilton, 1987.

Kermina, F. *Madame Roland ou la passion révolutionnaire.* Paris: Perrin, 1976.

Lamartine, Alphonse de. *Histoire des Girondins.* 8 vols. Paris: Furne, Coquebert, 1847.

Lloyd, Tom. "Madame Roland and Schiller's Aesthetics: Carlyle's *The French Revolution.*" *Prose Studies* (Great Britain) 9, no. 3. (1986): 39–53.

Loomis, Stanley. *Paris in the Terror: June 1793-July 1794.* London: Cape, 1965.

May, Gita. *Madame Roland and the Age of Revolution.* New York: Columbia University Press, 1970.

Michelet, Jules. *Les Femmes de la Révolution française.* Ed. F. Giroud. Paris: Carrère, 1989.

———. *Histoire de la Révolution française.* 2 vols. Ed. G. Walter. Paris: Gallimard, 1952.

Mullaney, Marie M. "Madame Roland: The Paradoxical Feminism of an Eighteenth-Century 'Loophole Woman.' " *Maryland Historian* 14, no. 1 (1983): 1–10.

Pope-Hennessy, Una. *Madame Roland: A Study in Revolution.* London: Nisbet, 1917.

Sainte-Beuve, Charles-Augustin. *Oeuvres.* 2 vols. Ed. M. Leroy. Paris: Gallimard, 1951.

Tarbell, Ida M. *Madame Roland.* London: Lawrence and Bullen, 1896.

Taylor, I. A. *Life of Madame Roland.* London: Hutchinson, 1911.

Willcocks, M. P. *Madame Roland or the Mirror of Men's Dreams.* London: Hutchinson, 1936.

FRANÇOISE SAGAN
(1935–   )

Judith Graves Miller

BIOGRAPHY

Born to affluent and socially prominent parents in 1935, Françoise Sagan (née Quoirez) spent her early childhood traveling happily between her parents' opulent apartment in Paris's sixteenth arrondissement and her grandparents' rural estate in the Lot. In 1940, at the onset of the German Occupation of France, her industrialist father moved her, her mother, and two siblings to the ostensibly calmer outlying region around Lyons, where they nevertheless experienced the anxiety of frequent machine-gun strafings and ongoing surveillance. The end of the war in 1945 brought the family back to Paris, at which time Sagan, permanently affected by both the beauty of the Burgundian countryside and the horrors of the war, embarked on a picaresque educational career, bouncing from one convent school to another, proclaiming jauntily her metaphysical skepticism and her preference for café life over religious devotions. While preparing for the entrance exams to the Sorbonne in the summer of 1953, she began work on *Bonjour Tristesse* (1954), the novel whose publication one year later would catapult her into the intoxicating firmament of media stardom. With nary a hiatus, Sagan has remained in the public eye ever since, her ingenuousness, wit, and audacity helping to transform her life and works into a legend.

In the case of Françoise Sagan, attempting to separate reality from myth in order to understand her young adult years proves almost counterproductive. Sagan consciously chose to construct herself as a feminine dandy, opting for glitter, high style, and outrageous behavior as a way of coping with the moral chaos of the postwar period. She drove fast cars, spent her evenings drinking Scotch and jitterbugging in the flourishing jazz clubs of St. Germain des Prés, and, with a gang of actors, filmmakers, models, and publicists, helped metamorphose St. Tropez from a pokey fishing village into the most sought-after vacation spot on the Mediterranean. The intellectual counterpart to her friend and contemporary, "sex goddess" Brigitte Bardot, Sagan refused to bow down to bourgeois conventions and the patriarchal norm of the primacy of the family. She also created characters who embodied her rebelliousness.

Her fast-paced existence led her into some precarious situations (notably gambling debts) and narrow escapes (a car crash in 1957 that left her addicted to a morphine-based painkiller), but it did not preclude her commitment to a number of progressive social actions. In 1960, she courted death when O.A.S. (Secret Army) supporters bombed her apartment because she had proclaimed solidarity with the Algerian independence movement. In 1971, she risked incarceration by signing the now famous "Manifesto of the 343," which called for state-subsidized abortions on demand. More recently, she campaigned vociferously for the presidency of François Mitterrand, alienating in the process a number of international jet-setters who make up her social set.

Now in her later middle years, with sixteen novels, nine plays, two volumes of short stories, four autobiographical texts, and myriad reportages, interviews, scenarios, lyrics to songs, and even two ballets behind her, Sagan has settled into a somewhat less disordered lifestyle. She still spends generously of her time and money on longtime friends, two ex-husbands, and grown son Denis. She still chooses to rent every few years a new flat in Paris rather than put down roots by buying a home. She still claims cockily, as in her lyrical 1984 memoirs *Avec mon meilleur souvenir* (*With Fondest Regards*), that "the person who has not felt . . . the prestigious and fascinating silence of an imminent death . . . has never loved speed nor . . . life" (85–86).[1] However, she also accepts with measure and pride—befitting an author who has entered (and recently left) the Gallimard pantheon—official invitations to tour Japan (1980), to participate in the jury of the Cannes film festival (1979), or to receive the Prix de Monaco for the overall quality of her work (1985).

Her work is, indeed, one aspect of her life that she has never mocked, while nonetheless cunningly underplaying her talents: "I am an accident which keeps on happening" (Jean-Louis Echine). Although her nonchalance has earned her avuncular scoldings from critics who complain about her overuse of adjectives or sometimes questionable grammar, her obvious ease in creating pithy images and seductive rhythms has also prompted a plethora of positive comments about her special music. To this appreciation, Antoine Blondin adds a telling corrective encapsulating Sagan's appeal, an appeal that has kept her texts on the best-seller lists for over forty years: "The captivating quality of what has been rather grotesquely called 'the famous little voice' and what is [in fact] her style and her tone comes from the marvelous precision of an instrument that de-banalizes the real" (277).

MAJOR THEMES

A writer who imbues the everyday with magic, Sagan takes her place among the company of popular storytellers who transport their readers to a glamorous world of moneyed cosmopolites. Children, old people, material concerns, career worries do not disturb their existence. Her characters, for the most part, spend their time falling in and out of love. Sagan's romances, however, by refusing a happy ending, by clothing themselves in pleasurable melancholy, and by introducing female characters who counter the romance stereotype, convey subtly the limits of women's possibilities within patriarchy. As such they can be read, along with the works of contemporaries such as Françoise *Mallet-Joris, Christiane *Rochefort, Geneviève Dormann, or Marie Cardinal, as reflecting the nascent and nonmilitant feminism of the 1960s. Rachel Brownstein's comments about feminist reading stategies apply well to the Saganian canon: her texts ''are full of useful information [if women] would try to change'' (*Becoming a Heroine: Reading about Women in Novels* [New York: Viking, 1982], 297).

Of all Sagan's novels, *Bonjour Tristesse* proves in many ways the most transgressive. François Mauriac was quite aware of this when he dubbed Sagan ''a charming monster'' (*Le Figaro*, June 6, 1954) after she won the prestigious Prix des Critiques for her initial publishing effort. Heroine and first-person narrator Cécile, like a Gidean innocent, seduces the reader into identifying with her as she plots and quite inexorably realizes the collapse of her widowed father's first serious liaison. Cécile's scheming ultimately results in the violent death of Raymond's mistress, Anne. Attracted to the adolescent Cécile through her outbursts of lucidity and humor as well as through her efforts to establish sexual autonomy, the reader also discovers something perverse in an attachment to this child who manipulates her irresponsible father, her own young but highly responsible lover, and the intelligent, powerful, and admirable Anne.

In this first of the many triangular intrigues that propel her novels, Sagan takes the contours of the ''family romance'' and distorts its prescribed ending. Cécile neither enters adulthood as a well-rehearsed ''woman'' nor suffers the consequences of a precocious sexuality. She thrives in an insouciance of her own choosing, positioning herself outside of all conventional constraints through her unorthodox victory toward selfhood. In *Bonjour Tristesse*—as in her second novel, *Un Certain Sourire* (*A Certain Smile*, 1956)—Sagan suggests the desirability of self-conscious solitude. By keeping the romance within the family she also, as in several later texts that hint at incestuous affections, in particular her play *Château en Suède* (A Castle in Sweden, 1960) and autobiographical musings *Des bleus à l'âme* (*Scars on the Soul*, 1972), subverts the sex-gender system. In her deconstruction of the family romance, Sagan challenges the continuation of a society based on the exchange of women.

In her third-person love fantasies, the form that dominates her novelistic production, Sagan indirectly targets the mentality that locks women into preordained roles. If her main female characters do not fathom their way out of behavior that they know to be self-defeating, the reader is not so handicapped. The middle-aged beauty Paule in *Aimez-vous Brahms . . .* (1959), for example, returns to her narcissistic and philandering lover Roger after a brief fling with the younger and completely devoted Simon. Paule cannot see in Simon's dependency and abjection the doubling of her own rapport with Roger. To her Roger is the acceptable, "the normal," "her master," "conforming to certain moral or aesthetic rules" (170), both because he is slightly older and because she is his precious rock: lovely and unconscious. To the question, "Aimez-vous Brahms?" (Are you free to take on life and adventure?), Paule seems to respond resignedly, "No, time is killing the 'woman' in me."

Lucile, in *La Chamade* (1965), similarly recognizes her boundaries by re-entering, after a passionate affair, the luxurious cocoon in which her wealthy protector has encased her. Unlike either of her male lovers, Lucile cannot engage with the world in any meaningful combat. As is true of most of Sagan's female characters in her third-person romances, Lucile perceives her exclusive battlefield in terms of an entrancing but ultimately stifling bedroom. Like Paule, she is trapped in a projection of patriarchal making.

Nathalie Sylvener, the most profound and sensitive of Sagan's heroines, in *Un Peu de soleil dans l'eau froide* (*A Few Hours of Sunlight*, 1969), takes love addiction beyond the metaphorical "lostness" of Paule and Lucile to a real and fatal encounter with death, the hidden partner in her love triangle. In *Un Peu de soleil dans l'eau froide*—in which the novel of manners component latent in all of Sagan's work occupies a central place—a superficial but enticing Paris rivals the provincial Nathalie for the attention of a high-rolling journalist, Gilles. Gilles lacks the moral fiber to respond to Nathalie's desperation. Much like those characters of Marguerite ˙Duras who are also unable to create an identity for themselves through erotic attachments, Nathalie embraces death as the only partner able to fill the vacuum of her existence.

A fourth and much jauntier variation on the ways in which a patriarchal mind-set conditions women to live out men's scripts is Sagan's 1977 novel *Le Lit défait* (*The Unmade Bed*). In this work, which reframes characters from three previous novels—*Dans un mois, dans un an* (*Those Without Shadows*, 1957), *Les Merveilleux Nuages* (*The Wonderful Clouds*, 1962), and *Un Profil perdu* (*Lost Profile*, 1974)—Sagan seems to reverse the dependency pattern, with the avant-garde playwright Edouard Maligrasse drawing his emotional and creative sustenance from Béatrice Valmont, the leading actress of the Parisian Boulevards. On closer inspection, however, it becomes clear that Béatrice, despite her feistiness and personal ambition, has had to accept performing the role of the "sadistic wanton" Edouard needs her to be. In this novel Sagan suggests that having the imagination required for play may lessen the burden of combining intimacy with identity. But even with this talent there is no enduring transcendence in a love affair.

Sagan's theater pieces, on the whole less successful and more predictably articulated than her novels, nevertheless also invert the prevailing social and moral codes. Two long-running productions in particular, *Château en Suède* and *Le Cheval évanoui* (The Stunned Horse, 1966), while qualified as Boulevard drama, that is, light drawing-room comedy, use whimsy to undercut the comforting resolutions fundamental to type. Thus the former, irreverently parodying aspects of Tchekovian and Ibsenian realism, introduces enchanting characters who nonetheless cannibalize the outside world in order to preserve their own privileged space of fantasy. The latter, reminiscent of Noël Coward's fast-paced and clever verbal sparring matches, exposes the compromises and hypocrisy underlying the traditional "happily-ever-after" ending. Like Georges Feydeau's, Sagan's dramatic world inscribes on stage a structureless reality held together by a socially deviant code of behavior. It therefore uncovers and releases the repression inherent in a bourgeois and patriarchal order.

Of late, Sagan has moved away from the romance to invent what might best be termed fantasies of revolt. Especially in her second collection of short stories, *Musiques de scènes* (*Incidental Music*, 1981), and her 1983 version of a nineteenth-century confessional novel, *Un Orage immobile* (*The Still Storm*), she creates strong mythic heroines who bask in their own glory and refute any clear-cut opposition between masculinity and femininity. These works express forbidden yearnings and deal in physical impossibilities. They transport the reader to a literary realm far removed from the realistic conventions underpinning most of her romances.

In Sagan's story "La Futura," for example, a high-priced and well-connected courtesan takes revenge on an aristocratic and brutal Neopolitan client. She refuses to protect his son from the Austrian army, thereby saving in his stead a guileless and handsome peasant. In this way La Futura recoils from being bought one last time. Rather, she chooses her own sexual desires over sexual commodification.

Likewise in "L'Echange," the energetic middle-aged wife of a prosperous, proper, and extremely jealous English gentleman elects to turn a would-be thief into an evening's adventure. Rejecting any sense of propriety, she takes the invader to her bed and informs him the next morning that the painting he had attempted to steal is a fake. Unbeknownst to her husband, she had already sold the original to help maintain her own larcenous freedom. Like La Futura, and the various Minervas, Medusas, and Amazons in *Incidental Music*, the heroine of "L'Echange" represents what women find divine and demonic in themselves.

Un Orage immobile goes further than any of Sagan's texts in giving form to suppressed anger. In it Sagan cleverly establishes a composite hero/ine, a doubled principal character—male and female—who transfers sex both into a rifle and a pen. Nicolas Lomont (narrator and character) disappears into Marthe (the revolutionary heroine) in the act of writing her story. He thus releases his own pent-up fury in Marthe's willful destruction of the status quo. It may well be that this fragmented character camouflages Sagan's embedding of herself (or her authorial persona) in the narrative. Nicolas-Marthe can then be understood as the materialization of the dream of escape of a female consciousness locked into a male narrator.

In complementary fashion, Sagan paints in her memoirs *Avec mon meilleur souvenir*, which appeared the year after the novel, a portrait of herself as an uncontainable figure whose best revenge against the prisons hemming her in is her own literary imagination. Thinking of herself as daughter to Sartre, whom she eulogizes in the chapter "Lettre d'amour à Jean-Paul Sartre" (A Love Letter to Jean-Paul Sartre), and to Proust, whose character the Duchess of Sagan inspired her pen name ("Lectures" ["Readings"]), Sagan situates herself through association among those twentieth-century artists and writers who share an unmediated and impassioned profile. For Sagan, as becomes obvious in her treatment of the personalities and themes of her memoirs, art—in this instance, writing—allows her to live out fantasies of control and domination denied her, and women in general, in life.

SURVEY OF CRITICISM

As media phenomenon, Sagan has attracted the attention of so many journalists that her combined press dossier from the publishing houses of Julliard, J-J. Pauvert, Flammarion, and Gallimard fills an entire filing cabinet. The quality of these pieces, however, tends to range from the sensationalistic to the hagiographic. The eighty best of the many interviews she has accorded have been compiled by Jean-Jacques Pauvert in *Réponses 1954–1974* (*Nightbird: Conversations with Françoise Sagan*, 1974). In these exchanges, she both builds her persona as "undutiful daughter of the bourgeoisie" and pokes fun at her efforts to shake up the establishment. She also evokes convincingly her disciplined but effortless writing habits.

Three other interviews are of particular note. In autumn 1956 Sagan spoke with Blair Fuller and Robert Silvers of the *Paris Review*: in "The Art of Fiction XV: Françoise Sagan," she seriously attempts to depict how she structures and finds the rhythm for her novels. A 1977 interview with Jean-Louis Echine, "Entretien: Sagan sans clichés," tries and partially succeeds in demystifying the author. Echine discusses cogently the real originality of Sagan's later works. Jean-François Josselin in "Les Années Sagan" (1983) coaxes Sagan into concentrating her remarks on the nostalgia evident in the parodic style of *Un Orage immobile*.

Several authors, doubtless fascinated by the overnight sensation of *Bonjour Tristesse*, which was translated into twenty-seven languages in the first year after its publication, wrote immediate appraisals of the book and its author. Jean Lignière in *Françoise Sagan et le succès* (1957) describes condescendingly the complex, possibly homosexual relationship between Cécile and Anne in *Bonjour Tristesse*. He also implies that Sagan may not have written the novel alone. Gérard Gohier-Marvier, less treacherous but just as demeaning, effusively traces Sagan's life up until the writing of *Bonjour Tristesse* (*Bonjour Françoise!*, 1957). He specializes in interviews with her classmates from secondary school as well as conversations with childhood friends who "knew her when."

Taking a different tack, Georges Hourdin in *Le Cas Françoise Sagan* (1958) attacks Sagan's raucous lifestyle and immorality. From his perspective as a fervent Catholic, Hourdin reads *Bonjour Tristesse* as evidence of the ethical slothfulness of contemporary youth. He begs Sagan to return to the Church.

Of these early and overtly biased studies, the least objectionable is Gérard Mourgue's *Françoise Sagan* (1958). Mourgue dissects Sagan's first three novels from an existentialist point of view, understanding her characters' actions as attempts to fill the void left by their apprehension of an absurd universe. In a similar vein, Alfred Cismaru in his 1965 article, "Françoise Sagan's Theory of Complicity," gives deft plot summaries of her works up to and including her play *Bonheur, impair et passe* (Win, Draw, and Pass, 1964) and reviews each according to the thematics of freedom's limits and imperatives.

All the monographs from the 1950s confirm Sagan's ability to startle, confound, even threaten male readers of her texts. A close analysis of these studies reveals a great deal about a certain critical fringe in France during the Cold War years. About Sagan, writer or person, very little of any value is said.

With the exception of Pol Vandromme's *Françoise Sagan ou l'élégance de survivre* (1977), no book-length discussion of Sagan appeared for a period of almost twenty years after the flurry created by her early triumphs. In fact, Vandromme's impressionistic overview of her style and life echoes the tone of the many newspaper and magazine articles of the 1960s and 1970s, which routinely confuse Sagan with her characters. An exception to this is Brigid Brophy's article, "Françoise Sagan and the Art of the Beau Geste" (1964), which sympathetically and perceptively engages with the entirety of her work.

In 1985 Bertrand Poirot-Delpech, longtime drama and fiction critic for *Le Monde*, at last brought out a thorough biographical study of Sagan, which considers her work and the launching of her talents within the cultural context of the mid-1950s. His *Bonjour Sagan* also gathers excellent reproductions of illustrations and photographs that document her career throughout almost a half century. These feature the famous *Life* magazine photos of Sagan upon the occasion of her first visit to the United States in the spring of 1955. She is seen feted by Manhattan literati but preferring the company of Billie Holiday in Harlem and Tennessee Williams on Long Island. A recent biography, *Sagan*, by Jean-Claude Lamy (1988) rerecords her life—but in greater detail—as told many times in the past. Lamy's book is of special interest in the portrayal of the Parisian publishing world and, especially, of Sagan's working relationship with her remarkable editor at Gallimard.

Two scholarly works examine Sagan's production from within a feminist frame. Marian St. Onge in her 1984 doctoral dissertation, "Narrative Strategies and the Quest for Identity in the French Female Novel of Adolescence: Studies in Duras, Mallet-Joris, Sagan, and Rochefort," provocatively interprets *Bonjour Tristesse* from a revisionary psychoanalytical stance. Judith Graves Miller's general overview, *Françoise Sagan* (1988), uses insights gleaned from reading feminist theoreticians and critics (notably Rachel Blau DuPlessis, Janice Radway, Sandra Gilbert, Susan Gubar, Rachel Brownstein, Nancy Miller, Tania Modleski, and Joanna Russ) to understand Sagan against the grain. She assesses what is positive and challenging in Sagan's romances.

Only one collection of Sagan's texts and memorabilia exists in the United States. Housed in Rare Books and Special Collections of the Pennsylvania State University Library, the John Robert Kaiser collection of Françoise Sagan includes first and limited editions, several original manuscripts, theater programs, over 200 photographs of Sagan and the actors who starred in her films and plays, and books and articles on Sagan up to 1972. Kaiser has also compiled a very complete bibliography of her works (novels, plays, articles, translations, cinema criticism, lyrics to songs) from 1954 to 1972.

NOTE

1. All translations from the French are my own.

BIBLIOGRAPHY

Major Works by Françoise Sagan

Bonjour Tristesse. Paris: Julliard, 1954.
Un Certain Sourire. Paris: Julliard, 1956.
Dans un mois, dans un an. Paris: Julliard, 1957.
Aimez-vous Brahms . . . . Paris: Julliard, 1959.
Château en suède. Paris: Julliard, 1960.
Les Merveilleux Nuages. Paris: Julliard, 1961.
La Chamade. Paris: Julliard, 1965.
Le Cheval évanoui suivie de l'Echarde. Paris: Julliard, 1966.
Un Peu de soleil dans l'eau froide. Paris: Flammarion, 1969.
Des bleus à l'âme. Paris: Flammarion, 1972.
Un Profil perdu. Paris: Flammarion, 1974
Réponses 1954–1974. Paris: J.-J. Pauvert, 1974.
Des yeux de soie. Paris: Flammarion, 1975.
Le Lit défait. Paris: Flammarion, 1977
Musiques de scènes. Paris: Flammarion, 1981.
Un Orage immobile. Paris: J.-J. Pauvert, 1983.
Avec mon meilleur souvenir. Paris: Gallimard, 1984.
De guerre lasse. Paris: Gallimard, 1985.
Sarah Bernhardt: Le Rire incassable. Paris: Robert Laffont, 1987.
La Laisse. Paris: Julliard, 1989.

Translations of Françoise Sagan

Bonjour Tristesse. Trans. Irene Ash. New York: E. P. Dutton, 1955
A Certain Smile. Trans. Anne Green. New York: E. P. Dutton, 1956.
Aimez-vous Brahms? Trans. Peter Wiles. New York: E. P. Dutton, 1960.

La Chamade. Trans. Robert Westhoff. New York: E. P. Dutton, 1966.
A Few Hours of Sunlight. Trans. Terence Kilmartin. New York: Harper and Row, 1971.
Scars on the Soul. Trans. Joanna Kilmartin. New York: McGraw-Hill, 1974.
Silken Eyes and Other Stories. Trans. Joanna Kilmartin. New York: Delacorte, 1977.
Nightbird: Conversations with Françoise Sagan. Trans. David Macey. New York: Clarkson Potter, 1980.
Incidental Music. Trans. C. J. Richards. New York: E. P. Dutton, 1983.
The Unmade Bed. Trans. Abigail Israel. New York: Delacorte Press/Eleanor Fried, 1978.
The Still Storm. Trans. Christine Donougher. New York: E. P. Dutton, 1986.
With Fondest Regards. Trans. Christine Donougher. New York: E. P. Dutton, 1985.

Studies of Françoise Sagan

Blondin, Antoine. *Ma Vie entre des lignes.* Paris: Table Ronde, 1982.
Brophy, Brigid. "Françoise Sagan and the Art of the Beau Geste." *Texas Quarterly* 7, no. 4 (Winter 1964): 59–69.
Cismaru, Alfred. "Françoise Sagan's Theory of Complicity." *Dalhousie Review* (Winter 1965–66): 457–69.
Echine, Jean-Louis. "Entretien: Sagan sans clichés." *Nouvelles Littéraires*, (April 7, 1977): 5.
Fuller, Blair, and Robert Silvers. "The Art of Fiction XV: Françoise Sagan." *Paris Review* (Autumn 1956): 83–91.
Gohier-Marvier, Gérard. *Bonjour Françoise!* Paris: Editions du Grand Damier, 1957.
Hourdin, Georges. *Le Cas Françoise Sagan.* Paris: Editions du Cerf, 1958.
Josselin, Jean-François. "Les Années Sagan." *Nouvel Observateur* (March 18, 1983): 14–17.
Kaiser, John Robert. "Françoise Sagan." *Bulletin of Bibliography and Magazine Notes* 30, no. 3 (July-September 1973): 106–9.
Lamy, Jean-Claude. *Sagan.* Paris: Mercure de France, 1988.
Lignière, Jean. *Françoise Sagan et le succès.* Paris: Editions du Scorpion, 1957.
Miller, Judith Graves. *Françoise Sagan.* Boston: G. K. Hall, 1988.
Mourgue, Gérard. *Françoise Sagan.* Paris: Editions Universitaires, 1958.
Poirot-Delpech, Bertrand. *Bonjour Sagan.* Paris: Herscher, 1985.
St. Onge, Marian. "Narrative Strategies and the Quest for Identity in the French Female Novel of Adolescence: Studies in Duras, Mallet-Joris, Sagan, and Rochefort." Diss, Boston College, 1984.
Vandromme, Pol. *Françoise Sagan ou l'élégance de survivre.* Paris: S.E.C.L.E.-Régine Deforges, 1977.

GEORGE SAND
(1804–1876)

Annabelle M. Rea

BIOGRAPHY

The child who would become George Sand was born Amantine-Aurore-Lucile Dupin on July 1, 1804, less than a month after the marriage of her aristocratic father, descended from the Polish royal family and the French military hero the Maréchal de Saxe, to her proletarian mother, daughter of a Paris bird merchant. In fact, Aurore grew up with two mothers: Antoinette-Sophie-Victoire Delaborde Dupin, who gave birth to her, and her paternal grandmother, Marie-Aurore Dupin de Francueil, who educated her and with whom she lived in the country. With the early death of her father, Aurore, from age four on, was even more torn between the two women. George Sand would later, in her literary search for the ideal family, have much to say about the rivalry of two women for one man and women's relationships in general.

After private tutoring, a little more than two years of convent education in Paris, and a year and a half of intensive reading at Nohant during her grandmother's final months, Aurore Dupin married, at eighteen, Casimir Dudevant, a man far from her intellectual and cultural equal. Casimir's preference for hunting—both animal and female human—his drinking, and his lack of interest in his wife's musical or literary activities soon destroyed the couple. Without the private suffering and introspection inspired by the marital disunion and the public pain of the subsequent trial for separation, would we have had Sand the feminist writer or perhaps Sand the writer at all? Without the economic problems caused by this situation, would we have had the enormous literary output of this woman who supported herself, two children, and others, such as the social philosopher Pierre Leroux, through her writing?

Much has been made of Sand's amorous history, of the number of men with whom she hoped to create the ideal couple to realize her lifelong dream. None of these men was more romantic than the dashing magistrate of her youth, Aurelien de Sèze, nor more devoted than the artist Alexandre Manceau, her longtime companion in later years; several others were, however, more famous. Jules Sandeau, for instance, wrote with her under the name J. Sand, lived with her during her earliest days in Paris, and helped her gain access to the literary establishment. His writing career led to membership in the Académie Française and to relative oblivion today, while hers was to lead to widespread admiration in her time and an impressive and still growing reputation in the twentieth century. The experience of both sublime passion and great suffering with the poet and dramatist Alfred de Musset enriched the work of both writers, and their travel to Italy provided thematic material that Sand would exploit throughout her career. With Frédéric Chopin she shared over eight years of family life and mutual inspiration. The quest pursued by Sand in her own life to find the missing half of the androgyne in ideal companionship—it has been suggested that her relationship with her adored son Maurice was an extension of this search—forms one of the richest of the thematic resources of her work.

Sand devoted much of her lifetime to helping others. Supported and furthered by her republican lawyer-lover Louis-Chrysostome Michel, called Michel de Bourges; the religious reformer, her spiritual advisor Abbé Félicité de Lamennais; and especially Pierre Leroux, she championed many social causes in her writing. She aided financially, inspired, and counseled several worker-poets, such as Agricol Perdiguier, and ministered to the poor and ailing of her Berry countryside. In March 1848 she took on an unpaid position as unofficial Minister of Propaganda, writing editorials for the *Bulletin de la République*, for the provisional government that she expected to realize her ideal republic. Her bitter disillusionment at the violent suppression of popular uprisings in May and June caused her to retreat from such direct but behind-the-scene involvement in political affairs. Sand had eschewed a more active participation, refusing, for example, to accept a nomination for office supported by the newspaper *La Voix des Femmes*, for she rejected political roles for women until they had the education to enable them to act independently of priests and husbands. Women and their rights were, however, a constant source of concern, if not always in her life— we must acknowledge severely strained relationships with certain women, especially her daughter Solange—at least in her works. The social vein, reflecting her commitment to reform, continued in her writings until the end of her literary career.

The myth of George Sand as the young rebel who wore pants, smoked, lived with a number of different lovers—doing in public things allowed only to males in her time—has elements of truth, as does that of the mature, altruistic "Bonne Dame de Nohant." The real George Sand, a woman with strengths and weaknesses, lived a long, full life as a writer, a lover, a mother and grandmother, a good friend to many, and a social reformer. Because of her enormous energy, her intellectual and emotional searching, her financial need, and her refusal to succumb to discouragement, she succeeded brilliantly in her career, despite the restrictions imposed upon women in nineteenth-century France by the Napoleonic Code and public opinion.

MAJOR THEMES

To discuss briefly the major themes of George Sand's work is a daunting task. She left more than sixty novels, twenty-five plays (far less than the total figure, this represents only plays actually produced on the Paris stage), twenty-six short stories and novellas, well over 16,000 letters (many have not survived), a lengthy autobiography (1,600 pages in the Pléiade edition), several collections of travel pieces, plus numerous prefaces and political, social, literary, artistic, or musical essays.

A critic writing this piece before the feminist movement of the late twentieth century would have analyzed Sand's thematics quite differently. Today we recognize, underneath the surface simplicity of many of her tales, beyond the familiar motifs drawn from mythology or literature, some very radical ideas, particularly concerning male and female roles in society, radical for her time and still relevant, if no longer radical, for ours as well. Sand took these motifs from many sources. As she herself stated, for example, *Léone Léoni* is a revision of the Abbé Prévost's tale of obsessive, ruinous love, *Manon Lescaut*, with a change in gender. Critics have pointed out other remakes of familiar themes: the Pygmalion motif in *François le Champi* (*The Country Waif*), *André*, and *Lélia*; Beauty and the Beast in *Mauprat*; Persephone and Demeter in *Lélia*; Tristan and Iseult in *Valentine*; Goethe's treatment of the chemistry of love, *Elective Affinities*, in *Jacques*, his *Faust* in *Les Sept Cordes de la lyre* (*Seven Strings of the Lyre*); and Etienne Pivert de Senancour's introspective, tormented *Oberman* in a number of works, especially *Lélia*, with its female version of the Romantic world-weariness known as *le mal du siècle*. This familiarity frequently allowed her to pass her subversive ideas into her readers' consciousness without being discovered by the censor, whether parent or priest.

One of the most frequent of Sand's targets and one that was clearly understood by censors was that of marriage as it existed under the Napoleonic Code in nineteenth-century France. As Napoleon put it, the wife was to her husband as the fruit tree to the gardener: his property. Divorce, which had existed in France until 1816, was then abolished until 1884, when it was reinstated during a period of social reform under the Third Republic. Adultery by the husband was punishable by a small fine but only if he brought his concubine into the marital domicile, whereas the wife's penalty was three months to two years' imprisonment, for it was her fidelity that ensured the transfer of property to legitimate heirs. For Sand, marriage under conditions of such blatant inequality was a "prostitution jurée"—prostitution with vows (*La Comtesse de Rudolstadt* [The Countess de Rudolstadt] 492),[1] and she detailed its miseries in 1832 in the very early *Indiana*. In her numerous portraits of the ideal couple, she sought to explore differences of social status, age, and education. She wrote much about the transformation of the individual, in preparation for an egalitarian relationship, through education, hard work, and very often via travel. In *Mauprat* Edmée de Mauprat, through a lengthy process, tamed the beast in her cousin Bernard so that he finally became worthy of her love. But the most striking treatment of the theme comes in *François le Champi*, where an adopted foundling child is molded into an ideal husband by and for the woman who adopted him. Such shaping of the male into a sensitive, compassionate, and tender individual seems a fairly radical idea even today.

In her works, Sand often examined questions of gender. The recently re-edited dialogue-novel *Gabriel* poses the question more dramatically than other Sand texts through the use of a girl, isolated from others, raised by her grandfather as a boy, and then released into the world to deal with her female body, male education, and expectations for freedom of action. In *François le Champi* both Madeleine and François serve as caretakers for the ailing, and he attends to household tasks when she is ill. Fadette of *La Petite Fadette* (*Fanchon the Cricket*) transforms her fiancé through the depth of her thoughts and her practical medical knowledge while he helps her improve her appearance and social graces. Sand's exploration of the androgynous nature of human beings is frequent and thorough. Within Sand's ideal couple, then, there exists a sharing of characteristics between the male and the female but also a complementarity.

Sand created women characters who do not conform to their century's standards requiring them to be delicate and ill. Her physically strong women may ride horseback, sometimes in dangerous conditions, like Fiamma in *Simon*. Consuelo, whose travels have been compared to those of Ulysses, treks across Europe in the novel that bears her name. Often the voice, the beautiful voice with reasoned words, is the first-mentioned characteristic of Sand's women, not pretty hair or eyes or a graceful figure. Using the voice, for example, that of a singer in *Consuelo* (*Consuelo: A Romance of Venice*) or a traditional healer in *La Petite Fadette*, Sand plays with popular images of women, such as the siren or the witch, and explodes those stereotypes.

Her women are often more knowledgeable than others of their milieu. Sand maintained that women were as capable of learning as men, that society had to change to make room for the educated woman, and that it was equally necessary to revise male education. As she showed in *André*, the education that took a woman out of her station in a society that had remained the same could be poisonous. Sand looked at women's medical knowledge through Fadette and several others and saw the injustice of the 1803 law barring them from practice. She studied women artists such as Consuelo the singer-composer and Thérèse Jacques, the portraitist of *Elle et lui* (*She and He*). In *Nanon*, the title character, illiterate until age twelve, educated herself to write the novel we read. Because of the absence of the mother, Sand's women characters often lack maternal— or even parental—models so that, without the imprinting of past modes of behavior, they invent their lives, breaking new ground. In the world imagined by Sand, these strong women often receive male approval and even preference.

Men, as one of her male characters puts it, "love deeply only the woman who, through her character, seems to rise above the weakness and inaction of her sex" (*Mauprat*, 261).

However, despite the many examples of strongly positive female characters, Sand's women rarely get along well with each other for very long. Those who do share friendship communicate by letter or see each other only infrequently. Women friends, or a mother and daughter as in *Valentine*, are often torn apart by their love for the same man. Once a woman marries, female friendships dissolve. Although we find many cases of female jealousy and some even of hatred in Sand's work—and one may certainly fault her for this—she is increasingly seen as a feminist writer. It is not, however, in the purportedly feminist *Lettres à Marcie* (*Letters to Marcie*), truncated by the misogynistic editor Lamennais, but more in the fictional texts that one truly sees Sand's role as "the voice of women at a time when women were silent," to use the unattributed phrase cited by André Maurois in his biography many years ago.

Sand's writing should be seen as *engagé*, or literature committed to social change; she pleaded, for instance, for a greater understanding of the problems faced by women. We have touched upon her portraits of women; she wrote of aristocratic women, peasant women, working women, artists. She treated questions not discussed openly in her time, such as that of female sexuality in *Lélia*. This early novel, later radically revised, she termed "the most daring and honest action of my life" (*Letters d'un voyageur*, 754) for its treatment of the female psyche. She also courageously wrote of special social cases like that of the unwed mother. She spoke of the courtesan, especially in *Isidora*, where the biography of the "fallen woman" is related in full, from her beginnings in poverty, her status as an upper-class prostitute, her marriage to a count, through to her final fulfillment as an autonomous widow, the founder of a Voltairian village who has thrown off jewelry and other trappings of femininity. In *André*, with Geneviève and others around her, Sand explored the situation of the *grisette*, the poor, as yet unmarried working girl who was often suspect, merely because of her social status.

Not all of the social issues pertained exclusively to women. Among the first writers to do so, Sand expressed her concern for workers, artisans, and peasants of both sexes and all ages, for example in *Le Compagnon du Tour de France* (*The Journeyman Joiner, or The Companion of the Tour of France*), *La Ville noire* (The Black City), and *La Mare au diable* (*The Haunted Pool*). One of the first in literature to paint detailed portraits of children, she fought particularly against society's prejudice toward the foundling. A frequent subject of Sand's writings was society's failings toward its poor and marginal, especially in the area of education.

Sand was critical not only of specific social injustice but of many of the patriarchal institutions of her time. Throughout her works, she evaluates the educational system, especially as it deals with women—as she describes it in *Histoire de ma vie*, "the bad education you have sentenced us to" (2: 126)—

but even more generally blaming it for producing children incapable of reading. Her characters often serve as effective instructors outside the educational institutions. She saw the male medical establishment as frequently too materialistic, lacking in the necessary heart for effective care of the whole being, both physical and mental. Sand showed in a number of her works how "the great art of the sorceress" (*Correspondance* 7: 490), or folk remedies, could often serve more effectively to cure the ill, how women were skilled in medical or pharmaceutical techniques although officially barred from any kind of practice. Religion she criticized harshly for its dogma and, especially, its hierarchy, writing particularly anticlerical works in *La Daniella*, although the criticism was toned down in a revised version, and later, *Mademoiselle La Quintinie* (Miss La Quintinie). She was a staunch supporter of state-controlled, nonreligious education.

In place of the patriarchal structures, Sand substitutes superior individuals. The successful teachers, like Madeleine of *François le Champi*, work outside the institutions. Madeleine has taught her adopted son not only reading but also his catechism, thereby substituting herself for the Church as well. Sand's "superior" individuals—be they foundling, courtesan, bastard, adulterer, or "witch"—are not necessarily those recognized by society as such. Her reforms, small-scale and private, begin with the individual and move from there to the family unit, which serves as a kernel for social transformation. One family group builds a school; another couple devote themselves to poor and ailing slaves on the Ile Bourbon. As Sand puts it in *Le Meunier d'Angibault* (The Miller of Angibault, 141), "We can still do something for the family but, without being very rich, we cannot yet do anything for humankind."

Another major theme is that of travel. As Sand put it in her important *Lettres d'un voyageur*, the voyage provides the ideal metaphor for life. For Sand, the voyage of initiation, central in a text like the extraordinary *Consuelo*, for instance, is often required before a couple can come together. In *Isidora* we find an example of what has been termed the "mid-life re-birth journey."[2] Travel writing, defined by Sand as "a course in psychology and physiology in which I myself am the subject" (*Lettres d'un voyageur*, 893), was also an important genre for Sand, with texts like *Lettres d'un voyageur*, *Voyage en Auvergne* (A Trip to the Province of Auvergne), or *Un Hiver à Majorque* (*Winter in Majorca*). Important too is the use of certain locales as settings for her works, especially Italy and Berry. A number of Sand's texts can be classified as regionalist because of her use of authentic details of folklore, language, and costume of her native region, especially her pastoral novels. *La Mare au diable*, in fact, includes an appendix giving a wealth of details on the marriage customs of her region. Sand clearly wished to help preserve regional traditions threatened by the growing centralization and consequent uniformity of nineteenth-century France.

In this rapid thematic survey we have of necessity neglected certain of Sand's major texts and several other important themes. We might have mentioned her skillful use of history, with the seventeenth-century Protestant-Catholic struggles of *Les Beaux Messieurs de Bois-Doré* (The Handsome Men of Bois-Doré), for example; or her expert treatment of music in many works, or her texts on actors and the theater. We must also mention the great variety of techniques she explored—epistolary form, the dialogue novel, the journal, the Berry oral tale. As we shall see, critics have begun to discuss the significant contributions made by Sand in her experimentation with literary form. Sand's androgeneity in writing or, as a recent dissertation by Leyla Ezdinli has called it, her "literary transvestism," her "double-gendered identity," must also be saluted as an original contribution to her art.

Writing, for Sand, was indeed an art, despite her pressing need to earn her living with her pen. Although in encouraging Marie *d'Agoult to write, she advised her to write quickly, as she did, it is a mistake to conclude that Sand tossed off her works without revising them. As Jean Courrier has shown in the analysis of the manuscript of *Le Marquis de Villemer* in his recently completed dissertation, Sand's corrections came to no less than 3,249. In her early years, she had considered other ways of earning a living, such as painting decorative objects. As she grew into the writing profession, and however difficult it sometimes was to strive to reform society—she termed these reforms "remedies one prepares for others" (*Correspondance* 3: 773)—she learned to love her work. As early as 1831 she wrote to her son's tutor Jules Boucoiran that writing had given her life a purpose; it had become a passion.

SURVEY OF CRITICISM

In Sand's time some readers were profoundly shocked by her criticism of the social status quo, by her definition of marriage as a partnership of equals, or her discussion of female sexuality. The Church, for example, reacted in a number of ways, especially to the anticlerical outbursts, but also to other threats seen in her writing. As one priest put it, Sand's work was considered dangerous "not because it stirs the senses a great deal but because it leads the heart and the mind astray" (Tricotel, 19). Her works were removed from the curriculum of convent schools and also placed on the Index of books prohibited to all Catholics, selected volumes in the 1840s and her complete works in 1863. Sand rarely responded to criticism, but Letter 12 of *Lettres d'un voyageur*, where she replies to the literary critic Jean-Marie-Napoléon Nisard, who had accused her of hating the institution of marriage, and certain of her prefaces provide exceptions to that rule, giving us insight into the kinds of objections put forth.

Sand's writings also had enormous influence in her time, from Russia to North America. In Russia, Sand, considered a "touchstone"—from a title of a short novel published in 1862 by S. V. (Sofia) Englehart, inspired by the French writer—gained the admiration of great figures such as Bakunin, Dostoyevsky, and Turgenev. In England, George Henry Lewes sang her praises in his critical pieces, while Sand's namesake, his companion George Eliot, acknowledged the influence of her French sister. Elizabeth Barrett Browning and the Brontë sisters too expressed their admiration for Sand and her works, as did John Stuart Mill.

In the field of politics, Italy's Giuseppi Mazzini told of his respect for her ideas. The American Henry James wrote thoughtful pieces analyzing her fiction, and Walt Whitman's work gave evidence of his debt to her. Margaret Fuller, the social reformer, also expressed her admiration. Our century has done much to document this influence; Patricia Thompson's *George Sand and the Victorians*, which outlines how widely Sand's ideas were taken up and incorporated on the other side of the Channel, provides one excellent example.

In France, Sand was broadly respected by major intellectuals of her time, as the circle of her friendships shows. For example, she frequented the painter Eugène Delacroix, the musicians Frédéric Chopin, Franz Liszt, and Pauline Garcia Viardot, the historian Jules Michelet, the actress Marie Dorval, the critic Charles-Augustin Sainte-Beuve, as well as fellow novelists Honoré de Balzac, Alexandre Dumas fils, and especially Gustave Flaubert, with whom she carried on one of the most fascinating correspondences in print.

After the great influence and respect enjoyed during her lifetime, Sand fell into a period of purgatory, as so often happens, but hers was longer than most. For many years she was remembered primarily for her "notorious" lifestyle and her pastoral novels, especially *La Mare au diable*, considered appropriate for children, not adults. The celebration of the centennial of Sand's death in 1976, coinciding with the development of the feminist movement, did much to renew scholars' interest in Sand's writing.

Many are still fascinated by Sand's life. Although a number of good biographies have appeared in recent years, such as those by Barry, Cate, and Winegarten, it is interesting that many scholars still return to Wladimir Karénine's *George Sand, sa vie et ses oeuvres*, published between 1899 and 1912. New editions of Sand's works by the Editions de l'Aurore (twenty-two volumes to date), the Editions des femmes, the "Introuvables" series of the Editions d'Aujourd'hui (twenty-six works), and Slatkine's thirty-two–volume set of reprints have done much to nurture the scholarly productivity and to allow for the study of lesser-known texts, such as *Gabriel, Isidora, Jeanne, Nanon*, and *Valentine*.

One cannot speak of Sand criticism today without acknowledging the monumental accomplishments, over almost fifty years, of Georges Lubin, with the help of his wife Maddy Lubin. Lubin's most important contribution has been his impeccable editions of Sand's writing. The *Oeuvres autobiographiques* (Autobiographical Works) include two of her finest works, *Histoire de ma vie* and *Lettres d'un voyageur*. It is the twenty-four–volume series of her correspondence that will stand as Lubin's greatest achievement, however. It has contributed appreciably to the revival of the interest in Sand, and the wealth of information on Sand's writing and on the cultural history of the nineteenth century in the extensive notes has earned the admiration and gratitude of Sandistes the world over.

Many others are now writing about Sand. In French universities, Simone Vierne of Grenoble's Centre de Recherches sur l'Imaginaire has carried on Léon Cellier's study of the Orphic voyage of initiation and has recently done outstanding work on Sand and revolution. Béatrice Didier's incisive writings and her research group in Paris have also made significant additions. Theses, indicating the presence of future scholars, appear regularly in France. One example of the kind of work being done is Anne Chevereau's study of Sand's lifelong spiritual quest, from the imaginary god-figure of her childhood, Corambé, to the "paraprotestantism" developed from her interest in the most progressive ideas of the Protestant movement. Perspectives such as this from outside the field of literature have done much to enrich Sand studies. Similarly, the collaboration of psychologist Jean-Louis Bonnat with the literary scholar Mireille Bossis has produced a valuable volume on epistolarity that emphasizes the contributions of Sand.

Sand scholarship in the United States has exploded in recent years. Sand is in the process of "recanonization," as Naomi Schor has put it. That Sand has returned to canonical status may be symbolized by David Powell's Sand volume in the Twayne World Authors series, where Sand joins some thirty-five other French writers, including ten other women.

Several additional studies require mention. In a pioneering work in 1977, Janis Glasgow explored the relationship between Sand and Balzac. Kathryn Crecelius's book *Family Romances* shows the honing of the writer's tools in Sand's explorations of form in her very earliest pieces. Gay Manifold's important investigation of Sand's theatrical career points out Sand's attention to staging, her scenic innovations, such as the free movement of the actors, her concern with realistic details of costumes and properties in folk drama, for instance, and the instructional intent of her popular theater. Isabelle Naginski's study is one of the most significant to date because she shows Sand to be an innovative writer, through an in-depth examination of Sand's experiments with form. Naginski treats in a most original manner several much-studied texts, but also the less well known, like *Spiridion*, which she sees as Sand's first attempt at a novel of initiation.

The renewed interest in Sand's works in the twentieth century has led to many other developments. Associations have been formed in France; the Paris-based Amis de George Sand publishes an annual bulletin, and the group led by Jean Courrier in Grenoble produced excellent issues of the *Présence de George Sand* until the review's demise in 1990. In the United States, the Friends of George Sand, under the leadership of Natalie Datlof of Hofstra University, have periodically published *George Sand Studies* as well as volumes of Sand conference papers.

It is clear that Sand studies have come of age in the late twentieth century. With the texts outlined above, and others promised, Sand scholarship is moving into the mainstream of criticism of nineteenth-century literature to regain for George Sand the place she so richly deserves as one of France's great female writers and one of the nineteenth century's most important figures.

NOTES

1. All translations from Sand's works are my own.
2. Annis Pratt, *Archetypal Patterns in Women's Fiction*. Bloomington: Indiana University Press, 1981, 17.

BIBLIOGRAPHY

Major Works by George Sand

Indiana. Paris: Roret, 1832.

Valentine. Paris: Dupuy, 1832.

Lélia. Paris: Dupuy, 1833; revised ed., Bonnaire, 1839.

Jacques. Paris: Bonnaire, 1834.

Léone Léoni. Paris: Bonnaire, 1835.

André. Paris: Bonnaire, 1835.

Simon. Paris: Bonnaire, 1836.

Lettres à Marcie. Paris: Le Monde, 1837; In *Mélanges*. Paris: Perrotin, 1843, 157–219.

Lettres d'un voyageur. Paris: Bonnaire, 1837.

Mauprat. Paris: Bonnaire, 1837. (Edition cited: Paris: Nelson/Callmann-Lévy, n.d.)

Spiridion. Paris: Bonnaire, 1839.

Gabriel. Paris: Bonnaire, 1840.

Les Sept Cordes de la lyre. Paris: Bonnaire, 1840.

Le Compagnon du Tour de France. Paris: Perrotin, 1840.

Un Hiver à Majorque. Paris: Souverain, 1842.

Horace. Paris: Potter, 1842.

Consuelo. Paris: Potter, 1842–1843; *La Comtesse de Rudolstadt*. Paris: Potter, 1843–
     1844.

Jeanne. Paris: Potter, 1844.

Le Meunier d'Angibault. Paris: Desessart, 1845. (Edition cited: Plan de la Tour, France:
     Editions d'Aujourd'hui, 1976.)

Isidora. Paris: Souverain, 1846.

La Mare au diable. Paris: Desessart, 1846.

Lucrezia Floriani. Paris: Desessart, 1847.

La Petite Fadette. Paris: Lévy, 1849.

François le Champi. Paris: Cadot, 1850.

Mont-Revêche. Paris: Cadot, 1853.

Les Maîtres sonneurs. Paris: Cadot, 1853.

Histoire de ma vie. Paris: Lecou-Cadot, 1854–1855.

La Daniella. Paris: Librairie Nouvelle, 1857.

Les Beaux Messieurs de Bois-Doré. Paris: Cadot, 1858.

Elle et lui. Paris: Hachette, 1859.

Jean de la Roche. Paris: Hachette, 1860.

La Ville noire. Paris: Lévy, 1861.

Le Marquis de Villemer. Paris: Lévy, 1861.

Nouvelles (*La Marquise*, 1832; *Lavinia*, 1833; *Metella*, 1833; *Mattea*, 1835; *Pauline*,
     1841). Paris: Lévy, 1861.

Mademoiselle La Quintinie. Paris: Lévy, 1863.

Mademoiselle Merquem. Paris: Lévy, 1868.

Nanon. Paris: Lévy, 1872.

Contes d'une grand-mère. Paris: Lévy, 1873.

Questions d'art et de littérature. Paris: Calmann-Lévy, 1879.

Questions politiques et sociales. Paris: Calmann-Lévy, 1879.

Correspondance. 6 vols. Paris: Calmann-Lévy, 1881–1884.
Correspondance entre George Sand et Gustave Flaubert. Paris: Calmann-Lévy, 1904.

Modern Editions

Indiana. Ed. Pierre Salomon. Paris: Garnier, 1985.
Valentine. Ed. Aline Alquier. Meylan: Aurore, 1988.
Lélia. Ed. Béatrice Didier. 2 vols. Meylan: Aurore, 1987.
André. Ed. Huguette Burine and Michel Gilot. Meylan: Aurore, 1987.
Lettres d'un voyageur, in *Oeuvres autobiographiques,* vol. 2. Ed. Georges Lubin. Paris: Gallimard, 1971.
Mauprat. Ed. Claude Sicard. Paris: Garnier-Flammarion, 1985.
Spiridion. Intro. Georges Lubin. Paris: Aujourd'hui, 1976.
Gabriel. Ed. Janis Glasgow. Paris: Edition des femmes, 1988.
Les Sept Cordes de la lyre. Intro. René Bourgeois. Paris: Flammarion, 1973.
Le Compagnon du Tour de France. Intro. René Bourgeois. Grenoble: Grenoble University Press, 1988.
Un Hiver à Majorque. Ed. Jean Mallion and Pierre Salomon. Meylan: Aurore, 1985.
Horace. Ed. Nicole Courrier and Thierry Bodin. Meylan: Aurore, 1982.
Consuelo. Ed. Simone Vierne and René Bourgeois. 3 vols. Meylan: Aurore, 1983.
Jeanne. Ed. Simone Vierne. Grenoble: Grenoble University Press, 1978; Meylan: Aurore, 1986.
Le Meunier d'Angibault. Ed. Marielle Caors. Meylan: Aurore, 1990.
Isidora. Ed. Eve Sourian. Paris: Editions des femmes, 1990.
La Mare au diable. Ed. Pierre Salomon and Jean Mallion. Paris: Garnier, 1981.
Lucrezia Floriani. Paris: La Sphère, 1981.
La Petite Fadette. Intro. Pierre Salomon and Jean Mallion. Paris: Garnier, 1981.
François le Champi. Ed. Pierre Salomon and Jean Mallion. Paris: Garnier, 1981.
Les Maîtres sonneurs. Ed. Jean Mallion and Pierre Salomon. Paris: Garnier, 1981.
Histoire de ma vie, in *Oeuvres autobiographiques,* vols. 1 and 2. Ed. Georges Lubin. Paris: Gallimard, 1970–1971.
La Daniella. Geneva: Slatkine, 1979.
Les Beaux Messieurs de Bois-Doré. Paris: Albin-Michel, 1976.
Elle et lui. Ed. Thierry Bodin. Intro. Joseph Barry. Meylan: Aurore, 1986.
Jean de la Roche. Ed. Claude Tricotel. Meylan: Aurore, 1988.
La Ville noire. Ed. Jean Courrier. Grenoble: Grenoble University Press, 1978; Meylan: Aurore, 1989.
Le Marquis de Villemer. Ed. Jean Courrier. Meylan: Aurore, 1988.
Nouvelles (*La Marquise,* 1832; *Lavinia,* 1833; *Metella,* 1833; *Mattea,* 1835; *Pauline,* 1841). Ed. Eve Sourian. Paris: Edition des femmes, 1986.
Mademoiselle la Quintinie. Intro. Simone Balayé. Paris: Ressources, 1979.
Mademoiselle Merquem. Ed. Raymond Rheault. Ottawa: Ottawa University Press, 1981.
Nanon. Ed. Nicole Mozet. Maylan: Aurore, 1987.
Contes d'une grand-mère. Ed. Philippe Berthier (with Christiane Smeet-Sand for four tales). 2 vols. Meylan: Aurore, 1982–1983.
Correspondance. Ed. George Lubin. 24 vols. Paris: Gallimard, 1964–1990.
Correspondance entre George Sand et Gustave Flaubert. Ed. Alphonse Jacobs. Paris: Flammarion, 1981.

Voyage en Auvergne, in *Oeuvres autobiographiques*, vol. 2. Ed. Georges Lubin. Paris: Gallimard, 1971.
Souvenirs de 1848. Plan de la Tour, France: Aujourd'hui, 1976.

Translations of George Sand

Indiana. Trans. George Burnham Ives. Chicago: Academy, 1978.
Valentine. Trans. George Burnham Ives. Chicago: Academy, 1978.
Lelia. Trans. Maria Espinosa. Bloomington: Indiana University Press, 1978.
Leone Leoni. Trans. George Burnham Ives. Chicago: Academy, 1978.
Letters to Marcie. Trans. Betsy Wing. Chicago: Academy, 1989.
Lettres d'un voyageur. Trans. Sacha Rabinovich. Intro. Patricia Thompson. London: Penguin, 1987.
Mauprat. Trans. Stanley Young. Intro. Diane Johnson. New York: Da Capo, 1977.
Seven Strings of the Lyre. Trans. George A. Kennedy. Chapel Hill: North Carolina University Press, 1989.
The Journeyman Joiner, or The Companion of the Tour of France. Trans. Francis G. Shaw. New York: Fertig, 1976.
Winter in Majorca. Trans. Robert Graves. Chicago: Academy, 1989.
Consuelo: A Romance of Venice. Trans. Fayette Robinson. New York: Da Capo, 1979.
The Haunted Pool. Trans. Frank H. Potter. Berkeley: Shameless Hussy, 1976.
Lucrezia Floriani. Trans. Julius Eker. Chicago: Academy, 1985.
Fanchon the Cricket. Trans. unknown. Chicago: Cassandra, 1977.
The Country Waif. Trans. Eirene Collis. Intro. Dorothy Zimmerman. Lincoln: Nebraska University Press, 1977.
The Bagpipers. Trans. K. P. Wormeley. Chicago: Academy, 1977.
The Story of My Life. Multiple trans. Ed. Thelma Jurgrau. Albany: SUNY, 1990.
She and He. Trans. George Burnham Ives. Chicago: Academy, 1978.
Letters of George Sand. Trans. Raphael L. Beaufort. 3 vols. New York: AMS (rpt. of 1886 ed.).
The George Sand-Flaubert Letters. Trans. Aimée L. McKenzie. New York: Liveright, 1970.

Studies of George Sand

Album Sand. Ed. Georges Lubin. Paris: Gallimard, 1973.
Barry, Joseph. *Infamous Woman: The Life of George Sand*. Garden City, N.Y.: Doubleday, 1977.
Bossis, Mireille, and Jean-Louis Bonnat, eds. *Ecrire, publier, lire les correspondances*. Nantes: Nantes University Press, 1982.
Bulletin des Amis de George Sand (formerly *Bulletin de Liaison*). Paris: 1976- .
Cate, Curtis. *George Sand: A Biography*. Boston: Houghton Mifflin, 1975.
Chevereau, Anne. *Du Catholicisme au paraprotestantisme?* Paris: Privately printed, 1988.
Coars, Marielle. *Le Berry de George Sand*. Issoudun: Privately printed, 1989.
Crecelius, Kathryn J. *Family Romances: George Sand's Early Novels*. Bloomington: Indiana University Press, 1987.
Datlof, Natalie, ed. *George Sand Papers: Conference proceedings, 1976*. New York: AMS Press, 1980.

————. *George Sand Papers: Conference proceedings, 1978*. New York: AMS Press, 1982.

Dickenson, Donna. *George Sand: A Brave Man—The Most Womanly Woman*. Oxford: Berg, 1988.

Didier, Béatrice. *L'Ecriture-femme*. Paris: PUF, 1981.

Ezdinli, Leyla. *George Sand's Literary Transvestism: Pre-texts and contexts*. Diss. Princeton University, 1988.

Europe. Special Issue: "George Sand," March 1978.

George Sand Studies (formerly *Friends of George Sand Newsletter*). Hempstead, N.Y.: 1978.

Glasgow, Janis. *Une Esthétique de comparaison: Balzac et George Sand: "La Femme abandonnée" et "Metella."* Paris: Nizet, 1977.

————, ed. *George Sand: Collected Essays*. Troy, N.Y.: Whitston, 1985.

Karénine, Wladimir [Vavara Komarova Stassova]. *George Sand, sa vie et ses oeuvres*. 4 vols. Paris: Ollendorff and Plon-Nourrit, 1899–1912.

Manifold, Gay. *George Sand's Theatre Career*. Ann Arbor: UMI, 1985.

Marix-Spire, Thérèse. *Les Romantiques et la musique: le cas George Sand 1804–1838*. Paris: Nouvelles Editions Latines, 1954.

Maurois, André. *George Sand*. Trans. Gerard Hopkins. New York: Harper, 1953.

Miller, Nancy K. *Subject to Change: Reading Feminist Writing*. New York: Columbia University Press, 1988.

Naginski, Isabelle. *George Sand: Writing for Her Life*. New Brunswick, N.J.: Rutgers University Press, 1990.

Poli, Annarosa. *L'Italie dans la vie et l'oeuvre de George Sand*. Paris: Colin, 1960.

Powell, David. *George Sand*. Boston: Twayne, 1990.

Présence de George Sand. 36 vols. Echirolles: Association pour l'Etude et la Diffusion de l'Oeuvre de George Sand, 1978–1990.

Schlientz, Gisela. *George Sand, Leben und Werk in Texten und Bildern*. Frankfurt-am-Main: Insel Verlag, 1987.

Schor, Naomi. "Idealism in the Novel: Recanonizing Sand." *Yale French Studies* 75 (1988): 56–73.

Thompson, Patricia. *George Sand and the Victorians: Her Influence and Reputation in Nineteenth Century England*. New York: Columbia University Press, 1977.

Tricotel, Claude. *Comme deux troubadours: Histoire de l'amitié Flaubert-Sand*. Paris: Société de l'Edition de l'Enseignement Supérieur, 1978.

Van Rossum-Guyon, Françoise. *George Sand: Recherches nouvelles*. Amsterdam: C.R.I.N., 1983.

Vierne, Simone, ed. *George Sand: Colloque de Cerisy*. Paris: Sedes, 1983.

Winegarten, Renee. *The Double Life of George Sand, Woman and Writer: A Critical Biography*. New York: Basic Books, 1978.

Wingard Vareille, Kristina. *Socialité, sexualité et les impasses de l'histoire: Evolution de la thématique sandienne d' "Indiana" (1832) à "Mauprat" (1837)*. Uppsala: Acta Universitatis Upsalensis, 1987.

NATHALIE SARRAUTE
(1900–   )

Ann Cothran

Nathalie Sarraute has claimed an area of investigation unique in fiction: the exploration of our inner, mental reality as the source of human external behavior. Sarraute focuses on those fleeting sensations of which we are only vaguely aware but which make up the very fabric of our psychological existence. Her entire work is the effort to capture and to translate these internal, largely nonverbal dramas into language. Her pioneering exploration of an uncharted area has required her simultaneously to find equally new forms of expression. Although she began developing her new forms and subjects as early as the 1930s, she is inevitably associated with the "New Novelists," a group of writers of the 1950s and 1960s. Although these writers have little in common other than the desire to renew the techniques of the traditional novel, many of them in so doing are able, as is Sarraute, to achieve a new kind of realism, which has nothing in common with traditional realism in literature. The nineteenth-century novel's exact rendering of external detail and concern for social conditions is replaced by a psychological realism, more representative of the modern view of the world as fragmented, incoherent, and unknowable; but because of the revolution in form, these texts are initially difficult. Learning to read Sarraute is like learning a new language or following a piece of music that has no melody: the familiar points of orientation have been removed. The uninitiated reader is uncomfortable in a fictional world of nameless characters who are indistinguishable one from another, where there is no sequence of events to form a recognizable plot, where scenes may be repeated a number of times from different angles of vision, with no indication that they are being repeated, leaving the reader to ask: "Who is speaking?" "Where am I?" "What is happening?" or "*Is* anything happening?" The effort to learn this new language, however, is amply rewarded as one gains access to a universe that offers an extraordinary representation of human relationships.

BIOGRAPHY

Nathalie Tcherniak was born in Ivanovo-Voznessensk, Russia, on July 18, 1900. Her parents, who had been forced by Tsar Nicholas II's anti-Semitic repression to leave Russia in order to pursue university studies, had met in Switzerland, and returned to Russia after her father completed his degree. They were divorced when Nathalie was two. Because she spent much of her childhood between France and Russia, she was fluent in both French and Russian at an early age. When she was seven years old, she attempted to write her first novel, only to be crushed when a family friend to whom it had been given for approval dismissed it summarily with the advice that she first learn how to spell if she wanted to become a writer.

Sarraute eventually settled permanently in Paris with her remarried father and stepmother. Thanks to the latter's mother, she learned English and German, and to read French and Russian literature. After the *baccalauréat*, she took a degree in English at the Sorbonne, studied for a B.A. in Oxford, where she was captain of the punting team, and studied sociology in Berlin. She then returned to Paris to study law. In 1923 she met Raymond Sarraute, whom she married two years later. They have three daughters, one of whom, Claude, writes for *Le Monde*. Nathalie Sarraute practiced law for twelve years. In 1932 she composed two short sketches which were eventually to appear in her first work, *Tropismes* (*Tropisms*). After being refused by Gallimard and Grasset, it was accepted by Denoël in 1937, but received only one review, in *La Gazette de Liège*. She began her second work, *Portrait d'un inconnu* (*Portrait of a Man Unknown*), in 1941. During the Nazi occupation of France, she was forced to take refuge at the country home of a French woman, posing as the governess of her own children. *Portrait*, finished in 1946, was finally published in 1948 by Robert Marin. In spite of a laudatory preface by Sartre, in which he coined the term *anti-novel*, the book did not sell well. Sarraute then began to write critical essays, mainly to explain what she was trying to do in fiction.

In 1953 a second novel, *Martereau*, was published, followed by *L'Ere du soupçon* (*The Age of Suspicion*, 1956), a collection of previously published critical essays. *Portrait* was reissued in 1957 by Gallimard and *Tropismes* reprinted in the same year by Editions de Minuit. Her third novel, *Le Planétarium* (*The Planetarium*, 1959), was well received and is perhaps still the best known of her works. A fourth novel, *Les Fruits d'or* (*The Golden Fruits*, 1963), won the International Prize for Literature in 1964, the same year she published her first radio play, *Le Silence* (*Silence*). A second radio play, *Le Mensonge* (*The Lie*), was broadcast in 1966. Her fifth novel, *Entre la vie et la mort* (*Between Life and Death*, 1968), was followed by a third radio play, *Isma* (1970), a novel, *Vous les entendez?* (*Do You Hear Them?*, 1972), a play, *C'est beau* (*It's Beau-*

tiful, 1973), her most recent novel, *"disent les imbéciles"* (*"fools say"*, 1976), and another play, *Elle est là* (*She's There*, 1978). Her most recent texts include a work of prose fiction, *L'Usage de la parole* (*The Use of Speech*, 1980), a radio play, *Pour un oui ou pour un non* (*For a Yes or a No*, 1982), and an autobiographical account of her childhood, *Enfance* (*Childhood*, 1983).

In spite of the long time it took to gain critical recognition, Sarraute is today one of the best known writers in France. She is invariably mentioned whenever the modern novel is discussed. Her works have been translated into numerous languages, including Finnish and Japanese. Sarraute has traveled extensively and lectured widely. She is relatively unknown outside of the university in the United States, where she has been a frequent visitor to college campuses. She still lives in Paris, where she is very generous in granting interviews to students and critics.

MAJOR THEMES

In a modest statement in *L'Ere du soupçon* (141), Sarraute explains that the duty of the writer is to bring to expression that "parcel" of reality which the writer alone is first to recognize. Sarraute's own "parcel" of reality is composed of microscopic, fleeting impulses—intense, inner reactions to other people's speech, gestures, and visible feelings, the existence of which she became aware at a very early age. From her very first work, *Tropismes*, she has never stopped exploring this domain and the various ways in which these pre-language impulses could be expressed. The term *tropism* refers to a biological organism's involuntary reaction to an external stimulus. Sarraute chose this term because it perfectly describes the types of human interactions (or, more accurately, action-reaction-reaction) found in all of her works. A typical segment of narration, particularly in the early works, might consist of a remark, question, or slight change of expression on the part of one character, which causes a second character suddenly to feel a strong swell of resentment, which itself is translated into a repulsion image. This sudden sensation—the tropism—in turn provokes a reaction manifesting itself externally as a word or gesture in reply, which then creates a tropistic response in the first character. Thus there is a constant interplay between the banal surface world of the commonplace and the cliché and the inner, often violent world of the tropisms, between "consciousnesses" and "subconsciousnesses."

On a large scale, these reactions reveal the human need for approval, the desire to dominate, a terrible fear of rejection or ridicule, anxiety over the judgment of others, anger and contempt for how others behave in interactions, the desire to conform, self-doubt where one's own opinions and values are concerned. (In Sarraute's work, it must be remembered, these "motivations" are all examined at the microscopic level.) She tends to explore them in middle-class settings among family, friends, and acquaintances. Occasionally, she has been criticized for never deviating from this setting, for not representing other classes or social issues. But Sarraute is not interested in social issues as the subject of her fiction, rather in the in-depth representation of that "matter as anonymous as blood" that we all share (*L'Ere du soupçon*, 74).

Perhaps in no other writer is technique as inseparable from content as in Sarraute. Like other authors associated with the New Novel, she has all but eliminated the traditional structures of character, plot, external description, and the like. For Sarraute, it is necessary to remove everything that would detract attention from the subsurface activities of the tropisms. Her major formal contribution is in the area of language. Since Rimbaud, the problem of "finding a language" appropriate to their vision has been crucial for writers, particularly for poetic writers like Sarraute (for whom the term poetic refers to "that which makes the invisible appear"; cited in Minogue, 28).

If the tropism can be termed Sarraute's basic unit of psychological content, then "sub-conversation" is the basic unit of formal expression. This designation—sub-*conversation*—is somewhat misleading. It does not so much refer to a type of conversation or dialogue as call attention to the verbal expression of the psychological movement of tropisms, the translation into words of the internal dramas. Sometimes the translation does resemble dialogue, or the recorded thoughts of a character, but the most essential representation of the tropistic sensations is the image. Metaphors are frequently the only means through which a sensation analogous to that of the tropism can be transmitted to the reader. Simple images are often taken from the animal and vegetable world to capture instinctive reactions of attraction and repulsion. Other metaphors describe the sensation of walls crumbling or miasmas rising. Characters are enveloped by sucker-laden tentacles or filled with swollen pouches of acrid liquid on the verge of bursting open. A special feature of Sarraute's technique is the greatly extended metaphor, which she develops to the point that frequently a lengthy segment of narration becomes a kind of novel in miniature, with its own plot and characters. If a character lets a chance remark drop, only to regret it instantly, the text suddenly gives an account of a group of soldiers ambushed, taken prisoner, and brought into the enemy camp as an analogy (battles, invading Hun-like hordes, and fairy tale recreations are very frequent). The primacy of the tropism and sub-conversation are directly responsible for Sarraute's attenuation of the traditional structures of the novel. Plot, a carefully articulated sequence of causally linked events, is replaced by the rapid succession of tropistic responses whose only connection is the action-reaction sequence and the internal logic of the image. In Sarraute, nothing happens on the surface, whereas the regions below swarm with activity. Chronological time is replaced by memory (reviewing of scenes) and anticipation (imagined scenes); and "real" time is greatly slowed down in order to examine at narrative length the instantaneous moment of the tropism. Perhaps the most disconcerting change for the reader is the evolution in Sarraute's representation of characters. Even in the early novels, they are for the most part nameless, never physically described, while the narration shifts constantly from inside to outside, from speaker to reaction, with little or no indication of the shift. In later novels, she all but eliminates the surface representation, concentrating instead on the internal in such a way that it is as though disembodied "voices" are speaking to each other without the intermediary of surface dialogue.

Such is the result of Sarraute's desire to detach the psychological element from its subject, just as modern painting has removed the pictorial element (*L'Ere du soupçon*, 75). With no familiar guideposts, it is not surprising that the reader new to Sarraute feels initially lost and bewildered. Guideposts are present, however, and eventually the once strange universe grows familiar—all too familiar, in fact, for Sarraute forces us to recognize in ourselves the existence of these very common movements.

All of Sarraute's works are set in the same universe, and thus this description applies generally to each of the individual works. Over the course of her career, however, a very definite evolution can be observed, primarily in her technique and, to an extent, in her specific subject matter. A brief survey of her works will introduce some aspects of this evolution.

Sarraute's first published work, *Tropismes*, consists of twenty-four short texts (one to three pages each) that show people engaged on the surface in everyday activities, while beneath the surface their unconscious reactions to each other are revealed through tropisms. *Tropismes* contains in germ all of her future work, as she was to say later in *L'Ere du soupçon* (iv). Indeed, all the basic elements of the fiction to come are present: banal, outer reality, tropistic movements, and anonymous characters.

Sarraute's first two novels, *Portrait d'un inconnu* and *Martereau*, both use first-person narrators as tropism recorders. In *Portrait d'un inconnu*, the hypersensitive narrator observes a Balzacian couple, a miserly father and his unmarried daughter, in their reactions to each other, going so far as to imagine scenes between them (a typical and, over time, frequent Sarraute device) when he cannot physically observe them. His search for tropisms comes to an abrupt halt at the end of the novel when the daughter's fiancé appears as a character, complete with name and a physical description, too solid for tropisms to be revealed. In *Martereau*, the situation is rather reversed. Here the hypersensitive nephew-narrator hopes that nothing (i.e., tropisms) will shatter the calm, reassuring outer appearance of a family acquaintance, Martereau. When the narrator's uncle arranges for Martereau to "purchase" a country house for him in order for the uncle to avoid paying taxes, and Martereau not only refuses to give a receipt, but also moves into the house, intense suspicions arise about Martereau, forcing the nephew to investigate the tropistic possibilities. In one major part of the novel he "replays" a scene from a variety of points of view. At the end the suspicions are put to rest, only to reawaken when a seemingly innocent remark of Martereau's suddenly calls everything into question again.

Le Planétarium, in many respects central to Sarraute's work, is the best known of her novels. Here she eliminates the first-person narrator, allowing freer movement into the tropistic world from consciousness to consciousness, more frequent reviewed and imagined scenes. The plot is all but eliminated: will Alain and Gisèle Guimier get Aunt Bertha's apartment? (They do at the end, an almost unnoticed fact.) Subplots swirl around family struggles, grated carrots, taste in furniture, reactions to a well-known writer.

Sarraute's next three novels, *Les Fruits d'or*, *Entre la vie et la mort*, and *Vous les entendez?*, are explicitly concerned with the theme of artistic creation. In *Les Fruits d'or*, the main "character" is a novel of the same name. The plot traces its rise to fame and subsequent fall, and the tropistic investigation of the anonymous admirers and detractors of the novel focuses on the inauthenticity of critical reception, the desire to belong to the group, and doubt of one's own judgment. The protagonist of *Entre la vie et la mort* is a writer who in various ways reveals his relationship to the creative process. His hopes, fears, and insecurities are examined in his childhood fascination with words, the way in which he composes, and his reaction to critical reception. The catalyst of *Vous les entendez?* is a pre-Columbian statue. This object, much loved by a father and his visiting friend, is seemingly ridiculed by the adolescent children whose peals of laughter can be heard from upstairs, provoking tropistic reactions in the adults and vice versa.

Critics agree that *"disent les imbéciles"* is by far Sarraute's most difficult novel, and even though the universe of tropisms remains the foundation, it seems to introduce a theme that has, in retrospect, been implicit all along in Sarraute's work: the terribly destructive power of words. The novel opens on a non-threatening scene of a grandmother surrounded by her loving grandchildren. Over the course of the novel, the notion emerges that language, through its propensity to categorize and its capacity to attach labels to ideas, is destructive to thought. In particular, the "voices" seem concerned with protecting their ideas from the recurring, crushing remark: "That's what fools say." By the end of the novel, the totalitarian possibilities inherent in language are frighteningly revealed. In her most recent fictional work, *L'Usage de la parole*, Sarraute returns to the short sketch. Like *Tropismes*, *L'Usage de la parole* cannot be called a novel. Unlike *Tropismes*, where the investigation centers on inner behavior, in this work Sarraute probes the everyday use of trite, seemingly harmless expressions that conceal (or sterilize) the negative tropistic world beneath. In both *"disent les imbéciles"* and *L'Usage de la parole*, a series of disembodied "voices" replace all vestiges of plot and character in order to allow unimpeded concentration on language itself.

In addition to her novels, Sarraute is the author of six radio plays, the first published in 1964 and the most recent in 1982. Typically, she writes a radio play after completing a novel in order to wrap up some question of theme left unfinished in the novel. This genre posed a very difficult problem for her at first. Because the plays consist purely of dialogue, she had to find a means of incorporating sub-conversation in that dialogue. Otherwise, the plays are typical of her work: anonymous characters discuss banal problems that provoke intense reactions, or in some cases, unlike the novels, silences are generators of tropisms.

In 1956, when the New Novelists were attracting the attention of the literary world, four previously published essays were united in *L'Ere du soupçon*. This short volume is by far the best introduction to Sarraute's aims and methods. The essays raise and discuss questions of the psychological forces that the modern novel must account for, the how and why of the novel's evolution, the question of literary realism as it changes over time.

In 1983, she published an autobiographical account of her childhood, *Enfance*, completely unlike traditional autobiography. As a Sarraute "voice" talks to another Sarraute "voice," the child's experience is fragmented, in order to examine and question it from the tropistic perspective. It seems appropriate that toward the end of a long career spent investigating tropistic behavior, Sarraute has returned to the source of the "parcel of reality."

From *Tropismes* to *L'Usage de la parole* and *Enfance*, the universe of tropisms and the commonplace remains the focus of her investigation, though its contours change. Her work has constantly evolved as her further explorations into the unknown give rise to increasingly refined techniques. Inner "landscapes" occupy greater and greater textual space as the surface world all but disappears, and concomitantly, relatively recognizable characters dissolve into inner "voices," centers of consciousness in tropistic communication with each other. What emerges from these explorations are fundamental issues of human concern such as our relationships with others, the formation and holding of values, the fate of the individual in the collective mentality, and, more recently, the terrible power of language itself (see Besser, 172). Sarraute is not recognizably topical or political. It is difficult to call her a feminist writer—certainly in comparison to Simone de *Beauvoir and Monique *Wittig. But like many women writers, she writes in those *so-called* marginal areas—in her case, those inner sensations that provoke all of our outer behavior, which she considers fundamental to understanding human existence. Like all marginal explorations that women make, and know must be made, Sarraute's "parcel" forms the boundless underpinning of the human experience.

SURVEY OF CRITICISM

The famous Sartre preface to *Portrait d'un inconnu* notwithstanding, Sarraute received virtually no critical attention until the publication of *L'Ere du soupçon*. Thereafter books, articles, and doctoral dissertations began to appear in rapidly growing numbers. Almost without exception, once critics began to write about Sarraute, she has been very favorably received. Her enthusiastic readers are legion, and most enthusiastic among them is Claude Mauriac, who claims that she has contributed more than anyone else in modern times to our understanding of human beings (*L'Allittérature contemporaine*, 324). Sarraute has had her detractors, among the most surprising of whom must be Jean-Paul Sartre. His earlier praise for Sarraute was based on her innovations in the novel, but by 1960, Sartre had changed his opinion of her work, finding it insufficiently attentive to social and historical concerns. Perhaps more unfortunate are the number of severe misreadings of Sarraute, which seem to be the result of critics interpreting the surface reality rather than the underneath world of tropisms. (For a representative sample, see Minogue, 166–67.)

The first works on Sarraute are found in studies of the contemporary novel and the New Novel that devote a chapter to her works. In the mid–1960s, the first two general studies devoted exclusively to Sarraute appeared: Cranaki and Belaval's *Nathalie Sarraute* and Micha's *Nathalie Sarraute*. These are recommended to the reader new to Sarraute as solid introductions and as first lessons in learning her language. For nonreaders of French, Ruth Temple's *Nathalie Sarraute* offers summaries of her works and discussion of tropisms and subconversation up through the 1963 *Les Fruits d'or*. Some of the important early articles on Sarraute treat the fundamental elements of her work, tropisms, subconversation, the narrator, characters, and her special use of metaphor (see Blot, Cismaru, Cohn, Finas, Minor, Pingaud). As Sarraute began to attract wider critical attention, studies of her work became more technical in focus. The following summary is limited to selected book-length studies (important articles treating individual works and particular subjects are included in the bibliography).

Two excellent studies in French are Micheline Tison Braun's *Nathalie Sarraute ou la recherche de l'authenticité* (1971) and André Allemand's *L'Oeuvre romanesque de Nathalie Sarraute* (1980). Tison Braun proposes the authentic and inauthentic as the two fundamental psychological, behavioral oppositions in Sarraute's work and sees Sarraute as the likely successor to French moralists in the seventeenth-century tradition. Tison Braun also focuses on artistic creation as an important theme in Sarraute, considering it a symbolic form of the creation of the personality. This is an excellent study of the psychology of human relations fundamental to Sarraute's work. André Allemand's analysis of Sarraute's novels considers them from the narrative perspectives of character, discourse, and time. A given Sarraute novel illustrates the main thesis of each chapter. This detailed study relies to an extent on the reader's familiarity with Sarraute's work, with the New Novel, and with contemporary approaches to poetics and linguistics. Françoise Calin, in *La Vie retrouvée: étude de l'oeuvre romanesque de Nathalie Sarraute*, chooses to isolate various thematic elements that make up Sarraute's universe, such as the mask. Anthony Newman's *Une Poésie des discours* (1976) is the only truly formalist book-length study of Sarraute to date. He proposes a poetics of the novel derived from a formal and systematic analysis of Sarraute's novels. This very technical but rewarding work draws on contemporary (at the time of its writing) theories of narration to develop a reading of the discourses of Sarraute, stressing in particular the fundamental irony of Sarraute's writing, which grows from the confrontation of the tropisms with the surface.

Until 1979 no full-length study of Nathalie Sarraute had appeared in English. The first was Gretchen Rous Besser's *Nathalie Sarraute* in the Twayne World Authors series. In addition to providing a solid, up-to-date overview of Sarraute's work, it has an annotated bibliography and is one of the few critical works to discuss the radio plays. Helen Watson-Williams's 1981 study of Sarraute's novels considers them exclusively from the aesthetic point of view, affirming that from *Tropismes* to *"disent les imbéciles"* Sarraute is concerned with the work of art—its nature, its appreciation and reception, and, most recently, its place and value in human life.

Once the reader has become somewhat familiar with Sarraute, perhaps the most rewarding study of all is Minogue's *Nathalie Sarraute and the War of the Words*. As her title indicates, Minogue sees language as the heart of the Sarrautian enterprise, her works an "exploration of the ways and wars of words as manipulated by humankind" (22). Minogue's study is aware of and sensitive to Sarraute's language and the role words play in her work. The fundamental concepts of tropisms and sub-conversation are useful distinctions in understanding the innovations in form and content that Sarraute has never ceased to elaborate, but works such as these provide a much-needed analysis of that most basic yet complex of Sarraute's elements: words.

BIBLIOGRAPHY

Works by Nathalie Sarraute

Tropismes. Paris: Robert Denoël, 1939.
Portrait d'un inconnu. Paris: Robert Marin, 1948.
Martereau. Paris: Gallimard, 1953.
L'Ere du soupçon. Paris: Gallimard, 1956.
Le Planétarium. Paris: Gallimard, 1959.
Les Fruits d'or. Paris: Gallimard, 1963.
Entre la vie et la mort. Paris: Gallimard, 1968.
Vous les entendez? Paris: Gallimard, 1972.
"disent les imbéciles." Paris: Gallimard, 1976.
Théâtre: Elle est là. C'est beau. Isma. Le Mensonge. Le Silence. Paris: Gallimard, 1978.
L'Usage de la Parole. Paris: Gallimard, 1980.
Pour un oui ou pour un non. Paris: Gallimard, 1982.
Enfance. Paris: Gallimard, 1983.

Translations of Nathalie Sarraute

Tropisms. Trans. Maria Jolas. New York: George Braziller, 1963.
Portrait of a Man Unknown. Trans. Maria Jolas. New York: George Braziller, 1958.
Martereau. Trans. Maria Jolas. New York: George Braziller, 1959.
The Age of Suspicion. Trans. Maria Jolas. New York: George Braziller, 1963.
The Planetarium. Trans. Maria Jolas. New York: George Braziller, 1960.
The Golden Fruits. Trans. Maria Jolas. New York: George Braziller, 1964.
Between Life and Death. Trans. Maria Jolas. New York: George Braziller, 1969.
"fools say." Trans. Maria Jolas. New York: George Braziller, 1977.
Collected Plays. Trans Maria Jolas and Barbara Wright. London: Calder, 1981.

The Use of Speech. Trans. Barbara Wright. London: Calder, 1983.
Childhood. Trans. Barbara Wright. London: Calder, 1984.

Studies of Nathalie Sarraute

Allemand, André. *L'Oeuvre romanesque de Nathalie Sarraute.* Neuchâtel: Editions de la Baconnière, 1980.

Belaval, Yvon. "*Tropismes.*" *Nouvelle Nouvelle Revue Française* 62 (1958): 335–37.

Bell, Sheila M. *Nathalie Sarraute: A Bibliography.* London: Grant and Cutler, 1982.

Besser, Gretchen Rous. *Nathalie Sarraute.* Boston: Twayne, 1979.

Bloch-Michel, Jean. *Le Présent de l'indicatif: essai sur le nouveau roman.* Paris: Gallimard, 1963.

Blot, Jean. "Nathalie Sarraute: une fine buée." *Nouvelle Nouvelle Revue Française* 188 (1968): 111–18.

Bouraoui, H. A. "Sarraute's Narrative Portraiture: The Artist in Search of a Voice." *Critique: Studies in Modern Fiction* 14 (1972): 77–89.

Brée, Germaine. *Women Writers in France.* New Brunswick, N.J.: Rutgers University Press, 1973.

Britton, Celia. "The Self and Language in the Novels of Nathalie Sarraute." *Modern Language Review* 77 (1982): 577–84.

Cagnon, Maurice. "*Le Planétarium*: quelques aspects stylistiques." *French Review* 40 (1967): 620–26.

Calin, Françoise. *La Vie retrouvée: étude de l'oeuvre romanesque de Nathalie Sarraute.* Paris: Minard, 1976.

Cismaru, Alfred. "The Reader as Co-Creator in Nathalie Sarraute's Novels." *Renascence* 16 (1964): 201–7, 218.

Cohn, Ruby. "A Diminishing Difference." *Yale French Studies* 27 (1961): 99–105.

———. "Nathalie Sarraute's Sub-conversations." *Modern Language Notes* 78 (1963): 261–70.

Cothran, Ann. "Reporting and Commentary in Sarraute's Novels." *L'Esprit Créateur* 17 (1977): 245–69.

Cranaki, Mimica, and Yvon Belaval. *Nathalie Sarraute.* Paris: Gallimard, 1965.

Eliez-Ruëgg, Elisabeth. *La Conscience d'autrui et la conscience des objets dans l'oeuvre de Nathalie Sarraute.* Berne: Lang, 1972.

Finas, Lucette. "Nathalie Sarraute ou les métamorphoses du verbe." *Tel Quel* 20 (1965): 68–77.

Goldmann, Lucien. *Pour une sociologie du roman.* Paris: Gallimard, 1964.

Greene, Robert. "Nathalie Sarraute's *L'Usage de la parole*, or Re(en)trop(iz)ing *Tropismes.*" *Novel* 16 (1983): 197–214.

Heath, Stephen. *The Nouveau Roman: A Study in the Practice of Writing.* Philadelphia: Temple University Press, 1972.

Jaeger, Patricia J. "Three Authors in Search of an Elusive Reality: Butor, Sarraute, Robbe-Grillet." *Critique: Studies in Modern Fiction* 6 (1963): 65–85.

Janvier, Ludovic. *Une Parole exigeante: le nouveau roman.* Paris: Minuit, 1964.

Jefferson, Ann. "Imagery Versus Description: The Problematics of Representation in the Novels of Nathalie Sarraute." *Modern Language Review* 73 (1978): 513–24.

Magny, Olivier de. "Nathalie Sarraute ou l'astronomie intérieure." *Les Lettres Nouvelles* 41 (1963): 139–53.

Mauriac, Claude. *L'Allittérature contemporaine*. Paris: A. Michel, 1969.

Mercier, Vivian. *The New Novel from Queneau to Pinget*. New York: Farrar, Straus and Giroux, 1971.

Micha, René. "Des rires jeunes, des rires cristallins." *Critique* 299 (1972): 295–98.

———. *Nathalie Sarraute*. Paris: Editions Universitaires, 1966.

Minogue, Valerie. *Nathalie Sarraute and the War of the Words*. Edinburgh: Edinburgh University Press, 1981.

Minor, Ann. "Nathalie Sarraute: *Le Planétarium*." *Yale French Studies* 24 (1959): 96–100.

Morot-Sir, Edouard. "L'Art des pronoms et le nommé dans l'oeuvre de Nathalie Sarraute." *Romanic Review* 72 (1981): 204–14.

Nadeau, Maurice. *Le Roman français depuis la guerre*. Paris: Gallimard, 1970.

Newman, A. S. *Une Poésie des discours: essai sur les romans de Nathalie Sarraute*. Geneva: Droz, 1976.

Picon, Gaëtan. "Sur *Les Fruits d'or*." *Mercure de France* 1197 (1963): 485–93.

Pingaud, Bernard. "Le Personnage dans l'oeuvre de Nathalie Sarraute." *Preuves* 154 (1963): 19–34.

Racevskis, Karlis. "Irony as a Creative and Critical Force in Three Novels of Nathalie Sarraute." *French Review* 51 (1977): 37–44.

Ricardou, Jean. *Le Nouveau Roman*. Paris: Seuil, 1973.

Ricardou, Jean, and Françoise Rossum-Guyon, eds. *Nouveau Roman: hier, aujour-d'hui*. 2 vols. Paris: Union Générale d'Editions 10/18, 1972.

Robbe-Grillet. *Pour un nouveau roman*. Paris: Minuit, 1963.

Roudiez, Léon S. "A Glance at the Vocabulary of Nathalie Sarraute." *Yale French Studies* 27 (1961): 90–98.

Sartre, Jean-Paul. Preface to *Portrait d'un inconnu*, by Nathalie Sarraute. Paris: Union Générale d'Editions 10/18, 1964. 7–14.

Temple, Ruth Z. *Nathalie Sarraute*. New York: Columbia University Press, 1968.

Tison Braun, Micheline. *Nathalie Sarraute ou la recherche de l'authenticité*. Paris: Gallimard, 1971.

Watson-Williams, Helen. *The Novels of Nathalie Sarraute: Towards an Aesthetic*. Amsterdam: Rodopi, 1981.

Zeltner, Gerda. "Nathalie Sarraute et l'impossible réalisme." *Mercure de France* 1188 (1962): 593–608.

ALBERTINE SARRAZIN
(1937–1967)

Warren F. Motte, Jr.

BIOGRAPHY

On September 17, 1937, a newborn baby girl was left at the Welfare Office in Algiers, where the name Albertine Damien was given to her. At the age of two, she was adopted by an older couple, a doctor in the colonial army and his wife; they renamed the child Anne-Marie R——. In 1947 the family left Algeria for Aix-en-Provence where, on September 27, Albertine was raped by a forty-year-old member of the R—— family named Albert.

For the next five years, Albertine proved herself a capable student, even a brilliant one, in literary studies, art, and music. During this period, she began to keep a diary. Relations with her family becoming more and more difficult, she asked to be allowed to board at her secondary school, a request her parents refused. In 1952, faced with her lack of discipline, her parents subjected Albertine to a psychiatric evaluation: she was declared "normal," and the psychiatrist prescribed a separation from her parents. The director of Aix's secondary school expressed her willingness to take Albertine into the school, but her parents disregarded both the psychiatrist's advice and the director's offer. On November 20, 1952, on her adoptive father's initiative, the police took Albertine to the Refuge of the Good Shepherd in Marseilles, a reform school where, according to Albertine's later testimony, the carceral regime rivaled that of any prison she subsequently came to know. During this period, her adoptive father began to take the legal steps that would eventually result (in October 1956) in the annulment of the original adoption.

During her detention at the Good Shepherd, Albertine met Emilienne, with whom she became intimate, and studied for the secondary school terminal examination, the *baccalauréat*. Transferred under guard from the Good Shepherd to another school on July 11, 1953, in order to take part of that exam, Albertine escaped through the kitchen of the school and hitchhiked to Paris. There she discovered the capital's attractions, supporting herself through prostitution. On November 11, Emilienne, having likewise escaped from the Good Shepherd, joined Albertine in Paris. Together they attempted a holdup on December 21, during the course of which Emilienne wounded a woman. Two days later the police found and arrested them, transferring them to the Fresnes prison. Albertine's adoptive parents refused to provide a lawyer for her.

In July 1955 Albertine was escorted from Fresnes to take the second part of her *baccalauréat*, which she passed. In November she and Emilienne appeared before the juvenile court where, for their holdup, they were condemned to seven and five years of prison, respectively. Albertine was transferred in January 1956 to the Doullens reform school in Picardy. There she took home economics classes as well as first-year university studies, including literature and Latin. At Doullens she met and became friendly with Madame Gogois-Myquel, a psychiatrist at the school, to whom Albertine would later dedicate *La Cavale* (*The Runaway*). On April 19, 1957, while escaping from Doullens, Albertine jumped from a thirty-foot wall and broke her ankle. A passing motorist, Julien Sarrazin, picked her up and cared for her.

Julien in turn was arrested and incarcerated in March 1958. He was released in June and rejoined Albertine; together they carried out several burglaries. On September 8 they were arrested; Julien was released, but Albertine was remanded in custody to finish the sentence imposed in 1955. She was imprisoned in Amiens, then transferred to Soissons. Julien and Albertine were married on February 7, 1959, while Albertine was still in prison: she took the name Albertine Sarrazin. In June, Julien was again arrested; condemned to the Pontoise prison, he was afterwards transferred to Soissons.

In the fall of 1960 both were freed, Julien on September 23, Albertine on October 5. The following January they were the victims of an automobile accident in which both were seriously injured and Julien's mother was killed. Returning to burglary as a way of life, Albertine and Julien were arrested once again in April. Imprisoned at Versailles, Albertine began to write *La Cavale*. Freed on June 6, 1963, she took a job in a department store in Troyes, visiting Madame Gogois-Myquel from time to time. Julien was transferred in November of that year to the prison in Nîmes. During that same month, the injuries sustained in the car accident continuing to trouble her, Albertine was operated on in Marseilles.

In January 1964 she went to live in Alès and took a job freelancing for a local newspaper. She was arrested on April 9 for stealing a bottle of whiskey and condemned to four months in prison. During that time she wrote *L'Astragale* (*Astragal*). Julien was freed in May; the following August Albertine left prison for the last time. They moved to the Cévennes, a sparsely populated region in central France, in November of that year. There they took a house with a friend named Maurice.

In April 1965 Albertine Sarrazin received word from Jean-Pierre Castelnau, literary director of the Editions Jean-Jacques Pauvert, of his intention to publish her manuscripts. She prepared at his request a revised version of *La Cavale*. In June Albertine and Julien moved to Montpellier. *L'Astragale* and *La Cavale* were published in October; both were received very favorably by the press and the public. Although legally forbidden to visit Paris, Albertine nonetheless obtained special authorization to go there for a series of interviews and promotional engagements. On February 28, 1966, in Tunis, she was awarded the Four Jury Prize. The following May she and Julien bought an old farmhouse near Montpellier, ''The Oratory.'' Her third novel, *La Traversière* (The Crossing), was published in November to great acclaim.

In January 1967 Albertine underwent an operation on her ankle. The following June she was again hospitalized, undergoing a salpingectomy as well as an appendectomy. She returned to the hospital in July where, in the course of a nephrectomy on July 10, she died. Julien Sarrazin brought a malpractice suit against Albertine's doctors, which he eventually won. He used the damage award to found a publishing house, the Editions Sarrazin, devoted to the publication of his late wife's work.

MAJOR THEMES

In spite of their formal heterogeneity, Albertine Sarrazin's writings display a remarkable similarity of theme. Throughout her work she elaborates sustained and mutually complementary discourses on power and its uses, the limits and possibilities of love and sexuality, the dialectic of freedom and constraint, and the nature of language, especially as it is deployed in the gesture that tests it most rigorously, writing.

It is useful, as Elissa Gelfand has suggested, to view Sarrazin's writing as two rather distinct modes of expression. The first is the highly personal, almost hermetic mode that characterizes most of her early production (approximately 1949 to 1961). Here should be noted the diaries, such as *Le Passe-peine, 1949–1967* (Pass-Time, 1949–1967) and the *Journal de prison, 1959* (Prison Journal); the letters, including *Lettres à Julien, 1958–60* (Letters to Julien), *Lettres de la vie littéraire* (Letters from the Literary Life), and *Biftons de prison* (Prison Notes); and the poems. In the other, later mode, a far more polished, public voice makes itself heard. This is the voice of the novels, *La Cavale*, *L'Astragale*, and *La Traversière*; and of the short stories appearing in *La Crèche* (The Cradle).

The early writings, the diaries in particular, are marked by a highly subjectivist, impressionist narration wherein (apparently, at least) little attention is given to structure and style. As in her later works, Sarrazin evokes prison as the organizing experience of life; yet the order of this experience is amorphous. In contrast to the novels, there seems to be no clear structural distinction between the regime of the inside and that of the outside, between constraint and liberty. That sort of opposition appears to be inoperative in the early writings, where Sarrazin seems cannily to reduce commonly held antinomies and hierarchies in an attempt to elaborate a flat, homogeneous discursive world. This technique finds its analogues in other aspects of Sarrazin's early work: chronology (apart from the minimal, literal chronology of the diaries and the letters) is fixed and static; the carceral space is opaque and ill-defined; the narration (in stark contrast to that of the prose fiction) is free of discernible teleology.

The early writings constitute nonetheless a very powerful discourse, arguably more powerful as *statement* than the highly mediated, relatively conventionalist language of the novels. Addressing largely the same issues in both modes of her writing, Albertine Sarrazin refuses any sort of closure or resolution in the first; here, power is a constant, and there is no real possibility for the disenfranchised of eventually acceding to it. Its locus is distant and unattainable; power manifests itself in the world capriciously, but with an authority that cannot be put into question. Sexuality becomes radically abstracted from its accomplishment: like the other human relations it comes to symbolize, it is the object of impossible longing and nostalgia. The prisoner, here, is exemplary. Her world is *the* world, her condition the human condition; existence and the experience of existence are reduced and collapsed. The shape of Sarrazin's writing in the early work is thus precisely figural of the shape of the world she projects: her minimalist technique corresponds to a vision of a starkly truncated, bleakly circumscribed world. In this perspective, Sarrazin offers her early works as the direct, unmediated transcription of incarceration.

In the prose fiction, that radical stance is attenuated. The language, both in the literal and the figurative sense, is no longer that of the diaries, of the letters. It is far more colored by the use of *argot*, of slang; in many passages the incidence of the latter is so strong as to give the impression of artificiality, of a fragile, heavily stylized, and (most important) *written* language. In a sense, Sarrazin borrows this lexicon without actually appropriating it; it remains foreign and significantly male, a language elaborated by men for men. This linguistic change testifies to a more ample formal shift: Sarrazin in fact comes to embrace the form of the contemporary novel. Her adoption of the novel, granted the institutionalization of that genre, leads her to confront problems analogous to those that arise as she modifies her lexicon. The norms and conventions that the novel imposes exercise an imperial influence on the issues central to Sarrazin's thought, recasting them (by comparison to the early writings) in a most significant manner. The world of prose fiction is hierarchical rather than flat: as Elissa Gelfand has pointed out, Sarrazin's discourse in the later work is consistently mediated by metaphor. In support of this, a rigorous regime is installed, one in which effects of prominencing, fullness of detail, and a deliberately conventional spatio-temporal order figure strongly. The whole is dominated by a starkly etched teleology, providing a grid in which each element of the textual fabric takes its place, assuming pertinence: in the novels, significance (and signification) is predetermined and *coerced*.

Inevitably, this phenomenon entails (or testifies to, more appropriately) an ideological shift. In contrast to the static, carceral wasteland of the early work, the narrator's world in the novels is sharply divided in terms of inside and outside. The barrier between those two topographies is porous, and the subject's displacement from one to the other moreover defines a precise and ineluctable progression, a novelistic teleology, in short. Within this teleology, the literal and the figurative complement each other in strict parallel. Thus, the *cavale*, the escape, is both the actual escape from prison and the more abstract salvation from the carceral condition that writing offers. The itinerary that Sarrazin's novels propose, from prison, to conditional freedom, to full and definitive liberation through literature, testifies to a deliberate scripting of desire: taken together, they trace a story of apprenticeship, transcendence, and apotheosis whose principal figure is Albertine Sarrazin herself.

SURVEY OF CRITICISM

Although Albertine Sarrazin's writings elicited an impressive critical response in the middle and late 1960s, the vast majority of the latter came in the form of reviews and brief appreciations; to date, there has been very little sustained analysis of Sarrazin's literary production. The most ample readings of her work have been those provided by Elissa Gelfand, an American academic, and Josane Duranteau, a French journalist and novelist.

Elissa Gelfand examines Sarrazin in a feminist perspective, although she is careful to point out that Sarrazin's writings—unlike those of contemporary writers outside of prison such as *Beauvoir, *Duras, and Christiane *Rochefort—are not animated by overtly feminist consciousness and intent. Gelfand's own purpose is twofold: first, on a local level, she offers an analysis of Sarrazin as an evolving writer; on a broader political and cultural ground, she proposes Sarrazin as a recent example of the imprisoned French woman writer, a tradition that she traces back to the eighteenth-century figure of Madame *Roland.

Postulating the construct of "femininity in form," which she defines as the presence of certain libidinal, unconscious, nontraditional elements in texts, and further evoking the "feminine," defined as the "bisexual," the "nonmasculine" principle which valorizes rather than represses sexual differences within the self, Gelfand argues that Sarrazin's writing traces an identifiable itinerary from prisoner to author. Gelfand focuses her analysis upon two texts, *Journal de prison, 1959* and *La Cavale*. She suggests that the *Journal* is characterized by "sincere discourse and raw imagery," by a sort of "natural language"; in short, Gelfand argues that in the *Journal* Sarrazin "speaks herself." It is, moreover, nontraditional in form, stylistically fragmented and telegraphic, impressionistic in its presentation of the world of experience. *La Cavale*, on the other hand, is far more formally traditionalist and is marked by a rigorous organization: in three parts and forty-five chapters, the novel recounts eighteen months of imprisonment in three different institutions. A precise chronological structure and a rigorous spatial order form the foundation of the text's ortholinear narration.

Gelfand argues the significance of these differences, suggesting that the *Jour-*

nal testifies to an unmediated desire for freedom, deploying a direct discourse; in *La Cavale*, on the contrary, that desire is constantly mediated (and attenuated) by metaphor. Changing terms, Gelfand relocates this difference in the subject's relation to the body, the *Journal* demonstrating a positive, essentially feminine attitude toward the body, *La Cavale* testifying to a masculine alienation therefrom. The evolution she sees is one where language and experience are progressively constrained, and thus brought under control.

Gelfand's argument, both at the local level and in its broader implications, is canny and persuasive. The liberation that Sarrazin wished for may be expressed as the displacement from "prisoner" to "author": it is through this function that Sarrazin sought to be empowered, and it is for this reason, as Elissa Gelfand lucidly points out, that Sarrazin's writings become increasingly specular. More and more, that is, the story that they tell is the chronicle of their own genesis.

Josane Duranteau's *Albertine Sarrazin* bears distinct traces of both journalistic and novelistic style. Locating her analysis in a resolutely biographical mode, Duranteau reads Sarrazin's books through her life, and vice versa. This can be disconcerting, as in the first part of the book, written in the second person and directed toward Sarrazin herself, whom Duranteau by her own admission had met just twice. These two meetings serve as the point of departure for Duranteau's book, followed shortly by her account of Julien Sarrazin's malpractice suit, which she covered for *Combat* in the fall of 1970.

Granted access by Julien Sarrazin to a significant body of unpublished material, Duranteau relies heavily upon the latter, interpolating it into her book. (Subsequently, moreover, Josane Duranteau would edit much of this material for publication, including *Lettres à Julien 1958–60*, *Journal de prison, 1959*, *Lettres de la vie littéraire*, and *Le Passe-peine, 1949–1967*.)

The short portion of *Women of Iron and Velvet* that Margaret Crosland devotes to Albertine Sarrazin serves to locate the latter in a canon of French women writers from George *Sand to the present. She offers a biographical sketch, insisting upon the themes of social marginality, incarceration, and liberation. Unfortunately, Crosland devotes little or no attention to Sarrazin's writing *as writing*.

Ann Cothran's essay, "Narrative Structure as Expression of Self in Sarrazin's *L'Astragale*," approaches that text as a novel of apprenticeship and offers a provocative analysis of the formal devices that Sarrazin uses to tell "the story of a woman's life as she searches for psychic wholeness" (13). Cothran focuses upon Anne's ankle, suggesting that the passages in the novel dealing with it must be read on two levels, both literally and as commentary on Anne's self-image, broken but nonetheless on the mend. Cothran says that Sarrazin indulges in a literary impressionism, through the restriction of information given to the reader, and through a distortion of temporal structures. These effects are intended to allow the reader to identify with Anne and her struggle in the present moment of the narration, and contribute to the elaboration, Cothran argues, of a new kind of mimesis.

BIBLIOGRAPHY

Works by Albertine Sarrazin

L'Astragale. Paris: Jean-Jacques Pauvert, 1965.
La Cavale. Paris: Jean-Jacques Pauvert, 1965.
La Traversière. Paris: Jean-Jacques Pauvert, 1966.
Romans, lettres et poèmes. Paris: Jean-Jacques Pauvert, 1967.
Poèmes. Paris: Jean-Jacques Pauvert, 1969.
Lettres à Julien, 1958–60. Ed. Josane Duranteau. Paris: Jean-Jacques Pauvert, 1971.
Lettres et poèmes. Paris: Livre de Poche, 1971.
Journal de prison, 1959. Preface by Josane Duranteau. Paris: Editions Sarrazin, 1972.
La Crèche. Paris: Sarrazin, 1973.
Lettres de la vie littéraire. Ed. Josane Duranteau. Paris: Jean-Jacques Pauvert, 1974.
Le Passe-peine, 1949–1967. Ed. Josane Duranteau. Paris: Julliard, 1976.
Biftons de prison. Intro. Brigitte Duc. Paris: Jean-Jacques Pauvert, 1977.

Translations of Albertine Sarrazin

Astragal. Trans. Patsy Southgate. New York: Grove, 1967.
The Runaway. Trans. Charles Lam Markmann. New York: Grove, 1967.

Studies of Albertine Sarrazin

Bost, Pierre. *Albertine mon amie*. Béziers: Editions Vision sur les Arts, n.d.
Cothran, Ann. "Narrative Structure as Expression of the Self in Sarrazin's *L'Astragale*." *L'Esprit Créateur* 19, no. 2 (1979): 13–22.
Crosland, Margaret. *Women of Iron and Velvet: French Women Writers After George Sand*. New York: Taplinger, 1976.
Duranteau, Josane. *Albertine Sarrazin*. Paris: Editions Sarrazin, 1971.
Gelfand, Elissa Deborah. "Albertine Sarrazin: A Control Case for Femininity in Form." *French Review* 51, no. 2 (1977): 245–51.
———. "Albertine Sarrazin: The Confined Imagination." *L'Esprit Créateur* 19, no. 2 (1979): 47–57.
———. *"Imagination in Confinement: Women's Writings from French Prisons*. Ithaca: Cornell University Press, 1983.
———. "Women Prison Authors in France: Twice Criminal." *Modern Language Studies* 11, no. 1 (1980–81): 57–63.
Meyer, Ursula. *Albertine Sarrazin. Pathetische und ironische Elemente im Gesellschaftsbild der Autorin und in ihrer Selbstdarstellung*. Constance: Hartung-Gorre Verlag, 1984.
Willemart, Philippe. "Gamberge en cavale," *Língua e Literatura* 8, no. 8 (1979): 287–91.

MADELEINE DE SCUDÉRY (1607–1701)

Katharine Ann Jensen

BIOGRAPHY

Born in 1607, Madeleine de Scudéry was orphaned early in childhood. She and her older brother, Georges, inherited nothing when their parents died. The aristocratic origin of the Scudéry family was obscure, and an ambiguous nobility combined with financial insecurity were a liability in seventeenth-century France. Although social hierarchies shifted throughout the century, an appearance of nobility backed by the reality of money made for privileged conditions leading to social and political power. In their adulthood, both Georges and Madeleine were said to exaggerate their noble status, an exaggeration that may have been designed to mask how hard they—especially Madeleine—were writing to make ends meet.

Scudéry was raised by an uncle in Rouen who gave her the standard education for a girl of her class and time. She learned writing, spelling, dancing, drawing, and painting. However, on her own initiative, it seems, she also learned Italian and Spanish as well as how to garden, cook, doctor, and run a country household. When her uncle died, she went to Paris at age thirty to live with her brother. Georges, by this time, had made a name for himself both in the military and in letters. Through him, Scudéry became connected to the social and literary elite of the day, frequenting the Hôtel de Rambouillet, the most famous salon in the first half of the century.

Four years after moving to Paris, Scudéry published her first novel, the four-volume *Ibrahim ou l'Illustre Bassa* (*Ibrahim or the Illustrious Bassa, an Excellent New Romance*) under her brother's name, in 1641. Despite the pseudonymous publication, Madeleine was recognized as the author of the immensely popular work. Indeed, throughout her life she openly acknowledged authorship of her works in her correspondence, although she always published under her brother's name or anonymously after his death. Scudéry's public denial of authorship indicates the enormous degree to which maintaining appearances of propriety mattered in the elite world. A person of the nobility was not supposed to write "seriously," for a living, which Scudéry did, and, even more important, a noblewoman, an honnête femme, the model of feminine virtue, piety, and morality, was not supposed to write at all—and certainly not about love, which, again, Scudéry did.

Writing under Georges's name may also have had to do, initially, with his previous literary renown, his signature boding well for book sales (Tallémant des Réaux, Historiettes II [Paris: Gallimard, 1960]; 686). In any event, Georges did collaborate in his sister's work: he wrote the battle scenes, the prefaces, and the dedicatory letters. This, in some sense, was the "least" he could do, since he made free with the money earned from the books and spent it frivolously, adding to the Scudérys' financial difficulties. To what degree Georges exploited his sister—financially and emotionally—is difficult to determine. In 1660, however, after six years on her own, she refused to allow him to live with her, and from that time on she never mentioned his name in any of her correspondence (Aronson, Mademoiselle de Scudéry, 36). Yet before this break in 1660, Scudéry was Georges's faithful companion. Thus in 1642, when he was awarded the governorship of Notre-Dame-de-la-Garde at Marseille, she accompanied him. As her letters reveal, she felt very much in exile, far from Paris and her friends. Two years later, she and her brother returned to Paris because Georges had lost the governorship.

Before moving to Marseille, Scudéry published Les Femmes illustres ou Les Harangues héroïques (Illustrious Women, 1642), fictional portraits of women in history, myth, and legend. When back in Paris, she published her second novel, Artamène ou le Grand Cyrus (Artamenes, or The Grand Cyrus, an Excellent New Romance), in ten volumes, from 1649 to 1653, which met with enormous success. The work went through five French editions and was translated into English, German, Italian, and Arabic. This novel is generally seen as representing, under the guise of the historical Cyrus's heroic exploits, a spectrum of contemporary social milieux. Certain characters are believed to portray the nobility, Cyrus is the Prince de Condé, while others similarly correspond to guests of the Hôtel de Rambouillet. A key linking the real-life people to their fictional and idealized characterizations was said to have circulated in unpublished form. Scudéry depicts herself as "Sapho," whose wit, liveliness, and deep love for friends are among her outstanding qualities.

Scudéry's popularity within elite coteries led to her opening her own salon, around 1653, known as the Samedi (Saturday) for the day she received her guests. Due to Scudéry's presence as well as that of Valentin Conrart and Paul Pellisson, members of the Académie française, the Samedi had a literary reputation that distinguished it from other salons. Pellisson gained special attention from Scudéry and became her lifetime emotional and spiritual lover, though not, apparently, "more" than that. She portrays him as one of the heroes both in

Cyrus and in her second ten-volume novel, *Clélie, Histoire romaine* (*Clelia, an Excellent New Romance*), published from 1654 to 1660—also a representation of an ideal elite society, which was another best-seller.

After the publication of *Clélie*, and in reaction to the changing literary tastes of the day, Scudéry turned from the writing of heroic and multivolume novels to that of *nouvelles* (short stories) and collected *Conversations* (*Conversations upon Several Subjects*). She wrote two *nouvelles*, *Célinte, Nouvelle première* (Celinte, First Nouvelle) and *Mathilde d'Aguilar*, in 1661 and 1667, respectively. Then, in the last dozen years of her life, from 1680 to 1692, she wrote eight volumes of conversations, all dedicated to the king. Many of these conversations were culled from her long novels in which a number of friends meet to discuss questions concerning appropriate and ideal behavior in society.

Scudéry was the only woman in her century to be acknowledged by the Académie française. She received first prize for her *Discours surla gloire* (*Discourse on Glory*) in 1671. In 1683 Scudéry was awarded a royal pension; she would be one of two women in the seventeenth century to receive such distinction (the other being Marie-Catherine Desjardins de *Villedieu). A year later, she was elected to the Academia dei Ricovrati of Padua, which recognized other prominent women of seventeenth-century France, such as Rambouillet and the poet Henriette de la Suze.

MAJOR THEMES

Scudéry's three long novels, *Ibrahim*, *Cyrus*, and *Clélie*, conform in many ways to the genre in vogue in the first half of the century, the heroic novel. The plots of these novels, according to convention, begin *in medias res* and unfold through a labyrinthine course winding through many subplots. Each novel has ancient history as a backdrop, but the heroes and heroines, like those of other heroic novels, are endowed with seventeenth-century French virtues. The wars that the heroes fight in order to prove their valor are partly historically accurate and partly fabricated. While wars, abductions, shipwrecks, and various other calamities earn these novels their reputation for adventure, their real subject is love and its anatomizing. The Scuderian plot stages several pairs of lovers who are repeatedly separated and united, repeatedly forced to surmount obstacles that allow them repeatedly (!) to prove their excellent characters and their fidelity to love; after long ordeals, the lovers are reunited once and for all for a happy ending. This happy ending, moreover, in line with the traditional didacticism of epic, includes the punishment of the wicked as well as the reward of the virtuous.

The innovation that Scudéry brings to this schematic plot and to the novel genre in general is the characters' analysis of their amorous feelings and conduct; these analyses, which become ever more prominent from one novel to the next, take the form of conversations. Salon society itself was predicated on the art of conversation, and Scudéry reflects, reinforces, and inflects this art in her writings, laying particular emphasis on the art of *galant* conversation. According to the elite social ideal of *honnêteté* ("decency," "courtesy," "gallantry"), men, who were used to the vulgarity of war, must seek the company of women, who concerned themselves with the gentility of social interaction, in order to gain cultivation. It is precisely women's conversation that instills in a man the sought-after politeness and *honnêteté* that make him a desirable social being. The conversations in Scudéry's novels are a *mise-en-abîme* ("infinite mirroring") of polite society as it was (ideally) lived in the salons. She brings characters together in secluded, privileged spaces (like the salons) in order to discourse about the rules regulating elite behavior, especially between the sexes. Her novels, with their emphasis on the conversations that analyze and dictate behavior, are very much reference guides for her worldly readers. *Galanterie*, the term defining the ideal relationship between the sexes in polite society, is a neo-Petrarchan version of love. It positions the lover as passionately yet respectfully in thrall to a virtuous and inaccessible mistress. She, meanwhile, protecting her virtue and honor, demands ever more signs of her lover's obeisance before indicating, through discreet indirection, that he has pleased her and may continue to love her. Scudéry's novels elaborate the highly sophisticated code of *galanterie*. The characters debate questions such as the following: Can a woman accept a lover's passion without loving him? Should a woman hope to inspire love for men she cannot love in return? Who, between the lover who declares his love and the lover who lets it show discreetly, deserves the title of true lover? Who is most to be pitied: the lover who lives far from his mistress, he who is not loved by his mistress, he who has lost her, or he whom she makes jealous?

The emphasis of *galanterie* is on a spiritual love, one that transcends carnal desire and is in harmony with honor and reason. To this spiritual extent, love can exist, indeed, thrives much better, outside of marriage than within it. In *Cyrus*, for example, Sapho, under pressure from Phaon to marry him, demands that he desire nothing from her but to possess her heart. She argues that marriage, that is, physical possession, diminishes desire and that those who want always to love passionately must never marry. Phaon agrees and finds that his love and happiness increase as Sapho's affection becomes more violent through her recognition of the superior—nonphysically based—quality of his love for her.

What we will anachronistically term Scudéry's feminism is evident throughout her writings in their privileging of *galanterie*. She was writing at a time when marriages were arranged without the woman's consent and when women had virtually no reproductive rights. So while women might find lovers outside marriage, the potential consequences of consummated desire, if not disastrous for the woman's reputation and good name, were at the very least encumbering. *Galanterie*, then, is proposed as a way for women to engage in love while controlling both it and the man involved. It promises women power and independence.

Galanterie, in the Scuderian universe, is not diametrically opposed to marriage and its sexual implications, for the heroes and heroines of the main plots do marry. But these marriages, as the obstacles to the lovers' union are designed to prove, are above all marriages of souls, based on mutual esteem and respect. Love as it is defined and portrayed in Scudéry's oeuvre displaces physical desire as a primary attraction between the sexes and legal marriage as the goal. For example, the first book of *Clélie* presents the *Carte de Tendre* (Map of Tendre), which maps out four kinds of spiritual love: tenderness, appreciation, esteem, and inclination. Each kind of love can lead to Tendre, a platonic paradise, but the beloved woman must make access to Tendre difficult for her lover; before arriving, he should prove his perseverance and devotion. The most direct path to Tendre is to go through the River of Inclination; few men, however, can take this route, as it depends on a *mutual* and immediate consonance of souls and a reciprocity of desire. Most lovers, therefore, must pass through towns like "Submission," "Obedience," and "Constant Friendship" to arrive at Tendre, where they will be loved as a result of appreciation. Other arduous paths will result in arrival at Tendre, where the mistress will accord love based, for example, on esteem. Legal marriage, on the other hand, should it take place, implicating as it does a male power structure of husbandly rule and physical domination, leads to the "Dangerous Sea" and "Unknown Lands."

As the *Carte de Tendre* illustrates, *galanterie* offers a number of subtle ways to express love other than through physical passion. Scudéry's novels detail such means; poetry and letters are two of them. In *Clélie*, there are various models of love letters, and they themselves are pretexts for conversations on the art of love-letter writing. The characters distinguish between galant letters, which are witty and playful, and love letters, which are tender and passionate. They further distinguish between love letters penned by men, who may express their passion openly and therefore rather tediously, and those penned—more artfully—by women, who must simultaneously conceal and imply their tenderness.

As this emphasis on women's epistolary expertise in contrast to men's implies, the feminism of Scudéry's novels extends beyond the value placed on spiritual marriage. The primary role that women characters play, implicitly and explicitly, in the novels' conversations highlights the feminine qualities of intelligence, subtlety, and grace, as well as designating women's social and linguistic power. At a time when many of her contemporaries saw woman as little better than an animal, prey to her body and her blind emotions, Scudéry's advocacy of feminine reason and reasonableness was a subversive sexual ideology. In *Cyrus*, furthermore, Scudéry argues on behalf of women's education. Taking account of present conditions of instruction—a clear reference to conditions outside the novel— Sapho finds that girls are taught little more than how to dance, sing, and keep a neat appearance. As a result, they turn into vacuous, ignorant women, concerned only with trivial matters. Sapho thus calls for an instruction that would strengthen women's virtue while allowing them to use their minds, an instruction that would verge neither toward ignorance nor toward the "scholarly." Specifically, women should be allowed to learn foreign languages, they should be able to read Hesiod and Homer and "modestly" give their opinions of them, they should be able to take part in serious conversations—but not too great a part, lest they risk their modesty and delicacy.

In summary, Scudéry's long novels, as well as her excerpted "Conversations," offer models and reflections for life in an elite, polite, worldly society. Such a life centers around gracious and intelligent women who exercise power over language and enjoy a privileged position in love.

SURVEY OF CRITICISM

As the multiple editions of Scudéry's works testify, she was, during her lifetime, one of the most-read novelists of the day. Her popularity lasted throughout the century, and many contemporary men and women of letters wrote their enthusiastic praise both of the writer and of the woman. Exceptions to this rule, however, include the novelist Antoine Furetière and the satirist Nicolas Boileau. In *Le Roman bourgeois* Furetière makes fun of Scudéry's physical unattractiveness and commitment to learning. Boileau, meanwhile, takes her to task in several texts. The most damaging for Scudéry as a woman is *Satire X*, which is a devotedly misogynistic work even beyond its reference to her. The perils of being a woman writer—regardless of a carefully kept appearance of anonymity—are readable through Boileau's attack on Scudéry's immorality. Because her novels are about love, she will lead her women readers down the road to ruin; if women follow the models presented in the fictions, they will allow themselves platonic lovers. And the next and inevitable step, in Boileau's topography, is into bed. In his *Dialogue des héros de roman* and in *L'Art poétique*, he turns his criticism to Scudéry the writer, decrying, among other things, the overwhelming length of the novels, their ahistoricism, and their devirilization of real, that is, historical heroes like Cyrus (who certainly did not win all his battles for reasons of love!). Boileau, in effect, holds Scudéry responsible for a genre that was in demand when she wrote but which had fallen out of vogue in his generation.

As of 1731, a new edition of the novels was published, indicating that the early part of the eighteenth century, despite changes in the novel genre, still boasted a readership. By the end of the century, however, the critical consensus was aligned with Boileau, classifying Scudéry's novels as unreadable and implausible (Aronson, *Mademoiselle de Scudéry*, 152).

Victor Cousin, in the nineteenth century, worked to save Scudéry from oblivion in his two-volume *La Société française au XVIIème siècle d'après Le Grand Cyrus*. Proceeding from a patriotic fervor to remind Frenchmen of their great and glorious history, Cousin argues for *Le Grand Cyrus* on the basis of what it tells us about "the most beautiful epoch of French society" (vi). He condemns the novel at the same time for its excessive length and assures his readers that, far from proposing they ever read the work, he has provided quotations from it which will be more than sufficient (v). Cousin's interest in *Cyrus* stems from his discovery of a printed key dated 1657, found in the Arsenal library in Paris, in the last volume of the novel. He is unsure whether it corresponds to the original key that circulated in the seventeenth century and also faults it for its preoccupation with people and matters from an "inferior" level of society—a preoccupation that betrays the key's bourgeois origin, as well as Scudéry's (20). Despite this disappointing "lower-class cast," the key is invaluable, Cousin maintains, in identifying for the reader the aristocratic characters in the novel, "so many eminent and different personages, artists, poets, men of letters, . . . all of whom . . . honored the fatherland!" (21). It is this key that saves the novel from being insipid, a fate from which *Clélie*, however, cannot be spared. In *Clélie*, moreover, Scudéry was especially interested in depicting her own rather than high society, and so is "incessantly occupied with small galanteries, small poetry, small wit" (11).

Significantly less class-biased than Cousin, Sainte-Beuve in his *Causeries du lundi (Monday Chats)* judges Scudéry in historical terms. He appreciates her long novels as part of a vogue and lauds them for their value in instructing readers about society ideals. The early seventeenth-century taste in novels, however, makes them unreadable to the nineteenth.

It is Emile Faguet, however, more than Sainte-Beuve or Cousin, who seems to have pronounced the death sentence on Scudéry, the woman and the writer, in his *Histoire de la poésie française*. He describes her as a "Précieuse ridicule," explicitly associating her with Molière's and other seventeenth-century writers' satires of learned and empowered women. The derogatory title, "Précieuse ridicule," connoting a pretentious, frivolous, humorless, sexually repressed, pedantic, and arrogant woman, remains with Scudéry today. Yet she never referred to herself as a *précieuse*, nor did her contemporaries. It is highly doubtful that Molière had her as the target of his "Précieuses ridicules" or "Les Femmes savantes"; he alludes to her novels to satirize misreadings of them, not their writing or their author (Aronson, *Mademoiselle de Scudéry*, 47–48, 141–43). Furthermore, as Domna C. Stanton has argued in "The Fiction of *Préciosité* and the Fear of Women," the referential, female specificity of the *précieuse* has been effaced in literary history, beginning in the seventeenth century: "The only reality that can be claimed for the précieuse is her representation in a body of mid-seventeenth-century texts which are designed to chastise her pervasive faults" (113). Not only is the epithet *précieuse (ridicule)* inappropriate for Scudéry, it is a general misnomer, designating a male fantasy, not a female reality.

Various studies in the past decade or so have worked to liberate Scudéry and her works from the previous two centuries' social and literary condemnations. Alain Niderst's *Madeleine de Scudéry, Paul Pellisson et leur monde* (1976) is a social history and biography that seeks to reconstruct the context within which Scudéry wrote. Niderst reads her novels both as depicting historical figures— an aspect he emphasizes—and as presenting an ideal vision of society for emulation. Niderst sees Scudéry's emphasis on the ideal and the possibility of attaining it as an extension of sixteenth-century humanism.

Like Niderst, Nicole Aronson in *Mademoiselle de Scudéry* (1978) focuses on biography and social history to contextualize Scudéry's writings. In addition to plot summaries and thematic analyses of the author's works, from the novels to the conversations, Aronson reviews literary history. Thus she presents and interprets the varying receptions, misreadings, and misconceptions of Scudéry as woman and writer from the seventeenth century to our own.

In contrast to both Aronson and Niderst, René Godenne in *Les Romans de Mademoiselle de Scudéry* (1983) concentrates on the literary aspects of the novels. Godenne is avowedly committed to separating the woman's life from her works and analyzes them from a structuralist approach, denouncing traditional interpretations of the *à clef* variety. His study is systematic and exhaustive, breaking down plots and subplots, grouping character types, highlighting recurrent themes within and among the novels. He sees an evolution in Scudéry's three heroic works from *Ibrahim* to *Clélie*: the latter's focus on female characters (the only one of the heroic novels to have a woman's name as title) represents a thematic culmination. In *Clélie*, the masculine exploits and heroics as well as the less than perfect characters that existed in the earlier novels are absent. Instead, almost all action and conversation center around women's interests: love and its analysis.

Shorter studies of Scudéry include those of Elizabeth C. Goldsmith, Donna Kuizenga, and Caren Greenberg. Using social history and speech act theory, Goldsmith analyzes the specificity of Scudéry's conversations within the context of absolutism to reveal her influence on the reorganization of social hierarchies. Motivated by feminist critical concerns, Greenberg studies Scudéry's *Les Femmes illustres* to argue for a blurring of boundaries between fiction and reality, a blurring that signifies the inscription of the woman writer. Kuizenga, also working from a feminist perspective, analyzes in *Clélie* the relationship between the status of the novel as a feminine and feminized genre and Scudéry's concept of verisimilitude.

Given the size of her oeuvre and her under- and misrepresentation in literary history, Scudéry remains a rich source for continued readings and teachings. Such activities should be facilitated by recent reprintings (Slatkine) of the novels and *nouvelles*.

BIBLIOGRAPHY

Works by Mlle de Scudéry

Ibrahim ou L'Illustre Bassa. 4 vols. Paris: Sommaville, 1641.

Les Femmes illustres ou Les Harangues héroïques. Part I: Paris: Sommaville et Courbé, 1642. Part II: Paris: Quinet et de Sercy, 1644.

Artamène ou Le Grand Cyrus. 10 vols. Paris: Courbé, 1649–1653. Rpt. Geneva: Slatkine, 1972.

Clélie, Histoire romaine. 10 vols. Paris: Courbé, 1654–1660. Rpt. Geneva: Slatkine, 1973.

Célinte, Nouvelle première. Paris: Courbé, 1661. Rpt. Paris: Nizet, 1979.
Mathilde d'Aguilar. Paris: Martin et Eschart, 1667. Rpt. Geneva: Slatkine, 1979.
La Promenade de Versailles. Paris: Barbin, 1669. Rpt. Geneva: Slatkine, 1980.
Discours sur la gloire. Paris: Le Petit, 1671.
Conversations sur divers sujets. 2 vols. Paris: Barbin, 1680.
Conversations nouvelles sur divers sujets. 2 vols. Paris: Barbin, 1684.
La Morale du monde ou Conversations. 2 vols. Paris: Mortier, 1686.
Nouvelles Conversations de morale. 2 vols. Paris: Veuve de Sebastien Mabre, 1686.
Entretiens de morale. 2 vols. Paris: Anisson, 1692.

English Translations of Mlle de Scudéry

Ibrahim or the Illustrious Bassa, an Excellent New Romance. Trans. Henry Cogan.
London: J. R., 1652.
Artamenes, or The Grand Cyrus, an Excellent New Romance. Trans. F. G. London,
1653–1655.
Clelia, an Excellent New Romance. Trans. J. Davies and Havers. London, 1678.
An Essay upon Glory. Trans. by a person of the same sex. London, 1708.
Conversations upon Several Subjects. 2 vols. Trans. F. Spence. London, 1683.

Selected Studies of Mlle de Scudéry

Aronson, Nicole. "L'Illustre Romaniste et le misérable satirique." *Oeuvres et Critiques*
12 (1987): 85–92.
———. *Mademoiselle de Scudéry*. Boston: G. K. Hall, 1978.
Boursier, Nicole. "Avatars de l'héroïne chez Madeleine de Scudéry." *Biblio 17* 36 (1987):
261–89.
Cousin, Victor. *La Société française au XVIIème siècle d'après Le Grand Cyrus*. 2 vols.
Paris: Perrin, 186?.
Dalla Valle, Daniela. "Le Merveilleux et la vraisemblable dans la description des romans
baroques: *La Promenade de Versailles* de Madeleine de Scudéry." *Dix-septième
Siècle* 153 (1986): 223–30.
DeJean, Joan. "La Lettre amoureuse revue et corrigée. Un texte oublié de Madeleine de
Scudéry." *Revue d'histoire littéraire de la France* 88 (1988): 17–22.
Godenne, René. *Les Romans de Mademoiselle de Scudéry*. Geneva: Droz, 1983.
Goldsmith, Elizabeth C. "Excess and Euphoria in Madeleine de Scudéry's 'Conver-
sations.'" In *Exclusive Conversations: The Art of Interaction in Seventeenth-
Century France*. Philadelphia: University of Pennsylvania Press, 1988. 41–75.
Greenberg, Caren. "The World of Prose and Female Self-Inscription: Scudéry's *Les
Femmes illustres*." *L'Esprit créateur* 23 (1983): 37–43.
Guénoun, Solange. "*Clélie*: Terres inconnues et imaginaires: Pour une épistémologie du
transport." *Biblio 17* 11 (1984): 81–100.
Kuizenga, Donna. "*Des choses heureusement inventées*: Verisimilitude in *Clélie*." *Ca-
hiers du Dix-septième Siècle* 3 no. 1 (Spring 1989): 77–87.
Magendie, Maurice. "Les Romans de Mlle de Scudéry." In *La Politesse mondaine et*

les théories de l'honnêteté en France au XVIIème, de 1600 à 1660. Paris: Alcan, 1925. 629–92.

Niderst, Alain. *Madeleine de Scudéry, Paul Pellisson et leur monde.* Paris: PUF, 1976.

Stanton, Domna C. "The Fiction of *Préciosité* and the Fear of Women." *Yale French Studies* 62 (1981): 107–34.

SOPHIE ROSTOPCHINE, COMTESSE DE SÉGUR (1799–1874)

Christine Lac

BIOGRAPHY

Sophie de Ségur, née Rostopchine, was born in 1799, the third child of Tsar Paul I's personal advisor, Count Feodor Rostopchine. Since Count Rostopchine was forced into exile following the ascension of Tsar Alexander I, Ségur's childhood was not spent in the midst of courtly life, but rather on her family's provincial estate, Voronovo. Most of the childhood memories Ségur would draw upon in her novels came from the period she spent in Voronovo between 1801 and 1812.

Voronovo was a little world of its own, stretching over 60,000 acres and supporting 1,700 people, including doctors, tailors, weavers, shoemakers, cabinetmakers, poor relatives, a multinational teaching corps, and moujiks. In this rural setting, she fed the horses, went on long walks in the woods, rode donkeys, and learned her lessons under her mother's supervision.

Because the family lived quite independently and in isolation from any outside social structures, Ségur's father and mother provided her only contact with authority. Both parents had strong personalities and deeply influenced her development. Her father, Feodor Rostopchine, was a colorful character, as quick-tempered as he was generous. He was the warm-hearted accomplice who listened to Sophie's first tales when she was only his Sophaletta and smuggled candies and cookies for his children in spite of his wife's veto; historians and writers like Tolstoy, however, remember him as the man who gave the order to burn Moscow to prevent Napoleon I from conquering it.

Just as stubborn and defiant as Sophie's father was her mother, Catherine Pratassoff Rostopchine. Catherine Pratassoff was raised by an aunt at the court of Catherine II, never learning Russian and speaking only French. She married

Feodor Rostopchine in 1794. During the family's exile in Voronovo she converted from Russian Orthodoxy to Roman Catholicism. Her apostasy is historically meaningful as it recalls the Jesuits' influence in Russia, and also reveals the tsar's difficulties with the Catholic converts, who defied him openly by practicing a forbidden religion. Catherine went so far as to write the tsar a letter warning him of her activities and showing her determination to be arrested rather than relent. Sophie, under her mother's influence, would be the only one of her children to convert to Catholicism.

Under such a mother's supervision, Sophie was not pampered during her childhood. In her novels, she would describe some of the rules her mother made up for the children. Like her brothers and sisters, Sophie had to clean her own room, sew her own clothes, and sleep on a board with newspapers for covers. Her wardrobe consisted of a white short-sleeved percale dress summers as well as winters. The strict mother forbade any eating or drinking between meals, forcing the children to steal water from the dog's dish and bread from the horses' basket.

These very strict measures were the source of much conflict between parent and child, and between the mother and father as well. Ségur's novels would reveal how much these conflicts fueled the imagination of the child and later of the writer. Most of her works revolved around parental figures who behaved like her own mother and father. Even though she was very critical of both and depicted their faults without indulgence, she nonetheless admired their strength of character, emulated it in her life, and described it in fiction.

After the burning of Moscow, life as she knew it changed. Rostopchine left Russia in disgrace in 1814 and came back and left again in 1816 for a lengthy sojourn in Germany and later France. For a few years Sophie, her mother, and the rest of the family remained in Moscow and in St. Petersburg, where they socialized with prominent Russian Catholics like the Swetchine and the Galitzine, but the whole family moved to France in 1817 to be reunited with Feodor.

As a young woman of marriageable age, Sophie went to balls, plays, and parties. Her letters to her cousin Lise Galitzine showed her ambivalence toward these activities, which thrilled her passionate and jovial nature yet frightened her idealistic sense of humility. In 1819, Sophie married the young French aristocrat Eugène de Ségur. Although he had dazzled her at first with his good looks and manners, the marriage was not entirely satisfactory. Eugène's love of women was not restricted to his wife, and his mother did not approve of Sophie's manners, which she harshly criticized as countrified and uncouth. In order to save his daughter from total unhappiness, Feodor Rostopchine gave her her own estate, Les Nouettes, in 1820 before he left France to return to Russia.

Les Nouettes was reminiscent of Voronovo in its vastness and organization. Situated in Normandy, it comprised a large mansion and enough land to support the family. Ségur would spend most of the summers there as a gentlewoman farmer, the head of her own household. There, her seemingly eccentric personality could flourish without public disdain or mockery. She was far from the people who described her as "the canary lady with purple bows," an allusion to her fondness for vivid colors, far from those who decried her loud laughter, her peasant-like rolled "r's," and the boots she wore for her long walks in the country.

During the winters she lived with her husband in their Parisian home, where they each had their own apartment. Eugène de Ségur was busy with his position as president of the Chemins de Fer de l'Est (Eastern Railroad), and Sophie de Ségur took care of the household and family matters. The Ségur-Rostopchine marriage was more of a partnership than a romantic relationship, a partnership that produced eight children, including twins, between 1820 and 1835.

During her childbearing years, Ségur's life revolved around her children. She experienced sorrow at the loss of her second baby, but also the joy of adoption as she requested that her nephew Woldemar come live with her at his father's death (c. 1842). A tender-hearted mother, she raised her children according to her own principles, inventing games for them, playing with them, sharing her passion for sweets while teaching them love, respect, generosity, and independence, rather than using stark discipline. It was therefore quite an ordeal for her little brood when this beloved mother became bedridden after her last pregnancy. The nature of the illness has never been very well defined, and the symptoms may have been intermittent; her children wrote of severe back pains, bouts of laryngitis, and terrible migraine. She spent almost thirteen years with these ailments, recovering slowly by 1847.

By that time her children were beginning to leave the nest. Starting with her daughter Nathalie's wedding in 1846 and her son Gaston's ordination, Ségur started a new phase of her life, ready to try her wings after her thirteen years of confinement. She became very active, traveling constantly either to be with her daughters when they had babies or to set up her son's household when he was a church envoy in Rome. Her son had rekindled her faith, which had become dormant after her parents left France, and she was very active in charity work and an ardent advocate of papal authority.

In some ways she appears to have been quite conservative: a supporter of the pope, and a monarchist by conviction, she described events in her letters from that specific point of view, calling Thiers "a hateful little man" and blaming Napoleon III for not defending the Vatican more forcefully. However, she was interested in political events mostly when they affected her family, commenting, for instance, that the "Reds" during the Commune would prevent her daughter from coming to Paris from Brittany, or worrying about which son-in-law would be awarded which political position. Personally, however, she was a nonconformist. She preferred country life to courtly life, swore by homeopathy, tried all new inventions and gadgets (rubber boots or new methods of drying hay, for example), and allowed dissenting opinions and lively discussions in her household (her husband and son-in-laws did not agree with her or with each other).

She soon became a grandmother, the title by which she would become famous as the author who wrote for grandchildren. She started spending a large part of her day writing letters, sometimes three to the same household on the same day (for instance, to her daughter, her son-in-law, and her grandson), and also novels. Her first books were published in the Bibliothèque des Chemins de Fer (Railroad Library), a collection Hachette was selling in train stations like those controlled by the Compagnie des Chemins de Fer de l'Est of which Ségur's husband was president. Then Hachette bought her works for their children's collection, the Bibliothèque Rose (Pink Library), whose star writer she became.

Her early works had a practical purpose. Her book of first aid for children was meant to help her child-bearing daughters, and her fairy tales were supposed to entertain her granddaughters while they were in England because of their father's diplomatic mission. Yet she abandoned these conventional genres very early in her career and created her own brand of stories, which became instant best-sellers on the children's literature market. She published one to three books a year almost up to her death in 1874, forced into this prolific output more because of her editor's requests than by financial need, although she would use her added income to help her progeny in times of crisis.

Her last years were rather sorrowful. She lost her daughter Sabine to consumption; several of her grandchildren also died, and her son Gaston became blind. Worried by the Prussian war in 1870, disappointed at the establishment of the Third Republic, she became more and more devout, entering the Tiers Ordre (an association of lay people wishing to live by the rules of a religious order) as Sister Marie-Françoise. She sold Les Nouettes in 1872 and moved to Paris to a small apartment, partly to live in simpler surroundings, partly because her resources had dwindled while she helped her children or grandchildren in their difficulties. She died in 1874 of a heart attack and was buried with these words, "God and my children," on her tombstone.

MAJOR THEMES

Marie-Louise Audiberty argues that Ségur's life as well as her works constitute the "family romance of reconciliation." More than a theme in itself, the idea of reconciliation gives Ségur's writing a structure and a style that is distinctive in its attempt to analyze what opposing characters or situations have in common. Her works show the slow chronological progression of her system of values toward the integration of worldly power and heavenly good as she explores the maturation of a character within the family in the earlier novels, within the community in her middle period, or finally, in the latest novels, within the complex web of a whole society.

It is important to note that Ségur dedicated each of her books to a specific grandchild, because this reveals a crucial aspect of her writing: her works addressed specific children, using their names and characteristics within the text. Thus, as her grandchildren grew and moved away, the characters in the novels became older and their fictional territory broader. Moreover, as Ségur became more established, her intended audience also became larger, until she had to visualize a whole society as her reading public.

Dedicated to her granddaughters Camille and Madeleine, her first book, *Nouveaux Contes de fées pour les petits enfants* (New Fairy Tales for Little Folks), contains all her major themes in embryonic form. Not a novel but a collection of fairy tales, it is written in very literary French and follows the formulaic plot of the genre. However, Ségur adds a new dimension to the fairy tale that bridges the gap between classical tales (by Perrault, the Grimms, or even Andersen) and modern children's stories to come as she creates realistic child characters who are faced with real children's problems (to eat candy or not) in a magical setting. The most famous of the collection, *Histoire de Blondine, Bonne-Biche et Beau Minon* (often translated as ''The Lilac Forest'') can be used as an example of Ségur's renovation of the genre.

Blondine, the main protagonist, has to decide whom to trust in the story: the beautiful entertaining parrot who claims he is a victim, or the sweet-talking doe who is accused of enchanting the parrot. When she listens to the parrot and wanders in a forbidden forest, Blondine makes a mistake, but she redeems herself as she resists further temptations, not for her own sake but to save her friends. The tale exhibits three features characteristic of Ségur's oeuvre: first, the power of eliciting empathy (the characters' empathy for the powerless, as well as the author's, or the reader's); second, the protean nature of good, which needs to be defined by the characters through experience; and third, the interconnectedness of the characters' actions or values, presented in a tightly woven sociocultural fabric which is destroyed or restored by the hero's actions, much as in classical tragedy.

Ségur's next three books, semi-autobiographical novels about the daily life of contemporary little girls and little boys, set on its course her career as a writer of children's literature. Childhood became a theme in itself in all of Ségur's work. No author before her had addressed the young as a readership in its own right, and this new voice became an instant success. Stylistically, she was an innovator, using direct dialogue that reads like the lines in a play, or using dialects and foreign speech in children's literature. And she was among the first to abandon the tradition of didactic allegories in favor of realistic stories. But, most important, she respected her audience and characters enough to let them develop outside of formulaic plots and moralistic clichés.

Written as a trilogy between 1858 and 1859, her first three novels focus on a little girl, Sophie, who goes through three mothers before she learns to tame her temper in order to grow up as a worthy adult. *Les Petites Filles modèles* (Model Little Girls, 1858) narrates six-year-old Sophie's troubles at the mercy of Mme Fichini, an abusive and obnoxious stepmother. Mme Fichini finally gives her stepdaughter away to her worthy neighbor, Mme de Fleurville, who raises her own daughters Camille and Madeleine as model little girls. *Les Malheurs de Sophie* (*The Misfortunes of Sophy*, 1859) goes back to the time when Sophie was a very curious four-year-old who met with several mishaps while exploring her surroundings under the supervision of her mother, Mme de Réan. In the last book of the trilogy, *Les Vacances* (Vacation, 1859), Sophie continues her quest for a good mother, but her cousin Paul is the center of attention as he spins a tale of shipwreck, a desert island, and savages.

These three novels reinforce the structure of Ségur's thematics. Both Mme de Réan and Mme Fichini represent the boundaries of poor parenting; Réan's lack of empathy for the child's desires nullifies her attempts at curbing little Sophie's misbehavior; Fichini's own ambition and greed void her efforts at parenting. In contrast, Fleurville understands the child's motivations and appeals to her integrity and her desire for social integration and positive socialization. A typology of punishment offers more insights into Ségur's attitude toward her characters: when Sophie cuts up a bee to punish the insect for stinging people, Réan strings the pieces of the bee on a ribbon and makes Sophie wear them until they fall to dust; when Sophie falls in a pond and wets her dress, Fichini thrashes her until her arm gets tired; but when Sophie taunts her friends for their charity work and fights with them physically, Fleurville sends her to a detention room to copy a prayer until she is calm enough to analyze her actions. Fleurville as the good mother exemplifies what she preaches by not punishing the child in anger, or shaming her, but by addressing only her faulty behavior. Thus the child's integrity is preserved, while her character is shaped into that of a future matriarch.

In this trilogy Ségur strongly emphasizes the power women have over the household. The leading characters are husbandless: Fichini and Fleurville are widows; Réan's husband is attending to his business in Paris. Women supervise the land, manage the personnel, and raise the children alone. In this matriarchal setting, it seems paradoxical that little girls are the naughtiest and are punished more than their male cousins, yet even this pattern falls into Ségur's general scheme, because mothers are sternest while they groom their daughters to take their place, much like Catherine Rostopchine with her daughter Sophie, as well as Ségur with her own daughters.

The autobiographical elements reappear in *L'Auberge de l'Ange-Gardien* (*The Inn of the Guardian Angel*) and its sequel, *Le Général Dourakine* (General Dourakine). Published in 1863, these two books narrate the story of a wealthy Russian general, first as a prisoner of war in France in the custody of his French captor, and then as a landlord on his estate in Russia. In Dourakine, Ségur has created a formidable character based on her own father. Childish and powerful, he represents the average soul struggling between his quick temper, which leads him to extremes, and his compassion. Like the children in her other novels, he too had to undergo the process of socialization, with the added responsibility of learning how to master the power imparted to him by his status as an adult and a wealthy aristocrat.

With the above-mentioned trilogy, these two novels represent Ségur's attempt at "rewriting" her father and mother. This autobiographical series must have exorcised Ségur's family demons, because in a second group of novels her themes and characterization become broader in scope as she depicts common people as well as their community.

The eight novels published between 1860 and 1866 analyze the shifting position of the individuals within their community. Ségur presents characters who must follow the Christian doctrine of humility and yet follow the social creed of self-improvement. Between these two poles she introduces a wide array of characters. *Les Mémoires d'un âne* (A Donkey's Memoirs), *La Soeur de Gribouille* (Gribouille's Sister), *Pauvre Blaise* (Poor Blaise), *Les Deux Nigauds* (Two Fools), *François le Bossu* (François the Hunchback), *Comédies et proverbes* (Comedies and Proverbs), and also *Jean qui Grogne et Jean qui Rit* (Scowling John and Laughing John) all present characters who better their social position while staying humble and meek to the point of being defenseless. Yet, in *Un Bon Petit Diable* (A Good Little Devil), the hero Charles becomes much more active than the heroes of the preceding novel, while Ségur expands her battery of stylistic devices to include farce as well as drama in her writing. The author also probes the importance of money in a society experiencing a gradual shift of power from the nobility to the bourgeoisie. Ségur's last books all touch on this theme, as the writer tries to integrate her religious creed within a political and social scene that tends to reject her values.

Ségur's last five novels share certain characteristics that set them apart from her other books. They address an audience of young adults, not children; they describe characters growing from childhood into adulthood and study the young adults' trials and errors as they must make the choices that will enable them to fit into the complex fabric of their society; and, most important of all, they depict the redemption, thanks to their renewed faith in God, of characters caught in the evils of ruthless industrialism, class prejudices, arranged marriages, or military conscription.

La Fortune de Gaspard (Gaspard's Fortune) is a landmark book in Ségur's work because it is the first novel in which Ségur examines conflicting values and allows her character to mature socially as well as psychologically. From Sophie's misfortunes to Gaspard's fortune, Ségur changes her method of observation to include a social study of the environment in which her character evolves. She both praises and censures her hero as she follows his social ascension to the top; ambition and greed are part of his make-up, yet intelligence, probity, and industry are among the qualities that enable Gaspard to attain the success denied by Stendhal to Julien Sorel. Gaspard's greatest achievement is not to have risen from a peasant to a magnate, but to have been touched by divine grace. He is then able to transform his world in turn, by giving his workers Sunday off and not allowing young children to work (and making it unnecessary for them to do so), and by supporting the village parish hospital and school, for example. In Ségur's mind religion, far from being an opiate, gives the individual the strength to better his or her position and reform society.

For Ségur religion is not so much a source of inner strength that enables the individual to reach righteousness as well as bliss as it is a powerful medicine able to contain upper-class arrogance as well as lower-class violence. She exposes this idea in *Diloy le Chemineau* (Diloy the Laborer), which describes the shameful bond between Diloy the laborer and Félicie the aristocrat. Both have trespassed over the boundaries of their class: Félicie, because she insulted him and refused to be helped by him; Diloy, because he punished her by spanking her. Both must remain silent for fear of social reprisal, as they have broken the unspoken taboos of the social order, which dictate that the upper class not deny human status to the lower class, and that the lower class not use physical force to regain that lost status. To restore this order, Félicie and Diloy must reassess their values from a religious point of view, obeying the principle that all people are brothers and sisters no matter what position they hold in the hierarchy of social power. Thus Diloy must redeem himself by saving Félicie from drowning, while she must redeem herself by providing him with employment. They are able to forgive each other with the help of their faith in God, and thus they can mend their spiritual selves as well as the social fabric that links them.

Ségur is not so optimistic in her last novel, *Après la pluie le beau temps* (After the Rain Comes Sunshine), which is the only book she did not proofread herself. The novel describes at length the problems with legal guardianship, inheritance laws, and women's fate in a society that allows their emancipation from their parents or guardians only through marriage. Whereas Ségur is able to realize the integration of religious and social changes in the previous books, she cannot save her heroine Geneviève by faith alone. Geneviève prays and faints a lot when she learns that she may have to marry her guardian's son, who wants her money, but her faith is only a solace for her unhappiness, and it is bold and brash Miss Primrose, her unconventional cousin, who deals with the lawyers in a concrete way in order to set the young damsel free. Thus, although Ségur was able to offer religion as a source of power for the peasants, the workers, and the soldiers, she knew from experience that prayer alone would not emancipate a young woman, and she showed that she had a thorough knowledge of the laws that could.

Ségur's works were not considered part of the nineteenth-century literary canon, but she never aspired to belong to it and created her own genre. Although she was not the first to write for children, she was the first to create stories for them as a writer and not an educator. A stylistic innovator, she introduced realistic speech in literature for children, manipulating the subjunctive imperfect as well as country slang; she valued entertainment before edification, describing her characters' bad deeds in as much detail as their redemption. Thus, her books have appealed to generations of readers, boys or girls, from all classes and religions, in France and many other countries. Her style, characterization, setting, and plot exuded such energy and probed life with such candor that her novels reached the universality of classics.

Several authors referred to her in their novels and correspondence. In *Le Temps retrouvé*, in the scene where all of the characters meet again at the princesse de Guermantes's, Proust describes one of his characters, d'Agencourt,

as a senile General Dourakine, so certain is he that the metaphor will be understood by his French readership; Henry de Montherlant in his correspondence
with Roger Peyrefitte uses the general in much the same fashion. Sartre explains
that Lucien in *Le Mur* does not eat much because he had read that a famished
man should eat lightly in *The Inn of the Guardian Angel*. In *La Robe prétexte*,
Mauriac describes reading Ségur with relish as a child, imagining life with Paul,
Sophie, and their servants; in his journal he writes of his favorite passage in
"Gribouille's Sister" where an angry servant breaks all of the household dishes.
Freud himself was aware (and disapproved) of the Bibliothèque Rose because
the books were too violent (Kreyder, 219). All these allusions prove the far-
reaching influence Ségur exerted and still exerts on her French readers.

SURVEY OF CRITICISM

In the nineteenth century Ségur became the signature writer of the Bibliothèque
Rose. Her success was immediate: Ségur mentioned in one of her letters that
children recognized her in the street and wanted to kiss her; her name became
a household word, from the imperial palace where Napoleon III's son kept her
collected works to the various charitable institutions where Ségur donated her
works. Her fame spilled over geographic and linguistic boundaries rapidly as
her works were translated into English or transposed as textbooks for French
lessons as early as 1869. After Ségur's death, her son Gaston de Ségur and her
daughter Olga de Simard de Pitray each published laudatory biographies, and
Olga edited her mother's letters to herself and to her son Jacques.

In the twentieth century, critics started examining her work, mainly in the
form of critical biographies. In an article for *Le Figaro* (1907), Robert de
Montesquiou called her "le Balzac de l'Enfance" (the children's Balzac). She
became controversial: Zeiller (1913), for example, deplores her aristocratic tone
and the fact that children always win against the parents in her stories.

A few good biographies were written in the 1930s, by her great-granddaughter
Arlette de Pitray, by Jacques Chenevière, and the most detailed by Marthe de
Hédouville. In 1956, Edith Killip in Bristol, England, produced an interesting
dissertation on Ségur, a forerunner of the studies that flourished in the seventies
and eighties. Killip analyzed Ségur's place within children's literature up to
1956, considering the stylistic innovations as well as the biographical and cultural
elements that contributed to her success in spite of her definite religious bias,
which Killip described as a flaw.

Interest in Ségur was rekindled by Pierre Bléton's sociological essay in which
he produced a catalogue of information about nineteenth-century daily life in
France based on her work. Although he cautioned that not all literary work could
provide such data, he praised Ségur for the wealth of realistic details that enabled
him to discover the price of a loaf of bread or a servant's wages during the
Second Empire. Other historians and sociologists, following Bléton's lead, have
used Ségur's texts as support for their theses. Gilles Bollenot, for instance,

studied the influence of adoption on inheritance laws in "Gaspard's Fortune," and Jean-Marie Roux gathered evidence of generalized fear of water and of the slow emergence of swimming as a sport from Ségur's stories.

Jacques Laurent started a critical controversy when he described the frequent flogging in her novels as sadomasochistic. Pierre Berger, to defend Ségur, wrote an apology in the manner of *Beauvoir's "Must We Burn Sade?," and Jean Chalon denied that any child could be traumatized by Ségur's stories, while advising adults to reconsider her works as worthy of mature attention. Micheline Herz also analyzed Ségur's not-so-angelical angelism, which she qualified as Anglo-Saxon in the way it "looks on wealth as the outer sign of divine approval" (21), and Richard Laden focused on terror and sacrifice as the writer's means to contain nature.

The centennial of Ségur's death in 1974 saw a renewal in Segurian studies. In his scholarly preface to "Gaspard's Fortune" for Pauvert's new edition, Marc Soriano argued that the novel described with "relentless meticulousness one of the most important processes of [society's] metamorphosis; that is the annexation by the dominant class of an intellectual [Gaspard] who belonged originally to a dominated class" (lix). According to him, such a novel deserved to be reevaluated by an adult audience for its prophetic description of a society deteriorating into our consumer society.

Such analyses gave Ségur more credibility as a nineteenth-century writer. In the 1980s critics began to consider her as a woman writer as well. New biographies were published from a female if not feminist point of view for special collections in women's literature: Marie-Louise Audiberti wrote on Ségur for the series Femmes dans leur temps, and Beaussant's fictionalized first-person biography appeared in *Elle était une fois* in 1988. One of the most recent and the best book-length essay to date is by Laura Kreyder (1987), who studies Ségur as a literary as well as historical and social phenomenon.

With such essays, Ségur is becoming a topic of scholarly research. Her name even appears in Henri Mitterand's collection *Littérature* in the nineteenth century volume. And in 1989, her name resurfaced on the American scene with an article by Marie-France Doray in the reputable journal *Children's Literature*. Ségur, who was among the twenty most translated French authors of the year in 1955, whose first editor Hachette boasted sales of over 28 million of her books by 1981 (not counting the other twenty-three publishers re-editing her), may well be on her way to canonization.

BIBLIOGRAPHY

Works by Mme de Ségur

Nouveaux Contes de fées. 1857. Paris: Hachette, 1920.
La Santé des enfants. 1855. Paris: Hachette, 1857.
Les Petites Filles modèles. 1858. Paris: Hachette, 1920.

Les Malheurs de Sophie. 1859. Paris: Hachette, 1920.
Les Vacances. 1859. Paris: Hachette, 1919.
Mémoires d'un âne. 1860. Paris: Hachette, 1920.
La Sœur de Gribouille. 1862. Paris: Hachette, 1920.
Les Bons Enfants. 1862. Paris: Hachette, 1919.
Les Deux Nigauds. 1862. Paris: Hachette, 1919.
Pauvre Blaise. 1862. Paris: Hachette, 1920.
L'Auberge de l'Ange-Gardien. 1863. Paris: Hachette, 1920.
Le Général Dourakine. 1863. Paris: Hachette, 1919.
François le Bossu. 1864. Paris: Hachette, 1919.
Évangile d'une grand-mère. 1865, 1869. Paris: Société Liturgique, 1926.
Comédies et proverbes. 1865. Paris: Hachette, 1920.
Jean qui Grogne et Jean qui Rit. 1865. Paris: Hachette, 1920.
Un Bon Petit Diable. 1865. Paris: Hachette, 1920.
Les Actes des Apôtres. Paris: Hachette, 1866.
La Fortune de Gaspard. 1866. Paris: Hachette, 1920.
Quel amour d'enfant! 1866. Paris: Hachette, 1867.
Le Mauvais Génie. 1867. Paris: Hachette, 1920.
Diloy le Chemineau. 1868. Paris: Hachette, 1913.
La Bible d'une grand-mère. Paris: Hachette, 1869.
Après la pluie le beau temps. 1871. Paris: Hachette, 1920.
Lettres au vicomte et à la vicomtesse de Simard de Pitray. Paris: Gaume, 1891.
Lettres d'une grandmère. Paris: Oudin, 1898.

Selected Translations of Major Works by Mme de Ségur

Fairy Tales for Little Folks. Trans. Mrs. Chapman Coleman and her daughter. Philadelphia: Porter and Coates, 1869.
The Inn of the Guardian Angel. Illus. Foulquier: Trans. H. I. Adams. Boston: Lee and Shepard, 1871.
Sophie's Troubles. Trans. P.P.S. New York: P. J. Kenedy and Sons, 1889.
The Story of a Donkey. Abridged by Charles Welsh. Ed. Charles Dolel. Illus. E. H. Saunders. Boston: D. C. Heath, 1901. Revised 1930.
A Life of Christ for Children as Told by a Grandmother. Adapted by Mary Virginia Merrick. St. Louis: B. Herder, 1909.
Sophie. Adapted by Charles Welsh. Intro. Ada Van Stone. Illus. Eugène Prand. Boston: D. C. Heath, 1910.
Old French Fairy Tales. Illus. Virginia Frances Sterrett. Philadelphia: Penn Publishing Co., 1920.
Memoirs of a Donkey. Trans. Marguerite Fellows Melcher. New York: Macmillan, 1924.
Happy Surprises. Adapted by Julia Olcott from *Les Malheurs de Sophie, Les Petites Filles modèles,* and *Les Vacances.* Chicago: Albert Whitman and Co., 1929.
Sophie, the Story of a Bad Little Girl. Trans. Marguerite Fellows Melcher. New York: Knopf, 1929.
Princess Rosette and Other Fairy Tales. Trans. Virginia Olcott. Illus. Ben Kutcher. Philadelphia: Macre Smith Co., 1930.
The Inn of the Guardian Angel. Retold by Anna Pendleton. Illus. Margaret Freeman. Boston: Houghton Mifflin, 1931.

The Misfortunes of Sophy. Trans. Honor and Edgar Skinner. Illus. Marie Madeleine Franc-Nohain. New York: Putnam's Sons, 1936.

Contes de Fées. Henry's Kindness. Princess Rose. The Little Grey Mouse. Illus. Claire Marchal. London and Melbourne: Ward Lock and Co., 1964.

Forest of Lilacs. Pictures by Nicole Claveloux. New York: Harlan Quist, 1969.

The Angel Inn. Trans. Joan Aiken. Owings Mills, Md: Stemmer House, 1978.

Studies of Mme de Ségur

Audiberti, Marie-Louise. *Sophie de Ségur, née Rostopchine, l'inoubliable Comtesse*. Paris: Stock, 1981.

Beaussant, Claudine. *La Comtesse de Ségur ou l'enfance de l'art*. Paris: Robert Laffont, 1988.

Berger, Pierre. "Faut-il brûler la comtesse de Ségur?" *Lettres Françaises*, February 27, 1964.

Bléton, Pierre. *La Vie sociale sous le Second Empire; un étonnant témoignage de la Comtesse de Ségur*. Paris: Les Editions Ouvrières, 1963.

Bluche, François. *Le Petit Monde de la Comtesse de Ségur*. Paris: Hachette, 1988.

Bollenot, Gilles. "L'Adoption au XIXe siècle: 'La Fortune de Gaspard' de la Comtesse de Ségur." *Revue Historique* 550 (1984): 311–37.

Chalon, Jean. "Pour adultes seulement, la comtesse de Ségur." *Figaro Littéraire*, February 9, 1974.

Chenevière, Jacques. *La Comtesse de Ségur, née Rostopchine*. Paris: NRF, Gallimard, 1932.

Doray, Marie-France. "Cleanliness and Class in the Countess de Ségur." *Children's Literature* 17 (1989): 64–80.

Guérande, Paul. *Le Petit Monde de la Comtesse de Ségur*. Paris: Editions du Palais Royal, 1964.

Hédouville, Marthe de. *La Comtesse de Ségur et les siens*. Paris: Conquistador, 1953.

Herz, Micheline. "The Angelism of Mme de Ségur." *Yale French Studies: Women Writers* 27 (1961): 12–21.

Killip, Edith. "The Stories of the Comtesse de Ségur and Her Contribution to Children's Literature." Diss., Bristol University, 1956.

Kreyder, Laura. *L'Enfance des saints et des autres. Essai sur la Comtesse de Ségur*. Fasano, Italy: Schena-Nizet, 1987.

Lac, Christine. "Women and Children First: A Comparative Study of Louisa May Alcott and Sophie de Ségur (Rostopchine)." Diss., University of Nebraska, 1988.

Laden, Richard. "Terror, Nature, and the Sacrifice in the Comtesse de Ségur's *Les Petites Filles modèles*." *MLN* 94 (1979): 742–56.

Laurent, Jacques. "Etrennes noires." In *Au Contraire*. Paris: La Table Ronde, 1967.

Mathé, Sylvie. "La Poupée perdue: Ordre et désordre dans *Les Petites Filles modèles* de la Comtesse de Ségur." In *Theory and Practice of Feminist Literary Criticism*. Ed. Gabriela Mora and Karen S. Van Hooft. Ypsilanti, Mich.: Bilingual Press/ Editorial bilingüe, 1982. 117–30.

Montesquiou, Robert de. "Le Balzac de l'Enfance." *Le Figaro*, September 7, 1907.

Nières, Isabelle. "De la métamorphose à l'anamorphose: Quelques adaptations des *Malheurs de Sophie*." *La Revue des livres pour enfants* 101 (1985): 52–60.

Pitray, Arlette de. *Sophie Rostopchine*. Paris: Albin Michel, 1939.

Pitray, Olga, vicomtesse de Simard de. *Ma Chère Maman*. Paris: Gaume, 1891.

Roux, Jean-Marie. "La Comtesse de Ségur ou la peur de l'eau." *Revue d'histoire moderne et contemporaine* 30, no. 8 (1983): 154–62.

Ségur, Mgr. Louis-Gaston de. *Ma Mère. Souvenir de sa vie et de sa sainte mort*. Paris: Tobra, 1876.

Soriano, Marc. "Bibliothèque rose et Série noire." Preface to *La Fortune de Gaspard*, ix-lxiii. 1964. Paris: J. J. Pauvert, 1972.

Vinson, Marie-Christine. *L'Education des petites filles chez la Comtesse de Ségur*. Lyon: Presses Universitaires de Lyon, 1987.

Zeiller, Jacques. *La comtesse de Ségur*. Paris: Bloud, 1913.

MARIE DE RABUTIN-CHANTAL, MARQUISE DE SÉVIGNÉ (1626–1696)

Michèle L. Farrell

BIOGRAPHY

Marie de Rabutin-Chantal, Mme de Sévigné, was born in Paris on February 5, 1626, of Marie de Coulanges and Celse-Bénigne de Rabutin-Chantal. She was an only child and was orphaned at an early age: her father died when she was one, her mother when she was seven. She was brought up mainly by the maternal side of her family; her uncle Philippe de Coulanges was appointed her official guardian in 1637, but the paternal Rabutins demonstrated an ongoing interest in her welfare. Little is known of her early years or her education. She was married in 1644, at the age of eighteen, to Henri de Sévigné, of the minor nobility. Indeed, although she was to become known as "marquise," this was merely a courtesy title, since her husband held the title of 'baron.' They had two children: Françoise-Marguerite was born in Paris in 1646, and their son Charles in 1648. Henri de Sévigné was killed in a duel over his mistress in 1651, and Sévigné embraced her new status of widowhood, despite various offers of marriage. In later years, she wrote categorically: "le nom de *veuve* emporte avec lui celui *de liberté*" (the word widow connotes that of freedom; II, 1.781, p. 999).[1] She relied heavily on her uncle, Christophe, the abbé of Livry, for guidance in financial matters, and on her various relations for a sense of social and familial identity. Sévigné divided her time between her husband's estate of Les Rochers in Brittany, Livry, her uncle the abbé's country seat, and her native Paris, where she lived at various addresses, finally settling at l'Hôtel de Carnavalet in the Marais district. She made occasional visits as well to various properties in Burgundy inherited from the Rabutin side of her family. She also traveled to Vichy and Bourbon to take the waters for her rheumatic condition. Upon her daughter's marriage and move to Grignan in Provence, she began to visit the south of France, and it is there that she died.

Sévigné was a sociable, energetic woman of great charm and wit who held that one could not have enough friends. Occupying an interstitial social position, with a foothold both in the bourgeoisie through her maternal Coulanges relations and in the nobility through the paternal Rabutin side of the family, she had access to Louis XIV's court and made visits to Versailles, but was more at home in the salon milieus of Paris. Unlike most of her contemporaries, she also appeared genuinely to enjoy life in the country, and when she repaired to her estate of Les Rochers, as she did regularly to tend to her finances, she thrived on her relationship to nature. She was a close friend of Mme de *Lafayette as well as an occasional member of Mlle de *Scudéry's circle. She cultivated her many relations and well-placed friends, representing family interests in her capacity as head of household, and evidenced a great capacity for friendship. She corresponded loyally with her older cousin Roger de Rabutin, count of Bussy (1618–1693) throughout his years of exile following his fall from grace with the king, despite his caustic wit, occasionally directed against her. Another frequent correspondent was her younger maternal cousin Philippe-Emmanuel de Coulanges (1633–1716), fondly known as ''le petit Coulanges.'' She also remained a faithful friend to the Cardinal de Retz and to Foucquet through their political tribulations and loss of power.

In 1669, Sévigné's daughter Françoise-Marguerite was twenty-three; it was time not only to heed the conventions of the day, but also to silence rumors of the king's interest in her, a favored dancing partner. After the failure of a few tentative engagements, Sévigné raised the requisite dowry and arranged her marriage to the distinguished François, count of Grignan. He was, at the time, already twice widowed, with two daughters, in need of another dowry as well as an heir. Upon their departure in 1670–1671 to his native Provence, where he had been named the king's Lieutenant Governor, she initiated the correspondence with her daughter that was to last twenty-three years and would constitute the bulk of the literary corpus for which she is known. Her son Charles remained nearby and was a companion to his mother when he was not serving in military campaigns or indulging in mild debauchery. He married Marie de Mauron in 1684 and settled into a quiet life of piety in Brittany.

Mme de Sévigné's *Correspondance* represents the totality of her writings. The first letter in the most complete collection available today, Roger Duchêne's edition featuring 1,371 letters, is dated 1648; the last one, 1696. Forty-eight years are spanned in this writing; but, for the most part, the letters, in their chronology and focus, coincide with and are profoundly marked by the reign of Louis XIV (1661–1715). While Sévigné corresponded with her cousins Coulanges and Bussy, and with a number of friends, her most intense epistolary relationship was with her married daughter. Over a period of twenty-three years, from the moment of her daughter's departure from Paris to Provence, until their final reunion there, Sévigné wrote copiously to her at least twice a week. The only interruptions in the exchange of letters occurred when the two women found themselves together. She produced no other sorts of texts, nor is she known for any other accomplishment beyond the reputation she acquired as a brilliant conversationalist. What can be known of Sévigné, except for minor references here and there in the writings of her contemporaries, is available only through her letters. However, unlike Virginia Woolf's hypothetical Elizabethan woman, whose entire self-inscription consisted only of a "handful of . . . letters" (*A Room of One's Own* [New York: Harcourt, Brace and World, 1929], 47), the Sévigné corpus is enormous and offers a wealth of autobiographical material to the reader interested in studying how a seventeenth-century woman assigned meaning to her life through writing. Indeed, that very enormity is indicative of the meaning that was both imposed on and embraced by her: she herself inscribed her own excess, at once subscriptively and oppositionally, internalizing and writing out the position of superfluity she occupied as a woman in the affective and social economy—orphaned, widowed, and, finally, bereft of her daughter. In a reading of this abundant correspondence, it is easy to lose sight of the fact that, although the mother-daughter exchange spans twenty-three years, Sévigné and Françoise-Marguerite were separated for only eight years and four months during that period. This fact highlights the intensity of Sévigné's writing activity during the periods of separation.

Sévigné's letters were much admired, read aloud, copied, and circulated during her own lifetime. She wrote frequently in the company of others, and addressed messages in her letters to Françoise-Marguerite to members of her daughter's family and entourage. Thus her writing activity can be understood as doubly performative: she invented and projected her maternal writing self not only within her text, but also in the salons where she penned her letters and where they were received. Beyond this deliberate public display, however, she found herself with readers she had not envisaged. When Foucquet was arrested in 1661, letters she had written to him were seized along with his papers, and she worried throughout his trial that these purportedly innocent letters of friendship might be used against her. Then, in 1680, Bussy announced to Sévigné that he was forwarding to the king copies of letters they had exchanged between 1673 and 1675, this in the hope of reingratiating himself, and with little concern for his cousin's feelings in the matter. While Sévigné expressed discomfort and concern upon learning of his tactless behavior, she worried more about his fate with the king than her own. In her exchange with her daughter, a note of flirtation with the idea of eventual publication is regularly sounded, so that although she might not have anticipated the eventual actual book form her letters would find, it is clear that she wrote not only with her immediate addressees in mind but for a greater public as well.

In 1725 a pirate edition of her letters came out, and in 1726 yet two others appeared. To put an end to these unauthorized versions, Sévigné's granddaughter, Pauline de Simiane, undertook to publish an official collection, engaging the chevalier Perrin to edit the letters. At this time not only was censorship in the name of style and decorum exercised on Sévigné's letters, but the daughter's half of the correspondence was destroyed, "sacrificed," as Roger Duchêne puts it, to a "scruple" of the granddaughter's "conscience" (I, p. 765). Very few of Françoise-Marguerite's letters remain, and these are addressed to people other than her mother. By the same token, Pauline de Simiane had exacted a promise from Perrin that, upon completion of his edition of her grandmother's letters, these also would be destroyed. He was faithful to his promise, so that today only eight autographs remain. However, during the editing process, and with the involvement of other relatives from the Rabutin side of the family, various copies of the correspondence were generated. These have surfaced over time, the most recent discovery taking place in 1873 when Charles Capmas, a law professor in Dijon, happened upon and bought six manuscript volumes of Sévigné's letters (I, p. 770). All of the existing manuscripts as well as the printed editions of the correspondence were finally carefully dated, analyzed, and their relationship established by Roger Duchêne in the 1970s, so that today readers of his edition have at hand the most definitive one possible. It takes into account all earlier versions in circulation, scrupulously noting variants, discrepancies, inaccuracies, and undecidable passages, demonstrating how little of all that remains is assuredly Sévigné's very words, but provides at the same time a very readable text of the letters. The proliferation both of manuscript copies and of successive editions of the *Correspondance* attests to the enduring status Sévigné's writing enjoys in the French world of letters.

MAJOR THEMES

Sévigné prided herself on her spontaneity and imagination; she wrote on whatever struck her fancy and systematically refused categorization. She poured her writing into that accommodating epistolary form; hence, a great variety of themes can be identified and traced through the corpus of the correspondence. Indeed, the fluidity of her thinking and the diversity of her interests have given rise to all sorts of theme studies: Sévigné and medicine—and travel—and fashion,—and Jansenism, etc. This chapter will not attempt an exhaustive list, but will concentrate on the major themes that shape the correspondence. These are reflections on the epistolary genre as Sévigné elaborates her own relation to that tradition; intertextuality, as Sévigné draws on discourses circulating in her milieu to forge her own; and, finally, her construction of a textual maternal persona in the epistolary privileging of her relationship with her daughter.

Sévigné repeatedly insisted on the novelty of her enterprise. Although letter writing was much in fashion during her day, she claimed to be at once ignorant and disdainful of the many available manuals purporting to teach and provide models for the art of letter writing. She expressed admiration for the letters of Voiture, whose voice resembled her own, as well as for Pascal's *Lettres provinciales*, but acknowledged no actual influences on her own writing. She submitted tactfully to an unspoken tutelage in the practice of correspondence with her cousin Bussy. He fancied himself an authority on matters of style, as on most other subjects, and encouraged his cousin to write, commending her lively wit and turn of phrase as much with an eye to sustaining the correspondence through requisite doses of flattery as to actually shaping her style. Much that she learned from this tacit power relation Sévigné would pass on to her daughter, assuming with her the role Bussy played in their exchange.

From Paris, Sévigné was in a position to keep her exiled cousin, other friends, and her married daughter in Provence abreast of court and city news. Thus many of her letters have an almost journalistic quality as she reports her version of events and gossip. Social, political, and literary historians, including Voltaire, have tapped her letters over the centuries for perspective on well-known episodes from her time as well as for details on daily life: Foucquet's trial, the ordeals of the "witches" La Brinvilliers and La Voisin, the death of Turenne, the king's crossing of the Rhine and his affairs, birthing practices, the reception of plays and novels, the rise and fall of various ministers, etc. Often Sévigné's renderings of bits of news were measured by her correspondents against reports in *La Gazette* and *Le Mercure galant*; she had to enliven hers with insight, humor, and inside knowledge in order to compete successfully with these other purveyors of news.

Once the correspondence with her departed daughter was established (1671), Sévigné's writing took on a regular rhythm dictated by the postal system organized under Louvois. She received and sent letters twice a week, but she wrote to her daughter incessantly. She distinguished between "letters of response," which took up the thread of conversation from letters just received, and "letters of provision," which were more inventive, filling in the void of the wait. She had only contempt for the formulaic greetings and closures recommended in the manuals of her day, but she came to understand their function as she experienced the constraints of her writing situation and came to grips with the facts of absence, delay, and separation. This led to rhetorical experimentation and innovation in and around the epistolary form. Thus the material conditions of the correspondence frequently determined both the form of a letter and its content.

The protocol of the letter posited a polarity between the sender and the addressee; etiquette dictated that hyperbole be addressed to the receiver and modesty assumed by the person writing. This general axiom accounts for Sévigné's constant praise of her correspondent and her own posture of self-effacement. In exchanges with her daughter, she was also intent upon encouraging Françoise-Marguerite to feel a greater confidence about her writing ability, so necessary to the continuance of the correspondence. This dependable writing framework was necessary to Sévigné's well-being; for she needed to be writing just as urgently as she needed to be in contact with her absent daughter. Her drive to write was at once a function of her talent, of her class, and of her status as widow. Of the leisure class, and with social obligations only of her own choosing, Sévigné was free to cultivate her gift for writing. Indeed, she had great stretches of time that called for activity suitable to her station. What is not so readily explained is why, as opposed to her friend Mme de Lafayette and others of her female contemporaries who experimented with various fiction forms, Sévigné devoted her talent exclusively to letter writing. This can be understood perhaps as a sign of her conservatism, of her reluctance to challenge the status quo, since, during the period that she wrote, the epistolary genre was increasingly identified as a domain in which women might claim pride of place. This association of women with letter writing was emblematic of a generalized tendency among seventeenth-century literary authorities and educators to define them as essentially relational beings. Thus Sévigné's ready assimilation into the canon can at least in part be understood as a consequence of her subscription to a prescribed feminine comportment.

Sévigné was as avid a reader as she was a writer. She was also a brilliant conversationalist, frequenting the lively salons of Paris, and always up to date on the latest literary works, dramatic productions, religious sermons, and controversies. Frequently she read in the company of others and participated in the collective critiquing that was the hallmark of aristocratic cultural intercourse. Thus her discourse is permeated with that of others in circulation, and her opinions are more of a consensual than of an original nature. But her flair for expressing them—for capturing tones, lessons, detail, humor—is uniquely hers. She readily cites La Fontaine, Tasso, Voiture, Molière, Corneille, Racine, Quinault, Pascal, and others of her time, weaving them into her own thoughts so dexterously as to produce almost seamless prose, and, at the same time, reminding her correspondents through this practice of gentle allusion of their cultural commonality.

Although Sévigné was not particularly religious, she was thoughtful on the subject. Along with her friends she read regularly the lives of various saints, religious tracts, treatises, and devotion books, and listened attentively to sermons delivered by some of the great orators of her day such as Louis Bourdaloue and Jacques Bénigne Bossuet, and she reflected frequently, if despairingly, on her relationship to God. Incapable of embracing in practice the austere Jansenist tenets of her day, she remained nevertheless in admiration of their integrity and had great respect for those devout souls, for example, Pierre Nicole and Antoine Arnauld, who submitted to a life of self-abnegation. She tended to reroute the rhetoric of religious devotion to her daughter, just as she readdressed to her the various discourses of love she came across in her reading, this to the consternation of those concerned for her salvation. As often as she wrote of God, she wrote of a more generalized "Providence," and, especially in her later years, deferred humbly to this greater power. Nor was she particularly given to philosophy. She deplored her daughter's enthusiasm for Descartes and saw little value in isolated, abstract thinking. She was much more inclined to concrete observations about the people immediately surrounding her and to meditation inspired by nature. She enjoyed strolling through her gardens and woods in Brittany, and took an active interest in the health of her trees and the state of her grounds. She would pause to read and write in favorite corners, and would carefully inscribe the scenes before her, the reflections they gave rise to, in letters to her daughter. Memories of the past, combined with forays of imagination into the future inspired by her surroundings, helped her to fill the void of her present, which was generally experienced as a period of absence to be endured between past and future reunions with her daughter. By writing out what she saw before her, she endeavored to make herself present in her letter, and exacted the same sort of effort from her daughter, hoping to compensate through description for their absence from each other.

Indeed, it is around her daughter that Sévigné organized her life and her writing. Very little is known of their relationship prior to Françoise-Marguerite's marriage; Sévigné does not dwell on that past in her letters. But the daughter's departure unleashed a torrent of maternal feeling that channeled itself into letter form. With the exception of the Ceres-Proserpine myth, mother-daughter relations had not been culturally encoded at the time of Sévigné's writing, so she is to be credited for drawing on the amorous discourses available to her (religious, neo-Platonic, heterosexual, as well as mythological) and forging out of them a new one: that of a mother's love for her daughter. In the process of addressing herself to her daughter, she engaged in the act of self-construction that gave her a visible identity, and introduced the role of *mater* to the public sphere. She valorized herself as mother and came to be known by her social world as the mother who loved her daughter.

The privileging of this role was not without complications. The fictive ''I'' through which Sévigné gave voice to her maternal persona required the daughter's constant compliance in order to sustain that role. And Françoise-Marguerite resisted being permanently cast in the supporting role of the mother's daughter. The letters indicate that their relationship was strained, that they did not get along well when together and were on better terms with each other apart. In her writing, Sévigné was able to address an idealized daughter, so that the ''you'' of the letters also became a fictionalized pole that enabled the self-inventing ''I'' to write. Many of the themes that traverse the mother-daughter exchange—such as identity confusion, separation anxiety, neediness, vicarious experience—echo those of the discourses Sévigné drew on. Reinscribed in her epistolary frame and rerouted to the daughter, they have resonance for contemporary theorists interrogating maternality, attempting to sort out the nuances between, as Adrienne Rich puts it, the ''experience'' and the ''institution'' of motherhood (*Of Woman Born: Motherhood as Experience and Institution* [New York: Norton, 1976]).

SURVEY OF CRITICISM

Through the centuries, Sévigné has continued to enjoy the acclaim in which she delighted during her own time. She has a faithful following not only among the literati, but among amateurs of reading as well, and her name in France is a household synonym for ''mother'' as well as for ''letter.'' In the eighteenth century, her letters held the attention of historians such as Voltaire, intent upon recording in detail the reign of Louis XIV. In the nineteenth century, her style and her intellectual qualities were much vaunted by arbiters of the canon and shapers of pedagogy such as Sainte-Beuve, Gustave Lanson, and Brunetière. Proust signaled his great admiration for her maternal passion by characterizing Marcel's venerated grandmother as her devotee, and he praised her style by describing the painter Elstir as endowed with the same gift as hers—a flair for "present[ing] things in the order of our perceptions rather than explaining them first by their cause" (*A la recherche du temps perdu, A l'ombre des jeunes filles en fleurs* [Paris: Pléiade] I, 653–654; my translation).

In recent years Sévigné studies have flourished. In part this is due to the exhaustive work done by Roger Duchêne to produce a definitive edition of her letters and to document extensively the history of the correspondence, thus providing a stable corpus from which to read, available in its entirety only since 1978. It is also due to the fact that the Sévigné letters lend themselves to considerations of problematics of particular interest to critics today: Eva Avigdor has reconstructed an intellectual and moral portrait of Sévigné; Bernard Bray gives a structuralist reading of the epistolary situation as it is encoded in the letters; Jean Cordelier analyzes the relationship between living and writing in the Sévigné project; Nicole Bonvalet and Fritz Nies have, in very different ways, interrogated the correspondence from a perspective of reader reception, Nies offering a diachronic and synchronic study of reception of the letters, and Bonvalet focusing on ways in which women have tended to read Sévigné. Louise Horowitz and Marie-Odile Sweetser have considered Sévigné's aspiration beyond a vocation of intimate writing to one of authorship. Elizabeth Goldsmith has studied Sévigné's letter-writing activity in the context of the seventeenth-century epistolary vogue. Frances Mossiker has produced a highly readable and insightful biography of Sévigné for a general readership. Most important, renewal of interest in the *Correspondance* comes from feminist critics who have looked to the letters for historical perspective on theories of the maternal, and have done revisionist readings of the epistolary mother-daughter relationship: Harriet Ray Allentuch has studied the personality of Sévigné and the effects of her motherless upbringing on her later relationship with her daughter; Solange Guénoun has studied the relationship between the mother-daughter bond and Sévigné's inscription of that biological tie in her epistolary activity. Katharine Jensen celebrates the articulation of mother love in the letters. Interestingly, juxtaposed to her husband Roger Duchêne's *Madame de Sévigné, ou la chance d'être femme*, Jacqueline Duchêne has written a work that privileges instead the role of the daughter in the correspondence, *Françoise de Grignan, ou le mal d'amour*. My own work interrogates the self-construction and representation of Sévigné's maternal identity through discourses available to her and considers the consequences for the mother-daughter relationship as it is played out through the letters in light of that linguistic filtering process.

There is need for further work on the reception of the Sévigné letters by women readers over the centuries that would take into account the influence of the maternal lesson on their lives and study the process of role transmission. The *Correspondance* is a rich text that lends itself to many varied and even contradictory readings; it is far from exhausted, and will undoubtedly continue to generate new interpretations.

NOTE

1. My translation. References in the text are to Duchêne's edition (volume, letter, page).

BIBLIOGRAPHY

Works by Mme de Sévigné

Correspondance. Ed. and annotated by Roger Duchêne. 3 vols. Paris: Bibliothèque de la Pléiade, Editions Gallimard, 1972–1978.
Lettres. Edit. and introduced by Emile Gérard-Gailly. 3 vols. Paris: Bibliothèque de la Pléiade, 1953–1957.

Selected Letters

Lettres, Choix. Ed. Jacqueline Duchêne. Preface by Roger Duchêne. Paris: Librairie générale française, Le livre de poche, 1987.
Lettres. Ed. Bernard Raffali. Paris: Garnier-Flammarion, 1976.

Translations of Mme de Sévigné's Correspondence

Selected Letters. Intro. Leonard Tancock. Middlesex: Penguin Classics, 1982.
Letters of Madame de Sévigné to Her Daughter and Friends. Intro. Richard Aldington. New York: Dutton, 1937.

Studies of Mme de Sévigné

Allentuch, Harriet Ray. *Madame de Sévigné: A Portrait in Letters.* 1963. Rpt. Westport, Conn.: Greenwood Press, 1978.
———. "My Daughter/Myself: Emotional Roots of Madame de Sévigné's Art." *Modern Language Quarterly* 43, no. 2 (June 1982): 121–37.
Avigdor, Eva. *Madame de Sévigné: un portrait intellectuel et moral.* Paris: Nizet, 1975.
Bonvalet, Nicole. "Etudes parallèles: lorsque les femmes lisent Mme de Sévigné." *Oeuvres et critiques* 5 (1980): 121–42.
Bray, Bernard. "L'Epistolière au miroir: Réciprocité, réponse et rivalité dans les lettres de Madame de Sévigné à sa fille." *Marseille* 95, 4th trimester (1973): 23–29.
———. "Quelques aspects du système épistolaire de Madame de Sévigné." *Revue d'histoire littéraire de la France* 69 (1969): 491–505.
Cordelier, Jean. *Madame de Sévigné par elle même.* Paris: Seuil, 1967.
Duchêne, Jacqueline. *Françoise de Grignan ou le mal d'amour.* Paris: Fayard, 1985.
Duchêne, Roger. *Madame de Sévigné et la lettre d'amour: Réalité vécue et art épistolaire.* Paris: Bordas, 1970.
———. *Madame de Sévigné ou la chance d'être femme.* Paris: Fayard, 1982.

Farrell, Michèle L. "Grandmother Sévigné: Shaping Relationships." *Stanford French Review* 11, no. 3 (Fall 1987): 279–96.

———. "Patterns of Excellence: Sévigné in the Classical Maternal Tradition." *Papers in French Seventeenth Century Literature* 13, no. 25 (1986): 27–38.

———. "Praise, in Theory . . . and in Practice: The Case of La Bruyère and Sévigné." *Cahiers du dix-septième: An Interdisciplinary Journal* 1, no. 1 (Spring 1987): 203–11.

———. "Sévigné: The Art of Vicarious Living." In *Women in French Literature*. Ed. Michel Guggenheim. Saratoga, Calif.: Anma Libri, 1988. 65–75.

Gérard-Gailly, Emile. *Madame de Sévigné*. Paris: Hachette, 1971.

Goldsmith, Elizabeth C. *Exclusive Conversations: The Art of Interaction in Seventeenth-Century France*. Philadelphia: University of Pennsylvania Press, 1988.

———. "Giving Weight to Words: Madame de Sévigné's Letters to Her Daughter." In *The Female Autograph*. Ed. Domna C. Stanton. New York: New York Literary Forum, 1984.

———. "Madame de Sévigné's Epistolary Retreat." *L'Esprit Créateur* 23, no. 2 (Summer 1983): 70–79.

———. "Proust on Madame de Sévigné's Letters: Some Aspects of Epistolary Writing." *Papers on French Seventeenth Century Literature* 8, no. 15 (1981): 128–35.

Guénoun, Solange. "La Correspondance de Madame de Sévigné: une séparation littéraire." Diss., Princeton University, 1980.

Horowitz, Louise K. "The Correspondence of Madame de Sévigné: Letters or Belles-Lettres?" *French Forum* 6 (1981): 13–27.

Jensen, Katharine A. "Writing and Mother Love: The Letters of Mme de Sévigné." *French Literature Series* 16 (1989): 38–52.

Mossiker, Frances. *Madame de Sévigné: A Life and Letters*. New York: Knopf, 1983.

Nies, Fritz. *Gattungspoëtik und publikumsstruktur: sur Geschichte der Sévignébriefe*. Munich: Verlag, 1972.

Papers on French Seventeenth Century Literature 8, no. 15 (1981) includes proceedings of the North American Society for Seventeenth-Century French Literature conference (1981, San Francisco) on Madame de Sévigné by Harriet Allentuch, Roger Duchêne, Elizabeth Goldsmith, Solange Guénoun, Catherine Howard, Fritz Nies, Domna Stanton, Gabrielle Verdier, and Patricia Weed.

Sweetser, Marie-Odile. "La Lettre comme instance autobiographique: le cas de Madame de Sévigné." *French Literature Series* 12 (1985): 32–40.

———. "Madame de Sévigné, écrivain sans le savoir?" *Cahiers de l'Association internationale des études françaises* 39 (May 1987): 141–57.

Williams, Charles G. S. *Madame de Sévigné*. Boston: Twayne, 1981.

GERMAINE NECKER, BARONNE DE STAËL (1766–1817)

Karyna Szmurlo

"What an intoxicating pleasure it is to fill the universe with our name, to live so far beyond ourselves that we may entertain illusions about life's limits in time and space."

On the Influence of the Passions

Staël's literary work is coextensive with the desire to live intensely and to escape all existential closure. An aggressive expansiveness reveals itself in everything she did: her bursting into the political arena, her intellectual curiosity, and above all, her passionate commitment to writing and to being recognized as a writer. The contrast between aspirations and the lack of existential fulfillment made her both "alive and sad," as she described herself (Balayé, *Lumières et liberté*, 11).[1] The enthusiasm that drove her was combined always with a conviction of life's precariousness and its inevitable obstacles. It is the capacity to transform defeat into strength, to extract glory from frustration, that is Staël's most striking characteristic. She lived during the Revolution and was exiled twice, once by the Jacobin terror and later by Napoleon. Nonetheless, she became the most complete author of her time. Few women in history can claim a success equal to hers.

BIOGRAPHY

Louise Germaine de Staël was born in Paris into an exceptional milieu. The daughter of Jacques Necker, Louis XVI's First Finance Minister, and of Suzanne Curchod, an enlightened Protestant and well-known *salonnière*, from earliest youth she was surrounded by the best literary minds: Encyclopedists, people of the court and government, and a cosmopolitan society. At twelve, she began to read Montesquieu, Rousseau, and Voltaire. Among her friends were Diderot, d'Alembert, Helvétius, and Buffon. Grimm included one of her first compositions in his *Correspondance*, and the Count de Guibert called her "Apollo's priestess," charming all with her intellectual brilliance and talent for conversation. Born with features too pronounced to be deemed pretty, she surprised people with her vivacity, sparkling gaze, and a petulance which could unnerve the conventional. Mme Necker bore hard feelings because Germaine chose Jacques Necker as the object of her most intense affections, and later abandoned the strict existence of wife and mother; she would dismiss her daughter's success, saying, "That is nothing, absolutely nothing, compared to what I wanted to make of her" (Balayé, *Lumières et liberté*, 15). In addition to such maternal restrictions, Germaine had to endure the mockery of her beloved father, who disapproved of feminine self-expression and would call the little girl scribbling her first essays "Monsieur de Sainte-Escritoire" (Lord Holy-Desk). Early on Germaine became aware of the limits imposed on women, especially in the world of letters. From her youthful attempts the progress of the writer-to-be was marked by the compunction of authorship anxiety and followed an antithetical pattern in which a temptation to self-affirmation was always combined with fear of repression.

Staël's destiny is curiously interwoven with that of two powerful men, both of whom took on mythic proportions in her writings: Necker and Napoleon. Whereas the latter caused her suffering and inspired hatred, she idolized Necker as an unsurpassable statesman. When, following the vicissitudes of his prestigious position, Necker returned to Paris at Louis XVI's behest, enthusiastic crowds acclaimed him the savior of France on the eve of the Revolution and urged his carriage on toward the capital. The intensity of this glorious moment continued to resound in Germaine's imagination, and she avidly desired the same adulation for herself and her heroines. But the father was also the ideal man in private—a gentle and sensitive husband, the very "model of marital virtue and bliss," a perfect lord of the manor at Coppet, where he escaped the revolutionary furors (Herold, 21). His daughter openly admitted that "of all the men of earth, he is the one I would have most hoped for as a lover" (*Mon Journal* [My Journal], 67). She sought in vain her whole life for a passion capable of replacing this peculiar attachment.

In 1786 Germaine agreed to marry the Swedish ambassador to the French court, Baron Eric-Magnus de Staël-Holstein, chosen by the Neckers. In marrying a nobleman and the holder of an important diplomatic post, Staël managed both to escape the incessant parental criticism and to assure herself a brilliant place in Parisian society. And yet the union dissolved quickly; the couple lived separately and had only one child, Gustavine, who died before she was two. Staël's affective freedom disquieted those around her, especially in the era of progressive moral reproof of women's sexuality. As Herold notes: "Her unforgivable sins were her independence, her defiance of public opinion, her ruthless pursuit of happiness, and her conscious superiority. In a woman these were sins only exceptional minds could forgive" (69). Many lovers and suitors followed.

Among those who had a strong influence on her life were Count Louis de Narbonne, a libertine charmer, with whom she had two sons, Auguste and Albert; Count Adolphe Ribbing, responsible for assassinating the King of Sweden; and Benjamin Constant, the writer and a man of politics, who was the father of Albertine, the future Duchess of Broglie. There were others who either hated her, like Charles-Maurice de Talleyrand, the powerful bishop of Autun, or else remained her faithful, inseparable companions, like Mathieu de Montmorency or August Wilhelm Schlegel. Nevertheless, all of Staël's love affairs followed inevitably the same pattern of painful disintegration: an ardent generosity with a demand for total devotion and acceptance, withdrawal of the male partner, despair, and suicide threats. Germaine recreates this repetitive experience and relives the fear of rejection in all her fictional writings, where the marriage is impossible without perfect reciprocated passion, and the weakness or perfidy of men clashes with an exemplary feminine goodness. Only toward the end of her life did she enjoy the boundless devotion of a young Hussar, John Rocca, whom she secretly married shortly before her death.

Staël's keen need to influence others in her private life and to take an active part in political life led her into adventures of expatriation. Napoleon was not one to accept passively a woman's power. At the start, the enthusiastic Staël would admire in him a warrior-hero whose noble moderation contrasted admirably with the military violence of revolutionary leaders. But this portrait changed when she became aware that the First Consul's monarchical appetites were progressively compromising parliamentary rules and freedom. Consistently demystified, Napoleon will, for her, turn into an evil demon forcing the woman of genius into silence. *De la littérature dans ses rapports avec les institutions sociales (On Literature Considered in Its Relationship to Social Institutions, 1800)*, which praised the forces of progress, drew attacks from Bonaparte's press. With the publication of *Delphine* (1802), the first great novel in which a sentimental plot is the cover for revolutionary experience, Paris became off limits for her. The next novel, *Corinne ou l'Italie (Corinne, or Italy, 1807)*, which then replaced the military conquests of the Emperor in Italy with the independence of the Woman/Nation, was received coldly. *De l'Allemagne (On Germany, 1810)*, with its cosmopolitan sympathies, was literally destroyed, the plates broken at the printing press. Between 1802 and 1814 Staël was condemned to exile by interdictions of varying cruelty, which were intensified in the year 1810. Napoleon considered her truly dangerous: first in her Parisian salon, frequented by ambassadors, politicians, even Joseph and Lucien Bonaparte; then in her retreat at Coppet in Switzerland, which sheltered an international elite of European romanticism and became the fortress of intellectual opposition elaborating theories of democracy. Whereas the journeys to Germany (1803) and Italy (1804) still provided inspiration for research and guaranteed Staël a literary glory refused her in Paris, her 1812 escape from Coppet was nonetheless that of a political prisoner. On May 23, Staël began her flight across the continent with the Grande Armée marching toward Moscow at her heels. The memoirs *Dix années d'exil*

(*Ten Years of Exile*), published posthumously in 1820, relate this traverse through Germany, Poland, Russia, Scandinavia, and England, during which Staël incited the strongest European courts to battle against tyranny. Even the United States, which she described in her letter to George Ticknor as "the avant-garde of the human race . . . the future of the world," tempted her, but her plans to cross the Atlantic were never realized (Balayé, *Lumières et liberté*, 199–200). The project for establishing Bernadotte, the republican general, on the throne did not succeed either. After Napoleon's downfall, Staël returned to Paris and worked on an apologetic treatise devoted to Jacques Necker, *Les Considérations sur les principaux événements de la Révolution française* (*Considerations on the Principal Events of the French Revolution*, 1818), but her weakened health left her only two years to live. She died paralyzed on July 14, 1817, summing up her life on her deathbed: "I loved God, my father and freedom" (Balayé, *Lumières et liberté*, 11).

MAJOR THEMES

Liberty, understood as "the greatest happiness, the single glory of the social order," is the pivotal concept in Staël's works (*Delphine*, Part 5, Letter 14, 222). The most striking elements of her thought are trust in the inevitable progress of enlightenment and reason, and the dialectical relationship between a nation's sociopolitical basis and its culture. From *De la littérature* through *Considérations*, Staël stresses the interdependence of institutions and literature, which provide mutual guarantees for each other. With unquenchable zeal, she proclaims the republican order, especially the English model with its unwritten constitution, and insists on the social responsibility of the writer, who, thrown into action, is capable of reaching and moving the masses. A master of words, it is he who "maintains and increases the enlightenment necessary for democracy" (*De la littérature*, 1: 29). Staël herself provided considerable proofs of such engagement. Whether in her *Réflexions sur la paix adressées à M. Pitt* (Reflections on Peace Addressed to M. Pitt) or in the *Réflexions sur la paix intérieure* (Reflections on Peace at Home), or even in the *Circonstances actuelles* (On the Present Circumstances), all published in 1795, she promotes peace and mercy rather than political utilitarianism, and sets herself up against anarchy, the terrorist mentality, fanaticism, and violence. Her treatise *De l'influence des passions sur le bonheur des individus et des nations* (*On the Influence of the Passions on the Happiness of Individuals and Nations*, 1796) seeks remedies for post-Revolutionary sufferings: "The only real system for avoiding pain is to direct one's life solely in accordance with what one is able to do for others. . . . Existence must start from the self rather than return to it, and without ever being the center, one must always be the force propelling one's own destiny" (*Passions*, 177). Identification with others' misfortunes is most particularly apparent in the *Réflexions sur le procès de la reine* (Reflections on the Queen's Trial), where Staël takes up Marie-Antoinette's defense. "The liberty of a nation is not worth the life of an innocent soul" (*Circonstances*, 205). Later, this respect for humanity will develop into a powerful antimilitarism on an international level, the best example of which is the memoirs *Dix années d'exil*, a monument erected for all the nations that endured the scourge of Napoleonic imperialism.

Political imperatives consequently engender aesthetic principles. Full of an almost cosmic sympathy, Staël's activist thought opens up onto a diversity of cultures, to admire what is original about them and to find there new sources of inspiration. The desire to "walk freely through nature, without, however, belonging to any country or to any situation" gives birth to an entire poetics of the South and of the North that calls for an unfettered blossoming of national literatures, creation free of restrictions, and unrestricted textual dissemination by means of translation and criticism, which are interpreted as gestures of warm recognition (*De l'Allemagne*, 3: 268). These trends appear vividly not only in the novels and the major theoretical works, but also in the short texts of criticism such as the *Lettres sur les ouvrages et le caractère de J. J. Rousseau* (Letters on Rousseau, 1788) or even *De l'esprit des traductions* (On the Spirit of Translations, 1816). The coexistence of multinationalism in which individuality can be preserved and regenerated by reciprocal influences is at the heart of the Staëlian credo of cosmopolitanism/modernism.

As the proclaimer of progressive ideas on the independence of individuals and nations, Staël was naturally interested in the intellectual emancipation of women. Her reflections are concerned, above all, with the paradoxical aspect of the feminine destiny. In a historical perspective women exercise a powerful, civilizing role, thanks to their creativity and moral influence over society; however, on the existential level they "have no way at all of revealing the truth or of shedding light on their life" (*De la littérature*, 2: 341). Deprived in advance of all means of self-affirmation, they are condemned to permanent diminution. The very same society that exalts their faculties turns them away from real power. This antinomy of expansion/restriction provides the basic structure for the novellas of Staël's youth: *Histoire de Pauline* (Story of Pauline), *Adélaïde et Théodore* (Adelaide and Theodore), *Mirza*, and *Zulma*, and the two proto-feminist novels, *Delphine* and *Corinne*, whose heroines with mythological names herald great missions, yet are rejected and annihilated by the patriarchal world in its fear of feminine superiority. Staëlian protagonists want to live up to their potential and attain the maximum of self-achievement. For them, happiness means "the possession of a destiny related to their faculties," a true consciousness of existence through a continual process of heightening intellectual exchanges (*Sur le suicide* [On Suicide], *Oeuvres complètes* 3: 308). Their profusion of talents makes them so impatient to communicate their ideas that they may become both a source of self-contemplation and an object of public adulation. Yet, far from positing an autarchy, feminine advancement is associated here with a persistent quest for visibility.

Staël's work, however, also demonstrates the serious peril of the outpouring of the self. Confronting these young believers in natural instinct as the guarantor of happiness, a rigid world of unbending principles keeps such enthusiasm in check. Depicted as ridiculous and invalid in the wry mirror of the plays performed at Coppet (*Le Capitaine Kernadec* [Captain Kernadec], *La Signora Fantastici* [Signora Fantastici]), this corruptive system changes, in the great novels, into a despotic machine set in motion by tactics of self-interest. Its jaws, a miniature of Napoleonic Machiavellianism, distort the truth about Delphine's generosity or attempt to silence Corinne's literary talents in their mutilation of the spiritual. Unlike the theoretical texts, the fictional writing turns from red to black, from optimism to death, and fragmentation of every type (suicide, ruins, lack of communication, aphasia, etc.) is its overwhelming feature. Though Staël excels in the representation of the suffering of abandoned woman, the leitmotiv of weakness implies, paradoxically, the liberation/renaissance of the feminine self for posterity, and functions as a rebellion against a crushing order. Not only does Staël politicize the content of her fiction by emphasizing women's aspirations in their menace to patriarchy; she also adopts the textual strategies of patriarchal tradition to reach feminist goals.

SURVEY OF CRITICISM

Immensely popular during her lifetime, Staël was assured of a permanent place in literary anthologies as a founder of comparative literature and a precursor of romanticism. An author marginalized by the canon, her work has been underread. Literary historians have sought in it primarily transitional elements between the Enlightenment and romanticism, not seeing its own originality. Already considered by her literary admirers (Goethe, Humboldt, Schiller, Sismondi, Lamartine, Chateaubriand, and even Sainte-Beuve) as an exceptional phenomenon, a being hard to reconcile with traditional notions about the modesty expected of her sex, Staël more than any other woman author was subjected to antifeminist attacks and incited an active tradition of patriarchal polemics against her. For two centuries, biographers, moralists, literary critics, and historians, sustained by the scandals of her private life, repeated the clichés widespread in Napoleon's day and systematically loosed their fury against the writer who had dared step out of her socially assigned position to put all her energy into a transcendent body of work. Variations of this same hostile tendency may be seen over the centuries from "the prophetic sexism of Jacques Necker in 1785, through the patronizing chauvinism of Le Breton in 1901, to the misogynous hysteria of Anthony West in 1975" (Swallow, "The Weapon of Personality," 79). Whether in the provocatively titled *Mistress to an Age* (1958)—the bestselling biography by Christopher Herold—or in Ghislain de Diesbach's *Madame de Staël* (1983), or even in Julia Kristeva's 1988 article in *Romantisme*, we find the same method of "contravention," defined by Madelyn Gutwirth in sociological terms as "the systematic use of mockery and denigration by one group in its efforts to hamper the progress of another" (*Madame de Staël, Novelist*, 295).

Interest in Staël has revived considerably in the second half of our century, characterized by increasingly revisionist insights. This renaissance would never have been possible without the activities of the Société des Etudes Staëliennes in Paris and the erudition of its president, Simone Balayé. It is she who has pursued critical and textual research energetically, providing new editions, publishing the *inédits*, and, above all, encouraging international research. Her apologia, *Madame de Staël: Lumières et liberté* (1979), nourished by a profound knowledge of the period, puts this most powerful body of work conceived after the Revolution into its proper perspective. Staël emerges there as a political writer, a literary critic, a novelist, a philosopher, a playwright, and an actress whose creative efforts were deeply rooted in the rifts of history.

Feminist criticism has joined this movement to correct the interpretative exclusions of the past by placing Staël in the feminine tradition and reestablishing the reputation of her fiction, which had been dismissed *en bloc* by the canon. The search for Anglo-Saxon affiliations (Elizabeth Barrett Browning, Margaret Fuller, Maria Edgeworth, George Eliot, etc.) begun by Ellen Moers in her *Literary Women: The Great Writers* (1976) has been extended to other French women writers by Helen Borowitz (Mlle de *Scudéry), Madelyn Gutwirth (Madame de *Krüdener and Madame de *Charrière), and Joanna Kitchin (Madame *Cottin, Madame de Souza, and Madame de *Genlis). It was, however, the revolutionary work by Madelyn Gutwirth, *Madame de Staël, Novelist: The Emergence of the Artist as Woman* (1978), that revealed the feminist dimensions of Staëlian fiction. Here Staël's novels are no longer judged in terms of preceding masculine models, or as dramatized autobiography, but rather as a reply of a woman novelist to the feminine condition.

This critical initiative is carried forward in new studies of Staël's literary voice. *The Literary Existence of Germaine de Staël* by Charlotte Hogsett associates the writer's career with a struggle against the masculine/feminine roles, and the development of the tactical skill which gains her a voice within patriarchal discourse. Staël's fiction is seen by Marie-Claire Vallois in *Fictions féminines: Mme de Staël et les voix de la Sibylle* (1987) as a privileged realm of writing about herself that is, however, endlessly repressed by fear of censorship. From the same perspective, Nancy K. Miller, in the chapter on *Corinne* in her *Subject to Change* (1988), analyzes the novel as the site of tensions and social transformations, a battle of gazes in which the patriarchal gaze appropriates and fixes, while the feminine other sets itself free to live elsewhere. All these texts demonstrate a rich awareness of the multilayering of Staël's discourse as it moves simultaneously between self-assertion and self-regression. Consequently, despite their diverse approaches, the essays collected in the 1991 volume edited by Goldberger, Gutwirth, and Szmurlo, *Germaine de Staël: Crossing the Borders*, all pursue the textual dynamics of Staëlian assertion. In addition to its contribution to feminine poetics/politics and to the description of her voice as historian, the volume includes new documents on the impact of Staël's work on the Transcendentalists and on the formation of an American national literature.

Recent major works of criticism alluded to here have been ably supplemented by numerous articles and translations. In 1987 Vivian Folkenflik published the first English "general reader," *An Extraordinary Woman: Selected Writings of Germaine de Staël*, and Avriel Goldberger provided an exquisite translation, the first in a hundred years, of *Corinne, or Italy*. Publication of its companion, the voluminous novel *Delphine*, is to follow. Thanks to the growing research in women's studies, Staël's work now provides a rich terrain for new interpretation as it enters the twenty-first century at the height of its popularity.

NOTE

1. All translations are my own.

BIBLIOGRAPHY

Works by Germaine de Staël

Early Editions

Oeuvres complètes. 17 vols. Paris: Treuttel et Würtz, 1820–1821. Geneva: Slatkine, 1836.

Modern Editions

De la littérature. Ed. Paul Van Tieghem. Geneva: Droz; Paris: Minard, 1959.
Delphine. Une édition féministe de Claudine Herrmann. Paris: Editions des femmes, 1981.
Corinne ou l'Italie. Une édition féministe de Claudine Herrmann. Paris: Editions des femmes, 1979.
De l'Allemagne. Ed. Jean de Pange. Intro. Simone Balayé. 5 vols. Paris: Hachette, 1958–1960.
Considérations sur la Révolution française. Ed. and intro. Jacques Godechot. Paris: Tallandier, 1983.
Dix années d'exil. Intro. Simone Balayé. Paris: Union générale d'éditions, 1966.
Correspondance générale. Ed. Béatrice W. Jasinski. Paris: Pauvert, 1960–1978; Hachette, 1982–1985.
Mon Journal. Ed. Simone Balayé in *Cahiers staëliens* 28 (1980): 55–79.
Des circonstances actuelles qui peuvent terminer la Révolution et des principes qui doivent fonder la république en France. Ed. Lucia Omacini. Geneva: Droz, 1979.

Modern Translations of Germaine de Staël

An Extraordinary Woman: Selected Writings of Germaine de Staël. Trans. and with an introduction by Vivian Folkenflik. New York: Columbia University Press, 1987.
Corinne, or Italy. Trans. Avriel H. Goldberger. New Brunswick, N.J.: Rutgers University Press, 1987.

Ten Years of Exile. Trans. Doris Beik. Intro. Peter Gay. New York: Saturday Review Press, 1972.

Studies of Germaine de Staël

Balayé, Simone. *Les Carnets de voyage de Madame de Staël: Contribution à la genèse de ses oeuvres.* Genève: Droz, 1971.

———. *Madame de Staël: Lumières et liberté.* Paris: Klincksieck, 1979.

Borowitz, Helen. "The Unconfessed Précieuse: Madame de Staël's Debt to Mademoiselle Scudéry." *Nineteenth-Century French Studies* 1, no. 2 (Fall-Winter 1982): 32–59.

Diesbach, Ghislain de. *Madame de Staël.* Paris: Librairie Acadèmique Perrin, 1983.

Goldberger, Auriel, Madelyn Gutwirth, and Karyna Szmurlo, eds. *Germaine de Staël: Crossing the Borders.* New Brunswick, N.J.: Rutgers University Press, 1991

Groupe de Coppet. Actes et documents du deuxième Colloque de Coppet, July 10–13, 1974. Geneva: Slatkine; Paris: Champion, 1977.

Groupe de Coppet et la Révolution française. Actes du quatrième Colloque de Coppet, July 20–23, 1988. Lausanne: Institut Benjamin Constant, 1988.

Gutwirth, Madelyn. "Forging a Vocation: Germaine de Staël on Fiction, Power, and Passion." *Bulletin of Research in the Humanities* 86 (1983–1985): 242–54.

———. "La *Delphine* de Madame de Staël: femme, révolution, et mode épistolaire." *Cahiers Staëliens* 26–27 (1979): 151–65.

———. *Madame de Staël, Novelist: The Emergence of the Artist as Woman.* Urbana: University of Illinois Press, 1978.

———. "Madame de Staël, Rousseau, and the Woman Question." *PMLA* 86 (January 1971): 100–109.

———. "Woman as Mediatrix: From Jean-Jacques Rousseau to Germaine de Staël." In *Woman as Mediatrix: Nineteenth-Century Women Writers.* Ed. Avriel Goldberger. Westport, Conn.: Greenwood Press, 1987.

Gwynne, G. E. *Mme de Staël: femme, la Révolution française, politique, philosophie, littérature.* Paris: Nizet, 1969.

Herold, Christopher. *Mistress to an Age: A Life of Madame de Staël.* New York: Bobbs-Merrill, 1958.

Hogsett, Charlotte. *The Literary Existence of Germaine de Staël.* Carbondale: Southern Illinois University Press, 1987.

Kitchin, Joanna. "La littérature et les femmes selon Madame de Staël." In *Benjamin Constant, Madame de Staël, et le Groupe de Coppet.* Ed. Etienne Hofmann. Oxford: Voltaire Foundation; Lausanne: Institut Benjamin Constant, 1980.

Kristeva, Julia. "Gloire, deuil et écriture. Lettre à un 'romantique' sur Mme de Staël." *Romantisme* 62 (1988): 7–14.

Madame de Staël et l'Europe. Actes du Colloque de Coppet, July 18–24, 1966. Preface by Jean Fabre and Simone Balayé. Paris: Klincksieck, 1970.

Miller, Nancy K. "Performances of the Gaze: Staël's *Corinne, or Italy.*" In *Subject to Change: Reading Feminist Writing.* New York: Columbia University Press, 1988.

Moers, Ellen. "Performing Heroinism: The Myth of Corinne." In *Literary Women: The Great Writers.* Garden City, N.Y.: Doubleday, 1976.

Petterson, Carla L. "*Corinne* and *Louis Lambert*: Romantic Myth Making." In *The

Determined Reader: Gender and Culture in the Novel from Napoleon to Victoria. New Brunswick, N.J.: Rutgers University Press, 1986.

Poulet, George. "La Pensée critique de Madame de Staël." *Preuves* 190 (December 1966): 27–35.

Starobinski, Jean. "Suicide et mélancolie chez Mme de Staël." In *Madame de Staël et l'Europe: Colloque de Coppet.* Paris: Klincksieck, 1970.

Swallow, Noreen J. "The Weapon of Personality: A Review of Sexist Criticism of Madame de Staël." *Atlantis* 8, no. 1 (Fall 1982) : 79.

Szmurlo, Karyna. "Le Jeu et le discours féminin: la danse de l'héroïne staëlienne." *Nineteenth-Century French Studies* 15 (Fall-Winter 1986/87): 1–13.

Vallois, Marie-Claire. *Fictions féminines: Mme de Staël et les voix de la Sibylle.* Stanford Calif.: Anma Libri, 1987.

Winegarten, Renee. *Madame de Staël.* Lemington Spa, UK; Dover, N. H.: Berg, 1985.

CLAUDINE-ALEXANDRINE GUÉRIN DE TENCIN (1682–1749)

Eva Martin Sartori

BIOGRAPHY

Claudine-Alexandrine Guérin de Tencin was born in 1682 in Grenoble, the last of the five children of Antoine Guérin de Tencin and Louise de Buffevent. The Guérin de Tencin were a family of lawyers and administrators who had prospered in the Dauphiné since the sixteenth century. Mme de Tencin's biographers always begin with her great-grandfather, a peddler who settled in the town of Romans in the Dauphiné and became a jeweler. The reference to the peddler-jeweler is important, for Mme de Tencin's life was much affected by the family's relentless climb up the social and financial ladder. Her ancestors had prospered by marrying well, working hard, buying posts in the judiciary, and accommodating themselves to the existing power structure. The price of this prosperity was the sacrifice of some of the children to the Church. The family's resources had to be conserved for the oldest males, who would advance the family's fortune by buying land and positions. Of Mme de Tencin's six aunts and uncles, only one escaped the Church. Her father seemed determined to follow the same course with his children but was successful with only two of the four. The youngest son, Pierre, entered the Church, in which he pursued a successful career. The youngest daughter, Claudine-Alexandrine, was placed in Montfleury, a Dominican convent, at the age of eight in the hope that this early exposure would make it easy for her to take the veil.

What little is known of Mme de Tencin's life in the convent comes from the document drawn up by the ecclesiastical court that later annulled her vows. Although Montfleury was one of the most relaxed French convents, the young Claudine-Alexandrine felt clearly that she was unsuited to convent life. Her father rejected her pleas to be allowed to come home and threatened her variously with a worse convent, prison, or marriage to a poor rural nobleman. To thwart her attempts at escape, he bribed nuns to spy on her and intercepted her correspondence. She resisted by making herself ill with emetics and perhaps other medications. She also became deeply depressed; doctors later testified that she had experienced violent "vapors," which made them fear for her life. They believed these vapors were caused by a profound melancholy brought on by her dislike of the convent.

Finally she submitted to her father's orders and took the veil, but was resourceful enough to begin immediately the procedure that fourteen years later would lead to the annulment of her vows: the day after the ceremony she declared before a lawyer and two witnesses that she had been coerced into becoming a nun. This formal statement was repeated periodically to keep her appeal alive. Her father died in 1705, but it was not until 1712 that she succeeded in obtaining an annulment. At the age of thirty, Claudine-Alexandrine de Tencin was free, in the words of the papal brief, to "re-enter the century and dispose of her person as she saw fit" (quoted by Decottignies in his introduction to *Les Mémoires du Comte de Comminge*, 38). In spite of her secular status, her enemies referred to her all her life as a "defrocked nun" or as the "canoness Tencin." But Mme de Tencin seems to have put behind her this period of her life and never to have held a grudge against her family. On the contrary, she remained devoted to the advancement of her brothers and sisters and their families.

In Paris Mme de Tencin established a salon in which she received an international group of diplomats, writers, philosophers, and financiers. Soon after the death of Louis XIV she became the mistress of the abbé Dubois, the most powerful minister in the Regent's cabinet. The abbé was much older than she and ugly as well and in poor health. But this relationship gave her access to political power and the possibility of increasing her wealth during the period when John Law was controlling the finances and stock market of France. Her contemporaries believed that she acted as a spy for Dubois in her (possible) liaisons with the British diplomats Lord Bolingbroke and Matthew Prior. It was also rumored that she had had numerous other love affairs, with the ex-chief of police d'Argenson and the Regent himself among others. Her love affair with the artillery officer Louis Camus Destouches resulted in the birth of Jean Le Rond d'Alembert, the mathematician, philosopher, and contributor to the *Encyclopédie*. But the child played no role in her life. Within hours of the birth, she abandoned the infant on the steps of the church Saint-Jean Le Rond (whence his name) and never afterwards gave any sign that she knew he existed.

Mme de Tencin's notoriety reached a peak in 1726 when an ex-lover, Charles de la Fresnaye, committed suicide in her apartment in broad daylight. La Fresnaye left behind a statement in which he accused Mme de Tencin of trying to rob and assassinate him, and of having affairs with the elderly Fontenelle and with her nephew d'Argental. She was immediately imprisoned and not released until her acquittal four months later.

In 1727 her brother Pierre, by now an archbishop, took his turn in the limelight when, at the instigation of the cardinal Fleury and to further his own rise in the

Church, he convened a council in his diocese of Embrun to judge the Jansenist teachings of Jean Soanen, bishop of Senez. As expected, the bishop was found guilty and exiled. Voltaire expressed the general sentiment when he wrote: "Soanen was considered a saint in his province. The man guilty of simony (Pierre de Tencin had engaged in some shady dealings involving the priory of Merlou) condemned the saint, forbade him to exercise his duties as bishop and priest, and relegated him to a Benedictine convent" (quoted by Sareil, 174; this and subsequent translations from the French are mine). It was believed that Mme de Tencin had some of her friends write her brother's speeches and published articles and pamphlets favorable to his cause.

As she continued to aid her brother in his agitations against the Jansenists, Mme de Tencin was exiled to Passy in 1730 and warned by Cardinal Fleury to avoid taking part in activities unbecoming to her sex. "Your sex naturally confines you within certain boundaries of which I need not remind you," he wrote to her (quoted by Decottignies, 1969, 31). After her return to Paris five months later she concentrated her energy on the development of her salon which, at this period, took on a more literary character, although philosophic and scientific questions continued to be discussed. The "seven wise men" who constituted the permanent nucleus of her salon included the physicist Jean-Jacques Dortous de Mairan, the physician Jean Astruc, the historian, grammarian, and novelist Charles Duclos, the translator Jean-Baptiste de Mirabaud, and the archeologist Claude Gros de Boze, as well as its stars, the wit and popularizer of science Fontenelle, and the playwright, novelist, and essayist Marivaux, both "acquired" at the death of Madame de Lambert in 1733. The intimates were held together by certain rituals. For instance, she called her friends her "beasts" (bêtes) and referred to her salon as her menagerie. Every year she gave each of the men enough black velvet for a pair of breeches. Although her guests were mostly men, she also invited actresses like Mimi Dancourt and intellectual society women like Mme du Châtelet and Mme Geoffrin. There were also occasional visitors, among them the abbé Prévost and Montesquieu, who came to read from their works and solicit opinions.

Mme de Tencin was a consummate hostess. According to Marivaux, who is reported to have used her as a model for the character of Madame Dorsin in La Vie de Marianne, she had the ability to make others feel intelligent and witty. One of her close friends, Alexis Piron, saw her as combining male and female characteristics. Capable of "delicate" taste and feeling ("Goût et sentiment delicat"), she also had strength and courage, a woman but also a "statesman" (quoted by Masson, 230). She was a devoted and energetic friend, championing the admission of her intimates into the Académie française, lending them money when necessary, and promoting their works. One of the very last acts of her life was to pay for the printing of the errata pages of Montesquieu's Esprit des lois. Some found the atmosphere of her salon too contrived, but for others it epitomized the wit and grace of French social life.

Stimulated by the literary discussions in her salon, Mme de Tencin began to write novels. Because it was unseemly for an aristocratic woman to write, and perhaps because she wanted to avoid any further notoriety, all of her works were published anonymously. The first, the *Mémoires du Comte de Comminge* (*Memoirs of the Count of Comminge*), was published in 1735, followed by *Le Siège de Calais* (*The Siege of Calais*) in 1739 and by the *Les Malheurs de l'amour* (The Sorrows of Love, translated as *The Female Adventurers*) in 1747. Her last novel, *Anecdotes de la cour et du règne d'Edouard II* (Anecdotes from the Court and Reign of Edward II), was finished by Mme Elie de Beaumont and published posthumously in 1767. It is also possible that she wrote the novel *L'Histoire d'une religieuse écrite par elle-même* (A Nun's Story, Written by Herself), but neither her biographer Jean Sareil nor the critic Jean Decottignies, both of whom have studied her work carefully, think so. Her novels were highly praised and extremely popular in all of Europe. They inspired plays, a poem, an opera, and paintings and etchings. Some contemporaries attributed her works to her two nephews, Pont-de-Veyle and d'Argental, but her biographers find little to support these claims. There was no reason for either nephew to deny authorship of these very popular works and no reason for either to have left the last novel unfinished. It was not until the end of the century that her complete works were published under her name.

Although forbidden to "meddle" in politics, Mme de Tencin continued to intrigue at court. In 1742 her brother, who had finally succeeded in becoming a cardinal, was appointed a minister of state, but he was disliked by the king and had little influence. Mme de Tencin's solution was to manipulate the king through his mistress, the Duchess of Châteauroux. The Duchess's death in 1744 effectively ended Mme de Tencin's hopes for a political role. However, her attempt to establish ties with the king's mistress was the occasion of a fascinating correspondence with the Duke of Richelieu on the subject of the governance of France and the role that they envisaged for Mme de Châteauroux. It reveals a total lack of principle, an inability to see beyond the personal, but also a very keen psychological intelligence.

On the surface, at least, Mme de Tencin's last years were spent quietly. She had become a "mother of the Church," in the words of Saint-Simon, and the pope's portrait hung in her salon. But her last act again provoked a flurry of condemnation. Much of her property had already been siphoned off by her lover Astruc, but what was left was willed to her brother. The impoverished d'Alembert received nothing.

MAJOR THEMES

Although Tencin's contemporaries were primarily interested in the subtle analyses of love in her novels and in the conflicts her characters experienced between love and what they perceived to be their duty, modern readers are more likely to respond to the external power relations between her protagonists and between the lovers and those around them. The reader is witness to the plight of the young, especially young women, confronted by abusive and greedy parents and husbands and by a social code that makes any attempt at self-definition a dangerous enterprise. In the face of these obstacles her characters manage to find concrete, although mostly limited, ways to exercise their autonomy. And in one of her historical novels, *Le Siège de Calais*, the heroine's action extends to the political sphere, as it is she, rather than the warring noblemen, who successfully negotiates the release of the burghers of Calais.

Jean Sareil has lamented the complete absence of autobiographical elements in Mme de Tencin's fiction. Yet surely the coercive and violent parents obsessed with money and caste were drawn from models close to home. These figures recur in all of her novels. The action of *Les Mémoires du Comte de Comminge* is triggered by the father's pursuit of an inheritance he seeks to wrest from his cousin, M. de Lussan. Because of his father's enmity toward his cousin's family, Comminge is forbidden to marry Adélaïde de Lussan. In *Le Siège de Calais* the vindictive parent is the stepmother, Mme de Mailly, who wants to force Mlle de Mailly to marry her son, M. de Boulai, because she covets Mlle de Mailly's fortune. The parents of both Pauline and Eugénie, the heroines of *Les Malheurs*, are interested in their daughters only as pawns in their desire for social and financial advancement. Pauline's bourgeois mother, a social climber who puts on silly airs as she attempts to ape the nobility, manages to arrange a marriage with a duke for her daughter. Eugénie's family places her in a convent in order to pass on the undivided fortune to her brother. These parents are often choleric and violent. M. de Comminge attacks his son with a sword when he learns that the young man has destroyed the papers necessary to defeat Lussan's claim, then throws him into a dungeon, which he will be allowed to leave only when Adélaïde is safely married to someone else. Mme de Mailly conspires to have Mlle de Mailly's lover assassinated. M. de N . . . , who marries Pauline's mother, tries to have Pauline's lover assassinated and at the end makes an attempt on her life. In light of Mme de Tencin's history, it is surprising that monks and nuns are portrayed as sympathetic, tolerant, and compassionate parent substitutes, and that convents and monasteries are viewed as refuges rather than prisons.

When the heroine marries she often finds that she has but exchanged one tyrant for another. M. de Benavides, whom Adélaïde de Lussan marries, imprisons her, and Lancastre in the *Anecdotes* is known to have locked up and perhaps caused the death of his first wife. M. de N . . . in *Les Malheurs* allows his wife to die in childbirth so that he can collect her inheritance. But it is not only the women who suffer from marriage. The meek M. de Mailly is bullied by his intemperate and vindictive wife.

Constrained by parental authority and social conventions, it is only in her choice of a lover that the heroine can express her will and her moral principles. Mme de Tencin's heroines choose men whose manners exemplify the aristocratic ideal, but they also choose men who will allow them some measure of control over the relationship. The first sign of a lover's worthiness is the timidity and respect he shows the woman. Early in *Le Siège*, Mme de Tencin makes it clear that Canaple is worthy of Mme de Granson's love because, unlike her libertine husband, who thinks of women as conquests, he is sympathetic to the plight of women. "He is far from believing that a man of principle can be untrue to a woman; on the contrary, he is convinced that you can't be scrupulous enough in a relationship which often disturbs the entire life of someone you have convinced you would love forever," says his sister (91). (This and all subsequent quotations are translations from the 1832 edition of the *Oeuvres* published by Moutardier.)

To marry the men they love, the heroines' range of activity extends from determined stalling to energetic and resourceful action. In *Les Malheurs*, Pauline refuses her mother's choice of a husband, arranges for her lover's escape to Germany, and follows him disguised as a man. In the same novel, the jailer's daughter Hippolyte also falls in love with Barbasan, dresses in men's clothes so that she can act as his keeper, and then seduces him and bears his child. In *Les Mémoires* Adélaïde does not flaunt convention outright by running away with her lover (as Comminge asks her to do). But she only seems to opt for virtue over passion when she declares, "I have been mistress of my conduct if not of my feelings" (67). Her subsequent actions express her own values, not those of society, as Jean Decottignies was the first to point out. Thus she chooses to marry so that Comminge will be freed, and she chooses to marry the repulsive Benavides in order to remain true, at least emotionally, to Comminge. Her loveless marriage and her presence at the Trappist monastery are nothing short of sacrilegious: the lovers' burial in the same tomb expresses the author's belief in the supremacy of romantic love and in the heroine's right to make a choice.

But it is in *Le Siège de Calais* that Mme de Tencin's heroines are most fully empowered. Her contemporaries report that the novel was born of a wager: Tencin maintained that she could begin with the situation with which novels usually end. Canaple's love is the consequence of a fortuitous sexual encounter with his best friend's wife, which is the first episode of the novel. Like a medieval knight, Canaple must then win the heroine's love by continued submission and respect, while at the same time denying the equation between virtue and chastity on which courtly love is based. Mme de Granson's authority in the realm of the personal is translated into political power as it is she, supported by the warrior queen of England, and not the French knights, who saves the town of Calais. *Le Siège de Calais* is the only one of Mme de Tencin's novels that has a happy ending.

While Mme de Tencin has been criticized for the awkward structure of her novels, this very awkwardness can be viewed as evidence of a deeply subversive intent. Only the *Mémoires du Comte de Comminge* can be considered classical in form, as all the episodes bear on the story of Comminge and Adélaïde. But even this novel tends toward a bipolar structure as Adélaïde's voice begins to displace Comminge's, so that at the end Adélaïde, at first reticent and circumspect, flowers into an impassioned and vocal heroine. Tencin's later novels are much more complex and involve telling the stories of two or even three couples.

In *Les Malheurs* and in *Anecdotes* the stories are told serially, while in *Le Siège* three stories are interwoven. This multiplication is perhaps evidence of a need to escape aesthetic strictures as well as a moral compulsion to accumulate warnings and cautions against the perils that await untutored, unsuspecting, and vulnerable young women.

It is impossible to neatly categorize Mme de Tencin's fiction. An opportunist in her work as well as in her life, she drew from a number of literary currents. Like the "précieux" characters a century earlier, her heroes and heroines lack any recognizable features: the women are full of charm and grace, the lovers are all handsome. Of Eugénie, Blanchefort remarks, "Her simple beauty, so artless that she seemed not to even be aware of it, made her so touching that the count of Blanchefort could not resist so many charms" (*Malheurs*, 92). Her medieval knights sometimes sound either like visitors from a *Scudéry novel (Canaple, for instance) or as cynical as an eighteenth-century roué (M. de Granson). But in their self-indulgence and in the internal conflicts they articulate, her febrile characters are perhaps closer to those of the abbé Prévost than to Mme de *Lafayette's. Her plots also announce Romantic conventions. Her characters are always in motion, crisscrossing France and sometimes traveling abroad. Some of the most important events (the chance meetings of the hero and heroine in both the *Mémoires* and the *Siège*, for instance) occur on the road. She makes heavy use of coincidences, disguises (including cross-dressing), substitutions, secret marriages, nocturnal births, and unlikely reunions. Wild and somber settings objectify the characters' moods.

But the basic tension is between the characters' anarchic passions and the author's belief in an orderly and intelligible universe. She shared her contemporaries' belief that human behavior was knowable and that its laws could be generalized. This belief is evident in the numerous generalizations and maxims that punctuate her novels, for instance: "When the heart is truly touched, it takes pleasure in everything which proves to itself its own sensibility" (*Mémoires*, 172); "Most men mistake a strong feeling of vanity for love" (*Anecdotes*, 219); "The heart furnishes us with all the errors we need" (*Malheurs*, 39); "It is true that a woman doesn't have any lovers when she doesn't want to have any" (*Anecdotes*, 221).

Most of her maxims concern love and the different ways in which men and women love. In *Malheurs* she writes, "Women in general are always indulgent when it is a question of tender feelings" (65), while in *Anecdotes* she reflects that "men have convinced themselves that love doesn't obligate them to be very scrupulous; and, in any case, they believe that they must remain faithful only in their heart" (224). Occasionally, however, her observations range farther. For instance, she explains that the nobility remains worthy of respect because noble families were originally more estimable than others, and since there must be some distinction among people, this one remains the easiest (*Malheurs*, 10). The implication of these observations is that, if human nature follows certain laws, then human behavior can be manipulated and controlled. Yet, as her novels also show, she was far from believing that human beings are creatures of reason alone. The signature of her fiction is the tension between these two poles, metaphorically expressed by the constrained, coercive space of the convent or the dungeon and the open road with its promise of adventure.

SURVEY OF CRITICISM

Mme de Tencin's novels were extremely popular and highly praised by her contemporaries. Reviewing *Les Mémoires du Comte de Comminge* in 1735 in *Le Pour et contre*, Prévost reported that "it is the unanimous judgment of the public as well as mine that the book is very well written" (7:77). Voltaire also admired the purity of style of *Le Siège de Calais* (letter of July 27, 1739). While her contemporaries commented mainly on the style and the characters, later critics emphasized its "morality." Baculard d'Arnaud was the first to capitalize on the emotional sensuality of the last scene in the *Mémoires*, on which he based his very successful play, *Les Amants malheureux, ou le Comte de Comminge* (1764). In 1769 the abbé de La Porte saw the *Mémoires* as the portrayal of "virtuous love" (3: 273). At the end of the eighteenth century critics compared Tencin to Mme de Lafayette because both were concerned with the conflict between love and duty. "Madame de Tencin appeared. . . . She and Madame de Lafayette must serve as models," wrote Delandine in 1786 (quoted by Decottignies in his introduction to *Les Mémoires*, 126).

Early in the nineteenth century the critic La Harpe described the *Mémoires* as the "pendant" of the *Princesse de Clèves* (7: 306) and praised *Le Siège* and *Les Malheurs* as absorbing and stylish works. Tencin's novels continued to be edited in scholarly and popular editions throughout the century. Toward the end of the nineteenth century, however, the Goncourt brothers in *La Femme au dix-huitième siècle* shifted the public's interest to her life rather than her fiction. In their hands, she became the consummate intriguer, the prototype of the brilliant and willful woman of the world, her intelligence and self-control allowing her to manipulate others at will—a Madame de Merteuil *avant la lettre*.

At the beginning of the twentieth century scholars continued to show more interest in Mme de Tencin's life than in her work. Pierre-Maurice Masson was the first to write a biography based on existing documents. His is still the best account of her life. More recently, Jean Sareil has written a biography of the family but has focused much more on Pierre than on Claudine-Alexandrine, perhaps because as a Church and state dignitary the cardinal left much more of a paper trail than did his sister. Masson is the only one of her biographers with more than a passing interest in her work, which, however, he finds "unreal and dry" (126) and uninteresting because it lacks the "shiver of a personal temperament or character" (179). There is a need for a new biography which would carefully assess her life as a woman and the extent of her political and literary influence.

Current interest in women's fiction has stimulated a number of scholars to interpret her novels as reflective of a woman author's concerns. Jean Decottignies, who has published an excellent critical edition of *Les Mémoires du Comte de Comminge*, has compared Mme de Tencin's novels with those of her contemporaries. He concludes that though Mme de Tencin used stock themes (children in revolt against parental authority, unhappy marriages, the convent as setting, love as an occasion for rebellion, etc.), her plots were structured in such a way as to subvert conventional notions of morality. Decottignies emphasizes the choices Adélaïde makes after her separation from Comminge. Comminge's and Adélaïde's preoccupation with their profane love in a setting devoted to the worship of God, and the establishment's acquiescence (in the person of the charitable monk), are final evidence that, contrary to eighteenth-century interpretations, it is not virtue but rather love that triumphs in this novel. In *Le Siège de Calais* the very fact that the novel begins where novels normally end challenges the validity of ordinary modes of discourse.

Shirley Jones, in "Madame de Tencin: An Eighteenth-Century Novelist" (1979), sees conservatism where Decottignies sees subversion. She compares Tencin's novels with those of male writers such as Duclos, Crébillon, and Marivaux, and finds that Tencin's are, like all the novels written by women at the time, characterized by "rigorous moral conservatism." She attributes Tencin's choice of the historical novel to women's desire to rewrite history to make it a "a chronicle of female domination" (212) and the medieval background of some of the novels to an interest in resuscitating the chivalric tradition. Jones believes that the historical transposition only helped women avoid the moral and political issues they faced in real life.

In "Madame de Tencin and the 'Mascarade' of Female Impersonation" (1985) Alice Parker looks to the novelist's life for clues to the meaning of her work. In her life Tencin had to hide behind her brother and lovers to exercise power, behind religious respectability to maintain her social life, and behind the veil of anonymity to publish her novels. Parker argues that in her fiction she also uses a conventional framework to "mask radical departures from prescribed patterns of gender difference" (69). Thus plot and structure are used to denounce the victimization and humiliation of women by authoritarian parents and husbands. Men and women who transgress are treated with indulgence, among them young women escaping forced marriages or rebelling against forced religious vocations. Frequent cross-dressing and plot reversals, such as in *Le Siège*, represent attempts to divorce psychological from sexual identity. In their portrayal of unhappy couples, her novels are cautionary tales warning the reader against seeking escape in romantic love or even marriages of reason. Parker agrees that Tencin was not interested in changing fictional forms. Rather "her strategy was to inflect inherited tropes and images in a subtle way so that all the pieces of the code are reshuffled and acquire new meaning" (73).

In *A New History of French Literature* (1989) Nancy K. Miller compares Tencin's *Mémoires* with the abbé Prévost's *Manon Lescaut*, both written in the form of a memoir. She notes that, while des Grieux rejoins the world of men at the conclusion of *Manon Lescaut*, Comminge, blind to the real woman he had loved, is left in the monastery with only a few objects to remind him of the woman he has lost. For Miller, "the novel sharpens the critique of patriarchy by showing the ways in which the sons as men prove to be as blind as the fathers to the fatal embodiment of human relations" (442).

BIBLIOGRAPHY

Works by Mme de Tencin

Oeuvres de Madame de Tencin. Amsterdam; Paris, 1786. (Contains the Delandine edition
    of the *Mémoires du Comte de Comminges; Le Siège de Calais; Les Malheures de
    l'amour;* and *Anecdotes de la cour et du règne de' Edouard II, rio de'Angleterre.*)
Oeuvres complètes des Mesdames de la Fayette, de Tencin et de Fontaines. New ed.
    Paris: Moutardier, 1832. (Also contains her letters to the Duc de Richelieu.)

Modern Editions

Mémoires du Comte de Comminge. Ed. Jean Decottignies. Lille: Giard, 1969.
Le Siège de Calais. Paris: Editions Desjonquères, 1983.
Letters of Madame de Tencin and the Cardinal de Tencin to the Duc de Richelieu. Paris:
    Editions Mazarine, 1967.

Translations of Mme de Tencin

Memoirs of the Count of Comminge. London: G. Kearsley, 1774.
The Female Adventurers. 2 vols. Dublin: P. Wilson and J. Potts, 1776.
The Siege of Calais by Edward of England. An Historical Novel. T. Woodward and Paul
    Vaillant, 1740. Rpt. New York: Garland, 1974.

Studies of Mme de Tencin

Bollmann, Martina. *Madame de Tencin romancière*. Thèse de doctorat de 3e cycle.
    Université de la Sorbonne Nouvelle, Paris III, 1982.
Coynart, Charles de. *Les Guérin de Tencin (1520–1758)*. Paris: Hachette, 1910.
Decottignies, Jean. Introduction to *Mémoires du Comte de Comminge*, by Madame de
    Tencin. Lille: Giard, 1969.
——. "Roman et revendication féminine, d'après les *Mémoires du Comte de Comminge*
    de Madame de Tencin." In *Roman et lumières au 18e siècle*. Paris: Editions
    sociales, 1970.
——. "Les Romans de Madame de Tencin: fable et fiction." In *La Littérature des
    Lumières en France et en Pologne: esthétique, terminologie, échanges*. Acta
    Universitatis Wratislaviensis, no. 330. Wroclaw, 1976, pp. 249–64.
Dewey, Pascale. *Mesdames de Tencin et de Graffigny, deux romancières oubliées des
    coeurs sensibles*. Diss., Rice University, 1976.

Goncourt, Jules de, and Edmond de Goncourt. *La Femme au dix-huitième siecle*. 2 vols. Paris: Flammarion et Fasquelle, 1882.

Jones, Shirley. "Madame de Tencin: An Eighteenth-Century Novelist." In *Woman and Society in Eighteenth-Century France: Essays in Honour of John Stepehenson Spink*. Ed. Eva Jacobs et al. London: Athlone Press, 1979.

Kavaliunas, Jojita Elijana Jurate. *Passions and the Search for Happiness, as Manifested in Certain French Novels of the 18th Century*. Diss., Case Western Reserve University, 1972.

La Harpe, J.-F. *Lycée ou Cours de littérature ancienne et moderne*. New ed. 16 vols. Paris: Chez Agasse, 1799–1805.

La Porte, abbé de. *Histoire littéraire des femmes françaises*. 5 vols. Paris: Lacombe, 1769.

Masson, Pierre-Maurice. *Une Vie de femme au XVIIIe siècle: Madame de Tencin (1682–1749)*. 3rd ed. Paris: Hachette, 1910. Rpt. Geneva: Slatkine, 1970.

Miller, Nancy K. "The Gender of the Memoir-Novel." In *A New History of French Literature*. Ed. Denis Hollier. Cambridge, Mass.: Harvard University Press, 1989.

Parker, Alice. "Madame de Tencin and the 'Mascarade' of Female Impersonation." *Eighteenth Century Life* 9, no. 2 (1985): 65–77.

Prévost, abbé. *Le Pour et contre*. 20 vols. Paris: Didot, 1735.

Sadler Moore, Patricia A. *The Birth of the Corrupt Heroine: Gestation in the Novels of Madame de Tencin*. Diss., University of Florida, 1980.

Sareil, Jean. *Les Tencin*. Geneva: Droz, 1969.

Vachon, Marie-Françoise. *Les Romans de Madame de Tencin*. Diss., Columbia University, 1975.

FLORA TRISTAN (1803–1844)

Mary Rice-DeFosse

BIOGRAPHY

Treated as a pariah by an unjust and repressive society, Tristan, in the words of her spiritual daughter, Eléonore Blanc, "accepted this name and made of it her own title of nobility" (23).[1] Tristan transformed her personal struggle against oppression into an international crusade for the emancipation of workers and women alike. Her contribution, wrote the poet André Breton, was one "in which a boldness which knows no bounds placed itself in the service of extreme generosity" (*Arcane* 17 [1945]: 69). Tristan's life and works are inextricably entwined: her own experience informed her writing, while at the same time she tried to implement the ideas presented in her works through positive action.

Born in Paris in 1803, Flore Céleste Thérèse Henriette Tristan y Moscoso was the first-born child of an irregular union between Don Mariano Tristan y Moscoso, a Peruvian nobleman, and Anne-Pierre Laisnay, a French émigrée he met in Bilbao, Spain, where the two were married in a religious ceremony that was never legitimated by the required civil formalities. Her father's sudden death in 1807 shattered the family's happy life together, for Tristan and her mother, never officially recognized as Mariano Tristan's heirs, were left not only bereft, but stripped of their home, former social position, and income. In desperation, Anne-Pierre Tristan used a small inheritance to move her family, which now included a son born after his father's death, to the country. There Tristan probably received only a sporadic education. Back in Paris after her younger brother's death, she was apprenticed at age seventeen and soon earned her way as a lithographic colorist. In February 1821, she married her employer, the engraver André Chazal who, unlike previous suitors, accepted her despite her illegitimate status. After four years of marriage, Flora Chazal, pregnant with the couple's third child, left her indebted and abusive husband, but since divorce was no longer permitted in

France after 1816, she was unable to free herself completely. She did, however, obtain a *séparation de biens* (separation of income and property) from Chazal in 1828. Refusing the name Madame Chazal and all it connoted, she reverted to her maiden name and supported herself and her family during this obscure period of her life as a ladies' maid or companion, traveling to England, Switzerland, and Italy while her children remained with her mother in France. Tristan found herself without a civil status, for she was neither single nor a widow, although she sometimes passed as one or the other. In truth she felt herself even more a pariah than when she had first discovered the irregular nature of her parents' marriage.

Humiliated that the daughter of a nobleman should earn her living as a servant, the young woman sustained herself with memories of her happy childhood years before her father's death, a time when figures like the dashing Simón Bolívar had frequented the family's home in Paris, and when Flora herself had been considered a member of the powerful Tristan y Moscoso family of Peru. On her thirtieth birthday, April 7, 1833, Tristan embarked on a voyage to her father's homeland in an attempt to claim what was, in her eyes, her rightful position and inheritance. On shipboard, the beautiful and passionate woman attracted the amorous attentions of the captain, Zacharie Chabrié, who, believing Tristan was a single mother, proposed marriage, an offer she obviously could not accept given her true circumstances. Although she was received warmly by her father's family in Peru, introduced into Peruvian society in Aréquipa and Lima, and granted a small pension, Tristan was never acknowledged as the legitimate daughter of Don Mariano Tristan. Even if she had been frustrated in her initial purpose, however, her adventurous journey marked an important turning point, for through her travels she came to realize that she was not alone in her plight, that others suffered far greater subjugation and mistreatment than she did. Moreover, it was during this voyage that Flora Tristan began to write, keeping a journal that would later become *Pérégrinations d'une paria* (*Peregrinations of a Pariah*).

Upon her return to France in late 1834, Tristan began a new phase of her life. With a modest income from her uncle, Pio Tristan, she was able to live independently in Paris, where she published her first work, a pamphlet entitled *Nécessité de faire bon accueil aux femmes étrangères* (On the Necessity of Welcoming Foreign Women), undoubtedly a reflection of her travel experiences, in 1835. She thus entered the literary and artistic circles of the 1830s, coming into contact with such visionaries and social reformers as Charles Fourier and Victor Considérant. She attended meetings of the *Gazette des Femmes*, where she met Eugénie Niboyet and other writers for this women's journal. She also established close relationships with Olympe Chodzko, a Polish patriot and intellectual, and the painter Jules Laure, and through these connections was introduced into the circle that included the actress Marie Dorval and the most celebrated woman writer of the day, George *Sand. Sand and Tristan expressed their mutual dislike, but nonetheless shared similar concerns about women's subordinate position in marriage, evidenced on Tristan's part by an 1837 petition to the Chamber of Deputies to reinstitute divorce.

At the same time Tristan was making a name for herself in journalism and literature, her domestic troubles once more began to escalate. When their eldest son had died in 1832, Tristan's husband had agreed to allow her to keep their daughter, Aline, "in exchange" for their second child, Ernest. Mother and daughter were reunited in 1835 once Tristan established herself in Paris, but Chazal soon claimed his paternal right to sole custody of the child. After repeated abductions of the recalcitrant girl, who wished to remain with her mother, several violent scenes between the estranged husband and wife, and a failed lawsuit brought by Chazal against the boarding school from which Aline had fled, a court order forced the girl to join her father. Next Chazal was accused of incest, and although he was acquitted, Aline was at last remanded to her mother's care. This was not the end of it, however.

André Chazal grew ever more incensed over his wife's new life and literary success, especially after her confessional *Pérégrinations d'une paria* appeared in January 1838. In June he purchased a set of pistols, and on September 10, as Tristan was approaching her lodging in the rue du Bac, he fired at her. She was hit in the left shoulder, the bullet lodged near her heart, but she made a swift recovery. Within ten days she was back at work, producing by the year's end short pieces for the *Revue de Paris*, *L'Artiste*, and *Le Voleur*, a melodramatic novel entitled *Méphis*, and, ironically enough in the circumstances, a petition calling for the abolition of the death penalty.

Tristan's literary reputation grew with her notoriety. During Chazal's sensational trial, his lawyer, Jules Favre, attempted to cast blame for his client's crime of passion on the victim, but the would-be assassin was nevertheless sentenced to twenty years in prison. Finally free, Tristan had her name and those of her children legally changed to her patronym.

Once she had apprenticed Ernest and Aline in skilled trades and thus secured their futures, the writer left for London in order to study English society and social problems. She spent four months in the spring and summer of 1839 in England, where she visited the Houses of Parliament (disguised as a Turkish man, since women were not permitted entry), a prison, the slums, the races, the "finishes" or gin palaces, where she observed the cruel misuse of prostitutes, and the insane asylum at Bedlam. This last had special significance for Tristan, for there she encountered a madman named Chabrier, who she at first feared might be her old seafaring friend, Chabrié. This inmate announced to her that she was destined to save the world with a new social order. Whether Tristan believed this portent or not, from this point on her work displayed an increased religious fervor. Indeed, in the following years she even used the title "Woman Messiah," bestowed on her by the madman, as she became even more involved in agitation for social change.

In 1840 Tristan published a scathing exposé of the social conditions she had observed in England in her *Promenades dans Londres* (*Flora Tristan's London*

Journal). A less expensive version dedicated to workers was issued in 1842 as *La Ville monstre* (The Monster City). Now preoccupied with the working classes, she read or corresponded with artisan leaders who were trying to reform the traditional French guild system, men like Adolphe Boyer, Pierre Moreau, Agricol Perdiguier, and Jean Gosset. Due to the lack of cooperation she received from artisan leaders as she moved away from the fragmented artisan groups, Tristan proposed a radical alternative, an international association for all workers, regardless of trade, degree of skill, nationality, or gender. She outlined its features in *L'Union ouvrière* (*The Workers' Union*), first published through self-subscription in 1843, five years before *The Communist Manifesto*.

The writer spent the last months of her life spreading her message among French workers. In the spring of 1844, she undertook her own *tour de France*, the traditional journeyman's circuit around the country. From April to September, she visited seventeen cities from Auxerre to Bordeaux, trying to win support for her union, speaking in workshops, taverns, and rented halls, and noting the workers' living and working conditions in great detail. She recorded her activities and observations in the diary she kept of the journey, also admitting her horror, despair, and fatigue. In a weakened state ever since Chazal's attempt on her life, Tristan was tormented by illness, police surveillance, and harassment by local authorities, but labored on. She finally succumbed to typhoid fever in Bordeaux in September 1844, and died there in November, her mission unfinished. Her death was mourned by those she had reached all over France; in 1848 they erected a monument to this apostle for their cause in the city where she had died and was buried.

MAJOR THEMES

Flora Tristan's fight for social justice is the touchstone of her works. Her early experiences as an illegitimate child, an abused wife, and a social outcast prepared her to perceive oppression and combat it. Despite an initial alienation from the powerless and the downtrodden, writing about their lives enabled Tristan to transcend her personal situation, to identify with other oppressed human beings, and to champion their cause. This process is most graphically encoded in *Pérégrinations d'une paria*, the autobiographical journal that takes the author from France to the Cape Verde Islands, then to South America as well as to the realization of her own potential. Her precise descriptions of black slaves, native Americans, and especially the women of Peru, subjugated in marriage or the convent, carry with them a forceful indictment of nineteenth-century society and its institutions.

Indeed, Tristan's detailed portraits of women lie at the core of the social critique that threads through her major works. As in her account of her South American voyage, the impact of her *Promenades dans Londres* stems from the writer's ability to document the concrete realities of women's lives as prostitutes, prisoners, workers, slum dwellers, and ignorant daughters of the middle class.

The emancipation of working-class women through education, vocational training, and appropriate work is a key component in the program for social change
she puts forth in *L'Union ouvrière*, but it should be noted that its author was
also criticized for the brutal honesty with which she represented the ignorance
and cruelty of women when denied intellectual, moral, and material equality,
including the right to work. In her petition for the reestablishment of divorce,
Tristan characterizes marriage as then practiced as a perverse form of slavery
detrimental to both tyrant and victim. She cogently argues that it is unnatural to
preserve a union that God has already destroyed, for a couple's tendency to
change and grow incompatible is a natural one. The writer thus reveals a Romantic sensibility in opposing nature and culture in order to condemn the latter.
She maintains in her petition to abolish the death penalty that even when society
attempts to act with justice it can err: the taking of an innocent life is a wrong
that can never be redressed.

Tristan's only novel, *Méphis*, develops these same themes in the form of a
melodramatic fiction. In the meandering plot line of a romance between a mag-
netic Latin beauty and the proletarian artist-prophet who falls in love with her,
Tristan implicates church and state in the continued oppression of women and
workers. The hero and heroine function as mouthpieces for the writer's own
ideas, while other characters illustrate the decadence and corruption of the idle
rich and the megalomania of the clergy. John Lysberry, otherwise known as
Méphis or Mephistopheles because he is a rebel and pariah, tries to liberate the
suffering Maréquita from her conventional notions of love just as he works to
free workers from exploitation at the hands of the bourgeoisie. In this and other,
shorter pieces devoted to art itself, Tristan makes it clear that she views the artist
as a divine messenger who reveals truth to the world in terms of his or her own
historical context. Maréquita, a composer and singer, is such a figure, as is
Méphis, whose masterpiece is a painting of the Woman-Guide who leads humanity on the path of progress.

In her conception of the Woman Messiah, the writer was obviously influenced
by the Saint-Simonian doctrine of a messianic couple destined to establish a new
social order, but when Tristan herself adopted the role of female apostle to the
working classes, she served alone. Her stance toward the workers recalls the
conviction expressed in her writings that women embody the critical moralizing
force within the family; in her own case, she extended the maternal metaphor
to the universal human family.

In her earliest piece, *Nécessité de faire bon accueil aux femmes étrangères*,
the writer proposes a practical organization aimed at helping to overcome the
difficulties women face in a foreign land. This pamphlet, with its internation-
alism, its emphasis on women's pivotal role as society's mothers, and its pragmatic solutions to social problems, prefigures *L'Union ouvrière*, often considered
Tristan's masterwork. *L'Union ouvrière* elaborates in its most extensive form
Flora Tristan's vision of the peaceful means through which to restructure society.
The writer anticipated a world in which every human being would enjoy rights

to education, work, and political voice. She saw her workers' union, an association that would not recognize distinctions of trade, skill, or sex for membership or limit itself within France's national boundaries, as a pragmatic, nonviolent step toward social justice and universal peace. The structure Tristan projected included local committees of correspondence in France and abroad, with a central committee in Paris or Lyons. The organization would be represented by a Defender who would speak on behalf of the laboring classes in the French Chamber of Deputies. Contributions from workers and other interested persons would go to support the union's programs, notably a series of workers' "palaces," similar in conception to community residences described by Robert Owen and Charles Fourier, where the old and infirm could still lead productive lives according to their capacities and the young would receive education and practical training. Although Tristan borrowed freely from "utopian" socialist thinkers like Louis Blanc, Owen, Fourier, the Saint-Simonians, and the Chartists, she offered a practicable plan for workers to emancipate themselves within the immediate social context and the family unit. She called on working-class men to unite in order to effect, in their own self-interest, the liberation of their wives, sisters, and daughters as well. Tristan's insistence on equal rights for women, however, provoked considerable resistance from workers.

As Tristan gained a greater sense of her own mission, her writings took on increasingly religious overtones, especially evident in her unpublished works, letters, and the Tour de France journal, in which she compares her own sufferings to those of Christ and Christian martyrs. Yet, where Christianity, in her eyes, had merely fulfilled humankind's spiritual needs, she believed that eventually progressive reforms could effectively address all aspects—intellectual, moral, and material—of life on earth. Although L'Emancipation de la femme (The Emancipation of Woman) continues to preach Tristan's principal message, this posthumous work, supposedly based on the writer's notes, is considered to be so heavily edited by Alphonse Constant that its language no longer remains hers. The recently published Tour de France, on the other hand, manifests the same lucid commentary blended with spiritual inspiration as had earlier works.

SURVEY OF CRITICISM

Most studies of Flora Tristan reflect the integral link between her life and works; they devote attention to both her experiences and literary achievements. There were many early responses to Tristan during her lifetime and immediately following her death, but with the repression of the political left after the Revolution of 1848, she fell into relative obscurity. Among the early homages to the writer are articles by Jules Janin and Eugène Stourm and a biography by her close friend and disciple, Eléonore Blanc. Blanc's version of Tristan's life, brief but faithful to its subject, also represents an effort to continue Tristan's mission and is consequently addressed to workers.

Although Aline's son, the artist Paul Gauguin, mentions Tristan in Avant et *après*, it is clear that he had little direct knowledge of the grandmother he never knew. In fact, it was Eléonore Blanc who received the writer's papers at her deathbed. The manuscripts were passed down through the Blanc family to Jules Puech, whose 1925 book, *La Vie et l'oeuvre de Flora Tristan*, still remains the definitive work on the writer because of its extensive documentation and its thorough treatment of Tristan's philosophical, political, and literary contributions as well as her biography. Puech attributes her essential importance to the action she took. His work, like that of Hélène Brion, Marguerite Thibert, and also Léon Abensour, reflects the resurgence of interest in the history of socialism and of feminism that occurred in France in the early twentieth century, an interest that naturally included Tristan. Latin American writers like Magda Portal and Alberto Sanchez helped to raise consciousness in their works about this revolutionary precursor somewhat later in the century. More recent biographies by Jean Baelen, Dominique Desanti, and Pierre Leprohon approach Tristan as an extraordinary woman whose thought and writings complement her experience. These last rely heavily on Tristan's own autobiographical works and letters, but also include interpretations of her life and ideas.

Among the most important contributions to scholarship on Tristan in recent years are a number of renditions and translations of her works, beginning with Lucien Scheler's *Morceaux choisis* (Selections) in 1947. Since then new editions of *Pérégrinations d'une paria*, *Promenades dans Londres*, *L'Union ouvrière*, and *Nécessité de faire bon accueil aux femmes étrangères* have all appeared, as well as translations of the first three, although both the new edition of *Pérégrinations d'une paria* and its translation are somewhat abridged. The hitherto unpublished *Lettres* (Letters) and *Le Tour de France* round out this group of major publications, which all contain notes and commentary, but unfortunately *Méphis* is still out of print and largely unavailable.

Contemporary historians, especially two specialists in women's history, S. Joan Moon and Laura S. Strumingher, have added significantly to the existing scholarship with new data and new historical methodologies. Moon presents Tristan's achievement as a unique synthesis of feminism and utopian socialism with comparisons to other reformers of the period. Strumingher's more extensive, biographical study also elaborates Tristan's place within the historical context, with particular emphasis on her many relationships with women, but differs from Moon in that she finds Tristan's ideas more practical than utopian.

In the field of literary criticism, Sandra K. Djikstra examines Tristan's literary aesthetics in relation to her Romantic psychology and historical context. Her approach thus overlaps with the biographical and historical studies previously mentioned, but treats the linguistic, semantic, and structural characteristics of Tristan's texts in greater depth using Marxist criticism. By far the best literary analysis of Tristan's works is found in Leslie Rabine's unpublished dissertation on four women writers of the Romantic period including Tristan. In this comparative study, Rabine explores the narrative strategies through which each woman writer developed her own literary voice. As she traces Tristan's growth as a writer, Rabine notes the changes Tristan effected in Romantic literary forms and themes. Other short critical pieces by a variety of literary scholars in several languages tend to focus on a specific work such as *Méphis*. The only major collection of essays on Tristan, *Un Fabuleux Destin: Flora Tristan*, contains the proceedings of the first international conference on the writer, edited by Stéphane Michaud.

Yet there is still much to be said about Tristan in the field of literary scholarship using the newly developed tools of feminist criticism. As Strumingher suggests, the writer's works reveal a "feminist approach," for the author's close personal involvement with her subject matter undermines conventional criteria used in judging objectivity, but does not diminish the force of her realism. The surrealist André Breton's fascination with Tristan's freshness of style as well as her political views is telling. She is able to infuse clear-sighted, well-reasoned social critiques with a discourse that seems to surge directly from the unconscious, lending her texts an opacity that threatens traditional literary codes. These characteristics may account for Tristan's position outside the literary canon, but they also underscore the writer's significance as a forerunner in women's writing as well as in feminism and socialism.

NOTE

1. All translations are my own.

BIBLIOGRAPHY

Works by Flora Tristan

First Editions

Nécessité de faire bon accueil aux femmes étrangères. Paris: Delaunay, 1835.
"Les Couvens d'Aréquipa." *Revue de Paris*, 2nd series 32 (1836): 227–259.
"Lettres à un architecte anglais." *Revue de Paris*, 2nd series 37 (1837): 134–139, 38 (1837): 280–290.
"Pétition pour le rétablissement du divorce à Messieurs les députés." Paris: Archives Nationales, pétition no. 133, dossier 71, December 20, 1837.
"De l'Art et de l'artiste dans l'antiquité et à la Renaissance." *L'Artiste*, 3rd ser. 9 (1838): 117–21.
"Episode de la vie de Ribera dit l'Espagnolet." *L'Artiste*, 3rd ser. 13 (1838): 192–96.
"De l'Art depuis la Renaissance." *L'Artiste*, 3rd ser. 24 (1838): 345–48.
"Lettres de Bolivar, publiées avec commentaires par Flora Tristan." *Le Voleur* (July 31, 1838): 90–94.
Pérégrinations d'une paria (1833–1834). 2 vols. Paris: Arthus Bertrand, 1838.
Pétition pour l'abolition de la peine de la mort. Paris: Huzard, 1838.
Méphis. 2 vols. Paris: Ladvocat, 1838.
Promenades dans Londres. Paris: H.-L. Delloye, 1840.

La Ville monstre. 2nd ed. of *Promenades dans Londres*. Paris: H.-L. Delloye, 1842.
L'Union ouvrière. Paris: Prévot, 1843.
L'Union ouvrière. 3rd ed. Paris and Lyons: chez tous les libraires, 1844.
L'Emancipation de la femme, ou le testament de la paria. Posthumous work completed according to the author's notes and published by A. Constant. Paris: Au bureau de *La Vérité*, 1846.

Modern Editions

Nécessité de faire bon accueil aux femmes étrangères. Ed. Denys Cuche. Paris: L'Harmattan, 1988.
Pérégrinations d'une paria. Paris: Maspero, 1979.
Promenades dans Londres. Ed. François Bédarida. Paris: Maspero, 1978.
L'Union ouvrière. Ed. Daniel Armogathe and Jacques Grandjonc. Paris: Des Femmes, 1986.
Le Tour de France. Preface by Michel Collinet. Ed. J. L. Puech. Paris: Editions Tête de Feuilles, 1973.
Le Tour de France. Ed. J. L. Puech. Intro. Stéphane Michaud. 2 vols. Paris: Seuil, 1980.
Lettres. Ed. Stéphane Michaud. Paris: Seuil, 1980.

Translations of Flora Tristan

Peregrinations of a Pariah. Ed. and trans. Jean Hawkes. London: Virago, 1986.
Peregrinations of a Pariah. Trans. Charles de Salis. Intro. Joanna Richardson. London: Folio Society, 1986.
Flora Tristan's London Journal. Trans. Dennis Palmer and Giselle Pincetl. London: G. Prior; Cambridge, Mass.: Charles River Books, 1980. Trans. of *Promenades dans Londres*.
The London Journal of Flora Tristan or the Aristocracy and the Working Classes of England. Trans. Jean Hawkes. London: Virago, 1982. Trans. of *Promenades dans Londres*.
The Workers' Union. Trans. and intro. Beverly Livingston. Urbana: University of Illinois Press, 1983.

Studies of Flora Tristan

Abensour, Léon. *Le Feminisme sour le règne de Louis-Philippe et en 1848*. Paris: Plon, 1913.
Baelen, Jean. "Une Romantique oubliée." *Bulletin Guillaume Budé* 29 (1970): 504–601.
———. *La Vie de Flora Tristan: Socialisme et féminisme au XIXe siècle*. Paris: Seuil, 1972.
Benhamou, Paul. "Flora Tristan, pionnière du socialisme et du féminisme." *Selecta* 7 (1986): 53–59.
Blanc, Eléonore. *Biographie de Flora Tristan*. Lyons: Privately printed, 1845.
Brion, Hélène. *La Voie féministe: Une Méconnue, Flora Tristan*. Epône: Société de l'édition de l'avenir social, 1919.

Bullrich, Silvina. *Flora Tristan la visionaria.* Buenos Aires: Riesa Ediciones, 1982.

Desanti, Dominique. *Flora Tristan: Oeuvres et vie mêlées.* Paris: Union Générale d'Editions, 1973.

―――. *A Woman in Revolt: A Biography of Flora Tristan.* Trans. Elizabeth Zelvin. New York: Crown, 1976. Trans. of *Flora Tristan: La Femme révoltée.* Paris: Hachette, 1972.

Djikstra, Sandra K. "The City as Catalyst for Flora Tristan's Vision of Social Change." In *Women Writers and the City: Essays in Feminist Literary Criticism.* Ed. Susan Merrill Squier. Knoxville: University of Tennessee Press, 1984.

―――. *Flora Tristan: Pioneer Feminist and Socialist.* Berkeley, Calif.: Center for Socialist History, 1984.

Garland-Jackson, Mary. "La Formulación de la *Mujer-Mesis* en *Méphis, ou le prolétaire de Flora Tristan.*" *Discurso Literario* 4 (1987): 601–11.

Gattey, Charles Neilson. *Gauguin's Astonishing Grandmother: A Biography of Flora Tristan.* London: Femina, 1970.

Goldsmith, Margaret L. *Seven Women Against the World.* London: Methuen, 1935.

Janin, Jules. "Madame Flora Tristan." *La Sylphide* 1, 2nd ser. (January 1845): 3–8ff.

LeJeune, Paule. *Flora Tristan: Réalisations, oeuvres.* Paris: Collection "Le Peuple Prend la Parole," 1975.

Leprohon, Pierre. *Flora Tristan.* Paris: Editions Corymbe, 1979.

Levitta-Baldi, Margareth. "Education et société dans l'oeuvre de Flora Tristan." *Studii del' Instituto Linguistico* 6 (1983): 223–43.

Livingston, Beverly. "George Sand and Flora Tristan." *Topic* 35 (1981): 38–44.

Michaud, Stéphane. *Flora Tristan (1803–1844).* Paris: Editions Ouvrières, 1984.

―――, ed. *Un Fabuleux Destin: Flora Tristan.* Proceedings of the First International Colloquium on Flora Tristan, May 3–4, 1984. Dijon: Editions Universitaires de Dijon, 1985.

Moon, S. Joan. "Feminism and Socialism: The Utopian Synthesis of Flora Tristan." In *Socialist Women: European Socialist Feminism in the Nineteenth and Early Twentieth Centuries.* Ed. Marilyn J. Boxer and Jean H. Quataert. New York: Elsevier, 1978. 19–50.

Portal, Magda. *Flora Tristan, precursora.* Lima: Editorial La Equidad, 1983.

Puech, Jules L. *Flora Tristan et le Saint-Simonisme.* Paris: Marcel Rivière, 1925.

―――. *La Vie et l'oeuvre de Flora Tristan.* Paris: Marcel Rivière. 1925.

Rabine, Leslie. "Feminist Writers in French Romanticism." *Studies in Romanticism* 16 (1977): 491–507.

―――. "The Other Side of the Ideal: Women Writers of Mid-Nineteenth-Century France (George Sand, Daniel Stern, Hortense Allart, Flora Tristan). Diss., Stanford University, 1973.

Randow, Bettina von. "Melancholie und Sozialismus: Flora Tristan." *Die Französiche Autorin vom Mittelalter bis zur Gegenwart.* Ed. Renate Baader and Dietmar Fricke. Wiesbaden: Akademische Verlagsgesellschaft Athenion, 1979.

Sanchez, Luis Alberto. *Una Mujer sola contra el mundo.* Lima: Juan Mejia Baca and P. O. Villanueva, 1957.

Scheler, Lucien. *Morceaux choisis précédés de la geste romantique de Flora Tristan.* Paris: La Bibliothèque Française, 1947.

Stourm, Eugène. "Madame Flora Tristan." *L'Union* (December 1844): 4.

Strumingher, Laura S. "The Legacy of Flora Tristan." *International Journal of Women's Studies* 7 (1984): 232–47.

———. *The Odyssey of Flora Tristan.* New York: Peter Lang, 1988.

Thibert, Marguérite. "Féministe et socialisme d'après Flora Tristan." *Revue d'histoire économique et sociale* 9 (1921): 115–36.

Tisoc Lindley, Hilda. *La Agonia de Flora Tristan y el movimiento feminista.* Lima: N.p., 1971.

THE TROBAIRITZ
(c. 1170–1260)

Anne Callahan

BIOGRAPHY

The trobairitz were women poets who lived in the South of France during the twelfth and thirteenth centuries. The term "trobairitz" in medieval Occitan (sometimes referred to as Provençal) combines the root of *trobar* (to compose) with the suffix *airitz*, which refers to a female agent in contrast to the masculine *ador*. The term has not been used frequently in English since many scholars have chosen to refer to these poets as "the women troubadours." However, "trobairitz" is now being adopted by feminist scholars interested in recovering a tradition of women writers with its own language. The number of trobairitz whose names are known is small (approximately twenty), and there are slight variations in the attribution of individual poems by medieval scholars (see Bogin, Paden). There are also several anonymous poems attributed to women. There is every reason to believe that there were more trobairitz than those whose work has been recovered to date, and it is also likely that the extant work of the known trobairitz represents only a portion of their actual writings. One thing seems certain, however: despite the rapid spread of troubadour poetry to all neighboring areas, as far north as London and as far south as Sicily, only Occitania, where the courtly lyric originated, produced women poets.

Scholars have advanced several possible historical factors to account for the existence of women poets in Occitania, including inheritance laws, which were favorable to women in the South of France for a period known as "the golden interlude" (c. 1180–1230), the absence of men from their fiefdoms during the Crusades, the education and high degree of literacy of women of nobility, and the relatively privileged position of women of aristocratic birth (all of the trobairitz were aristocrats, three of them countesses) in the South of France. This latter factor, the privileged status of the aristocratic woman in Occitania, was due in part to the sexual power given to women by the twelfth-century philosophy of love, *fin'amors* (the Provençal precursor of "courtly love.") *Fin'amors* was a highly ritualistic code of love that elevated women to sexual equality with men in romantic relationships between the sexes; its codes and practices centered on female sexuality. As *fin'amors* moved to the North the rituals, which were highly erotic in Occitania, became more and more symbolic; it evolved into that philosophy of love which has been known as courtly love since Gaston Paris created that term in 1883. The end of trobairitz activity corresponds to the move from the erotic to the ethereal and the resulting idealization of women in courtly love lyrics.

The best source of the scant information available on the lives of the trobairitz is the *vidas*, brief biographies that precede the poems in manuscripts, and *razos*, prose commentaries on the poems that were presented to the audience by *jongleurs* (performers, minstrels) to introduce the song. Only four of the trobairitz can be named with certainty: the Countess of Die, Castelloza, Azalais de Porcairagues, and Clara d'Anduza (Zufferey). (Following the "Major Themes" section of this chapter is a section of biographical notes on all of the trobairitz named in the scholarship, including those whose identity as actual historical women has not been clearly established.)

The poetic forms used by the trobairitz can be divided into two general categories: love poetry in a single voice and poetic dialogues. Verses in a single voice are called either *canso*, a love poem or song, or *sirventes*, a moralizing poem, political, personal, or didactic in tone, dealing with subjects other than love; the most common form of poetic dialogue was the *tenso*, a dialogue or debate poem in which two speakers express their points of view on one subject in alternating strophes of identical rhyme-schemes. The translations of the trobairitz lyrics in this chapter are from Meg Bogin's *The Women Troubadours*.

MAJOR THEMES

Love, desire, female sexuality, and the arbitrary power given to women by the codes of *fin'amors* are strong thematic lines traversing the trobairitz texts. The points at which these lines converge mark early moments in the history of what contemporary French feminists call *écriture feminine* (feminine writing), where women as writing subjects represent themselves and question, by the act of writing itself, the representations of female desire that have traditionally been the products of the male imagination. The trobairitz style is direct. The poems read like letters, journals, or diaries of lived experience: Alais says that "making babies doesn't seem so good, and it's too anguishing to be a wife"; Carenza answers that she would "like to have a husband," but that "making babies is a huge penitence: your breasts hang way down." The most fascinating aspect of trobairitz writing is the different perspective it brings to our understanding of the art of courtly love, which until the appearance of Meg Bogin's book in 1976 was always considered from the point of view of the troubadours.

The history of romantic love can be traced to twelfth-century Occitania, where male poets, the troubadours, created a philosophy of love, *fin'amors*, which gave women sexual power over men. However, as described by the trobairitz, this power was artificial and arbitrary; its rituals lifted a woman to the position of absolute sovereign when in reality she was the slave to a master who sometimes agreed to play the chivalric game, to reverse the roles. The lady was always socially superior to the knight; this social superiority was exchanged against a "natural" sexual inferiority. Equality was symbolically established through this exchange. The *tenson* between Marie de Ventadorn and Gui d'Ussel clearly indicates that for Marie, while the man has everything to gain by insisting on equality in love, for the woman this equality is a regression. Also, the reasons for the elevation, empowerment, and equality of women in *fin'amors* undermine the benefits an individual woman might derive from the new code of love. In *fin'amors*, the woman is represented as sovereign only so that she might become an object worthy of a man's love and a worthy subject for his songs, in other words, a means to a higher good. This representation is complicated by the fact that by virtue of her sex the woman was considered inferior to the socially inferior lover. In order to give her the value as a person that her rank would give her were she a man, the rituals of *fin'amors* transform her symbolically into a man. She is called *midon* (my lord), and the love test (the *asag*) is modeled on a ritual that was enacted between male *compagnons* (companions) according to the codes of *amitié virile* (male friendship). In other words, in order to be celebrated in heterosexual love lyrics, the woman had to be conceived of in the male imagination as the equal of his male lord or companion.

It is important to keep this ambiguity in mind when trying to understand the anguish and confusion expressed in the trobairitz lyrics (Furber and Callahan, Nelli). The verses of Castelloza, for example, are representative of the consistent complaint that although in theory *fin'amors* celebrates female sexuality and grants women a power they have not previously enjoyed, their sexual relationships were far from satisfying, and their power arbitrary and fleeting: "Handsome friend, as a lover true I loved you for you pleased me, but now I see I was a fool, for I've barely seen you since." Garsenda states the case of the real woman who has been turned into an idol in explicit terms: "You're so well-suited as a lover, I wish you wouldn't be so hesitant; . . . For a lady doesn't dare uncover her true will, lest those around her think her base." That the truth of the lady's will is sexual desire is revealed by Tibors: "I can tell you truly that I've never been without desire since it pleased you that I have you as my courtly lover"; and Domna H. complains quite frankly about lovers who take the *asag* (love test, which involves the lovers sleeping chastely side by side partially dressed with a sword between them) too seriously. She poses the situation of a lady who has asked each of two lovers to swear that he would do no more than hug or kiss her. One immediately breaks his oath; the other doesn't dare. The lady prefers the lover who is so blinded by passion "that he can't hear or see or know if he does wrong or right."

Another point of view is expressed by the Countess of Die: "Now I see I've been betrayed because I wouldn't sleep with him; night and day my mind won't rest to think of the mistake I made." It seems that the erotic pleasure (the term used in the lyrics is "joy") celebrated by *fin'amors* comes into direct conflict with rituals such as the *asag*; the woman is consequently confused and frustrated.

Fin'amors is not only a celebration of the joy of love, however; it also celebrates the joy of singing (in the poetry the term used is *trobar)*, that is, it revels in the pleasure of creating poetry. And although the poetic content of *fin'amors* is not wholly suitable to women poets, they want to share in the pleasure of writing. They want to participate in the pleasure that writing about their own desire can bring, but they do not want writing to be the only pleasure available to them; they also want to love and be loved as flesh and blood women who desire real relationships with men, both as sex partners and valued friends. Their common desire to be acknowledged as individuals, to enjoy real, not merely symbolic equality with men is articulated in Guillelma's *tenson* with Lanfrancs Cigala. And although some trobairitz demand the ritualistic authority and power over the lover that is accorded to the woman in the rules of *fin'amors* (Marie de Ventadorn and the Countess of Die), this is not the dominant attitude. For the most part they refuse the role of imperious mistress who commands a humble slave with the artificial and arbitrary power bestowed on women by the codes of courtly love. For them, the capacity to love and to suffer, roles traditionally assigned to the male in courtly lyrics, is tied not to one's sex but to one's position as lover and singer: "God knows I should have had my fill of song—the more I sing the worse I fare in love" (Castelloza).

Thus, the gender assignments of the roles of sovereign and subject are exchanged when the woman becomes the lover through her song: "I'd gladly stay forever in your service" (Azalais). Evidence that the trobairitz were aware of the importance of writing in the appropriation of subjectivity and in controlling the representation of women in these early texts of love and desire is found in the strong poem by Lombarda called "I'm Glad I Wasn't Called Bernarda for Bernart." In this poem Lombarda rejoices in the fact that she did not take the name of her husband, but has her own name and identity. If she were represented merely as the feminine version of a man's name, his reflection in a mirror, so to speak, she herself would have no image when she looked in the mirror. The poem recognizes the power of representation and celebrates women's right to represent themselves: "For the mirror with no image so disrupts my rhyme that it almost interrupts it; but then when I remember what my name records, all my thoughts unite in one accord."

NAMES OF TROBAIRITZ AND SUMMARY OF AVAILABLE BIOGRAPHICAL INFORMATION

Alais: No available biographical information. She composed with Iselda, her sister, and Carenza. *Known works:* One poem: "Na Carenza al bel cors avinen" (Lady Carenza, with the lovely, gracious body).

Alamanda: She lived in the second half of the twelfth century and was perhaps Gascon. She wrote a poetic dialogue with Giraut de Borhelh, one of the most celebrated troubadours of the period. *Known works:* One *tenson* with Giraut de Borhelh: "S'ie.us quier conseill, bel'almig'Alamanda" (If I seek your advice, pretty friend Alamanda).

Almucs de Castelnou: She lived in the first half of the thirteenth century, the wife of Guigue de Châteauneuf-de-Randon (arrondissement of Mende, Lozère). *Known works:* One poem answering Iseut de Capio: "Domna n'Iseutz, s'ieu saubes" (Lady Iseut, if he showed some contrition).

Azalais d'Altier: She is addressed in a song by Uc de Saint-Circ. Altier is in the canton of Villefort, an arrondissement of Mende (Lozère), about forty-seven kilometers from Anduze (Gard). *Known works:* None.

Azalais de Porcairagues: She was born around 1140 and was from the city of Portiragnes, not far from Béziers in the Montpellier region. She is associated romantically with both Gui Guerrejat, son of Guillaume VI of Montpellier, and Rimbaut d'Orange, a celebrated troubadour. *Known works:* One *canso:* "Ar em al freg temps vengut" (Now we are come to the cold time).

Beatritz de Romans: The only information we have on Beatritz is that she was from Romans, northeast of Montélimar, and lived probably in the first half of the thirteenth century. *Known works:* One *canso:* "Na Maria, pretz e fina valors" (Lady Maria, in you merit and distinction).

Carenza: No available biographical information. She composed with Alais and Iselda. *Known works:* One poem answering Alais and Iselda: "N'Alais e n'Iselda, ensanhamen" (Lady Alais and Lady Iselda).

Castelloza: She was born around 1200 and was from the region of Puy in the Auvergne. She was probably the wife of a noble who fought in the Fourth Crusade. *Known works:* Three *cansos:* "Amics, s'ie.us trobes avinen" (Friend, if you had shown consideration), "Ja de chantar non degr'aver talen" (God knows I should have had my fill of song), and "Mout avetz faich long estatge" (You stayed a long time, friend).

Clara d'Anduza: She was born in the first half of the thirteenth century and was from Anduze, one of the most important cities of Languedoc. She was most likely the wife or the daughter of Bernard d'Anduze, lord of the city. *Known works:* One *canso:* "En greu esmay et en greu pessamen" (The *lauzengiers* [spy, gossip, enemy] and the deceitful spies).

Countess of Die: The theory has been ventured that she was one of the twin daughters of Marguerite de Bourgogne (d. 1163) and Guigues IV, dauphin of Viennois and the Count of Albon, who died in battle in 1142. She married Guillem de Poitiers, Count of Valentinois. The conjecture is that her son was the Count of Die (north of Montélimar) and that she took the title of Countess of Die after his death. The *vidas* indicate that her lover was Rimbaut d'Orange (1146–1173), the brother of the trobairitz Tibors. *Known works:* Four *cansos:* "Ab joi et ab joven m'apais" (I thrive on youth and joy), "A chantar m'er de so qu'ieu non volria" (Of things I'd rather keep in silence I must sing), "Estat ai en greu cossirier'' (I've lately been in great distress), and ''Fin ioi me don'alegranssa'' (Fine joy brings me great happiness).

Garsenda (Countess of Proensa): She was born around 1170 and belonged by both birth and marriage to two of the most powerful families of Provence. Her husband, Alphonse II, was lord of Provence and the brother of the King of Aragon. After his death she governed Provence; she entered a religious order in 1225. *Known works:* One *tenson:* ''Vos que.m semblatz dels corals amadors'' (You're so well-suited as a lover).

Gaudairenca: She is thought to have been the wife of Raimon de Miraval, whose period of activity was 1191–1229. According to a *razo*, she ''knows very well how to compose songs and dances.'' *Known works:* None.

Gormonda de Monpeslier: Her work is dated 1228 or 1229. She was from Montpellier. *Known works:* One *sirventes:* ''Greu m'es a durar'' (It is so difficult to endure).

Guillelma de Rosers: She lived during the first half of the thirteenth century and was undoubtedly from Rougiers, near Monaco. She composed a poetic dialogue with Lanfrancs Cigala, a troubadour from Genoa. *Known works:* One *tenson* with Lanfrancs Cigala: ''Na Guillelma, man cavalier arratge'' (Dame Guillelma, several knights traveling by dark).

H. (Domna): Nothing is known of the trobairitz called Domna H. Her work has been dated between 1220 and 1240. *Known works:* One poem with Rosin: ''Rosin, digatz m'ades de cors'' (Rosin, tell me from the heart).

Isabella: She was born around 1180 and was perhaps the daughter of a noble of one of the Christian empires of the East. She composed a poetic dialogue with Elias Cairel, a troubadour from Périgord. *Known works:* One *tenson* with Elias Cairel: ''N'Elias Cairel, de l'amor'' (Elias Cairel, I want to know).

Iselda: No available biographical information. She composed with Alais and Carenza. *Known works: See* Alais.

Iseut de Capio: She composed with Almucs de Castelnou (first half of thirteenth century) and probably lived in the same vicinity of Mende (Lozère). *Known works:* One poem with Almucs de Castelnou: ''Domna n'Almucs, si.us plages'' (Lady Almucs, with your permission).

Lombarda: She was born around 1190 and was most likely from Toulouse. She composed a poetic dialogue with Bernard Arnaut, Count of Armagnac. *Known works: Tenson* with Bernard Arnaut: ''No.m volgr'aver per Bernard na Bernards'' (I'm glad I wasn't called Bernarda for Bernart).

Maria de Ventadorn: She was born around 1165 in Limousina, the daughter of a viscount and wife of Ebles V of Ventadour, lord of a neighboring viscounty. *Known works:* One *tenson* with Gui d'Ussel: ''Gui d'Ussel, be.m pesa de vos'' (Gui d'Ussel, because of you I'm quite distraught).

Tibors: She was born around 1130, the sister of the troubadour Rimbaut d'Orange and daughter of Guilhem d'Omelas and Tibors d'Orange, whose château was called Sarenom, known today as Sérignan, near Grasse in the Alpes-Maritimes. Her first marriage was to Gaufroy de Mornas, her second to Bertrand des Baux, a great patron of the troubadours. Her second husband was assassinated on the order of Raimon V of Toulouse in 1181, and Tibors died in 1182. They had three sons. *Known works:* One *canso*: "Bels dous amics, ben vos posc en ver dir" (Sweet handsome friend, I can tell you truly).

SURVEY OF CRITICISM

There are only two complete extant editions of the poems of the trobairitz. The first is Oskar Schultz-Gora, *Die provenzalischen Dichterinnen*. The other is Jules Véran, *Les Poétesses provençales du moyen âge*, which draws almost entirely from Schultz-Gora. Information on the lives of the trobairitz comes mainly from the *vidas*, the brief biographies that precede the poems in manuscripts. The earliest collections of poems with *vidas* date from the middle to the late thirteenth century. Few translations of the *vidas* are available to the modern reader. The first critical edition of the *vidas* (Boutière and Schutz) provided French translations, and a few other French and Spanish versions appear in anthologies (see Riquer, *Los trovadores*). There was only one English translation (Ida Farnell, 1896) before Margarita Egan's modern version of 1984.

Meg Bogin's *The Women Troubadours* (1976) is the first full-length study of the trobairitz and includes the first edition of their works in English translation. Bogin provides a historical background and a cursory introduction to the form and themes of the poetry; the chief value of Bogin's book lies in the translations of the poems and in her sketchy but provocative discussion of the ambiguous role of women in the philosophy of *fin'amors*. In a 1978 article in *Signs* Marianne Shapiro explores the issues raised by Bogin in her discussion of *fin'amors* and raises several others in her rigorous feminist reading, which focuses on strategies for finding a voice in courtly love poetry revealed in the trobairitz lyrics. She elaborates a theory of the essential paradox of the trobairitz poet as a desiring subject who would be, in potentia, a desired object.

The most extensive, serious scholarly criticism to date can be found in the 1989 collection of essays, *The Voice of the Trobairitz*, edited by William D. Paden, who has also contributed an invaluable general introduction. The volume includes essays by twelve American and European scholars who view the trobairitz in perspectives ranging from philological to Bakhtinian, Derridean to feminist. Of special interest for students of women's writing are the articles by Joan Ferrante, who argues, albeit tentatively, that there is a female rhetoric in the poetry of the trobairitz, and Tilde Sankovitch, who reads Lombarda's poetry in the perspective of feminist psychoanalysis.

BIBLIOGRAPHY

Collections of Works by the Trobairitz

Schultz-Gora, Oscar. *Die provenzalischen Dichterinnen. Biographien und Texte nebst Anmerkungen und einer Einleitung*. Leipzig: Fock, 1888. Rpt. Geneva: Slatkine, 1975.

Véran, Jules, ed. *Les Poétesses provençales du moyen âge et de nos jours*. Paris: A. Quillet, 1946.

Translations of Works by the Trobairitz

Bogin, Meg. *The Women Troubadours*. New York: Paddington Press, 1976. French translation by Jeanne Faure-Cousin with the collaboration of Anne Richou. *Les Femmes troubadours*. Paris: Denoel/Gonthier, 1978.

Perkal-Balinsky, Deborah. *The Minor Trobairitz: An Edition with Translation and Commentary*. Diss., Northwestern University, 1986.

Riquer, Martin de. *Los trovadores: Historia literaria y textos*. 3 vols. Barcelona: Planeta, 1975.

Stanton, Domna C., ed. *The Defiant Muse: French Feminist Poems from the Middle Ages to the Present*. New York: Feminist Press, 1986.

Critical Studies of the Trobairitz

Boutière, Jean, and A. H. Schutz. *Biographies des troubadours*. 1st ed. Toulouse:, E. Privat, 1950; 2nd ed. Paris: Nizet, 1964. Rpt. New York: B. Franklin, 1972 (based on 1950 ed.)

Bruckner, Matilda Tomaryn. "Na Castelloza, Trobairitz, and the Troubadour Lyric." *Romance Notes* 25 (1985): 239–53.

Dronke, Peter. "The Provençal Trobairitz: Castelloza." In *Medieval Women Writers*. Ed. Katharina M. Wilson. Athens: University of Georgia Press, 1984. 131–52.

Egan, Margarita. *The Vidas of the Troubadours*. New York and London: Garland, 1984.

Farnell, Ida. *The Lives of the Troubadours: Translated from the Mediaeval Provencal, with Introductory Matter and Notes, and with Specimens of Their Poetry Rendered into English*. London, 1896.

Furber, Donald, and Anne Callahan. *Erotic Love in Literature from Medieval Legend to Romantic Illusion*. Troy, N.Y.: Whitston, 1982.

Giraudon, Liliane, and Jacques Roubaud, eds. *Les Trobairitz: Les Femmes dans la lyrique occitane*. *Action poétique* 75 (1978).

Jeanroy, Alfred. *Jongleurs et troubadours gascons des XIIe et XIIIe siècles*. Paris: H. Champion, 1923.

Nelli, René. *L'Erotique des troubadours*. Toulouse: Edouard Privat, 1963. Rpt. 2 vols. Paris: Union Générale d'Editions, 1974.

Paden, William D., ed. *The Voice of the Trobairitz: Perspectives on the Women Troubadours*. Philadelphia: University of Pennsylvania Press, 1989.

Robbins, Kittye Delle. "Woman/Poet: Problem and Promise in Studying the 'Trobairitz' and Their Friends." *Economia* 1, no. 3 (1977): 12–14.

Sarde, Michèle. *Regards sur les françaises*. Paris: Stock, 1983.

Shapiro, Marianne. "The Provençal Trobairitz and the Limits of Courtly Love." *Signs* 3 (1978): 560–71.

Zufferey, François. "Toward a Delineation of the Trobairitz Corpus." In *The Voice of the Trobairitz*. Ed. William D. Paden. Philadelphia: University of Pennsylvania Press, 1989.

MARIE-CATHERINE DESJARDINS DE VILLEDIEU (1640?–1683)

Katharine Ann Jensen

BIOGRAPHY

Marie-Catherine Desjardins was the daughter of bourgeois parents; her mother worked as a ladies' maid for the prominent and noble Rohan family, and her father was in charge of timber revenue for the Perseigne forest in Normandy. The exact date and place of Desjardins's birth is not verifiable, but she probably spent her childhood in Normandy. At the age of fifteen, she fell in love with a cousin and intended to marry him. For reasons that are unclear, her father was incensed by the proposed marriage and issued a writ against the fiancé, accusing his own daughter of "criminal disobedience." This excessive behavior prompted Desjardins's mother to file for a separation from the father. The separation was obtained, and the mother moved to Paris with Desjardins and an older daughter.

In Paris, although a minor, Desjardins lived on her own and received guests, which was, of course, exceptional behavior for a woman and not apt to earn her a reputation for flawless feminity. Yet, offsetting this questionable independence, Desjardins was received within the circle of women her mother served. If she was received as less than an equal, she was definitely more than a servant. The noblewomen admired Desjardins for her wit and spirit, and within this encouraging milieu she began composing and reciting poetry. Her poems began appearing in published collections as of 1659.

At the time she began composing poetry, around 1658, she met a nobleman and lieutenant of a prestigious regiment, Antoine de Villedieu. Their meeting apparently kindled the "grand passion" for both of them, and they lived together openly; they signed a marriage contract in 1660 but did not exchange vows. Their marriage became a bone of some contention, for Villedieu tired of Desjardins and carried on sexual conquests elsewhere. While she maintained publicly that they were married, he denied it. He eventually had her sign a declaration denying that they had ever entered into a marriage contract. This forced re-nunciation was not, however, the end of the story. In 1664, several years after they had separated, Desjardins learned that Villedieu's regiment was about to be sent on a dangerous expedition. Fearing for her former lover's life, she hurried to join the regiment before it left France. She persuaded Villedieu to exchange vows with her, which they did, but again the result was only an official promise to marry pending completion of all the legal and religious formalities. When he returned from his expedition, Villedieu was not inclined to follow through on these marital formalities, and in 1667, after officially declaring himself unfaith-ful, he once more had Desjardins sign a document annulling any promises of marriage between them. He then married a young widow more financially at-tractive than Desjardins, who, for her part, continued to call herself and to sign her works "Madame de Villedieu," something she had done since her first promised marriage. Villedieu was killed in battle shortly after his new marriage, and when his widow remarried, Desjardins obtained permission from his family to continue to call herself by his name.

If meeting Villedieu launched Desjardins into a tumultuous and all-too-familiar story of passion and female sexual dispossession, his advent in her life did not, on the other hand, vitiate her textual productivity. Because she lived by her pen, she was obliged to write and publish prolifically. Her first prose publication appeared in 1660 and was a retelling in narrative form of Molière's play *Les Précieuses ridicules*, called *Récit de la Farce des Prècieuses* (Story of the Farce of *the Précieuses*). Desjardins had composed the *Récit* for a friend who had been unable to see Molière's play and wanted an account of it. The *Récit* circulated widely in manuscript form, and an unfaithful copy of it was published, along with one of Desjardins's celebrated sonnets, without her consent. To regain textual control, Desjardins brought the original version of the *Récit* to a publisher of her choosing, Claude Barbin, who specialized in social literature, or *mondain* genres.

Eager to make a profit from this newly popular writer, Barbin offered to publish a novel Desjardins had started, *Alcidamie*. The first two volumes appeared in 1661, but the remaining volumes were never written, possibly because *Al-cidamie* was a *roman à clé*, purportedly about the Rohan family and Marguerite de Rohan's attempt to do in her brother in order to be sole family heiress. Marguerite de Rohan put pressure on Desjardins not to publish the novel at all; by leaving the work unfinished, Desjardins may have been conceding to this pressure.

In the following four years, until 1665, in addition to publishing collections of her poetry, Desjardins turned her talents to the theater—a unique choice for a woman writer of the day—writing both tragedies and tragicomedies. Her plays were presented with varying success; her last play, *Le Favory* (The Favorite), was presented by Molière and his troupe for Louis XIV. After this performance, Hugues de Lionne, one of Desjardins's supporters and one of the king's ministers, requested a royal pension for the writer. The pension was promised, but the promise was not kept until eleven years later, and then, due to budgetary constraints, Desjardins was awarded only half of the original sum. In the meantime, she abandoned the dramatic genre to return to the novel in its developing shorter form, which would be where her greatest success lay.

In 1667, while in the Netherlands after her definitive break with Villedieu, Desjardins's novel *Carmente* was published, dedicated to her protectress, the Duchess of Nemours. At this same time, Desjardins learned that Villedieu had sold her private love letters to Barbin (Villedieu needed money for a military campaign). She wrote to her publisher to stop the unauthorized exposure of her private life to the public eye, but to no avail. *Lettres et billets galants* (Galant Letters and Notes) was published in 1668. In the Netherlands, Desjardins was enthusiastically received within aristocratic circles with the exception of the Belgian women, who ostracized her, a woman so deviant from the feminine norm as to be openly a writer *qua* adventuress. Desjardins wrote a short story, *Anaxandre*, dedicated to the women of Brussels in a gesture of self-demystification and -disculpation. The heroine of the story, like Desjardins, is a poet, but far from being the product of self-conscious ambition, her poetry is born of her enduring, virtuous, and faithful love for Clidamis, a military officer, who (unlike Villedieu) reciprocates her passion. Through this fictionalized autobiography and romantic plot, Desjardins sought to present her case to her female judges as one with which they could identify and therefore accept. During her stay abroad, she also wrote many letters to friends, and Barbin quickly published these—again contrary to the author's wishes—as *Recueil de quelques lettres et relations galantes* (Collection of Some Galant Letters and Relations, 1668).

Upon her return to Paris, Desjardins, now officially Villedieu, entered a difficult financial period, although she was otherwise supported by people well connected in social, literary, and political circles. Under financial pressure, Desjardins de Villedieu was susceptible to Barbin's exploitative solicitations, and as she was one of the most popular writers of the day, he was determined to maintain her popularity by ensuring that she wrote according to current vogues and by publishing her works at a constant rhythm. In three years, 1669–1672, Desjardins de Villedieu wrote and published six novels, a collection of poetry, and a collection of fables; this amounted to approximately one-third of her entire oeuvre. After these taxing years, Desjardins de Villedieu withdrew to a convent for some time but eventually returned to Paris, still writing and publishing. She published her last novel, *Les Désordres de l'amour* (The Disorders of Love) in 1675; it was the following year that she obtained her royal pension.

Subsequent to this award, at the age of thirty-seven, Desjardins de Villedieu married a nobleman, Claude-Nicolas de Chaste. A year later, she had a son. Chaste died unexpectedly in 1679, and Desjardins de Villedieu, with her son, went to live with her mother and sister in the provinces. It seems that she adopted a pious, religious life, though she must have continued to write, or at least had written after her marriage; for when she died in 1683, Barbin discovered two finished manuscripts of novels, which he published several years later. Various editions of her complete works were published in 1696.

MAJOR THEMES

The material necessity that underlay Desjardins de Villedieu's literary production determined to a great extent not only its quantity but also its thematic content. Barbin, as earlier mentioned, was interested in Desjardins de Villedieu's adaptability to the mercurial social literature of the day. Indeed, her sole literary apprenticeship was carried out in the salons; she was not, that is, "taught" to write, nor is it likely that, as a bourgeoise, she received more than a rudimentary education to start with. Consequently, much of her poetry, as well as some of her prose, were composed as "circumstantial pieces," written for a particular person or occasion, usually in an effort to amuse or flatter. Given the aristocratic world's fascination with seeing itself as art, such circumstantial literature had continual publishing appeal. Conversely, while much of her poetry has been seen to be imitative, she gained early recognition—and condemnation—for her innovative sonnet "Jouissance." Written in 1658 and published a year later, the sonnet is a celebration of the sexual pleasure the female poet persona enjoys with "Tircis." Desjardins shocked many with this poem, first for violating genre—only men wrote sonnets—and then for presenting, as a woman, such clearly sexual material. Yet the genre to which Desjardins de Villedieu brought most innovations as a woman, although not in the form of sexually explicit subject matter, was the novel, specifically, the developing genre of the historical novel.

She began and subsequently punctuated her career as a novelist by adhering to the heroic mode; five of her novels are cast within this mold, made popular in the early seventeenth century by Honoré d'Urfé's *L'Astrée* and carried on by Marin Le Roy de Gomberville and Madeleine de *Scudéry among others. Desjardins de Villedieu's *Alcidamie* (1661), *Carmente* (1667), *Les Exilés de la Cour d'Auguste* (*The Exiles of the Court of Augustus Caesar*) (1672–1673), *Les Galanteries grenadines* (The Grenadine Galantries, 1673), and *Les Annales galantes de Grèce* (The Galant Annals of Greece [posthumous], 1687) all take place in remote historical times or pastoral settings. These vague and therefore utopic times and places form, according to convention, the context for the representation of an ideal love. Tested by a series of cataclysmic adventures such as shipwrecks, kidnappings, and wars, Desjardins de Villedieu's heroes and heroines, usually of the nobility, prove themselves to be gloriously good and true both to their beloved and to the crown, for virtue and honor are predicated on allegiance to the sovereign. Commensurate with such allegiance, virtuous and faithful love unites, in the end, the heroes and heroines who had been torn apart by external forces. In the heroic tradition, love is based on an idealization of woman such that heroines often seem virtual abstractions of purity and power in contrast to the suffering and supplicating heroes. Yet here Desjardins de Villedieu deviates from tradition by humanizing her heroines. The eponymous heroines Carmente and Cléonice, for example, are shown to be constrained by laws of state, which they as princesses must serve. Although they capitulate to these laws by giving up a love that (provisionally) contradicts their duty, their amorous sacrifice is poignant rather than "heroically" or narcissistically self-glorifying (Cuénin, 407–10).

While Desjardins de Villedieu marks her heroic novels with a new inflection of feminine love, she virtually rewrites history in her historical novels by focusing on the primacy of passion in human actions. This rewriting of history, while radical in its emphasis on the dialectic between personal psychology and public event (see Beasley, Stanton), was prepared for in part by mid-seventeenth-century views of history. Historians came to be seen as mere compilers of events. What was increasingly desired was the explanation of events in light of underlying motives. Whereas historical events were understood to be the military exploits and political feats of great men, the telling of this "true" history in relation to the motives underlying it was complicated by the concept of plausibility (*vraisemblance*). What was "plausible" was determined by contemporary mores, such that the motives behind past political events were to be written in terms of present-day ideologies. Thus the historical novel inhabited a space between the past and the present, between the (purely) "factual" and the (purely) "fictional."

In her first historical novel, *Le Journal amoureux* (*Love Journals*, 1669–1670), Desjardins de Villedieu uses the framework of sixteenth-century France to tell an explicitly fabricated story, or rather, stories, for the novel is divided into six parts. The separate sections illustrate a common, and anti-heroic, theme: love, understood as passion and fatality, not reason and choice, subjugates men and women and is the prime mover of both personal and political actions. The conception of love as irrational and ungovernable is not original to Desjardins de Villedieu but characterizes the second half of the century, also found, for example, in Racine, La Rochefoucauld, and *Lafayette. This conception of love, culled from contemporary ideology, constitutes, then, a portion of the plausibility with which Desjardins de Villedieu endows "history." Her originality lies precisely in linking love, the domain of the private, to politics, the domain of the public.

In her next novel, *Les Annales galantes* (The Galant Annals, 1670), Desjardins de Villedieu makes a bolder claim for her thematics of passion as public ruler by building her story around *recognizable* historical events and characters. She contrasts this project with her previous novel, whose story she fully fabricated, having borrowed from history only the names of characters and places. In locating her new narrative within a historically "real" context, thereby writing political, as opposed to "purely" fictional history, Desjardins de Villedieu asserts both the plausibility and the veracity of her interpretation of human motivations. That ambitions are born of sexual desire, power, and jealousy becomes a way to understand political history, not only a means to characterize human psychology.

Radical in its implications, Desjardins de Villedieu's version of political events completely undermines the nobility of "true" history wherein "great" men's actions were understood as separate from and superior to personal intrigue.

By the time she writes *Les Désordres de l'amour* (*The Disorders of Love*, 1675), Desjardins de Villedieu binds political history all the more tightly within the thematics of private passion. Closely following the authoritative writings of true historians, she tells the story of sixteenth-century France as one in which external matters of state are inextricably linked to internal plottings. The novel opens, for example, with the assertion that "love is the moving force of all the other passions of the soul." The author punctuates her narrative of historical events with such *exempla* or longer, poetic maxims that explicitly uncover love/passion as the seductive and destructive force behind and within political actions. The narrative each time expands the maxim.

While the emphasis added by the maxim posits the determinative interrelation of private and public domains, it is in this interrelation itself that Desjardins de Villedieu signals a feminine and "feminist" view of history. For when the public acts of powerful men have their source in amorous interests, then women take a place in political history. Thus, by rewriting "official" history in her novels, Desjardins de Villedieu weaves women into the fabric of public life and into the web of her readers' (un)consciousness. Moreover, as a necessary part of her thematics, she represents women "in love" as women who are also, often, politically ambitious: queens and princesses and mistresses who seduce in the quest for power. What these ambitious women "lose" in ideal femininity they gain in subject status, as active agents of their own, albeit nefarious, plots, not passive victims of men's conquests.

Yet the female sufferer does have a place in Desjardins de Villedieu's oeuvre, even a privileged one. Madame de Maugiron in the *Désordres*—the only entirely fictional character in the novel—represents this type of heroine as well as the theme of unreturned love. Although betrayed by her lover, Madame de Maugiron makes it her ambition to continue to love him passionately, faithfully, and masochistically until she herself dies, unable to sustain herself after his death. In the love letters Desjardins wrote to Villedieu over the course of six years and throughout his repeated infidelities, letters which he had published (*Lettres et billets galants*), she represents herself as just this sort of eternally faithful and emotionally dependent "heroine." While the first-person protagonist of *Les Mémoires de la vie d'Henriette Sylvie de Molière* (*The Memoires of the Life and Rare Adventures of Henrietta Sylvia Moliere*) finds a happy ending in marriage and reciprocated love, her narrative is that of a woman who remains sublimely faithful despite suffering the emotional betrayal of her beloved's misapprehensions of her. By portraying as central figures these women who love better than they are loved, Desjardins de Villedieu points, on the one hand, to a gendered discrepancy in amorous relations—an insistence that corresponds to a feminine/feminist perspective of history and fiction (see Miller). On the other hand, by placing positive value on these heroines' fidelity and single-minded commitment to what they perceive as true passion, Desjardins de Villedieu asserts a "heroinism" of the second sexed and underclassed, for Maugiron and Molière are, as Desjardins herself was, of dubious origin in contrast to their noble lovers. Still, the costs of such "sublimity," the price of loving better and beyond the privileged male/victimizer, might yet be measured by the female authorial voice at the end of Part II of the *Désordres*: "I do not doubt that at this point more than one reader will say . . . that I haven't always spoken of love [in this pessimistic way], but it's on that very basis I speak so ill of it; for having had such a perfect experience of love, I find myself authorized to paint it in such black colors."

SURVEY OF CRITICISM

Because they conformed and adapted to the changing tastes of an elite society of readers, Desjardins de Villedieu's writings were extremely popular in her lifetime and enjoyed numerous reprintings. Her historical novels, particularly the *Désordres*, received praise from contemporary literary critics. The reason the *Désordres* was praised, however, stems from the critical furor surrounding Lafayette's 1678 *La Princesse de Clèves*. Both Lafayette's and Desjardins de Villedieu's novels feature a woman's confession to her husband of her love for another man. Representative of Lafayette's detractors, Jean-Baptiste de Valincour in his 1678 *Lettres à Madame la Marquise de *** sur le sujet de La Princesse de Clèves* attacks the novel's heroine for implausible, that is, inappropriate, feminine behavior while favorably contrasting the conduct of Desjardins's confessional heroine.

The charge of implausibility levelled at the Princess of Clèves concerned, in general terms, her desire to gain a singular virtue, to be "better" than other women—a desire fulfilled by the novel's ending. In his 1685 *Nouvelles Lettres de l'auteur de la critique générale de l'histoire du calvinisme*, Pierre Bayle disapproves of the "pure" fictitiousness of Lafayette's extraordinary heroine (and hero), cast as they are within a real historical context. He later lauds, by contrast, Desjardins de Villedieu's *Annales galantes* and *Journal amoureux* for portraying heroines who are "no better" than ordinary women. Elsewhere, Bayle praises Desjardins de Villedieu at the expense of Scudéry, also on the grounds that the former author paints a more "faithful," therefore plausible, image of contemporary customs and mores than the latter.

Whereas Valincour and Bayle affirm Desjardins de Villedieu's expertise in the historical novel, at least in distinction to Lafayette, their contemporary, Jean de La Bruyère, indicts her works in this genre. In *Les Caractères* (1696), he cites the *Annales galantes* and the *Journal amoureux* in a general castigation of readers of such social literature, whom he finds lazy, stupid, and insipid ("De la ville," no. 13). The charge of frivolity, here levelled at readers, came to apply to Desjardins de Villedieu's works in general in the eighteenth century and, indeed, up to our own. The *Désordres* is the single work that received consistent critical attention beyond the seventeenth century. Yet, whatever attention literary history has bestowed on the *Désordres*, it has until the last decade been almost exclusively in relation to *La Princesse de Clèves* and the confession scenes. Not only does the comparison reduce the intricate *Désordres* to a single episode, it minimizes Desjardins de Villedieu in light of the canonical Lafayette.

In 1947, however, in *The Life and Works of Marie-Catherine Desjardins*, Bruce Morrissette took up the cause of what he nonetheless calls "this second- or third-rate writer" in the interest of placing her in literary history. He studies the scope of her textual production from the standpoint of its composition, style, and sources. Morrissette emphasizes the author's position as one of the most popular writers of the century as well as one of the most influential in the development of French fiction. Some thirty years after this study, Micheline Cuénin published her two-volume doctoral thesis, *Roman et société sous Louis XIV: Madame de Villedieu (Marie-Catherine Desjardins 1640–1683)* (1979). This exhaustive scholarly work has as its explicit aim, like Morrissette's pioneering enterprise, to put Desjardins de Villedieu back on the map of literary history. Through extensive and invaluable documentation, Cuénin contextualizes the author's life and work within the history and sociology of seventeenth-century France. She studies all the oeuvre in detail from perspectives of its production, reception, genre, style, and themes. Cuénin focuses especially on Desjardins de Villedieu's treatment of love in relation to the various contemporary ideologies of love.

The third full-length study to date, Arthur Flannigan's *Mme de Villedieu's "Les Désordres de l'Amour": History, Literature, and the Nouvelle Historique* (1982), analyzes the novel through a structuralist technique. Through close textual analysis, Flannigan studies the shifts in the novel from the historical event (*énoncé*) to its representation as literature (*énonciation*) in order to elucidate the development and specificity of the *nouvelle historique* as a genre. In a shorter piece, "Madame de Villedieu's *Les Désordres de l'Amour*: The Feminization of History," Flannigan contends that Desjardins de Villedieu's use of history for the illustration of universal truths traces "a specifically 'feminine' presence within the text" (95). For Flannigan, however, this feminine presence is metaphoric and not bound to the gender of the author.

Conversely, in "Tender Economies: Mme de Villedieu and the Costs of Indifference," also about the *Désordres*, Nancy K. Miller postulates the woman writer's presence within her text. Through her staging of the inequitable relation between men's "public" history and women's "private" history, Desjardins de Villedieu encodes her "self-consciousness about writing as a woman about the costs of love" (91).

Other recent articles that similarly argue for Desjardins de Villedieu's self-conscious textual inscription of her gender or for her radical revision of history as dialectic—too numerous to summarize here—are collected in a special volume of *Papers on French Seventeenth-Century Literature—Actes de Wakeforest—* devoted to the various works of this writer.

With the exception of Arthur Flannigan's paperback edition of the *Désordres*,

Desjardins de Villedieu's works remain difficult to obtain for either teaching or scholarly purposes. One hopes that the current concern to rewrite literary history and the increased critical attention to this long-obscured woman writer will put her works back on public and private shelves.

BIBLIOGRAPHY

Major Works by Mme de Villedieu

Alcidamie. 2 vols. Paris: Barbin, 1661.
Lisandre, Nouvelle par Mlle des Jardins. Paris: Barbin, 1663.
Recueil de poésies de Mlle des Jardins, augmenté de plusieurs pièces et lettres en cette dernière édition. Paris: Barbin, 1664.
Le Favory, Tragi-comédie par Mlle des Jardins. Paris: Billaine, 1665.
Anaxandre, Nouvelle par Mlle des Jardins. Paris: Barbin, 1667.
Carmente, Histoire grecque par Mlle des Jardins. 2 vols. Paris: Barbin, 1667.
Lettres et billets galants. Paris: Barbin, 1668. Rpt. Paris: Publications de la Société d'Etude du XVIIe Siècle, 1975.
Recueil de quelques lettres et relations galantes. Paris: Barbin, 1668.
Cléonice, ou le roman galant. Paris: Barbin, 1669.
Le Journal amoureux. 6 vols. Paris: Barbin, 1669–1670.
Annales galantes. Paris: Barbin, 1670.
Les Amours des grands hommes. 4 vols. Paris: Barbin, 1671.
Les Exilés. 6 vols. Paris: Barbin, 1672–1673.
Les Galanteries grenadines. 2 vols. Paris: Barbin, 1673.
Mémoires de la vie d'Henriette Sylvie de Molière. 6 vols. Paris: Barbin, 1674. Rpt. Tours: Publication du Groupe d'Etude du XVIIe Siècle, 1977.
Les Désordres de l'amour. Paris: Barbin, 1675. Rpt. Geneva: Droz, 1970. Rpt. Washington, D.C.: University Press of America, 1982.
Portrait des faiblesses humaines. Paris: Barbin, 1685.
Annales galantes de Grèce. 2 vols. Paris: Barbin, 1687.

English Translations of Mme de Villedieu

Love Journals. London: T. Ratcliff and M. Daniel, 1671.
The Loves of Sundry Philosophers and Other Great Men. Savoy: Herringman and Starkey, 1673.
The Memoires of the Life and Rare Adventures of Henrietta Sylvia Moliere. London: W. Crooke, 1677.
The Disorders of Love. London: James Magnes and Richard Bentley, 1677.

Selected Studies of Mme de Villedieu

Assaf, Francis. ''Mme de Villedieu et le picaresque au féminin: *Les Mémoires d'Henriette Sylvie de Molière*.'' *Biblio 17* 37 (1987): 361–78.
Beasley, Faith. ''Villedieu's Metamorphosis of Judicious History: *Les Désordres de l'Amour*.'' *Biblio 17* 37 (1987): 393–406.

Cuénin, Micheline. *Roman et société sous Louis XIV: Madame de Villedieu*. 2 vols. Paris: Champion, 1979.

Decker, Roxanne Lalande. *"Les Désordres de l'amour* ou le pouvoir au féminin." *Biblio 17* 37 (1987): 501–10.

Flannigan, Arthur. *Mme de Villedieu's "Les Désordres de l'Amour": History, Literature, and the Nouvelle Historique*. Washington, D.C.: University Press of America, 1982.

———. "Mme de Villedieu's *Les Désordres de l'Amour:* The Feminization of History." *L'Esprit créateur* 23 (1983): 94–106.

Gethner, Perry. "Love, Self-Love and the Court in *Le Favory.*" *Biblio 17* 37 (1987): 407–20.

Goldsmith, Elizabeth. "Private Expression and Public Domain in the *Lettres et billets galants.*" *Biblio 17* 37 (1987): 439–50.

Goldwyn, Harriet. *"Manlius*, l'héroisme inversé." *Biblio 17* 37 (1987): 421–38.

Jensen, Katharine A. "The Love Letter and the Female Writing Self: Masochist or Narcissist? The Case of Mme de Villedieu." *Biblio 17* 37 (1987): 451–68.

Lafouge, Jean-Pierre. "Mme de Villedieu dans ses Fables." *Biblio 17* 37 (1987): 469–82.

Leggett, Carleen. "The Woman and the Novelistic Maxims." *Biblio 17* 37 (1987): 483–500.

Miller, Nancy K. "Tender Economies: Mme de Villedieu and the Costs of Indifference." *L'Esprit créateur* 23 (1983): 80–93.

Morrissette, Bruce. *The Life and Works of Marie-Catherine Desjardins (Mme de Villedieu), 1632–1683*. St. Louis: Washington University Studies, 1947.

Rowan, Mary. "Patterns of Imprisonment and Escape in the Prose Fiction and Poetry of Mme de Villedieu." *Biblio 17* 37 (1987): 379–92.

Stanton, Domna C. "Villedieu's *Nouvelles* on the History of Fiction and the Fiction of History." *Biblio 17* 37 (1987): 339–60.

Verdier, Gabrielle. "Gender and Rhetoric in Some Seventeenth-Century Love Letters." *L'Esprit créateur* 23 (1983): 45–57.

———. "Madame de Villedieu and the Critics: Toward a Brighter Future." *Biblio 17* 37 (1987): 323–38.

SIMONE WEIL
(1909–1943)

J. P. Little

Nearly half a century after her death, Simone Weil's reputation continues to grow. Recognized as a highly original thinker in the field of religious philosophy from the publication of *La Pesanteur et la grâce* (*Gravity and Grace,* 1947) onwards, her social and political thought as elaborated in *L'Enracinement* (*The Need for Roots*, 1949) was recognized by Albert Camus, among others, as essential to the reconstruction of France after World War II. Her extraordinary life has always attracted attention, indeed notoriety, and the need has frequently been felt to label her as either saint or subversive. But a proper understanding of her contribution to twentieth-century thought has been obscured at times by her very diversity, the unclassifiable nature of her writing, and by the mistrust, if not downright hostility, engendered by her tendency to reject all orthodoxies in her pursuit of truth at all costs. The fact that she is not a systematic philosopher has made other philosophers wary of her too, although there are signs that she is being taken more and more seriously in this area. There seems little doubt that she will continue to attract well-deserved attention and acquire an increasingly solidly based reputation.

BIOGRAPHY

Simone Weil was born on February 3, 1909, into a comfortable middle-class Jewish family. The main influences of her childhood were her mother, a strong-minded and intelligent woman of Austrian extraction, who supervised every detail of her children's education and continued to follow and attempt to protect her daughter to the end of her life, and her brother André, three years her senior, who became a renowned mathematician, and whose precocious intellectual gifts caused Simone in early adolescence to compare unfavorably what she considered to be her own mediocre gifts with his undoubted genius. The rivalry between the two was on the whole fruitful, however, and it was a happy and enriching childhood, disrupted nevertheless by World War I. Simone's outrage at the humiliation imposed on Germany under the terms of the Armistice marks what is perhaps her first explicit social statement.

Her highly successful school career terminated at the Lycée Henri-IV in the decisive meeting with Alain, the philosopher and teacher who exercised a formative influence on a whole generation of French youth. From there she went to the Ecole Normale in the rue d'Ulm, from which she graduated in 1931 with the *agrégation* and her *diplôme d'etudes supérieures* on Descartes. During this period she was becoming more and more aware of social issues, participating in a workers' educational scheme, teaching French and political philosophy, and forming increasingly clear views on, for example, the colonial question, which was to preoccupy her to the end of her life.

The intensely competitive world of the Ecole Normale was also a very masculine one, and it is not difficult to see why Simone had by this time rejected the more overtly feminine side to her nature, paying little or no attention to dress or appearance. This process had already begun in her mother's attitude toward her, since she made no distinction in her treatment of her son and daughter, preferring anyway boyish behavior in children.

The reputation for political militancy that she acquired at this time followed her in the various teaching posts she held over the next few years. In the first, at Le Puy, she became unofficial spokesperson for the unemployed, causing great scandal among the local population, and involved herself with trade union affairs in the nearby mining community at St-Etienne. Although considered a Marxist by some—and her talent for provocation did not discourage such rumors—she never joined the Communist Party, and in fact became rapidly disillusioned both with the Party and with the capacities of the trade union movement to bring about a more just system for its members. Her relationship with organized labor was always a stormy one, and the articles she wrote for various journals at this time show her highly critical of the self-interest and capacity for self-delusion of much of the left. Her final disillusionment with the Communist Party came in 1933, during a visit to Germany, where she realized its incapacity to stand up to the rising tide of Nazism. This visit marks the effective end of her period of political militancy, although she continued to the end of her life to be preoccupied with sociopolitical questions.

Her uneasy relationship with the educational establishment resulted in her moving from Le Puy to Auxerre after only one year, and then to Roanne, after which, anxious to study at first hand the factory conditions upon which much of her increasingly mature thought on the nature of work and social organization was based, she took a job as a factory hand, spending the period between December 1934 and August 1935 in a variety of manual jobs, the appalling rigors of which she records with great objectivity in her "Journal d'usine" (Factory Journal), published as part of *La Condition ouvrière* (The Worker's

Condition, 1951). Her none-too-robust health—she had suffered from crippling headaches since her time at the Ecole Normale—finally broke under the experience, and it was in a state of total mental and physical exhaustion that she went that summer with her parents for a short holiday to Portugal.

In Portugal she had the first of her mystical experiences, where she suddenly realized the relationship between the Christian religion and affliction, and hence her implicit allegiance to it. After this crucial break she took up a teaching post in Bourges, where she continued to occupy herself with the problems of factory organization and also the conditions of agricultural workers, spending a short period helping a family of local peasants on their farm.

When the Spanish Civil War broke out in 1936, Simone, although holding pacifist views, decided that where others were giving their lives in what she felt to be a just cause, there her duty lay also, and she duly enlisted with the Republican forces. She was invalided out after an accident in the kitchen that caused serious leg burns, but not before she had realized that no one side in the conflict had the monopoly of truth or justice. The experience increased her pessimism with regard to the inescapable forces bearing upon individuals in society.

In the autumn of 1937 Simone took up a teaching post at St-Quentin, but in fact taught there for only one term because of continued ill health. She continued to write on social questions, however, campaigning for justice with regard to the colonial question, for example. She was increasingly preoccupied with spiritual matters, and the following Easter attended all the Easter Week services at the Abbey of Solesmes, renowned for its plain-chant. A further mystical experience occurred there, again related to her state of extreme affliction. It was at Solesmes that she was introduced to the English Metaphysical poets, and in particular George Herbert, whose poem "Love" she later learnt by heart, reciting it when her headaches were particularly intense. It was during one of these recitations that she first encountered the mystical presence of Christ. One of the most noteworthy features of these experiences was their total unexpectedness, and indeed a mark of their authenticity can be seen in the way in which she neither sought them nor prepared herself in any way for them. It is also of note that she spoke to no one about them at the time: we learn of them only through letters to Fr. Joseph-Marie Perrin, a Dominican priest who was to become a close friend, and to the poet Joë Bousquet, written much later, and in any case not destined for publication. Few people if any seem to have realized the development that was going on within her at this time.

The outbreak of war in September 1939 caused Simone great anguish, not least because of her pacifist views. Having done all in her power to prevent a war, however, she decided that, since war was declared, she must oppose the evil of Nazism with all her being. After fleeing with her family from Paris, she spent some months in Marseille, where she joined in Resistance activity, worked for the improvement in the conditions of a local camp of Indochinese workers brought over for the war effort, continued her writing with remarkable intensity, and also explored further her own spiritual position, particularly her relationship with the Catholic church, to which she felt increasingly drawn but never in fact entered. It was here that she conducted an intense dialogue with Fr. Perrin, who also put her in touch with the self-taught philosopher-farmer Gustave Thibon, allowing her to participate in the agricultural work which was of such significance to her.

Desperate to play a real part in the war, she was persuaded that access to England, and hence to a mission in occupied France, would be easier from the United States, and accordingly she arrived in New York in July 1942. There followed several months of extraordinarily intense intellectual creativity, but immense frustration at what she saw to be her betrayal of France through inactivity. She was able finally to persuade the authorities to get her to England, however, and in November 1942 arrived there to work with the Free French forces. This did not ultimately satisfy her, though, since instead of being given the dangerous mission that she longed for, she was put to work writing reports, the most extended of which was to be published under the title *L'Enracinement*. Years of self-imposed privation had taken their toll, however, and her refusal to eat more than the barest rations available to the French in France finally undermined her frail constitution and prevented her from fighting the tuberculosis which had by then been diagnosed. She died in a sanatorium at Ashford, Kent, on August 24, 1943, consumed by despair at not being able to participate adequately in the affliction of the times.

MAJOR THEMES

In addressing the question of Simone Weil's philosophy, it is important to bear in mind the particularly close relationship that she saw between philosophy and lived experience. As we have seen, she had from an early age an acute sensitivity to the problems of human existence in general, and the problems of the age in particular. This was reinforced by her study of Plato, for whom the aim of philosophy was to bring about "a change in the soul." It is natural, therefore, that all her writing has a strong moral content: she came to see philosophy as the analysis of the principles underlying all human activity, and its purpose to establish the bases of a more just society. Her concern for justice springs largely from the injustice and oppression she saw around her, which forms the central theme of an early major essay, "Reflexions sur les causes de la liberté et de l'oppression sociale" (Reflections on the Causes of Liberty and Oppression in Society). This analysis was enriched by her subsequent factory experience, which gave rise not only to the "Journal d'usine" but also to essays and notes that she continued to produce to the end of her life on that central question of human activity, manual labor. While throughout she considered that work is free only when grasped by the intelligence, she came increasingly to realize that whereas the harshness of the work experience could never fully be overcome, this could be turned to positive effect through consent. In fact, the manual worker was among the most privileged of beings, since his labor allowed him a contact with matter, with the laws of the universe, and hence with reality itself.

This is a particular application of the general idea of the universe and all that operates in it being composed of a network of immutable relationships which, following Plato, Simone Weil terms necessity. Necessity is seen equally in the laws governing the waves on the sea and in human conduct, for example in the desire for revenge when one is wronged, or the human need to exploit the power that circumstances give one over others. Using an image from physical law, she terms this "gravity," and holds that even the most apparently powerful tyrant is almost totally in its control.

This is clearly a pessimistic assessment of human relationships, and leaves little scope for individual freedom. She is saved from mechanistic determinism, however, by her positing a radically other supernatural realm in opposition to necessity, which she terms, in the manner of Plato, the Good. It is the intervention of this supernatural element that is responsible for all that we know of true goodness, beauty, and justice, and human beings have the power, firstly, to provoke its descent by attention fixed tirelessly on the possibility of that descent, against all probability, and then to consent to it, even when this means a total destruction of the natural self with its haphazard mixture of relative good and evil. Consent is thus for Simone Weil the most important and perhaps the only manifestation of human freedom.

The irruption of the supernatural into the mechanical world of necessary relationships is often seen by Simone Weil as a means of breaking the cycle of evil, which has a natural tendency to expand and perpetuate itself. This function is performed by certain perfectly pure beings, historical or mythological, whose sacrifice of self permits the dissolution of evil. Christ was for her the supreme example of such a being, although she moves effortlessly across other religious traditions, finding incarnations of mediating purity in various Greek deities—Prometheus and Dionysos, for instance—in the Hindu god Krishna, and also in the biblical figure of Job and in Plato's perfectly just man.

If such mediation is necessary, it is because of Simone Weil's firm conviction that the absolute, be it termed God or the Good, can have no direct relationship with the natural world. Simone Weil's radical dualism is evident in her concept of creation as being the withdrawal of God in order that something other might exist. She stresses the importance of the impersonal element of the deity, and of negative definitions of God as ultimately unknowable. This concept of God lies at the heart of much of her rejection of Judaism with its Old Testament manifestation of a Lord of Hosts who was powerful rather than good. It underlies, too, many features of the Catholic Church that she found unacceptable: the Crusades were possible because the Church saw itself as a temporal, totalitarian power, determined to impose universal recognition of Christianity by temporal means. In this respect, the Church simply took over from the Roman Empire, another object of Simone Weil's fierce condemnation. Her sense of the operation of necessity in human relationships meant that she saw most of history to have operated in this way. History is the record of relationsips of force within society, and, not surprisingly, is therefore full of atrocities.

She recognizes the possibility of another form of social organization, however, and its occasional incarnation in, for example, the Languedoc civilization of the twelfth century. The essays "L'Agonie d'une civilization vue à travers un poème épique" (A Medieval Epic Poem) and "En quoi consiste l'inspiration occitanienne?" (The Romanesque Renaissance) manifest her enthusiasm for this society, based, in her view, on the notions of legitimacy and consent to a social order, a hierarchy which involved no humiliation but mutual respect as between equals. It was also on a relatively small scale—she frequently evokes the notion of "city," derived from the Greek city-state—and compares it to the potentially limitless totalitarian state in its manifestation as Empire—Roman, French, and so forth—which, borrowing Plato's image, she terms "the Great Beast."

It is, however, entirely consistent with her thinking on natural relationships in society that the twelfth-century Languedoc civilization should ultimately have perished, destroyed by the totalitarian Great Beast in the form of the Church allied to secular forces. There is an inevitable logic to this destruction: what is spiritually rich is in Simone Weil's view necessarily physically vulnerable and a prey to superior force. In the same way there is also a necessary relationship in her thinking between suffering and the revelation of reality, that absolute which, as I have already indicated, embraces in Platonic fashion goodness, truth, and beauty. The way to absolute goodness and the abolition of evil is Christ's way of the Cross; the way to Simone Weil's own personal revelation of absolute truth was, she became convinced, the way of affliction, of sharing to the maximum degree possible in the horror brought about by the war. It is noteworthy in this respect also that her first mystical experiences took place in a state of extreme physical and moral distress. Even the way to truth through beauty has a relationship with suffering: the beauty created by the greatest poets—Homer in *The Iliad*, Shakespeare in *King Lear*, Racine in *Phèdre*—results from the steady contemplation of human wretchedness, with no attempt to hide that wretchedness by recourse to evasion or lies. Her fine essay, "*L'Iliade* ou le poème de la force" (*The Iliad* or the Poem of Force), illustrates clearly the way in which truthful contemplation produces beauty. Such an act of attention involves a complete emptying of self, a rejection of the personal, what Simone Weil called "decreation," which is ultimately a human image of the Creator's withdrawal at the moment of creation. The great artist and the saint both partake in this way of an impersonal perspective on human reality.

From the perspective of the decreated self, the world order is revealed as beautiful in the manner of the Stoic's perception of it. Beauty, in Simone Weil's view, is not a partial selection of reality in conformity with individual human desires, it is the tangible reflection of the whole of reality itself. In this way it becomes, when properly assumed, a source of joy since, for Simone Weil, nothing was ultimately more joyful than to live in the truth, nothing filled her with more horror than the thought of living a lie. The fact that the world order embraced necessarily the humanly unacceptable, appalling, inexplicable suffering, was clearly beyond comprehension on one level, but from the superior perspective of the decreated self the path to true knowledge.

Even in this extreme, the view of Simone Weil as preoccupied with suffering to the exclusion of a more joyful way to truth must therefore be modified. She also has very positive things to say, at least potentially, on the ordering of society, particularly in *L'Enracinement*, where she analyses social organization in terms of the needs of humanity rather than the rights of individuals. One of the most basic spiritual needs, in her view, is the need for roots, for that sense of community, conveyed by a common tradition, which draws nourishment from the past in order to project into the future. The sense of patriotism in such a culture has nothing to do with the chauvinism and desire for prestige and false glory that has often gone under that name, from Louis XIV onwards. A truly rooted society relies on the consent of its members for its sustenance, and in relationships between the different groups that compose it, as in the workplace, appeals to the individual intelligence rather than authority to gain this consent. Given the right environment, every human being was capable of understanding the universe, since that understanding depended not on what is normally considered to be intelligence, but on a certain quality of attention.

The complexity of Simone Weil's thought is evident, but the contradictions— between her espousal of tradition and her radical reappraisal of social organization, between a profound egalitarianism and an equally real sense of hierarchy, between her mysticism and her sociopolitical activism—only apparent. In her passionate concern for truth she will continue to stimulate and to provoke, turning our attention to those questions we prefer normally to leave unspoken.

SURVEY OF CRITICISM

Criticism of Simone Weil's writings has followed in large measure the particularly haphazard nature of the publication of those writings. Since she left no full-length text, collections have been put together according to the enthusiasms of those who discovered her. In the early publications, at least, her mother's hand is strongly present. Gustave Thibon's personal selection from Simone Weil's notebooks, which appeared in 1947 under the title *La Pesanteur et la grâce* (*Gravity and Grace*), emphasized the religious dimension to her thought, as did *Attente de Dieu* (*Waiting on God, 1950*), while *L'Enracinement* (*The Need for Roots*, 1949) gave a religious perspective to her political philosophy. Early criticism in French, such as the two works by Marie-Magdeleine Davy, *Introduction au message de Simone Weil* (1954) and *Simone Weil* in the Collection Témoins du XXe siècle (1956), emphasized the spiritual dimension, as did, in German, Karl Epting's *Der Geistliche Weg der Simone Weils* (1955) and, in French, Bernard Halda's later *L'Evolution spirituelle de Simone Weil* (1964). Serious philosophical attention combined with this religious perspective is given to her thought in François Heidsieck's *Simone Weil: une étude avec choix de textes* in 1965, and in 1967 in Michel Narcy's *Simone Weil: malheur et beauté du monde*, while the most thorough philosophical approach remains Miklos Vetös *La Métaphysique religieuse de Simone Weil* (1971). The volume issuing from the Colloque de Cerisy-la-Salle in 1975, *Simone Weil philosophe, historienne et mystique* (1978), ranges widely over essential aspects of Simone Weil's thought, as do the very considerable number of articles published by the *Cahiers Simone Weil* which, since their appearance in 1978 (preceded by the *Bulletin de l'Association pour l'étude de la pensée de Simone Weil*), have constituted an essential reference.

Important also because of their concentration on the social and political thought of Simone Weil are Philippe Dujardin's *Simone Weil: idéologie et politique* (1975) and the long article in *Les Temps Modernes* (March 1983) by Robert Chenavier, "Relire Simone Weil."

In the English-speaking world, Sir Richard Rees's fine translations that appeared in the sixties (*Selected Essays*, 1962, and *Seventy Letters*, 1965) contributed to a wider understanding of Simone Weil's thought, and his *Brave Men: A Study of D. H. Lawrence and Simone Weil* (1958) and *Simone Weil: A Sketch for a Portrait* (1966) gave a refreshingly direct perspective unmarred by any hagiography. More recent studies of note include the essays in *Simone Weil: Interpretations of a Life*, edited by George Abbott White (1981), which combine critical viewpoints with biography, John Hellman's *Simone Weil: An Introduction to Her Thought* (1982), Eric O. Springsted's *Simone Weil and the Suffering of Love* (1986), and J. P. Little's *Simone Weil: Waiting on Truth* (1988).

Given the interest aroused by Simone Weil's extraordinary life, it is not surprising that biography has played an important part in studies concerning her. Excellent early work was done by Jacques Cabaud in his *L'Expérience vécue de Simone Weil* (1957), complemented by his *Simone Weil: A Fellowship in Love* (1964) and the German version, *Simone Weil: Die Logik der Liebe* (1968). Joseph-Marie Perrin and Gustave Thibon presented a combined portrait under the title *Simone Weil telle que nous l'avons connue* (1952), whereas a friend from her Ecole Normale days, Maurice Schumann, who was one of the last people to see her during those anguished weeks in London before her death, gives an individual and sensitive interpretation in *La Mort née de leur propre vie (Péguy, Simone Weil, Gandhi)* (1974). The essential reference for Simone Weil's biography is, however, the two-volume account written by her fellow-student and lifelong friend Simone Petrement, *La Vie de Simone Weil* (1973).

Simone Weil's complete works are now being reissued by Gallimard in an entirely revised form, under the general editorship of André-A. Devaux and Florence de Lussy. Two volumes have so far appeared, and it is to be hoped that their systematic and meticulous handling of Simone Weil's diverse writings will stimulate an ever more coherent critical approach.

BIBLIOGRAPHY

Works by Simone Weil

La Pesanteur et la grâce. Paris: Plon, 1947.
L'Enracinement. Paris: Gallimard, 1949.
Attente de Dieu. 2nd ed. Paris: La Colombe, 1950.
La Condition ouvrière. Paris: Gallimard, 1950.
La Connaissance surnaturelle. Paris: Gallimard, 1950.
Intuitions pré-chrètiennes. Paris: La Colombe, 1951.
Lettre à un religieux. Paris: Gallimard, 1951.
La Source grecque. Paris: Gallimard, 1953.
Oppression et liberté. Paris: Gallimard, 1955.
Écrits de Londres et dernières lettres. Paris: Gallimard, 1957.
Leçons de philosophie de Simone Weil (Roanne 1933–1934) (presented by Anne Reynaud). Paris: Plon, 1959.
Écrits historiques et politiques. Paris: Gallimard, 1960.
Pensées sans ordre concernant l'amour de Dieu. Paris: Gallimard, 1962.
Sur la science. Paris: Gallimard, 1965.
Poèmes, suivis de 'Venise sauvée,' Lettre de Paul Valéry. Paris: Gallimard, 1968.
Cahiers. Vol. 1. New rev. and aug. ed. Paris: Plon, 1970.
Cahiers. Vol. 2. New rev. and aug. ed. Paris: Plon, 1972.
Cahiers. Vol. 3. New rev. and aug. ed. Paris: Plon, 1974.
Réflexions sur les causes de la liberté et de l'oppression sociale. Paris: Gallimard, 1980.
Œuvres complètes. New ed. Tome I, *Premiers essais philosophiques.* Paris: Gallimard, 1988.
Œuvres complètes. New ed. Tome II, *Ecrits historiques et politiques,* vol. 1, *L'Engagement syndical.* Paris: Gallimard, 1988.

Translations of Simone Weil

Complete Editions

Gravity and Grace (La Pesanteur et la grâce). Trans. Emma Craufurd. London: Routledge and Kegan Paul, 1952.
Waiting on God (Attente de Dieu). Trans. Emma Craufurd. London: Routledge and Kegan Paul, 1951.
The Need for Roots (L'Enracinement). Trans. Arthur F. Wills. London: Routledge and Kegan Paul, 1952; New York: Putnam's Sons, 1953.
Intimations of Christianity (Intuitions pré-chrétiennes). Trans. Elizabeth Chase Geissbühler. London: Routledge and Kegan Paul, 1957.
Letter to a Priest (Lettre à un religieux). Trans. Arthur F. Wills. London: Routledge and Kegan Paul, 1953. New York: Putnam's Sons, 1954.
On Science, Necessity, and the Love of God (includes *La Source grecque*). Trans. Richard Rees. London: New York, Toronto: Oxford University Press, 1968.

Oppression and Liberty ((Oppression et liberté). Trans. Arthur F. Wills and John Petrie. London: Routledge and Kegan Paul, 1958.

Lectures on Philosophy (Leçons de philosophie de Simone Weil). Trans. Hugh Price. Intro. Peter Winch. Cambridge: Cambridge University Press, 1978.

Collections of Weil's Writings

First and Last Notebooks (Cahiers). Trans. Richard Rees. London, New York, and Toronto: Oxford University Press, 1970.

Formative Writings, 1929–1941. Ed. and intro. Dorothy Tuck McFarland and Wilhelmina Van Ness. Amherst: University of Massachusetts Press, 1987.

Gateway to God. Ed. David Raper. Glasgow: Wm. Collins (Fontana Books), 1974.

Selected Essays (1934–43). Trans. Richard Rees. London: Oxford University Press, 1962.

Seventy Letters. Trans. Richard Rees. London: Oxford University Press, 1965.

Simone Weil: An Anthology. Ed. Siân Miles. London: Virago Books, 1986.

The Simone Weil Reader. Ed. with an intro. by George A. Panichas. New York: David McKay, 1977.

Individual Essays

"The Iliad or the Poem of Force." Trans. Mary McCarthy. *Politics* 2, no.11 (November 1945): 321–31. (Also rpt. in *Simone Weil: An Anthology*, ed. Miles, 182–215).

"Reflections on War." Trans. unspecified. *Politics* 2, no.2, (February 1943): 51–55.

"Words and War." Trans. Bowden Broadwater. *Politics* 3, no. 3 (March 1946): 69–73.

Studies of Simone Weil

Anderson, David. *Simone Weil*. London: S.C.M. Press, 1971.

Cabaud, Jacques. *L'Expérience vécue de Simone Weil*. Paris: Plon, 1957.

———. *Simone Weil: A Fellowship in Love*. London: Harvill, 1964; New York: Channel Press, 1965.

———. *Simone Weil: Die Logik der Liebe*. Trans. from the author's English and French by Franziska Maria Marbach, and revised by the author. Freiburg/Munich: Karl Auber, 1968.

Chenavier, Robert. "Relire Simone Weil." *Les Temps Modernes*, no. 440 (March 1983): 1677–1714.

Davy, Marie-Magdeleine. *The Mysticism of Simone Weil* (Trans. by Cynthia Rowland of *Introduction au message de Simone Weil*, Paris: Plon, 1954). London: Rockliff; Boston: Beacon Press, 1951.

———. *Simone Weil*. Preface by Gabriel Marcel. Paris: Editions Universitaires, 1956.

Dujardin, Philippe. *Simone Weil, idéologie et politique*. Grenoble: Presses Universitaires de Grenoble, 1975.

Epting, Karl. *Der Geistliche Weg der Simone Weils*. Stuttgart: Friederich Vorwerk Verlag, 1955.

Halda, Bernard. *L'Evolution spirituelle de Simone Weil*. Paris: Beauchesne, 1964.

Heidsieck, François. *Simone Weil: une étude avec un choix de textes*. Paris: Seghers, 1965.

Hellman, John. *Simone Weil: An Introduction to Her Thought*. Philadelphia: Fortress Press, 1982.

Kahn, Gilbert, ed. *Simone Weil, philosophe, historienne et mystique*. Paris: Aubier Montaigne, 1978.

Little, J. P. *Simone Weil: Waiting on Truth*. Oxford: Berg, 1988.

Little, J. P., ed. and André Ughetto. Special issue of *Sud* (1990).

Narcy, Michel. *Simone Weil: malheur et beauté du monde*. Paris: Editions du Centurion, 1967.

Perrin, Joseph-Marie. *Mon Dialogue avec Simone Weil*. Preface by André-A. Devaux. Paris: Nouvelle Cité, 1984.

Perrin, Joseph-Marie, and Gustave Thibon. *Simone Weil as We Knew Her* (trans. by Emma Craufurd in *Simone Weil telle que nous l'avons connue*, Paris: La Colombe, 1952). London: Routledge and Kegan Paul, 1953.

Pétrement, Simone. *La Vie de Simone Weil*. 2 vols. Paris: Fayard, 1973 (trans. by Raymond Rosenthal under the title *Simone Weil: A Life*, New York: Pantheon Books, 1977).

Rees, Richard. *Brave Men: A Study of D. H. Lawrence and Simone Weil*. London: Gollancz, 1958; Carbondale: Southern Illinois University Press, 1959.

———. *Simone Weil: A Sketch for a Portrait*. London: Oxford University Press, 1966; Carbondale: Southern Illinois University Press, 1966.

Schumann, Maurice. *La Mort née de leur propre vie (Péguy, Simone Weil, Gandhi)*. Paris: Fayard, 1974.

Springsted, Eric O. *Simone Weil and the Suffering of Love*. Preface by Robert Coles. Cambridge, Mass.: Cowley Publications, 1986.

Vetö, Miklos. *La Métaphysique religieuse de Simone Weil*. Paris: Vrin, 1971.

White, George Abbott, ed. *Simone Weil: Interpretations of a Life*. Amherst: University of Massachusetts Press, 1981.

For a more extended bibliography, including secondary material up to the end of 1978, the reader is referred to my *Simone Weil: A Bibliography* (London: Grant and Cutler, 1973), and Supplement 1 (1979). Other bibliographical material is to be found in:

Marchetti, A. *Simone Weil, con una Bibliografia sistematica*. Bologna: Tipografia Compositori, 1977.

White, George Abbott. "Simone Weil's Bibliography: Some Reflections on Publishing and Criticism," in White, ed., *Simone Weil: Interpretations of a Life*. Amherst: University of Massachusetts Press, 1981.

MONIQUE WITTIG
(1935–)

Diane Griffin Crowder

BIOGRAPHY

Monique Wittig was born in the Haut Rhin department in Alsace. She moved to Paris in the 1950s, where she studied Oriental languages. Her first novel, *L'Opoponax* (*The Opoponax*, 1964), immediately drew attention to her when it was awarded the Prix Médicis by a jury including Nathalie *Sarraute, Claude Simon, and Alain Robbe-Grillet. Praised by such influential writers, the novel was quickly translated into English, where it won critical acclaim as well. Her play, *L'Amant vert* (The Green Lover), was produced in Bolivia in 1969, and several short stories were published in the late 1960s as well.

Wittig was a major figure in the revolt of students and workers in May 1968. She quickly realized that the radical men leading the revolt were not inclined to share the limelight with women. Wittig was one of the first leading feminist theoreticians and activists and an important participant in the early meetings out of which grew the various groups of the women's movement. It was in this heady atmosphere of radical political action that she completed what may be her most influential work to date, *Les Guérillères* (1969). Revolutionary both in form and content, this novel has been widely translated, debated, and used as a source of ideas by major feminist and lesbian thinkers around the world.

Monique Wittig believed that action was necessary to awaken the public to the oppression of women. In August 1970, in sympathy with the national women's strike called by American feminists, Wittig and others decided upon a dramatic demonstration. Marching to that most sacred of French national shrines, the Tomb of the Unknown Soldier at the Arc de Triomphe, they carried wreaths of flowers with banners bearing such slogans as "There is one who is even more unknown than the Soldier: his wife." The press reported the incident in front-page stories which, for the first time, gave a name to the movement. The media dubbed it the MLF, or Mouvement pour la libération des femmes, in imitation of the American media's label, the women's liberation movement.

Throughout the early 1970s, Wittig was a central figure in the radical lesbian and feminist movements in France. She was a founding member of such groups as the Petites Marguérites, the Gouines rouges, and the Féministes révolutionnaires. The period 1964–1975 was also her most productive in terms of fiction, with four long works, several short stories, criticism, and radio dramas. In 1973 she published *Le Corps lesbien* (*The Lesbian Body*), and in 1975, with coauthor Sande Zeig, *Brouillon pour un dictionnaire des amantes* (*Lesbian Peoples: Material for a Dictionary*). But the intensity of the debates between divergent tendencies within the movement, which at times became personal attacks on activists like Wittig, took its toll. Wittig has described the political process which tends to turn on one's own comrades in her parable "Paris-la-politique" (Paris-the-Political). In 1976 Wittig moved to the United States.

Although living outside France, Wittig did not cease to be involved in the French movement. She turned her attention increasingly toward theoretical works, and a number of her most famous essays date from the late seventies and early eighties. In a variety of genres ranging from the philosophical essay ("The Straight Mind") to the parable ("Les Tchiches et les Tchouches") she explored the intersections of lesbianism, feminism, and literary form. She became part of the editorial collective of France's major theoretical feminist journal, *Questions féministes*, and she is advisory editor to an American journal, *Feminist Issues*, founded in part to make available in English the important works being published in France. Most of her essays were published in these two journals. She has become truly bilingual, as she translates her own work from English into French and vice versa. She also translated Djuna Barnes's *Spillway* as *La Passion*, as well as Herbert Marcuse and the Portuguese "Three Marias."

In the eighties, she returned to drama and fiction. In a stunning fulfillment of her goal of recreating culture, Wittig wrote two works that take as their pre-texts classics of male literature. Her play, produced by Zeig first in English as *The Constant Journey* (1984) and later in Paris as *Le Voyage sans fin* (1985), is a reworking of *Don Quixote* in which all major characters are female. Her latest novel, *Virgile, non* (*Across the Acheron*), uses Dante's *Divine Comedy* as the structuring metaphor. But now paradise, hell, and limbo are all situated in contemporary San Francisco, and all the angels, the lost souls, and those in limbo are female.

In 1986 she completed a doctoral dissertation on "le chanteur littéraire" under the direction of Gérard Genette. Wittig currently serves as a visiting professor at various American universities, maintains her close ties to the French movement, and is working on several projects, including a collection of her essays, a book on language, and a film script.

MAJOR THEMES

"With writing, words are everything" ("Trojan Horse," 47). Wittig insists on the materiality of words, as she insists on the materiality of the body or of women's oppression. The relation of women to language and to the culture expressed in it is the overarching theme of her work. Unlike the Nouveau Roman writers (especially Nathalie Sarraute) who influenced her style, Wittig's exploration of language has an expressly political goal. She intends to create a lesbian language, in which the categories of sex are abolished. Like Simone de *Beauvoir, Wittig recognizes that "one is not born a woman." Believing that biological differences have no meaning outside a (hetero)sexist discourse, she maintains that the very concepts of "woman" and "man" are political constructs whose function is to keep women subordinate to men. Rejecting the categorizing of people by sex is a necessary stage in eliminating the oppression of women; hence, her near-total suppression of the words "woman" and "man" in her fiction.

Wittig's style is especially dense and requires the reader to pay attention to words and phrases in a new way. Her ambition is nothing less than to appropriate all cultural symbolic systems, to make them a tool for the abolition of gender itself. This explains a number of striking features of her work.

All of her works consist of short passages (many only a paragraph in length), seemingly juxtaposed arbitrarily. The reader must look for ways to connect the passages into a coherent narrative. Often a single word, repeated in several passages, accumulates layers of meaning as the text progresses. A good example of this is the word "amazons" in *Brouillon*, or the multiple meanings of the symbol 0 in *Les Guérillères*. By the end of the work, each of these has been defined and refined by the shifting contexts of the short passages. They become complex symbols that reshape the reader's consciousness in often subtle ways.

Wittig has said: "Any important literary work is like the Trojan Horse at the time it is produced. Any work with a new form operates as a war machine, because its design and its goal is to pulverize the old forms and formal conventions" ("Trojan Horse," 45). Wittig's writings all make war on traditional forms because her primary goal is to alter our perspective on the world through transformations of both literary and cultural codes. She accomplishes this by consistently subverting existing language, myths, and forms—deconstructing our culture in order to reveal its hidden meanings, then using the pieces to construct a new vision of daring freedom.

Wittig's five novels and last play can be seen as anticipating and influencing movements within feminist thought of the past two decades. In *L'Opoponax* we find the young girl struggling to create an autonomous identity that can call itself "I." *Les Guérillères* shows us powerful female warriors meeting the challenge of overthrowing all of male culture and creating the first of the great utopian visions of the neofeminist movement. Having won the war and eliminated the concept of "man," they can turn to explorations of sensuality and love for the lesbian body (*Le Corps lesbien*). They exuberantly appropriate the power of naming and thereby create a new dictionary and history of the companion lovers (*Brouillon*). But resistance is great, and the patriarchy continues to claim its victims. So the Wittigian hero's ardent love leads her to become a new female

Quixote fighting injustice, even if the world calls her mad (*Le Voyage sans fin*), and her rage that injustice still reigns plunges her into that most epic of all voyages, through hell and limbo, seeking paradise like Dante before her (*Virgile, non*).

Each of Wittig's novels seeks to appropriate for female use an existing genre. *L'Opoponax* is the quintessential *bildungsroman*. Told from the perspective of Catherine Legrand, a little girl growing up in a provincial village, the clear, simple sentences plunge us again into the world of childhood, its delights, torments, and fears. Wittig uses the third-person indefinite pronoun "on" (one), rather than "je" (I), to create a neutral space in which Catherine Legrand can formulate a self outside gender.

A major theme of the work is the creation of identity through language. When she falls in love with a schoolmate, Valerie Borges, she creates for herself an imaginary being, the opoponax, who is to blame for anything that goes wrong and who, conveniently, writes the love notes to Valerie Borges that Catherine Legrand cannot write. She appropriates this strange word for a plant and redefines it as the source of mischief. Only as the opoponax can Catherine say "I" ("I am the opoponax") until the end of the novel. When Valerie finally reciprocates Catherine's love, Catherine can speak authoritatively. In sentences beginning with "On dit" (one says), Catherine's lyrical love turns the beloved into a figure of mythical proportions.

The epic *Les Guérillères* embodies Wittig's concept of language as both the means of oppressing women and the tool for liberation. "[They] say, unhappy one, men have expelled you from the world of symbols and yet they have given you names, they have called you slave, you unhappy slave. . . . [They] say, the language you speak poisons your glottis tongue palate lips. They say, the language you speak is made up of words that are killing you" (113–14). It is in the gaps of male language that female experience and knowledge must be inscribed, and this novel is in fact that inscription.

Moreover, it is the dismantling of our familiar culture and the depiction of a totally new one in which the artificial division of the sexes into social classes is abolished. It uses war as a structuring theme, but this war is fought by the collective heroine, "elles" (they), against male culture. Wittig uses the third-person plural feminine as a universal pronoun, in place of the masculine "ils." She has stated that her goal was "not to feminize the world but to make the categories of sex obsolete in language" ("The Mark of Gender," 9). Unfortunately, the English translations of this and most later works err, substituting "the women" for "they."

In *Les Guérillères* Wittig fully develops her most striking weapon against androcentric culture—the reworking of myths and allusions. Already in *L'O-poponax* Catherine Legrand appropriated male poets like Baudelaire and Scève in her private language of love. In *Les Guérillères* a series of passages recall both classical and modern texts (i.e., Freud, the Arthurian cycle), but with a twist. In the latter case, Arthur and his knights are in quest of the "spherical cup containing the blood," or the vulva. The quest was unsuccessful because Arthur and the Round Table did not understand what the symbol meant, but the reader has been given the key in many passages linking the circle with the female principle.

In such deconstructive passages, Wittig uses her typical economy of style. She includes only a few details of the old myth to guide the reader in interpreting the dramatic quality of the difference between our world and that of the *guérillères*. The shock of defamiliarization forces the reader to question our own meaning structures, as well as to interpret the meaning given to the stories by the characters. Like her subsequent novels, the text is an elaborate tissue of allusions to be unravelled and rewoven by the reader.

Lists, often unpunctuated, are a frequent device for getting rid of the binary "either/or" mentality of male language. Wittig uses them especially to appeal to the senses. The long lists of perfumes used by the *guérillères*, like the lists of fruits or birds in the paradise of *Virgile, non*, evoke a sense of richness and overflowing abundance in this new world of lesbian language. The lists of names in *Les Guérillères* is a particularly powerful example of this technique. Here, each forename (women have no surname) is a shorthand for an entire universe of stories and of women. The reader may know women with these names, and can tell their (real-life) stories. Since the names represent all parts of the world, no single reader can know all the myths and stories behind all the names. Thus, a collective multicultural readership mirrors the collective, multicultural heroes in the novel. Together, the names incorporate all aspects of culture—mythology, history, art, and science.

Le Corps lesbien transforms Western love poetry completely. The poetic "I" has been a male poet addressing a female "thou." Wittig marks her separation from the male poetic tradition by splitting the male "I" of literary tradition. This "j/e" is so powerful that it can "attack the order of heterosexuality in texts" and "lesbianize the symbols" ("Mark of Gender," 11). The couple becomes all the mythical characters in love poetry. Here we have Orphea saving her Euridice, and here the passion of "Christa the much-crucified." And her couple is not alone, but integrated into a community of other lesbians who live and love under the sign of Sappho.

Wittig asserts the materiality of the lesbian body by reversing the major technique of poetry—metaphor. Whereas male literature erases the female body by replacing it with other terms (lips become rubies, etc.), Wittig insists on the integrity of the body. Every part is loved here. Not just the breasts and genitals of male poetry, but the very bones become invested with erotic power. Interspersed in the text are lists of parts of the body, until by the end of the novel, the violently fragmented female body has been entirely reconstructed.

In *Brouillon pour un dictionnaire des amantes*, Wittig and coauthor Zeig tackle the problem of language directly. Written in standard dictionary format, the novel depicts the history of the world as if men had not existed. Alternately humorous and serious, it exalts heroines from the past and present. The page for Sappho is left blank, presumably so the reader can write her own definition (or perhaps Sappho is beyond description). The definitions proposed tie words to a female history and culture. Some definitions are taken from feminist works, others from classical texts, but all presume a female point of view.

Wittig's two most recent works challenge male culture in an even more subversive way, by taking as their structuring devices *Don Quixote* and *The Divine Comedy*. Wittig returns to the epic quest genre, completing a cycle begun with the war epic of *Les Guérillères*.

The mock-epic *Le Voyage sans fin* is an attempt to use certain cinematic effects in theater. The actors play out each short scene on stage, while a taped sound track features dialogues that often do not match the action. Wittig's marvelous wit and sense of irony, often overlooked by critics, serve to heighten the absurdity of a world that views female heroes as mad. The major themes of the play revolve around the nature of writing and fiction as they relate to women's social roles. The books that gave Quichotte her "mad" ideas are ones she has herself written. The titles of the books—*L'Artémisiade*, *La Geste des Amazones*, *Phyllis de Flandres*—parody male literature, but of course none of them has ever been published.

The other major theme of the play concerns the relation between "reality" and "fiction." As in Cervantes, Wittig's Quichotte tilts at windmills, but in the name of righting real injustices. If knights errant are rarely successful, it is because they are a real threat to the absolute tyranny of the powerful, who hate and persecute them. If Quichotte slays puppets portraying the capture of Amazon lovers, it is because Wittig considers the representation of the degradation of women to contribute to their material subordination.

In *Virgile, non*, as in Dante, the author becomes a character (here, Wittig) and narrator who is guided through the hell of women's oppression, the limbo of lesbian marginalization, and the vision of a paradise beyond our imagining. But in place of the kindly Virgil we have a stern lesbian guide, Manastabal, and throughout the reader is reminded that Wittig is playing against Dante's male vision, subverting it.

Wittig's use of Dante as a structuring device allows her to intertwine a number of important themes. The most obvious is the relationship among hell, limbo, and paradise. All three coexist simultaneously in an eternal present, set in San Francisco. Unlike Dante, Wittig does not make an orderly journey through a hierarchical series of circles of hell, then move to purgatory and finally to heaven. Instead, Manastabal tells Wittig that the circles of hell are not numbered, and, in any case, they will not visit them in any particular order. Wittig responds, "Let's go in disorder, then."

The various circles of hell describe the reality of women's lives in a patriarchal society. Wittig uses many devices to "defamiliarize" this reality so as to render apparent the hidden horror of our culture. Some passages are extremely funny. Other circles of hell are so ghastly that Wittig faints, or must bathe in the Acheron, river of forgetfulness. The two "Parade" sequences are truly horrifying because

Wittig does not have to invent any monsters. In the first, the parade begins with women used in commercial advertising and descends to women used in pornography. In the second, the women on parade represent literally the physical cruelties done to women in various cultures. Chinese footbinding, genital mutilation, forced starvation, beatings, and other tortures are graphically displayed. Wittig can barely stand to watch, but Manastabal tells Wittig her suffering at *seeing* the damned souls is an insult to those who suffer physically and in silence.

Limbo is set in a lesbian bar. Periodically, Wittig and Manastabal arrive there, where they drink tequila, watch those playing pool, and talk. These scenes function as a respite from hell, as a depiction of lesbian life, and as a time when Manastabal can further instruct Wittig on the relation between lesbian culture and the hell of heterosexuality. The lesbians in limbo are "outlaws," "runaway slaves" whom Wittig admires.

Naked golden and black "dyke" angels on motorcycles appear to the astonished Wittig when she first visits paradise. But she must win her way there by finding the language to describe paradise. Yet again, the major theme is the creation of a lesbian language which will permit us to imagine a new world. An exuberant feast of words awaits Wittig when she finally arrives at "The Kitchen of the Angels" at the end of her long quest.

As a lesbian, Wittig is very aware of the problem she faces in being taken seriously as a writer. She threatens the status quo politically and poetically. Her goal is to render the lesbian point of view universal, to make her lesbian language as universally understood as any literary language. Her insistence, therefore, on suppressing the marks of gender in language by annihilating or reversing them forces the reader to become aware of the political effects of the universalization of the heterosexual male point of view. It is this wrenching apart of the norm that creates the tension and violence of her texts.

SURVEY OF CRITICISM

Monique Wittig is clearly one of the most original thinkers and writers of her generation. She has created what Hawkesworth calls a "rhetoric of vision" which has already transformed feminist thought.

Yet attempting to alter radically the structure of our mythic languages and doing so in such a deliberate fashion is an enormously risky undertaking for any writer. To what extent has Wittig succeeded? Individual critical judgments aside, it is clear that her work has had an enormous impact upon the feminist and lesbian communities in both France and the United States. *Les Guérillères* in particular has influenced an entire generation of feminist and lesbian utopian novels in France, England, Quebec, and the United States. It is indeed difficult to find a collection of critical writings on feminist or lesbian literature where she is not mentioned. Yet her political position has not always endeared her to the popular press.

L'Opoponax was warmly greeted by most reviewers, praised highly by such influential writers as Marguerite *Duras, Claude Simon, and Mary McCarthy, whose "Everybody's Childhood" ensured the book serious attention in England and the United States.

Such near-unanimity came to an abrupt end with the publication of *Les Guérillères*. Coming as it did when the women's movement was in its infancy, the book received very different reviews in France than in England and the United States. French reviewers like André Dalmas immediately recognized the importance of the linguistic and cultural revolution in the work and praised Wittig for her extraordinary ability to create a new language that bridged the gap between "saying" and "doing." Claude Cluny found the work one of beauty and genius.

In England and the United States, most male reviewers attacked the book savagely, while most female reviewers found it a lyrical expression of women's aspirations and determination to eliminate sexism. The transparent rage of many male reviewers at the idea of a feminist revolution was clearly a reaction to the politics, rather than to the style, of the text. The split among critics was evident as well in reviews of *Le Corps lesbien*, with some English and American critics accusing the work of sadism, while many French critics (male and female) again found the work beautiful. Clearly, her works provoked strong reactions in some critics.

Scholarly critics were generally impressed by her innovations. Like *L'Opoponax*, *Les Guérillères* received serious critical appreciation almost from the beginning. Critics recognized the importance of Wittig's creation of a new language in which to express new visions of a world beyond gender divisions. Science fictional and utopian aspects of the text also received considerable attention. Many aspects of the world of the *guérillères* have inspired feminist utopian writers such as Joanna Russ and Françoise d'Eaubonne. It has become one of the most frequently cited works among feminist critics in both France and the United States.

Les Guérillères is a central work in the canon of modern writing. Scholars have given important critical attention to her later works as well. Elaine Marks, Hélène Wenzel, Marthe Rosenfeld, and Diane Crowder have all written on the radical break with tradition in the creation of a lesbian language in *Le Corps lesbien*, and *Brouillon* provides a key to Wittig's linguistic universe. The newest works will no doubt inspire much theoretical interest in the reworking of male traditions and the use of epic forms. *Virgile, non* deserves serious study also for its philosophical return to key themes of *Les Guérillères*.

Wittig's essays have had a major impact upon critical theory as well. Her analysis of the relation between language and politics transcends the tensions between "cultural" and "political" feminism. Sometimes erroneously grouped with *Cixous and *Irigaray under the rubric of "l'écriture féminine" (female writing), she is adamantly opposed to exalting female difference. She advocates "lesbian writing" in which the category of sex will be eliminated and language freed from its fetters of male domination.

BIBLIOGRAPHY

Works by Monique Wittig

L'Opoponax. Paris: Minuit, 1964.
"Banlieues." *Nouveau Commerce* 5 (1965): 113–17.
"Lacunary Films." *New Statesman*, July 15, 1966, 102.
L'Amant vert. unpublished 1967.
"Bouvard et Pécuchet." *Les Cahiers Madeleine Renaud-Barrault* 59 (1967): 113–122.
"Voyage: Yallankoro." *Nouveau Commerce* 177 (1967): 558–63.
[Trans.] *L'Homme unidimensional*. Paris: Minuit, 1968. (Trans. of *One Dimensional Man*, by Herbert Marcuse.)
Les Guérillères. Paris: Minuit, 1969.
[With Gilles Wittig, Marcia Rothenburg, and Margaret Stephenson] "Combat pour la libération de la femme." *L'Idiot international* 6 (1970): 13–16.
"Le Grand-Cric-Jules," "Récréation," "Dialogue pour les deux frères et la soeur." Radio plays. Radio Stuttgart, 1972.
Le Corps lesbien. Paris: Minuit, 1973.
"Une Partie de campagne." *Le Nouveau Commerce* 26 (1973): 13–31.
[Trans., with Evelyne Le Garrec and Vera Prado] *Nouvelles lettres portugaises*. Paris: Seuil, 1974. (Trans. of *Novas Cartas Portuguesas*, by the Three Marias [Isabel Barreno, Teresa Horta, and Fatima Velho Da Costa].)
[With Sande Zeig] *Brouillon pour un dictionnaire des amantes*. Paris: Grasset, 1976.
"Un Jour mon prince viendra." *Questions féministes* 2 (1978): 31–39.
"Paradigm." In *Homosexualities and French Literature*. Ed. Elaine Marks and George Stambolian. Ithaca, N.Y.: Cornell University Press, 1979. 114–21.
"The Straight Mind." *Feminist Issues* 1, no. 1 (1980): 103–11. "La Pensée straight." *Questions féministes* 7 (1980). Rpt. in *Amazones d'hier, lesbiennes d'aujourd'hui* 3, no. 4 (1985): 5–18.
"On ne naît pas femme." *Questions féministes* 8 (1980): 75–84. Rpt. in *Amazones d'hier, lesbiennes d'aujourd'hui* 4, no. 1 (1985): 103–18. Translated as "One is not born a woman." *Feminist Issues* 1 no. 2 (1981): 47–54.
[Trans., with "Avant-Note"] *La Passion*. Paris: Flammarion, 1982. (Trans. of *Spillway*, by Djuna Barnes.)
"Les Questions féministes ne sont pas des questions lesbiennes." *Amazones d'hier, lesbiennes d'aujourd'hui* 2, no. 1 (1983): 10–14.
"Les Tchiches et les Tchouches." *Le Genre humaine* 6 (1983): 136–47.
"Le Lieu de l'action." *Digraphe* 32 (1984): 69–75.
"The Trojan Horse." *Feminist Issues* 4, no. 2 (1984): 45–49. "Le Cheval de Troie." *Vlasta* 4 (1985): 36–41.
"The Mark of Gender." *Feminist Issues* 5, no. 2 (1985): 3–12. Rpt. in *The Poetics of Gender*. Ed. Nancy Miller. New York: Columbia University Press, 1986. 63–73.
"Paris-la-Politique." *Vlasta* 4 (1985): 8–35.
Virgile, non. Paris: Minuit, 1985.
Le Voyage sans fin. Vlasta 4 supplement, 1985.
"On the Social Contract." *Feminist Issues* 9, no. 1 (1989): 3–12.

Translations of Monique Wittig

The Opoponax. Trans. H. Weaver. New York: Simon and Schuster, 1976.

Les Guérillères. Trans. David LeVay. London: Peter Owen, 1971. New York: Avon, 1973. Boston: Beacon, 1985.

The Lesbian Body. Trans. David LeVay. London: Peter Owen, 1975. New York: Avon, 1976.

[With Sande Zeig] *Lesbian Peoples: Material for a Dictionary.* New York: Avon, 1979.

"One Is Not Born a Woman." *Feminist Issues* 1, no. 2 (1981): 47–54.

"The Place of Action." In *Three Decades of the New French Novel.* Champaign: University of Illinois Press, 1986.

"The Point of View: Universal or Particular?" *Feminist Issues* 3, no. 2 (1983): 63–69. (Trans. of "Avant-Note" de *La Passion.*)

Across the Acheron. Trans. Margaret Crosland and David LeVay. London: Peter Owen, 1987. (Trans. of *Virgile, non.*)

Studies of Monique Wittig

Bourdet, Denise. "Monique Wittig." *Revue de Paris* 71 (1964): 115–119.

Cluny, Claude-Michel. "La Longue Marche des jeunes filles en fleurs." *Les Lettres françaises* 130 (November 22, 1969): 5–6.

Crosland, Margaret. "The Two-Breasted Amazon." In *Women of Iron and Velvet.* New York: Taplinger, 1976. 211–17.

Crowder, Diane Griffin. "Amazones de . . . demain?: la fiction utopique féministe et lesbienne." *Amazones d'hier, lesbiennes d'aujourd'hui* 2, no. 4 (1984): 19–27.

———. "Amazons or Mothers? Monique Wittig, Hélène Cixous and Theories of Women's Writing." *Contemporary Literature* 24, no. 2 (1983): 117–44.

———. "Une Armée d'amantes: l'image de l'Amazone dans l'oeuvre de Monique Wittig." *Vlasta* 4 (1985): 79–87.

Dalmas, André. "Un Langage nouveau." *Quinzaine littéraire* 83 (November 16–30, 1969): 9.

Duffy, Jean. "Language and Childhood: *L'Opoponax* by Monique Wittig." *Forum for Modern Language Studies* 19, no. 4 (1983): 289–300.

———. "Women and Language in *Les Guérillères* by Monique Wittig." *Stanford French Review* 7, no. 3 (1983): 399–412.

Durand, Laura. "Heroic Feminism as Art." *Novel* 8, no. 1 (1974): 71–77.

Duras, Marguerite. "Une Oeuvre éclatante." *Le Nouvel Observateur* 757 (November 5, 1964): 18–19.

Hawkesworth, Mary E. "Feminist Rhetoric: Discourses on the Male Monopoly of Thought." *Political Theory* 16, no. 3 (1988): 444–67.

Higgins, Lynn. "Nouvelle Nouvelle Autobiography: Monique Wittig's *Le Corps lesbien.*" *Sub-Stance* 14 (1976): 160–66.

Hokenson, Jan. "The Pronouns of Gomorrha: A Lesbian Prose Tradition." *Frontiers* 10, no. 1 (1988): 62–69.

Jean, Raymond. "Le 'Féminaire' de Monique Wittig." In *Pratique de la littérature: roman/poésie.* Ed. Raymond Jean. Paris: Seuil, 1978. 130–32.

Lindsay, Cecile. "Body/Language: French Feminist Utopias." *French Review* 60, no. 1 (1986): 46–55.

Marks, Elaine. "Lesbian Intertextuality." In *Homosexualities and French Literature.* Ed. Elaine Marks and George Stambolian. Ithaca, N.Y.: Cornell University Press, 1979. 353–77.

McCarthy, Mary. "Everybody's Childhood." *New Statesman* (July 15, 1966): 90–94.

Ostrovsky, Erika. "A Cosmogony of O: Monique Wittig's *Les Guérillères.*" In *Twentieth Century French Fiction.* Ed. George Stambolian. New Brunswick, N.J.: Rutgers University Press, 1975. 241–51.

Rosenfeld, Marthe. "Language and the Vision of a Lesbian-Feminist Utopia in Wittig's *Les Guérillères.*" *Frontiers* 6, no. 1 (1981): 6–9.

———. "The Linguistic Aspect of Sexual Conflict: Monique Wittig's *Le Corps lesbien.*" *Mosaic* 17, no. 2 (1984): 235–41.

Shaktini, Namascar. "Displacing the Phallic Subject: Monique Wittig's Lesbian Writing." *Signs* 8 (1982): 29–44.

Simon, Claude. "Pour Monique Wittig." *L'Express* 702 (November 30, 1964): 69–71.

Spraggins, Mary Pringle. "Myth and Liberation in Monique Wittig's *Les Guérillères.*" *International Fiction Review* 3 (1976): 47–51.

Stampanoni, Susanna. "Un Nom pour tout le monde: *L'Opoponax* de Monique Wittig." *Vlasta* 4 (1985): 89–95.

Suleiman, Susan Rubin. "(Re)Writing the Body: The Politics and Poetics of Female Eroticism." In *The Female Body in Western Culture.* Ed. S. R. Suleiman. Cambridge, Mass.: Harvard University Press, 1986. 7–29.

Thiébaux, Marcelle. "A Mythology for Women: Monique Wittig's *Les Guérillères.*" In *The Analysis of Literary Texts.* Ed. Randolph Pope. Third and Fourth York Colloque, Ypsilanti, Mich., 1980. 89–99.

Vlasta 4 (1985). Special issue on Monique Wittig.

Waelti-Walters, Jennifer. "Circle Games in Monique Wittig's *Les Guérillères.*" *Perspectives on Contemporary Literature* 6 (1980): 56–64.

Wenzel, Hélène Vivienne. "Le Discours radical de Monique Wittig." *Vlasta* 4 (1985): 43–52.

———. "The Text as Body/Politics: An Appreciation of Monique Wittig's Writings in Context." *Feminist Studies* 7, no. 2 (1981): 264–87.

MARGUERITE YOURCENAR
(1903–1987)

C. Frederick Farrell, Jr.,
and Edith R. Farrell

Marguerite Yourcenar's value lies in her exemplary style, her many works in all of the major genres, and her success as a role model for twentieth-century readers; her fame was assured by her election to the French Academy as the first woman member in its more than 350-year history.

BIOGRAPHY

Marguerite Antoinette Jeanne Marie Ghislaine Cleenewerke de Crayencour was born on June 8, 1903, and her mother died only ten days later. She spent her first summers on the family estate of Mont Noir near Lille, where she learned, not class consciousness, but an appreciation for the land, the farm animals, and people who live simple lives. About the age of nine, she and her father moved to Paris, where the books, art, and history in its libraries and museums expanded her horizons. Her education was private, directed by tutors and by her father, who taught her Latin at ten and Greek at twelve in addition to an appreciation of the great authors of the world, whose works they read aloud together.

Her first experience of war and exile came in 1914, when she and her father fled and spent a year in England. For the rest of her teens and early twenties, they traveled together, while she read voraciously, especially in history, politics, and the philosophy and literature of the Far East, and began her career as a writer. Her first two books, published privately under her anagram pen name, Yourcenar, show, in embryo form, the themes and images of her opus. In her twenties, she undertook two major projects whose subjects would be the basis for much of her later work. One was a life of the Emperor Hadrian; the other a vast saga covering four centuries of European history, tentatively entitled "Remous" (Eddies). The year 1929 was decisive: her first novel, *Alexis,* a letter from a young bisexual musician to the wife he was leaving, was accepted and published; her father died, penniless; and the Wall Street crash decimated the personal fortune left her by her mother. She had the choice of conserving her remaining money or continuing her leisured life for ten more years. With her habitual disdain for material worries, she decided to spend the 1930s exploring love, Greece, and her abilities as a writer, as she published nine books in six different genres.

La Mort conduit l'attelage (Death Drives the Team, 1934), consisting of segments taken from "Remous," was later to be rewritten into major novels. She has described *Denier du rêve* (*A Coin in Nine Hands*, 1934) as a modern *commedia dell'arte*. It explores daily life in Fascist Italy and centers around Marcella's attempted assassination of "Caesar." *Feux* (*Fires*, 1936) narrates and conceals, in baroque prose poetry, the author's own unhappy love affair, while *Nouvelles orientales* (*Oriental Tales*, 1938) explores other aspects of love. *Le Coup de grâce* (*Coup de Grace*, 1939) depicts Sophie's doomed love for Erick, who in turn loves Conrad, and is set against the somber background of war.

The year 1939 marks another crossroads. Her wealth was gone; World War II prevented her living in Greece; and what had once seemed a stable civilization was being overturned. A friend, Grace Frick, invited Yourcenar to come to America for a six-month lecture tour, and it was here that she made her home for the rest of her life.

Once more an exile, and forced to earn her living for the first time, Yourcenar tried commercial writing and taught, primarily at Sarah Lawrence College. She has called the 1940s a night of the soul and experienced at that time "the despair of a writer who does not write" (*Memoirs of Hadrian*, 323). During this period, she read and reread the classics; participated in Hartford's Athenaeum Theater; translated poetry, including Negro spirituals; and became acquainted with Mt. Desert Island, in Maine. All of her life, up to this time, had been a preparation for the work of her maturity.

She formalized her break with the past in 1947 when she became an American citizen and took her pen name, Yourcenar, as her legal name. In 1948, a trunk she had left in Switzerland before the war arrived, containing, among other things, an almost forgotten effort to write the life of the Emperor Hadrian. This sparked a three-year effort to recreate history from within, using the mystical techniques of Loyola and intense historical investigation in order to give a true picture of the second century.

The result was *Mémoires d'Hadrien* (*Memoirs of Hadrian*, 1951), and it brought Yourcenar onto the international literary scene. It is a compendium of the classical world as well as an account of the accomplishments and thoughts of one outstanding individual who brought peace to the world.

Following this unexpected success and the fame that it brought, Yourcenar devoted herself in the 1950s to rewriting and publishing work that she had done earlier: in the novel, *Denier du rêve*; in poetry, *Charités d'Alcippe* (*The Alms of Alcippe*); in the theater, *Electre* (*Electra*); and in the essay notes published on *Hadrien* and *Electre* that marked the beginning of a new tendency to discuss ideas and literary creation with her readers. She and Grace Frick settled into a modest white house, Petite Plaisance, on Mt. Desert Island, and its rugged ocean coast became part of the rhythm of her life. But it was a time of travel, too, a time to collect the impressions and the material that she would need for the works of the sixties and seventies.

Intending to revise *La Mort conduit l'attelage*, she was again inspired by her philosopher-alchemist, Zeno, who became the hero of *L'Œuvre au noir* (*The Abyss*, 1968), in which the sixteenth century, with its beauty and its violence, its excitement and its fear, its discoveries and its religious and political persecutions, was recreated. Yourcenar wrote this novel about the turmoil of a changing world in the midst of the disruptions of the sixties. And Yourcenar joined in them—as always on the side of the oppressed. She protested the war in Vietnam and the dangers of overpopulation, supported consumer-protection groups, and, especially, worked for the conservation of the earth and its wildlife. In part due to this, her voice became known as a voice of wisdom and her life as a model for life in our century.

Her first collection of essays, *Sous bénéfice d'inventaire* (*The Dark Brain of Piranesi and Other Essays*), was published in 1962. Two more plays appeared, of which *Qui n'a pas son Minotaure?* (*To Each His Minotaur*, 1963) is most clearly the result of the war years, with its scenes evoking deported prisoners and a devouring monster. Her collection of Negro spirituals, *Fleuve profond, sombre rivière* (Deep River, Dark River), was completed, and sections of it were performed and recorded. Finally, translations of the poems of her American friend, Hortense Flexner, testify to her ever-growing attachment to the landscape of Maine.

During the 1970s, Yourcenar continued her work of consolidation, with two volumes of theater in 1971 and a monumental work covering thirteen centuries of Greek poetry, *La Couronne et la lyre* (The Crown and the Lyre, 1979). She also completed two volumes, *Souvenirs Pieux* (Dear Departed, 1973) and *Archives du Nord* (The Archives of Nord, 1979), of a new kind of autobiography, one that begins, "The being I call myself." In it, she traces both lines of her family in Flanders, venturing far back into prehistory, commenting on the world before human beings and then on the history, the ideas, and the art that they have brought into being. Although she was confined to her home by the lingering illness of Grace Frick, who died in November 1979, she continued to expand her own horizons and those of her readers with her translations of James Baldwin, *Le Coin des Amen* (*The Amen Corner*, 1982); a modern Indian woman, "Amrita Pritam: Poèmes" (1983); and Yukio Mishima, *Cinq Nô Modernes* (*Five Modern Nô Plays*, 1984).

In 1980, Yourcenar was already seventy-six years old, but she was entering the period of her greatest productivity—twelve books to date—and the one in which she was most in the public eye. The debate over her (or any woman's) election to the French Academy raged through both the popular and the literary press, finally creating such a scandal that her election was virtually assured by public opinion before the Academicians took their vote.

During her last years she began to travel again as she had during other periods of her life, visiting the Americas, Europe, Africa, and Asia, usually with her new traveling companion, Jerry Wilson. She completed her recasting of *La Mort* with *Comme l'eau qui coule* (*Two Lives and a Dream*), containing *Anna, Soror*, a story of incestuous love in sixteenth-century Naples, *Un Homme obscur* (An Obscure Man) and "Une Belle Matinée" (A Lovely Morning). The last two have protagonists who are neither powerful nor intellectual: Nathanaël, the "obscure man," accepts life's gifts and trials as he finds them, while his son, Lazare, in the last story, sets out to be a strolling actor. Both have an ability that Yourcenar prized: to see the world as it is and still to marvel at it.

She wrote both at home and while she traveled, publishing a collection of some of her best essays, *Le Temps, ce grand sculpteur* (*That Mighty Sculptor, Time*), *Blues et gospels* (Blues and Gospel Songs), an expanded volume of original poetry, and *La Voix des choses* (The Voices of Things), a collection of readings that had guided her in her life, illustrated with photographs by Jerry Wilson. She also worked on the last volume of her autobiography, *Quoi? L'Éternité* (What? Eternity), dealing with her early life with her father. Never finished, it was brought out posthumously in 1988. Still other work remains to be published.

This output was not accomplished easily. Marguerite Yourcenar continued her interests and her work until the end, despite injuries from an automobile accident and the recurrent bronchial and heart problems from which she had suffered for years. In the fall of 1987, she gave two major addresses, one on "superpollution" in Canada and one at Harvard on Jorge Luis Borges, a close personal friend whose work she admired. On November 8 she suffered the stroke that ultimately caused her death on December 17.

She will be remembered for the purity of her language; the breadth of her interests; the steadfastness of her support for the oppressed; the open-mindedness that allowed her to see the value in all peoples and beliefs; and for a life in which the petty and the selfish were subordinated to what she saw as the greater good.

MAJOR THEMES

The themes in Marguerite Yourcenar's work combine to form a picture of a universe, not merely a world. Like her subjects, they have remained remarkably constant. Her classical education focused her attention early on the individual's potential for good or evil as depicted in Greek literature and on the organization, functioning, and changes of society as seen by the Romans. To this was added Oriental thought and direct experiences with many countries. The result was an author who considered herself a citizen of the world, open to all that it had to offer in any place and from any time. Not only did she consider nothing human to be alien to her, but the natural universe, in its extent and evolution, and the many conceptions of the supernatural were accepted and incorporated into her worldview.

Despite the presence of these constants, we find a shift in her treatment of them. Beginning with abstracts, she moved to a more differentiated view of her subjects; her optimistic view of society became more pessimistic. Going beyond the human, she turned to the earth in its geological reality and to a contemplation of the infinite that causes a reordering of human values.

All of her works are informed and enriched by the extent of her interests and knowledge. Her characters and milieus always carry with them references, implicit or explicit, to humanity in general, to the arts, and to the sweep of history. Specific beliefs or customs are seen in a cross-cultural context that makes of human wisdom or folly an accumulation of the ages.

Marguerite Yourcenar's view that life is sacred led her to an appreciation for every individual, and this feeling permeates her works. She insisted that she made no distinction of class, education, or talent among her friends; some of her characters of whose value she spoke most eloquently are those of humble origins or limited abilities who celebrate life in the living of it. They include Lina, the prostitute in *Denier du rêve;* Nathanaël, the protagonist of *Comme l'eau qui coule*; and the many ancestors whom she knew only by name, if that, in her autobiography. In *Les Yeux ouverts (With Open Eyes)*, she quotes the Chinese monk who wrote, "What a miracle! I sweep the courtyard and go to the well for water" (238).

This sense of the "infinitely sacred" often led her, particularly in *Feux* and *Denier du rêve*, to make of her characters human avatars of their mythical or divine prototypes. Such a view also made of her a champion of the oppressed and of victims of prejudice, a theme that recurs in most of her works. Zeno, of *L'Œuvre au noir*, a character that she said she loved like a brother, is perhaps the best-rounded example. He runs counter to the norm in that he is bisexual in a rigid society; intellectually curious in a seminary whose students' only goal is to meet the minimum requirements; and a free-thinker at a time when that was dangerous. He is actively oppressed for his medical research, including dissection, which was illegal; for his books, which were banned and burned; and for his heresy, for which he himself was sentenced to be burned at the stake.

Other groups of oppressed people who play important roles in her work include the citizens of Fascist Italy in *Denier du rêve*, innocent victims of war in *Coup de grâce*, and slaves in *Hadrien*. Women are usually not treated as any more oppressed than their male counterparts, although in *Labyrinthe du monde* (The World's Labyrinth) Yourcenar does stress the dangers of unrestrained childbearing.

Her concern for life extends to animals, considered as worthy of respect and dignity as human beings in such novels as *Denier* and, expressed even more forcefully, in her essays. She advocates actively caring for the earth, a theme she associates particularly with humble people.

She has been criticized for dwelling over-much on death, especially since Hadrian tells his story while on his deathbed, but she defended herself by saying that only at the end of a life can one see the whole picture. She shared Hadrian's view that death is the beginning of another adventure, and that one should try to enter it "with open eyes."

The desire to die with dignity or for a purpose implies the theme of suicide, which is present either in reality or symbolically in many of her works: Icarus's death, in *Le Jardin des chimères* (The Garden of the Chimeras, 1921), is a kind of suicide, as is the failed assassination attempt in *Denier* and Antigone's defiance in *Feux*; Hadrian considers suicide and gives it up because of a conflict with his duty as emperor; Rémo, in *Souvenir Pieux*, is a historical example; and Zeno uses his death as a means of accomplishing his alchemical Great Work instead of providing a spectacle for his enemies.

Love, in a wide range of forms—heterosexual, bisexual, homosexual, incestuous, maternal, and divine—is one of Yourcenar's primary themes and a sufficient justification of many of her characters' lives. In her lexicon, love is not necessarily for another human being. *Feux* gives the best expression of this multiplicity, for in the nine sketches, the characters, nearly all women, dedicate their lives to another human being, man or woman, to God, or an absolute, such as justice or wisdom.

She makes a careful distinction between love and pleasure—or the soul and the body. Both of them have a rightful place in life, and Yourcenar considers that the modern idea of sublimation is "an unfortunate term and one that insults the body" (*Fires*, xxii). Many of her characters—Alexis is the first—do not consider them to be necessarily linked. The large number of bisexual or homosexual characters, men and women, makes this distinction easier. It also allows her to extend her theme of oppression to those who are persecuted or disdained because of their sexual orientation or practices.

Marriage is a subordinate theme, and its images are nearly always negative: "When you talk about a hearth, sometimes you are talking about burning coals" (*Archives du Nord*, 80). She had, in fact, an extremely exalted view of marriage and motherhood, as shown by the legendary young wife in "Le Lait de la mort" (The Milk of Death) in *Nouvelles orientales*, but she saw only too clearly that most do not measure up to these standards. Real marriages have often involved inequality—even servitude—for the wife in addition to the dangers of childbirth. The ideal relationship, in her view, is the Hindu maithuma, in which the woman plays the role of goddess for the man. The lover as god is a major theme of *Feux*.

The traditional images of woman as Mary or Eve are made explicit by the old priest Campanus in *L'Œuvre*, but are also illustrated elsewhere. The commentary on love in *Denier* contrasts Marcella, who is capable of great love, and Angiola, who tempts men in order to profit from them, while Rosalia and Dida each represent the nurturing woman on two different levels of society and understanding. Women who are cold, egocentric, and self-serving are always condemned, perhaps even more than men with these same characteristics; those representing Mary Magdalene are prized. The most valued women, like Plotina in *Hadrien* and the Lady of Froso in *L'Œuvre*, are called *parèdres* (consorts of a god).

Yourcenar has been considered a moralist, and it is certain that ethical values and religious themes play a dominant role in her opus. She values and promotes understanding among every people and time in order to avoid the conflicts caused by narrow-mindedness. Her great historical novels paint exact pictures of their times so that readers can realize how the characters are unconsciously shaped by the dominant views of their age and how universal understanding can reduce these prejudices.

She is staunchly opposed to the abuse of any kind of power: individual, as Conrad, in *Coup de grâce*, abuses the power that love gives him over Sophie; social, as the "right-thinking" citizens of *Labyrinthe* condemn all who disagree with them; religious, as the church leaders in *L'Œuvre* condemn Zeno; or political, as the Fascist state cripples its people in *Denier*.

This sympathy for the downtrodden applies even to people with whom she does not agree. She sympathizes with a group of witches in *Archives du Nord* because they have no other interest in a life of very hard work, and she compares the satisfactions they get from their secret meetings to our release through dancing and drugs (73).

Themes of purity, especially among small groups like the revolutionaries in *Denier* or the conspirators in *Electre;* justice, as it is seen in "Antigone" in *Feux*; freedom, not only political freedom, but detachment from material possessions; peace, to allow the free development of one's life; generosity; and renunciation underlie many of her plots and characters.

In one of many forms, the divine is ever-present in her works, and union with it is the goal of the author and many of her characters, who search for ways of going beyond personal or human limitations. Love is one of the primary means. Various forms of initiation, both actual, like Hadrian's experiences with the cults of Mithra and Eleusis, for example, or symbolic, like her grandfather's ascent of Mt. Etna in *Labyrinthe*, or the rites surrounding childbirth, are among the common means of finding the universal in life. Meditation, like her own use of St. Ignatius of Loyola's methods to participate with her historical characters, is cultivated by her characters as a means of rising above the human condition, as are other paths, like Zeno's study of alchemy.

Dreams—her own, in *Les Songes et les sorts* (Dreams and Destinies), and those of her characters—are a means of contact with the beyond. A major device of *Denier* is the contrast between the characters as they view themselves in dream and the limitations they face in their everyday lives. Dreams are sources of images that can inspire a life or great works of art, which, with myths, are repositories of the dreams of a people or the highest points that its civilization has attained.

Much of the richness of Yourcenar's work lies in this multilayered perspective on the world. On the one hand, the realistic lives of her people are portrayed with ever more specific and telling detail. At the other end of the spectrum are the ideals they espouse, the dreams that enrich their thinking and emotional responses, the values that they support, and the form of the divine that they worship. In the course of reading the opus, Yourcenar's readers can find the conditions of life in many times and places by which they can better judge their own. They find, too, an indication of new sources of inspiration and enjoyment that allow them to move beyond the limitations of their historical period.

SURVEY OF CRITICISM

Marguerite Yourcenar did not receive a great deal of critical attention during the first three decades of her career. It was not until *Mémoires d'Hadrien* that she captured the attention of the general public in France, and academic criticism lagged almost another three decades behind. The esteem in which she was held is more visible in the honors, awards, and prizes that she received than in the critical studies that were devoted to her.

Those who did admire her work, however, were extremely loyal, and often eminent artists and critics. Her first work, *Le Jardin des chimères*, was labeled by one French critic as very long and very dull, but the Nobel laureate Rabindranath Tagore was so impressed with the work of the eighteen-year-old author that he invited her to come and live in India.

Her father served as her early critic: his paying for the publication of her first two works was indicative of his faith in her. The only novel that he lived to read, however, was *Alexis*. After his death, Yourcenar found a note in his copy saying that he had never read anything as clear as *Alexis*.

None of her books in the 1930s attracted a great deal of critical acclaim at the time, but Edmond Jaloux stands out among those who recognized her early. He wrote very perceptive and laudatory reviews of her early books, and, in appreciation, Yourcenar dedicated *Denier du rêve* to him. Her reputation might have grown more quickly if Jaloux had not been accused of collaboration and discredited after World War II.

It is particularly unfortunate that Yourcenar's work was not reviewed more, since she was an author who took the reactions of readers and critics very seriously, to the point of calling a book that had been through multiple editions a kind of collaboration between author and reader. Late in life she spoke of her gratitude toward reviewers of *La Mort*, who encouraged her, and expressed her regret that *Denier* lacked the "patina" acquired by others' reactions. *Coup de grâce*, now considered one of her best works, came out in the summer of 1939, when the world's attention was elsewhere.

It was not until *Hadrien* that critics began to notice her. Even then, many thought it a unique masterpiece, at a level that the author could never match. It was much admired by Thomas Mann, however, won the Femina-Vacaressco Prize, and was crowned by the French Academy; its English translation received the *New York Times'* Page One Award. Later in the decade, *Sous bénéfice*, and her entire opus, received the Prix Combat.

The 1960s and early 1970s saw an increasing number of honors: honorary doctorates from Smith, Bowdoin, and Colby, and election to the *Académie royale belge de langue et de littérature françaises*. One of the best early overviews of her work was the address by Carlo Bronne on the occasion of her reception.

Her work was regularly reviewed by such critics as Robert Kanters in *Le Figaro littéraire*, Mathieu Galey in *L'Express*, Yvon Bernier in *Il Faut Lire* (Canada), and Stephen Koch in the *New York Times* and the *Saturday Review*. Interviews, both in print and on radio and television, became common. They include an edition of *"L'Express* va plus loin avec . . . "* ("L'Express* goes further with . . . "*) and "Radioscopie," for which Jacques Chancel devoted an entire week instead of the usual day. There have also been a number of special issues of journals in France and other countries devoted to her work.

Until about 1980, the majority of critics tended to follow certain well-worn lines. Yourcenar was routinely praised for her great learning, her outstanding re-creations of characters and historical periods, and her classical style. She was just as regularly criticized for spending too much of her time rewriting instead of creating new works, for "burying herself" in the past, for not giving an important enough place to women, and for concealing personal experiences that had contributed to her work.

Some critics were also somewhat shocked by the amount of homosexuality in her books and by Yourcenar's refusal to give preference to French artists over those of other countries and to Christianity over other religions in her books and interviews. It was not until late in her career that critics considered that her inclinations in these matters were justifiable and justified.

She was elected to the Legion of Honor (1971) and awarded the Prix littéraire de Monaco (1972), the Grand prix national de la culture (1974), the Grand prix de l'Académie française (1977), and an honorary doctorate from Harvard (1981). Yourcenar also received a distinction rarer than any of the preceding: her works were collected in a Pléiade edition, an acknowledgment that they are destined to become classics. She was nominated for the Nobel Prize in literature.

Jean Blot wrote the first book on Yourcenar. In it he gives a broad overview of her career, although his remarks are occasionally patronizing. Three books on her have come out since 1983 in the United States: Farrell and Farrell's collection of essays in 1983; Horn's Twayne series book (1985) and Schurr's volume (1987), which provide introductions to her work; and such well-known scholars and critics as Moses Hades, Joseph Epstein, Wallace Fowlie, and Henri Peyre have written on her work.

Important European contributions include the studies of Maurice Delcroix

(Belgium), Biondi and Rosso (Italy), and Elena Real (Spain); Poignault's thesis
on Hadrian; Spencer-Noël's work on the theme of alchemy; and Andersson's
study of death in four of Yourcenar's novels.

Much of the current critical effort is being orchestrated by the International
Yourcenar Society, which publishes a *Bulletin* and holds colloquia about every
two years in which leading Yourcenar specialists contribute papers on the specific
theme chosen for the conference. These collections are in the process of being
published by the universities of Valencia, Pavia, and Tours.

Now that overviews have been established and broad subject areas explored,
the second generation of academic critics is beginning to reexamine Yourcenar's
works in the light of a number of different critical perspectives. The large
collection of manuscripts and correspondence currently being sorted and cata-
logued at the Houghton Library of Harvard University will allow more extensive
and informed stylistic studies than have been possible up to now.

Although some predicted that interest in Yourcenar would diminish after her
death, because they thought that her personality was stronger than the appeal of
her books, this has not proved to be the case. Rather, critical attention is growing
just as her reputation did—a little slowly, but at an increasing pace.

BIBLIOGRAPHY

Major Works by Marguerite Yourcenar

Le Jardin des chimères. Paris: Perrin, 1921.

Les Dieux ne sont pas morts. Paris: Sansot, 1922.

Alexis; ou, Le Traité du vain combat. Paris: Sans Pareil, 1929. Rev. ed. Plon, 1965.
    With *Coup de grâce*, Gallimard, 1978.

La Nouvelle Eurydice. Paris: Grasset, 1931.

Pindare. Paris: Grasset, 1932.

La Mort conduit l'attelage. Paris: Grasset, 1934.

Denier du rêve. Paris: Grasset, 1934. Rev. ed. Plon, 1959. Defin. ed. Gallimard, 1971.

Feux. Paris: Grasset, 1936. Rev. ed. Gallimard, 1974.

[Trans.] *Les Vagues*. Paris: Stock, 1937. (Trans. of *The Waves*, by Virginia Woolf.)

Les Songes et les sorts. Paris: Grasset, 1938.

Nouvelles orientales. Paris: Gallimard, 1938. Rev. eds. 1963, 1975.

Le Coup de grâce. Paris: Gallimard, 1939. Rev. ed. with *Alexis*, 1978.

[Trans.] *Ce que savait Maisie*. Paris: Laffont, 1947. (Trans. of *What Maisie Knew*, by
    Henry James.)

Mémoires d'Hadrien. Paris: Plon, 1951. With "Carnets." Paris: Club du Meilleur Livre,
    1953. Rev. ed. illus. Paris: Gallimard, 1971.

L'Écrivain devant l'histoire. Paris: Centre National de Documentation Pédagogique, 1954.

Électre: ou La Chute des masques. Paris: Plon, 1954.

"Carnets de notes d'*Electre*." *Théâtre de France* (1954): n.p.

"Carnet de notes 1942–1948." *Table Ronde* (1955): 83–90.

Les Charités d'Alcippe & autres poèmes. Liège: Flûte Enchantée, 1956. Rev. ed. ex-
    panded. Paris: Gallimard, 1984.

Preface to *Gita Govinda*, by Jayadeva. Trans. François D. Dio. Paris: Emile-Paul, 1957.

Présentation critique de Constantin Cavafy, 1863–1933. Paris: Gallimard, 1958. Rev. ed., 1978.

Sous bénéfice d'inventaire. Paris: Gallimard, 1962. Rev. ed. 1978.

Le Mystère d'Alceste, suivi de Qui n'a pas son Minotaure? Paris: Plon, 1963.

Preface to *Les Prisons imaginaires*, by Giovanni Battista Piranesi. Paris: Kieffer, 1964.

[Trans., comp., and ed.] *Fleuve profond, sombre rivière: Les Negro Spirituals*. Paris: Gallimard, 1964.

L'Œuvre au noir. Paris: Gallimard, 1968.

Présentation critique d'Hortense Flexner. Paris: Gallimard, 1968.

Théâtre. 2 vols. Paris: Gallimard, 1971.

Discours de réception à l'Académie royale belge de langue et de littérature françaises, 19 mars 1971. Includes the speech of Carlo Bronne. Paris: Gallimard, 1971.

Souvenirs pieux, suivi de L'Album de Fernande. Monaco: Editions Alphée, 1973. Paris: Gallimard, 1974. First volume of *Le Labyrinthe du monde*.

Archives du Nord. Paris: Gallimard, 1977. Second volume of *Labyrinthe*.

[Trans., comp., and ed.] *La Couronne et la lyre: Poèmes traduits du grec*. Paris: Gallimard, 1979.

Mishima, ou la vision du vide. Paris: Gallimard, 1980.

Les Yeux ouverts, entretiens avec Matthieu Galey. Paris: Editions du Centurion, 1980.

Discours de réception de Mme Marguerite Yourcenar à l'Académie française et réponse de M. Jean D'Ormesson. Paris: Gallimard, 1981.

Comme l'eau qui coule. Paris: Gallimard, 1982. Contains "Anna Soror . . . ," "Un Homme obscur," and "Une Belle Matinée."

[Trans.] *Le Coin des "Amen,"* by James Baldwin. Paris: Gallimard, 1982. (Trans. of *The Amen Corner*.)

Œuvres romanesques. Paris: Gallimard, 1982. The first of two volumes of complete works.

Le Temps, ce grand sculpteur. Paris: Gallimard, 1983.

[Trans., with Rajesh Sharma and Charles Brasch] "Amrita Pritam: Poèmes." *Nouvelle Revue Française* 365 (1983): 166–78.

[Comp. and trans.] *Blues et gospels*. Paris: Gallimard, 1984.

[Trans. with Jun Shiragi.] *Cinq Nô modernes*. Paris: Gallimard, 1985.

[Comp. and trans.] *Le Cheval noir à tête blanche*. Paris: Gallimard, 1985.

"Les Trente-trois noms de Dieu." *Nouvelle Revue Française* 401 (1986): 101–17.

[Comp. and ed.] *La Voix des choses*. Paris: Gallimard, 1987.

Quoi? L'Éternité. Paris: Gallimard, 1988.

Translations of Marguerite Yourcenar

Alexis. Trans. Walter Kaiser in collaboration with the author. New York: Farrar, Straus and Giroux, 1984.

A Coin in Nine Hands. Trans. Dori Katz in collaboration with the author. New York: Farrar, Straus and Giroux, 1982; Henley-on-Thames: Ellis, 1984. (Trans. of *Denier du rêve*.)

Fires. Trans. Dori Katz in collaboration with the author. New York: Farrar, Straus and Giroux, 1981; Henley-on Thames: Ellis, 1982. (Trans. of *Feux*.)

Oriental Tales. Trans. Alberto Manguel in collaboration with the author. New York:

Farrar, Straus and Giroux, 1985; Henley-on-Thames: Ellis, 1985. (Trans. of *Nouvelles orientales.*)

Coup de Grace. Trans. Grace Frick in collaboration with the author. New York: Farrar, Straus and Cudahy, 1957; London: Secker and Warburg, 1957. Rev. ed. New York: Farrar, Straus and Giroux, 1981; Henley-on-Thames: Ellis, 1983.

Memoirs of Hadrian. Trans. Grace Frick in collaboration with the author. New York: Farrar, Straus and Young, 1954; London: Secker and Warburg, 1955. Rev. ed. *Memoirs of Hadrian and Reflections on the Composition of "Memoirs of Hadrian."* New York: Farrar, Straus, 1963; London: Secker and Warburg, 1974.

The Alms of Alcippe. Trans. Edith R. Farrell. New York: Targ Editions, 1982. (Trans. of *Les Charités d'Alcippe.*)

The Dark Brain of Piranesi and Other Essays. Trans. Richard Howard and Grace Frick in collaboration with the author. New York: Farrar, Straus and Giroux, 1984; Henley-on-Thames: Ellis, 1985. (Trans. of *Sous bénéfice d'inventaire.*)

The Abyss. Trans. Grace Frick in collaboration with the author. New York: Farrar, Straus and Giroux, 1976; London: Weidenfeld and Nicolson, 1976. (Trans. of *L'Œuvre au noir.*)

Plays. Trans. Dori Katz in collaboration with the author. New York: Performing Arts Journal Publications, 1984. Contains only four of the plays: *Render unto Caesar, The Little Mermaid, Electra,* and *To Each His Minotaur.*

Mishima: A Vision of the Void. Trans. Alberto Manguel. Henley-on-Thames: Ellis, 1986; New York: Farrar, Straus and Giroux, 1987.

With Open Eyes: Conversations with Matthieu Galey. Trans. Arthur Goldhammer. Boston: Beacon Press, 1984. (Trans. of *Les Yeux ouverts.*)

Two Lives and a Dream. Trans. Walter Kaiser in collaboration with the author. New York: Farrar, Straus and Giroux, 1987; Henley-on-Thames: Ellis, 1987. (Trans. of *Comme l'eau qui coule.*)

That Mighty Sculptor, Time. Trans. Walter Kaiser in collaboration with the author. Henley-on-Thames: Ellis, 1987; New York: Farrar, Straus and Giroux, 1988. (Trans. of *Le Temps, ce grand sculpteur.*)

Studies of Marguerite Yourcenar

Andersson, Kaysa. *Le Don sombre: le thème de la mort dans quatre romans de Marguerite Yourcenar.* Uppsala, Sweden: Acta Universitatis Upsaliensis, 1989.

Biondi, C., and C. Russo, eds. *Voyage et connaissance dans l'œuvre de Marguerite Yourcenar.* Pisa: Editrice Libreria Goliardica, 1988.

Blot, Jean. *Marguerite Yourcenar.* 1971. Paris: Séghers, 1976.

Bossuges, Madeleine. *Sagesse et mystique.* Grenoble: Editions des Cahiers de l'Alpe-Société des Écrivains Dauphinois, 1987.

Bronne, Carlo. See *Discours de réception à l'Académie royale belge de langue et de littérature française* in "Major Works" section, above.

Delacroix, Maurice. "Clair de femme dans *Un Homme obscur* de Marguerite Yourcenar." *Ouverture et Dialogue*, Mélanges offerts à W. Leiner. Tübingen: Gunter Narr Verlag, 1988. 639–51.

———. "La Mort dans l'œuvre narrative de Marguerite Yourcenar." In *La Mort en toutes lettres.* Ed. Gilles Ernst. Nancy: Presses Universitaires de Nancy, 1983. 205–15.

Epstein, Joseph. "Read Marguerite Yourcenar." *Commentary* 74, no. 2 (1982): 60–65.

Farrell, C. Frederick Jr., and Edith R. Farrell. *Marguerite Yourcenar in Counterpoint.* Lanham, Md.: University Press of America, 1983.

———. "Title as Image: Le Chef rouge/La Veuve Aphrodissia." *Romanic Review* 74, no. 2 (1983): 233–44.

Gaudin, Colette. "Marguerite Yourcenar's Prefaces: Genesis as Self-Effacement." *Studies in Twentieth-Century Literature* 10, no. 1 (1985): 31–55.

Harris, Nadia. "Les 'Jeux de construction' dans l'œuvre de Marguerite Yourcenar." *French Review* 62, no. (1988): 292–99.

Horn, Pierre. *Marguerite Yourcenar.* Boston: Twayne, 1985.

Nunn, R. R., and E. J. Geary. *The Yourcenar Collection: A Descriptive Catalogue.* Brunswick, M.: Bowdoin College, 1984.

Peyre, Henri. "Marguerite Yourcenar: Independent, Imaginative and 'Immortal.' " *World Literature Today* 57 (1983): 191–94.

Poignault, Rémy. *Le Personnage d'Hadrien dans "Mémoires d'Hadrien" de Marguerite Yourcenar.* In *Littérature et Histoire.* 2 vols. Tours: L'Université de Tours, n.d.

Real, Elena, ed. *Marguerite Yourcenar, actes du colloque international. Valencia (Espagna) 1984.* Valencia: Universitat de Valencia, 1986.

———, ed. *Marguerite Yourcenar. Biographie, Autobiographie, Actes du IIᵉ colloque international, Valencia, October, 1986.* Valencia: Universitat de Valencia, 1988.

Rutledge, H. C. "Marguerite Yourcenar: The Classicism of *Feux* and *Mémoires d'Hadrien*." *Classical and Modern Literature: A Quarterly* 4, no. 2 (1984): 87–99.

Shurr, Georgia Hooks. *Marguerite Yourcenar: A Reader's Guide.* Lanham, Md.: University Press of America, 1987.

Soos, Emese. "The Only Motion Is Returning: The Metaphor of Alchemy in Mallet-Joris and Yourcenar." *French Forum* 4 (1970): 3–16.

Spencer-Noël, Geneviève. *Zénon ou le thème de l'alchimie dans "L'Œuvre au noir" de Marguerite Yourcenar.* Paris: Éditions A.-G. Nizet, 1981.

Stillman, Linda Klieger. " 'L'Amour au noir' de Marguerite Yourcenar." In *Le Récit amoureux.* Ed. Didier Coste et al. Paris: Champ Vallon, 1984.

Watson-Williams, Helen. "Hadrian's Story Recalled." *Nottingham French Studies* 23 (1984): 35–48.

Whatley, Janet. "*Mémoires d'Hadrien*: A Manual for Princes." *University of Toronto Quarterly* 50 (1980–81): 221–37.

Interviews, Tributes, and Special Editions of Journals

Bernier, Yvon. Presentation. *Les Adieux du Québec à Marguerite Yourcenar.* Quebec: Les Presses Laurentiennes, 1988.

Bernier, Yvon, and Vincent Nadeau, eds. *Marguerite Yourcenar.* Special issue of *Etudes littéraires* 12, no. 1 (1979): 7–116.

" 'L'Express' va plus loin avec Marguerite Yourcenar." *L'Express* 917 (1969): 47–52.

Livres de France 5 (1964): 2–14.

Marguerite Yourcenar. Mont Noir, France, n.d. A small volume done by the village of Mont Noir.

Marguerite Yourcenar. Special issue of *Sud* 55 (1984): 5–87.

Radioscopie. Created by Jacques Chancel. Radio-France. Paris. June 11–15, 1979.

Rosbo, Patrick de. *Entretiens radiophoniques avec Marguerite Yourcenar*. Paris: Mercure de France, 1972.

Société Internationale D'Études Yourcenariennes. *Bulletin*. Tours: Caesarodunum, 1987–

Addendum to Studies of Marguerite Yourcenar

Savigneau, Josyane. *Marguerite Yourcenar: l'Invention d'une vie*. Gallimard, 1990.

APPENDIX A: SITUATING WOMEN WRITERS IN FRENCH HISTORY: A CHRONOLOGY

Julia Lauer-Chéenne

An asterisk indicates that a chapter on this writer is included in this volume.

406	Gaul invaded by the Franks.
507	Clovis establishes Paris as the capital of France. Salic law enacted which, in the fourteenth century, will be interpreted to mean that women cannot accede to the throne of France.
8th and 9th centuries	Women acquire property and inheritance rights.
800	Charlemagne crowned emperor and creates office of queen consort whereby crowned women actively participate in royal rule.
829	Council of Paris prohibits divorce except in cases of impotence and physiological incapacity.
10th and 11th centuries	Churchmen encourage antifeminist attitudes and blame Eve for evil in the world. Roger de Caen writes *Carmen de mundi contemptu* (Song of Contempt for the World) in which he states that women should be avoided because they are a great danger.
1031	Council of Bourges reiterates prohibitions against priests and deacons having wives or concubines.
1066	Norman conquest of England.
1095–99	First Crusade.
	La Chanson de Roland.
1071–1127	Guillaume IX d'Aquitaine, the earliest known troubadour, writes lyrics that celebrate courtly love and others that are erotic and licentious.

1101   Fontevrault is founded by Robert d'Arbrissel, who preaches a new spiritualism. Women and men who belong to this order are placed under the supreme authority of an abbess.

               Birth of Héloïse.

1128–34   Abélard-Héloïse correspondence.

1152   Louis VII repudiates Aliénor d'Aquitaine, who marries Henri Plantagenet, the future Henry II of England.

1165   Chrétien de Troyes begins his series of Arthurian romances.

1170–1260   The trobairitz, women troubadours, flourish in the south of France.

1175   Comical animal satires and parodies are collected in *Le Roman de renart*.

1180?   ˙Marie de France: *Lais*.

1185   André le Chapelain writes *De amore* and other courtly literature in which he lists female vices.

1190   First fabliaux. This genre continues through the thirteenth century and characterizes women as crafty, sensual, and perverted in their relationships with men.

13th century   Creation of the universities.

               Founding of University of Paris by statutes of the Fourth Lateran Council.

1215   Inquisition created to question and identify suspected heretics.

1220   Guillaume de Lorris writes the first part of the *Roman de la rose*.

1226–52   Blanche of Castile, Queen of France, acts as Regent for her son, Louis IX; crusades launched against the Albigensians.

1275   Part Two of *Roman de la rose* by Jean de Meung has a misogynistic stance.

1293   Pope Boniface VIII issues decree cloistering all nuns.

1310   Marguerite Porete's *Mirror of Simple Souls* is declared heretical, and she is burned to death.

1348   Bubonic plague devastates Europe.

1364   ˙Birth of Christine de Pizan.

1370   Froissart: *Chroniques*.

1399   Christine de Pizan's *Epître au dieu d'amour* lays groundwork for her defense of women against the misogynism of the *Roman de la rose*.

1400–1403   Christine de Pizan responds to misogynistic elements of *Roman de la rose* in a series of letters to early humanists Jean de Montreuil and Jean and Pierre Col, thus becoming the first woman known to have participated in a literary controversy in France. This dispute concerning the nature of women and their relationships with men and society became known as the *querelle des femmes*.

Early 15th century	*Les Quinze Joyes du mariage*, which portrays woman as a matrimonial demon, fuels the *querelle*.
1429	Joan of Arc defeats English at Orléans. Christine de Pizan writes poem in her honor.
1431	Joan of Arc is burned at the stake in Rouen. Gutenberg invents the printing press in Strasbourg.
1440–42	Martin le Franc supports women in *Le Champion des dames*.
1461	Villon: *Le Grand Testament*.
1486	Jacob Sprenger, a German inquisitor, and Heinrich Kramer, write *Malleus Maleficarum* (The Hammer of Witchcraft), a manual promoting witchhunting and the idea of women as satanic agents.
1492	*Birth of Marguerite de Navarre.
1510	*Birth of Hélisenne de Crenne.
1520	*Birth of Pernette du Guillet.
1522	*Birth of Louise Labé.
1526	Erasmus disparages women in *Institutis Christiani Matrimonii* (*The Institution of Christian Marriage*).
1528	Castiglione's *Il Corteggiano* (*The Courtier*), a manual of courtly behavior, becomes popular and is translated into French in 1537.
1530	François Ier creates the first educational institution outside the university, which will become the Collége de France.
1532	Rabelais: *Pantagruel*.
1537	Translation into French of Henry Cornélius Agrippa's *De nobilitate et praecellentia foeminei sexus* (*Of the Nobility and Excellence of the Feminine Sex*), which extols women.
1538	Hélisenne de Crenne: *Les Angoisses douloureuses qui procèdent d'amours*.
1539	Hélisenne de Crenne: *Epîtres invectives de madame Helisenne*.
1541	Jean Calvin's *Institution chrétienne* translated into French.
1542	Antoine Héroët writes *La Parfaite Amye*, a poem that describes the perfect court woman.
1544	Maurice Scève: *Délie*.
1545	Pernette du Guillet: *Rimes*.
1546	Rabelais: *Tiers Livre*.
1549	Du Bellay: *Défense et illustration de la langue française*.
1550	Ronsard: *Odes*.
1553	Guillaume Postel's *Les Très Merveilleuses Victoires des femmes du nouveau monde* is a mystical presentation of women's virtues.

1555	François de Billon in *Le Fort inexpugnable de l'honneur du sexe féminin* preaches equality of the sexes.
	Louise Labé: *Débat de folie et d'amour*.
1555–56	Ronsard: *Amours de Marie*; *Hymnes*.
1558	Publication of Marguerite de Navarre's *Heptaméron* (written between 1546 and 1549), a collection of stories that present, among other subjects, the personal and social concerns of women.
1559	Henri II is killed in a tournament in Paris.
	Amyot: Translation of *Vies Parallèles de Plutarque*.
1560	Catherine de Médici becomes Regent.
1562	Wars of Religion begin.
1572	At the Saint Barthélémy massacre thousands of Protestants are killed in Paris. The responsibility falls on Catherine de Médici.
1580	Jean Bodin, the distinguished humanist, promotes witch hunting in *La Démonomanie des sorciers*.
	Montaigne: first edition of his *Essais*.
1589	Assassination of Henri III. The Catholic majority distrust his Protestant heir, Henri IV. After converting to Catholicism Henri IV is crowned king.
1595	*Marie de Gournay publishes her edition of Montaigne's *Essais* with coeditor Pierre de Brach.
1598	Edict of Nantes grants freedom of worship to Protestants.
1607	*Birth of Madeleine de Scudéry.
1609	Angélique Arnauld reforms the convent of Port-Royal, which will become a center of Jansenism in the middle of the century.
1610	The Marquise de Rambouillet creates the *chambre bleue*, the inner sanctum of her suite of salons, which for decades functions as an alternative court where power is exercised through conversation. After the assassination of Henri IV, Marie de Médici is Regent for her son, Louis XIII.
1619	Honoré d'Urfé publishes Part I of *L'Astrée*, a popular pastoral novel.
1622	Marie de Gournay: *Egalité des hommes et des femmes* (*Of the Equality of Men and Women*).
1626	Marie de Gournay rejects the notion of female inferiority in *Le Grief des dames* (*The Complaint of the Ladies*).
	*Birth of Marie de Rabutin-Chantal, marquise de Sévigné.
1632	Théophraste Renaudot organizes La Société des conférences to educate women by means of oral lectures.

1634	Académie française founded by Richelieu.
	*Birth of Marie-Madeleine Pioche de La Vergne, comtesse de Lafayette.
1637	Corneille: *Le Cid*.
	Descartes: *Discours de la méthode*.
1640	*Birth of Marie-Catherine Desjardins de Villedieu.
1642	Madeleine de Scudéry publishes *Les Femmes illustres ou les Harangues héroïques* under her brother's name.
1643	Death of Louis XIII.
	Anne d'Autriche becomes Regent for her son, Louis XIV.
	Vaugelas: *Remarques sur la langue française*.
1649–53	Madeleine de Scudéry: *Arthamène ou le Grand Cyrus*.
1651	*Birth of Marie-Catherine Le Jumel de Barneville, comtesse d'Aulnoy.
1654	Madeleine de Scudéry's influential novel, *Clélie*, marks the resurgence of salon activity after the unrest of the Fronde.
1655	Louise de Morillac, with Saint Vincent de Paul, organizes and becomes Mother General of the Sisters of Charity.
	Les Conférences de l'Hôtel d'Anjou (lectures about philosophy, literature, geography, music) aim to educate middle-class women.
1656–57	Pascal: *Lettres provinciales*.
1659	Molière: *Les Précieuses ridicules*.
1660	Somaize in *Le Grand Dictionnaire des précieuses* names widows, women separated from husbands, and independent young women as realistic examples of women experiencing new freedoms.
1661	Beginning of Louis XIV's personal reign (1661–1715).
1662	Molière: *L'Ecole des femmes*.
1663–71	The Academies of Inscriptions and Letters, of Sciences, of Music and of Architecture are founded by Jean-Baptiste Colbert, minister of Louis XIV.
1664	La Rochefoucauld: *Maximes*.
1667	Racine: *Andromaque*.
1668	Marguerite Buffet, an early pedagogue, publishes *L'Eloge des illustres savantes*.
1670	Pascal: *Pensées* (published posthumously).
1670–96	Mme de Sévigné writes letters to her daughter in Provence.
1672	Molière: *Les Femmes savantes*.
	Louis XIV establishes his court at Versailles.

1673	Poullain de la Barre's *De l'égalité des deux sexes* applies a Cartesian approach to the question of equality for women and concludes that cultural conditioning accounts for the status of women.
	Boileau: *L'Art poétique*.
1675	Mme de Villedieu: *Les Désordres de l'amour*.
1677	Racine: *Phèdre*.
1678	Mme de Lafayette: *La Princesse de Clèves*.
1680	Founding of the Comédie-Française.
1680–92	Madeleine de Scudéry: *Conversations morales*.
1682	*Birth of Claudine Alexandrine Guérin de Tencin.
1685	Revocation of the Edict of Nantes by Louis XIV.
1686	Saint-Cyr is founded by Mme de Maintenon for the education of young women of the aristocracy.
1687	Fénelon's *Traité de l'éducation des filles* describes a limited educational program suitable for young women.
1690	Locke: *Essay Concerning Human Understanding*.
	Marie-Catherine d'Aulnoy: *L'Ile de la félicité*.
1694	Boileau's *Satire X* (*Against Women*) exhorts the young to avoid contact with the new breed of independent women. Charles Perrault counters in his *Apologie des femmes*.
1695	*Birth of Françoise d'Issembourg d'Happoncourt de Graffigny.
1697–98	Mme d'Aulnoy publishes four volumes of fairy tales.
1697	Bayle: *Dictionnaire historique et critique*.
	*Birth of Marie de Vichy-Chamronnd, marquise du Deffand.
1713	*Birth of Marie Jeanne Riccoboni.
1715	Accession to the throne of Louis XV with the Duc d'Orléans as Regent (1715–23).
1721	Montesquieu: *Lettres persanes*.
1727	Mme de Lambert: *Réflexions nouvelles sur les femmes*.
1731	Prévost: *Manon Lescaut*.
1731–41	Marivaux: *La Vie de Marianne*.
1732	*Birth of Julie de Lespinasse.
1734	Voltaire: *Lettres philosophiques*.
1735	Tencin: *Les Mémoires du Comte de Comminge*.
1740	*Birth of Isabelle de Charrière.
1741	Duclos: *Les Confessions du Comte de ***.
1745	Mme de Pompadour becomes Louis XV's titular mistress.
1746	*Birth of Stephanie-Félicité, comtesse de Genlis.

1747	Voltaire: *Zadig*.
	Mme de Graffigny: *Lettres d'une Péruvienne*.
	Marivaux: *La Colonie*.
1751–72	Publication of Diderot and D'Alembert's *Encyclopédie*.
	*Birth of Marie Jeanne Phlipon (Manon) Roland de la Platière.
1757	Mme Riccoboni: *Lettres de Mistriss Fanni Butlerd*.
1759	Voltaire: *Candide*.
	Le Journal des dames, first women's magazine, is published.
	Mme du Châtelet's translation of Newton (published posthumously).
1761	Rousseau: *Julie, ou la Nouvelle Héloïse*.
1762	Rousseau writes *Emile*, in which he advocates a "natural" hierarchy where women submit to motherhood and men.
1764	*Birth of Juliane von Krüdener.
1766	*Birth of Germaine Necker de Staël.
1767–80	Abbé de la Porte: *Histoire littéraire des femmes françaises*.
1770	*Birth of Sophie Cottin.
1774	Accession of Louis XVI.
	Beaumarchais: *Le Barbier de Séville*.
1776	Adam Smith: *The Wealth of Nations*.
	American colonies issue Declaration of Independence.
1778	*Birth of Claire de Duras, novelist.
1779	Mme de Genlis becomes tutor of the children of the Duc and Duchesse de Chartres.
1781	Kant: *Critique of Pure Reason*.
1781–88	Louis-Sébatien Mercier publishes *Le Tableau de Paris*, in which he addresses the advantages of divorce over separation and demands that women be allowed to choose their own profession.
1782	Laclos: *Les Liaisons dangereuses*.
	Mme de Genlis: *Adèle et Théodore ou Lettres sur l'éducation*.
1783	Laclos argues that women should be better educated, but not in excess, in *De l'éducation des femmes*.
1784	Mme de Charrière: *Lettres neuchâteloises*.
1786	*Birth of Marceline Desbordes-Valmore.
1787	Bernardin de Saint-Pierre: *Paul et Virginie*.
	Condorcet supports women's right to vote in *Sur l'admission des femmes au droit de cité*.
1787–88	French nobility meet in the Assembly of Notables and force the king to call the Estates General in order to deal with reforms and financial problems.

1789   Estates General convened.

                Women of the Third Estate petition the king with grievances in
                January. Fall of Bastille and the *Déclaration des droits de
                l'homme* (Declaration of the Rights of Man) signal the beginning
                of the Revolution. Market women march to Versailles in October
                demanding bread and force the royal family to move to Paris.

1790   Théroigne de Méricourt founds the first women's political club
                and defends the right of women to bear arms.

1791   Birth of the first feminist magazine, *Etrennes nationales des
                dames*.

                Olympe de Gouges writes the *Déclaration des droits de la femme
                et de la citoyenne*, stating that the rights of women correspond
                to the rights of men.

                Sade: *Justine ou les malheurs de la vertu*.

1792   Mary Wollstonecraft publishes *Vindication of the Rights of Woman*
                in response to Rousseau's ideas and in reaction to events in
                France.

                Use of the guillotine adopted. Abolition of the monarchy.

                Legislative Assembly legalizes divorce.

1793   Early in the year the Society of Revolutionary Republican Women
                is founded by Pauline Léon and Claire Lacombe. The society
                is closed down by the government in October.

                Royalists revolt in the Vendée. Reign of Terror begins.

                Assassination of Marat by Charlotte Corday.

                Execution of Marie-Antoinette, Mme Roland, and Olympe de
                Gouges; public beating of Théroigne de Méricourt.

1794   The government of the ''Terror'' bans women's clubs and bars
                women from popular assemblies. Reaction and ''coup'' end
                ''Terror'' in July.

1795   Rule of more moderate five-man Directory begins, but restrictions
                and curfews on women remain.

                Mme de Staël: *Essai sur les fictions*.

1796   Publication of Diderot's *La Religieuse* (written in 1760).

                Mme de Charrière: *Les Trois Femmes*.

1798   French expedition to Egypt led by Bonaparte.

                Malthus: *An Essay on the Principle of Population*.

1799   Bonaparte seizes power in France.

                Sophie Cottin: *Claire d'Albe*.

                ˙Birth of Sophie Rostopchine, comtesse de Ségur.

1800   Women are not allowed to wear the patriotic tricolor *cocarde*.

                Mme de Staël: *De la littérature*.

1801	Concordat signed by Bonaparte and the pope, restoring Catholicism.
	Chateaubriand: *Atala*.
1802	Bonaparte elected First Consul for life.
	Mme de Genlis publishes the first of a series of popular historical novels.
	Chateaubriand: *Le Génie du christianisme*.
1803	England declares war on France.
	*Birth of Flora Tristan.
	Mme de Staël: *Delphine*.
	Mme de Krüdener: *Valérie*.
1804	*Birth of Delphine Gay de Girardin.
	*Birth of George Sand.
	Promulgation of the Civil Code (later known as the Napoleonic Code) situates women as inferiors who must completely submit to masculine authority. Bonaparte crowned emperor.
1805	*Birth of Marie d'Agoult (pseudonym Daniel Stern).
1807	Marceline Desbordes-Valmore begins to publish her poems.
	Mme de Staël: *Corinne*.
1808	Sophie de Senneterre founds *L'Athénée des dames*, a journal that treats women's issues.
	Charles Fourier in *Théorie des quatre mouvements* writes that women's rights and social progress go hand in hand.
1810	Napoleon divorces Josephine to marry the Austrian princess Marie-Louise.
1814	Napoleon abdicates and is exiled on Elba.
	Bourbon dynasty is restored with Louis XVIII.
	Saint-Simon publishes *Réorganisation de la société européenne*, which advocates a communal reorganization of society and forms the basis of the early Saint-Simonian feminist movement.
1815	Napoleon returns to Paris and rules for one hundred days until his army is defeated at Waterloo; Louis XVIII regains the throne.
	Mme de Genlis: *Les Battuécas*.
1816	Divorce is abolished.
1820	Lamartine: *Méditations poétiques*.
1822	Hugo: *Odes et poésies diverses*.
	Vigny: *Poèmes* (1822 and 1829).
1824	Death of Louis XVIII and accession of Charles X to the throne.
	Mme de Duras: *Ourika*.

1825	Mme de Genlis: *Mémoires*.
	Saint-Simon: *Le Nouveau Christianisme*.
1827	Hugo's preface to *Cromwell*.
1828	Nerval: *Faust*.
1829	Correspondence exchanged between Prosper L'Enfantin, Olinde Rodrigues, Charles Duveyrier, and Pierre Buchez elaborates the feminist theory of the Saint-Simonian school.
1830	French conquest and occupation of Algeria begins. July Revolution installs Louis-Philippe as "Citizen King."
	Musset: *Contes d'Espagne et d'Italie*.
1831	Stendhal: *Le Rouge et le Noir*.
	Michelet: *Histoire romaine*.
1832	Publication of *Indiana* makes George Sand famous.
	Théophile Gautier: *Poésies*.
	Sainte-Beuve: *Critiques et portraits littéraires*.
	La Tribune des femmes, a feminist newspaper directed by Suzanne Volquin, is founded.
1833	George Sand: *Lélia*.
	Balzac: *Eugénie Grandet*.
1834	Flora Tristan: *Nécessité de faire bon acceuil aux femmes étrangères*.
	Balzac: *Le Père Goriot*.
	De Tocqueville: *La Démocratie en Amérique*.
1836–38	*Gazette des femmes*, a bourgeois magazine, advocates women's right to petition the government.
1836–48	Delphine Gay de Girardin: *Lettres parisiennes*.
1837	Accession of Queen Victoria to British throne.
1838	Louis Daguerre develops Niepce's invention of photography.
	Tristan: *Pérégrinations d'une paria*.
1839	Stendhal: *La Chartreuse de Parme*.
1842	George Sand: *Consuelo*.
1843	Flora Tristan publishes *Union ouvrière*, which calls for the common liberation of women and workers.
1844	Sainte-Beuve: *Portraits des femmes*.
1845	Mérimée: *Carmen*.
	*Birth of Judith Gautier.
1846	Sand: *La Mare au diable*.
1847	Marie d'Agoult (Daniel Stern): *Essai sur la liberté*.

1848	Revolution of 1848; fall of Louis-Philippe. French males over the age of twenty-one given the right to vote. Parisian workers revolt against the bourgeois Republic. Louis-Napoleon, nephew of Napoleon, elected president.
	La Voix des Femmes, first daily feminist newspaper inspired by Saint-Simonian ideals, is organized by Eugénie Niboyet, Suzanne Voilquin, Elisa Lemonnier, and Désirée Gay.
	Marx and Engels: *The Communist Manifesto*. Mill: *Principles of Political Economy*.
	Jeanne Deroin's candidacy for Legislative Assembly is declared unconstitutional.
1849	The Legislative Assembly suspends the right of assembly, prohibits strikes, restricts freedom of the press, and abolishes universal suffrage.
1850	Falloux Law decrees the creation of a girls' school in every community of 800 inhabitants and allows religious orders to open schools.
	Laws bar women from political activities, and Pauline Roland, Saint-Simonian journalist and feminist, and others are arrested for conducting political meetings and are sentenced to six-month prison terms.
1850–53	Marie d'Agoult: *Histoire de la Révolution de 1848*.
1851	Persecution of socialist and feminist leaders continues through deportation, imprisonment, and exile.
1852	Louis-Napoleon proclaims himself emperor.
	Haussmann begins redesigning Paris, destroying some old quarters and opening the *grands boulevards*.
1857	Flaubert: *Madame Bovary*.
	Baudelaire: *Les Fleurs du mal*.
1858	Ségur: *Les Petites Filles modèles*.
	Proudhon attacks women in *La Justice dans la Révolution et dans l'Église*.
1859	Ferdinand de Lesseps begins construction of the Suez Canal.
	Darwin: *On the Origin of Species*.
	George Sand: *Elle et lui*.
1860	Jenny d'Héricourt writes *La Femme affranchie*, in which she challenges Proudhon to update his analysis of women's abilities on the basis of current scientific information.
	*Birth of Rachilde (pseud. for Marguerite Valette).
1861	Juliette Lamber criticizes Proudhon's pseudo-scientific analyses of women's inferiority in *Idées anti-proudhoniennes*.

1862	Flaubert: *Salammbô*.
	Hugo: *Les Misérables*.
	Ségur: *L'Auberge de l'Ange-Gardien*.
1865	The painter Rosa Bonheur is the first woman awarded the Cross of the Legion of Honor.
1866	Verlaine: *Poèmes saturniens*.
	Ségur: *La Fortune de Gaspard*.
1867	Claude Bernard: *Introduction à la médicine expérimentale*.
	Marx: *Das Kapital* (1867–94).
	Judith Gautier: *Le Livre de jade*.
1868–69	Censorship of press is relaxed and moves are made toward a parliamentary system in France.
	Baudelaire: *L'Art romantique* published posthumously.
1869	Verlaine: *Fêtes galantes*.
	Mill: *The Subjection of Women*.
	Author/lecturer Maria Deraismes supports the Society to Claim the Rights of Women and, with Léon Richer, publishes *Le Droit des femmes*, a journal advocating legal equality for women.
	Franco-Prussian War begins.
1871	Capitulation of Paris is followed by the Paris Commune, March through May. French lose Alsace and Lorraine.
	Louise Michel and other women active in the Commune (*les pétroleuses*) are sentenced to death, exile, or prison. L'Union des femmes pour la défense de Paris et les soins aux blessés formed to protect the civil population, care for the wounded, and teach and organize female workers.
1873	Rimbaud: *Une Saison en enfer* (written 1873).
	*Birth of Colette.
1874	Claude Monet's paintings mark the beginning of Impressionism.
	Flaubert: *La Tentation de Saint Antoine*.
	Verlaine: *Romances sans paroles*.
	*Birth of Lucie Delarue-Mardrus.
1875	Constitutional laws establish the Third Republic.
	Judith Gautier: *L'Usurpateur*.
	Taine: *Les Origines de la France contemporaine* (1875–93).
1876	Mallarmé: *L'Après-midi d'un faune*.
	*Birth of Anna de Noailles.
1877	Zola: *L'Assommoir*.

1878	Maria Deraismes presides over the Congrès international du droit des femmes.
1879	Louis Pasteur discovers the principle of vaccination.
1880	Rachilde: *Monsieur de la nouveauté.*
	Camille Sée Law provides secondary school education to girls.
1881	Militant suffragist Hubertine Auclert, who had already refused to pay taxes, saying, "I don't vote. I don't pay," publishes the newspaper *La Citoyenne*, which calls for women's political rights. Primary education in France becomes free, lay, and compulsory.
1882	La Ligue française pour le droit des femmes founded by Léon Richer.
	Blanche Edwards becomes the first woman to receive a medical degree in France.
	Judith Gautier: *Richard Wagner et son oeuvre poétique depuis "Rienzi" jusqu'à "Persifal."*
1883	August Bebel's *Woman under Socialism* is published.
1884	Clémence Royer, a mathematician, is the first woman to teach at the Sorbonne.
	Divorce law reestablished which favors men.
	Huysmans: *A Rebours.*
	Verlaine: *Les Poètes maudits.*
	Rachilde: *Monsieur Vénus.*
1887	Mallarmé: *Poésies.*
	Rachilde: *La Marquise de Sade.*
1889	Marya Chéliga founds the Union universelle des femmes, a feminist association which affirms women's civil and political rights. Construction of the Eiffel Tower for the World's Fair.
	Barrès: *Un Homme libre.*
	Claudel: *Tête d'or.*
1891	Rachilde: *Théâtre: Le Vendeur du soleil, La Voix du sang.*
1893	Aline Valette's brochure, *Socialisme et sexualisme*, situates the women's rights struggle within the class struggle and states that only economic reform can effect emancipation on a social and sexual scale.
1894	Condemnation of Dreyfus for treason and subsequent campaign to establish his innocence.
1895	Cinematography invented by Auguste and Louis Lumière in Lyons.
	Founding of the Confédération Générale du Travail.
1896	Jarry: *Ubu Roi.*
	Bergson: *Matière et mémoire.*

1897   Mlle Chauvin, first woman lawyer admitted to bar.

Marguerite Durand, a middle-class republican feminist, publishes *La Fronde*, the first daily completely organized and controlled by women.

Péguy: *Jeanne d'Arc*.

Gide: *Les Nourritures terrestres*.

1898   Marie and Pierre Curie discover radium.

Founding of reactionary movement Action Française.

Construction of the Paris metro begins.

1899   Seamstress Louise Saumoneau and Elisabeth Renaud found the short-lived Feminist Socialist Group.

1900   Freud: *The Interpretation of Dreams*.

Colette: *Claudine à l'ècole*.

Rachilde: *La Jongleuse*.

1901   Anna de Noailles: *Le Coeur innombrable*.

1902   Founding of the Goncourt Academy.

*Birth of Nathalie Sarraute.

1903   *Birth of Marguerite Yourcenar.

1904   Paul Lafargue discusses women's oppression using Marxist theory in *La Question de la femme*.

First meeting of the International Woman's Suffrage Alliance held in Berlin.

1905   Founding of French Socialist Party.

Separation of church and state established in France.

Sigmund Freud's *Dora* is published.

1906   Dreyfus declared innocent.

1907   Marguerite Durand presides over Congrès du travail féminin, attended by numerous union representatives and organized by her association, L'Office du travail féminin.

Married women gain the right to control their own salary.

Lydia Pissarjevsky expresses doubt that Marxism will liberate women in *Socialisme et féminisme*.

Picasso's *Les Demoiselles d'Avignon* signals departure toward abstraction in painting.

*Birth of Violette Leduc.

1908   *Birth of Simone de Beauvoir.

1909   *Birth of Simone Weil.

1910   Marguerite Durand and Hubertine Auclert unsuccessfully attempt to run for the National Assembly.

1911	Colette: *La Vagabonde.*
	Lanson: *La Méthode de l'histoire littéraire.*
1912	Jung: *The Psychology of the Unconscious.*
1913	Apollinaire: *Alcools.*
	Proust: *A la recherche du temps perdu* (1913–22).
1914	*Birth of Marguerite Duras.
	French mobilization and outbreak of World War I.
1916	Battles of Verdun and the Somme.
	Hélène Brion criticizes socialists and trade unions for not attending to women's problems in *La Voie féministe: femme, ose être!*
	Joyce: *Portrait of the Artist as a Young Man.*
	Kafka: *Metamorphosis.*
1917	*La Voix des femmes*, founded by Colette Reynaud, originally has the issue of suffrage for its *raison d'être.*
	Engineering schools open to women.
	Russian Revolution begins.
	Valéry: *La Jeune Parque.*
	Apollinaire: *Les Mamelles de Tirésias.*
	*Birth of Christiane Rochefort.
1918	Feminist schoolteacher Hélène Brion is tried for treason and loses teaching license for distributing pacifist literature.
	Armistice ends World War I.
1919	Treaty of Versailles.
	Senate refuses to consider a proposal for women's suffrage.
1920	Contraceptives banned and abortion is made a capital crime.
	Colette: *Chéri.*
	Freud: *Beyond the Pleasure Principle.*
	*Birth of Benoîte Groult.
	*Birth of Andrée Chedid.
1921	Wittgenstein: *Tractatus logico-philosophicus.*
	Yourcenar: *Le Jardin des chimères.*
1922	Victor Margueritte's *La Garconne* (The Bachelor Girl) is published and sells 300,000 copies its first year.
	Mauriac: *Le Baiser au lépreux.*
	Colette: *La Maison de Claudine.*
	Thibaudet: *Physiologie de la critique.*
	Delarue-Mardrus: *L'Ex-voto.*
	Italian Fascists march on Rome. Mussolini is appointed Prime Minister.

1924	Breton: *Manifeste du surréalisme*.
1925	Exhibition of Art Deco in Paris.
	Hitler: *Mein Kampf* (1925–27).
	Delarue-Mardrus: *Graine au vent*.
1926	Colette: *La Fin de Chéri*.
	Bernanos: *Sous le soleil de Satan*.
	Eluard: *Capitale de la douleur*.
1927	Lindbergh makes first solo crossing of Atlantic.
1928	Aragon: *Le Traité du style*.
	Maginot Line, a fortification system to protect France from Germany, is built.
1929	Wall Street crash ushers in worldwide economic depression.
	Jean Larnac: *Histoire de la littérature féminine en France*.
	Cocteau: *Les Enfants terribles*.
193?	*Birth of Luce Irigaray.
1930	Malraux: *La Voie royale*.
	Colette: *Histoire pour Bel-Gazou*.
	*Birth of Françoise Mallet-Joris.
1932	Céline: *Voyage au bout de la nuit*.
	Noailles: *Le Livre de ma vie*.
1933	Roosevelt's New Deal begins in America.
	Hitler comes to power in Germany.
	Stein: *Autobiography of Alice B. Toklas*.
1934	Gabrielle Duchêne, feminist pacifist, presides over Worldwide Committee of Women Against War and Fascism, and their International Congress is held in Paris.
	Anti-republican riots in France.
	Yourcenar: *Denier du rêve*.
1935	Italian invasion of Abyssinia.
	*Birth of Françoise Sagan.
	*Birth of Monique Wittig.
1936	Spanish Civil War begins.
	Popular Front government under Léon Blum initiates social reforms including the forty–hour work week. Blum appoints three women to positions in his government.
	Germany reoccupies Rhineland.

1937	Fall of Blum government.
	Identical educational programs instituted in both girls' and boys' lycées.
	*Birth of Hélène Cixous.
	*Birth of Albertine Sarrazin.
1938	Anschluss: Austria declared part of Germany.
	Munich agreement with Hitler and Mussolini signed by Chamberlain and Daladier.
	Married women declared legal majors.
	Sartre: *La Nausée*.
	Artaud: *Le Théâtre et son double*.
	Bachelard: *La Psychanalyse du feu*.
1939	Germans occupy Czechoslovakia. Italy and Germany sign a formal military alliance. French Communist Party supports Nazi-Soviet NonAggression Pact. Hitler invades Poland and World War II begins.
	Code de la famille creates government payments for the birth of the first child and a system of family allowances.
	Dr. Madeleine Pelletier, socialist physician and longtime activist for women's reproductive rights, is arrested for performing abortions.
	Sarraute: *Tropismes*.
	Sartre: *Le Mur*.
1940	Germans enter Paris and occupy half the country.
	French government moves to Vichy, and Pétain becomes chief of state. De Gaulle heads the Free French forces.
1941	Japanese attack Pearl Harbor.
	Hitler invades the Soviet Union.
	Beginnings of French Resistance.
	*Birth of Julia Kristeva.
1942	Allies land in North Africa. French fleet scuttled at Toulon. Germans occupy Free Zone.
	Camus: *L'Etranger*.
1942–44	Large number of French women are active in Resistance groups.
1943	Allied invasion of Sicily.
	Germans surrender at Stalingrad.
	De Gaulle and Giraud form Committee of National Liberation in Algiers.
	Beauvoir: *L'Invitée*.

1944	Women gain the right to vote in April.
	Colette: *Gigi et autres nouvelles*.
	Allies land in Normandy and liberate Paris.
1945	Unconditional surrender of German army.
	French Third Republic ended by referendum; De Gaulle becomes head of state.
	Beauvoir: *Le Sang des autres*.
1946	Resignation of De Gaulle.
	Constitution of Fourth Republic declares women's equality in most areas.
	First film festival at Cannes.
	Genet: *Miracle de la rose*.
	Sartre: *L'Existentialisme est un humanisme*.
	Leduc: *L'Asphyxie*.
1947	Camus: *La Peste*.
	Sarraute: *Portrait d'un inconnu*.
	Weil: *La Pesanteur et la grâce*.
	Merleau-Ponty: *Humanisme et terreur*.
1949	Council of Europe established.
	Beauvoir: *Le Deuxième Sexe*.
	Lévi-Strauss: *Les Structures élémentaires de la parenté*.
1950	Ionesco: *La Cantatrice chauve*.
	Duras: *Un Barrage contre le Pacifique*.
	Weil: *Attente de Dieu*.
1951	Beckett: *Molloy* and *Malone meurt*.
	Weil: *La Condition ouvrière*.
	Yourcenar: *Mémoires d'Hadrien*.
	Mallet-Joris: *Le Rempart des béguines*.
1952	Beckett: *En attendant Godot*.
1953	Robbe-Grillet: *Les Gommes*.
	Barthes: *Le Degré zéro de l'écriture*.
1954	Fall of Dien Bien Phu; Laos and Cambodia become independent.
	National rebellion against France begins in Algeria.
	Sarraute: *Martereau*.
	Beauvoir: *Les Mandarins*.
	Butor: *Passage de Milan*.

1955	Duras: *Le Square*.
	Lévi-Strauss: *Tristes Tropiques*.
	Mallet-Joris: *La Chambre rouge*.
	Sagan: *Bonjour tristesse*.
1956	Morocco granted independence.
	Dr. Marie-Andrée Weill-Hallé founds the French Movement for Family Planning, thereby confronting the restrictive law of 1920 banning contraception.
	Genet: *Le Balcon*.
	Sarraute: *L'Ere du soupçon*.
	Robbe-Grillet: *Pour un nouveau roman*.
	Sagan: *Un Certain Sourire*.
1957	French Assembly ratifies Rome treaties for Common Market.
	Delarue-Mardrus: *Nos Secrètes Amours*.
1958	De Gaulle elected French president of Fifth Republic.
	Duras: *Moderato cantabile*.
	Rochefort: *Le Repos du guerrier*.
	Beauvoir: *Mémoires d'une jeune fille rangée*.
	Sarrazin: *Journal de prison*.
1959	Sarraute: *Le Planétarium*.
	Queneau: *Zazie dans le métro*.
	Vian: *Les Bâtisseurs d'empire*.
1960	Introduction of the "new franc."
	Explosion of first French nuclear bomb.
	Founding of *Tel Quel*, avant-garde literary magazine headed by Philippe Sollers.
	Simon: *La Route des Flandres*.
	Beauvoir: *La Force de l'âge*.
1961	Army revolt collapses in Algeria.
	Gagarin orbits the earth.
	First European summit meets in Paris.
	Berlin Wall is constructed.
	Rochefort: *Les Petits Enfants du siècle*.
1962	Independence of Algeria proclaimed.
	Char: *La Parole en archipel*.
	Benoîte and Flora Groult: *Ainsi soit-elle*.

1963   De Gaulle opposes Great Britain's participation in the Common
                Market.

                President Kennedy assassinated.

                Beauvoir: *La Force des choses*.

                Sarraute: *Les Fruits d'or*.

1964   Colette Audry founds Le Mouvement démocratique féminin,
                which fights for democracy in the family and the workplace.

                Andrée Michel and Geneviève Texier: *La Condition de la Fran-
                çaise d'aujourd'hui*.

                Jacques Lacan founds Freudian school in Paris.

                Sartre: *Les Mots*.

                Leduc: *La Bâtarde*.

                Beauvoir: *Une Mort très douce*.

                Wittig: *L'Opoponax*.

1965   De Gaulle is reelected president.

                American raids on North Vietnam begin.

                Anachronistic features of the Napoleonic Code revoked.

                Perec: *Les Choses*.

                Sagan: *La Chamade*.

                Chedid: *Double-Pays*.

                Sarrazin: *L'Astragale*.

1966   France withdraws its forces from NATO command.

                China begins cultural revolution.

                Lacan: *Ecrits*.

                Barthes: *Critique et vérité*.

                Foucault: *Les Mots et les Choses*.

                Greimas: *Sémantique structurale*.

                Yourcenar: *Fleuve profond, sombre rivière*.

1967   Neuwirth Law liberalizes rules on contraception.

                Cixous: *Le Prénom de Dieu*.

1968   May-June: Students riot in the Latin Quarter demanding educa-
                tional, social, and political reform.

                Le Mouvement de libération des femmes seeks to organize women.

                Universities are given administrative autonomy.

                Explosion of French H-bomb.

                Yourcenar: *L'Oeuvre au noir*.

                Modiano: *La Place de l'Etoile*.

1969   De Gaulle resigns. Georges Pompidou is elected president.

Duras: *Détruire dit-elle*.

Wittig: *Les Guérillères*.

Cixous: *Dedans*.

Kristeva: *Séméiotiké: Recherches pour une sémanalyse*.

1970   Barthes: *L'Empire des signes*.

Partisan, année zéro publishes first entire issue on works of women about women.

The radical group Féministes révolutionnaires declares its objective to disrupt the patriarchal order.

1971   In *Le Nouvel Observateur* 343 well-known women sign a declaration in support of abortion, noting that they have had abortions themselves.

"Paternal" authority is replaced by "parental" authority within family law.

Women march for contraception and free abortion in Paris.

Gisèle Halimi founds *Choisir*, which fights for contraception, sexual education, and repeal of the law of 1920.

Le Torchon brûlé, a radical feminist paper, is founded.

1972   Spirale, a movement created by Catherine Valabrègue, explores feminine culture and has for its objective to liberate women's creativity.

Bonnefoy: *L'Arrière-Pays*.

Char: *La Nuit talismanique*.

Cixous: *Neutre*.

Sollers: *Lois*.

Jabès: *Le Livre des questions*.

Chedid: *Visage premier*.

1973   Le mouvement pour la liberté de l'avortement et pour la contraception (MLAC) is organized.

The bookstore des femmes promotes the sole publication of women's writing.

Mallet-Joris: *La Maison de papier*.

Irigaray: *Le Langage des déments*.

Wittig: *Le Corps lesbien*.

1974   Death of Georges Pompidou. Giscard d'Estaing is elected president.

The Simone Veil Law legalizes abortion.

Voting age lowered to eighteen.

Secretariat of State for the Status of Women created, headed by Françoise Giroud.

Publication of *Les Pétroleuses*, a feminist Communist paper.

Ligue du droit des femmes is founded, with Simone de Beauvoir as sponsor.

Le Quotidien des femmes, a women's daily, is created.

Irigaray: *Speculum de l'autre femme*.

Leclerc: *Parole de femme*.

Chawaf: *Retable-Rêverie*.

Chedid: *Néfertité et le rêve d'Akhnaton*.

Kristeva: *Des chinoises*.

Kristeva: *La Révolution du langage poétique*.

1975   Divorce by mutual consent made possible.

Foucault: *Surveiller et punir*.

Cardinal: *Les Mots pour le dire*.

Duras: *India Song*.

Cixous: "Le Rire de la Méduse."

1976   Strike by prostitutes.

The journal *Sorcières*, edited by Xavière Gauthier, is published.

Cixous: *Portrait de Dora*.

1977   Contraception made legal and decreed "a medical act like another."

Georges Pompidou National Center of Art and Culture opens in Paris.

Maïté Albistur and Daniel Armogathe: *Histoire du féminisme français*.

Questions féministes, a journal edited by Simone de Beauvior, is published.

Leclerc: *Autrement dit*.

Cixous: *Souffles*.

Yourcenar: *Archives du nord*.

Irigaray: *Ce Sexe qui n'en est pas un*.

1978   Several feminist journals started, including *Des femmes en mouvements*, edited by Des Femmes publishing house; *F Magazine*, edited by Claude Servan-Schreiber; and *Le Fait féminin*, edited by Evelyne Sullerot.

Perec: *La Vie mode d'emploi*.

1979	Char: *Fenêtres dormantes et porte sur le toit.*
	Yourcenar: *La Couronne et la lyre.*
	Chawaf: *Maternité.*
1980	Marguerite Yourcenar becomes the first woman elected to the Académie Française.
	Blanchot: *L'Ecriture du désastre.*
1981	Socialist François Mitterrand elected president.
	Capital punishment is abolished.
	Beauvoir: *La Cérémonie des adieux.*
1983	Sartre: *Carnets de la drôle de guerre.*
1984	Duras: *L'Amant.*
	Blanchot: *La Communauté inavouable.*
	Sagan: *Avec mon meilleur souvenir.*
	Cixous: *L'Histoire terrible mais inachevée de Norodom Sihanouk roi du Cambodge.*
1986	Deguy: *Brevets.*
	Michaux: *Affrontments.*
1987	Bonnefoy: *Ce qui fut sans lumière.*
	Kristeva: *Soleil noir.*
1988	François Mitterrand is reelected president.
1989	France celebrates the bicentennial of the storming of the Bastille.
1990	Kristeva: *Lettre Ouverte à Harlem Dèsir.*
	Kristeva: *Les Samouraïs.*
	Irigaray: *Je, tu, nous.*
	Irigaray: *Sexes et genres à travers les langues.*
	Beauvoir: *Lettres à Sartre.*
1991	Edith Cresson appointed prime minister.
	Kristeva: *Le Vieil homme et les loups.*
1992	Marie-Christine Blandin is the first woman to head an entire French "region"—Le Nord-Pas-de-Calais.
	Irigaray: *J'aime à toi.*
	Cixous: *Déluge.*

APPENDIX B: LIST OF AUTHORS BY DATE OF BIRTH

c. 1170–1260	The trobairitz
fl. 1160–78	Marie de France
c. 1365–c. 1430	Christine de Pizan
1492–1549	Marguerite de Navarre
c. 1510–c. 1560	Hélisenne de Crenne
1520?–45	Pernette du Guillet
1520–66	Louise Labé
1565–1645	Marie Le Jars de Gournay
1607–1701	Madeleine de Scudéry
1626–96	Marie de Rabutin-Chantal, Marquise de Sévigné
1634–93	Marie-Madeleine Pioche de La Vergne, Comtesse de Lafayette
1640?–83	Marie-Catherine Desjardins de Villedieu
1650?–1705	Marie-Catherine Le Jumel de Barneville, Comtesse d'Aulnoy
1682–1749	Claudine Alexandrine Guérin de Tencin
1695–1753	Françoise d'Issembourg d'Happoncourt de Graffigny
1697–1780	Marie de Vichy-Chamrond, Marquise du Deffand
1713–92	Marie Jeanne Riccoboni
1732–76	Julie de Lespinasse
1740–1805	Isabelle de Charrière
1746–1830	Stephanie-Félicité, Comtesse de Genlis
1754–93	Marie Jeanne Phlipon (Manon) Roland de la Platière
1764–1824	Juliane von Krüdener
1766–1817	Germaine Necker, Baronne de Staël

1770–1807	Sophie Cottin
1777–1828	Claire de Duras
1786–1859	Marceline Desbordes-Valmore
1799–1874	Sophie Rostopchine, Comtesse de Ségur
1803–44	Flora Tristan
1804–76	George Sand
1804–55	Delphine Gay de Girardin
1805–76	Marie, Comtesse d'Agoult
1845–1917	Judith Gautier
1860–1953	Rachilde
1873–1954	Colette
1874–1945	Lucie Delarue-Mardrus
1876–1933	Anna de Noailles
1900-	Nathalie Sarraute
1903–87	Marguerite Yourcenar
1907–72	Violette Leduc
1908–86	Simone de Beauvoir
1909–43	Simone Weil
1914-	Marguerite Duras
1917-	Christiane Rochefort
1920-	Andrée Chedid
1920-	Benoîte Groult
193?-	Luce Irigaray
1930-	Françoise Mallet-Joris
1935-	Françoise Sagan
1935-	Monique Wittig
1937-	Hélène Cixous
1937–67	Albertine Sarrazin
1941-	Julia Kristeva

TITLE INDEX

SUBJECT INDEX

Note: Pages in **boldface** indicate dictionary entries.

CONTRIBUTORS

Marianna Mustacchi Archambault is Professor of French at Bucknell University, where she chairs the Department of Modern Languages. She is coauthor, with Paul J. Archambault, of *A Renaissance Woman: Helisenne's Personal and Invective Letters* (1986)

Paul J. Archambault is Professor of French at Syracuse University. Coauthor of *A Renaissance Woman*, he is the author of *Camus' Hellenic Sources* (1972) and *Seven French Chroniclers* (1974). He also edits *Symposium: A Quarterly Journal in Modern Foreign Literatures*.

Faith E. Beasley is Assistant Professor of French at Dartmouth College. Her book, *Revising Memory: Women's Fiction and Memoirs in Seventeenth-Century France* (1990), examines the memoirs and novels of Lafayette, Villedieu, and Montpensier, among others, and their relationship to history. She has published articles on women writers, the concept of *vraisemblance*, and the quarrel surrounding *La Princesse de Clèves*.

Lucille F. Becker is a member of the French Department at Drew University. Her articles and reviews have appeared in the *Nation, Colliers Encyclopedia, Yale French Studies, Romanic Review, French Review, Modern Language Journal, Romance Notes, World Literature Today, Encyclopedia of World Literature in the Twentieth Century, Major World Writers*, and *Contemporary World Writers*. She contributed a chapter to the book *Montherlant vu par des jeunes de 17 à 27 ans* (1959) and edited a critical text of Montherlant's play, *Le Maître de*

Santiago (1965). Her books include *Henry de Montherlant* (1970), as well as *Louis Aragon* (1971), *Georges Simenon* (1977), *Françoise Mallet-Joris* (1985), and *Twentieth-Century French Women Novelists* (1989), which were published in Twayne's World Authors Series.

Thomas F. Broden is Assistant Professor of French at Purdue University. He has published on theory in the *American Journal of Semiotics, Recherches Sémiotiques/Semiotic Inquiry,* and the *French Review.* His work with Duras is part of a larger book project on the presence of social questions in contemporary literature in French.

Matilda Tomaryn Bruckner, Associate Professor of French at Boston College, has published books and articles on twelfth- and thirteenth-century French romance and troubadour lyric (including the trobairitz or female troubadours). She is currently working on the "Poetics of Continuation" in the *Perceval* Continuations and the *Romance of the Rose.*

Anne Callahan is Professor of French at Loyola University of Chicago. She is the author, with Donald Furber, of *Erotic Love in Literature from Medieval Legend to Romantic Illusion* and has published articles on George Sand and Marguerite Duras. She is currently completing a critical study of George Sand's fictional and autobiographical writing.

Verena Andermatt Conley is Professor of French and Women's Studies at Miami University in Ohio. She is the author of *Hélène Cixous: Writing the Feminine* and the editor of Hélène Cixous's *Reading with Clarice Lispector* and *Readings.*

Ann Cothran is Associate Professor of Foreign Languages and Literature at Wittenberg University. She has published articles on Sarraute, Sarrazin, and Colette.

Isabelle de Courtivron is Associate Professor of French and Head of Foreign Languages and Literatures at MIT, where she teaches courses in French language, literature, and culture as well as in Women's Studies. She is coeditor, with Elaine Marks, of *New French Feminisms* (1982), and, with Margery Resnick, of *Women Writers in Translation: An International Bibliography* (1983). She is the author of *Violette Leduc* (1985) and has written articles on Violette Leduc, Simone de Beauvoir, Christiane Rochefort, George Sand, and Clara Malraux. She has just completed a biography of Clara Malraux and is coediting, with Shari Benstock, a collection of essays about couples and creativity in the arts and literature.

Kathryn J. Crecelius is the author of *Family Romances: George Sand's Early Novels* (1987). Her articles on literature, theory, and culture have appeared in *Nineteenth-Century French Studies, Présence de George Sand,* and *L'Esprit Créateur,* among other journals.

Diane Griffin Crowder, Associate Professor of French at Cornell College, has published several previous articles on Monique Wittig. She has also researched and published on feminist utopian fiction, feminist semiotics, and pedagogy. She founded and chairs the Women's Studies program, has been chair of the Department of Classical and Modern Languages, and recently spent a year teaching at Smith College.

Judith Curtis, Associate Professor of French at Scarborough College, University of Toronto, has published in the fields of eighteenth-century French theater and women letter-writers. She is a member of the team editing the correspondence of Mme de Graffigny.

Michael Danahy is Head of the Department of Foreign Languages at the University of Wisconsin-Stevens Point, where he teaches French language, literature, and culture. He has published poetry, as well as research on literary and pedagogical subjects. His books include an intermediate reader, *Plaisir de lire* (1990) and *The Feminization of the Novel* (1991), winner of the Gilbert Chinard Prize for the best manuscript of 1989. The National Endowment for the Humanities has sponsored his research in France on Marceline Desbordes-Valmore. He is preparing the first modern verse translation of the poet's work in English.

Elyane Dezon-Jones teaches French literature at Barnard College in New York. She has published *Proust et l'Amérique* (1982), a critical edition of *Le Côté des Guermantes,* and many articles on Proust. The author of an anthology of French women writers, *Les Ecritures féminines* (1983), and of a book on Marie de Gournay, *Fragments d'un discours féminin* (1988), she is currently working on a theory of genetic criticism.

Tama Lea Engelking is Assistant Professor of French at Cleveland State University. She earned her degree from the University of Wisconsin-Madison. Her main research interests include feminist criticism and French women writers, specifically turn-of-the-century poets. In addition to her work on Anna de Noailles, she has written on Renée Vivien, Gérard d'Houville, Lucie Delarue-Mardrus, and Natalie Clifford Barney.

C. Frederick Farrell, Jr., and **Edith R. Farrell** both teach at the University of Minnesota, Morris, where he is Chair of the Division of the Humanities. Their books deal with Marguerite Yourcenar, Louise Labé, Éméric Crucé, and

Gaston Bachelard. They are on the Board of Directors of the Société Internationale d'Études Yourcenariennes.

Michèle L. Farrell is Assistant Professor of French Literature at Duke University. In addition to her work on Sévigné, she has published articles on Poullain de la Barre, Marie de Gournay, Mme d'Aulnoy, and Charles Perrault.

Nicole Fouletier-Smith is an Associate Professor of French at the University of Nebraska-Lincoln. She has published articles in the *French Review*, *Romance Notes*, and *Lettres Romanes*, and is now pursuing research in the area of French civilization.

Melanie Hawthorne is Assistant Professor of French at Texas A&M University. Her interests include nineteenth-century prose fiction, women writers, and feminist criticism. She is currently writing a book about Rachilde, having translated *The Juggler* into English.

Micheline Herz was Professor of French at Rutgers University. She published on topics in seventeenth- and twentieth-century French literature and the literature of Québec. At her death in 1992 she was working on a book about the idea of Europe in seventeenth-century French literature.

Lynne Huffer, Assistant Professor of French at Yale University, is currently completing a book on Colette. She has also published articles on Nerval, Montaigne, Christine de Pizan, Proust, and feminist writing. Her most recent work examines the maternal metaphor in twentieth-century French writing. She is the author of *The (En)gendered Text: Colette and the Problem of Writing*.

Katharine Ann Jensen is Assistant Professor of French at Louisiana State University. She is currently writing a book entitled *Writing Love: Letters, Women, and the Novel (1669–1776)*.

Nicole Ward Jouve is Professor of English and Related Literature and Women's Studies at the University of York, Great Britain. She is the author of *Le Spectre du gris* (fiction, 1977), translated by the author as *Shades of Grey* (1981); *L'Entremise* (fiction, 1980); *Un Homme nomme Zapolski* (1983), reworked into English as *The Streetcleaner: The Yorkshire Ripper Case on Trial* (1986); *Baudelaire: A Fire to Conquer Darkness* (1980); *Colette* (1987), and *White Woman Speaks with Forked Tongue: Criticism as Autobiography* (1990).

Dorothy Kelly teaches French language and literature at Boston University. She has written several studies that relate to feminist and gender issues, including *Fictional Genders: Role and Representation in Nineteenth-Century French Nar-*

rative (1989) and "Gender, Metaphor, and Machine: *La Bête humaine*" (1989). She is currently working on a book on voyeurism in the French novel.

Bettina L. Knapp is Professor of Romance Languages and Comparative Literature at Hunter College and the Graduate Center of the City University of New York. She is the author of numerous critical studies, including *Louis Jouvet: Man of the Theatre*; *That Was Yvette*; *Aristide Bruant*; *Jean Racine: Mythos and Renewal in Modern Theatre*; *Gérard de Nerval: The Mystic's Dilemma*; *Antonin Artaud: Man of Vision*; *A Jungian Approach to Literature*; *Architecture, Archetype, and the Writer*; *Dance, Archetype, and the Writer*; *Women in Twentieth-Century Literature*; and *Music, Metaphor, and the Writer*.

Christine Lac is Assistant Professor in the Department of Romance Languages at St. Olaf College.

Julia Lauer-Chéenne is affiliated with the University of Nebraska-Lincoln. Dr. Lauer-Chéenne is active in the visual arts and is a specialist in photo-montage.

J. P. Little has held lecturing posts in England (universities of Sussex and Southampton, and the Open University), in Africa (Ghana and Sierra Leone), and since 1980 has been at St. Patrick's College, Dublin, Ireland. Her publications include *Simone Weil: A Bibliography* (1973); *Supplement No. 1* to the foregoing (1979); *Beckett: "En attendant Godot" and "Fin de partie"* (1981); *Simone Weil: Waiting on Truth* (1988); *Genet: "Les Nègres"* (1990); guest editor, special number on Simone Weil of the French literary review *Sud* (1990); numerous articles on Simone Weil and on the *théâtre de l'absurde*.

Caryl L. Lloyd, Associate Professor of French at the University of South Alabama, has written on eighteenth- and nineteenth-century topics in *The French Review*, *Studies on Voltaire and the Eighteenth Century*, the *Revue Jules Vallès* and other journals.

Gita May is Professor of French and Department Chair at Columbia University. She is the author of a number of books, notably *Diderot et Baudelaire, critiques d'art*; *De Jean-Jacques Rousseau à Madame Roland: Essai sur la sensibilité preéromantique et révolutionnaire*; *Madame Roland and the Age of Revolution* (winner of Columbia University's Van Amringe Distinguished Book Award); and *Stendhal and the Age of Napoleon*. She has also published numerous articles, extensive essays, contributions to books and festschrifts, as well as reviews and review articles. She edited Diderot's *Essais sur la peinture* and *Pensées détachées sur la peinture* for the complete critical edition of Diderot's works, and coedited *Diderot Studies III*. She is a past President of the American Society for Eighteenth-Century Studies and has served on the Executive Council of the Modern Language Association of America.

Danielle Mihram is Head of the Reference Center at Doheny Memorial Library, University of Southern California. In addition to French literature and librarianship, her research and publications also include cybernetics and the interface between the science and the social sciences.

Judith Graves Miller is Professor of French at the University of Wisconsin-Madison, where she teaches courses in contemporary literature, particularly French theater, and directs and produces annually a play in French with her students. She has written extensively on modern theater and dramatic techniques for *Theatre Journal*, *Theater*, and *Modern Drama* and is the author of two monographs: *Theatre and Revolution in France Since 1968* (1977) and *Françoise Sagan* (1988).

Warren F. Motte, Jr., teaches French and Comparative Literature at the University of Colorado. He is the author of *The Poetics of Experiment: A Study of the Work of Georges Perec*, and the editor and translator of *Oulipo: A Primer of Potential Literature*. His most recent book is entitled *Questioning Edmond Jabès*.

Marie Naudin is Associate Professor at the University of Connecticut. She is the author of *L'Evolution parallèle de la poèsie et de la musique en France* (1968) and articles dealing with the nineteenth century (France) and the twentieth century (France and Québec).

Pauline Newman-Gordon is Professor of French Literature at Stanford University. She has published books and articles on modern French literature, many devoted to Proust, and a collection of poems entitled *Mooring to France*.

Yolanda Astarita Patterson is Professor of French and Women's Studies at California University, Hayward. She is a founding member of the International Simone de Beauvoir Society and has served as its president since 1983. She has lectured and published extensively on Simone de Beauvoir. Her book entitled *Simone de Beauvoir and the Demystification of Motherhood* was published in 1989.

Catherine Portuges is Director of the Interdepartmental Program in Film Studies and Associate Professor of Comparative Literature at the University of Massachusetts, Amherst, where she also teaches in the French Department. She is coauthor of *Gendered Subjects: The Dynamics of Feminist Teaching* (1985), and her book *Screen Memories: The Hungarian Cinema of Marta Meszaros* is forthcoming. She has published articles on autobiography, cinema, and women writers including "Seeing Subjects: Women Directors and Cinematic Autobiography" in *Life/Lines: Theories of Women's Autobiography* (1988); "Love and Mourning in Duras's *Aurelia Steiner''* in *L'Esprit Créateur (1990); and "Attachment and Separation in La Jeune Fille rangée* (1987).

Annabelle M. Rea is Professor of French at Occidental College. She has published on George Sand and contemporary Québec writer Anne Hébert.

Mary Rice-DeFosse is Assistant Professor of French at Bates College. She has published on nineteenth- and twentieth-century French literature. Rice-DeFosse was able to pursue her research on Flora Tristan as a participant in a 1989 NEH Summer Seminar on the "Woman Question," held at Stanford University.

François Rigolot is Meredith Howland Pyne Professor of French literature at Princeton University. A specialist in Renaissance poetics, he has written extensively on Rabelais (*Les Langages de Rabelais*, 1972), Montaigne (*Les Métamorphoses de Montaigne*, 1988), and problems of linguistics and poetics (*Poétique et Onomastique: L'Exemple de la Renaissance*, 1977) and textuality (*Le Texte de la Renaissance*, 1984). He is the editor of Louise Labé's complete works (*Oeuvres complètes de Louise Labé*, 1986) and is currently preparing a new edition of Montaigne's *Journal de voyage* and Montaigne's translation of Sebond's *Theologia naturalis* for the Presses Universitaires de France.

Marian Rothstein teaches French at Grinnel College. Her published research deals with Jean Lemaire de Belges, Robert Garnier, and Maurice Scève, among others. She is currently working on the French Renaissance novel.

Eva Martin Sartori is Associate Professor in the University Libraries of the University of Nebraska-Lincoln. She has written on topics in French literature and library science. With Stephen Lehmann, she coedited *Women's Studies in Western Europe: A Resource Guide* (1986).

Lucy M. Schwartz is Professor of French Literature at the University of North Dakota. She has published articles on Mme de Duras, Sainte-Beuve, Christiane Rochefort, George Sand, and Nathalie Sarraute.

Lewis C. Seifert, Assistant Professor of French Studies at Brown University, has published articles on French literature of the sixteenth and seventeenth centuries and is currently working on a study of gender and fairy tales. His research interests also include feminist criticism, theory of theater, and social history.

Samia I. Spencer is Professor of French and Director of French Graduate Studies at Auburn University. In addition to her publications on eighteenth-century French literature, women and politics, and French and Quebecois literature and culture, she is the editor of *French Women and the Age of Enlightenment* (1984) and *Foreign Languages and International Trade: A Global Perspective* (1987).

Katherine Stephenson is Assistant Professor of French and Women's Studies at the University of North Carolina at Charlotte. She has published semiotic studies of Voltaire, Camus, and Irigaray, and is currently collaborating with Irigaray on empirical research into sexual differentiation in language use.

Karyna Szmurlo, Assistant Professor of French at Clemson University, is coeditor of *Germaine de Staël: Crossing the Borders*. She publishes extensively on Staël and is currently preparing a book entitled *Performative Discourses: Germaine de Staël*.

Ruth P. Thomas is Professor of French at Temple University and Director of the Temple Sorbonne Summer Program. She has published articles on Mme de Lafayette, Marivaux, Diderot, and others, as well as the heroines of eighteenth-century French novels.

Janet Whatley teaches French literature at the University of Vermont. She has published essays on Marivaux, Diderot, Colette, Yourcenar, and the eighteenth-century French literary canon. She has also published articles on Renaissance French voyage accounts and has translated Jean de Léry's *Histoire d'un voyage fait en la terre du Brésil*.

Charity Cannon Willard has written extensively on Christine de Pizan, especially since her retirement from her career as a college professor. She and her husband are preparing a critical edition of Christine de Pizan's *Fais d'armes et de chevalerie*.

Renee Winegarten is a literary critic and author. She lives in London and is a frequent contributor to journals in the United States. Her works include *Writers and Revolution, The Double Life of George Sand, Madame de Staël*, and *Simone de Beauvior: A Critical View*.

Colette H. Winn is Associate Professor of French at Washington University in St. Louis. In addition to a book on the Death Sonnets of Jean de Sponde, she has published works on Bonaventure des Périers, Marguerite de Navarre, Hélisenne de Crenne, Jeanne Flore, and Pernette du Guillet in *Neophilologus, Orbis Litterarum, Poétique, Romance Notes, Romance Quarterly, Romanic Review, Symposium*, and other journals. Her book *L'Esthétique de jeu dans l'Heptaméron de Marguerite de Navarre* is forthcoming.

Dorothy Zimmerman is a Professor Emerita at the University of Nebraska-Lincoln, where, until recently, she taught courses in comparative literature and women's studies. She has edited a translation of George Sand's *François le Champi* (*The Country Waif*) and May Wynne Lamb's *Life in Alaska: The Reminiscences of a Kansas Woman 1916–19*, and has published on Sand, Germaine de Staël, and others.